A History of
The Expansion of Christianity

Volume VI

THE GREAT CENTURY
IN NORTHERN AFRICA AND ASIA
A.D. 1800-A.D. 1914

A History of
THE EXPANSION OF CHRISTIANITY
(*Volume VI*)

THE
GREAT CENTURY
IN NORTHERN AFRICA AND ASIA
A.D. 1800-A.D. 1914

by
KENNETH SCOTT LATOURETTE

THE PATERNOSTER PRESS

ISBN: 0 85364 119 6

THE GREAT CENTURY

Copyright © 1944 by Harper and Row, Publishers
Published by special arrangement with Harper and Row, Publishers,
New York
Printed in the United States of America
This edition is distributed by The Paternoster Press
Paternoster House, 3 Mount Radford Crescent
Exeter, Devon, by arrangement with
The Zondervan Publishing House, Grand Rapids, Mich., U.S.A.

This Edition 1971

AUSTRALIA:
Emu Book Agencies Pty., Ltd., 511 Kent Street, Sydney, N.S.W.

SOUTH AFRICA:
Oxford University Press, P.O. Box 1141, Oxford House,
11, Buitencingle Street, Cape Town

In memory of

HARLAN PAGE BEACH

1854–1933

Contents

Chapter I

Chapter II

Chapter III

Chapter IV

Chapter V

Chapter VI

Chapter VII

CONTENTS

Chapter VIII

The assembling of the materials for the present volume has entailed the consultation of libraries in several different parts of the world. Use has been made especially of the large collection of the Congregation for the Propagation of the Faith, in Rome, of the British Museum, of the Wason collection (now in Cornell University), of the Morrison library on China (now in Tokyo), of the library of the North China Branch of the Royal Asiatic Society, in Shanghai, of the Missionary Research Library, in New York City, and, above all, of the libraries of Yale University, especially the Day Missions Library. To the librarians and their assistants of each of these collections the author is under a heavy and a very pleasant debt. The courtesy and efficiency which he has invariably met make happy the memories of the long days of research. Many other friends along the way, in Europe, the Near East, India, China, Korea, Japan, and the United States, have contributed generously in counsel and from their stores of knowledge. To enumerate them all would prolong this page unduly. The author must, however, especially record his grateful obligation to members of the Society of the Divine Word and of the Catholic Foreign Mission Society of America (the Maryknollers), and particularly to the Reverend J. J. Considine of the latter goodly fellowship, for giving him some insight into the attitudes and achievements of a great Christian communion which is not his own. The author cannot hope to have freed his pages from all error. However, had it not been for the generous help of these many friends the following chapters would have been guilty of far more mistakes than they now contain. As in the earlier volumes, the author is under a peculiar debt of gratitude to Mrs. Charles T. Lincoln. She has turned into all but flawless typescript what in many places has been an extraordinarily difficult first draft and has made invaluable suggestions for improving the literary style. Last but by no means least is the obligation to the publishers and their staff who in the face of war conditions have put the volume into print and have given it its highly satisfactory typographical dress and binding.

A History of
The Expansion of Christianity

Volume VI
THE GREAT CENTURY
IN NORTHERN AFRICA AND ASIA
A.D. 1800-A.D. 1914

Chapter I

BY WAY OF INTRODUCTION

A S WE pass from Africa south of the Sahara to the north coast of Africa and Asia in our geographic pilgrimage of the expansion of Christianity in the nineteenth century, we come into a very different world.

In the preceding volume we dealt with areas in which for the most part Westerners and their culture impinged upon peoples of primitive cultures. Here at the outset of the nineteenth century vast regions were but sparsely settled. In the temperate zones new nations of predominantly European descent arose. The primitive cultures offered but feeble and short-lived resistance to the invading complex civilization of the whites, made powerful by the machine and the technique of a scientific age. Vigorous through the great revivals of the nineteenth century, Christianity accompanied the expansion of Europeans. It was the dominant faith of the new white communities and nations which arose. It made rapid progress among primitive peoples. It was the vehicle through which much of white civilization was brought to the dusky and black-skinned races. Through it languages were reduced to writing, literature was prepared, modern medical skill was summoned to attack disease, and fresh handicrafts and methods of agriculture were introduced. Profound changes were made in social customs and moral standards. Revolutionary spiritual horizons were given to life. In the Americas and most of the smaller groups of the islands of the Pacific the majority of the population professed acceptance of the Christian faith. In all but a few of the larger areas Christianity made very rapid advance. When the outbreak of the war of 1914-1918 brought the era to an end, the assimilation of these primitive folk to the white man's culture and to the associated religious faith was proceeding apace.

In North Africa and Asia Christianity was confronted by a very different situation. Here as a rule it was in contact with ancient and advanced cultures and religions. Here it came face to face with its traditional rival, Islam, before which in earlier centuries it had suffered its most severe losses. The advanced cultures and faiths did not yield so readily as did those of the primitive folk, either to Western civilization or to Christianity. This was to be expected. It was

1

not merely to the impact of the Occident that the high civilizations of Asia proved resistant. It has usually been characteristic of advanced cultures and their religions that they have been much slower to disintegrate before an invading civilization and the propagation of a new faith than have primitive cultures with their animism or polytheism.

Although in the nineteenth century Christianity did not make proportionately as rapid progress in northern Africa and Asia as it did in the Americas, the islands and lands in the South Pacific, and Africa south of the Sahara, a number of factors facilitated its spread in these areas. Indeed, in these brief decades it achieved more widespread gains in Asia than it had ever previously enjoyed.

In northern Africa and Asia, as elsewhere on the globe, western European peoples were becoming the masters. In the course of the nineteenth century practically all the peoples of these vast regions had either become politically subject to the Occident or were in process of preserving their political independence by the sacrifice of their cultural independence. Most of the northern shore of Africa either passed directly under European control or, as in the case of Egypt, did not preserve its full autonomy. The Turkish Empire survived, but with boundaries which were sadly shrunken since the days when the eastern Mediterranean had been a Turkish sea. Persia continued intact, but Great Britain and Russia had carved out rival spheres of influence. Protected by its mountain barriers, Afghanistan proudly remained self-governing, but it was a minor state. The British completed their conquest of India, subdued Burma, and extended their sway over much of the Malay Peninsula. France acquired most of Indo-China. Siam owed its survival to Anglo-French jealousy which kept it as a buffer state. In disdain and distrust of the encroaching Occident, the vast Chinese Empire strove to maintain both its political and its cultural aloofness, but was compelled to compromise them both. Of the nations of Asia, only the Japanese succeeded in enlarging their borders and defeating the European, and they owed that achievement chiefly to their foresight and promptitude in reorganizing their life according to Western patterns and adopting the mechanical devices of the Occident. Except for a few remote corners, all the civilizations of Asia, even in lands which perpetuated their political independence, were being modified by the impact of the Occident. In some, as in Japan, the cultural revolution had gone far. In China it had only recently begun, but with a shattering violence which was unprecedented in the history of that land. Christianity, accompanying the Occidental invasion, found the walls of cultural resistance weakened. Being, in the minds of the vanquished, so closely associated with the powerful conqueror, it was given a hearing. As the century progressed the rate of Occidental penetration was accelerated. With it the growth of Christianity also gathered momentum.

We must recall, moreover, what we have found again and again in the past two volumes, that in the nineteenth century the Christianity of Western peoples, Protestantism and Roman Catholicism, experienced a striking revival. The advance of Occidental power in Asia was paralleled by an hitherto unequaled growth in the movements for the propagation of the Christian faith. These found in Asia both their greatest challenge and a major field for their energies.

Then, too, the nineteenth century expansion of Europe and of Christianity coincided with a period of political weakness in Asia. No Asiatic people except the Japanese were building an empire, and the Japanese effort was only getting under way when the events of the year 1914 brought the era to an end. The Ottoman and Mogul empires had been in decay for several generations. The one was now dubbed the Sick Man of Europe and was clearly nearing its death. The other finally faded out about the middle of the century. In China the Manchu (Ch'ing) Dynasty was declining from the brilliant apex which it had reached in the eighteenth century and its days were obviously numbered. In Japan the dawn of the nineteenth century found a regime, the Tokugawa Shogunate, which by its very success was digging its own grave: the feudalism of which it was the embodiment and upon which it depended was suffering from a fatal dry rot induced by the peace whereby the Tokugawa had sought to make their power secure. In other words, the empires which had held chief place in Asia in the period immediately preceding the nineteenth century were moribund and no new ones had arisen to take their places. The continent was ripe for change.

Political decrepitude had as company a religious somnolence which in some instances was decay. To be sure, new stirrings were afoot in Islam. The Wahabi movement, arising in the eighteenth century, in the nineteenth century was in full tide. It was in part the source, in the nineteenth century, of the brotherhood or order of the Senussi. In Shiite Persia, in that same century, arose the Babist revival and the Bahais. From the Indian Sunnites sprang the Ahmadiya movement. In Hinduism, moreover, fresh sects came into being. Even when these were in part the effect of contact with Christianity, they gave evidence of a vitality sufficient to respond to competition. Yet the majority of Moslems and of Hindus were but little if any affected by these awakenings. Shinto was experiencing a marked access of vigour, but its hold was limited to one nation, Japan. Buddhism, moreover, while here and there putting forth new shoots, for several centuries had been in waning health. For generations Confucianism had developed no new school of outstanding significance. Shortly before 1914 the structure of the imperial state and the educational system by which it was buttressed were swept aside. It was clear that the great non-Christian faiths of Asia would not yield as quickly to Christianity as the animism of primitive peoples was doing. Yet all Asiatic religions had been more robust in previous times, and none was as vital as nineteenth century Christianity. Some, moreover, were being honeycombed by the acids of Occidental modernity.

It must be added that the weakening of the cultures of Asia under the impact of the Occident and the adoption of some phases of Occidental civilization were not necessarily followed by the acceptance of Christianity. Asiatic peoples might pay Occidental culture the sincere flattery of imitation, but it was the mechanical devices through which the Occident had achieved its mastery which won their grudging admiration and which they sought to acquire, together with the science and the type of education necessary to the creation and operation of the machine. They were inclined to hold to their traditional religions and to view Christianity with scornful and hostile eyes as the faith of the aggressive and disliked Westerner.

The Christianity propagated in Asia in the nineteenth century was not that of the churches which had their historic seats in Asia. These ancient bodies were on the defensive, mainly against Islam, but also against the forms of Christianity introduced from the West and, in India, against Hinduism. The Christianity which spread was chiefly that of the Occident, Roman Catholicism and Protestantism.

In proportion to the population this Western Christianity made much less headway in Asia in the nineteenth century than it did among the primitive folk which engaged so much of our attention in the preceding volume. This was in part because of greater resistance offered by the more advanced faiths and cultures of Asia. It was also because, in proportion to the population, fewer missionaries were sent to Asia than to these other lands.

Such accessions as came to Christianity in Asia in the nineteenth century were for the most part from special groups. Large numbers were from primitive or near-primitive tribes in India and Burma which, like primitive folk elsewhere, were more inclined than were peoples of advanced civilizations to adopt a new religion if it was brought to them in connexion with a high culture. In India the chief gains were among the outcastes, underprivileged millions who were often not far from primitive peoples in culture and who also saw in Christianity a possible door of escape from their unhappy hereditary lot. Fairly extensive growth was registered among those who were uprooted by the revolutions brought by the coming of the West. In Japan numbers of the early converts were from the *samurai*, whose traditional position and livelihood were a sacrifice to the new order. In more than one Asiatic land many converts were recruited from those elements in the urban communities which had received an education of an Occidental type and who were in occupations associated with the Western invasion.[1] Some were from those who were dazzled by the power and the wealth of the Occident and who sought the secret in Christianity. A few were religiously hungry souls who found in the Christian faith the goal and the satisfaction of their quest. In spite of notable gains, in 1914 professing Christians in every country in Asia constituted a small minority. In nearly every land this minority was rapidly growing, but it was still only a minute fraction of the population. The effects upon civilization were widely spread, but they were merely at their beginning.

When consideration is given to the difficulties which faced it, in the nineteenth century Christianity made amazing progress in northern Africa and Asia. As elsewhere in most of the world it came to the end of the period on a rapidly ascending curve. Its influence upon cultures was out of all proportion to its numerical strength. It had an outstanding role as a pioneer in new types of education, in movements for the relief and prevention of human suffering, and in disseminating ideas. In spite of the world-wide upheavals of the ensuing decades, after 1914 it was to have a striking growth both in numbers and in influence.

[1] Davis, *The Economic and Social Environment of the Younger Churches*, pp. 38, 39.

Chapter II

THE NORTHERN SHORES OF AFRICA AND THE NEAR EAST. THE CANARY ISLANDS AND RIO DE ORO: THE MADEIRAS MOROCCO: ALGERIA: TUNIS: CYRENAICA: EGYPT: THE ANGLO-EGYPTIAN SUDAN: ABYSSINIA: ITALIAN SOMALILAND: BRITISH SOMALILAND: FRENCH SOMALILAND: ERITREA: PALESTINE: SYRIA: ASIA MINOR AND ARMENIA: MESOPO-TAMIA: PERSIA: ARABIA: AFGHANISTAN

WE COME first of all to the northern shores of Africa and the western portions of Asia.

Here was the region which saw the birth of Christianity and in which Christianity registered its first great advances. It included Palestine, where the founder of Christianity lived and taught. It embraced Syria, in whose former capital, Antioch, had been an early centre of non-Jewish Christianity. In it was Asia Minor, the first large area where Christianity became the dominant faith. It was the home of the Armenians, the first professedly Christian nation. North Africa had been the scene of an early marked development of Latin Christianity and was the birthplace of Augustine, the most influential of the Latin-using church fathers.

This was also the region in which Christianity had suffered its greatest territorial losses. Although Islam was to be found elsewhere, here was the heart of the Moslem world. Here Mohammed had lived. Here was Mecca, to the Moslem the most sacred of holy sites. Here, in Cairo, were the intellectual headquarters of the faith. Here had long been most of the chief strongholds of Moslem political power. Christianity survived, but in minority groups which for centuries had continued to lose ground before the ascendant Crescent.

In the nineteenth century efforts were made to regain for the Cross at least some of the territory which had been sacrificed. However, they faced numerous obstacles. Converts could come from Christianity to Islam, but under the Moslem law death was the penalty of defection from the Prophet. In their prolonged losing struggle against Islam, the churches of the region had developed unlovely characteristics or had accentuated obnoxious traits which had been

6

theirs in pre-Islamic days. The different churches formed distinct communities which quarreled with one another. Many of the clergy were ignorant and crude. Since Christians were on the defensive and were regarded by the Moslems as inferior, they tended to depend upon their wits to maintain their position and to many of the Moslems appeared tricky. Moreover, Christianity was distrusted because it was associated with western European imperialism. The Crusades had helped to fix this suspicion in the Near Eastern mind. In the nineteenth century the territorial ambitions of supposedly Christian European nations had revived and reinforced it. Russia used its Orthodox faith as an excuse for intervention in behalf of its co-religionists who were under the Turk. France and Italy supported Roman Catholic enterprises as entering wedges and bulwarks of their political designs. Moreover, in the Eastern churches ritual and the Bible were in older literary forms of the languages of their constituencies, or, as in Egypt, were in a tongue which their constituencies had abandoned. They were therefore largely unintelligible to the masses and even to some of the priests. The masses of Christians were ignorant and superstitious. They themselves had first to be educated and their faith purified and revived before they could propagate their religion. In consequence of these various difficulties nineteenth century attempts to spread Christianity among non-Christians in North Africa and the Near East made little direct headway.

The nineteenth century endeavours to propagate Christianity in North Africa and western Asia were chiefly by Christians from the West—Roman Catholics and Protestants. There was a large Roman Catholic migration from France and Italy to the northern shores of Africa. As a result Christianity reappeared in a region in which it had been strong before the Moslem conquest but from which, except for a few merchants and captives, it had disappeared centuries before. Quite apart from these settlers, Roman Catholic and Protestant missionaries were widely scattered. Both groups sought to revive the existing Christianity of the region. Roman Catholics strove to do this by bringing the Eastern Christians into communion with their church. As late as 1840 Roman Catholic missions in the Near East which had formerly flourished under French protection were in a sad state of decay.[1] However, not long after the middle of the century a revival began. In the 1850's there was inaugurated at Paris *L'Œuvre des Écoles d'Orient* whose purpose it was to encourage the Oriental Christians to become Roman Catholics.[2] In 1862 Pope Pius IX founded the *Congregatio pro Negotiis Ritus Orientalis* to specialize on the Eastern churches.[3] As the numbers

---

[1] Baudrillart in Descamps, *Histoire Générale Comparée des Missions*, p. 540.
[2] Lesourd, *L'Année Missionnaire*, pp. 325, 326.
[3] Berg, *Die katholische Heidenmission als Kulturträger*, Vol. I, p. 172.

of converts from these churches increased, Rome created dioceses for them. Many of them were in Uniate bodies, and for each of these a patriarch was appointed. In the latter part of the century Pope Leo XIII was particularly active in behalf of the Uniates. To provide a clergy for them he established several seminaries in Rome.[4] In 1901 there was begun *Les Amis de la Syrie et du Levant* to strengthen French influence in the Near East by assisting French Roman Catholic missions in that area.[5] Some Protestants laboured to build up branches of their respective denominations. Others strove by schools, personal contacts, and translations of the Bible into the current vernaculars to bring about an awakening within existing churches without creating a schism. Nearly always, however, the groups who responded to this latter type of Protestant programme were forced out by the conservatives and found themselves under the necessity of organizing into separate communities which were usually termed Evangelical. Since under Turkish law the Christian churches had corporate relations with the government, the Evangelicals constituted themselves into legal bodies and obtained official recognition. Both Roman Catholics and Protestants conducted schools to which non-Christians as well as Christians were admitted. Both maintained orphanages and engaged in works of mercy which included medical service. Through these channels contacts were made with non-Christians and something of Christian moral idealism was spread by precept and example. Yet very few formal converts from Islam were won by either Roman Catholics or Protestants.

Since in these volumes we are concerned with the expansion of Christianity and have therefore passed rapidly over the spread of one form of Christianity at the expense of another and since so much of the effort of Roman Catholic and Christian missionaries in northern Africa and western Asia was directed towards other Christian bodies, we will not devote as much space to these areas as their size and populations might seem to demand. However, we must not ignore them, for some spread of Christianity took place through immigration and the chief ultimate objective of both Roman Catholic and Protestant missions was the Moslem. Jews were also widely scattered and numerous attempts were made to reach them. Here and there were pagans, largely animists, especially in areas in contact with the Africa south of the Sahara and of Egypt.

Following our logical course from where the last volume paused in our geographic survey, Senegal, Upper Senegal, and Niger, we come to the Canary

[4] Schwager, *Die katholische Heidenmission der Gegenwart*, pp. 228, 229.
[5] Lesourd, *op. cit.*, pp. 326-329.

Islands and to the adjacent Rio de Oro, or Spanish Sahara. Neither need detain us. The former had been Spanish and Roman Catholic since the fifteenth century [6] and the latter, sparsely settled, was predominantly Moslem, with a few resident Spaniards, Roman Catholics, and some Christian fisher folk from the Canaries.[7]

Nor must the Madeiras long engage us. Since the fifteenth century they had been Portuguese and Roman Catholic. In the 1830's the active propagation of Protestantism was begun, chiefly by a clergyman of the Free Church of Scotland. The movement spread rapidly, but aroused bitter persecution. Several hundred of the converts sought refuge in the British West Indies and the United States. Their flight brought a subsidence of the trend toward Protestantism.[8]

Morocco, a combination of high and broken mountains, desert, and fertile valleys, was ethnologically a mixture with Berber stock predominating. Religiously it was prevailingly Moslem, but with traces of pre-Islamic beliefs and local developments. Jews of more than one strain were fairly numerous. The Christianity, largely superficial, which had existed before the Arab conquest in the seventh and eighth centuries, disappeared before the triumphant Islam. In the long interval before the nineteenth century it was represented only by Spanish and Portuguese footholds on the shore and the adjacent islands and by Christian captives. In the nineteenth century Spanish activities increased and the French, from the vantage-ground won in Algeria through their conquest of that region in the 1830's and 1840's, made their influence felt. Between 1900 and 1914, through diplomatic crises in which Germany was active and which threatened a European war, Spain and France extended and confirmed their interests. The Spanish zones were a narrow strip along the northern coast opposite Gibraltar and an enclave on the south-west coast. In 1912 France obtained what in effect was recognition by the leading native government in Morocco of a protectorate over the remainder of the country.[9]

Christianity achieved but slight progress in Morocco in the nineteenth century. The jealous loyalty of the populace to Islam and the hostility to foreigners proved effective obstacles.

[6] Vol. II, p. 342.

[7] *Spanish Sahara* (London, H. M. Stationery Office, 1920, pp. 35), pp. 7, 8, 16-19.

[8] Herman Norton, *Record of Facts Concerning the Persecutions at Madeira in 1843 and 1846* (New York, The American and Foreign Christian Union, 1850, pp. 285), *passim;* C. Carus Wilson, *The Madeira Persecutions* (London, The Religious Tract Society, no date, pp. viii, 149), *passim.*

[9] *French Morocco* (London, H. M. Stationery Office, 1920, pp. 98), pp. 1-35; *Spanish Morocco* (London, H. M. Stationery Office, 1920, pp. 42), pp. 1-15.

In spite of its tenaciously held footholds in the Spanish-controlled cities on the northern shore of Morocco, Roman Catholicism made but little headway in Morocco. It was chiefly confined to the European population who were of that faith. The responsibility for its propagation had long been entrusted to the Spanish Franciscans, but in 1853 their staff was reduced to one man.[10] In the latter half of the nineteenth century reinforcements came. The chief of these was José Lerchundi, who was appointed in 1862 and died in 1896. With head-quarters in Tangier, Lerchundi did much to develop schools, to open new centres, to build a hospital, to promote the study of Arabic, to create and print literature, and to found, in Spain, a college for the training of missionaries for the Holy Land and Morocco.[11] In 1908 the prefecture apostolic under which the enterprise was administered was raised to a vicariate apostolic. In that year, too, French Brothers Minor arrived. Between 1911 and 1914 immigrants who came from Europe made possible and necessary an increase in the numbers of parishes.[12]

Protestant Christianity also entered Morocco. Its chief agency was the North Africa Mission. This enterprise was inaugurated in the 1880's by a group which centered in London and which had among its leaders George Pearse, then in his late sixties, Grattan Guinness, whom we have already met in the preceding volume in connexion with Africa, and Edward H. Glenny. It was of the family of what were usually termed "faith missions," of which the China Inland Mission, whose story we are to tell later in this volume, was a pioneer and the leading exemplar. It was undenominational, but was described as "orthodox, evangelical, and evangelistic." Begun first for the Kabyles of Algeria, before the middle of the 1880's the North Africa Mission had extended its field into Morocco. The first station was in Tangier, a Spanish possession. There, because of the need for that kind of service and because it was a means of removing prejudice, chief emphasis was placed upon a hospital, but other activities were undertaken among Moslems, Jews, and Spanish Roman Catholics. Before 1900 several other cities were entered, among them the capital, Fez. Converts were few.[13] Other Protestant organizations represented were the British and Foreign

[10] Lemmens, *Geschichte der Franziskanermissionen*, pp. 15, 16; Schwager, *Die katholische Heidenmission der Gegenwart*, pp. 209, 210.

[11] José María López, *El P. José Lerchundi* (Madrid, Imprenta Clásica Española, 1927, pp. xx, 523, xii), *passim*.

[12] Pons, *La Nouvelle Église d'Afrique*, pp. 284-292.

[13] Glenny in Rutherford and Glenny, *The Gospel in North Africa*, pp. 135-159, 177-202; Albert A. Isaacs, *A Biographical Sketch Relative to the Missionary Labors of Emma Herdman of the Empire of Morocco* (London, S. W. Partridge & Co., 1900, pp. 134), *passim*.

Bible Society, which was there many years before the North Africa Mission;[14] The London Society for Promoting Christianity amongst the Jews, whose first contact with Moroccan Jews was in Marseilles in 1834 and which had a resident representative in Morocco as early as 1844;[15] the Southern Morocco Mission, with headquarters in Scotland and which sent its first two missionaries in 1888 and by 1913 had a staff of nineteen and was conducting dispensaries, schools, and an orphanage and was distributing and translating the Bible;[16] the Mildmay Mission to the Jews; the Central Morocco Mission, founded by the English Presbyterians; the Gospel Union, from the United States; and the Plymouth Brethren.[17] Protestants were, therefore, more active among the non-Christian population than were Roman Catholics. Yet they, too, had few converts.

To the east of Morocco were two regions which in 1914 were French territory, Algeria and Tunisia. They were brought into the French Empire by conquest in the nineteenth century. The French extended their authority over Algeria in the 1830's and 1840's, and in succeeding decades pushed their frontier southward. A French protectorate over Tunisia was effected in 1881 and 1883, to the great discontent of Italy, which had ambitions in that area, and of Turkey, which claimed suzerainty. The population of both Algeria and Tunisia, like that of Morocco, was predominantly Berber of several strains. To this were added Arab elements through earlier conquests and migrations. Berbers and Arabs were Moslems. Jews were also present in considerable numbers and held to their hereditary faith. The Christianity which before the Arab conquest had been so strong had, except for a few merchants and captives from Europe, disappeared long before the nineteenth century.

In the course of the nineteenth century, Christianity was reintroduced. It came partly by an extensive immigration, in Algeria chiefly from France and Spain and into Tunisia mainly from Italy and France. This immigrant Christianity was predominantly Roman Catholic, but had in it some Protestantism as well. Christianity also spread partly through missions. These likewise were chiefly

[14] *The Sixty-Fifth Report of the British and Foreign Bible Society* (1869), pp. 172, 173; *The One Hundred & Second Report of the British and Foreign Bible Society* (1906), p. 162.
[15] Gidney, *The History of the London Society for Promoting Christianity amongst the Jews*, pp. 168, 260, 262, 309, 393, 488-492, 570, 617, 618.
[16] Kerr, *Morocco after Twenty-Five Years*, pp. 222-263; *Southern Morocco Mission; Founded 1888: Review of the Work* (Glasgow, Pickering & Inglis, c. 1913, pp. 12), *passim;* James Haldane, *Missionary Romance in Morocco* (London, Pickering & Inglis, no date, pp. 189), *passim.*
[17] Kerr, *op. cit.,* pp. 267-273; Rutherford and Glenny, *op cit.,* p. 203.

Roman Catholic, but they were not quite so overwhelmingly so as was the immigration. The predominance of Roman Catholic Christianity was to be anticipated. By tradition France was prevailingly of that faith and in the nineteenth century the French led in the Roman Catholic missionary enterprise among non-Christians.

For many years before the French conquest French Lazarists had been caring for the Christian captives. In 1645 they had established themselves in Tunis and the following year they had gained entrance to Algiers. The King of France had a consulate in each of these ports and the Duchesse d'Aiguillon, niece of Richelieu and patroness of Vincent de Paul, the founder of the Lazarists, acquired them for the superior general of that order. Vincent de Paul and his successors saw that the posts were filled with devout laymen, lay brothers, or priests.[18] The last of the Lazarists left in 1827, when relations between France and Algiers were broken off.[19]

The French conquest was hailed by the Roman Catholic Church as an opportunity for the revival of its ancient strength in North Africa. The Holy See had made vows in behalf of the French arms and on the news of the victory the *Te Deum* was chanted in Rome.[20] However, the Revolution of 1830 in France overthrew the Bourbons with their traditional support of the Church and the ensuing regime of Louis Philippe hesitated to build an ecclesiastical establishment in North Africa for fear that by so doing the Moslem population would take offence and that thus the uncompleted French occupation would be jeopardized.[21] For a number of years very little religious care was given either to the French soldiers or to the colonists.[22] In 1838, when a bishop was finally appointed for Algiers, there were in all the colony only four priests, a few sisters, and one church.[23] The first bishop, Antoine Adolphe Dupuch, encountered difficulties with the civil and military authorities, partly because he wished to begin missions among the Moslems, and was dismissed in 1845.[24] The new bishop, Pavy, had better success. In 1856 there was reported a well organized

[18] Coste, *La Congrégation de la Mission*, pp. 211-213; Repeticci, *L'Algérie Chrétienne*, pp. 13, 14. On one of the early priest-consuls, see *En Mémoire du Vicaire Apostolique et Consul de France, Jean le Vacher, l'Illustre Martyr d'Alger, Solennités Religieuses et Civiles du Juillet 1927 à Ecouen, sa Ville Natale. Compte-Rendu & Discours* (Imprimerie de Balan-Sedan, 1928, pp. 78), *passim*.
[19] Repeticci, *op. cit.*, pp. 10, 11.
[20] Descamps, *Histoire Générale Comparée des Missions*, p. 561.
[21] Pons, *La Nouvelle Église d'Afrique*, p. 12.
[22] Repeticci, *op. cit.*, pp. 26, 27. For documents for this period and leading up to the creation of a diocese, see *Revue d'Histoire des Missions*, Vol. VIII, pp. 85-122.
[23] Tournier, *La Nouvelle Église d'Afrique. La Conquête Religieuse de l'Algérie, 1830-1845*, p. 99.
[24] Pons, *op. cit.*, pp. 48-59.

diocese, with sixty churches, chapels, and oratories, ninety-one priests, and fifty-three parishes. Some mosques were transformed into churches. Extensive financial assistance was given by the state and funds were also contributed by the Society for the Propagation of the Faith.[25] Priests of the Holy Cross, Lazarists, Jesuits, and Trappists had entered, Brothers of St. Joseph were in charge of schools, there were several scores of sisters, and a seminary was beginning the training of a body of clergy.[26] In 1865 Pavy was given the title of Archbishop of Algiers and two suffragan sees were created.[27] From 1846 to 1850 forty-three new parishes were erected, between 1850 and 1858 seventy-eight were added, and between 1858 and 1862 these were augmented by thirty-one.[28] When, in 1866, Pavy died, there were 187 parishes and the number of secular priests had increased from the 29 whom he found when he came to 273.[29] Pavy was succeeded by Charles Martial Allemand Lavigerie (1825-1892), the most famous of the episcopate of the revived North African church. He was later made cardinal and, in 1884, after French authority had been extended over Tunisia, he was given the title of Archbishop of Carthage and Primate of Africa.[30] Thus Rome, by restoring what had once been the foremost see in North Africa, sought to dramatize the recovery of the Church in this scene of some of its most notable former triumphs.

Tunisia for a time presented a special problem. Both France and Italy were interested in it. Ecclesiastical rivalry reflected the contending political ambitions. In 1665 a treaty between the Bey of Tunis and the powerful Louis XIV of France had declared that the Capuchins and other Roman Catholic missionaries in Tunis should be regarded as French subjects and be under French protection.[31] In 1830, however, the prefecture apostolic of Tunis seems to have had as clergy only two Italian Capuchins and one Spaniard, a Trinitarian.[32] Early in the 1840's there were said to be 8,000 Roman Catholics in Tunisia, of whom three-fourths were in the capital. There appear then to have been only one priest, a Spaniard, and a Capuchin hospital.[33] After the French conquest of Algeria, European colonists, chiefly Italians, French, and Maltese, and mostly Roman Catholic, began coming by the hundreds.[34] In 1843, largely at the instance of France,

[25] Tournier, op. cit., p. 99.
[26] Pons, op. cit., pp. 39-45.
[27] Pons, op. cit., pp. 78, 79.
[28] Pons, op. cit., pp. 76, 77.
[29] Pons, op. cit., p. 77.
[30] Pons, op. cit., pp. 252, 253.
[31] Pons, op. cit., p. 210.
[32] Pons, op. cit., p. 206.
[33] Notizie Statistiche delle Missioni di Tutto il Mondo Dipendenti dalla S. C. de Propaganda Fide (1844), pp. 580-585.
[34] Pons, op. cit., p. 208.

Tunisia was made a vicariate apostolic.[35] In 1867 there were said to be 15,055 Roman Catholics and in 1877, 16,286, under the care of Italian Capuchins.[36] In 1840 there arrived French Sisters of St. Joseph of the Apparition who gave themselves to schools and the sick.[37] In 1855 there also came French Brothers of Christian Schools.[38] In 1875 Lavigerie, then Archbishop of Algiers, proposed the setting up of a French college in Tunis. Within a few years this was accomplished. Lavigerie was also active in seeking to bring Tunisia under French authority.[39] After the reduction of Tunisia to a French protectorate, Lavigerie introduced additional French sisters.[40] It was he, moreover, who was chiefly responsible for the revival of the Archbishopric of Carthage with himself as the first incumbent.[41] The Italian Capuchins were not happy over these political and ecclesiastical developments. Some of them were anti-French. The head of the Capuchins withdrew them. The last of them left in 1891.[42] The French were now clearly in control.

The anti-clerical trend of the French state under the Third Republic brought embarrassment to the young church in Algeria and Tunisia. Lavigerie lost the favour of the governor general.[43] In 1880 the secularization of the communal schools was begun and the Jesuits were expelled from the college of Notre Dame. Some public religious processions were forbidden. In 1904 the Trinitarians were dismissed from the military hospital at Oran. In 1909 the laws of 1901, 1902, and 1904 were ordered enforced and the schools established by the various religious congregations were closed. Not far from the same time the state alienated the episcopal funds and the palace of the archbishop. Government financial support was withdrawn.[44] These measures, to be sure, were simply the extension of those being taken in France, but here as in the mother country they worked distress.

Yet the Roman Catholic Church survived these adversities. Funds were obtained from Europe to aid in the construction of at least one cathedral.[45] There was sufficient vigour to show itself in the creation of new parishes.[46] Roman Catholic Christianity was firmly rooted in the new communities of European blood which had arisen by migration from Europe. In 1906 Algeria had 278,976

[35] Pons, op. cit., pp. 211, 212.
[36] Pons, op. cit., p. 219.
[37] Pons, op. cit., pp. 222-224.
[38] Pons, op. cit., p. 233.
[39] Pons, op. cit., pp. 239, 240; Phillips, The Church in France, 1848-1907, p. 325.
[40] Pons, op. cit., p. 247.
[41] Pons, op. cit., p. 252.
[42] Pons, op. cit., pp. 257-261.
[43] Pons, op. cit., p. 133.
[44] Pons, op. cit., pp. 140, 150-177, 271-273.
[45] Pons, op. cit., pp. 169, 170.
[46] Pons, op. cit., p. 192.

French settlers and their descendants, 117,475 Spaniards, 33,153 Italians, and 6,217 Maltese.[47] Tunisia had 81,156 Italians, 34,610 French, and 10,330 Maltese.[48] The large majority of these were at least nominally Roman Catholic and some were loyally so. In 1890 it is said that 450,567 were registered as Roman Catholics and that there were 308 churches and chapels and 407 priests. About 1930 the numbers of Roman Catholics are reported to have been 805,000.[49]

The Roman Catholics were not content merely to care for the immigrants who were of their faith. They reached out to the non-Christians.

There were efforts to win the Jews. Thus the Sisters of Our Lady of Sion and the Fathers of Sion, who owed their origin to the Ratisbonne brothers, converted Jews,[50] found one of their fields among the Jews of Tunisia.[51]

The major efforts to reach the non-Christians were among the Moslems. Very early in the French occupation some of the clergy wished to seek converts from Islam. In his initial pastoral letter the first Bishop of Algiers, Dupuch, stressed the duty of instructing the inhabitants in the Christian faith. To this the civil officials objected, for they feared that the populace would take umbrage and that French rule would suffer. Indeed, lest Moslem susceptibilities be offended, they ordered crucifixes removed from the hospitals in which Roman Catholic sisters served. The second bishop, Pavy, introduced in his seminaries the study of Arabic and ordered his clergy to read the Koran that they might the more intelligently approach Moslems. Yet the government forbade the latter even to enter the cathedral.[52] Indeed, some of the French adopted Islam.[53] For years the French state interpreted the promise to preserve religious liberty to mean that the Moslems must remain Moslems.[54] When, at the behest of Pavy, a Lazarist began the religious instruction of Arab orphans, the Minister of War ordered him to return to France.[55] However, by 1845 a few Arabs had been baptized. Some sought baptism in the effort to become French.[56] In 1855 four students preparing for the priesthood banded themselves together to undertake missions to the Moslems and obtained the papal blessing for their project, but officials compelled the abandonment of the project.[57]

Aggressive continuous efforts to reach the Moslems were to wait until the

[47] The Encyclopædia Britannica, 11th ed., Vol. I, p. 645.
[48] The Encyclopædia Britannica, 11th ed., Vol. XXVII, p. 396.
[49] Baudrillart in Descamps, Histoire Générale Comparée des Missions, p. 562.
[50] Vol. IV, p. 112.
[51] Marie, Historie des Institutes Religieux et Missionnaires, pp. 309-313.
[52] Bouniol, The White Fathers and Their Missions, pp. 18, 19.
[53] Pons, La Nouvelle Église d'Afrique, p. 101.
[54] Pons, op. cit., p. 106.
[55] Piolet, Les Missions Catholiques Françaises au XIXe Siècle, Vol. V, p. 61.
[56] Pons, op. cit., pp. 112, 113.
[57] Bouniol, op. cit., p. 20.

episcopate of Lavigerie. Lavigerie was by conviction a missionary. That purpose is said to have been formed in his seminary days as the result of an address by a bishop from China. While still in his thirties Lavigerie had been active in promoting missions to the non-Roman Catholic churches in the Near East. For a time he was in Rome as adviser to the Propaganda on questions related to these bodies.[58] It is not strange, therefore, that he should have been chosen as Archbishop of Algiers. Nor was it remarkable that when he assumed that post he saw it not only as the head of an ecclesiastical structure for shepherding the European colonists but also as a call to carry his faith to non-Christians. His kindling imagination pictured the French foothold in North Africa as an open door for the Christian Gospel to all the continent. In a discourse in his cathedral on the inauguration of religious services in the army in Africa he declared that "Providence who has destined us to civilize Africa has given us the victory." [59] To the evangelization of Africa he brought his great gifts of leadership, promotion, and organization. Within a few months after he assumed office he began to assemble children who had been orphaned through natural disasters which had visited Algeria and placed them in the care of sisters.[60] He openly dissented from the attitude of the government and claimed freedom for missionary activity.[61] He required the study of Arabic in the theological seminaries of his see. Late in 1867, less than a year after he had taken office, three of the seminary students offered themselves as missionaries. They were the nucleus for what became the White Fathers. In 1868 Lavigerie opened a novitiate for the new body with these three and four others. The better to approach the Arabs, he required them to conform as far as possible to Arab ways and gave them a modified form of Arab dress as their official garb. From this came their name, the White Fathers.[62] In 1872 the first twelve took life vows and the following year the rules of the new society were approved by a provincial council.[63] White Sisters were later added for enterprises appropriate for women.

The White Fathers did not restrict their field to Moslems and Arabs. Indeed, it was south of the Sahara that they had their most notable numerical successes.

However, the new society did not neglect the region in which it had its birth. In 1872 some of its members ventured into the Sahara.[64] The following year they opened a station among the Kabyles, a people who lived in the mountains

[58] Bouniol, op. cit., pp. 21-23.
[59] Lavigerie, Œuvres Choises, Vol. I, pp. 23-83.
[60] Bouniol, op. cit., pp. 24-28.
[61] Lavigerie, op. cit., Vol. I, pp. 157-172.
[62] Bouniol, op. cit., pp. 28-32.
[63] Bouniol, op. cit., pp. 37, 38.
[64] Bouniol, op. cit., pp. 41ff.

between Tunisia and Morocco and whose ancestors are said to have been Christians in their pre-Moslem days. Jesuits had preceded the White Fathers and had made useful studies of the language and customs.[65] Lavigerie strictly forbade his missionaries to administer baptism to any non-Christians, whether children or adults, without his express permission.[66] He wished them to win the friendship of the Kabyles before even introducing the subject of religion. Thus, presumably, bitter antagonism would be prevented. Not until 1887 did Lavigerie allow religious instruction in the mission schools and then only if the local constituency asked for it. The first baptisms of Kabyle boys were administered in Rome in 1903 to pilgrims who had gone to that city for the jubilee of Pope Leo XIII.[67] Converts remained few. As late as 1930 there were not 700 among the Kabyles and less than 100 in the Sahara.[68] The Sahara had cost the lives, through violence, of a number of missionaries.[69] A Moslem did not easily become a Christian. Moslem law and custom presented solid obstacles. Of the converts, at least among the Kabyles, the majority sought and obtained naturalization as French citizens.[70] Yet a beginning had been made. Here and there Christian villages came into being.[71] To be sure, these were made up chiefly of those who, as orphans, had been reared by the missionaries and looked to the latter for guidance. However, a slight dent had been made in the prevailing Islam.

A heroic and picturesque figure was Charles Eugène de Foucauld (1858-1916). A scion of an aristocratic family, pampered and spoiled as a youth and frail of body, he entered the army. In the 1880's he was an intrepid explorer in the back parts of Morocco, Algeria, and Tunis. In 1886, in his late twenties, he had a profound religious experience which culminated in his conversion. After visiting the sacred sites in Palestine he joined the Trappists. Later he was ordained priest. Eventually (1901) with the approval of the Holy See, to satisfy his inward urge to a missionary career and to the life of a hermit, he went to the Sahara. There he conceived the idea of a new order vowed to penitence, prayer, and perpetual adoration of the Holy Sacrament for the glory of God and the salvation of souls and whose members should live among non-Christian populations. Although this dream was not realized, he succeeded in founding an association to labour

---

[65] Bouniol, *op. cit.*, pp. 141, 142.

[66] Lavigerie, *op. cit.*, Vol. II, pp. 523-526.

[67] Bouniol, *op. cit.*, pp. 142-144.

[68] Antony Philippe, *Missions des Pères Blancs en Tunisie, Algérie, Kabylie, Sahara* (Paris, Dillen & Cie, 1931, pp. 146), pp. 143, 145.

[69] Bouniol, *op. cit.*, pp. 54-56, 150, 151. For the life of one of these martyrs see Brébion, *Alexis Pouplard des Pères Blancs (1854-1881)* (Algiers, Maison-Carrée, 1925, pp. 206), *passim*.

[70] André Bonnichon, *La Conversion au Christianisme de l'Indigène Musulman Algérien et ses Effets Juridiques* (Paris, Librairie du Recueil Sirey, 1931, pp. 152), p. 12.

[71] Bouniol, *op. cit.*, pp. 135, 136, 139.

for missions among the Moslems. In his beloved Sahara, in 1916, he was killed by Tuaregs.[72]

Protestantism, while not as prominent in Algeria and Tunisia as was Roman Catholicism, was present and active. Numbers of the European immigrants were of that faith. Some were Reformed. Others, principally from Alsace, were Lutherans. Pastors for these came from Europe and for years state financial aid was given to the Protestant congregations. In Algeria Protestant care for the immigrants began in the 1830's.[73] In Tunis a French Protestant church was erected in 1889 as the outgrowth of the labours of a chaplain who had come with the army of occupation.[74] The McCall Mission [75] opened a number of halls in Algeria, primarily for the French, but eventually it withdrew.[76] We also hear of efforts for the Spanish immigrants, one of them by a former Roman Catholic priest.[77] Although its chief objective was the Moslems, the North Africa Mission, in spite of the fear of French colonial officials that its members were British agents, made approaches to Roman Catholics.[78] The British and Foreign Bible Society was active and by 1914 had a number of colporteurs in its employ and was distributing the Bible among the French, Spaniards, and Italians.[79] From the United States the Methodist Episcopal Church entered North Africa in 1908. By 1914 it had gathered some French churches and was reaching out towards the Arabs and the Kabyles as well.[80] As early as the 1830's the Basel Mission sent a man to Algeria to serve the German settlers.[81]

The numerous Jews in Algeria and Tunis constituted an appeal to the Protestant forces. In the 1830's the London Society for Promoting Christianity amongst the Jews began a mission in Tunis and but for the opposition of the French authorities would have inaugurated one in Algiers.[82] In the 1850's

[72] René Bazin, Charles de Foucauld, Hermit and Explorer, translated by Peter Keelan (London, Burns Oates & Washbourne, 1923, pp. viii, 356). There is also a German translation, by M. A. Attenberger, Der Wüstenheilige (Lucerne, Räber & Cie, no date, pp. 352); George Gorrée, Memoires of Charles de Foucauld, Explorer and Hermit. Seen in his Letters. Translated by Donald Attwater (London, Burns Oates & Washbourne, 1938, pp. ix, 167); A. Boucher, La Vie Heroique de Charles de Foucauld (Librairie, Bloud & Gay, 1931, pp. 55).
[73] Cooksey, The Land of the Vanished Church, p. 70.
[74] Cooksey, op. cit., p. 49.
[75] See Vol. IV, pp. 132, 133.
[76] Rutherford and Glenny, The Gospel in North Africa, p. 173.
[77] Rutherford and Glenny, op. cit., pp. 174, 175.
[78] Rutherford and Glenny, op. cit., pp. 160, 165, 166.
[79] The Hundred and Tenth Report of the British and Foreign Bible Society, 1914, pp. 169-174.
[80] Annual Report of the Board of Foreign Missions of the Methodist Episcopal Church for the year 1914, pp. 241-247.
[81] Schlatter, Geschichte der Basler Mission 1815-1915, Vol. I, p. 93.
[82] Gidney, The History of the London Society for Promoting Christianity amongst the Jews, pp. 188-195. For a picture of the mission see Davis, A Voice from North Africa,

marked interest was found by a missionary in Oran and Tunisia.[83] In 1889 a representative of the society reported that in Algiers a number of Jews belonged to the Roman Catholic Church and that there were two Protestant converts.[84] In the 1880's and 1890's the society was active among the Jews of Algeria and Tunis.[85]

The Moslem majority in Algeria and Tunis also proved a challenge to Protestants. In the 1850's and 1860's J. Furniss Ogle, an English clergyman, after a period in Patagonia with the South American Missionary Society, conducted a mission, chiefly for Moslems, and sought to support it by farming. His death through shipwreck, in 1865, brought the enterprise to an end.[86] The North Africa Mission laboured among the Kabyles and some other groups, and that in spite of French opposition. The New Testament was put into the Kabyle tongue.[87] The American Methodists had a mission to the Kabyles[88] and addressed themselves also to the Arabs.[89] French Wesleyans concerned themselves with the Kabyles.[90] In the 1880's came the Plymouth Brethren.[91] There was a Swiss mission, led by H. S. Mayor, chiefly for the Kabyles.[92] The Algiers Missions Band arose out of the efforts of I. Lilias Trotter, an Englishwoman of marked artistic talent, a friend of Ruskin, who went to Algeria in 1888, in her middle thirties, and spent there most of the remainder of a long life.[93] Not many converts were won by these various enterprises, but there was much of heroism on the part of the missionaries.

We hear of Greek Orthodox Christians, immigrants, with at least one church.[94]

pp. 199-202. On the travels of an early missionary of the society, see *Paulus Ewald,* editor, *Reise des evangelischen Missionar Christian Ferdinand Ewald, von Tunis nach Tripolis und wieder zurück* (Nuremberg, Ferdinand v. Ebner, 1842, pp. 240), *passim.*
[83] Gidney, *op. cit.,* pp. 307, 308.
[84] Gidney, *op. cit.,* pp. 487, 488.
[85] Gidney, *op. cit.,* pp. 567-569.
[86] *Life and Missionary Travels of the Rev. J. Furniss Ogle, M.A., from his Letters. Selected by his Sister, and edited by Rev. J. A. Wylie* (London, Longmans, Green, and Co., 1873, pp. viii, 414), *passim.*
[87] Rutherford and Glenny, *op. cit.,* pp. 162-172.
[88] Paulus Scharpff, editor, *Mit der Seele erschaut. Briefe und Tagebuchblätter des Kabylenmissionars Dr. Fritz Rösch* (Nuremberg, J. Koezle, 1920, pp. 171), *passim.*
[89] *Annual Report of the Board of Foreign Missions of the Methodist Episcopal Church for the year 1914,* pp. 243, 245, 246.
[90] Rutherford and Glenny, *op. cit.,* p. 175.
[91] Rutherford and Glenny, *op. cit.,* p. 245.
[92] H. S. Mayor, *L'Evangile chez les Musulmans* (Lausanne, Imprimeries Réunies, 1912, pp. 45), *passim.*
[93] Blanche A. F. Pigott, *I. Lilias Trotter* (London, Marshall, Morgan & Scott, no date, pp. ix, 245), *passim.*
[94] Davis, *op. cit.,* p. 199.

East of Tunisia, Tripolitania and Cyrenaica, embraced in what eventually was known as Libya, constituted a sparsely settled, largely desert region. It had long been nominally part of the Ottoman Empire when, in 1911, Italy, wishing compensation for the recent French advances in Morocco, began its occupation. This was at the cost of a war with Turkey. By 1914 Italian authority had been fairly well established in the coast of Tripolitania, but farther to the east it was precarious and was later seriously threatened by an uprising of Moslem zealots. By 1914 some Italian immigration had entered, chiefly in Tripolitania.

Italian rule had so recently been established and the land had previously been so overwhelmingly Moslem that by the year 1914 Christianity had made very little progress. The Italian and Maltese immigrants were Roman Catholics. Among what must be called the foreign population there were a few Greek Orthodox and Egyptian Copts.[95] In the seventeenth century Tripolitania had been a prefecture apostolic entrusted to the Franciscans.[96] In 1914 it became the vicariate apostolic of Libya.[97] Protestantism was but slightly represented. In 1829 agents of the London Society for Promoting Christianity amongst the Jews sought to distribute Bibles among the Jews of Tripoli.[98] In the 1870's and 1890's the Jews of Tripoli were repeatedly visited by representatives of that society.[99] In the 1890's the North Africa Mission established a centre at Tripoli.[100] In 1913 or 1914 an Italian Baptist pastor organized what was said to be the first Protestant church of any denomination among the Italians of Tripoli.[101] Christianity was weak in this vast area.

In the ancient land of the Pharaohs the nineteenth century added other chapters to the already long political and religious history. As the eighteenth century drew toward its close Egypt was theoretically under the Sultan of Turkey. Near the end of that century Napoleon led his famous invasion of Egypt, but in 1801 the French occupation was terminated. In 1803 the British forces which had aided in the expulsion of the French also evacuated the country, although for a time in 1807 the British returned. Out of the internal conflicts which followed, Mohammed Ali, an Albanian, made himself master

---

[95] *Italian Libya* (London, H. M. Stationery Office, 1920, pp. 68), p. 37.
[96] Streit, *Atlas Hierarchicus*, p. 101.
[97] Baudrillart in Descamps, *Historie Générale Comparée des Missions*, p. 563.
[98] Gibney, *History of the London Society for Promoting Christianity amongst the Jews*, p. 190.
[99] Gibney, *op. cit.*, pp. 381, 567.
[100] Cooksey, *The Land of the Vanished Church*, p. 60; Rutherford and Glenny, *The Gospel in North Africa*, p. 245.
[101] *Sixty-ninth Annual Report of the Foreign Mission Board of the Southern Baptist Convention*, 1914, p. 60.

of the land and established a ruling line which continued into the twentieth century. As the nineteenth century progressed, Egypt more and more felt the pressure of the expanding Europe. In the 1850's permission was given the French Ferdinand de Lesseps to dig the Suez Canal. The English obtained concessions for a telegraph company and the establishment of the Bank of Egypt. Railways, telegraphs, and post offices were introduced. In 1869 the Suez Canal was opened. In the 1870's, when the national finances had badly deteriorated, the English and the French set up a dual control in the interest of their bondholders. Revolt followed and in 1882 the English stepped in and suppressed it by armed force. They were now in control. The Egyptian reigning line was continued, but under British supervision administrative and judicial reforms were carried out, extensive irrigation works were constructed, and by 1914 the land was more prosperous than it had been in many centuries, perhaps ever. Through capitulations which came as a result of the Turkish connexion, foreigners enjoyed extraterritorial privileges. A nationalist movement arose in protest against the subservience to the English, but the British protectorate continued.

Religiously Egypt presented a picture which could be understood only in light of its history. The pre-Christian cults had long since vanished, erased by the conquering faith of the Cross, but they had left their traces in popular beliefs and customs. Islam was dominant both politically and numerically. The foundations for its primacy had been laid by the Arab conquest in the seventh century. At the close of the nineteenth century 92 per cent. of the people were Moslems.

However, the Christianity of earlier days survived. The majority of the Christians were Copts. They constituted a larger proportion of the population in Upper than in Lower Egypt. At the close of the nineteenth century they numbered over half a million.[102] They were Monophysite in belief. Although Arabic had become the vernacular of the land, in their services the Copts preserved the pre-Islamic language of the land.[103] The Coptic church had long displayed effects of its Egyptian environment. Its calendar was based upon the course of the Nile's flood and it said prayers for the rise of the water which brought life to Egypt's fields and upon which the very existence of the country depended.[104] Circumcision, a pre-Christian custom, was widely practised, although the Church forbade it after baptism.[105] Under a Christian veneer many

---

[102] Watson, *Egypt and the Christian Crusade*, pp. 99, 100; Richter, *A History of Protestant Missions in the Near East*, p. 340.

[103] For a description of some of the Coptic church buildings, the ritual, and some of the customs in the fourth quarter of the nineteenth century, see Alfred J. Butler, *The Ancient Coptic Churches of Egypt* (Oxford, The Clarendon Press, 2 vols., 1884).

[104] Leeder, *Modern Sons of the Pharaohs*, pp. 66, 69.

[105] Leeder, *op. cit.*, p. 102; Blackman, *The Fellahin of Upper Egypt*, pp. 87-89.

pre-Christian burial customs and beliefs survived.[106] The Copts were, moreover, influenced by their Moslem *milieu*. Their long struggle for existence against the conquering Islam made them tenacious of their old customs and prevented continuing growth in theology or structure. They veiled their women and held them in seclusion.[107] Many of them paid reverence to Moslem saints.[108] It must be recorded, however, that Moslems also held in honour some of the Christian saints [109] and joined with the Copts in greeting the Easter season.[110] Copts are said to have multiplied in the nineteenth century.[111] Yet they were in danger of being absorbed by the prevailing Islam. Their increase was reported to be chiefly in the cities and towns, for here regular clerical ministrations could be maintained. In the rural villages the priest came but rarely, if ever, and while parents might take their children to a town for baptism, little religious instruction could be given and gradually, almost unconsciously, conformation to the surrounding Islam ensued.[112] Interestingly enough, Copts complained that the British occupation had worked against the Copts and for Islam, for the English, wishing to please the Moslem majority, kept Copts out of the high offices which had once been theirs, did not allow them representation on the provincial councils, taxed them to support schools in which Islam was taught, and, in deference to the Moslem observance of Friday, required them to work on the Christian Sunday.[113] Christians coming in from the West were critical of the Copts, partly on doctrinal grounds, but also for moral and intellectual reasons. They insisted that the priests were largely ignorant, that the average Christian could not understand the languages in which the services were said, and that in ethical practice the Copts were deceitful, grasping, intriguing, and, at times, addicted to drunkenness. The Coptic faith was reported to have little effect upon the morals of its adherents.[114] Yet the literacy rate was considerably higher among Copts than Moslems, the disparity being particularly marked among women.[115] Moreover, we hear of Moslem mothers who had lost several children asking for the blessing of a Coptic woman to preserve the life of a surviving

---

[106] Leeder, *op. cit.*, p. 132.
[107] Leeder, *op. cit.*, p. 22.
[108] Leeder, *op. cit.*, p. 136.
[109] *Ibid.*
[110] Leeder, *op. cit.*, p. 234.
[111] Leeder, *op. cit.*, p. 239.
[112] Leeder, *op. cit.*, p. 240.
[113] Leeder, *op. cit.*, pp. 329ff.; Kyriakos Mikhail, *Copts and Moslems under British Control. A Collection of Facts and a Résumé of Authoritative Opinions on the Coptic Question* (London, Smith, Elder & Co., 1911, pp. xiv, 146), pp. 19-30.
[114] Watson, *op. cit.*, pp. 111-116.
[115] Elizabeth Cooper, *The Women of Egypt* (New York, Frederick A. Stokes Co., 1914, pp. 380), p. 344.

child, saying that the Christians were good people.[116] In contrast with the Moslems, the Copts did not permit divorce.[117] In the second half of the nineteenth century and the fore part of the twentieth century there were attempts from within at reform. These arose partly from contacts with Protestants.[118] The Coptic church was far from dead.

Others of the ancient Eastern churches were also represented in Egypt. There were Syrian Christians, not very numerous, but augmented by immigration under the British regime. Many of them were in government employ. Others were village money-lenders, accused of being grasping and merciless. They had some of the vices of servitude, but were seldom corrupt and their intellectual level and adaptability were high.[119] There had been Armenian Christians in Egypt for centuries. They were few and were mostly shopkeepers, but under Mohammed Ali and his successors some of them held high government posts.[120] Greek Orthodox were also present, representatives of those who in pre-Moslem days had adhered to the Byzantine church. They were under the Patriarch of Alexandria, an official theoretically and often actually appointed by the Œcumenical Patriarch of Constantinople. Mohammed Ali, wishing to free his realm from Constantinople and its Turkish influence, himself chose a patriarch. In the latter half of the nineteenth century advance in the Greek Orthodox fold was registered. Numbers increased, largely by the immigration of Greeks and Syrians. In spite of dissensions due to rivalries between these two national groups, schools, hospitals, and other charitable works were begun.[121] There were a few Russian immigrants among the Orthodox.[122] From Syria came Jacobites, periodically torn by internal dissensions.[123] There were also a few Nestorians.[124]

Roman Catholic missions in Egypt had been continuous since the seventeenth century. Capuchins, Jesuits, and Franciscans had laboured there. In 1741 the Coptic Bishop of Jerusalem became a Roman Catholic and was placed at the head of a Uniate church made up of Copts who had submitted to the see of Peter. However, for many years the Roman Catholic enterprise did not flourish. In

---

[116] Blackman, *op. cit.*, p. 65.

[117] Blackman, *op. cit.*, p. 95.

[118] Fortescue, *The Lesser Eastern Churches*, pp. 258, 259; Adeney, *The Greek and Eastern Churches*, pp. 613, 614; Heyworth-Dunne, *An Introduction to the History of Education in Modern Egypt*, pp. 420, 421; Strothmann, *Die koptische Kirche der Neuzeit*, pp. 24-47.

[119] Cromer, *Modern Egypt*, Vol. II, pp. 214-218.

[120] Cromer, *op. cit.*, Vol. II, p. 219; Strothmann, *op. cit.*, pp. 62, 63.

[121] Attwater, *The Dissident Eastern Churches*, pp. 50, 51; Heyworth-Dunne, *op. cit.*, pp. 273-275.

[122] Richter, *A History of Protestant Missions in the Near East*, p. 340.

[123] Strothmann, *op. cit.*, pp. 55-62.

[124] Strothmann, *op. cit.*, pp. 63-65.

1840 church buildings were to be found in only Cairo and Alexandria, and this in spite of the fact that, compliant with the wish of Mohammed Ali, in 1824 the Pope had taken steps (not effective for several decades) towards giving the Coptic Uniates a patriarch of their own. In the latter half of the nineteenth century Roman Catholic Christianity enjoyed a marked growth. The Franciscans continued. The Jesuits once more appeared (1879), sent to establish schools to counteract the growing Protestant educational achievement. The Society of African Missions (Lyons) came. Teaching brothers and congregations of women arrived. Schools were multiplied and efforts for women increased. In 1859 the Franciscan Missionaries of Egypt launched charities for the Moslems. In 1895 the Patriarchate of Alexandria was erected with two suffragan bishoprics. Something of a mass movement from the Copts swelled the Uniate body, and in 1904 there were said to be 22,000 members in that church. Of these more than half were in Upper Egypt and almost all were from the very humblest social strata. Seminaries were opened for the training of a priesthood. The growth was facilitated, especially in Upper Egypt, by the large financial support given by the Emperor Francis Joseph of Austria in his role of protector of the Coptic mission. However, this assistance from a foreign monarch seemed to the Egyptian authorities to forebode political complications and for a time the trend toward the Uniate fold slowed down. Moreover, the decline of French influence and the increase of British power brought embarrassment to the Roman Catholic enterprise, staffed as it was largely by French personnel.[125]

In addition to the Coptic Uniates, Roman Catholic Christianity was reinforced by several thousands of the Latin rite.[126] These were mainly Italians, French, Austrians, Hungarians, and Spaniards.[127] It was also represented by Greek Uniates, Melchites, mostly Syro-Arabs, but with some Greek blood. They were under an ecclesiastical dignitary who bore the title of Patriarch of Antioch and All the East.[128] There were still other Roman Catholic Uniates. These included Chaldeans, or Uniates from the Nestorians, a few Armenians, Maronites (some of these were in Egypt at least as early as the eighteenth century), and Syrian Uniates of Jacobite spiritual ancestry.[129]

Protestant Christianity seems first to have come to Egypt in the seventeenth century in the person of Peter Heyling, who was seeking access to Abyssinia,

---

[125] Schwager, *Die katholische Heidenmission der Gegenwart*, pp. 255-258; Attwater, *The Catholic Eastern Churches*, pp. 136-138; Lemmens, *Geschichte der Franziskanermissionen*, pp. 22-24; *Fides Service*, Sep. 15, 1934.
[126] Schwager, *op. cit.*, pp. 258, 259.
[127] Richter, *op. cit.*, p. 340.
[128] Attwater, *op. cit.*, pp. 106-111.
[129] Strothmann, *op. cit.*, pp. 74-77.

but apparently he left no lasting trace of his presence.[130] For a time in the eighteenth century the Moravians had a mission in Egypt, chiefly among the Copts, but after a few years they deemed it wise to withdraw.[131]

The renewal of Protestant effort was through the Church Missionary Society. That body, while still young, dreamed of stimulating the Eastern churches in such fashion that they would become active in spreading the Christian faith among Moslems and pagans. In 1815 William Jowett, a Cambridge graduate, was sent to the Near East on a mission of inquiry. Among other countries, Jowett visited Egypt. He was cordially received by the Coptic Patriarch. A little later a printing establishment was set up on the island of Malta, by that time a British possession, and from it tracts and copies of the Scriptures were issued in a number of the languages of the Near East.[132] In 1825 the Church Missionary Society sent to Egypt five men who had been trained at Basel. Among them were Samuel Gobat, later Anglican Bishop of Jerusalem, and J. R. T. Lieder. Bibles and tracts were distributed among Christians and Moslems. Schools were opened, among them one for the training of Coptic clergy. The Coptic clergy were, in general, friendly.[133] In 1865 Lieder, the last of the original contingent, died, and Egypt was left without a foreign staff.[134] Towards the close of 1882, however, Egypt, now occupied by the English, was once more given a missionary.[135] In the meantime Mary Louisa Whately, daughter of an Anglican Archbishop of Dublin, who had first visited Egypt for her health (1856), had carried on schools, at the outset from her private means, later with financial assistance from the Society for Promoting Female Education in the East and from friends. She continued until her death, in 1889.[136] The Church Missionary Society developed hospitals and schools and sought primarily to reach Moslems. It gathered a small handful of converts from Islam. It also attracted a few Copts.[137]

[130] Richter, *Mission und Evangelisation im Orient*, pp. 56, 57.
[131] Watson, *Egypt and the Christian Crusade*, pp. 132-142; Hutton, *A History of Moravian Missions*, pp. 161-164.
[132] Stock, *The History of the Church Missionary Society*, Vol. I, pp. 222-228.
[133] Stock, *op. cit.*, Vol. I, pp. 350, 351.
[134] Stock, *op. cit.*, Vol. III, pp. 113, 114.
[135] Stock, *op. cit.*, Vol. III, p. 266.
[136] E. J. Whately, *The Life and Work of Mary Louisa Whately* (London, The Religious Tract Society, no date, pp. 159), *passim;* M. L. Whately, *Ragged Life in Egypt, and More about Ragged Life in Egypt* (London, Seeley, Jackson, and Halliday, new edition, 1870, pp. 276), *passim.*
[137] Stock, *op. cit.*, Vol. III, pp. 746-750; *Proceedings of the Church Missionary Society for Africa and the East . . . 1913-14*, pp. 82-86. For biographies of two leaders in the British Student Christian Movement who became members of the mission and sought especially to reach Moslems, see W. H. T. Gairdner, *D. M. Thornton* (London, Hodder and Stoughton, 1908, pp. xiv, 283), *passim;* Constance E. Padwick, *Temple Gairdner of Cairo* (London, Society for Promoting Christian Knowledge, 1929, pp. xvi, 330), *passim;*

Almost as early as the Church Missionary Society, the London Society for Promoting Christianity amongst the Jews became intermittently active in Egypt. One of its representatives, the much-travelled German Christian Jew, Joseph Wolff, visited Alexandria and Cairo in 1821.[138] In 1847 resident missionaries were placed in Cairo, but after a few years the enterprise was suspended. Later, however, missionaries were placed for longer and shorter intervals in Alexandria and Cairo.[139] The Church of Scotland long had a mission for the Jews in Alexandria.[140]

The leading Protestant mission in Egypt was that of the United Presbyterian Church of North America. It was usually known simply as the American Mission. It began in 1854 with an enterprise of the Associate Reformed Church of the West, one of the bodies which later joined to constitute the United Presbyterian Church.[141] By 1875 it had stations from Alexandria to Assiut and could count nearly 600 church members.[142] This was in spite of persecutions by Copts and the civil authorities. In 1878 a secular head of the Protestants was appointed and thus provision was made to place that group on the same legal basis with the other religious bodies of the land.[143] In 1895 church members had increased to 4,554.[144] This growth was almost entirely by accessions from the Copts. The mission was strongest in and around Assiut. Moslems were not neglected, but, because of popular feeling, conversions from among them were next to impossible. The American Mission had a number of schools, culminating in a college at Assiut. It trained a native clergy. It maintained hospitals. In 1895 the native church was given a presbyterial organization. In 1899 this was enlarged to the status of a synod with four presbyteries. Here was a rapidly growing, vigorous church with its own clergy.[145]

In addition, several smaller Protestant agencies, British and Continental, entered the country. In 1855 Spittler conceived a plan of a chain of twelve stations (the so-called Apostolic Highway) up the Nile to Abyssinia. Several of these

---

and *W. H. T. to his Friends. Some Letters and Informal Writings of Canon W. H. Temple Gairdner of Cairo 1873-1878* (London, Society for Promoting Christian Knowledge, 1930, pp. vii, 173), *passim.*

[138] Wolff, *Travels and Adventures*, pp. 107ff.

[139] Gidney, *History of the London Society for Promoting Christianity amongst the Jews,* pp. 102, 103, 121, 261, 262, 305, 306, 387, 388, 566, 615.

[140] *Reports on the Schemes of the Church of Scotland,* 1878, pp. 344ff.; 1911, pp. 392, 393.

[141] Watson, *The American Mission in Egypt,* pp. 61ff.

[142] Watson, *op. cit.,* pp. 279, 280.

[143] Watson, *op. cit.,* p. 327.

[144] Watson, *op. cit.,* p. 386.

[145] Watson, *Egypt and the Christian Crusade,* pp. 152-197; Rena L. Hogg, *A Master-Builder on the Nile. Being a Record of the Life and Aims of John Hogg, D.D.* (Chicago, Fleming H. Revell Co., 1914, pp. 204).

were inaugurated, three of them in Egypt, but altered conditions in Abyssinia led to the abandonment of the project.[146] In 1856 and 1857 Fliedner, the founder of the famous Kaiserswerth institutions,[147] while in Egypt for his health, began a hospital in Alexandria. In 1870 a hospital was commenced in Cairo and staffed with Kaiserswerth deaconesses.[148] In 1892 the North Africa Mission sent a representative to Egypt, primarily for Moslems.[149] Beginning with 1818 the British and Foreign Bible Society was active, although not continuously.[150] The Egypt General Mission, or the Egypt Mission Band, from Britain, came in 1898.[151] The Sudan Pioneer Mission, from Germany, was begun in 1901 and, until the Sudan should be opened, found a foothold in Upper Egypt.[152] The Canadian Holiness Mission and the Pentecostal Bands of the World were also present.[153] In 1865 or 1866 a Dutch mission was founded which centred about an orphanage.[154] The Nile Mission Press owed its existence to Annie Van Sommer, of England.[155] In Port Said the Peniel American Mission and the Bethel Orphanage laboured chiefly among children. Several organizations, including churches, the Young Women's Christian Association, and homes for sailors and soldiers, ministered to the European population.[156]

In the year 1914 Christianity was much stronger in Egypt than it had been at the outset of the nineteenth century. It had made numerical gains. These were presumably partly due to an increase of births over deaths in the Christian population, but they were certainly due in part to immigration. A few accessions had come from the Moslem community. There had probably been some losses to Islam. Christianity became more varied. Roman Catholic Christianity grew. Various forms of Protestantism entered and one, American Presbyterianism, registered a notable growth. This increase in variety was partly through immigration but was chiefly at the expense of the Coptic church. Yet if divisions in the Christian community multiplied, vitality increased. Missionaries from the West brought something of the vigour which marked the Christianity of western Europe and the United States in the nineteenth century. Nor were the Moslems

[146] Richter, *Mission und Evangelisation im Orient*, pp. 249ff.
[147] Vol. IV, p. 148.
[148] Richter, *op. cit.*, p. 252.
[149] Rutherford and Glenny, *The Gospel in North Africa*, p. 227.
[150] Canton, *The History of the British and Foreign Bible Society*, Vol. II, pp. 3, 26, 378.
[151] Watson, *Egypt and the Christian Crusade*, p. 202; W. J. W. Roome, *"Blessed be Egypt." A Missionary Story* (London, Marshall Brothers, 1898, pp. 100), *passim*.
[152] Watson, *op. cit.*, p. 202; Richter, *op. cit.*, pp. 250-252.
[153] Watson, *op. cit.*, p. 203.
[154] Richter, *op. cit.*, p. 249.
[155] Watson, *op. cit.*, pp. 203, 204; Arthur T. Upson, *High Lights in the Near East. Reminiscences of Nearly 40 Years' Service* (London, Marshall, Morgan & Scott, no date, pp. 128), *passim*.
[156] Watson, *op. cit.*, pp. 203, 204.

neglected. Almost all the missions had made some contact with them. Cairo was, moreover, becoming a centre for the preparation of missionaries for the Moslem world. The Nile Mission Press supplied Christian literature for Moslems in about thirty different countries.[157] In 1912 a school was opened to train Protestant missionaries for Moslem lands by the study of Arabic and Islam.[158] In the age-long struggle against Islam results which could be measured in statistics might be small. Yet momentum was being gathered.

Stretching southward from Egypt to Uganda and the Belgian Congo there was what in 1914 was known as the Anglo-Egyptian Sudan. As its unifying natural feature it had the valley of the Nile, but it was not entirely confined to the latter. Its peoples embraced a medley of races, with Hamites and Arabs prevailing in the North and Negroes in the South. There was much mixture of stocks. At the close of our period the population was estimated at something over three millions. In the last quarter of the nineteenth century it had declined by about three-fourths, but by 1914 it was recouping some of its losses. Mohammed Ali annexed the region to Egypt. Succeeding rulers of his line extended their inherited borders. In 1881 a fanatical Moslem movement led by one who claimed to be the Mahdi sought to extinguish Egyptian rule and drive out the foreigners. The English, in the early stages of their occupation of Egypt, at first decided to evacuate the Sudan and then, several years after the tragic death of the governor-general, the picturesque, deeply religious, and heroic Charles George Gordon, at Khartum (1885), undertook the reconquest of the land. The reconquest was accomplished between 1896 and 1899. An Egyptian-British condominium was set up. In the ensuing peace the rehabilitation of the region was begun. Religiously Islam prevailed in the North and animism among the blacks of the South.[159]

Christianity had been introduced into the country at least as early as the sixth century and possibly before that time. For many generations it had been very strong. Only slowly did it succumb to the aggressive Islam.[160] Even in the middle of the nineteenth century a few scattered Coptic and Armenian Christians were found.[161]

[157] Strong and Warnshuis, *Directory of Foreign Missions*, p. 32.
[158] *Proceedings of the Church Missionary Society for Africa and the East . . . 1913-14*, pp. 82, 83.
[159] *Anglo-Egyptian Sudan*, pp. 1-58.
[160] Vol. II, pp. 231-234, 303.
[161] *The Sixty-fourth Report of the British and Foreign Bible Society* (1868), p. 136; *The Sixty-fifth Report of the British and Foreign Bible Society* (1869), p. 175.

Attempts to strengthen and spread Christianity came in the nineteenth century in the course of that phenomenal expansion of Christian missions which was one of the outstanding features of the period. As was to be expected, Christianity had its chief growth in the animistic South rather than in the Moslem North. Indeed, after the English had subdued the country they forbade Christian missions in a North in which Moslem fanaticism had so recently been rampant and where it might readily once more raise its head. In the South they encouraged missions and, to prevent overlapping and competition, allocated a distinct area to each body that was represented.[162]

Roman Catholic Christianity was first on the field. In 1846 Rome created the vicariate apostolic of Central Africa or the Sudan, an ecclesiastical division which at the outset also embraced the Sahara. As pro-vicar the Holy See appointed a Jesuit, Ryllo, who when a missionary in Syria had become aware of the Sudan through a merchant and later, while rector of the College of the Propaganda in Rome, had revealed his dreams to the proper authorities in that city. Ryllo sailed in 1847, together with three Italian priests and Knoblecher, an Austrian priest under the Propaganda. In 1848 the party reached Khartum and there made its temporary home. Within a few months Ryllo died. Led by Knoblecher and reinforced by a few Jesuits, the saddened party went a sixty-four days' journey farther up the Nile, to found a mission in one of the most notorious centres of the slave trade. Knoblecher soon returned to Europe for help. There, in Austria, he organized an association for the support of the enterprise with branches in every diocese. The Emperor Francis Joseph I gave it his protection, backed it by a substantial financial grant, and on its behalf opened an Austrian consulate in Khartum. A station was founded on the White Nile south of Lado, not far from Uganda. Franciscans came from Venetia and the Tyrol. In 1867 Daniel Comboni founded in Verona a missionary institute for the Sudan. In that year he also inaugurated in Cairo a centre among the large Negro population of that city. There, he hoped, new recruits could become acclimated before going farther south. Sisters joined the enterprise. Gradually, beginning in 1873, Comboni opened various stations from Khartum southward. More deaths followed, and in the 1880's the storm let loose by the Mahdi brought great suffering to the mission. Comboni died in 1881. The mission survived in Cairo and spread to the Red Sea and up the Nile to Assuan. The Verona institute became a congregation under the name of the Sons of the Holy Heart. In 1900, after the British reconquest, the mission once more pushed up the Nile and established itself in the southern part of the Sudan, among the pagans.[163] Progress was

[162] *Anglo-Egyptian Sudan*, pp. 57, 58.
[163] Schwager, *Die katholische Heidenmission der Gegenwart*, pp. 178-184. On Comboni

slow. Not until 1911 were the first ten converts baptized. It was well after 1914 before the gains began to be rapid.[164]

Protestant Christianity came at least as early as the 1860's. In that decade a representative of the British and Foreign Bible Society was for a time in Khartum.[165] In 1865 Spittler, pursuing his plan of a chain of stations from Cairo to Abyssinia, founded a centre in Khartum.[166] Not long after the death of Gordon a fund was raised to bring into being a memorial mission.[167] However, continuous Protestant effort was to wait until the establishment of British rule.

In 1899 the Church Missionary Society fulfilled a long-cherished dream and moved into the Sudan. For a time the government did not allow it in the North, but assigned it a field in the South. By 1914, however, it had a hospital and schools in the North. Yet in that year it had only 6 communicants in the North and 105 in the South.[168]

The United Presbyterians, the "American Mission" in Egypt, for years looked longingly southward. In 1899 it sent a commission to visit the Sudan. In 1900 a party which included the first foreign missionary of the Egyptian church went south. In the North the United Presbyterians cared for their fellow church members who had moved in from Egypt. In the South they reached out to the non-Christians, pagans. By 1914 promising beginnings had been made in both sections.[169]

In 1913 the Sudan United Mission reached into the South.[170]

---

see *Il Servo di Dio. Mons. Daniele Comboni Vicario Apostolico dell'Africa Centrale, Fondatore delle Missioni Africane di Verona e delle Pie Madri della Nigrizia* (Verona, Istituto Missioni Africane, 1928, pp. viii, 330), *passim*. On sufferings under the Mahdi, see F. R. Wingate, *Ten Years' Captivity in the Mahdi's Camp, 1882-1892, from the Original Manuscripts of Father Joseph Ohrwalder* (London, Sampson Low, Marston & Co., 14th ed., no date, pp. xvi, 471), *passim*. On one of the priests of the renewed mission see Cesare Romano, *Un Apostolo Moderno dell'Africa Tenebrosa. Cenni biografici del P. Guiseppe M. Beduschi dei Figli del Sacro Cuore* (Verona, Istituto Missioni Africane, 1927, pp. vii, 344).

[164] Lesourd, *L'Année Missionnaire*, 1931, p. 224; Lemmens, *Geschichte der Franziskanermissionen*, p. 24.

[165] *The Sixty-third Report of the British and Foreign Bible Society* (1867), p. 151; *The Sixty-fourth Report of the British and Foreign Bible Society* (1868), p. 136; *The Sixty-fifth Report of the British and Foreign Bible Society* (1869), p. 175.

[166] Richter, *Mission und Evangelisation im Orient*, p. 249.

[167] Stock, *The History of the Church Missionary Society*, Vol. III, pp. 318, 319.

[168] W. Wilson Cash, *The Changing Sudan* (London, Church Missionary Society, 1930, pp. vii, 88), pp. 28-34, 46-55; Watson, *The Sorrow and Hope of the Egyptian Sudan*, pp. 132-134; *Proceedings of the Church Missionary Society for Africa and the East . . . 1913-14*, pp. 86-88.

[169] Watson, *op. cit.*, pp. 134-178; J. Kelly Giffen, *The Egyptian Sudan* (Chicago, Fleming H. Revell Co., 1905, pp. 252), pp. 56ff.; Ried F. Shields, *Behind the Garden of Allah* (Philadelphia, United Presbyterian Board of Foreign Missions, 1937, pp. 196), pp. 63ff.

[170] *Anglo-Egyptian Sudan*, p. 58.

East of the Sudan stretched Abyssinia, or, officially, Ethiopia. In 1914 it was a purely inland realm, shut off from the sea by British, French, and Italian possessions. Much of it was mountainous, with elevated plateaus broken by canyons. Topographically it was highly varied. The population, too, was far from uniform. While most of it was Hamitic, this term embraced several groups, among them the Abyssinians and the Gallas. On the western border there was a strong admixture of Negro blood. The monarchs claimed descent, on decidedly dubious historical grounds, from the kings of Aksum and ultimately from a son of Solomon and the Queen of Sheba. In the nineteenth century the most notable rulers were Theodore II, who reigned from 1855 to 1868, and Menelik, who reigned from 1889 to 1913. Menelik greatly extended the borders of his realm. He decisively defeated the Italians (1895-1896) and compelled them to surrender the protectorate which they had asserted in the 1880's. Under Menelik, moreover, the rising flood of European cultural influence made itself markedly felt. However, relatively secure in their remote fastnesses, in the main the people of the land pursued their traditional ways.[171]

Religiously the core of the realm was Christian and had been such for many centuries.[172] The church was Monophysite in creed. Ecclesiastically it was subordinate to the Coptic Patriarch. That dignitary consecrated its head, the Abuna, who was chosen from a Coptic monastery. The Abyssinian church had distinct local characteristics and had been profoundly influenced by its immediate environment. It had ceased to be actively missionary, although Menelik and one other of the rulers in their conquests required of some of the vanquished the nominal acceptance of the official faith. There were as well many Moslems. Judaism was the religion of the Falashas, an Hamitic group. Paganism, of several kinds, was present, especially among some of the Gallas and tribes in which Negro blood was strong.[173]

From the second quarter of the nineteenth century Roman Catholics were active in Abyssinia. As we saw in an earlier volume,[174] in the sixteenth and seventeenth centuries the Jesuits made persistent and for a time largely successful efforts to bring the Abyssinian church into fellowship with Rome. However, a violent reaction drove them from the country. The Franciscans attempted to renew Roman Catholic influence, but with no continuing results. In the second quarter of the nineteenth century Roman Catholic activity was

---

[171] For a good summary account of Abyssinia, see *Abyssinia* (London, H. M. Stationery Office, 1920, pp. 109), *passim*.

[172] Vol. I, pp. 236, 237.

[173] *Abyssinia*, pp. 57-61; Charles F. Rey, *Unconquered Abyssinia* (London, Seeley, Service & Co., 1923, pp. 312), pp. 122-143.

[174] Vol. III, pp. 79, 80.

renewed. In 1839 Italian Lazarists penetrated into Abyssinia. Conversions from the Abyssinian church followed. At times entire villages came over. A beginning was made in training native priests. Persecutions which broke out from time to time rendered the growth irregular, but by 1853 there were said to be 5,000 and by 1885, 30,000 Roman Catholics. French Lazarists were substituted for the Italians of that order. The international complications under the reign of Menelik brought embarrassment.[175] On the eve of 1914 the vicariate apostolic which embraced the heart of the country had only 1,500 Roman Catholics.[176] A numerically more successful mission was that of the Italian Capuchins in the southern part of the land, with its stronghold among the Gallas. Its great figure was Guglielmo Massaja (1809-1889). In 1849 Massaja was appointed head of the newly founded vicariate apostolic of Gallas. However, not until 1853 did he succeed in overcoming the various obstacles and actually reach his field. A few of his colleagues had arrived before him. French Capuchins came to his assistance and in 1863 the mission was transferred to them. Yet Massaja remained on. Considerable accessions came in more than one region. Provision was made for the training of a native clergy. For this purpose Massaja founded a seminary in Marseilles which was later moved to Kaffa, in the southern part of Abyssinia. In 1879 a turn in the political wheel in Abyssinia drove Massaja and his fellow missionaries into exile, but the orphaned flock was cared for by the native clergy. Massaja, now an old man, did not return, but went to Rome and was raised to the cardinalate.[177] In the 1880's partial success was had in re-entering the land from the West and also through French Somaliland, but the resurgent Moslem power constrained some of the Gallas to adopt Islam, and the Mahdi storm brought additional peril. The conquest of part of the land of the Gallas by Menelik in the latter part of the 1880's re-opened the door. Because of the influence of Massaja's successor, Taurin, with Menelik, Roman Catholicism enjoyed a certain amount of prestige. In the first decade of the twentieth century, however, persecution was again its lot. Yet the growing penetration of Abyssinia by Western culture faciliated the spread of Roman Catholicism.[178] In 1913 it counted 19,000 native adherents in

---

[175] Schwager, *Die katholische Heidenmission der Gegenwart*, pp. 260-262; Demimuid, *Vie du Vénérable Justin de Jacobis . . . Premier Vicaire Apostolique de l'Abyssinie* (Paris, Anciénne Maison Charles Douniol, 1906, pp. vi, 415), *passim;* Coste, *La Congregation de la Mission*, pp. 215ff.

[176] Streit, *Atlas Hierarchichus,* p. 101.

[177] Guglielmo Massaja, *I Miei Trentacinque Anni di Missione nell' Alta Etiopia* (Rome, Tipografia Poliglotta, 1895, pp. 287), *passim;* Schwager, *op. cit.,* pp. 174-176; Aurelius, *De Kapucijnen en de Missie,* pp. 54-59; Lady Herbert, *Abyssinia and Its Apostle* (London, Burns, Oates, & Co., no date, pp. vi, 200), *passim.*

[178] Schwager, *op. cit.,* pp. 176-178; Huonder, *Der einheimische Klerus in den Heidenländern,* pp. 239-245.

the vicariate apostolic which embraced the southern part of the country.[179]

The efforts of Protestant Christianity to reach Abyssinia dated from the seventeenth century. In the 1630's Peter Heyling arrived. He was in the land for a number of years, but he had no successor. In the eighteenth century the wide-ranging Moravians sought entrance through Egypt, but in vain.[180]

The nineteenth century renewal of Protestant endeavour slightly antedated the resumption of Roman Catholic missions. Of the group of young men from Basel whom the Church Missionary Society sent to Egypt in 1825, two, Samuel Gobat and Christian Kugler, were appointed with the hope that they might sometime make their way into Abyssinia. A few years earlier the Church Missionary Society and the British and Foreign Bible Society had interested themselves in the publication of portions of a translation of the Bible into Amharic, the vernacular of part of the country.[181] Gobat and Kugler reached Abyssinia in 1830. There they made some progress, but Kugler lost his life through an accident and Gobat was forced by illness to return to Europe. Later in the 1830's Gobat was in Abyssinia again for a few years, but poor health once more compelled his retirement.[182] Four other Basel men, among them J. L. Krapf, were sent to Abyssinia by the Church Missionary Society. The influence of Roman Catholic priests strengthened the opposition to them, and they left.[183] However, Krapf went into another part of the country and there was brought into touch with pagan Gallas. Out of this contact sprang his enterprise in East Africa whose heroically painful but successful course we noted in the preceding volume.[184]

In 1855 came four young men from Spittler's Pilgrim Mission of St. Chrishoma, where lay evangelists were being trained. They had studied in Jerusalem with Gobat, then bishop in that city, and Krapf introduced one of their number, Johann Flad, to their field. It was hoped that after the fashion of the Moravians they could quietly labour at handicrafts and gradually stimulate the emergence of small inner circles which would reform the Abyssinian church.

[179] Streit, op. cit., p. 101.

[180] Richter, Mission und Evangelisation im Orient, pp. 56-58.

[181] Stock, The History of the Church Missionary Society, Vol. I, pp. 227, 228, 351.

[182] Samuel Gobat, pp. 101-185; Samuel Gobat, Journal of a Three Years' Residence in Abyssinia, in Furtherance of the Objects of the Church Missionary Society (London, Hatchard & Son, 1834, pp. xxi, 371), passim; Stock, op. cit., Vol. I, pp. 351-353.

[183] Stock, op. cit., Vol. I, p. 353; Krapf, Travels, pp. 12-20; Journals of the Rev. Messrs. Isenberg and Krapf, Missionaries of the Church Missionary Society, Detailing their Proceedings in the Kingdom of Shoa, and Journeys in Other Parts of Abyssinia, in the Years 1839, 1840, 1841, and 1842 (London, Seeley, Burnside, and Seeley, 1853, pp. xxvii, 529), passim; Carl Wilhelm Isenberg, Abessinien . . . Tagebuch meiner dritten Missionsreise, von Mai 1842 bis December 1843 (Bonn, Adolph Marcus, 1844, pp. xx, 218), passim.

[184] Krapf, op. cit., pp. 20ff.; Stock, op. cit., Vol. I, p. 353.

Before long Flad, the outstanding member of this quartette, entered the service of the London Society for Promoting Christianity amongst the Jews. In 1860 that organization inaugurated an enterprise for the Falashas who, it will be recalled, were Jews by religion. For many years persecution rendered continuous residence of the missionaries impossible. Famous among the pioneers for his sufferings through long imprisonment was the converted German Jew, Henry Aaron Stern, who had travelled widely in the Near East as a missionary to his race. Yet Flad made visits to the country and native agents laboured so faithfully that by 1910 it was said that 18,000 Falashas had been baptized. For many years these baptisms were into membership in Abyssinian church.[185]

In 1866 came Swedish missionaries of the *Evangeliska Fosterlands-Stiftelsen*. Krapf had been largely instrumental in interesting that organization in Africa. A centre was established in Massawa on the coast, in what was later an Italian possession, Eritrea.[186] There the mission persevered. Eventually it extended its operations into Abyssinia proper, and into Jubaland, in the southern part of Italian Somaliland. Krapf directed its attention to the Gallas and it succeeded in reaching some of that group of peoples.[187]

Beginning in 1888 there was a movement to bring the Abyssinian church into union with the Russian Orthodox Church. The ruler of Abyssinia sought Russian assistance against the encroaching English, French, and Italians. There was an ambition, too, on the part of the ruler to free the Church from dependence on the Coptic Patriarch by forming a connexion with Russia. The effort, however, came to nought.[188]

[185] Gidney, *The History of the London Society for Promoting Christianity amongst the Jews*, pp. 366-375, 476-484, 562-565; Johann Martin Flad, *60 Jahre in der Mission unter den Falaschas in Abessinien* (Giessen, Brunnen-Verlag, 1922, pp. 442), *passim;* Martin Flad, *Ein Leben für Abessinien*, edited by Hans-Georg Feller (Giessen, Brunnen-Verlag, 2d ed., 1936, pp. 228), *passim;* M. Margoliouth, *Abyssinia* (London, W. Macintosh, 1866, pp. 117), pp. 39ff.; *The Autobiography of Theophilus Waldmeier*, pp. 3-82; T. Waldmeier and J. M. Flad, *Ons Zendingwerk in Abessinië* (Zwolle, Van Hoogstratten & Gorter, 1870, pp. 242), *passim;* Theophil Waldmeier, *Erlebnisse in Abessinien in den Jahren 1858-1868* (Basel, C. J. Spittler, 1869, pp. vi, 151), *passim;* Henry A. Stern, *The Captive Missionary* (London, Cassell, Peffer, and Galpin, no date, pp. xii, 397), *passim;* Isaacs, *Biography of the Rev. Henry Aaron Stern*, pp. 139-397; Pauline Flad, *Eine braune Perle. Erinnerungen aus dem Missionsleben in der afrikanischen Schweiz* (Giessen, Brunnen-Verlag, 1929, pp. 58).

[186] G. E. Beskow, *Den Svenska Missionen i Ost-Afrika* (Stockholm, Fosterlands-Stiftelsens Förlags-Expedition, 1884, pp. 271), *passim.*

[187] Nils Hylander, *Morgonljus. Femtioårigt Missionsarbete på Natthöljd Jord 1865-1916* (Stockholm, Evangeliska Fosterlands-Stiftelsens Förlags-Expedition, 1917, pp. 257), *passim;* Adolph Kolmodin, *Galla och Evangelium* (Stockholm, Fosterlands-Stiftelsens Förlags-Expedition, 1885, pp. 91); G. E. Beskow, *Den Svenska Missionen i Ost-Afrika* (Stockholm, Fosterlands-Stiftelsens Förlags-Expedition, 1887, pp. 187).

[188] Lübeck, *Die russischen Missionen*, p. 59.

Separating Abyssinia from the sea in 1914 were possessions of western European powers, the creations of the empire-building of the nineteenth century and chiefly of the 1880's. Proceeding from south to north these were Italian Somaliland, British Somaliland, French Somaliland, and Eritrea. The population was Hamitic, here and there with Negro and Negroid admixtures. In 1914 it probbly totalled less than a million and a half. The prevailing religion was Islam. European control was largely in the form of protectorates which permitted the native governments to continue.

Christianity was propagated in all four of these territories. From very early times it had been present in much of the area. It survived, notably in French Somaliland and Eritrea, in the Monophysite form which it had among the Copts of Egypt and in Abyssinia. The missions of the nineteenth century were from western Europe and were both Roman Catholic and Protestant. Roman Catholic Christianity came to Italian Somaliland in 1906 in the persons of Italian Trinitarians. Nearly two years earlier the Trinitarians had sought entrance but had been denied by the Italian governor on the ground of Moslem fanaticism. They waited near the border in British East Africa. When permission was gained to come to their chosen field they settled in the southern section, which, incidentally, was the most populous part of the country. They were given a substantial subsidy by the Italian colonization company. They engaged in the care of the sick and by the purchase and manumitting of youthful slaves, chiefly Negroes, built up a nucleus of a community which could be trained in the faith.[189] Also in the first decade of the twentieth century the Swedish Protestant mission which we mentioned two paragraphs above opened stations in British East Africa in the lower part of the valley of the Juba in a region which after 1914 was ceded to Italy.[190] In British Somaliland the Capuchins, coming from Aden, made a beginning in 1892. They concentrated their attention upon children and youths. Some of these were gathered in time of famine. By 1914 there were several hundred converts.[191] There seem to have been no Protestant missions in the British protectorate. French Somaliland was included in the field of the Capuchins. So, too, was Eritrea, where by 1914 there were more than 20,000 Roman Catholics, of whom about 2,700 were Europeans and the remainder mainly from the Monophysites.[192] In Eritrea was the chief strength of the Swedish Protestant mission.[193]

---

189 Schwager, *Die katholische Heidenmission der Gegenwart,* pp. 171, 172.
190 Hylander, *Morgenljus,* table in rear entitled "Historisk overblick över huvudmissionsstationerna i Ost-Afrika."
191 Schwager, *op. cit.,* pp. 172, 173; Streit, *Atlas Hierarchicus,* p. 101.
192 Schwager, *op. cit.,* p. 262; Streit, *op. cit.,* p. 101.
193 Hylander, *op. cit.,* pp. 11ff.

We must now turn from Africa to western Asia. First of all we must visit Palestine, not only because it was the birthplace of Christianity, but also because physically it is so closely connected with Africa. Although, at the dawn of the nineteenth century, the land was part of the Turkish Empire, was ruled by Moslems, and was predominantly Moslem by faith, it still had numbers of Christians. These were of many churches, for the Holy Land, especially Jerusalem, was a goal of pilgrims, as it had been for centuries. Here, too, were Jews, an appealing though stubborn field for the Christian missionary. In the 1830's Mohammed Ali of Egypt extended his rule into Palestine, but in the 1840's, assisted by British, Austrian, and Russian fleets and by internal revolt, the Turks re-established their authority. In the latter half of the nineteenth century the lot of the country improved. Some of the appliances of western European culture penetrated the land. Travellers and pilgrims from the West increased. The Zionist movement for the establishment of a Jewish state in Palestine contributed to the founding of Jewish colonies.

It was to be expected that, accompanying and even preceding the invasion of Western culture, missionaries from Europe and America would be attracted to Palestine. These came in great variety from the Russian Orthodox, Roman Catholic, and Protestant communions.

Russian Orthodox missions were late in arriving and were closely allied with the attempts of the Czars to extend their political influence. In her effort to gain territory, especially in the Balkans, at the expense of the decadent Ottoman Empire, Russia posed as the successor of the Byzantine emperors in a protectorate over all Greek Orthodox Christians. She tried to bring the Orthodox Patriarchs of Antioch and Jerusalem under her influence. In 1882 the Imperial Orthodox Palestine Association was constituted by the Grand Prince Sergius Alexandrovich to enhance the prestige of the Orthodox Church in Syria and Palestine. It collaborated with the Orthodox Missionary Society[194] and possessed ample financial resources. In 1898 the Russians had 64 schools and 213 teachers with 6,739 pupils in Syria and Palestine. Within the next six years the number of pupils almost doubled. Medical clinics and at least one hospital were also opened.[195] However, the Russian enterprises were insecure. They did not take firm root in Palestine and their backing in the mother country was more from imperial ambition than from religious conviction.

Roman Catholic missions were much earlier on the ground and were far more varied and extensive. For centuries the Franciscans had been present as cus-

[194] See Vol. IV, p. 107.
[195] Lübeck, *Die russischen Missionen*, pp. 31-45.

todians of the holy sites to which Roman Catholic pilgrims came.[196] They had made a few converts, chiefly from non-Roman Catholic churches. In the fore part of the nineteenth century accessions increased.[197] With the re-establishment of Turkish rule with European assistance, in the 1840's the Roman Catholic forces were augumented. In 1847 Pope Pius IX revived the long-lapsed Roman Catholic Patriarchate and appointed Joseph Valerga, a Genoese, who had had missionary experience in the Near East, as Patriarch of Jerusalem.[198] Valerga was energetic and was gifted in Oriental languages. Under him marked advance was registered. One of his first acts was to found a seminary for the training of a native clergy. Before many years his priests were seeking to bring non-Roman Catholic Christians into fellowship with Rome.[199] Fresh interest was aroused in Roman Catholic circles in Europe. In the 1850's an enterprise was begun in France for schools in the Near East, in Germany the Association of the Holy Sepulchre was constituted, and in Austria the Association of the Immaculate Conception was organized with the entire Near East as its objective.[200] In the 1880's the Palestine Association of Catholic Germany came into being, and in 1895 it was consolidated with the earlier Association of the Holy Sepulchre to form the German Association of the Holy Land.[201]

For a time the Franciscans sought to maintain their monopoly of the field. As late as the twentieth century about two-thirds of the Roman Catholics in Palestine were in parishes served by them.[202]

However, other orders entered. The break in the Franciscan monopoly seems to have been due to Lavigerie. Supported by French diplomacy which sought, in the interests of national prestige and power (albeit with only partial success), the assignment of the Holy Land to French clergy, Lavigerie obtained entrance to Jersualem (1878) for his recently founded White Fathers. They opened a seminary for the training of clergy for the Melchites, a Uniate body.[203] In the course of the next thirty-five years additional French bodies followed—brothers who gave themselves to teaching, Fathers of the Holy Heart of Betharram, Fathers of Sion, Dominicans, Assumptionists, Trappists, Bene-

[196] For a partial picture of the Franciscan mission in the 1770's by a German friar who served in Palestine in those years, see Salvius Obermayr, *Im Heiligen Lande!* edited by Erhard Schlund (Trier, Paulinus Druckerei, 1913, pp. 183), *passim.*

[197] Lemmens, *Geschichte der Franziskanermissionen*, pp. 76, 77.

[198] Lübeck, *Die katholische Orientmission*, p. 52.

[199] Schwager, *Die katholische Heidenmission der Gegenwart*, pp. 268, 269.

[200] Schwager, *op. cit.*, p. 269; Lübeck, *op. cit.*, p. 54.

[201] Berg, *Die katholische Heidenmission als Kulturträger*, Vol. I, pp. 183ff.

[202] Lemmens, *op. cit.*, p. 77.

[203] Lübeck, *op. cit.*, p. 55; Bouniol, *The White Fathers and Their Missions*, pp. 49-51, 288-296.

dictines, Carmelites, Passionists, and Lazarists. Many congregations of women also entered, most of them French, but at least one Italian and one German.[204] They conducted schools and ministered to the sick.[205] The presence of large numbers of French missionaries witnessed both to the prominence of France in nineteenth century Roman Catholic missions and to the French political influence in the Near East which sought to buttress itself through the French protectorate of Roman Catholic interests. Restive under the French predominance, Germans strove to offset it by new and special enterprises of their own.[206] Italian Salesians came and founded orphanages and an agricultural school.[207]

For many years Roman Catholic missions, led by the Franciscans, endeavoured to assimilate all their converts to the Latin rite. This had the effect of denationalizing their adherents and making them conform to Occidental ways. In the last quarter of the nineteenth century a different policy began to be pursued. It placed emphasis upon the Uniate bodies and thus sought to make Roman Catholic Christianity less exotic. The Uniate churches preserved many of the forms and much of the structure of the Eastern non-Roman Catholic churches. A convert from one of the latter would, therefore, presumably feel more at home in the Uniate church which had arisen from his own communion than in the Latin rite. By pioneering in the training of clergy for the Melchite Uniates, Lavigerie aided in the transition to the new emphasis. Others of the orders followed this precedent. Increasingly the Papacy encouraged the Uniate churches.[208] In doing so it believed that it was witnessing to the claim of the Roman Church to be catholic, the true fold of all Christians.

By the year 1914, then, Roman Catholicism in Palestine was varied. It embraced adherents of various rites. It was represented by numerous orders, congregations, and seculars. It was to be found on the east as well as the west side of the Jordan. It was not only at the sacred shrines of the faith. It also conducted schools, orphanages, and agricultural enterprises.

Protestant activity in Palestine began slightly earlier than did the revival of Roman Catholic missions. As the century progressed it increased both in numerical strength and in variety. Not only were some of the major missionary societies represented, but many small groups also appeared, some of them moved by the anticipation of the second coming of Christ. Protestant missions in Palestine were inaugurated in the 1820's at about the same time, by both the American Board of Commissioners for Foreign Missions and the London So-

[204] Lübeck, *op. cit.*, pp. 55, 56.
[205] Lübeck, *op. cit.*, pp. 64, 65.
[206] Lübeck, *op. cit.*, pp. 56-58.
[207] Lübeck, *op. cit.*, p. 63.
[208] Lübeck, *op. cit.*, pp. 58-62.

ciety for Promoting Christianity amongst the Jews. In 1818 the American Board appointed Levi Parsons and Pliny Fisk to go to Palestine and from there, as its first missionaries in the Near East, to survey the entire region. Parsons reached Jerusalem early in 1821 but died the following year in Alexandria, where he had gone for his health.[209] Other representatives of the American Board lived in Jerusalem for longer or shorter intervals, but in 1844 the decision was reached to concentrate on other areas as more promising and important.[210] Not far from 1820 the London Society for Promoting Christianity amongst the Jews had an agent in Jerusalem.[211] In 1821 and 1822 Joseph Wolff, who travelled from Gibraltar to Bokhara among Jewish communities, spent some time in Palestine.[212] After several intermittent visits of various agents to the city, in the 1830's a continuing centre was established in Jerusalem. It included a hospital, a school, and a church. In the course of the next seventy years several hundred conversions were reported and additional stations were opened in other parts of the Holy Land.[213]

It was partly in connexion with the mission of the London Society for Promoting Christianity amongst the Jews that a Protestant bishopric was instituted in Jerusalem. At the outset this was a joint British-German enterprise. The incumbent was to be an Anglican and was to be named alternately by the Crowns of England and Prussia.[214] The bishopric was founded in 1840. A converted Jew, Michael Solomon Alexander, was the first appointee.[215] He reached his post in 1842, soon confirmed several Hebrew Christians, baptized some others, and ordained two Jewish converts. Alexander died in 1845 and was succeeded by Samuel Gobat, whom we have previously met in Egypt and Abyssinia. Gobat had a long episcopate, from 1846 to 1879. He faced a number of grave difficulties—among them conflicts arising out of his jurisdiction over both Anglican and Prussian clergy and differences of conviction in Anglican circles between High-Churchmen, who looked askance at conversions from the Eastern churches and at such close co-operation with non-Anglicans, and Evangeli-

[209] Anderson, *History of the Missions of the American Board of Commissioners for Foreign Missions to the Oriental Churches*, Vol. I, pp. 1-15; Daniel O. Morton, *Memoir of Rev. Levi Parsons, First Missionary to Palestine from the United States* (Burlington, Chauncy Goodrich, 1830, pp. 408).

[210] Anderson, *op. cit.*, Vol. I, pp. 15-39.

[211] Gidney, *The History of the London Society for Promoting Christianity amongst the Jews*, p. 118.

[212] Wolff, *Travels and Adventures*, pp. 131ff.

[213] Gidney, *op. cit.*, pp. 117-122, 178-182, 246-251, 376-386, 605-612; Gidney, *Sites and Scenes*, pp. 45-72.

[214] Gidney, *The History of the London Society for Promoting Christianity amongst the Jews*, pp. 203-214, 232-245.

[215] J. F. A. de le Roi, *Michael Solomon Alexander, der erste evangelische Bischof in Jerusalem* (Gütersloh, C. Bertelsmann, 1897, pp. 230), *passim*.

cals who desired them. Yet under him marked advances were made in multiplying schools and in the gathering of congregations from accessions from the Eastern churches.[216] Gobat was succeeded by Joseph Barclay, who had come to the Near East as a missionary of the London Society for Promoting Christianity amongst the Jews and had served for a number of years under Gobat. Barclay had only about two years before death removed him.[217] The bishopric was then vacant for a time. When, in 1888, it was once more filled (by the appointment of G. F. Popham Blyth), co-operation with the Prussian church had lapsed (1886) (to the intense relief of Anglican High-Churchmen) through the withdrawal of the German Government. The Jerusalem episcopate was now only for Anglicans.[218] To assist various enterprises connected with the diocese, the Jerusalem Bishopric Mission Fund, later the Jerusalem and the East Mission, was constituted (1888).[219]

In addition to the London Society for Promoting Christianity amongst the Jews and the Jerusalem episcopate, Anglicanism was represented in Palestine by the Church Missionary Society. The Church Missionary Society, after an exploratory tour by a special representative, sent its first resident agent to Jerusalem in 1851.[220] In spite of criticisms from High-Churchmen that it was trespassing on the Eastern churches, the society continued its efforts, occupying new centres and building up schools and congregations.[221]

Among the numerous other Protestant enterprises inaugurated in Palestine before 1914 were the one begun in Nazareth by a physician, Vartan, trained through the Edinburgh Medical Missionary Society and which was continued through that organization;[222] that of the Free Church of Scotland, later the United Free Church, through its Jewish Mission Committee, which had as its most distinguished pioneer D. W. Torrance, a physician who developed a hospital at Tiberias on the Sea of Galilee and served both Jews and Moslems,[223] and which eventually had other centres;[224] the medical enterprise of the Mildmay Mission at Hebron, which had as its outstanding figure Alexander Paterson,

[216] *Samuel Gobat*, pp. 221-390.
[217] *Joseph Barclay, D.D., LL.D., Third Anglican Bishop of Jerusalem. A Missionary Biography* (London, S. W. Partridge & Co., 1883, pp. xii, 600), *passim*.
[218] Stock, *The History of the Church Missionary Society*, Vol. III, pp. 276-278.
[219] *The Jerusalem Bishopric Mission Fund*, Annual Reports, 1889ff.
[220] Stock, *op. cit.*, Vol. II, pp. 142, 143.
[221] Stock, *op. cit.*, Vol. II, pp. 143-148, Vol. III, pp. 115-117, 277, 341-343, 523-529, 661.
[222] Thomson, *Reminiscences of Medical Mission Work*, pp. 136-143; Norman C. Macfarlane, *Ian Macfarlane, Soldier and Medical Missionary* (London, The Religious Tract Society, no date, pp. 187), *passim*.
[223] W. P. Livingstone, *A Galilee Doctor. Being a Sketch of the Career of Dr. D. W. Torrance of Tiberias* (New York, George H. Doran Co., no date, pp. x, 283), *passim*.
[224] W. Ewing, *J. E. H. Thomson* (London, Hodder and Stoughton, no date, pp. xv, 292), *passim*.

which ministered to both Jews and Arabs, and which was later taken over by the United Free Church of Scotland; [225] an undertaking in Jerusalem which came from Spittler's Pilgrim Mission of St. Chrischona and whose best known member was Johann Ludwig Schneller who built up an important orphanage; [226] the *Evangelische Jerusalems Verein,* organized in the cathedral in Berlin in 1853, with an associated organization in Sweden formed in 1900; [227] the institutions inaugurated in Jerusalem in 1851 by Fliedner and his Kaiserswerth deaconesses; [228] a leper asylum in Jerusalem supported by the Moravians; [229] the Christian and Missionary Alliance, which by 1914 had three centres; [230] the Palestine Village Mission; [231] and the *Evangelische Karmelmission,* with which were associated a number of colonies of German farmers.[232]

Bordering on Palestine geographically and closely related to it in political and religious history was Syria. Here the name Christian is said to have been first applied to the followers of Jesus. Here, at the dawn of the nineteenth century, were communities of several of the Eastern churches, stubborn survivals of the successive waves of Moslem conquest. Greek Orthodox, Jacobites, and some Nestorians and Armenians were there. Roman Catholics, too, had been present for centuries. They were divided into several Uniate churches. The largest of these were the Maronites, who had an interesting history going back for many centuries and were chiefly a mountain folk, dwelling mainly in the Lebanon. Their liturgical language was Syriac, although the Scriptures and some of the prayers were read in Arabic, the vernacular. Ecclesiastically they were ruled by a patriarch whose election was confirmed by the Holy See.[233] There were Catholic Syrians, drawn from the Jacobites. While some Syrian Jacobites had united with Rome as early as the sixteenth century, the main movement dated from the 1780's, when one of the rival candidates for the Jacobite Patriarchate of Antioch, together with some of the bishops, made his

[225] W. Ewing, *Paterson of Hebron* (London, James Clarke & Co., no date, pp. 256), *passim.*
[226] Ludwig Schneller, *Vater Schneller. Ein Patriarch der Evangelischen Mission im Heiligen Lands* (Leipzig, H. G. Wallmann, 1898, pp. 197), *passim.*
[227] Richter, *Mission und Evangelisation im Orient,* pp. 172, 173.
[228] Richter, *op. cit.,* p. 177.
[229] *London Association in Aid of the Moravians. Seventy-Seventh Annual Report,* 1894-5, p. 12.
[230] *The Christian and Missionary Alliance. Annual Report,* 1913, p. 11.
[231] Wyon, *An Eastern Palimpsest,* p. 106.
[232] W. Sziel, *Zeugendienst im Heiligen Lande. Die Evangelische Karmelmission, ihr Werden und Wachsen* (Schorndorf, Ev. Karmelmission, pp. 144), *passim.*
[233] Attwater, *The Catholic Eastern Churches,* pp. 180-195; Silbernagl, *Verfassung und gegenwärtiger Bestand sämtlicher Kirchen des Orients,* pp. 361-385.

submission to the Pope.[234] There were Greek Uniates, Melchites.[235] There were also Armenian and Chaldean (Nestorian) Uniates and some Roman Catholics of the Latin rite.[236] In the thirteenth and fourteenth centuries Dominicans had laboured in Syria. In the fifteenth century came Franciscans, followed late in the following century by the Jesuits and in the seventeenth century by the Capuchins and Carmelites. The Jesuits were particularly active. When, in 1773, their society was dissolved by papal order, French Lazarists were substituted for them. However, the French Revolution dealt the Lazarists severe blows. In the first decade of the nineteenth century the French Capuchin mission came to an end.[237] In Syria, as elsewhere, the beginning of the nineteenth century found Roman Catholic missions at a low ebb.[238] Persecutions vexed some of the Uniates.[239]

In spite of the decline of the fortunes of Roman Catholicism at the end of the eighteenth century, numerically in 1800 Christianity was relatively stronger in Syria than in Palestine.

Yet even in Syria Christianity was a minority movement. Moslems were in the majority. There were also Druses, a closely knit group with a monotheistic faith which owed much to Islam but was distinct from it.[240] Moreover, while Arabic was the prevailing language, racially the land presented a great mixture, deposits from the many invasions which from prehistoric times had poured into the region. So closely were Christians and Moslems associated that on occasions of illness or other crisis each frequented the others' shrines to pray for deliverance.[241]

As in most of the rest of the Near East, the nineteenth century witnessed a progressive strengthening of Christianity, chiefly by Roman Catholic and Protestant missions from the West. These missions did not get really under way until the second quarter of the century and had their main development after 1850.

The occupation of Syria in the 1830's by the forces of Mohammed Ali brought something of an opportunity for Occidental missions. While the disorder at-

[234] Attwater, op. cit., pp. 165ff.; Silbernagl, op. cit., pp. 358, 359.
[235] Lübeck, Die katholische Orientmission, p. 83.
[236] Schwager, Die katholische Heidenmission der Gegenwart, p. 285.
[237] Hilaire de Barenton, La France Catholique en Orient, p. 206.
[238] Lübeck, op. cit., pp. 84-87.
[239] Lübeck, op. cit., pp. 87, 88.
[240] For a brief study with footnote references to authorities and with some sources in translation, see Philip K. Hitti, The Origins of the Druze People and Religion, with Extracts from their Sacred Writings (New York, Columbia University Press, 1928, pp. viii, 80), passim.
[241] Hasluck, Christianity and Islam under the Sultans, Vol. I, pp. 75-82.

tendant upon the expulsion of the Egyptian armies in the 1840's worked hard-ship, the fact that British and Austrian assistance facilitated the re-establishment of Turkish rule increased the openings for Westerners. Not even conflicts be-tween Maronites and Druses with the massacres of the Maronites which were especially marked in 1860 [242] more than momentarily embarrassed Roman Cath-olic and Protestant missions.

It was to be expected that, beginning with strong constituencies in the coun-try in 1800 and backed by French influence, Roman Catholic Christianity would enjoy a marked growth. In the second quarter of the century the Jesuits reap-peared (1831).[243] The Lazarists revived their enterprise. French nuns entered.[244] The massacres of Maronites in 1860 gave France the opportunity to intervene. That year, so full of terror for the Christians, marked the inception of rapid growth under French protection. By 1914 various orders, teaching brotherhoods, and sisterhoods were present, with their customary accompaniments of schools, hospitals, orphanages, and churches. The chief centres were Aleppo, Damascus, and Beirut.[245] Especially noteworthy was the great University of St. Joseph, at Beirut, developed by the Jesuits.[246] With all this assistance from Europe, Roman Catholic Christianity flourished, especially in the various Uniate bodies by which it was represented.[247]

The earliest attempt to propagate Protestant Christianity in Syria seems to have been by the London Society for Promoting Christianity amongst the Jews. On behalf of that society, Wolff visited several Syrian cities in 1822 and 1823.[248] The first continuing Protestant enterprise—and what proved eventually to be the largest—was that begun in 1823 by the American Board of Commissioners for Foreign Missions, and in 1870 assigned to the Presbyterians, after the with-drawal of the New School Presbyterians from this Congregational body, because of their reunion with the Old School Presbyterians. Two agents of the Ameri-can Board reached Beirut in 1823.[249] There, in 1825, one of the two pioneers of

[242] Jessup, *Fifty-Three Years in Syria*, Vol. I, pp. 157ff.
[243] Charles, *Jesuites Missionnaires, Syrie, Proche Orient*, p. 20.
[244] Lübeck, *op. cit.*, p. 90.
[245] Lübeck, *op. cit.*, pp. 94-98; *Missionnaires Capucins au Levant Syrien* (Beirut, Imp. Jeanne d'Arc, 1931, pp. 29), pp. 15ff.; Luce Camuzet, *L'Œuvre de Syrie de Soeurs de St. Joseph de l'Apparition* (Paris, La Nation, 1931, pp. 54), *passim*.
[246] Charles, *op. cit.*, pp. 20ff.
[247] On one of the heads of the Melchites see Konrad Lübeck, *Patriarch Maximos III Maslum* (Aachen, Xaverius-Verlag, 1919, pp. 139), *passim*.
[248] Wolff, *Travels and Adventures*, pp. 138-150, 168-172; Gidney, *Sites and Scenes*, pp. 114, 115.
[249] Anderson, *History of the Mission of the American Board of Commissioners for Foreign Missions to the Oriental Churches*, Vol. I, pp. 40ff.

the American Board in the Near East, Pliny Fisk, died.[250] Reinforcements came. Converts were gathered, chiefly from other Christian bodies. This entailed persecutions. The total membership was not large—only 2,744 in 1908.[251] It later suffered heavily from the migration of many of the Christians to America.[252] Yet Protestant churches were organized and the training of a native clergy was begun. The Bible was translated into Arabic under the leadership of Eli Smith and, after his death, of Cornelius V. A. Van Dyck. A printing establishment was set up in Beirut. From 1822 'to 1833 the American Board maintained a press at Malta. This island as a British possession seemed a convenient point for the printing of literature for the Near East. In 1834, however, part of the press was moved to Smyrna and part to Beirut.[253]

The American Board and its successors, the Presbyterians, conducted numbers of schools.[254] The most prominent of the educational institutions which arose from this effort was the Syrian Protestant College, later (beginning in 1920) the American University of Beirut. Its first and second presidents and chief creators were Daniel Bliss and his son, Howard S. Bliss. Inspired by the New England Congregational colleges, like them it had an independent board of trustees (incorporated in America in 1863). To it came students from several faiths and through them it exercised a leavening influence upon a wide constituency.[255]

To the large American mission there were added to the Protestant forces several other enterprises. The Church of Scotland had in Beirut a mission to the Jews.[256] In 1860 Mrs. Bowen-Thompson founded what grew into the British Syrian Mission. It was staffed mainly by women and concerned itself chiefly with schools.[257] English and American Friends undertook the support of Theophilus

[250] Alvan Bond, *Memoir of the Rev. Pliny Fisk* (Edinburgh, Waugh & Innes, 1829, pp. 399), pp. 288ff.
[251] Brown, *One Hundred Years*, p. 999.
[252] Jessup, *Fifty-Three Years in Syria, passim;* Anderson, *op. cit.,* Vol I, pp. 40-73, 224-278, 362-385, Vol. II, pp. 324-399; Brown, *op. cit.,* pp. 969ff. See also Edward W. Hooker, *Memoir of Mrs. Sarah L. Huntington Smith* (New York, American Tract Society, 3d ed., 1845, pp. 396), *passim;* Isaac Bird, *Bible Work in Bible Lands* (Philadelphia, Presbyterian Board of Publication, 1872, pp. 432), *passim; A Memorial of Theodosia Davenport Jessup, Wife of Rev. Henry Harris Jessup, D.D.* (Beirut, American Mission Press, no date, pp. 57), *passim.*
[253] Jessup, *op. cit.,* Vol. II, p. 814.
[254] Brown, *op. cit.,* pp. 981-988; Jessup, *op. cit.,* Vol. II, p. 814.
[255] *The Reminiscences of Daniel Bliss, Edited and Supplemented by His Eldest Son* (New York, Fleming H. Revell Co., 1920, pp. 259), *passim;* Stephen B. L. Penrose, Jr., *That They May Have Life. The Story of the American University of Beirut, 1866-1941* (New York, The Trustees of the American University of Beirut, 1941, pp. xviii, 347), *passim.*
[256] *Reports on the Schemes of the Church of Scotland, 1911,* p. 393.
[257] Pitman, *Missionary Heroines in Eastern Lands,* pp. 47-87; *Daughters of Syria* (a periodical, London).

Waldemeier, who had been a missionary in Abyssinia and Syria before becoming a Quaker. Out of this contact arose a continuing project of the English Friends.[258] In the 1890's Waldemeier resigned from the Friends' Mission and founded in the Lebanon a hospital for the insane to which patients came from much of western Asia and which drew its financial support from the United States, Great Britain, Switzerland, Holland, and Germany.[259] Deaconesses from Kaiserswerth, moved by the massacres of 1860, founded an orphanage in Beirut.[260] In 1861 the Prussian Order of St. John began a hospital in that city.[261] In Scotland the Lebanon School Society was organized. The Free Church of Scotland, too, had schools in Syria.[262] The Irish Presbyterians entered and continued after the Free Church of Scotland withdrew.[263] For a time in the 1870's and 1880's the Church Missionary Society conducted schools for the Druses, but they were peremptorily closed by the Moslem civil authorities.[264] The Reformed Presbyterians, or Covenanters, from the United States, were represented.[265] There were a few other small enterprises.[266]

As a result of these various Roman Catholic and Protestant missions, the already complex Syrian Christianity became even more variegated. A few converts were gathered from outside the Christian fold, but most of the new Christian communities arose at the expense of the older ones. Yet the European and American missions contributed greatly to the raising of the educational level of the Christians. By their orphanages and hospitals they cared for the suffering and friendless and witnessed to Christian charity. Indirectly they partly permeated some non-Christian circles with Christian ideals of morals and philanthropy. By their wide distribution of the Bible in the vernacular the Protestants helped to familiarize professing Christians with the Gospel story.

Russian influence was late in making itself felt in Syria. Not until the 1890's did it become strong. It sought a channel through the Greek Orthodox Church and endeavoured to place in the highest posts ecclesiastics friendly to Russia. Schools were founded and attempts were made to counteract the Roman Catholic and Protestant missions.[267]

[258] The Autobiography of Theophilus Waldemeier, pp. 199-260.
[259] The Autobiography of Theophilus Waldemeir, pp. 263ff.; Lebanon Hospital for the Insane. Annual Reports (London, 1899ff.).
[260] Richter, Mission und Evangelisation im Orient, p. 140.
[261] Ibid.
[262] Richter, op. cit., p. 142.
[263] Richter, op. cit., p. 143.
[264] Stock, The History of the Church Missionary Society, Vol. III, pp. 116, 119, 120, 518.
[265] Richter, op. cit., pp. 144, 145.
[266] Richter, op. cit., pp. 145, 146.
[267] Lübeck, Die russischen Missionen, pp. 36-43.

Cyprus, conquered by the Turks in the sixteenth century, remained a Turkish possession until 1914. In 1878 it was occupied and administered by the English, but it was under nominal Turkish suzerainty until its formal annexation by Great Britain in 1914.

Religiously, in the nineteenth century the majority of the population of Cyprus were adherents of the Greek Orthodox Church. In 1821 the Turks killed the four Greek bishops and large numbers of priests, monks, and laymen. Yet the episcopal posts thus tragically made vacant were filled and the church went on. Only a minority of the population were Moslems. Roman Catholic Christianity was represented, although slightly. The Turkish conquest had all but eliminated it. The Franciscans sought to keep it alive, but as late as the twentieth century could count only five churches and a few schools. Sisters of St. Joseph of the Apparition assisted with hospitals and orphanages. There were Maronites and there was a small Armenian minority.[268] Protestantism was almost negligible.[269] In 1891, out of a population of 209,286, 75 per cent. were Greek Orthodox, 22.9 per cent. were Moslems, 1,131 were Maronites, 915 were Roman Catholics of other rites, 269 were Armenians, and 201 Anglicans.[270]

We now come to Asia Minor and to the plateaus and mountains east of Asia Minor, west of Persia, south of the Black Sea and the Caucasus, and north of Mesopotamia, the area which was the ancient home of the Armenians and which often is made to bear their name. We must also include Constantinople, for, although it lies on the European shore of the Bosporus, it was the capital of the Turkish Empire.

In 1800 these regions had for centuries been under the rule of the Ottoman Turks. In the nineteenth century the empire was progressively decrepit. It retained its hold, but the aggressive Occident increasingly made itself felt. Under the capitulations, a system going back to the days of Turkish strength and even earlier, Westerners were *imperia in imperio,* subject to their own laws and consuls. Various European powers, notably Russia, Great Britain, France, Austria, and Italy, sought territorial gains at the expense of a realm which only a few generations before had been the terror of Christendom. Wars followed, famous among them being that in the 1850's which bore the name of Crimea. Various attempts were made to save the remnants of empire by adopting Occi-

---

[268] *The Catholic Encyclopedia,* Vol. IV, p. 591.
[269] Richter, *op. cit.,* p. 145; Strong, *The Story of the American Board,* p. 87.
[270] J. Hackett, *A History of the Orthodox Church of Cyprus from the Coming of the Apostles Paul and Barnabas to the Commencement of the British Occupation (A.D. 54- A.D. 1878)* (London, Methuen & Co., 1901, pp. xviii, 720), p. 280.

dental ways. Most notable of these was the revolution of 1908, in which the Young Turks, trained in Western ways and infected with the nationalism which prevailed in the Occident, seized power and strove for the rejuvenation of the land.

Religiously the region was overwhelmingly Moslem. However, strong Christian minorities existed, survivals of the days when Christianity was the prevailing faith. There were many Greek Orthodox, chiefly in the cities on the west coast. They acknowledged the headship of a patriarch at Constantinople who still bore the ambitious title of Œcumenical, reminiscent of the days when Constantinople had been the capital of the great Christian state of the East. There were tens of thousands of Armenians, most of them in the land of their ancestors, but many of them in the cities of Asia Minor and in Constantinople. There were also Jacobites and Nestorians. Roman Catholics, including more than one Uniate church, were represented. While a certain amount of intolerance existed between Moslems and Christians, as in Egypt and Syria, in time of emergency each might invoke the other's saints or share in the same religious procession.[271]

Racially the area was diverse. Those who bore the name of Turk were of many origins and were united chiefly by their Moslem faith. Kurds, largely hardy mountain dwellers in Armenia, were regarded by the Turks as Moslems but often denied that classification. Their religion, while in places displaying a Moslem veneer, was one of their own which in some of its ceremonies had a stronge resemblance to Christianity. Circassian minorities were originally from the Caucasus. Greeks were numerous in Constantinople and the cities of the western part of Asia Minor. Armenians were widely scattered. Like the Greeks, they tended to be more thrifty than the Turks and to be merchants. They and the Greeks were regarded by the Turks much as were Jews in prevailingly Christian lands—as clever and tricky and therefore to be distrusted and disliked. Stirred in part by the hope of European protection, for in the latter part of the nineteenth century Great Britain interested itself in the Armenians and, partly in an attempt to checkmate Russia and to exert an influence in Turkey, intermittently claimed a semi-protectorate over them, some of the Armenians began nationalistic agitation and plots. Thereupon the Ottoman Government, in an endeavour to preserve its authority, connived at and even ordered extensive massacres (1895-1896). These were by Turks and Kurds and wrought great destruction among the Armenian communities.[272]

[271] Hasluck, *Christianity and Islam under the Sultans*, Vol. I, pp. 63-67, 75-82.
[272] For one of the accounts of these massacres see William Nesbitt Chambers, *Yoljuluk. Random Thoughts on a Life in Imperial Turkey* (London, Simpkin Marshall, 1928, pp. xiv, 125), pp. 71ff.

Before the nineteenth century Roman Catholic Christianity had had a decidedly chequered history in Constantinople and Asia Minor. Under the Latin Empire which had been set up by the Crusaders in the thirteenth century an elaborate hierarchy had been created with a patriarch at its head. Imposed by force, it collapsed with the restoration of the Byzantine regime. Roman Catholicism continued as the faith of merchants from western Europe, chiefly Italians. In the eighteenth century the title of Patriarch of Constantinople still existed, but its holders resided in Rome and were represented in the East by vicars.[273] Dominicans entered Constantinople in the thirteenth century and despite the many political changes persisted into the twentieth century.[274] Also, there had long been Franciscans and Jesuits in Constantinople. Late in the eighteenth century the latter were replaced by the Lazarists.[275] French Capuchins were chaplains of the French Embassy from the seventeenth century until the French Revolution and then were followed by Italian members of their order.[276] There were missionaries of various orders in other parts of Asia Minor, notably Smyrna.[277]

In the nineteenth century Roman Catholic missions enjoyed a marked expansion. Orders and congregations already represented enlarged their staffs. New orders, such as the Assumptionists, the Salesians, and the Fathers of Sion, entered. Teaching brotherhoods and several organizations of sisters inaugurated enterprises. Some seculars also served.[278] New bishoprics and vicariates apostolic were created.[279] In spite of the fact that as a result of Franco-British cooperation with Turkey in the Crimean War the traditional death penalty for conversion from Islam to Christianity was abrogated by the Sultan and Moslems were legally permitted to receive baptism (1856),[280] popular feeling against such a change of religion was so strong that most of the accessions to the Roman Catholic fold were from other Christian bodies, mainly the Armenians. A large part of the growth was in the various Uniate bodies. There had long been Armenian Roman Catholics. In the nineteenth century their number increased. In 1830 French influence obtained their recognition by the Turkish Government as a distinct legal entity. The Armenian Uniates were headed by a patriarch. Difficulties arose with Rome over the attempt of the Papal See to regulate the

[273] Lübeck, *Die katholische Orientmission*, pp. 114-116.
[274] Lübeck, *op. cit.*, p. 117.
[275] Lübeck, *op. cit.*, pp. 117-119.
[276] *Capucins Missionnaires. Missions Françaises*, p. 11.
[277] Lübeck, *op. cit.*, p. 123.
[278] Lübeck, *op. cit.*, pp. 124, 125.
[279] Schwager, *Die katholische Heidenmission der Gegenwart*, p. 298.
[280] Schwager, *op. cit.*, p. 227.

election of the patriarch and bishops and to restrain the participation of the laity in ecclasiastical affairs. However, several dioceses existed and there was a fairly numerous body of parochial clergy, some of them trained in a college in Rome founded in 1883 for that purpose and some in seminaries in the Near East. There was at least one order of Armenian monks and one sisterhood, the latter founded in 1852. Moreover, numbers of Armenians conformed to the Latin rite.[281] A small body of Greek Uniates came into being in the second half of the nineteenth century. Eventually it was given its own bishop.[282] The extensive schools and medical service of missionaries from the Occident were widely influential, even when their beneficiaries did not become Roman Catholics.

Protestant Christianity had as its most numerous Occidental agents in Turkey and Armenia the representatives of the American Board of Commissioners for Foreign Missions. When, in 1870, its enterprises in Syria and Persia were transferred to the Presbyterians, the American Board, now become almost exclusively a Congregational society, retained Turkey and Armenia.

The American Board, like the Roman Catholics, found its chief openings among the existing Christian bodies, and particularly among the Armenians. At the outset, however, it wished not to win converts or to set up a new ecclesiastical structure, but, rather, to purify and bring new vigour to the Eastern churches.[283] It was to Smyrna that the pioneers, Fisk and Parsons, went, in 1820. From there they explored part of Asia Minor.[284] Interests in the United States was quickened by active sympathy for the Greek struggle for independence which was in progress in the 1820's.[285] In 1827 a journey was made from Smyrna into Cappadocia by a representative of the American Board.[286] It was not until the 1830's that the Board established continuing enterprises in Constantinople, Asia Minor, and Armenia. In 1830 and 1831 Eli Smith and H. G. O. Dwight made an extensive tour from Malta through Asia Minor, Armenia, as far as Persia, and back to Malta.[287] Before their return, William Goodell had begun, in June, 1831, a residence in Constantinople which, with some interruptions, was to be terminated only by old age, and which was to have as one of its out-

[281] Attwater, *The Catholic Eastern Churches*, pp. 205-209; Silbernagl, *Verfassung und gegenwärtiger Bestand sämtlicher Kirchen des Orients*, pp. 342-349.
[282] Attwater, *op. cit.*, pp. 118, 119.
[283] *Missionary Herald*, Vol. XXXIV (1838), pp. 117-126; Strong, *The Story of the American Board*, pp. 92, 93.
[284] Anderson, *History of the Missions of the American Board of Commissioners for Foreign Missions to the Oriental Churches*, Vol. I, pp. 11-14.
[285] Bacon, *Leonard Bacon*, pp. 148, 149.
[286] Smith, *Researches of the Rev. E. Smith and Rev. H. G. O. Dwight in Armenia*, Vol. I, p. iii.
[287] Smith, *op. cit.*, *passim*.

standing achievements the translation of the Bible into Armeno-Turkish.[288] New centres were opened in various cities of Asia Minor and Armenia.[289] Within the Armenian Church a following arose which favoured the missionaries and their message. This, quite understandably, led to persecution from the conservative majority. The conservatives disliked what seemed to them new and heretical doctrines and also feared that through them the unity of the Armenian communities would be disrupted and the opposition to the Turk and to Islam be weakened. Accordingly, those who followed the American missionaries were excommunicated. Some of those thus cast out organized what they called Evangelical churches. The first of these was formed in Constantinople in 1846.[290] In 1847 and, by a new imperial charter, in 1850 the Protestants were given legal status as a civil community.[291] As time passed, however, antagonism between the Gregorian (Armenian) Church and the Evangelicals declined. Evangelical pastors were often asked to preach in the old churches, and in the schools and theological seminaries maintained by the American Board were students preparing for ordination in the Gregorian body. As persecution dwindled, missionaries discouraged separation from the old church and the numbers of accessions to the Evangelical body became smaller.[292] The dreams of the pioneers of a transformation of the existing churches were in part being realized.

The American Board also made efforts to reach the Jews of Turkey.[293] Prominent in this phase of its programme was William G. Schauffler. Of German birth, Schauffler had spent his youth in Odessa in South Russia and had received his theological education in Andover. Most of his missionary career was in Constantinople, chiefly in translating the Bible. In later years he placed himself in the service of the American Bible Society and the British and Foreign Bible Society, the better to pursue an interest in the Turks which he had developed.[294]

---

[288] E. D. G. Prime, *Forty Years in the Turkish Empire: or, Memoirs of Rev. William Goodell, D.D.* (New York, Robert Carter and Brothers, 1876, pp. xii, 489), *passim*.

[289] For one of the pioneers at Smyrna see Daniel H. Temple, *Life and Letters of Rev. Daniel Temple* (Boston, Congregational Board of Publication, 1855, pp. xii, 492), *passim*.

[290] H. G. O. Dwight, *Christianity in Turkey: A Narrative of the Protestant Reformation in the Armenian Church* (London, James Nisbet and Co., 1854, pp. xiv, 360), *passim*. This is a revised edition of H. G. O. Dwight, *Christianity Revived in the East: or, a Narrative of the Work of God among the Armenians of Turkey* (New York, Baker and Scribner, 1850, pp. xii, 290). On some phases of the development of the Evangelical churches see James I. Good, *Life of Rev. Benjamin Schneider* (Board of Foreign Missions Reformed Church in the United States, no date, pp. 76), pp. 20ff.

[291] Barton, *Daybreak in Turkey*, p. 168.

[292] Barton, *op. cit.*, pp. 174, 175.

[293] Barton, *op. cit.*, pp. 140, 143.

[294] *Autobiography of William G. Schauffler* (New York, Anson D. F. Randolph & Co., 1887, pp. xxxv, 258), *passim*.

True to their New England heritage, the missionaries of the American Board stressed schools. Several of these were of college grade. Most of the students were Armenians, but some came from other Christian communities and gradually Turks began to enroll.[295] Most prominent of the schools were Robert College, on a commanding site overlooking the Bosporus, and the American College for Girls at Constantinople. Robert College owed its inception to Cyrus Hamlin. Hamlin, who had come to Turkey under the American Board and had been in charge of a school in Constantinople, resigned and founded Robert College, an institution which, like the Syrian Protestant College at Beirut, had an independent board of trustees incorporated in the United States. The college opened its doors in 1863.[296] Its students were from several different nationalities, but were chiefly Bulgarians and Armenians. As a pioneer in a Western type of higher education it had a profound effect through its graduates, especially in Bulgaria.[297] What became the American College for Girls was opened in 1871 in Constantinople and within a few years was moved to the Asiatic side of the Bosporus. In 1890 it was chartered as a college under the laws of Massachusetts. Later it received a Turkish charter. As an institution for the higher education of women in a land where that was a striking innovation, after 1908 it received the endorsement of the Young Turks.[298] The American schools were utilized chiefly by the racial minorities. The accusation was later made that, by producing able leadership dreaming of greater opportunities for their respective peoples, they increased the fear of the Turks that these minorities would rebel and thus helped to precipitate the violence by which the Turks sought, especially after 1914, to eliminate these groups.[299]

Not only were American Board missionaries active in developing new forms of education in Turkey and Armenia, they also were among the first to introduce Western medical practice. Numbers of them were living witnesses both to nine-

---

[295] Barton, *op. cit.*, pp. 181-193; *The Near East and American Philanthropy*, pp. 155-161. On one of these colleges see George E. White, *Charles Chapin Tracy, . . . First President of Anatolia College, Marsovan, Turkey* (Boston, The Pilgrim Press, 1918, pp. 79), *passim*.

[296] Cyrus Hamlin, *My Life and Times* (Boston, Sunday-School and Publishing Society, 2d ed., 1893, pp. 538), pp. 244ff.; *In Memoriam. Rev. Cyrus Hamlin* (Boston, privately printed, 1903, pp. 118), *passim*. For a biography which covered part of the years of the school which preceded Robert College, see Margarette Woods Lawrence, *Light on the Dark River; or Memorials of Mrs. Henrietta A. L. Hamlin* (Boston, Ticknor, Reed and Fields, 1854, pp. 321), pp. 165ff.

[297] Caleb Frank Gates, *Not to Me Only* (Princeton University Press, 1940, pp. x, 340), pp. 159ff.

[298] Mary Mills Patrick, *Under Five Sultans* (New York, The Century Co., 1929, pp. x, 357), *passim;* Mary Mills Patrick, *A Bosporus Adventure. Istanbul (Constantinople) Woman's College, 1871-1924* (Stanford University Press, 1934, pp. ix, 284), *passim;* L. J. Peet, *No Less Honor. The Biography of William Wheelock Peet* (privately printed, 1939, pp. 243), pp. 112ff.

[299] *The Near East and American Philanthropy*, p. 165.

teenth century progress in medical knowledge and to unselfish, devoted service to the sick.[300]

As was usual in nineteenth century missions, both Roman Catholic and Protestant, women had a large share in the enterprises of the American Board.[301] Although the American Board had the most extensive of the Protestant missions in Turkey and Armenia, it was by no means the only Protestant agency at work there. For a time the Boston Female Jews' Society supported a missionary in connexion with the American Board.[302] In the 1820's and 1830's the Basel Mission had men in the Caucasus. They were first sent to care for German settlers in that region, but they soon began to reach out toward Moslems and Armenians. On their staff was Karl Gottlieb Pfander, who was to become distinguished as a missionary to the Moslems in more than one land.[303] In the 1830's the London Society for Promoting Christianity amongst the Jews maintained a representative in Constantinople. There were a number of conversions, but during most of the 1840's the station was without a staff. In the 1820's agents of the society visited Smyrna and in 1829 a resident missionary was placed there.[304] During much of the nineteenth century centres were maintained in these two cities.[305] In the 1830's the Church Missionary Society appointed men to Smyrna. They were not content to confine their labours to that city but travelled extensively in Asia Minor.[306] Through most of the remainder of the nineteenth century Smyrna continued to be a station of the society.[307] When, in 1856, as an aftermath of their assistance in the Crimean War, the British obtained from the Turkish Govern-

[300] As some examples of these see Edward Mills Dodd, *The Beloved Physician. An Intimate Life of William Schauffler Dodd* (privately printed, 1931, pp. 108), *passim;* Clarence D. Ussher, *An American Physician in Turkey* (Boston, Houghton Mifflin Co., 1917, pp. xiii, 339), *passim;* Alice Shepard Riggs, *Shepard of Aintab* (New York, Interchurch Press, 1920, pp. xx, 200), *passim;* George F. Herrick, *An Intense Life. A Sketch of the Life and Works of Rev. Andrew T. Pratt, M. D., Missionary of the A. B. C. F. M., in Turkey 1852-1872* (New York, Fleming H. Revell, no date, pp. 83), *passim.*

[301] For a general sketch see Florence A. Fensham, *Mary I. Lyman and Mrs. H. B. Humphrey. A Modern Crusade in the Turkish Empire* (Chicago, Woman's Board of Missions of the Interior, 1908, pp. 101), *passim.* For some of the pioneers, see H. G. O. Dwight, *Memoir of Mrs. Elizabeth B. Dwight* (New York, M. W. Dodd, 1840, pp. 323), *Memoir of Mrs. Mary E. Van Lennep, by her Mother* (Hartford, Belknap & Hamersley, 1847, pp. 372), and Mrs. M. G. Benjamin, *The Missionary Sisters. A Memorial of Mrs. Seraphina Haynes Everett and Mrs. Harriet Martha Hamlin* (Boston, American Tract Society, 1860, pp. 335), *passim.*

[302] Josiah Brewer, *A Residence at Constantinople in the Year 1827 with Notes to the Present Time* (New Haven, Durrie and Peck, 1830, pp. 384), pp. 255ff.

[303] Schlatter, *Geschichte der Basler Mission*, Vol. I, pp. 93-118; Richter, *Mission und Evangelisation im Orient*, pp. 61-64, 110,111.

[304] Gidney, *The History of the London Society for Promoting Christianity amongst the Jews*, pp. 173-177.

[305] Gidney, *op. cit.*, pp. 299, 300, 363-365, 382-386, 448, 463, 464, 561, 604.

[306] Stock, *The History of the Church Missionary Society*, Vol. I, p. 350.

[307] Stock, *op. cit.*, Vol. III, pp. 115, 119.

ment the promise of religious toleration and what was tantamount to permission for Moslems to become Christians, the Church Missionary Society inaugurated in Constantinople an enterprise for Moslems. To it was appointed the gifted Pfander, who to his apprenticeship in the Balkans had added long experience among Moslems in Persia and India. Colleagues were given him. A few conversions were made, but a storm of persecution clouded the initially bright prospects.[308] Yet not until the 1870's, and then mainly because of shortness of funds, was the Constantinople station discontinued.[309] It was also in consequence of the Crimean War that the Society for the Propagation of the Gospel in Foreign Parts placed representatives in Constantinople. Persecution which followed the first few conversions from Islam led, in 1865, to the virtual suspension of the undertaking.[310] In 1896 J. Lepsius, son of a famous Egyptologist and son-in-law of Bishop Gobat, founded what eventually was called the *Deutsche Orient Mission*. In spite of the pro-Turkish policy of the German Government and press, Lepsius raised funds to care for Armenian children left orphaned by the massacres of that decade. Eventually the organization extended its activities to other countries and began work for Moslems.[311] Earlier, in 1844, the chaplain of the Prussian Embassy in Constantinople inaugurated the *Evangelisch-deutscher Wohltätigkeitsverein*. Out of it came a hospital, schools, and an orphanage.[312] We hear, too, of a German home for the blind,[313] of a hospital, an orphanage, and schools maintained by English Quakers, and of temporary undertakings by Disciples of Christ,[314] American Baptists,[315] and the (American) Church of the Brethren.[316] For a time the Church of Scotland was active in behalf of the Jews in Smyrna and Constantinople.[317] In the 1830's the Protestant Episcopal Church in the United States of America sent a representative on an exploring tour through much of western Asia.[318] There was also the Macedonian and Armenian Gospel Mission, begun in the twentieth century.[319]

---

[308] Stock, *op. cit.,* Vol. II, pp. 149-155.

[309] Stock, *op. cit.,* Vol. III, p. 119.

[310] Pascoe, *Two Hundred Years of the S. P. G.,* pp. 736, 737.

[311] Richard Schäfer, *Geschichte der Deutschen Orient-Mission* (Potsdam, Lepsius, Fleischmann, und Grauer, 1932, pp. 124), *passim.*

[312] Richter, *Mission und Evangelisation im Orient,* p. 113.

[313] *Ibid.*

[314] Richter, *op. cit.,* pp. 114-116.

[315] Shaw, *American Contacts with the Eastern Churches,* pp. 120ff.

[316] Moyer, *Missions of the Church of the Brethren,* pp. 159-165.

[317] *Reports of the Schemes of the Church of Scotland, 1911,* p. 390.

[318] Horatio Southgate, *Narrative of a Tour through Armenia, Kurdistan, Persia, and Mesopotamia* (New York, D. Appleton & Co., 2 vols., 1840).

[319] Jensine Oerts Peters, *Tests and Triumphs of Armenians in Turkey and Macedonia* (Grand Rapids, Zondervan Publishing House, 1940, pp. 95), *passim.*

From Turkey and Armenia we pass on to Mesopotamia. Mesopotamia is a district with vaguely defined natural boundaries and to which differing meanings have been given. We are using it here in its most inclusive sense—the entire Tigris-Euphrates Valley. In configuration the region is varied—from the mountainous northern districts, through plateaus in the centre, to the low-lying plains on the lower reaches of the valley. During the nineteenth century the region was part of the Turkish Empire. Its peoples were predominantly Moslem, but there were remnants of the Eastern churches, especially of the Nestorians who once had been so prominent and influential a minority. The entire area was sadly decayed. The days when it had been the proud centre of empires were in the far past. Population was scanty and poverty was chronic. During the fore part of the nineteenth century much of Mesopotamia was disturbed politically. Toward the end of the century conditions improved.

As in so much of western Asia, the nineteenth century missions from the Occident, both Roman Catholic and Protestant, were primarily among the adherents of the Eastern churches.

Roman Catholics had long been active in Mesopotamia. Since the sixteenth century some of the Nestorians had submitted to Rome. They were known as Chaldean Uniates.[320] The Chaldean patriarchate had a somewhat chequered history, but in 1830 it was revived through an appointee who was denominated the Patriarch of Babylon and had his seat at Mosul.[321] Syrian Uniates were under archbishops at Baghdad and Mosul who in turn were under the Patriarch of Antioch.[322] Carmelites with headquarters at Baghdad were in the region when the nineteenth century dawned. At the same time there were Italian Dominicans at Mosul. In the 1850's both enterprises were reinvigorated by transfer to French members of their respective orders.[323] The Carmelites had the southern portion of Mesopotamia. There by the year 1914 they had developed a number of centres with schools, a home for the aged, a home for the blind, and a dispensary. They were assisted by brothers of their third order and by sisters from Tours. The latter maintained schools and an orphanage.[324] The Dominicans were in the northern section of Mesopotamia. There they won thousands of Nestorians to the Chaldean body, other thousands of Jacobites to the Syrian Uniates, and a few hundred Armenians. They, too, were assisted by brothers of their third order and by sisters from Tours. They developed schools, among them a seminary for

[320] Vol. III, p. 80.
[321] Lübeck, Die katholische Orientmission, pp. 139, 140.
[322] Attwater, The Catholic Eastern Churches, p. 166.
[323] Lübeck, op. cit., p. 141.
[324] Lübeck, op. cit., p. 142.

the training of priests and an institution for the training of teachers. They had a press, a hospital, and dispensaries.[325] North of Mosul were Christian villages where a form of Syriac persisted as the vernacular.[326]

Protestant Christianity seems not to have appeared until the nineteenth century. In 1830 the Basel Mission reached south from the Caucasus and in Baghdad opened a school for Armenians.[327] In the 1820's the much travelled Joseph Wolff, missionary to the Jews, visited Mesopotamia.[328] In the 1840's Henry Aaron Stern, whom we met a few pages above in Abyssinia, was in Baghdad more than once in the course of extensive travels in Mesopotamia, Kurdistan, and Persia on behalf of the London Society for Promoting Christianity amongst the Jews.[329] There for about fifteen years his society maintained a station and could report a number of conversions.[330] For a time in the 1830's an English dentist had a mission among the Moslems in Baghdad.[331] The American Board of Commissioners for Foreign Missions extended its Armenian field into northern Mesopotamia. It long maintained a centre in Mosul.[332] In 1882 the Church Missionary Society placed two men at Baghdad.[333] There it continued.[334] Although represented, Protestantism was by no means so well rooted or so extensive in Mesopotamia as were the Eastern churches and Roman Catholic Christianity.

Persia, in the second quarter of the twentieth century known as Iran, was chiefly a mountainous and plateau country. Its population, possibly ten millions in number in 1910, was mixed, but was predominantly Iranian. Politically the country was governed by absolute monarchs. In the course of the nineteenth century Russian and British interests increased and were marked by rivalry. In 1907 a Russo-British convention divided the land into a Russian sphere of influence in the North, a British sphere in the South, and a neutral zone in the

[325] Lübeck, op. cit., pp. 142, 143.
[326] Lesourd, L'Année Missionnaire, 1931, p. 85.
[327] Schlatter, Geschichte der Basler Mission, Vol. I, p. 107.
[328] Wolff, Travels and Adventures, pp. 199ff.
[329] Henry A. Stern, Dawnings of Light in the East (London, Charles H. Purday, 1854, pp. x, 278), passim; Gidney, The History of the London Society for Promoting Christianity amongst the Jews, pp. 257-260.
[330] Gidney, op. cit., pp. 300-302, 384, 385.
[331] Richter, Mission und Evangelisation im Orient, p. 118.
[332] W. S. Tyler, Memoir of Rev. Henry Lobdell, M.D., Late Missionary of the American Board at Mosul (Boston, The American Tract Society, 1859, pp. 414), passim; C. H. Wheeler, Ten Years on the Euphrates (Boston, American Tract Society, 1868, pp. 330), pp. 29-32.
[333] Stock, The History of the Church Missionary Society, Vol. III, p. 515.
[334] Stock, op. cit., Vol. III, p. 752.

centre. Slowly Western ideas made their way into the land. In 1906, after the fashion of the Occident, a constitution was adopted with provision for representative institutions.

Religiously Persia was overwhelmingly Moslem, chiefly of the Shiite branch of Islam. There were, in addition, Kurds, in the North-west, with their peculiar faith, a few thousand who clung to the ancient Zoroastrianism, several thousand Jews, and numbers of Christians. The Christians were mainly Nestorians, but there were also Armenians and Greek Orthodox. As we shall see in a moment, the nineteenth century witnessed the growth of Roman Catholicism and the introduction of Protestantism. The Nestorians, numerically the leading Christian group, were mainly in the mountainous North-west, centring around Lake Urmia, in a region in which the political boundary between Persia and Turkey was topographically artificial. Some of them, therefore, were in parts of the mountains which had the Sultan for ruler. For neighbours they had the Kurds.[335]

In the course of the nineteenth century the Christian communities seem not to have displayed any marked numerical change, unless it may have been a slight growth due to natural increase. It is possible, indeed, that a decrease occurred, for the Nestorians were subject to recurring raids by the Kurds. However, the activity of foreign Christians, especially Roman Catholics, Protestants, and Russian Orthodox, wrought changes in the ecclesiastical complexion of the Christian groups.

Roman Catholic Christianity had been propagated in Persia before the nineteenth century. In the seventeenth and eighteenth centuries it had been represented by Jesuits, Carmelites, and Capuchins. By 1830, however, the Roman Catholic community was much reduced.[336] In the second quarter of the nineteenth century the field was entrusted to the Lazarists and by the close of the century the number of Roman Catholics is said to have risen to about 10,000.[337] Most of them had been won from the Nestorians. Schools and various charitable institutions had been developed.[338]

The introduction of Protestantism was chiefly the work of the American Board of Commissioners for Foreign Missions, its successor in that area, the Northern Presbyterians of the United States, and the Church Missionary Society.

Before these organizations had made their way to the country the saintly and linguistically gifted Henry Martyn, whom we are to meet in India in the next

---

[335] For a description of the Nestorians, see Arthur John Maclean and William Henry Browne, *The Catholics of the East and his People* (London, Society for Promoting Christian Knowledge, 1892, pp. xvi, 360), *passim*.
[336] Baudrillart in Descamps, *Histoire Générale Comparée des Missions*, p. 542.
[337] *Ibid*.
[338] Lübeck, *Die katholische Orientmission*, p. 143.

chapter, had spent several months (in the years 1811 and 1812) in the country, perfecting his translation of the New Testament and Psalms into the Persian tongue and presenting Christianity in debates with Moslems and Jews.[339] In the 1830's Joseph Wolff visited Persia.[340] The London Society for Promoting Christianity amongst the Jews followed up the openings thus revealed and sent emissaries who during much of the remainder of the century laboured in that land.[341] In 1833 the Basel Mission instituted a station in Tabriz. Pfander, prominent as a missionary to the Moslems, was for a time in Persia.[342]

It was in 1834 that the first resident missionaries of the American Board, Justin Perkins and his wife, reached Persia. They were sent to meet the opportunity disclosed among the Nestorians by the exploratory journey of Smith and Dwight earlier in the decade. In 1835 a central station was opened at Urmia. Reinforcements came. Schools were opened. Famous as a leader in education for girls was Fidelia Fiske, a graduate and at one time a faculty member of Mt. Holyoke College. Medical work was developed. A press issued quantities of Christian literature, chiefly in Syriac. The early missionaries prayed for revivals of the sort which they had known in the New England of their day. Gradually groups of Christians arose, Nestorian in background, which in time were constituted into the Assyrian Evangelical Church. Until about the year 1870 they also retained their membership in the old church. Eventually they numbered approximately 3,000.[343] The transfer of the enterprise to the Presbyterians, in 1870, brought no

[339] Smith, *Henry Martyn*, pp. 340ff.
[340] *Travels and Adventures of the Rev. Joseph Wolff*, pp. 283ff.; Wolff, *Researches*, pp. 43ff.
[341] Gidney, *The History of the London Society for Promoting Christianity amongst the Jews*, pp. 258-260, 300-302, 465-475, 555, 613, 614.
[342] Schlatter, *Geschichte der Basler Mission*, Vol. I, pp. 107, 108.
[343] S. G. Wilson, *Persia: Western Mission* (Philadelphia, Presbyterian Board of Publication and Sabbath-School Work, 1896, pp. 381), *passim;* Anderson, *History of the Missions of the American Board of Commissioners for Foreign Missions to the Oriental Churches*, Vol. I, pp. 164-223, Vol. II, pp. 107-149; Justin Perkins, *A Residence of Eight Years in Persia among the Nestorian Christians* (Andover, Allen, Morrill & Wardwell, 1843, pp. xviii, 512), *passim;* Justin Perkins, *Missionary Life in Persia* (Boston, American Tract Society, 1861, pp. 255), *passim;* Mary Lewis Shedd, *The Measure of a Man. The Life of William Ambrose Shedd, Missionary to Persia* (New York, George H. Doran Co., 1922, pp. xli, 280), pp. 1-90; Robert E. Speer, *The Foreign Doctor. A Biography of Joseph Plumb Cochran, M. D., of Persia* (Chicago, Fleming H. Revell Co., 1911, pp. 384), *passim;* Henry Martyn Perkins, *Life of Rev. Justin Perkins, D.D.,* (Chicago, Woman's Presbyterian Board of Missions of the Northwest, 1887, pp. 97), *passim; A Century of Mission Work in Iran*, pp. 1-5, 106-109; D. F. Fiske, *Faith Working by Love: as Exemplified in the Life of Fidelia Fiske* (Boston, Congregational Publishing Society, 1868, pp. 416); Dwight W. Marsh, *The Tennesseean in Persia and Koordistan. Being Scenes and Incidents in the Life of Samuel Audley Rhea* (Philadelphia, Presbyterian Publication Committee, 1869, pp. 380), *passim;* Joseph P. Thompson, *Memoir of Rev. David Tappan Stoddard, Missionary to the Nestorians* (New York, Sheldon, Blakeman & Co., 1858, pp. 422), *passim;* Thomas Laurie, *Dr. Grant and the Mountain Nestorians* (Boston, D. Lothrop & Co., 1874, pp. 418), *passim.*

serious interruption in the program or prosperity of the mission. Indeed, it was followed by expansion. In 1873 Tabriz, the chief city in north-west Persia, was made a station of the mission and a church arose which was primarily Armenian in race.[344] Moreover, in 1872 the Presbyterians extended their operations eastward and in the course of time had centres in various cities from Kermanshah in the west to Meshed in the east. At first a constituency was found among the Armenians, but the Moslems were not ignored. A few converts were made from among them. Schools, hospitals, and the printed page were important means of spreading the influence of the mission.[345]

In 1869 Robert Bruce, of the Church Missionary Society, began in Ispahan what was at first planned as a temporary residence. There, in 1871, on the eve of his intended departure for India, his earlier field, nine Moslems asked for baptism. He felt constrained to remain, and in 1875 his society, somewhat reluctantly, yielded to his importunity and made the enterprise a continuing one.[346] Reinforcements came. New centres were developed, chiefly in the south of Persia. Edward Craig Stuart, who had been in India and then had been bishop in New Zealand, came to Persia in 1894 to give himself to missions to Moslems and served until his retirement, in 1910. In 1912 a bishop was consecrated especially for Persia. Although much of the constituency was among Armenians, a number of converts were won from Islam.[347]

In the 1840's High Church Anglicans, through the Society for Promoting Christian Knowledge and the Society for the Propagation of the Gospel in Foreign Parts, maintained a mission among the Nestorians. In the 1870's and 1880's the mission was renewed. An Assyrian Christians Special Fund was raised.[348]

In 1911 Lutherans from the United States began a mission among the Kurds. Both the American and the British and Foreign Bible Society were long active in Persia.[349] In 1825 a Scottish missionary in southern Russia, William Glen, was engaged by the latter society to translate the Bible into Persian. Several years later Glen went to Persia as an agent of the United Associate Synod.[350]

[344] *A Century of Mission Work in Iran*, p. 113.
[345] *A Century of Mission Work in Iran*, pp. 5-14, 24-33; John G. Wishard, *Twenty Years in Persia* (Chicago, Fleming H. Revell Co., 1908, pp. 349), *passim*.
[346] Stock, *The History of the Church Missionary Society*, Vol. III, pp. 123-125.
[347] Stock, *op. cit.*, Vol. III, pp. 516, 517, 523, 530, 753, 786; Vol. IV, pp. 131-136; Napier Malcolm, *Five Years in a Persian Town* (New York, E. P. Dutton & Co., 1907, pp. xv, 272), *passim;* Florence S. Willmot, *Led Forth with Joy* (London, Marshall Brothers, no date, pp. 95), *passim;* Clara C. Rice, *Mary Bird in Persia* (London, Church Missionary Society, 1916, pp. iv, 200), *passim*.
[348] Pascoe, *Two Hundred Years of the S. P. G.*, pp. 728, 729; F. N. Heazell and Mrs. Margoliouth, *Kurds and Christians* (London, Wells Gardner, Darton & Co., 1913, pp. ix, 239), *passim*.
[349] *A Century of Mission Work in Iran*, p. 15.
[350] J. H. Baxter, *Scots in the Caucasus* (reprinted from *The Scots Magazine*, pp. 11), p. 9.

Late in the nineteenth century the Russian Orthodox Church reached south into Persia. Early in the century many Nestorians migrated into the Transcaucasus and South Russia, partly to escape from the Kurds or to find work. In 1859, to gain succour for his people, a Nestorian priest from Urmia journeyed to Constantinople to seek union with the Greek Orthodox Church. From there, at the advice of the head of the Russian mission in Jerusalem, he went to St. Petersburg. Nothing came of his journey immediately. In the 1880's some of the Nestorians, alarmed by the hostility of the Persian Government and by Kurdish raids, sought union with the Russian Orthodox Church to obtain the protection of the Russian state. In the 1890's a union was consummated and by 1900 over 20,000 Nestorians had entered into the Russian communion. Russian parishes and schools were opened and at Urmia a cathedral was erected. In Russia the Brotherhood of St. Cyril and Sergius was formed (1903) to support the mission. However, the defeat of Russia by Japan in 1905 was followed by a loss in Russian prestige and enthusiasm for the Russian church waned.[351]

The great peninsula of Arabia presented more formidable difficulties to the spread of Christianity in the nineteenth century than did any of the countries thus far traversed in this chapter. Christian missions were almost without a protecting outpost of European power. The strategic port of Aden was annexed by Great Britain in 1839 and placed administratively with British India. In 1857 the neighbouring island of Perim was acquired by the English. Early in the twentieth century the boundaries of a British protectorate inland from Aden were defined. Muscat, important for its command of the entrance to the Persian Gulf, had a British resident, but was under its own sultan. Aside from these slight enclaves, Arabia remained largely apart from the Occidental political power and culture which were flooding the rest of western Asia. In most of its vast area nineteenth century Europeans did not even so much as set foot. The Christian communities which once had fringed its shores had long since died out. The birthplace of Islam, Arabia was resolutely and almost solidly Moslem. The chief exceptions were a few thousand Jews who preserved their ancestral faith. Here and there were Christian aliens, largely Goanese and Europeans. It is not surprising, therefore, that the nineteenth century Christian missionary movement had little effect. Yet Christian missionaries from the Occident, both Roman Catholic and Protestant, made their way even to Arabia.

In the nineteenth century a few Roman Catholics settled in Jidda, the port on the Red Sea which commanded the road to Mecca. This was during the time that

[351] Lübeck, *Die russischen Missionen*, pp. 24-30.

Jidda was in the possession of Mohammed Ali, of Egypt. To serve these Roman Catholics the Propaganda sent, in 1840, a Servite. When Mohammed Ali withdrew his troops, the Roman Catholic mission station was removed to the British Aden. In 1850 Capuchins were substituted for the Servites and the mission was attached to the vicariate apostolic of Bombay. In 1859 Aden was made a prefecture apostolic. Later it was joined to the mission to the Gallas, in the adjacent section of Africa. In 1888 Aden became the seat of a vicar apostolic whose jurisdiction included British Somaliland, on the neighbouring African coast. Marist brothers and Franciscan sisters came to assist the Italian Capuchins. The numbers of Roman Catholics were very small, and presumably were almost entirely immigrants—Goanese, Abyssinians, and Europeans.[352]

Protestantism was somewhat later in obtaining a foothold in Arabia than was Roman Catholicism. In 1836 Joseph Wolff touched at Jidda and spent some time among the Jews of Yemen.[353] In 1856 Henry Aaron Stern devoted several months to Arabia, endeavouring to reach the Jews of the peninsula.[354] In 1885 General F. T. Haig, who had long been deeply interested in Christian missions, urged that an enterprise be begun at Aden. In response, Ion Keith-Falconer, son of a Scottish earl, a graduate of Cambridge, and a specialist in Arabic, went to Aden (1885), but died there in 1887. The Free Church of Scotland continued the enterprise thus tragically inaugurated, concentrating on medical service.[355] Some time after Keith-Falconer's death the Danes began a mission at Aden which specialized in education.[356] In 1885, in response to Haig's plea, the Church Missionary Society decided to open a centre at Aden, but in 1888, largely to avoid needless duplication of what the Free Church of Scotland was doing, it withdrew.[357] In 1891 Thomas Valpy French, then sixty-six years of age, ripe in experience as educator and bishop in India, responded to a plea for the spiritual need which Muscat presented and, although the Church Missionary Society, with which he had long been connected, was unable to support him in the venture, he began a residence in that striking and forbidding spot which in a little over four months was terminated by his death.[358] On the northern border of Arabia, across the Jordan from Palestine, the Church Missionary Society had

[352] Lübeck, *Die katholische Orientmission,* pp. 41, 42; *Capucins Missionnaires. Missions Françaises,* p. 65.
[353] Wolff, *Travels and Adventures,* pp. 496-512.
[354] Isaacs, *Biography of the Rev. Henry Aaron Stern,* pp. 101-138.
[355] Robert Sinker, *Memorials of the Hon. Ion Keith-Falconer* (Cambridge, Deighton, Bell and Co., 1888, pp. viii, 280), *passim;* James Robson, *Ion Keith-Falconer of Arabia* (London, Hodder and Stoughton, no date, pp. viii, 178), *passim.*
[356] Robson, *op. cit.,* p. 170; Richter, *Mission und Evangelisation im Orient,* p. 189.
[357] Stock, *The History of the Church Missionary Society,* Vol. III, pp. 521, 522.
[358] Stock, *op. cit.,* Vol. III, pp. 532-535; Birks, *Life and Correspondence of Thomas Valpy French,* Vol. II, pp. 361ff.

outposts.[359] In 1888 and 1889 three students in the Theological Seminary of the (Dutch) Reformed Church in America at New Brunswick, New Jersey, felt the burden of Arabia placed upon their hearts. They offered themselves to the foreign board of their denomination, but that body, hampered by debt, could not see its way clear to undertake a fresh enterprise. Accordingly they formed a new organization, the Arabian Mission. Funds were contributed by sympathetic friends. In 1889 one of three, James Cantine, sailed for Syria, there to study the language, followed in 1890 by a second, Samuel M. Zwemer. The mission's first centre was at Basrah, not far from the head of the Persian Gulf. Before many years other centres were established on the Bahrein Islands (where there had been a Christian bishopric as early as the third century,[360] but from which the faith had disappeared), and at Muscat. In 1894 the foreign board of the Reformed Church assumed the support of the mission. Reinforcements came, hospitals and schools were begun, and wide travel was undertaken to spread the Christian faith by spoken word, example, and printed page. In spite of the firm hold of Islam on the land, a few converts were made.[361] Zwemer became one of the most famous of Christian missionaries to Moslems, travelling over most of the Islamic world, arousing in Europe and America interest in bringing the faith to Moslems, and recruiting and training missionaries.

We must include in this chapter one other country, Afghanistan. Predominantly Moslem and ensconced in its mountains, Afghanistan jealously preserved its faith and its independence. So far as possible, except for the manufacture of armaments, it held itself aloof from the Westernizing forces and appliances which were penetrating its neighbours. The strong Christian communities, largely Nestorian, which had flourished in some of its caravan cities centuries before had vanished. Neither Roman Catholic nor Protestant missionaries were able to obtain a foothold. A few Armenian Christians lived in the country, but maintained their faith somewhat precariously.[362] In 1832 Joseph Wolff traversed the land and held converse with some of its Jews.[363] Now and again an Afghan became Christian through the missions on the Indian side of the border. Occa-

---

[359] Stock, *op. cit.,* Vol. III, pp. 116, 117, Vol. IV, p. 130.

[360] Vol. I, pp. 103, 234.

[361] Samuel M. Zwemer and James Cantine, *The Golden Milestone. Reminiscences of Pioneer Days Fifty Years Ago in Arabia* (New York, Fleming H. Revell Co., 1938, pp. 157), *passim;* Alfred DeWitt Mason and Frederick J. Barny, *History of the Arabian Mission* (New York, The Board of Foreign Missions, Reformed Church in America, 1926, pp. 256), pp. 57-165.

[362] Seth, *Armenians in India,* pp. 207-224.

[363] Wolff, *Travels and Adventures,* p. 351.

sionally a missionary made his way in from India.[364] However, Afghanistan was one of the few countries which in 1914 remained closed against the residence of Christian missionaries.

The nineteenth century witnessed marked changes in the status of Christianity in the northern sections of Africa and in western Asia. In these regions were the birthplace and the traditional stronghold of Islam. Although Christianity existed here at the dawn of the nineteenth century, it was in the form of survivals of ancient Eastern churches which were on the defensive. In the course of the nineteenth century Christianity was more actively and widely propagated than at any time since the Moslem conquest. This was by Roman Catholics from western Europe and by Protestants from western Europe, the British Isles, and the United States. The missionary advance was made in connexion with the penetration of Western culture and the growth of Occidental political power which were so marked a feature of the general history of the world in the nineteenth century. Roman Catholic Christianity had the support of France and, to a less extent, of Spain, Italy, and Austria, in their ambition to extend their empires. Russia used her Orthodox Church to reinforce her southward advance. Great Britain, while not so markedly employing Protestant missions as a tool of her imperialism, through some of her consular diplomatic officials gave assistance to Protestant enterprises. The extensive Protestant missions from the United States had no connexion with American political dreams, for these were non-existent in that region. Nor was American commerce sufficiently prominent to account for their presence. At times they were facilitated by British officials, but they were in no sense an adjunct to British imperial designs. The primary source of the spread of Roman Catholic and Protestant Christianity was neither economic nor political, but was to be found in the great revival of the Christian faith in the nineteenth century.

The main effects of Occidental Christian missions in Northern Africa and western Asia were not statistical. In northern Africa, to be sure, Christians were much more numerous in 1914 than in 1800. This, however, was mainly because of immigration, chiefly from France, Spain, and Italy. Relatively few converts came from non-Christian communities. In western Asia the totals of Christians may, indeed, have declined rather than increased. The massacres of Armenians and Maronites and the emigration to the Americas would seem to have had that as a result. In some respects the Occidental missions may have weakened the Christian communities. Certainly they added to the existing divisions. The

[364] Stock, *op. cit.*, Vol. IV, pp. 121, 209, 210; Lewis, *George Maxwell Gordon*, pp. 305ff.

growth of the various Uniate bodies and of Evangelical churches was at the expense of the existing Eastern churches. By educating Christians and arousing in them hopes of emancipation from the age-long contumely in which they had been held by Moslems, Occidental missions, although quite unintentionally, helped to precipitate the massacres. Yet through the missions from the West came notable contributions. Education was furthered. Modern medical science was brought to the alleviation and cure of disease. Loving, devoted care was given to orphans, the sick, and the victims of poverty and massacres. A purer standard of family life was inculcated by word and example. The Bible was put into many of the vernaculars and was widely distributed. The newer Christian communities which came into being were spiritually more vigorous than the communions from which they were drawn. New life became apparent in some portions of the Eastern churches. Moreover, a few converts were made from the Jews and the Moslems. As the century wore on towards its close, the solid wall of Islam began here and there to weaken. It had by no means crumbled, but it was giving evidence of the Christian impact. Christianity was having a greater effect upon the Moslem world as a whole than it had had since the first centuries of the Arab conquest.

The environment was placing its impress upon the Christianity of the region. The Eastern churches continued to reflect its influence. They were on the defensive, as they had been for centuries. So much of their energy was spent in preserving their existence that they had neither strength nor desire for innovations or advance in theology, ritual, organization, or methods. They were intensely conservative. Some of their members were being gradually absorbed by the Moslem communities in the midst of which they were set. Often the clergy were poorly educated and of inferior moral and spiritual quality. The body of the membership displayed the traits which a religious or cultural minority often develops in the struggle for survival—cleverness, suavity, fawning servility, secretiveness, skill in political manipulation, and duplicity.

The Christianity which was being propagated from the Occident was also modified by the environment. In the effort to win the Eastern churches, Roman Catholicism sought to make itself less alien by encouraging the growth of Uniate bodies which preserved the traditional ecclesiastical language and much of the distinctive customs and rituals of the East. It became, therefore, less exclusively Latin and Western and more varied and Oriental. Protestantism also freed itself from some of its Occidental denominationalism. Many of the new churches which arose from accessions from the Eastern bodies bore the simple name of Evangelical rather than the denominational labels of the Occident. To be sure, in creed, organization, and forms of worship they reproduced in large part what the missionaries had imported from the West. Yet the transfer was not complete. Moreover, confronted with ancient bodies which were professedly Christian and by the sturdy structure of Islam, some Protestant missionaries eschewed the desire to make formal converts. They sought, rather, to permeate existing communities with ideals of Christian origin without effecting a change in outward religious affiliation.[365] Those who most displayed this attitude were usually the missionaries who had been moulded by the liberalism which prevailed in some ecclesiastical circles in the Occident. We shall find the same tendency elsewhere in Asia, notably in India where Christianity confronted both Islam and a Hinduism which, while claiming to be tolerant and willing to adopt and adapt ideas and divinities from other systems, bitterly opposed any transfer of allegiance to another religious group. That some permeation of other religious bodies by Christian ethical and spiritual principles was achieved seems clear. Whether that modification would endure unless incorporated in avowedly Christian groups or unless reinforced by a continued influx of missionaries from the churches of the Occident was yet to be demonstrated. For the time being, through contact with the churches of the Occident, Christianity was undoubtedly gaining.

[365] For a very persuasive and widely read and approved presentation of this position, see Howard S. Bliss (President of the Syrian Protestant College of Beirut), *The Modern Missionary*, in *The Atlantic Monthly*, May, 1920. Reprinted by the American Board of Commissioners for Foreign Missions with the commendatory imprimatur of James L. Barton, the senior secretary of that body, it obviously represented the policy of more than one group.

Chapter III

INDIA. GENERAL SETTING: ROMAN CATHOLIC MISSIONS: PROTESTANT MISSIONS: EFFECT ON THE ENVIRONMENT: EFFECT OF THE ENVIRONMENT

IN INDIA Christianity was confronted by one of its greatest challenges. Here it registered some of its most striking gains of the nineteenth century. Progress was not only numerical, it lay also and possibly even more in the influence exerted upon Indian life both inside and outside the Church.

In India Christianity faced not so much a country as a continent, or, more properly, a subcontinent. In many ways India resembled western Europe. In area and in population it was not far from the size of Europe without Russia. Like western Europe, it was a land mass jutting out from the main body of the continent of Eurasia. Also like western Europe, it had a certain community of culture but was divided racially, linguistically, religiously, and politically. In Europe the cultural tie was Christianity and the Jewish-Greek-Latin heritage of which the Church had once been the main channel of transmission. In India the bond was also religious—Hinduism—and traditions, in part Indo-Aryan, which were closely associated with Hinduism. As in the case of Europe, wave after wave of conquest and immigration had flowed into India, largely from the great springs of population in the main mass of Eurasia. Each wave left a deposit and the result was great racial diversity. India was said to have more than two hundred languages. As Europe was predominantly Christian in professed religious allegiance, so the majority of the peoples of India were Hindu by faith. In both India and Europe there was a large Moslem minority. In India, however, that minority was politically more prominent than in Europe. Until the British conquest, most of the largest empires in India since A.D. 1000 had been built by Moslems. In both Europe and India Islam was strongest in the regions nearest to the historic centres of Moslem power—in Europe the South-east and in India the North-west. Politically India, like Europe, had never been entirely united under one rule. In both regions empires had arisen which for a time had brought together a large part of the whole. Always those empires had fallen apart and disunion had returned.

In a number of ways, however, India was very different from Europe. Hinduism and Christianity were so dissimilar as hardly to be comparable. India contained more diverse religious minorities than did Europe. In it were Sikhs, Buddhists, Jains, Parsees, and Christians, all of them communally self-conscious. There were, as well, several million animists. Europe had only Islam, Judaism, the numerous varieties of Christianity, and sprinklings of paganism. Moreover, the Indian social structure had caste as an outstanding characteristic. Caste made for a greater and more rigid stratification of society than anything Europe knew —although Europe also had its classes. Caste was to affect both the reception of Christianity and the structure of the Indian churches. A feature of the caste system was the lowest stratum, the depressed classes, or the outcastes. The depressed classes were condemned by the accident of birth to poverty and obloquy and to occupations shunned by the rest of the community, such as those of scavenger and leather worker. They, in turn, were divided into many groups.

Certain conditions in India in the closing decades of the eighteenth century require special mention, for they bore directly upon the spread of Christianity in the period with which this volume deals. One was the existence on the coast of footholds of European powers. It was largely in connexion with them that Christianity gained entrance to the land. The Portuguese had been present since the close of the fifteenth century. Of their various posts, the chief was Goa. In their settlements the population claimed the Portuguese name and in certain of its elements gave evidence of Portuguese blood. Many of these "Portuguese" were also found in non-Portuguese ports. The French were on the south-east coast, with Pondicherry as their main centre. At irregular intervals the Dutch held Chinsura, not far from Calcutta. The Danes had Tranquebar on the southeast coast and Serampore on the Hooghly near Calcutta. Through their East India Company, the British were the growing power. The East India Company's chief stations were in Bombay, Madras, and Calcutta, each of strategic importance for the control of important sections of the country.

It was also of significance for the spread of Christianity that before the year 1800 the British conquest was well under way. That conquest is usually said to have begun not far from the middle of the eighteenth century. At the outset the progress of British arms did not mean increased opportunities for Christianity. The East India Company was not entirely opposed to the spread of Christianity. It had long maintained chaplains for its employees and some of its officials had been friendly to the propagation of the faith. Yet in general it was religiously neutral.[1] Concerned primarily with commerce, it wished nothing to interfere with its profits. Toward the end of the eighteenth century, indeed, it

[1] Penny, *The Church in Madras*, Vol. I, *passim.*

sought to hinder the coming of missionaries to India, for these, it felt, with their efforts to win Indians would arouse enmities and so make it trouble.[2] Yet eventually the extension of British rule opened many doors to Christianity.

In the eighteenth century Christianity was represented in India by several of its major divisions.[3] The Syrian or St. Thomas Christians, long Nestorians but now predominantly (although not entirely) Jacobites, were numerous in the South. Roman Catholic Christianity was closely associated with Portuguese power. It was the faith of those who claimed the Portuguese name. The Portuguese Crown, under the padroado, insisted that it possessed the right to appoint the bishops, not only in territories which it actually controlled, but also in non-Portuguese domains. Here and there were Roman Catholic missions outside the Portuguese possessions. In the limited French enclaves there were French missions. Roman Catholic clergy were permitted to care for the "Portuguese" in the areas controlled by the English East India Company. Numbers of former Syrian Christians had become Roman Catholics. In the eighteenth century vigorous Protestant missions had been begun. They had been staffed by Germans of the Pietist strain, but they had been commenced under Danish auspices and had attracted financial assistance from Great Britain. There were scatterings of Armenians who held to their ancestral faith. In 1805 there were said to be seven Armenian churches in India, staffed by fourteen priests and one bishop. In that year there were also said to be two Greek churches with four priests.[4]

In the nineteenth century the completion of the British conquest brought changes which greatly affected the spread of Christianity. The conquest had been inaugurated for the purpose of protecting the East India Company's trading posts and with no thought of dominating all India. Once territory had been acquired, further wars and annexations became necessary to make secure the initial possessions. The pace was intensified by the Anglo-French rivalry which was chronic through much of the eighteenth century and which was peculiarly acute during the Napoleonic Wars. Among the British, moreover, were ambitious empire builders. The British advance was facilitated by the political divisions in India, accentuated as these were by the disintegration of the once powerful Mogul Empire which at its height had embraced most of the land. Because of Indian divisions, the British found allies among the native princes and effected the conquest of the land with relatively small forces of their own. Even the armies directly in the service of the East India Company were largely of Indian personnel, sepoys as they were called, drilled in European methods

[2] Richter, *Indische Missionsgeschichte*, pp. 141, 142.
[3] Vol. III, Chap. 8.
[4] Buchanan, *Memoir of the Expediency of an Ecclesiastial Establishment for British India*, p. 20. See also Seth, *Armenians in India, passim*.

and equipped with Western arms. By the middle of the nineteenth century most of India had been brought under British control, some of it directly administered by the East India Company, and some of it still governed by princes who were allied with the English or had submitted to them. In the years 1857-1858 came what was known as the Mutiny, an effort in which some of the sepoys, rebelling, were intent upon killing or expelling the foreigner. The Mutiny did not spread to all India but was confined chiefly to Bengal, Central India, and the Northwest. It was suppressed and was followed by the abolishment of the rule of the East India Company, now become an anomaly, and the transfer of the administration to the Crown. Before many years the designation Empress of India was added to the titles of Queen Victoria. From time to time the English still were constrained to fight, but the wars were henceforth on the periphery. India had been mastered.

Administratively the vast area thus incorporated into the British Empire was in two divisions. What was known as British India was governed directly by the foreigner through a bureaucracy heading up in a Viceroy and having as its core the Indian Civil Service, recruited from able graduates of British public schools and universities. The Indian states constituted the other division. These were governed by their own princes or chiefs. They were numerous and of varying size. The degree of British control also differed widely. The more powerful princes were almost independent except in foreign affairs and had their own armies and revenues. In area the Indian states were about two-thirds the extent of British India, but their population was only about thirty per cent. of the latter.

British rule was accompanied by the permeation of India by Occidental culture. Under its direction or with its encouragement systems of schools were developed which were largely based upon British models. The language of higher and much of secondary education became English. Through this Western education lay the road to official and most professional advancement. India's leaders were therefore familiarized with and in part moulded by Occidental civilization. The mechanical devices of the nineteenth century Occident were introduced. Railways, the telegraph, factory-made cottons, and, in time, factories became common. Under the British *raj* India was being welded into a self-conscious whole and was beginning to display the nationalism which was so prominent in nineteenth century Europe. Ideas of political independence entered, partly through the English literature which was taught in the schools. In 1885 the Indian National Congress was organized, soon to become the chief organ and spearhead for the movement for increased participation of Indians in government and, eventually, for independence. Gradually, although much less rapidly than the radicals demanded, the British rulers admitted Indians to a share in administration and began the shaping of representative institutions.

The cultural changes brought by the impact of the West were less spectacular in India than in many of the primitive peoples whom we met in the last volume or than in China and Japan. This was partly because of the nature of Indian civilization, which, while yielding and flexible in several of its aspects, was stubbornly tenacious of some of its essential features, notably caste and family. It was also because British administration provided a stability and an order within which change could take place without such explosive revolutions as were brought to some other peoples by the irruption of Western culture. Yet the acids of modernity were surely even though unobtrusively weakening the traditional structure of Indian life. Many of the Indian leaders, educated in Western learning and by Western methods, and under a government which, religiously neutral, gave the impression of being religiously indifferent, became thoroughly secularized. Increasingly they were without religious convictions. They adhered to their inherited faith outwardly, but from social inertia. They were intense nationalists and held to their ancestral religion as much because it was Indian as because it appealed to them as being true.

In some respects British rule was a handicap to the spread of Christianity in India. For a time the East India Company refused missionaries passage on its ships and forbade them to carry on their labours in its territories. This was especially the case in the 1790's and the early 1800's when the rising tide of missionary interest in Great Britain and America was beginning to issue in increased numbers of Protestant missionaries who were seeking access to India and when the company, engaged in the extension of its administration in India, was peculiarly apprehensive of an accretion of resistance because of antagonism among the Indians to the missionaries' activities.[5] These policies were transient. At the renewal of the company's charter by Parliament in 1813 friends of missions, largely Evangelicals, obtained modifications which granted more liberty to missionaries and provided for the establishment of an Anglican bishopric.[6] In 1833, at another renewal of the charter, other restrictions were withdrawn. For many years the East India Company, in succeeding to certain Indian governments, continued the practice of these régimes in maintaining and supervising some of the non-Christian shrines and festivals and in levying taxes for that purpose. This, too, was eventually brought to an end under pressure from British Christians who were scandalized by it.[7] To some extreme Indian na-

[5] Kaye, *Christianity in India*, pp. 244-256.
[6] Kaye, *op. cit.*, pp. 257ff.
[7] Kaye, *op. cit.*, pp. 372ff.; Richter, *Indische Missionsgeschichte*, pp. 199ff.; Allen and

tionalists, the fact that Christianity came in connexion with British rule made them regard the faith with jaundiced eyes. Probably more important was the habit of dependence of the Christians on the missionary bred by the supposed identification of the sahib with the all powerful and wealthy governing class of white men. Since during the latter part of the nineteenth century India was largely passive under the British *raj*, the churches nurtured by the foreigner also long tended to look to the foreigner for leadership and support.

In general, however, British rule facilitated rather than hindered the expansion of Christianity in India. The *pax Britannica* gave to the land more widespread peace and order than it had ever known and for the most part protected missionaries against physical violence. The British administered even-handed justice and by the policy of religious toleration which was eventually adopted accorded to converts some degree of security from persecution. Indeed, not far from the middle of the century the legal principle was established that in British territory a change of religious faith should not subject the convert to the forfeiture of his property which might be entailed under Hindu or Moslem law.[8] Although they did not single out Christians as such for assistance, the British authorities, by their policy of grants-in-aid to schools which met specified educational requirements, gave substantial support to educational institutions maintained by the Christian missions. Coming from the Occident, missionaries found it natural to develop the kind of schools which fitted into the British programme. The association of Christianity with the conquering European contributed to that faith a prestige which encouraged adherence, especially from classes which were underprivileged in the existing Indian order and which saw rosy opportunity in the friendship of the potent white sahib. Although many government officials were cool toward missions and at most maintained an attitude of frigidly correct courtesy towards the missionary, some sought to aid the spread of the faith in such ways as could be open to them without violating the religious neutrality enjoined by government policy.

So multiform and numerous were the Christian missions in India of the nineteenth century that the attempt to compress their story into one chapter, as the necessities of our space require, cannot be but painful. It will be by no means easy to steer a wise middle course between unsatisfactory general statements on the one hand and a confusing mass of detail on the other. In the endeavour to select the most significant events, individuals, and movements, we shall inevitably (although unintentionally) pass over some which deserve

---

McClure, *Two Hundred Years. The History of the Society for Promoting Christian Knowledge*, p. 291.
[8] Kaye, *op. cit.*, pp. 456-459; Pascoe, *Two Hundred Years of the S. P. G.*, p. 508.

mention and include others which a different chronicler would adjudge of minor importance. Moreover, in a land in which so many territorial, racial, and linguistic divisions were found, we cannot proceed state by state and province by province as a fuller account might do, but must content ourselves chiefly with the effort to reveal the chronological progress which the century witnessed in the country as a whole, to single out the more striking individuals, methods, and movements, and to portray the main outlines of the effects of Christianity upon India and of India upon Christianity.

In India, as in so many other parts of the world, Christianity acquired momentum as the nineteenth century progressed. Its gains, as was to be expected, were especially marked in the areas longest in close contact with Westerners. These were chiefly along the south coasts. They were mainly among those classes, the untouchables or outcastes, which suffered most from the existing social and economic order and among those, Eurasians (euphemistically Anglo-Indians) and so-called Portuguese, in whom European mingled with Indian blood and who wished to be identified with Europeans. However, some accessions came from the majority of the racial and social strata.

Christianity's expansion was almost entirely through Roman Catholic and Protestant missions from the Occident. The Christianity which spread was, therefore, chiefly Roman Catholic and Protestant. The Roman Catholicism was primarily from the continent of Europe. The Protestantism was almost a cross section of that multiform movement. Most of the denominations of the British Isles and the United States were represented, together with some from the British Dominions. Numbers of Continental European bodies, mainly Lutheran from Scandinavia and Germany, also sent missionaries.

The reasons for the spread of Christianity were to be found partly in the opportunity afforded by the control of India by Great Britain and the influx of Western culture and partly in the vigour in the churches of the Occident which gave rise to the nineteenth century missionary movement. We can best proceed in our narrative by first recounting the story of the Roman Catholic advance and then turning to the Protestants. After that we will seek to summarize the effects of Christianity in all its branches and the effects of India upon Christianity.

At the close of the eighteenth century Roman Catholic Christianity in India was in decay and the outlook for it was grim. The flourishing missions of the sixteenth and seventeenth centuries which had planted Christianity firmly in the Portuguese enclaves and had brought into being small Roman Catholic communities in several parts of the country, notably in the South, had declined. Roman Catholic Christianity was suffering from an ebb tide which was not to be halted until well along in the first half of the nineteenth century. Most discouraging pictures of the situation were being circulated in Europe.[9] Several factors had combined to bring about this unpromising condition.[10] The waning of Portuguese power was of primary importance, for it was in connexion with the building of the Portuguese Indian empire that Roman Catholic Christianity had enjoyed most of its growth. The Portuguese were being displaced by Protestant European powers, notably the English. A prolonged conflict between Rome and Portugal over the Portuguese right of patronage divided the Roman Catholic forces. Portugal insisted that the padroado, granted her by Rome in the days of her might, gave her the control of Roman Catholic enterprises not only in Portuguese possessions but also in all India. She was unable to supply clergy for that vast area and refused to permit Rome to do so unless the bishops were named by her and the missionaries obtained the permission of the Crown and went out by Lisbon. The attempt of the Papal See to side-step the issue by the appointment of vicars apostolic only aggravated the dispute. Other factors also contributed to the decline of Roman Catholic Christianity. The condemnation by Rome of some of the methods employed by the Jesuits was followed, a little later, by the expulsion of the Society of Jesus from the Portuguese and French domains and by the dissolution of the society by papal decree. In the eighteenth century the Maratha wars and the persecutions by the ardently Moslem Tipu Sultan wrought havoc in some of the Roman Catholic communities. Added to these were the French Revolution and the wars of Napoleon with their interruption of aid from Europe and with secularizing disturbances even in India.[11]

The sad state of Roman Catholic Christianity may be made more vivid by a few concrete illustrations. In the early part of the nineteenth century a professedly Roman Catholic community in Bengal had no public worship nor ad-

---

[9] The most famous of these discouraging pictures was by a former Roman Catholic missionary in India, J. A. Dubois, who, in *Letters on the State of Christianity in India; in which the Conversion of the Hindoos is Considered Impracticable* (London, Longman, Hurst, Rees, Orme, Brown, and Green, 1823, pp. viii, 222), declared (p. 2) that "under existing circumstances there is no human possibility of converting the Hindoos to any sect of Christianity" and that existing Christian communities were dwindling. The replies to this by Protestants agreed that Roman Catholic missions were a failure, but maintained that the Protestant enterprise was giving promise of success. See James Hough, *A Reply to the Letters of the Abbé Dubois on the State of Christianity in India* (London, R. Watts, 1824, pp. 322), and Henry Townley, *An Answer to the Abbé Dubois* (London, R. Clay, 1824, pp. viii, 214). On Dubois, who had been a missionary in India from 1799 to 1823, see Jenks, *Six Great Missionaries of the Sixteenth and Seventeenth Centuries*, p. 144.
[10] Vol. III, pp. 265-273.
[11] Josson, *La Mission du Bengale Occidental*, Vol. I, p. 139.

ministration of the sacraments, and gave no indication of its faith aside from the possession of a few images of the Virgin Mary and the saints.[12] Much the same report came from the adjacent Assam.[13] On the Fishery Coast, in the South, many of the nominal Christians reached old age without knowing how to make even the sign of the Cross. Sunday observance was neglected, and drunkenness and concubinage were frequent.[14] As late as the 1830's there was fear that Roman Catholic Christianity would disappear in Bengal through the decline in the number of Christians and the failure to give religious instruction to the youth.[15] In the fore part of the nineteenth century many of the native clergy from Portuguese Goa bought ordination and assignment to parishes.[16] Missionaries deteriorated in quality and were so engrossed in caring for existing Christian communities that they did not reach out to non-Christians.[17] All the bishops were Europeans, for the seventeenth century attempt to create a native episcopate had been disappointing.[18] In 1800 there were four dioceses in Portuguese hands. In them the lives of the Goanese priests were often scandalous. Outside these dioceses there are said to have been only four missions—that of Agra with six Capuchins, that of Pondicherry with five or six from the Missions Étrangères of Paris, the vicariate of Malabar with two Carmelites and a few native priests, and the vicariate of Bombay with two Carmelites.[19] The number of Roman Catholics in India is reported to have declined from 2,000,000 or 2,500,000 in 1700 to between 475,000 and 1,200,000 in 1800.[20] Christians were doing little to spread their faith among non-Christians. They were becoming, in effect, a kind of closed caste which was slowly losing ground. As in other parts of the world, at the dawn of the nineteenth century Roman Catholic missions were in the doldrums.

Recovery did not begin immediately with the new century. For many years the stubborn refusal of Portugal to relinquish the hold of its palsied hands upon

[12] Pascoe, *Two Hundred Years of the S. P. G.*, pp. 492, 493.
[13] Becker, *Im Stromtal des Brahmaputra*, p. 106; *Catholic Directory of India, Ceylon and Burma*, 1926, pp. 16ff.
[14] Hull, *Bombay Mission History*, Vol. I, p. 278.
[15] Becker, *op. cit.*, p. 104.
[16] Huonder, *Der einheimische Klerus in den Heidenländern*, p. 73.
[17] Hull, *op. cit.*, Vol. I, p. 215.
[18] Huonder, *op. cit.*, pp. 261, 262.
[19] Baudrillart in Descamps, *Histoire Générale Comparée des Missions*, p. 544. On Pondicherry, see Launay, *Histoire des Missions de l'Inde*, Vol. I, pp. 187ff. Between 1794 and 1806 seven from the seminary of the Missions Étrangères had been ordained as priests.—Launay, *op. cit.*, Vol. I, p. 209.
[20] Baudrillart in Descamps, *op. cit.*, p. 544; Schwager, *Die katholische Heidenmission der Gegenwart*, p. 343. An official estimate said that in 1808 there were 633,000 Roman Catholics in India.—*Notizie Statistiche delle Missioni di Tutto il Mondo Dipendenti dalla S. C. de Propaganda Fide* (1844), pp. 511-535.

the episcopate embarrassed efforts from other countries and from Rome to take advantage of the new day. Indeed, at no time in the nineteenth century was the dispute fully resolved. The struggle was long and painful and we have the space to give it only a brief summary.

The Portuguese authorities claimed that not far from the middle of the sixteenth century Pope Paul IV in creating the see of Cochin had clearly stated that the right of patronage should never be impaired for any cause whatever.[21] The issue was complicated by the pride of many of the Roman Catholics in India in the Portuguese name. Although the claim of many of these to Portuguese blood rested on dubious foundations, they insisted that they were Portuguese and saw in the padroado a bulwark of their position. Any attempt to weaken the padroado and to place them under the jurisdiction of bishops or vicars apostolic appointed without reference to Lisbon seemed to them a derogation from their dignity.[22]

The extent of the control of Portugal over the Roman Catholic Christianity of India in the fore part of the nineteenth century can be seen from a brief survey of the ecclesiastical organization. Under the Portuguese padroado were the archdiocese of Goa, with a large number of churches and monasteries in the Portuguese possessions, Goa, Damaun, and Diu, and with jurisdiction over churches and Catholic villages in and near Bombay, in the Deccan, and along the coast south of Goa; the archdiocese of Cranganore, on the south-west coast near Cochin, with jurisdiction chiefly over Syrian Christians in communion with Rome; the diocese of Cochin, with oversight of the Cochin and Tranvancore coasts and over the remnants of the once flourishing Jesuit missions in and near Madura and now served by a few Goanese priests and representatives of the Missions Étrangères of Paris; and the diocese of Mylapore (or Meliapur), with headquarters just south of Madras and with jurisdiction as well over a few churches in Bengal and Orissa.[23] The dioceses of Cochin and Mylapore had been vacant more than a third of the time since their founding and the archdiocese of Cranganore more than half the time.[24] In addition there were three vicariates apostolic, directly under the Propaganda, Verapoly (or Malabar), Pondicherry, Bombay, and the Tibetan-Hindustan Mission.[25]

In the 1830's the situation in the padroado dioceses became so deplorable that Rome felt it must take action. Civil strife in Portugal was accompanied by

[21] The Padroado Question, p. 23.
[22] The Padroado Question, pp. 2, 9.
[23] Hull, op. cit., Vol. I, pp. 220-222.
[24] The Padroado Question, pp. 19, 20.
[25] Hull, op. cit., Vol. I, pp. 220-222.

ecclesiastical disorder. In 1831 all four of the sees were vacant.[26] In 1833 the government suppressed the religious orders in Portugal and its colonies and the following year confiscated their property.[27] In 1832 the Propaganda asked the King of Portugal either to observe his duties and fill the dioceses or renounce his privileges. When no reply was vouchsafed, vicariates apostolic were created for Calcutta (1834), Madras (1834), Ceylon (1836), and Madura (1837).[28] The Portuguese clergy in India vigorously opposed these actions and soon were in open revolt.[29] Rome did not relent, but, on the contrary, came out in 1838 with the brief *multa praeclare* which abolished the sees of Cochin, Cranganore, and Mylapore, confirmed the vicariates apostolic, extended their jurisdiction, and deprived the padroado clergy of all power within their areas.[30]

Friendly relations between the Holy See and Portugal, broken off in 1833, were renewed in 1841.[31] Yet the controversy over the padroado continued.[32] Indeed, it was bitterest between 1839 and 1862.[33] The Mutiny and the new day which followed its suppression seemed an opportune time to effect a fresh arrangement. In 1857, 1860, and 1861 Pope Pius IX concluded agreements with Portugal whereby the latter recognized the jurisdiction of the vicars apostolic in all places in which they were in actual possession and Rome permitted Portugal to erect new dioceses with power of patronage over them. The three sees of Cochin, Mylapore, and Cranganore, suffragan to Goa, were reinstated, but their dimensions were reduced. The Archbishop of Goa was given jurisdiction over some communities outside his diocese.[34] The programme proved unworkable.[35]

[26] Josson, *La Mission du Bengale Occidental*, Vol. I, p. 162.
[27] D'Sa, *The History of the Diocese of Damaun*, p. 120; D'Sa, *History of the Catholic Church in India*, Vol. II, pp. 100ff.
[28] De Bussierre, *Histoire du Schisme Portugais dans les Indes*, pp. 63-66; Hull, *op. cit.*, Vol. I, p. 261.
[29] Hull, *op. cit.*, Vol. I, p. 261; *Väth, Die deutschen Jesuiten in Indien*, pp. 42ff.
[30] Hull, *op. cit.*, Vol. I, p. 222; D'Sa, *The History of the Diocese of Damaun*, pp. 94, 95; De Bussierre, *op. cit.*, pp. 258-265.
[31] D'Sa, *op. cit.*, p. 156.
[32] Among the controversial books and pamphlets, all four of them, as it happens, against the Portuguese position, are *Memoria sullo Scisma Indo-Portoghese che si Presenta al Pubblico da un Missionario delle Indie Orientali* (Italia, 1853, pp. 156); *Cenni sulla Questione del Patronato Indo-Portoghese Proposti da un Missionario dell' India. In Tre Memorie* (Genoa, 1853, pp. 160); Lorenzo Puccinelli, *Lo Scisma Indo-Portoghese al Giudizio degli Imparziali Memoire Tre* (Roma, Tipografia di Bernardo Morini, 1853, pp. 160); *The Portuguese Schism More Fully Investigated and the Danger of Adhering to it Plainly Explained . . . in a Few Words to the Rev. Philippe C. Piedade de Concecao . . .* (Colombo, The Catholic Press, 1846, pp. 33); De Bussierre, *op. cit.*, pp. 75-78.
[33] D'Sa, *The History of the Diocese of Damaun*, p. 64; De Bussierre, *op. cit.*, pp. 96ff.
[34] *The Padroado Question*, p. 37; D'Sa, *op. cit.*, p. 219; Hull, *Bombay Mission History*, Vol. II, pp. 1-19; Josson, *La Mission du Bengale Occidental*, Vol. II, pp. 1-3.
[35] Hull, *op. cit.*, Vol. II, pp. 94-96.

Complaints continued from both sides.[36] Non-Portuguese missions to India were growing rapidly and obviously must be freed from the burden of this chronic friction. In 1884 Rome appointed an Apostolic Delegate as its agent in India. Among his tasks was an adjustment of the padroado issue.[37] In 1886 a new settlement was negotiated. The Archbishopric of Goa was elevated to the Patriarchate of the East Indies (although in effect it had had this position since the sixteenth century) with the right to preside over national councils in the entire East Indies, and the Portuguese Crown retained the prerogative of patronage over the ancient sees of Goa, Cochin, Mylapore, and Cranganore (the title of Archbishop of Cranganore was to be borne by the Bishop of Damaun). The three padroado sees of Cochin, Mylapore, and Cranganore were to be suffragans of Goa. The King of Portugal was to have the privilege of presentation to the sees of Bombay, Mangalore, Quilon, and Madura. At about the same time (September, 1886) a hierarchy was created for India. The land was divided into seven ecclesiastical provinces—the archdioceses of Goa, Bombay, Agra, Calcutta, Madras, Verapoly, and Pondicherry—and various vicariates and prefectures apostolic were elevated to bishoprics.[38] This arrangement did not fully solve the issue. Portuguese national aspirations were not completely met. Preliminary steps taken by the Pope through the Apostolic Delegate had led to bitter debate in Portugal and the downfall of a ministry.[39] The compromise was in many ways advantageous to Portugal, for Rome could not afford, for the sake of the Church in Portugal itself, a drastic alienation of sympathy in the mother country. Not only was Portugal given a voice in more sees than before, but a larger number of Christians were transferred to the padroado districts than were lost to them.[40] Yet opposition was voiced in the Portuguese Chamber of Deputies.[41] In India in some places a double jurisdiction still existed and Christians who thought of themselves as under the padroado fiercely resented efforts to abridge

[36] *The Concordat Question*, p. 13; *Refutation of the Pastoral Address of the Right Rev. Dr. J. Fennelly* (Madras, The Lusitanian Press, 1860, pp. 118); *Memorials Submitted to the Holy See . . . by the Catholic Community of Canara* (Madras, C. Foster & Co., 1874, pp. 73, 6); Vindex [Mgr. Boujeau], *Blots Literary, Theological and Moral* (Jaffna, St. Joseph's Catholic Mission Press, pp. 110, xii).
[37] Schwager, *Die katholische Heidenmission der Gegenwart*, p. 351; Josson, *op. cit.*, Vol. II, pp. 1-3.
[38] Josson, *op. cit.*, Vol. II, pp. 1-3; D'Sa, *op. cit.*, pp. 1-3; Hull, *op. cit.*, Vol. II, pp. 130-192; Piolet and Vadot, *L'Église Catholiques aux Indes*, p. 23; Capuchin Mission Unit, *India and Its Missions*, p. 142. For the text of the bull erecting the hierarchy see Launay, *Histoire des Missions de l'Inde*, Vol. IV, pp. 559-564.
[39] Josson, *op. cit.*, Vol. II, pp. 1-3.
[40] Hull, *op. cit.*, Vol. II, p. 233.
[41] Henrique de Barros Gomes, *O Padroado da Coroa de Portugal nas Indias Orientaes e a Concordata de 23 de Junho de 1886. Discursos proferidos na Camara dos Senhores Deputados nas Sessões de 5, 6 e 7 de Maio de 1887* (Lisbon, Imprensa Nacional, 1887, pp. 107).

their ancient customs, even by Portuguese bishops.[42] Friction continued until after 1914 and, as we are to see in the next volume, in 1928 a fresh settlement was attempted. However, by the actions of 1886 the larger part of India was clearly removed from the hampering claims of the Portuguese.

Another set of problems inherited by Rome from the pre-nineteenth century and Portuguese periods was that of the Syrian Christians. Many of these Christians had united with Rome. Some were brought into full conformity and adopted the Latin rite. Others, while in communion with Rome, retained their ancient Malabar rites and were Uniates.[43] At times the Uniates were restive under their bishops. In 1861, at the request of some of them, the Roman Catholic Patriarch of Babylon (of the Chaldean or Nestorian Uniates) sent a bishop, Thomas Rocos, to whom most of the Malabar Uniates submitted. The missionaries persuaded him that he was creating a schism and he returned home. In 1874, again on the invitation of some of the Malabar Uniates, the Patriarch of Babylon sent another bishop, John Elias Mellus. By the following year about sixty churches were numbered among his adherents. Although, at the command of Rome, the Patriarch ordered him to leave, Mellus remained obdurate until 1881. Even after he became reconciled to the Patriarch and returned to his old see, several of the congregations remained aloof under the jurisdiction of two priests. Their numbers dwindled and by 1910 the priests had died.[44] In 1887, in accordance with his policy of strengthening the churches of the Oriental rites who were in communion with Rome and as part of the rearrangement and strengthening of the hierarchy, Pope Leo XIII separated the churches of the Syrian rite on the Malabar coast from those of the Latin rite and placed them under two vicariates apostolic. However, the first incumbents of these vicariates were Latins. In 1896 a new division of the Uniates was made among three vicariates apostolic which were filled by bishops of the Syrian rite and nationality.[45] In 1911 a fourth vicariate was created. In that year the Uniates in the 4 vicariates were said to number 665,084 served by 426 priests. Seminaries for the training of an indigenous priesthood were conducted by Carmelites. In the nineteenth century a congregation of Carmelite Tertiates for the men and two congregations for women came into being. There were two printing presses and several hundred schools. The Uniate communities were prospering.[46]

[42] C. A. Silveira of Manapad, *An Appeal for Liberty of Worship and Freedom from Arbitrary and Unjust Injunctions of the Toulouse Mission against Religious Processions in Public Streets* (Madras, 1920, pp. 132), *passim.*

[43] Vol. III, pp. 264, 265.

[44] *Catholic Directory of India, Ceylon, and Burma, 1926*, pp. 25, 26.

[45] Capuchin Mission Unit, *India and Its Missions*, p. 160; Lübeck, *Die katholische Orientmission*, p. 149.

[46] Lübeck, *op. cit.*, pp. 149, 150.

The Roman Catholic Church not only inherited from the preceding period embarrassing problems, it also suffered from the fact that in the nineteenth century the conquering power was Protestant. As between the various branches of the Christian Church the British *raj* maintained for the most part a correct neutrality. In 1833 the East India Company recognized as a matter of principle that provision should be made for the spiritual care of such of its servants as were Roman Catholics as well as of the Protestants in its employ. It made a monthly grant to four of the bishops, supported some children in Roman Catholic orphanages, and assigned grants-in-aid to Roman Catholic as well as to other schools.[47] Yet the government gave to the Church of England the preferred even though limited position of an establishment. More important was the fact that the British were predominantly Protestant. Quite apart from any overt steps, this fact gave to that wing of the faith a certain prestige, much as in the day of its might the Portuguese power helped to attract some Indians to Roman Catholic Christianity.

As a counterweight to these handicaps, the Roman Catholic Church could count as an asset the fairly large Indian communities attached to it, and numerous clergy.

Building on these foundations and reinforced by the growing enthusiasm of its adherents in Europe for the spread of their faith, Roman Catholic Christianity enjoyed a striking growth in nineteenth century India. By the year 1914 the missionary forces in India were largely augmented, partly by strengthening the staffs of orders already represented and partly by the re-introduction of the Society of Jesus and the coming of bodies not previously seen in the country. Yet even at the beginning of the twentieth century the time of the European priests was said to be so engrossed with schools and pastoral duties that there was little surplus energy for reaching out to non-Christians. Growth in numbers, presumably, was largely by the excess of births over deaths in the Roman Catholic communities.[48] We must not take the space for a detailed account of the growth. We can merely give a sketch which is not even a complete or well-rounded summary.

The half century or so before the years 1886 and 1887 when the fresh attempt to solve the padroado question and the creation of a hierarchy for India provided a landmark in the history of the Roman Catholic Church in India witnessed the coming of a number of orders. The revived Jesuits returned. Salesians,

---

[47] Anastasius Hartmann, *Remarks on the Resolutions of the Government of India upon the Catholic Affairs of India, 28th of February, 1856* (London, Burns and Lambert, 1857, pp. 50), *passim*.
[48] Schmidlin-Braun, *Catholic Mission History*, p. 596.

the Oblates of Mary Immaculate, the Holy Cross Fathers, the Society for Foreign Missions of Milan, and the Benedictines inaugurated enterprises.[49]

In the South, the seminary at Verapoly for the training of an indigenous clergy was developed by Francis Xavier of St. Anna, who arrived in 1832, later became vicar apostolic, and augmented the faculty, equipment, and student body. In 1866 the institution was moved to Puthenpally. In 1888, following the changes of 1886 in the structure of the Indian church, it was made a major seminary and was put directly under the Propaganda.[50]

In the field of the Missions Étrangères of Paris which centred at Pondicherry but extended outside French territory, advance was registered. Reinforcements were sent, additional Christian communities arose, and new churches were constructed.[51] In 1845 some limitations of the society's area were made because of the re-entry of the Jesuits into their former long-cultivated territory in Madura, memorable for Robert de Nobili and his daring experiment.[52] But three vicariates apostolic were created and the new heads were from the Missions Étrangères.[53] The seminaries for the training of the native clergy were given additional buildings and grew in the numbers of their students.[54] The schism over the Portuguese padroado brought difficulties,[55] but did not prevent the growth of the mission. With the creation of the hierarchy for India in the 1880's the area entrusted to the society became the archdiocese of Pondicherry with two suffragan dioceses.[56] Not far from 1897 the number of Roman Catholics was counted as 287,000 in a population of about 15,000,000.[57] This was a growth from about 170,000 twenty years before.[58]

Madura was restored to the Jesuits in 1836 or 1837. The society, from its Toulouse province, rapidly restaffed the field. By 1865 forty-four of its members had served in the renewed enterprise.[59] In a great famine in the 1870's the relief given by the Jesuits led to a large number of accessions, notably a mass movement of the Shanars, a caste depending upon the cultivation of the palm,

[49] Capuchin Mission Unit, op. cit., p. 130.
[50] History-Album of St. Joseph's Apostolic Central-Seminary, Verapoly-Puthenpally-Alwaye (1932, pp. 72), passim.
[51] Launay, Histoire des Missions de l'Inde, Vol. I, pp. 283ff., Vol. II, pp. 105ff.
[52] Vol. III, pp. 259-261.
[53] Launay, op. cit., Vol. II, pp. 312ff.
[54] Launay, op. cit., Vol. II, pp. 423-425.
[55] Launay, op. cit., Vol. III, pp. 289ff.
[56] Launay, op. cit., Vol. IV, p. 453.
[57] Launay, op. cit., Vol. IV, p. 454.
[58] Schwager, Die katholische Heidenmission der Gegenwart, p. 375.
[59] Louis Saint-Cyr, Les Nouveaux Jésuites Français dans l'Inde ou Vie du R. P. Pierre Perrin suivie de Notices sur quelques-uns de ses Compagnons (Paris, Librairie de P.-M. Laroche, 1865, pp. xii, 381)), pp. 373-378; Le Maduré, p. 5.

towards the Church.[60] With their customary emphasis upon education, the Jesuits developed at Trichinopoly St. Joseph's College, the outstanding Roman Catholic educational institution in South India.[61]

From 1836 to 1870 the Capuchins were allowed to retain their place, but only in the French settlements, under the device of a prefecture apostolic of Pondicherry. In 1879 that prefecture was transferred to the Congregation of the Holy Ghost and in 1886 it was merged with the newly created hierarchy.[62]

The vicariate apostolic which bore the name of Bombay was administered by the Discalced Carmelites from its erection in 1734 until past the middle of the nineteenth century.[63] In 1858, partly because of a shortage of staff and funds and in part in connexion with the rearrangement which followed the papal actions on the padroado issue near that time, the Capuchins surrendered the area and it was transferred to the Jesuits.[64] Most of the political division known as the Bombay Presidency was thus assigned to the Society of Jesus. It became the missionary territory of the German province. It was the earliest distinctively German Roman Catholic mission in India and, indeed, is said to have been the first German Roman Catholic mission in non-Christian lands in modern times. In 1886 when Bombay was created an archdiocese Poona was made a diocese. Both remained in Jesuit hands.[65] To the assistance of the Jesuits came the Daughters of the Cross of Liége.[66]

The Carmelites did not withdraw completely from India. They remained in charge of a portion of the south-west coast known as South Canara and for some years had their centre at Mangalore. The Christians of the region had suffered severely from the persecutions of Tipu Sultan and are said to have declined from 80,000 to 10,000. By 1860 they are reported to have risen again to a total of between 50,000 and 60,000 and to have rebuilt their churches.[67] One of the leaders of the enterprise was Lucien Garrelon, known better by his religious name, Father Marie-Ephrem. For a time he was head of a newly opened house of his order at Rennes, but he was sent to India. In 1868 he became Vicar Apostolic of Quilon. While attending the Vatican Council in 1870 he declined an offer to be coadjutor and successor to the Archbishop of Rennes, the Metro-

[60] Schwager, op. cit., p. 369.
[61] Schwager, op. cit., pp. 370, 371.
[62] Hull, Bombay Mission History, Vol. I, pp. 277, 278.
[63] Piolet and Vadot, L'Église Catholique aux Indes, p. 49.
[64] Hull, op. cit., Vol. I, pp. 488-493; Väth, Die deutschen Jesuiten in Indien, pp. 65, 66.
[65] Schwager, op. cit., p. 398; Schmidlin, Das Deutsche Missionswerk der Gegenwart, pp. 68ff; Streit, Atlas Hierarchicus, p. 99; Väth, op. cit., pp. 68ff.
[66] Laveille, Une Sœur Missionnaire. Sœur Théodorine de la Passion de la Congrégation des Filles de la Croix de Liége (1832-1911) (Louvain, É Desbarax, 1928, pp. x, 434), passim.
[67] Laouënan, Lettres sur l'Inde, p. 159.

politan of Brittany. Returning to India, he became bishop in the distracted see of Mangalore and died in 1873.[68] It was at the suggestion of Father Marie-Ephrem that Sophia Leeves, an English convert to Roman Catholicism, usually called by her religious name, Sister Teresa Veronica, became a member of the Third Regular Order of the Carmelites and inaugurated an institute known as the Apostolic Carmel, whose members were to give themselves chiefly to teaching. The first mother superior of the Apostolic Carmel was Sister Marie-des-Anges, whose mother is said to have died of a broken heart because her daughter went to India. It was at Mangalore that the Apostolic Carmel had its chief centre. Most of its pupils were Anglo-Indians. At Mangalore, too, were Discalced Carmelite Sisters. In 1878 Venetian Jesuits were substituted for Carmelite priests in Mangalore, but the Apostolic Carmel continued.[69] The Jesuits gained access to a group of aborigines very low on the social scale and established among them a catechumenate, schools, and one or two orphanages, and gave some medical care.[70] The Discalced Carmelites remained in charge in Quilon and Verapoly. In 1906, the first group of Sisters of the Holy Cross, founded in Switzerland in 1844, arrived in the diocese of Quilon. They and those who followed them were in charge of hospitals.[71] It was Bishop Benzier, himself a Swiss, who induced them to come. He made three trips to Europe to raise funds for his diocese. Funds came, too, through the steady correspondence which he maintained with Europe and America.[72]

Some indication of one of the motives leading to the acceptance of Christianity come from the Carmelite territory. On the Malabar coast a number of women of low caste were won to the Christian faith and wished to change their costume to that of women of higher castes. The non-Christians demurred and the government of Travancore, a native state, upheld them. When Roman Catholic and Protestant missionaries appealed the case to the British authorities, the latter ruled that each might dress as he or she wished. The Christians had gained their point.[73]

In the nineteenth century Madras and the adjoining regions witnessed a marked growth of Roman Catholic strength. In the first three or four decades

[68] *The Apostolic Carmel, Mangalore. A Retrospect of Sixty Years*, pp. 11, 12.

[69] *The Apostolic Carmel, Mangalore. A Retrospect of Sixty Years*, passim. On the Jesuit mission see S. F. Zanetti, *La Missione di Mangalore* (Milan, Tipografia Pontifica S. Giuseppe, 1895, pp. 30), *passim*, and *Status Missionis Mangalorensis ad Oram Canarensem et Malabaricam in Indiis Orientalibus ineunte Aprili, 1892* (Mangalore, Mission Press, 1892, pp. 14), *passim*.

[70] Alessandro Camiso, *I Korgàr. Nella Missione di Mangalore* (Milan, Tipografia Artigianelli, 1911, pp. 36), *passim*.

[71] J. V. F., *A Quarter Century of Progress, Diocese of Quilon, 1900-1925*, p. 38.

[72] J. V. F., *op. cit.*, p. 9.

[73] Laouënan, *op. cit.*, p. 138.

of the century the Roman Catholic cause was severely handicapped by the controversy over the Portuguese padroado. Protestant missions were very active in Madras and its vicinity and Roman Catholicism was under a cloud. When, in 1834, Rome took steps toward a solution by creating a vicariate apostolic of Madras, the new ecclesiastical division was made to include a vast territory on the north which later became the dioceses of Hyderabad, Vizagapatam, and Nagpur.

In its early years the vicariate apostolic of Madras was headed successively by bishops of various orders. Among them, too, were seculars. To enable the Roman Catholic Church to fit in with the British regime, Irish priests were appointed to the post. Notable among these were two brothers, John Fennelly, who served from 1842 to 1868 and became the real founder of the Madras Mission, and Stephen Fennelly. John Fennelly educated at his own cost clergy for the mission in the Irish college of Drumcondra, developed schools and various charitable institutions, and provided for the spiritual care of the Roman Catholics. Stephen placed the mission on a sound financial basis after the large expenditures under John and called in representatives of the recently founded English missionary organization, St. Joseph's Society of Mill Hill.[74]

The Mill Hill missionaries laboured primarily among the Telugus. When they arrived, in 1875, the Roman Catholics in their area numbered about 8,000.[75] There had been Christians among the Telugus at least as early as the fore part of the eighteenth century.[76] Under the care of the Mill Hillers mass movements towards the faith occurred. These were notable in and after the great famine year of 1878.[77] As a result of that tragedy thousands of those who had been given help joined either the Protestants or the Roman Catholics.

Earlier than the priests from Mill Hill, Oblates of Mary Immaculate from Turin arrived (1843) to share in the burden of the Madras vicariate.[78]

In 1851 the vicariate apostolic of Hyderabad, which included the larger part of the native state of that name in the heart of the Deccan, was carved out from the huge vicariate of Madras. In 1863 it was entrusted to the Milan Seminary. At the time of the arrival of the Italians the Roman Catholics of the region numbered between 7,000 and 8,000, mostly Goanese. The great numerical growth of the Milan enterprise began in the 1890's, and was chiefly among the

---

[74] Schwager, *Die katholische Heidenmission der Gegenwart*, pp. 380, 381; Piolet and Vadot, *L'Église Catholique aux Indes*, pp. 36ff.
[75] *Fides News Service*, Nov. 2, 1935, telling of the golden jubilee of the Mill Hill mission.
[76] Paul, *History of the Telugu Christians*, p. 16.
[77] Schwager, *op. cit.*, p. 381.
[78] Paul, *op. cit.*, p. 76.

Telugus. Various congregations of sisters, among them some recruited from the Italians, conducted schools in the vicariate.[79]

Vizagapatam and Nagpur, a large region north of the Godavari River, were separated from Madras as a new mission in 1850. Irish priests had been labouring there since 1839 among a few thousand Roman Catholics, remnants of the pre-nineteenth century Golconda Mission. In 1845 the area had been transferred to Salesians from Savoy, and that in spite of the protests of John Fennelly, who preferred his fellow Irish.[80] Protestants, already in Vizagapatam, also opposed their coming.[81] It was to the Salesians that the new vicariate was assigned. When, in 1886, Vizagapatam was made a diocese and when, in 1887, Nagpur, embracing the Central Provinces, was separated from it as a distinct diocese, the Salesians were continued in charge of them both.[82] In the early days of the Salesians in their area, one of them met with physical violence at the hands of a Goanese priest when he administered the sacraments in a Christian community which the latter had been serving.[83] The Salesians found one of their most fruitful fields among the Khonds, an aboriginal folk of primitive culture whose chief habitat, being in the hills, had kept them largely apart from Indo-Aryan and Dravidian civilization. The first contacts of the Salesians with the Khonds were made in the 1850's. The Khonds proved eager for instruction, but, since they were semi-nomadic, it was with difficulty that they could be brought together for continuous teaching.[84] Eventually several thousands of them were baptized and catechists were placed in their villages. Yet some of the catechists were prefunctory in fulfilling their duties and many of the parents distrusted the Christian schools on the ground that through them the children would be weaned from the traditions of their ancestors.[85] To Vizagapatam and Nagpur came representatives of several women's congregations. The first of these were the Sisters of St. Joseph of Annecy, from the centre from which the initial Salesians were derived.[86] They were followed by others.[87] As they developed,

[79] Schwager, op. cit., pp. 384, 385.

[80] [Domenge], La Mission de Vizagapatam, pp. 109-116.

[81] [Domenge], op. cit., p. 127.

[82] [Domenge], op. cit., pp. 511-515; Schwager, op. cit., p. 386.

[83] [Domenge], op. cit. p. 154.

[84] [Domenge], op. cit., p. 180; Rossillon, Sous les Palmiers du Coromandel, pp. 68-95.

[85] Rossillon, Les Moissonneuses du Coromandel, pp. 106-109.

[86] Rossillon, op. cit., pp. 19-32; I. de Cicé, La Grande Baptiseuse, Sœur Saint-Luce (1843-1929) des Sœurs de Saint-Joseph d'Annecy (Bar-le-duc, Imprimerie Saint-Paul, 1933, pp. 65), passim.

[87] [Domenge], op. cit., pp. 493-498. For the life of one of the Salesian sisters, see Feige, Hélène Touvé 1881-1915. Sœur Andre de Marie Immaculée, Catéchiste-Missionnaire aux Indes, d'apres sa Correspondénce (Paris, J. de Gigord, 1922, pp. xliii, 461).

the dioceses had, thanks largely to the aid of these sisters, the usual accompaniment of schools.

The populous Bengal had contained Roman Catholics long before the nineteenth century. At the dawn of the century, as we saw a few paragraphs above, their faith was deteriorating. After the dissolution of the Society of Jesus a few Portuguese Augustinians under the Bishop of Mylapore gave spiritual care to Roman Catholics in the south and east of the region.[88] In 1834, when Rome, cutting the Gordian knot in the padroado controversy, created a number of vicariates apostolic, Bengal was included as one of the new ecclesiastical divisions and was assigned to the English Jesuits. In the first party that came were also some Irish and French Jesuits.[89] Difficulty followed with the Augustinians, who resented what they regarded as an infringement on the authority of the padroado diocese of Mylapore.[90] The first vicar apostolic did not arrive until 1840.[91] A college, St. Xavier's, was begun. The Hindu College in Calcutta which was founded by a wealthy Calcutta merchant drew its faculty largely from the staff of St. Xavier's.[92] In the 1840's Irish Christian Brothers also came to Bengal as teachers.[93] In 1846 the English Jesuits were recalled from Bengal and St. Xavier's was discontinued.[94] In 1850 Bengal was divided into two vicariates. The western one included the chief city, Calcutta, and remained in Jesuit hands. The eastern one was entrusted (1853) to the Congregation of the Holy Cross of Mans. In 1870 a prefecture apostolic was carved out in Central Bengal and was given to the Milan Seminary.[95]

Western Bengal became a field of the Belgian Jesuits. The first Belgian contingent arrived in 1859.[96] St. Francis Xavier's College in Calcutta was reopened and soon was flourishing. Slowly beginnings were made in Orissa, in the southern part of the vicariate, and that in spite of an exhausting famine in the 1860's.[97] Late in the 1860's, at the suggestion of an English officer who had served in the plateau of Chota Nagpur immediately to the west of Bengal, the Jesuits began to reach out to the aborigines of that region. The Lutheran Gossner Mission, from Germany, was already there and had made hundreds of converts. Anglicans of the Society for the Propagation of the Gospel in Foreign Parts were soon

[88] Schwager, Die katholische Heidenmission der Gegenwart, p. 421.
[89] Josson, La Mission du Bengale Occidental, Vol. I, p. 163.
[90] Josson, op. cit., Vol. I, p. 170.
[91] Piolet and Vadot, L'Église Catholiques aux Indes, p. 28.
[92] Josson, op. cit., Vol. I, p. 207.
[93] Josson, op. cit., Vol. I, p. 241.
[94] Josson, op. cit., Vol. I, p. 233.
[95] Piolet and Vadot, op. cit., p. 28.
[96] Josson, op. cit., Vol. I, p. 276.
[97] Josson, op. cit., Vol. I, pp. 328-367.

to enter, profiting by a secession from the Lutheran ranks. The first Roman Catholic baptisms were in 1873 and not far from 1875 the first Roman Catholic village was formed.[98] In 1885 there came to Chota Nagpur a most remarkable Flemish Jesuit, Constant Lievens. When he reached his field Lievens found only 56 converts in his charge. Within about two years sickness and death among his colleagues left him the sole active priest in the area. Then began a mass movement from the aborigines. Thousands came over from Lutheranism, together with their catechists. Later other thousands came from paganism. The reason seems to have been the skill and the zeal of Lievens in championing the cause of the aborigines against the landlords (zamindars) and money-lenders and in helping the oppressed win their cases at court. In 1891 Lievens broke down with tuberculosis and the following year was forced by ill health to return to Belgium. In 1895 he died. Yet before his death reinforcements had begun to arrive. Three nephews of Lievens eventually came. The accessions from the aborigines continued. In 1921, 175,000 Roman Catholics were counted in the region. Needless to say, by no means all of these had first been Protestants.[99] Ranchi became the spiritual centre of the mission, with schools of various kinds in which both European and Indian sisters served.[100] Later one of the missionaries—by inducing the British officials to modify their laws in the light of the customs of one of the aboriginal groups, the Mundas—helped to allay unrest and augmented the esteem for the mission both among the Mundas and with the British raj.[101]

The progress of the Jesuits in Bengal proper was not so marked as among the susceptible aborigines. Military chaplains, in 1876 fixed at the total of forty-two, served the British troops in the Presidency of Bengal.[102] There were also a few railway chaplains.[103] Efforts were made to reach non-Christians through schools. A former Protestant missionary, William Wallace, who became a Jesuit, believed that if educated Hindus were to be successfully approached Hinduism must be known by the missionaries more fully and sympathetically. In spite of the handicap of frail health he persisted and won some of his younger colleagues to his ideals. The movement which he started sought to induce the theological seminaries in India to give more attention to the study of the traditional Hindu spiritual life and advocated setting aside at least one priest in each diocese to

[98] Josson, op. cit., Vol. I, pp. 398-408.
[99] Josson, op. cit., Vol. II, pp. 130-171, 379, 380; Van der Schueren, The Belgian Mission of Bengal, Part I, pp. 11-21, Part II, pp. 5-21. A brief life of Lievens is Francis J. Bowen, Father Constant Lievens, S. J., The Apostle of Chota-Nagpur (St. Louis, B. Herder Book Co., 1936, pp. 176).
[100] Schwager, Die katholische Heidenmission der Gegenwart, pp. 428, 429.
[101] Hoffmann, 37 Jahre Missionär in Indien, p. 14.
[102] Josson, op. cit., Vol. II, pp. 99, 100.
[103] Josson, op. cit., Vol. II, p. 106.

specialize in Indian thought. There was also talk of an order of Christian *sannyasis* who by conforming to some of the practices of the ascetic Hindu *sannyasis* would interpret Christianity in forms familiar to Hindus.[104] Obviously such a programme could not hope for extensive numerical results at any early time. We hear, too, at the other social extreme, of mass conversions among poverty-stricken farmers and fishermen south of Calcutta on the delta of the Ganges.[105] In spite, however, of the presence of several thousand "Portuguese" and Europeans who were Christians through heredity, Hinduism and Islam were so well entrenched in Bengal proper that any large number of conversions, except from the underprivileged, was not to be expected.

In central Bengal, later the diocese of Krishnagar, Roman Catholic progress was also slow. The Milan Seminary, to which the area was given in the 1850's, was not able to bring to the assignment sufficient resources in men or in money to take full advantage of it, even after (1870) it was made a separate prefecture apostolic.[106] Eventually a fairly extensive movement toward the faith began among the Santals, aborigines in the northern part of the district,[107] but in 1914 the entire diocese contained less than 10,000 Roman Catholics.[108]

In 1889, since the field was obviously too large for the resources of the Milan Seminary, most of Assam was separated from it and a recently founded German order, the Society of the Divine Saviour, or the Salvatorians, was induced to take it over. The first contingent, headed by Otto Hopfenmüller, then in his middle forties, arrived in 1890. Within a few months Hopfenmüller was dead.[109] For years results were very meagre. Only a few hundred Christians were there as a nucleus for expansion. Missionaries were slow in coming. Yet in 1915, when the World War of 1914-1918 led to a suspension of missionary activity, there were 13 missionaries, 5 missionary brothers, 5 religious communities, the beginnings of a congregation of native sisters, and over 5,000 Roman Catholics. More than two-fifths of the Christians were from an aboriginal hill people, the Khasis.[110] Here, as in so much of India and, indeed, of the nineteenth century world, some of Christianity's most rapid and extensive gains were among peoples of primitive culture.

The south-eastern portion of Bengal, together with the section of western Burma known as Arakan, the strip of coast which continued southward from

---

[104] Väth, *Im Kämpfe mit der Zauberwelt des Hinduismus*, p. 221.
[105] Schwager, *op. cit.*, p. 424.
[106] Becker, *Im Stromtal des Brahmaputra*, pp. 177, 206.
[107] Schwager, *op. cit.*, p. 430.
[108] Streit, *Atlas Hierarchicus*, p. 99.
[109] C. Becker, *P. Otto Hopfenmüller* (Aachen, Xaverius-Verlagsbuchhandlung, 1923, pp. 366), *passim*.
[110] Becker, *Im stromtal des Brahmaputra*, pp. 206-210, 251-284, 352, 353.

Bengal between the mountains and the sea, became an ecclesiastical division, after 1886 the diocese of Dacca. From early in the 1850's until 1875 eastern Bengal was a field of the Fathers of the Holy Cross. Misfortunes dogged the steps of the mission and in 1875 British-Belgian Benedictines took over the enterprise. In 1888 the field was returned to the Fathers of the Holy Cross. Some sisters came to the assistance of the men, schools were opened, and by 1914 not far from 10,000 Roman Catholics were served by the diocese. In addition there were several thousand Roman Catholics who called themselves Portuguese, in part descendants of the pre-nineteenth century Portuguese garrisons and settlements on the coast. They remained under the padroado and were within the jurisdiction of the Bishop of Mylapore.[111]

West of Bengal, embracing much of the Indo-Gangetic plain and reaching up into the Himalayas, was a vast area entrusted to the Capuchins. Early in the eighteenth century Italian Capuchins had made daring attempts to found a continuing enterprise in Tibet. These failed.[112] What for a time was a successful mission in Nepal was suspended because of the frequent wars.[113] However, the Capuchins were able to remain in parts of northern India, notably in Patna and Bettiah, not far from Nepal. Refugee Christian Nepalese preserved both their native tongue and their faith.[114] In Sardhana, north of Agra, the Moslem widow of a mercenary adventurer from Luxemburg who had been given the rule of the principality to support his troops had become a Christian in 1781, had stimulated the growth of a Roman Catholic community, and on her death (1836) had left a bequest for the maintenance of a church and a school. In 1838 an Italian Capuchin opened the school.[115] In 1808 an immense vicariate apostolic was created which was given the name of Tibet-Hindustan and which embraced the Capuchin mission. In 1845 the vicariate apostolic of Patna was hewn out of this ecclesiastical division, but was left in Capuchin hands. Its first head, Anastasius Hartmann, a Swiss, was a man of large learning as well as administrative gifts. Before his death from cholera (1866) he had helped to work out a plan for the entire Roman Catholic church in India.[116] In 1846 Tibet was assigned to the Missions Étrangères of Paris and what remained of the Tibet-Hindustan mission became the vicariate apostolic of Agra, still Capuchin.[117] The presence of many Irish Roman Catholics in the British forces which were the armies of conquest and occupation proved a field for Capuchin

[111] Schwager, op. cit., pp. 431, 432.
[112] Vol. III, p. 361; Capuchin Mission Unit, India and Its Missions, pp. 112-114.
[113] Capuchin Mission Unit, op. cit., pp. 113, 114.
[114] Capuchin Mission Unit, op. cit., p. 115.
[115] Josson, La Mission du Bengale Occidental, Vol. I, p. 181.
[116] Aurelius, De Kapucijnen en de Missie, pp. 59-66.
[117] Piolet and Vadot, L'Église Catholique aux Indes, pp. 23ff.

chaplains.[118] In 1886, at the time of the erection of the Indian hierarchy, Agra was made the seat of an archbishop with Allahabad-Patna and Lahore as suffragan sees.[119]

In the archdiocese of Agra the centre of the efforts for the Indians was long Sardhana with its well-established Christian community and its schools. The Rajah of Tajpur while on a sea voyage from Europe to India had long conversations with a Roman Catholic missionary. The conversion which followed opened wide the doors to his 50,000 subjects. There was also growth in the native state of Gwalior.[120] Yet on the eve of 1914 the number of Roman Catholics of Indian blood in the archdiocese was less than 2,000.[121]

In the diocese of Allahabad (from the former vicariate apostolic of Patna) the numerical strength of Roman Catholicism was not much greater.[122] To be sure, a Christian colony arose out of orphans saved from a famine in 1897 and nurtured in the faith.[123] Here, too, came English sisters, the first of them introduced to India by Hartmann.[124] Yet progress was much slower than in some other parts of India. In the year ending October 31, 1904, in the entire Allahabad Mission there were only twenty-seven conversions from paganism.[125]

In 1888 the diocese of Lahore, which embraced most of the Punjab, was assigned to the Belgian Capuchins. There were numbers of Irish Roman Catholics in the armed forces which guarded the North-west. Here and there gains were made, chiefly from outcaste groups and in agricultural colonies.[126] Yet in 1912 the total number of Roman Catholics in the diocese was only about 12,000.[127] In 1890 Rajputana was given to the Capuchins of the Paris province. In 1892 it was made a prefecture apostolic and in 1913 a diocese. Here the something over 3,000 Roman Catholics who in 1912 had been gathered from non-Christian faiths seem to have been chiefly from hill tribes of primitive culture.[128] In 1910 Simla was made an archdiocese. It was in the hands of English Capuchins.[129] In 1912 it had only a few hundred Indian Roman Catholics.[130]

[118] Capuchin Mission Unit, op. cit., p. 138.
[119] Schwager, op. cit., p. 410.
[120] Schwager, op. cit., p. 413.
[121] Streit, Atlas Hierarchicus, p. 99.
[122] Ibid.
[123] Schwager, op. cit., p. 415.
[124] Mission des Institutes Beatae Mariae Virginis der Englischen Fräulein in Ost-Indien (Das General-Mutterhaus München-Nymphenburg, c. 1925, pp. 83), passim.
[125] Catholic Calendar and Directory for the Archdiocese of Agra and Its Suffragan Dioceses of Allahabad and Lahore . . . for the year 1905 (Allahabad, Liddell's Press, pp. 74), p. 45.
[126] Schwager, op. cit., p. 411.
[127] Streit, op. cit., p. 99.
[128] Capucins Missionnaires, Missions Françaises, pp. 20-30.
[129] Schmidlin-Braun, Catholic Mission History, p. 601.
[130] Streit, op. cit., p. 99.

In the North-west, in Kashmir and Kafiristan, local opposition long proved an obstacle to the entrance of Christian missionaries. Capuchin chaplains cared for the Roman Catholics in the British garrisons, but not until the 1880's did resistance of the non-Christians begin to weaken. In 1887 the region was made a prefecture apostolic and was entrusted to St. Joseph's Society of Mill Hill. Although orphans were rescued in the famine of 1897, in 1912 not many hundred converts had been gathered.[131]

From this geographic survey of the Roman Catholic advance we now turn to the methods employed to win converts and to nourish the Christians in the faith.

A large proportion of the missionaries found their time and energies absorbed in shepherding the Christians and had little spare strength to reach out towards the non-Christians.[132] Thus in the 1880's in the Madura Mission a Jesuit missionary usually had the spiritual oversight of from 3,000 to 8,000 Christians scattered through 80 or more villages. He was, therefore, on the road most of the time, visiting his flock, caring for the ill, administering the sacraments, and defending the Roman Catholics in court against accusations brought by non-Christians and Protestants. As a rule he knew only a little of the prevailing vernacular, Tamil, and was dependent upon the catechists as intermediaries between himself and his flock.[133]

However, numbers of missionaries gave themselves exclusively to the winning of non-Christians. Beginning at least as early as 1890 the Propaganda made obligatory upon missions the setting aside of some missionaries to the task of conversion.[134]

We hear of at least one hard-working bishop who did much travelling through his diocese, preaching two or three times a day, personally catechizing candidates for confirmation, distributing the communion with his own hands, examining all parish records, and granting audiences to members of his flock.[135]

A substantial proportion of the converts came through mass movements.[136] Many of these were attracted in time of famine through the relief given by the missionaries.[137] Obviously large numbers would be brought in during or immediately after the famine months and from the classes which suffered most. Indians, moreover, tended to act by groups in religious as well as non-religious

[131] *Ibid.;* Schwager, *op. cit.,* pp. 407, 408.
[132] Capuchin Mission Unit, *op. cit.,* p. 216.
[133] *Le Maduré,* pp. 8, 16.
[134] Capuchin Mission Unit, *op. cit.,* p. 216.
[135] J. V. F., *A Quarter Century of Progress in the Diocese of Quilon, 1900-1925,* pp. 11-16.
[136] Pickett, *Christian Mass Movements in India,* p. 313.
[137] For some examples of this see Capuchin Mission Unit, *op. cit.,* pp. 157, 215; Schwager, *op. cit.,* pp. 415, 418.

matters. By tradition, therefore, they were inclined to adopt a new faith *en masse*.

As we have seen in our geographical survey, many converts were from the aboriginal tribes of primitive culture who had not yet been absorbed into any of the dominant faiths of India. Thousands, too, were from the depressed classes. Thus in one part of the archdiocese of Bombay the first converts were from the Mahars, a socially depressed group. The complaint was made that they played one Christian denomination against another, offering themselves to the highest bidder and threatening to go over to another Christian body if the help they demanded was refused. [138] In 1905 there came to the diocese of Mangalore Faustin Corti, a Jesuit, who in his earlier years sought to win the higher classes, especially the Brahmins and the Jains, hoping that if he succeeded the lower classes would follow their example. To this end he adopted Indian diet and Indian manners, walking barefoot from village to village, and seeking the friendship of landlords and community leaders. For five years he pursued this programme, but met with scarcely any success. Discouraged, he turned from the well-to-do to the Pariahs. He visited them in their homes, listened to their sorrows, and protected them against their landlords. For a time he hesitated to admit them to the Church, fearing disorder, but a newly consecrated bishop baptized them. The landlords persecuted them, but Corti held the confidence of the Pariahs and ultimately won several thousand of them. [139] In various parts of India numbers were gathered from the low castes through the help given them in drought and famine. [140]

By no means all the Roman Catholics were from tribes of primitive culture and the lower rungs of the caste structure. In that same diocese of Mangalore where so many outcastes became Christians there were a number of Roman Catholic families of Brahmin ancestry. [141] In that diocese, too, there were Anglo-Indian Christians. [142] The relative percentages of higher and lower castes in the Roman Catholic body varied from diocese to diocese. In the archdiocese of Verapoly five per cent. were said to be from the higher, thirty per cent. from the middle, and sixty-five per cent. from the lower castes. In Mysore the higher castes provided one-fourth of one per cent. of the Roman Catholics, the middle castes fifteen per cent. and the lower castes eighty-five per cent. In Calcutta the corresponding percentages were one, eight, and ninety-two. In Patna

[138] Hull, *Bombay Mission History*, Vol. II, pp. 451-466.
[139] Sequeira, *My Ramble Through the Missions of the Diocese of Mangalore*, pp. 1-19.
[140] Becker, *Indisches Kastenwesen und christliche Mission*, p. 54.
[141] Laouënan, *Lettres sur l'Inde*, p. 160.
[142] *Catholic Directory of India, 1915*, p. 61.

ninety-five per cent. were from the middle and four per cent. from the lower groups.[143]

The problem of the persistence of inherited caste divisions in the Christian community continued to vex the ecclesiastical authorities. When in 1870 the Vatican Council brought together the bishops of the Roman Catholic world, those from India made it the opportunity to consider the caste issue. They discovered no uniformity of practice. In some vicariates apostolic there was no recognition of caste within the Church, but Christians were regarded as forming in themselves a distinct caste. In others caste distinctions were observed. Some missionaries tolerated caste. Others wished to eradicate it. In Verapoly and part of Quilon the Syrian Christians, in two groups, constituted one caste and the fishers, very numerous, and of the Latin rite, another.[144] Rome attempted to insist on a common service for all castes and condemned the separation of castes in the same church building.[145] Yet in general Roman Catholics tended to regard caste as civil and social rather than religious and to tolerate it.[146] In the diocese of Cochin an effort was made to recruit priests from the fisher caste, but such a storm of protest arose among clergy and laity that the bishop felt constrained to desist.[147] In one place in the South a Parava found himself kept out of the priesthood by his low caste status but as a teacher and school inspector gave himself to a lay apostolate.[148] For many years in the archdiocese of Madras, although most of the Christian constituency was of low caste origin, only youths of higher caste were admitted to the seminary to prepare for the priesthood.[149] Early in the twentieth century when a new church was opened in the diocese of Pondicherry one-half the building was assigned to the Pariahs and one-half to the Sudras. A tumult arose which was resolved first by closing the building and then, upon its reopening, removing all distinction of place. At the same time, as a compromise, the old segregation was observed in the cathedral. As a result the cathedral was but scantily attended.[150] Mahars from the island of Salsette, who were originally sweepers, of a very low social status, had been won by Portuguese in pre-nineteenth century days. They were thereupon attached to the churches as musicians, and when not playing were occupied with such physical tasks as grave-digging, bell-ringing, and sweeping the

[143] *Missiones Cath. cura S. Cong. de Prop. Fide* (1927), pp. 78, 79.
[144] Becker, *op. cit.*, pp. 132ff.
[145] Schwager, *Die katholische Heidenmission der Gegenwart*, p. 332.
[146] Schmidlin, *Catholic Mission Theory*, p. 251.
[147] Becker, *op. cit.*, p. 102.
[148] Sigismund Freiherrn von Bischoffshausen, *Das höhere katholische Unterrichtswesen in Indien und die Bekehrung der Brahmanen*, p. 31.
[149] Becker, *op. cit.*, p. 100.
[150] Becker, *op. cit.*, p. 97.

church.[151] In other words, as Christians they still had an occupational status akin to that of a caste. In Assam the descendants of the pre-nineteenth century converts would not mingle with the new converts from the lower social strata.[152] In Assam, too, for at least a time Roman Catholics of European stock objected to having the same priests serve them and the "natives."[153] Many missionaries, especially in the South, sought to avoid offense to caste Christians by refraining from eating beef and usually had as cook one of the caste members who could be counted on to observe the same restrictions.[154] Partly because of the observance of caste, or so it was said, beginning with 1894 there were a number of conversions from the Brahmins in the Madura area,[155] the scene of the famous mission of Nobili to that caste. In Madura one of the Jesuits, Louis Lacombe, laboured among both low and high castes. The low caste converts he placed in a colony by themselves, sought to inculcate among them temperance, and endeavoured to free them from the oppression of the landlords. For Brahmin Christians he provided a home in which they might observe such practices of their caste—among them meals served by Brahmin hands—as were not deemed clearly contrary to the Christian faith.[156] Here in the stubborn caste system was a determinant of missionary methods. From it also came a palpable effect of the environment upon Christianity.

Very important in the Roman Catholic programme for the spread of the faith were the catechists. The catechists were recruited from among the Indians. It seems to have been generally agreed that the quality of the mission and of the Christian communities depended largely upon the character of the catechists.[157] Some catechists resided in villages. Others went from village to village where a foreign priest was rarely seen. Still others accompanied the missionary on his travels, acting as his clerk and secretary. It was chiefly through the catechists that the first approaches to non-Christians were made. It was by them that the preliminary instruction was given to catechumens, whether pagans or the children of Christians. It was the village catechists who visited the sick, cared for the poor, the aged, and the crippled, and helped the Christian farmers to better methods of agriculture.[158] Obviously the catechists held key positions in the life of the Church and in the growth of the Christian communities.

[151] Fernandes, *Bandra, Its Religious and Secular History*, p. 53.
[152] Becker, *op. cit.*, pp. 90, 91.
[153] Becker, *op. cit.*, pp. 56, 57.
[154] Becker, *op. cit.*, p. 87.
[155] Becker, *op. cit.*, p. 67; Berg, *Die katholische Heidenmission als Kulturträger*, Vol. I, p. 227.
[156] *Father Louis Lacombe, S. J.* (Trichinopoly, The Catholic Truth Society of India, 1930, pp. 80), *passim*.
[157] Van der Schueren, *The Belgian Mission of Bengal*, Pt. 1, p. 77.
[158] Capuchin Mission Unit, *India and Its Missions*, pp. 224-233.

Because of caste differences, instruction to catechumens was usually in private houses, and not in buildings erected for that purpose, as in some other lands. However, in the mass movement area in Chota Nagpur the Jesuits built great institutions for those who were coming over from the primitive folk. Often from 500 to 700 were brought together in such a compound.[159]

One method employed both for reaching non-Christians and for giving simple instruction to the Christians was the theatre. Because of the immorality of the plays presented and the connexion with non-Christian faiths, the native theatres were forbidden to Christians. However, mission theatres were set up in which Biblical themes were presented. The most popular of the plays is said to have been the Nativity.[160]

Much attention was given to the production of literature. We hear of a translation of the New Testament into Hindustani completed in 1864 by Bishop Pezzoni of Allahabad.[161] By the early part of the 1920's there were said to be more than 200 Roman Catholic books in Telugu and over 80 Roman Catholic periodicals in all India. About 45 of the latter were in English and at least 2 were dailies.[162] Dictionaries and grammars were compiled in several of the Indian languages to facilitate the approach of the missionary.[163]

Schools were emphasized. They could be multiplied because of the policy of the British Government which gave them grants-in-aid regardless of their religious affiliations. The place accorded to schools varied from diocese to diocese. In some, nearly a half of the stations had primary schools and there were a number of secondary schools. In others, a large majority of the stations did not even have a primary school.[164] Instructions from the Propaganda in 1845 directed that Roman Catholic schools be opened to all Indians without distinction of caste. In the classrooms Brahmin boys often sat side by side on the same benches with outcastes. In hospices, however, caste was observed in the eating and cooking arrangements.[165] Numbers of schools were conducted for girls by members of sisterhoods. For example, what is declared to have been the oldest school for girls on the Malabar coast was founded in 1862 by the Sisters of St. Joseph of the Apparition and was later served by the Apostolic Carmel. A large proportion of its pupils came from the families of Parsees

[159] Berg, op. cit., Vol. I, pp. 218, 219.
[160] Capuchin Mission Unit, op. cit., pp. 219-221.
[161] Schwager, Die katholische Heidenmission der Gegenwart, p. 415.
[162] Capuchin Mission Unit, op. cit., pp. 241-243; Hull, Bombay Mission History, Vol. II, p. 317.
[163] See A Short Sketch of Father A. F. X. Maffei, of the Society of Jesus (Mangalore, Codiabail Press, 1899, pp. 28) for some of these.
[164] Missiones Catholicae Cura S. Congregationis de Propaganda Fide, 1927, pp. 78-81.
[165] Becker, op. cit., p. 103.

and high caste Hindus.[166] Not far from the year 1867 Sisters of St. Joseph of Annecy began teaching, at the request of the Maharajah, in a school at Vizagapatam for Brahmins and Rajputs.[167] The Jesuits, famous educators that they were, had several colleges. These were said to be of excellent scholastic standing, but were reported to have won few converts. They gave no religious instruction to non-Christians. Their religious contribution was judged to be the nurturing in high caste Hindus, Parsees, and Moslems of a respect for Roman Catholicism.[168] Yet we hear of the conversion of Brahmins as the result of the work of St. Joseph's College of Trichinopoly.[169] At least one of the Jesuit colleges won a high reputation for its scientific attainments. It had a meteorological observatory [170] akin to the notable one maintained by the members of their society on the outskirts of Shanghai.

A great deal of energy was directed toward the education of Indian clergy. For many years a seminary on the British island of Penang, off the Malay Peninsula, attracted students from India and the Far East. As local seminaries were established elsewhere, its student body dwindled.[171] In the 1850's a seminary was founded by the bishop in the vicariate apostolic of Mangalore.[172] A seminary was maintained in Goa which in 1896 had 64 students in its theological course.[173] In 1890 Pope Leo XIII decided to found a pontifical seminary to train seculars for the different parts of India and Ceylon. It was his plan to have it maintain standards as high as those in the best seminaries in Europe. Belgian Jesuits were given charge. Kandy, Ceylon, was chosen as the site. By 1906 the institution had 86 students from 22 of the 40 dioceses of India and Ceylon.[174] By the close of 1914, 113 of the former students had been ordained.[175] Beginning in 1897, moreover, Rome insisted upon the preparation of a native clergy for the mass movement areas in Chota Nagpur. In 1903 a seminary was opened and by 1919, 12 of its former pupils had been ordained to the priest-

[166] *Golden Jubilee Memorial. St. Anna's High School Mangalore 1870-1920* (Mangalore, Kanarese Mission Press, 1920, pp. 95), p. 27.
[167] Rosillon, *Les Moissoneuses du Coromandel*, p. 176.
[168] *Il Penseiro Missionario*, Vol. IV, pp. 248-259; *Cinquant' Anni Mangalore sulla Costa Occidentale dell' India (1878-1928)* (Venice, "Le Missioni della Compagnia di Gesù," 1929, pp. 96), pp. 13-24; *Directory of the Diocese of Mangalore*, 1925, p. 21; Berg, *op. cit.*, Vol. I, pp. 361, 375.
[169] Sigismund Freiherrn von Bischoffshausen, *Das höhere katholische Unterrichtswesen in Indien und die Bekehrung der Brahmanen*, pp. 61-82.
[170] Josson, *La Mission du Bengale Occidental*, Vol. I, p. 384.
[171] Huonder, *Der einheimische Klerus in den Heidenländern*, pp. 142-144.
[172] *The Apostolic Carmel. Mangalore. A Retrospect*, p. 8.
[173] *Movimento Escolar do Seminario de Rachol, Goa* (1896), *passim*.
[174] J.-B. Van der Aa, *Lettres de Kandy. Souvenir du Seminaire Pontifical, 1906* (pp. 67), *passim*; Berg, *Die katholische Heidenmission als Kulturträger*, Vol. I, p. 342.
[175] *Catalogus Magistrorum et Alumnorum Pontificii Colegii Kandiensis, A.D. MCM-XXXII* (Trichinopoly, St. Joseph's Industrial School Press, 1932, pp. 30), pp. 10-28.

hood. Some of the student body were Eurasians.[176] Differences of opinion existed as to the quality of the Indian priesthood. Some held it not to be equal to that in the more advanced parts of Europe. Others maintained that it was very high.[177] In general the Indian priests seem to have been from the upper castes, but here and there were some from the lower social strata.[178]

The philanthropic institutions characteristic of the Roman Catholic Church in many lands and ages were represented in India. There were hospitals. The complaint was heard that although these were served by devoted sisters, most of the attending physicians were not practising Roman Catholics, but Protestants.[179] There were also refuges for widows, orphanages, homes for boys, homes for girls, and leper asylums.[180]

Often the missionary felt himself forced to devise means for enabling converts to make their living. Frequently converts by the act of becoming Christians lost their social standing and with it their accustomed occupations.[181] Converts from the lower classes were chronically poverty-stricken. In Chota Nagpur, to solve this problem and the ever-present one of debt, co-operative credit societies were formed to which only Roman Catholics were admitted.[182] In Chota Nagpur, moreover, the missionaries undertook for their converts co-operative stores, rice banks, produce banks, and industrial schools, and encouraged cottage industries and improved methods of agriculture. The Chota Nagpur Christians from the primitive groups regarded the missionaries as their *ma-bap,* or mother and father, and a paternalistic relationship developed not unlike that which we have found in Jesuit missions among aboriginal peoples in other countries and ages.[183] In Mangalore there was a Roman Catholic Provident Fund to encourage savings against the death of the head of the family, for expenses of weddings, and dowries.[184] In Mangalore, moreover, in 1913 a tract of waste land was acquired from the government and on it converts were settled.[185] In the Punjab the Capuchins obtained tracts of land and built on them Christian colonies recruited from low caste or outcaste groups. By the year 1916 there were said to be about 12,000 Roman Catholics in Chris-

[176] Josson, *La Mission du Bengale Occidental,* Vol. II, pp. 310-315.
[177] Huonder, *Der einheimische Klerus in den Heidenländern,* p. 89.
[178] Huonder, *op. cit.,* p. 86.
[179] Capuchin Mission Unit, *India and Its Missions,* pp. 246, 247.
[180] Capuchin Mission Unit, *op. cit.,* pp. 251-253; *The Madras Catholic Directory and General Annual Register,* 1906, p. 85.
[181] Berg, *op. cit.,* Vol. I, p. 287; *Le Maduré,* p. 23.
[182] Hoffman, *37 Jahre Missionär in Indien,* pp. 27-33; Josson, *op. cit.,* Vol. II, pp. 370-373.
[183] Van der Schueren, *The Belgian Mission of Bengal,* Part 2, pp. 22-28.
[184] *Catholic Directory of India, 1916,* pp. 435-440.
[185] *Directory of the Diocese of Mangalore, 1925,* pp. 78-81.

tian villages of from 10 to 80 families each. Gradually the requirement was enforced that Christian girls should be married only to Christians and not to pagans. While the criticism was sometimes made that converts were attracted from unworthy motives and were brought up in hot-house atmosphere, some missionaries stoutly defended the system.[186] In the Madras Presidency there were in 1914, 47 Roman Catholic co-operative credit societies organized under government acts with 3,375 members who were mainly Christian.[187]

An interesting insight into the methods and purpose of at least one missionary comes from the autobiographical record of a Jesuit of the Chota Nagpur mission. This priest told of his enthusiasm for spreading the co-operative programme and his energy in fighting the use of alcoholic beverages and in promoting temperance societies. He declared that he had two firm articles in his creed, one of them being belief in Jesus Christ, Son of God and man, our only true friend, and what he teaches through his Church, and the other a conviction that *Deus fecit hominem bonum* and that in youth we still find man as God made him. In conformity with this second guiding principle he paid little attention to the old but addressed himself to the young.[188]

Here and there efforts were made to reach Indians in ways that conformed to the indigenous cultural tradition. Thus we hear of a Bengali, Upadhyaya Brahmabandhav, who in his youth was attracted by the syncretistic Brahmo Samaj, then became a Roman Catholic, and at the end of his life found himself in conflict with the Church. He was an intense nationalist and was opposed to all Europeanizing tendencies in Indian life. He contemplated the founding of a purely Indian Roman Catholic monastery. He gave much thought to the effort to devise a theistic form of Vedanta and believed the goal of Vedanta to be faith in God and the Son of God. His pupil and biographer imitated him in living like a *sannyasi,* or Indian holy man, and for years conducted a Christian school for boys to which some of the more prominent families entrusted their sons.[189] In Bengal the Jesuits, instead of suppressing all pagan *mores,* Christianized, so far as possible, non-Christian feasts and customs. For the feast of cattle there was substituted the solemn blessing of the cattle by the priest. The Christian festivals, especially Christmas, were celebrated elaborately. When the bishop made his visit he was greeted with great

[186] *Catholic Directory of India, 1916,* pp. 423-435.
[187] *Catholic Directory of India, 1915,* pp. 58-60.
[188] Hoffmann, *op. cit.,* pp. 17, 18.
[189] Ohm, *Indien und Gott,* pp. 167-176; Macnicol, *India in the Dark Wood,* pp. 126, 127; Hoffmann, *op. cit.,* pp. 51-64; Alfons Väth, *Im Kämpfe mit der Zauberwelt des Hinduismus. Upadhyaya Brahmabandhav und das Problem der Überwindung des höheren Hinduismus durch das Christentum* (Berlin, Ferd. Dummlers Verlag, 1928, pp. 238), *passim.*

pomp.[190] Differences of opinion existed as to the desirability of the transfer of European traditions of church architecture as against the erection of ecclesiastical structures in Indian style. There was advocacy of the Gothic as best for India. On the other hand there were various attempts at buildings which incorporated Indian forms.[191]

In contrast with the desire to conform in non-essentials to the Indian environment was the trend of Indian Christians in Portuguese territories to become identified with the Portuguese in dress and by the assumption of Portuguese names.[192]

Many organizations were formed of the traditional Roman Catholic type, some of them for lay members who remained in the world and others made up of those who had renounced the world for the religious life. Thus among the old churches of Malabar there existed under various names confraternities of the Blessed Virgin Mary, some of which possessed endowments in the form of land.[193] There was the Men's Sodality of the Immaculate Conception of St. Peter's, Bandra. Its members made an annual pilgrimage to certain churches and it initiated a retreat for laymen.[194] The Sodality of the Blessed Virgin Mary which was established by the Jesuits at Mangalore in 1879 sought to strengthen the religious life of its members by weekly meetings, monthly general communions, retreats, and celebrations of the annual festivals. It also conducted picnics and excursions and eventually erected a recreation hall.[195] In Bombay there was a Society of St. Vincent de Paul whose members administered poor relief by personal visitation.[196] There were temperance societies.[197] In 1899 there was formed a Catholic Indian Association which covered much of South India and which endeavoured to promote communal solidarity among Roman Catholics.[198] In Calcutta attempts were made to do for Roman Catholics what the Young Men's and Young Women's Christian Associations were accomplishing

[190] Josson, La Mission du Bengal Occidental, Vol. II, p. 390.

[191] Berg, op. cit., Vol. II, pp. 149, 150; H. Heras, Shall We Build Churches in Indian Styles? (Reprinted from The Mangalorean Review, Bombay, 1928, pp. 4), passim.

[192] Laouënan, Lettres sur l'Inde, p. 160.

[193] J. V. F., A Quarter Century of Progress, Diocese of Quilon, 1900-1925, pp. 19, 20.

[194] Report of the Men's Sodality of the Immaculate Conception of St. Peter's, Bandra, 1873-1923 (Bombay, The Bowen Press, pp. 16), passim.

[195] Silver Jubilee 1879-1904. Sodality of the Immaculate Conception Codialbail, passim.

[196] Nineteenth Report of the Society of St. Vincent de Paul, from Dec. 1, 1875 to Nov. 30, 1876 (Bombay, 1877), passim.

[197] C. Dias, An Appeal on Behalf of St. Anne's Temperance Society by the Director (Bombay, 1907, pp. 8), passim; Ecclesiastical and Press Opinions on the Manual of Temperance (Calcutta, 1897, pp. 26), passim.

[198] Report of the Twenty-Eighth Annual General Meeting of the Catholic Indian Association of Southern India Held at Madras on the 29th September, 1929 (Madras, The N. M. S. Press, 1930, pp. 56, 4, 5), pp. 1-8.

under Protestant auspices. In 1903, too, the Catholic Association of Calcutta was formed.[199]

The most flourishing of the Indian men's orders—indeed, the only one which is said to have prospered—was a Carmelite congregation drawn from the Uniates. It was founded in 1831 and in 1885 received the approval of Rome. First planned as a branch of the Dominicans, it became, instead, affiliated with the Discalced Carmelites as a third order. Its chief purposes were to give retreats to lay folk in the churches and to seculars in the houses of the order, to educate youths for the priesthood, and to prepare and publish books. By 1910 it had fifteen monasteries, a study house, a high school, and several middle schools.[200] In 1857 another Indian community, the Brothers of the Immaculate Mother of God, was founded by one of the French missionaries of Pondicherry. By 1863 it had nine professed monks and three novices. It rendered excellent service in the memorable famine of 1878. By the year 1900, however, it had become extinct.[201]

Among Indian congregations of women were two in the Madura Mission. One was the Sisters of Our Lady of Seven Sorrows. At least some of its members gave themselves to teaching. The other, the Congregation of St. Anna, was for Hindu widows. Its members served in catechumenates for women, orphanages for girls, and hospitals.[202]

As a result of the missions of the pre-nineteenth century period supplemented by those of the nineteenth century, Roman Catholics were, in 1914, a noticeable part of the Indian population. In 1911, according to the figures gathered by the Church, there were 2,223,546 Roman Catholics in India. Of these 296,148 were in Portuguese territory, 25,918 were in the French possessions, and 364,660 were Uniates of the Syriac rite.[203] Not quite 100,000 were Europeans and Anglo-Indians.[204] These totals were confessedly inexact. They were slightly higher than the government census, a difference which would be more than accounted for by the fact that the figures gathered by the Church included not far from 90,000 catechumens.[205] The growth in the preceding half century had been striking. One set of figures gave the totals as 1,017,969 in 1861, 1,131,672 in 1871, 1,389,306 in 1881, 1,625,943 in 1891, and 1,860,876 in 1901.[206] Under the Archbishop of

[199] Josson, La Mission du Bengale Occidental, Vol. II, pp. 273-280.
[200] Berg, Die katholische Heidenmission als Kulturträger, Vol. I, p. 342; The Madras Catholic Directory and General Annual Register, 1906, pp. 272, 273.
[201] Paul, History of the Telugu Christians, pp. 97, 98.
[202] Berg, op. cit., Vol. I, p. 236.
[203] Catholic Directory of India, 1913, p. 435.
[204] Catholic Directory of India, 1913, pp. 424-426.
[205] Ibid.
[206] Catholic Directory of India, 1912, pp. 466-497.

Goa, and so under the Portuguese padroado, there were in 1914 about 294,442 Roman Catholics in Portuguese territory and 36,911 Roman Catholics in non-Portuguese territory.[207] The remainder, the vast majority, were under the hierarchy which was directly responsible to the Propaganda.

As a direct representative of Rome there was an Apostolic Delegate. Distinguished among those who held the post was Zaleski. Scion of an ancient aristocratic Lithuanian family, Zaleski was sent to Rome soon after his ordination to serve in the papal diplomatic service. He travelled in the Near East, was secretary to Agliardi, who inaugurated the hierarchy in India, and after appointments with the papal embassies in London and Paris he was commissioned with the task of founding the pontifical seminary in Kandy which was to train priests for India and Ceylon. In 1892 he became the third Apostolic Delegate for India and held the post until 1916, when he was created Latin Patriarch of Antioch and went to Rome.[208] As was natural because of the longer missionary contacts with that region, Roman Catholics were much more numerous along the west coast from Goa southward and on the east coast from Pondicherry southward.[209] In the fore part of the twentieth century the rate of increase was most rapid in the northern missions and slowest in the old centres, Goa, Pondicherry, Bombay, and Madras.[210] In 1912 India was ministered to by 966 European and 1,142 Indian priests, by 440 lay brothers, and by 2,778 sisters.[211] Roman Catholic Christianity had made notable strides in the nineteenth century, both in numbers and in morale.

Marked as was the growth of Roman Catholic Christianity in the nineteenth century, that of Protestant Christianity was proportionately more rapid. Since it had been introduced much later than Roman Catholic Christianity, Protestantism was not, in 1914, numerically as strong. In 1914 it counted only about 1,000,000 baptized members,[212] which was slightly less than half the strength of the Roman Catholic Church. Its staff, however, was considerably larger. Its missionaries from abroad numbered 5,465,[213] or slightly more than the entire

[207] *Annuario da Archdiocese de Goa para 1914*, statistical table after p. 165.
[208] *Catholic Directory of India, Ceylon and Burma, 1926*, pp. 535-537.
[209] Streit, *Atlas Hierarchicus*, p. 99.
[210] Capuchin Mission Unit, *India and Its Missions*, table II.
[211] Streit, *op. cit.*, p. 187.
[212] Beach and St. John, *World Statistics of Christian Missions*, p. 59.
[213] *Ibid.* Lists of Protestant missionaries were compiled from time to time. B. H. Badley, *Indian Missionary Directory and Memorial Volume* (Lucknow, American Methodist Mission Press, 1876, pp. xii, 279), contained lists of deceased as well as of living missionaries. One issued on the eve of 1914 but containing only living missionaries was James Inglis, *Protestant Missionary Directory of India for 1912-1913* (Ajmer, Scottish Missions Industries Co., pp. lxxxviii, 167).

total, Indian and foreign, of Roman Catholic priests, lay brothers, and sisters. Its native staff was between four and five times more numerous.[214] To India was directed about as large a proportion of the Protestant missionary energy of the nineteenth century as to any other one major non-Occidental section of the globe. It came from other portions of the British Empire, chiefly from the British Isles, and from the continent of Europe and the United States.

At the close of the eighteenth century, Protestantism was represented in India by British merchants and troops connected with the East India Company, most of them only passively of that faith, by the communities, mainly on the south-east coast, which had been founded by the Danish-German mission,[215] and by the beginnings of British missions.

Provision had long been made for the spiritual care of those from the British Isles who were in the service of the East India Company. In some of the chief centres of residence churches had been erected and clergymen of the Church of England had been stationed as chaplains.[216]

Towards the close of the eighteenth century and early in the nineteenth century there came to India chaplains who were committed to the Evangelical awakening. Some of them had been profoundly influenced by Charles Simeon, the famous Evangelical clergyman of Cambridge.[217] When, in 1793, the East India Company's charter was renewed, Wilberforce, one of the distinguished Clapham Evangelicals, saw to it that the House of Commons adopted a resolution making better provision for chaplaincies to Protestants in India in the service of the company.[218] Although the chaplains were in the pay of the East India Company and had the British employees of the company as their primary charge, some of them were also much interested in spreading their faith among non-Christians. One of them, David Brown, was in Calcutta and the vicinity from 1787 to 1812. A graduate of Cambridge, he owed much to Simeon. A man of prodigious energy, in India Brown was not only the garrison chaplain of Calcutta, a task which involved as well the supervision of an orphanage, but he also conducted a school for Hindus, was provost of the college which the East India Company began at Fort William, in Calcutta, for the training of its junior civil servants, and contributed to the movement which led to the formation of the Church Missionary Society.[219] Another, Claudius Buchanan, also a

[214] Beach and St. John, op. cit., p. 59; Streit, op. cit., p. 99.
[215] Vol. III, pp. 277-281.
[216] Chatterton, A History of the Church of England in India, pp. 1-93; Ashley-Brown, On the Bombay Coast and Deccan, pp. 60-114; Penny, The Church in Madras, Vol. I, passim.
[217] Chatterton, op. cit., pp. 108ff.
[218] Hole, The Early History of the Church Missionary Society, pp. 19, 20.
[219] Chatterton, op. cit., pp. 109-113; Memorial Sketches of the Rev. David Brown with

graduate of Cambridge, was in India from 1797 to 1809. He served in and near Calcutta and helped to initiate the project for an Anglican episcopate for India.[220] It was a sermon by him which had much to do with enlisting Adoniram Judson for the East.[221] In 1808 there arrived in Calcutta Thomas T. Thomason, also of the Cambridge Evangelicals. A brilliant scholar, he had been a curate to Simeon. He was deeply interested in promoting missions among non-Christian Indians.[222] Daniel Corrie, still another of the Cambridge Evangelicals, gave more than thirty years to India. In addition to his care for Europeans he had converts among the Indians. He was eventually archdeacon in Calcutta and then the first Anglican Bishop of Madras.[223]

Most notable of all the Evangelical chaplains was Henry Martyn. Martyn was born in 1781 in Cornwall of a father who was engaged in commercial pursuits and who was also deeply affected by the new religious life then stirring in England. While in Cambridge, Martyn, a sensitive soul, had a deep religious experience and took Simeon for a spiritual counsellor. He made an outstanding record as a scholar and graduated with the high honours of Senior Wrangler and first Smith's prizeman won in competition with unusually brilliant contemporaries. He became a fellow of St. John's College and decided to seek ordination and to become curate to Simeon. When still only barely turned twenty-one, Martyn came under the spell of the life of David Brainerd, the New England mystic and missionary to the North American Indians whose journals moved so profoundly many of that generation.[224] Inspired by Brainerd's example, Martyn determined to become a missionary. After a comparatively short tenure of his fellowship and curacy, he accepted a chaplaincy under the East India Company. In 1805 he sailed for India, leaving behind him the young lady of his love. Arriving in India in 1806 after a long voyage, Martyn exclaimed in his diary: "now let me burn out for God." He fulfilled that ambition. He was none too strong physically, and although impressing those who met him with the radiance of his inner life and a childlike happiness in the hours of his

a Selection of his Sermons. Preached at Calcutta (London, for T. Cadell and W. Davies, 1816, pp. xviii, 495), passim.

[220] Hugh Pearson, Memoirs of the Life and Writings of the Rev. Claudius Buchanan, D.D. (Boston, Samuel T. Armstrong, 1818, pp. 444), passim; Buchanan, Memoir of the Expediency of an Ecclesiastical Establishment for British India, passim; Chatterton, op. cit., pp. 113-115.

[221] Vol. IV, p. 81.

[222] J. Sargent, The Life of the Rev. T. T. Thomason (New York, D. Appleton and Co., 1843, pp. 356), passim.

[223] Memoirs of the Right Rev. Daniel Corrie, LL.D., First Bishop of Madras. Compiled chiefly from his own Letters and Journals, by his Brothers (London, Seeley, Burnside, and Seeley, 1847, pp. x, 640), passim.

[224] Vol. III, p. 220.

relaxation,[225] he was stern with himself. He lived with ascetic simplicity.[226] His journals reveal his exacting self-criticism. He found in a great predecessor, Francis Xavier, an ideal. Stationed at Patna (with its European suburbs Dinapore and Bankipore) and then at Cawnpore, he was faithful in his duties as chaplain. To these he added schools for the Indians, preaching to Hindus and Moslems,[227] and literary labours. For these latter he was peculiarly fitted, for they utilized his scholar's gifts. He familiarized himself with Hindustani, added Sanskrit, and increased his knowledge, already begun, of Arabic and Persian. He undertook the task of putting the New Testament into Arabic, Persian, and the Urdu form of Hindustani. In 1810, after only four years in India, Martyn had his Hindustani Testament ready for the press. In that year he left India, a sick man, wishing to go to Persia and then Arabia to perfect his translations of the New Testament into the tongues of those lands. In Persia he spent nearly a year at Shiraz, revising his Persian translation, studying Islam, and conversing and debating with Moslem scholars. He is said to have had one convert. In May 1812, his revision completed, he left Shiraz and journeyed overland, hoping to present a copy of his work to the Shah. This purpose was eventually accomplished, although not through his hands. From Persia he set out for England, but his frail body would not further sustain him and he died en route, at Tokat, in Asia Minor, October 16, 1812, when only thirty-one years of age.[228] No Protestant missionary to India was better remembered. The combination of rare ability and high devotion which he displayed in a day of pioneering had a profound effect on succeeding generations of missionaries. Interestingly enough, a convert from Islam who was a fruit of Martyn's preaching became the first Indian clergyman of the Church of England.

It must be added that the religious care of Europeans did not cease with the passing of these early chaplains. While we have space only to notice its existence, it went on. Churches were built and maintained and chaplains served the European garrisons, civil officials, and merchants. Moreover, provision was made, chiefly through private initiative, for Europeans not of the Anglican communion.

[225] *The Life and Times of Mrs. Sherwood,* pp. 313-315.
[226] *The Life and Times of Mrs. Sherwood,* p. 314.
[227] *The Life and Times of Mrs. Sherwood,* pp. 341, 374, 380.
[228] The early standard biography of Martyn is John Sargent, *A Memoir of Rev. Henry Martyn, B.D.* (New York, American Tract Society, from the 10th London edition, no date, pp. 442). The best printed source is *Journals and Letters of the Rev. Henry Martyn, B.D.,* edited by S. Wilberforce (London, R. B. Seeley and W. Burnside, 2 vols., 1837). The fullest biography is George Smith, *Henry Martyn* (London, The Religious Tract Society, 1892, pp. xii, 580). A readable more recent account is Constance E. Padwick, *Henry Martyn, Confessor of the Faith* (London, Student Christian Movement, 1922, pp. 302).

We hear, for example, of a Scots church (Presbyterian) in Bombay and of a Union Chapel in Calcutta.[229] Towards the end of the eighteenth century the Danish-German mission came to an end of one phase of its history. In Halle, the Pietist university centre in which so many of the staff had been trained, enthusiasm for spreading the Christian faith had ebbed. Recruits from that source dwindled. Moreover, the relation of Denmark to the mission changed. The Danish Crown took over the interests of the Danish East India Company and the missionaries were no longer directly under the King. The new Danish officials were out of sympathy with the enterprise and in the 1820's the Danish state decreed the discontinuation of missions as a means of conversion.[230]

However, no sharp break occurred. The foundations laid in the eighteenth century became the basis for a larger growth in the succeeding period. John Zachary Kiernander, a Swede who had been trained at Halle and had served in South India when the city where he had laboured was taken by the French, went to Calcutta. There he erected what was known as the Old Church, a building which became a centre of the Evangelicals.[231] The Society for Promoting Christian Knowledge had given financial support to some of the missionaries of the Danish-Halle enterprise.[232] It continued to maintain missionaries in South India. Its headquarters in the region were in Vepery, a suburb of Madras.[233] In 1825 it decided to support the missionaries in its employ for the remainder of their lives, but except for them transferred its interests to its sister organization, the Society for the Propagation of the Gospel in Foreign Parts.[234] By 1840 most of the stations which had once been manned by Lutherans from Halle had conformed in worship and organization to the Church of England.[235] The Christian communities which had been gathered continued. In the nineteenth century, partly

[229] As examples of the care for Anglicans see G. M. Davies, *A Chaplain in India* (London, Marshall, Morgan & Scott, no date, pp. xi, 321) and Penny, *The Church in Madras*, Vol. II, pp. 356-386, Vol. III, pp. 327-359. For the Union Chapel in Calcutta see an account of one of its pastors, an appointee of the London Missionary Society, *The Mission Pastor: Memorials of the Rev. Thomas Boaz, . . . by his Widow* (London, John Snow, 1862, pp. x, 470).
[230] Richter, *Indische Missionsgeschichte*, pp. 174-179.
[231] Chatterton, *A History of the Church of England in India*, pp. 79-83.
[232] Penny, *The Church in Madras*, Vol. I, pp. 180-200, 483-504; Allen and McClure, *Two Hundred Years. The History of the Society for Promoting Christian Knowledge, 1698-1898*, pp. 258ff.; *An Abstract of the Annual Reports and Correspondence of the Society for Promoting Christian Knowledge, passim.*
[233] Pascoe, *Two Hundred Years of the S. P. G.*, p. 505; *An Abstract of the Annual Reports and Correspondence of the Society for Promoting Christian Knowledge*, pp. 468ff.
[234] Pascoe, *op. cit.*, pp. 502-504.
[235] Richter, *op. cit.*, p. 179; Pascoe, *op. cit.*, p. 511.

because of them, the area attracted new missions from England, Germany, and Scandinavia.

The coming of William Carey to India in 1793 inaugurated a new era for Protestant missions in India. In an earlier volume [236] we traced the years of Carey's life before his embarkation for India. We saw how this son of a village schoolmaster, himself shoemaker, teacher, and Baptist clergyman, had dared to dream in terms of carrying the Christian message to the entire world and had inspired the formation of a society to enable his denomination to help fulfil that purpose. We saw something of his wide-ranging interests. The fascination which books of travel held for him presaged his comprehensive view of the world. His linguistic aptitude foreshadowed the prodigious accomplishments of himself and his colleagues in translating the Bible into the tongues of the East. His keen boyhood curiosity concerning everything living about him found an outlet in gardening and botanical studies which made him a pioneer of distinction in agriculture and the study of the plants of India. Moreover, he had the good fortune of a long life and was able to carry many of his plans to completion. His career was one of the most notable in the entire history of the expansion of Christianity.[237]

Carey's passage to India and his initial years in that country were beset with difficulties and discouragements which would have daunted a man of lesser faith and courage. John Thomas, the missionarily-minded physician who induced Carey to go to India rather than to the region of his first choice, the islands of the Pacific, proved to be of unsound judgment and financially irresponsible. Largely because of distrust for Thomas and the latter's debts, the voyage to India had to be by a Danish ship rather than one of the English East Indiamen on which passage had first been obtained. In an earlier sojourn in India, Thomas had lost the confidence of Charles Grant, who, influential in the East India Company and a loyal Evangelical, might have been of great help. Carey with his family and Thomas landed at Calcutta. Within a few weeks Thomas by his improvident ways had spent the sum that was designed to maintain the mission

[236] Vol. IV, pp. 66-69.

[237] Standard lives of Carey are John Clark Marshman, *The Life and Times of Carey, Marshman, and Ward, Embracing the History of the Serampore Mission* (London, Longmans, Green, Longmans, and Roberts, 2 vols., 1859); Eustace Carey, *Memoir of William Carey, D.D.* (Hartford, Canfield and Robins, 1837, pp. 468); George Smith, *The Life of William Carey, D.D.* (London, John Murray, 1885, pp. xiii, 463); S. Pearce Carey, *William Carey* (New York, George H. Doran Co., preface, 1923, pp. xvi, 428); and S. Pearce Carey, *Carey* (London, Marshall, Morgan & Scott, no date, pp. 127). There is also *Serampore Letters, Being the Unpublished Correspondence of William Carey and Others with John Williams 1800-1816* (New York, G. P. Putnam's Sons, 1892, pp. v, 150). It is upon these that the following paragraphs dealing with Carey, Marshman, and Ward are based.

for a year. Some of Carey's family were ill and Carey's wife, overburdened by the hardships and the difficulties of adjustment to the strange environment, developed a mental malady which proved a burden to him and to her for the dozen years or more which were to intervene before her death.

Soon, however, there came through Thomas the opportunity to superintend an indigo factory owned by a European. This provided the means of maintaining Carey and his family. Here Carey was occupied for six years. His industry and resourcefulness enabled him, in spite of frequent illness and his obligations to his business and employer, to pursue his acquisition of Bengali and Sanskrit, to translate most of the Bible into Bengali, and to engage in studies of Indian plants.

Undeterred by the insecurity brought by the Napoleonic Wars, reinforcements came from England. The indigo venture proved unprofitable to Carey's employer and other arrangements became necessary. The English East India Company proved adamant against permitting missionaries in the territories which it controlled. With the wars with France in progress and the dangers of intrigues against it in an India in which its foothold was still precarious, the company did not wish to risk the religious antagonism which might be aroused by the preaching of missionaries. Carey had thus far evaded that prohibition by being, so far as his source of income and main occupation were concerned, in business. Since the company resolutely forbade the newest additions to the Baptist mission access to its domains, refuge was found in Serampore, on the Hooghly a short distance above Calcutta. Here the Danish governor gave the missionaries sanctuary and resisted British pressure to expel them. Relations between Great Britain and Denmark were then none to amicable and the Danish authorities were not inclined to do the bidding of their powerful English neighbours. Carey joined the group at Serampore. Thenceforth the headquarters of Carey and his immeniate associates were to be under the tolerant Danish flag.

At Serampore the mission of Carey and the English Baptists had a striking development. The most prominent of Carey's Serampore colleagues were William Ward, a trained printer and experienced newspaper editor, and Joshua Marshman, a self-educated schoolmaster and as omnivorous a reader as Carey. Both arrived in 1799. Together with Carey they became known as the Serampore Trio.[238] Their co-operative endeavours were prolonged, for Ward lived until

---

[238] On the Serampore Trio see the books in the preceding footnote and also *Obituary Notice of the Life and Ministry of the Late Reverend John Mack of Serampore* (Newcastle, T. & J. Hodgson, 1846, pp. 25) ; and William Ward, *Farewell Letters to a Few Friends in Britain and America, on Returning to Bengal in 1821* (New York, E. Bliss and E. White, 1821, pp. 250).

For the biography of one who reached Serampore in 1803 but spent most of his eighteen

1823, Carey until 1834, and Marshman until 1837. Others were from time to time associated with them, but it was the Trio who made Serampore distinctive. At Serampore a printing press was set up, preaching to non-Christians was undertaken, and a school was opened for the children of Europeans. This last was partly for the purpose of obtaining income. In the year 1800 the first convert was baptized. At the friendly suggestion of David Brown and Claudius Buchanan, who had learned to trust him, Carey joined the staff of the newly founded college at Fort William which had been established for the training of the British civil staff of the East India Company. His assignment was the teaching of Bengali. His salary and the profits from the Serampore school were placed in the common purse and enabled the group to achieve one of their ambitions—financial independence from their home society. In his post at Fort William Carey developed written tools for the teaching of Bengali. Through these and his translation of the Bible he became a pioneer in the development of a prose literature in Bengali. A large part of the time and energy of the Serampore group was given to literary pursuits. Carey and Marshman translated the Bible in whole or in part into a number of the languages of India and South and East Asia. Marshman, indeed, put the Bible into Chinese. By 1832 portions or all of the Christian Scriptures in forty-four languages and dialects had been issued from the Serampore press. Ancillary to these undertakings was the preparation of grammars and dictionaries. The effort was made, too, to acquaint Occidental readers with Indian classics. For instance, Carey and Marshman translated the great epic poem the *Ramayana* and had a large portion printed on the mission press. In these herculean labours the Trio were assisted by native scholars, but theirs was the initiative. Mission stations were opened in various places, including Burma and the East Indies. Schools were begun, culminating in a college whose purpose it was to train Indians to reach their fellow countrymen with the Christian message. Both Christians and non-Christians were to be admitted. The curriculum was designed to include not only the Bible and Christian theology but also the philosophies and religions of India. For the college a dignified building was erected. By these various means the Serampore group attempted to implement the broad sweep of the vision which years before had inspired Carey's *Enquiry*. Carey, moreover, proposed that every ten years world conferences of all denominations be convened to co-ordinate plans for reaching all mankind with the Christian message. He suggested that the first be held at the Cape of Good Hope in 1810. The project proved too ambitious for Carey's friends in Great Britain, but a little over a century later it was to come to

years as a missionary elsewhere in India, see William Yates, *Memoirs of Mr. John Chamberlain* (London Wightman and Camp, 1826, pp. viii, 476).

fruition in the International Missionary Council. To these achievements and plans, at once intensive and far-reaching, for the spread of the Christian faith, Carey added attainments in the realm of agriculture and horticulture. Partly for his own recreation, he developed a garden in which he assembled plants from various parts of the East. His publications in that field were notable and he corresponded with like-minded savants in Europe. He organized what he called an agri-horticultural society for India for the purpose of improving the utilization of the soil and the food supply of his adopted land. Through Carey's initiative fruit trees were introduced from England and experiments were made in the culture of coffee, cotton, tobacco, sugar cane, and cereals. At few Christian mission centres had such comprehensive concrete steps ever before been taken for bringing the Christian message to bear upon so large a proportion of the earth's surface.

These amazing achievements had not been attained without overcoming grave obstacles and meeting painful reverses. Even after the mission was established at Serampore, attempts were made, especially from 1806 through 1812, to induce the English East India Company to curb and even to put a stop to all missionary enterprise in India. Their opponents asserted that by arousing religious animosities missions fomented rebellion and threatened British rule, and that the converts were of disreputable character. The storm blew over, but many critics remained. Added to these troubles and for the most part coming after their acute stage had passed, were dissensions within the ranks of the missionaries themselves and between the Trio on the one hand and the governing committee of the home society on the other. The controversy was partly between the younger additions to the mission and the Trio. The former felt that the latter had become dictatorial. Then, too, as the early associates of Carey in England who had joined in the formation of the society died and their places were taken by younger men, criticism of the methods of the Trio arose. The opposition was directed chiefly against Marshman, who was somewhat angular in disposition, but it also involved the other two. For a time the new arrivals maintained a separate mission. Eventually a division occurred between the home society and the survivors of the Trio, Carey and Marshman. The two men were left in control of the college and its grounds. The remainder of the property, although much of it had been gathered through the earnings and gifts of the Trio, was left under the direction of the society.

In spite of these difficulties, some of which clouded the later years of the Trio, Serampore's contributions continued to be outstanding. It was famous among the supporters of the Protestant missionary enterprise and its example did much to stimulate the rapid growth which Protestant missions were then displaying.

Moreover, the Baptist Missionary Society continued to reinforce its staff in Bengal. The mission did not die.[239]

As 1793 with the arrival of Carey proved a memorable year in the spread of Protestant Christianity in India, so 1813 witnessed the beginning of another important stage in the expansion in India of that form of the faith. In 1813, when the charter of the English East India Company was renewed, friends of Christian missions, among whom Wilberforce was prominent, obtained the insertion of a provision for an Anglican ecclesiastical establishment of a bishop and three archdeacons and for what had the effect of permission for missionaries to live and work in the territories controlled by the company.[240] This legislation was followed by the entrance of a number of new societies to India and the extension of undertakings already begun.

To be sure, between 1793 and 1813 a few societies had succeeded in establishing themselves in India, even in face of the unfriendly attitude of the East India Company. The Society for Promoting Christian Knowledge continued its support to survivors of the Danish-Halle mission.[241] In 1798 the London Missionary Society sent a representative to India, Nathaniel Forsyth. He went to Bengal, was self-supporting, and wore himself out with his labours, dying in 1816. Reinforcements reached him in 1812.[242] Forsyth had first planned to go to India in connexion with a project which the Haldanes, inspired by the example of Carey, had initiated for the establishment of a college in that country for the training of missionaries, but the opposition of the East India Company made that undertaking impossible.[243] The London Missionary Society, too, in 1803 appointed Ringeltaube, who had been educated in Halle and had first gone to India under the Society for Promoting Christian Knowledge. With other emissaries of the society he reached Tranquebar, on a Danish vessel, late in 1804. By the year 1813 missions of the London Missionary Society had been begun in a number of places in South India and as far north as Vizagapatam, 400 miles

[239] For one of Marshman's replies to his critics, see J. Marshman, *Statement Relative to Serampore, Supplementary to a "Brief Memoir"* (London, Parbury, Allen & Co., 1828, pp. lxxi, 172). For one of the staff who came in 1839 and who had much to do with a revision of the Bengali and Sanskrit versions of the Bible, see Edward Bean Underhill, *The Life of the Rev. John Wenger* (London, the Baptist Missionary Society, 1886, pp. xiv, 279).

[240] Penny, *The Church in Madras*, Vol. II, pp. 27-50; Kaye, *Christianity in India*, pp. 257ff. Not all that some had worked for was achieved. Claudius Buchanan had advocated bishops for Madras, Bombay, and Ceylon, and an archbishop for Calcutta. Buchanan, *Memoir of the Expediency of an Ecclesiastical Establishment for British India*, p. 20.

[241] Allen and McClure, *op. cit.*, pp. 276ff.

[242] *Reports of the* [London] *Missionary Society*, Vol. I, pp. 63, 77, 108; Gogerly, *The Pioneers*, pp. 59-61.

[243] Gogerly, *op. cit.*, pp. 59, 60. On Robert Haldane see Vol. IV, pp. 131, 133, and Mackickan, *The Missionary Ideal of the Scottish Churches*, p. 105.

north of Madras.[244] The Church Missionary Society had India among its earliest objectives. Henry Martyn had considered going out under its auspices, but because of family obligations believed his prospective salary under the society inadequate for his needs and received appointment, instead, to the better paid position of chaplain.[245] The first missionaries of the American Board of Commissioners for Foreign Missions [246] went to India, arriving in Calcutta in 1812. The opposition of the East India Company proved embarrassing and it was not until 1813 that permission was obtained to maintain a residence at Bombay.[247] Yet these scanty beginnings, except for the Serampore group, seemed of small moment.

The change effected in the East India Company's charter in 1813 was followed by a striking increase in Protestant missions in India. To this a number of factors contributed. The end of the Napoleonic Wars, coming as it did two years later, freed the seas for travel and the East India Company from the spectre of French rivalry. The continuation of the British advance in India presented new territories as a challenge to missionary effort. The growing interest of the Protestants of the British Isles, the United States, and Europe in foreign missions, reinforced as it was by the rising tide of religious revivals, was attracted to this vast subcontinent which was thus being opened to the spread of Christianity. It is not surprising that, after 1813, Protestant missions in India were augmented.

The establishment of the episcopate strengthened the Church of England, both among the Europeans and in its extension among the Indians. The first appointee to the new see of Calcutta was Thomas Fanshaw Middleton (1769-1822).[248] The son of a clergyman, a graduate of Cambridge, possessed of scholarly gifts, with experience as magistrate, prebend, archdeacon, and in local parishes, and an active supporter of the Society for Promoting Christian Knowledge, the new bishop was admirably qualified for his post. Sensitive, he was chagrined and annoyed by limitations in his ecclesiastical powers which failed to give him adequate jurisdiction over some of the chaplains. Dignified and with a sense of the importance of his office, to some he appeared haughty. Energetic, hard-working, and conscientious, he travelled widely in India,

---

[244] Lovett, *The History of the London Missionary Society*, Vol. II, pp. 18ff.
[245] Stock, *The History of the Church Missionary Society*, Vol. I, pp. 81, 82.
[246] Vol. IV, pp. 82, 83. For the life of one of these, who died in 1812, see Leonard Woods, *Memoirs of Mrs. Harriet Newell* (London, D. Jacques, 1820, pp. xii, 226).
[247] Strong, *The Story of the American Board*, p. 18; *Anecdotes of the Bombay Mission . . . extracted from the Letters and Journals of the Rev. Gordon Hall*, pp. 32-60.
[248] Charles Webb Le Bas, *The Life of the Right Reverend Thomas Fanshaw Middleton, D.D., Late Lord Bishop of Calcutta* (London, C. J. G. and F. Rivington, 2 vols., 1831), *passim*.

consecrating churches and giving stimulus to the erection of additional church structures. He named archdeacons for the three chief centres of British rule, Calcutta, Bombay, and Madras. He believed his first responsibility to be to those of European blood, professed Christians, but he also wished the appointment and ordination of missionaries for non-Christians. He encouraged schools and dreamed of a University of Calcutta, to emulate Oxford and Cambridge. In fulfilment of the latter project, he issued an appeal for funds and founded in Calcutta Bishop's College with the purpose of training preachers, catechists, and schoolmasters, of translating the Bible, of helping in their introduction to India missionaries of the Society for the Propagation of the Gospel in Foreign Parts, and of giving education to Moslems and Hindus. The institution thus founded quickly became a centre of active missionary operations in Bengal and into the twentieth century was the most important Anglical theological college in India. Middleton died in 1822, after about seven years in India, a victim of heavy labours and the difficulties of his new post in a trying climate.

The second Bishop of Calcutta was Reginald Heber (1783-1826).[249] The son of a rector, precocious, a graduate of Oxford, poet and saint, combining quick and broad sympathies with great charm and courtesy, before going to India Heber had already contributed to the Church the widely used hymns *Holy, Holy, Holy, From Greenland's Icy Mountains, The Son of God Goes Forth to War*, and *Brightest and Best of the Sons of the Morning*. Ardently missionary, a warm advocate of the British and Foreign Bible Society, a member of the Society for Promoting Christian Knowledge, and an early supporter of the Church Missionary Society, Heber, with his irenic temperament, had hoped to see a union of the various missionary societies of the Anglican communion. It was natural that he should be asked to become Middleton's successor. It was characteristic of him, too, that he turned his back upon probable ecclesiastical promotion in England and accepted the post. In India he travelled indefatigably over his huge diocese, encouraging both the chaplains to the Europeans and the missionaries to the non-Christians.[250] It was while on one of his journeys, and after less than three years in India, that Heber suddenly died.

[249] On Heber see *The Life of Reginald Heber, D.D., Lord Bishop of Calcutta, by his Widow* (London, John Murray, 2 vols., 1830), *passim;* a condensation of the above, *The Life and Writings of Bishop Heber* (Boston, Albert Colby & Co., 1861, pp. 348); and George Smith, *Bishop Heber* (London, John Murray, 1895, pp. xix, 370), *passim.*

[250] For an account of these journeys, an invaluable picture of India of the period, see Reginald Heber, *Narrative of a Journey through the Upper Provinces of India, from Calcutta to Bombay 1824-1825,* (*with notes upon Ceylon*), *an Account of a Journey to Madras and the Southern Provinces, 1826, and Letters Written from India* (London, John Murray, 3 vols., 2d ed., 1828).

Two short episcopates followed Heber's.[251] Then came, from 1832 to 1858, the long and able administration of Wilson.[252] Daniel Wilson (July 2, 1778-January 2, 1858), the son of a silk manufacturer, as a boy was designed by his father for a career in business. In his late teens, however, he had a striking conversion of the Evangelical type and decided to enter the ministry. At Oxford he was a contemporary of Heber. After service in various parishes and as tutor in Oxford, he was appointed, through the interest of the distinguished Evangelical, Charles Grant, to the see of Calcutta. He was then in his fifty-fourth year, at the age when many of his countrymen who held posts in India thought of retiring. He was a prodigious worker and an able organizer and was completely devoted to his calling. The more than a quarter of a century which he gave to India marked an epoch in the development of the Anglican communion in that land. A man of unflinching courage and uncompromising convictions, Wilson aroused a storm in the churches in South India by his sturdy opposition to the persistence of caste differences among Christians. An outspoken Evangelical, he minced no words in his criticism of the Tractarian movement. Under him many churches were built. Of deep religious faith and unrelenting with himself in prayer and spiritual discipline, he endeavoured to hold his clergy to his standards. He asserted his authority over Anglican missionaries as well as chaplains. He maintained his activity down to the last, in his eightieth year, and died, as he had wished, in harness.

In 1833, when the East India Company's charter was again renewed, Anglican bishoprics were created for Madras and Bombay. Wilson thereupon became metropolitan and in his travels still covered India and some adjacent regions. Thanks to Charles Grant, moreover, India was so opened that no missionary need obtain the permission of the company to enter or settle there.[253]

The development of an Anglican episcopate for India was accompanied by the growth of missions of the Church Missionary Society and the Society for the Propagation of the Gospel in Foreign Parts. In the decade after 1813 the Church Missionary Society sent twenty-six men to India. Of these, eleven were Germans in Lutheran orders and thirteen were English clergymen. Fourteen went to the

[251] Chatterton, *A History of the Church of England in India*, pp. 144-154. For the first of these see Edward James, *Brief Memoirs of the Late Reverend John Thomas James, D.D., Lord Bishop of Calcutta* (London, J. Hatchard and Son, 1830, pp. xxxix, 204), *passim.*

[252] Josiah Bateman, *The Life of Daniel Wilson, D.D., Bishop of Calcutta and Metropolitan of India* (Boston, Gould and Lincoln, 1860, pp. xiii, 744); *Bishop Wilson's Journal Letters Addressed to his Family, during the first nine years of his Episcopate, edited by his son, Daniel Wilson* (London, James Nisbet and Co., 1863, pp. xi, 371).

[253] Stock, *A History of the Church Missionary Society*, Vol. I, p. 294.

North, to Bengal and farther up the Ganges Valley. Eleven were assigned to the South, where some of them cared for the congregations which had been gathered by the Danish-Halle mission. One went to Bombay. An enterprise was developed in the Ganges Valley, beginning in Calcutta and Bengal, extending hundreds of miles north-westward and to the borders of Tibet.[254] In the years between 1823 and 1841 the staff of the Church Missionary Society was further increased. The numbers of Christians also multiplied, particularly in the South, in Tinnevelly and Travancore. The accessions were from several caste groups, including a middle one, the Sudras, but chiefly from the Shanars, who were of a somewhat humbler social stratum. The low castes were attracted in part by the protection and security and the opportunity for education and material improvement to be obtained through a connexion with the Church.[255] An enterprise was also begun among the Telugus. The Church Missionary Society further expanded its operations in the North. In Agra the famous German missionary to the Moslems, Pfander, served under its auspices from 1841 to 1854 (including a year of furlough) and through his writings and personal contacts made converts. The Punjab was annexed by the British in 1849 and not many years thereafter the Church Missionary Society, encouraged

[254] Josiah Pratt and John Henry Pratt, *Memoir of Rev. Josiah Pratt—for twenty-one years Secretary of the Church Missionary Society* (London, Seeleys, 1849, pp. xv, 501), pp. 89-105; Stock, *op. cit.*, Vol. I, pp. 191-202, Vol. II, p. 169. For the life of one of the most distinguished of the Germans, from Jänicke's school in Berlin, see *Memoir of the Rev. C. T. E. Rhenius, Comprising Extracts from his Journal and Correspondence, with Details of Missionary Proceedings in South India, by his Son* (London, James Nisbet and Co., 1841, pp. xii, 627). For the life of one who reached India in 1824 and who served north of Benares, see *Memorials of an Indian Missionary; or, a Memoir of the Rev. Michael Wilkinson* (London, Wertheim, Macintosh, & Hunt, 1859, pp. 279). A German trained at Basel, who reached India in 1830 and served for more than twenty years in the Bengal mission, is commemorated in *Memoir of the Rev. John James Weitbrecht . . . Compiled from his Journal and Letters, by his Widow* (New York, Protestant Episcopal Society for the Promotion of Evangelical Knowledge, 1856, pp. 542). See also *History of the Church Missionary Society in Bengal* (Calcutta, Church Mission Office, no date, pp. 216), and M. Wilkinson, *Sketches of Christianity in North India* (London, Seeley, Burnside, and Seeley, 1844, pp. x, 419), pp. 218ff.

[255] George Pettitt, *The Tinnevelly Mission of the Church Missionary Society* (London, Seeleys, 1851, pp. xii, 574), *passim*. On one who sailed for India in 1845 and served in the Tinnevelly mission, see Thomas Thomasan Perowne, *A Memoir of the Rev. Thomas Gajetan Ragland* (London, Seeley, Jackson, and Halliday, 1861, pp. viii, 356), *passim*. For an important narrative containing many documents, giving an account of the last days of the Danish-Halle mission and the transition to the Church Missionary Society and the Society for the Propagation of the Gospel in Foreign Parts, see W. Taylor, *A Memoir of the First Century of the Earliest Protestant Mission at Madras* (Madras, Joshua Higgenbotham, 1847, pp. xxiv, 370, lxvi). For one of the staff of the Tinnevelly mission see [Amy Wilson Carmichael], *Ragland Pioneer* (Madras, S. P. C. K., 1922, pp. 167). For a description of the South India enterprises of the Church Missionary Society see S[arah] T[ucker], *South Indian Sketches, Containing a Short Account of Some of the Mission Stations Connected with the Church Missionary Society in Southern India* (London, James Nisbet and Co., 2 vols., 1842, 1843).

and assisted by warmly sympathetic British officials, opened centres in the region.[256]

The transfer, in 1826, of the missions of the Society for Promoting Christian Knowledge to the Society for the Propagation of the Gospel in Foreign Parts was not followed immediately by any striking growth in the Christian communities which had been under the former. To be sure, we hear of the formation in Bombay, through the instance of Bishop Heber, in 1825, of a district committee of the Society for the Propagation of the Gospel in Foreign Parts,[257] but it was not until the 1840's that a marked movement towards Christianity began. In that decade, in the Tinnevelly region, where the Danish-Halle enterprise had laid the foundations, entire villages came over to the Christian faith. By 1858 the Shanars, who had been opposed to the reception into the Church of members of castes still lower than themselves, began to seek converts from such groups.[258] By 1846, moreover, the missionaries of the society had gathered a few hundred converts in Bengal, south of Calcutta, mainly from peasants of low caste stock.[259] In 1846 a mission was begun to the Gonds, an aboriginal tribe in what became known as the Central Provinces.[260] The Society for Promoting Christian Knowledge did not completely withdraw from India, but continued to assist with literature, grants for schools, and the building of churches.[261]

We must also record the efforts of the Church Missionary Society on behalf of the Syrian Christians in South India. Claudius Buchanan had helped draw the attention of the society to these fellow believers. In 1816 the society began an enterprise in Cochin and Travancore. Missionaries were sent whose purpose it was not to annex the Syrian church to the Anglican communion, but to awaken and purify it that it might, through a quickened life, undertake to spread its faith among the non-Christians around it. To this end a college was begun with the object of training clergy, a printing press was inaugurated,

---

[256] Stock, op. cit., Vol. I, p. 327, Vol. II, pp. 169, 198-213. For two of the staff of the Telugu mission, see John Noble, A Memoir of the Rev. Turlington Noble (London, Seeley, Jackson, and Halliday, 1867, pp. xv, 360), and George Townshend Fox, A Memoir of the Rev. Watson Fox . . . Missionary to the Teloogoo People, South India (London, Seeleys, 1853, pp. xxxiii, 382).

[257] Caldwell, Records of the Early History of the Tinnevelly Mission of the Society for Promoting Christian Knowledge and the Society for the Propagation of the Gospel in Foreign Parts, passim; Pascoe, Two Hundred Years of the S. P. G., pp. 569-575.

[258] Caldwell, op. cit., passim; Pascoe, op. cit., pp. 533ff.; Mullens, Missions in South India, pp. 91-118.

[259] James Long, Hand-book of Bengal Missions in Connexion with the Church of England (London, John Farquhar Shaw, 1848, pp. vii, 520), pp. 249ff.

[260] Pascoe, op. cit., pp. 604, 605.

[261] Allen and McClure, Two Hundred Years: the History of the Society for Promoting Christian Knowledge, 1698-1808, pp. 289-295.

translations into the vernacular, especially of the Bible, were undertaken, and religious services and preaching in the vernacular were commenced. For the first decade friendly relations were maintained with the head of the Syrian church. Then strains developed and a separation (1836) occurred between the mission and the church. The mission thereafter directed its efforts primarily to the non-Christians. However, some of the Syrian Christians, now unhappy in the old church, sought and received admission to the Anglican communion. Moreover, higher education in English of Syrian youths was continued by the missionaries, and some so trained became leaders in the Syrian body. Then, too, out of the influence of the Anglican mission there arose a division in the Syrian church. Those who incorporated the changes brought about by the contact called their body the Mar Thoma Church and claimed to be the true successors of the church founded by St. Thomas uncorrupted by what they declared to be the superstitious practices which had entered since apostolic days. In many ways, however, they closely resembled the parent body.[262]

Under the opportunities given by the revised charter of 1813, the London Missionary Society rapidly enlarged its staff in India. In general it developed from the centres which had been entered before 1813. It maintained what had been begun at Calcutta and pressed up the Ganges Valley to Benares, the holy city of the Hindus. In spite of discouragements, it held on in Vizagapatam. It was in Madras and had a station in Bellary, northwest of Madras. It was also in Bangalore, west of Madras, and in Salem, south of that city. It continued as well in the extreme South, in Travancore.[263]

The American Board of Commissioners for Foreign Missions developed the foothold it had acquired at Bombay and pushed inland from that port to

[262] W. S. Hunt, The Anglican Church in Travancore and Cochin, 1816-1916 (Kottayam, Church Missionary Society, Vol. I, 1920, pp. xi, 233), passim; P. Cheriyan, The Malabar Syrians and the Church Missionary Society, 1816-1840 (Kottayam, Church Missionary Society's Press, 1935, pp. x, 438), passim; Richard Collins, Missionary Enterprise in the East with Especial Reference to the Syrian Christians of Malabar and the Results of Modern Missions (London, Henry S. King & Co., 1873, pp. viii, 276), pp. 90ff.

[263] Lovett, The History of the London Missionary Society, Vol. II, pp. 46ff. On one of the staff in Bengal who had only a brief span of life in India, see Memoir of John Adam, Late Missionary at Calcutta (London, J. Cross, 1833, pp. 404). On a missionary in Bellary, who arrived in 1830 after that station was already well removed from the pioneer stage, see Ralph Wardlaw, Memoir of the Late Rev. John Reid, M.A., of Bellary, East Indies (Glasgow, James Maclehouse, 1845, pp. xvi, 468). For a Swiss who reached Chinsurah in 1821 under the London Missionary Society, and all of whose Indian career (he died in 1859) was spent in Bengal, see Joseph Mullens, Brief Memorials of the Rev. Alphonse Francois Lacroix (London, James Nisbet & Co., 1862, pp. xii, 483). There served for many years in Bangalore Benjamin Rice, who reached that city in 1837—Edward P. Rice, Benjamin Rice, or Fifty Years in the Master's Service (London, The Religious Tract Society, no date, pp. 192), passim. See also Kennedy, Life and Work in Benares and Kumaon, 1839-1877, pp. 27ff.

Ahmednagar. With the opportunity given by the charter of 1833, it likewise established itself at Madura, in the South.[264]

To India came, too, Presbyterian missionaries from Scotland. One of their number, Alexander Duff (1806-1878), by the methods which he devised began a new day for the Protestant enterprise in that country.[265] In 1829 Duff went to India as the first foreign missionary of the Church of Scotland. Duff had been reared in a home which was profoundly committed to the Evangelical awakening and which had felt the touch of Simeon. For his university course he had gone to St. Andrews. There he had been under the influence of a missionary society and of Thomas Chalmers, a kindling representative of the new life. In the Church of Scotland there was a small circle, led by John Inglis, which was planning a mission in India designed to centre around a system of schools. Duff was appointed as the first representative and, with his wife, reached India in 1830.

When Duff landed in India, Christian missions, particularly Protestant missions, were still being sharply questioned. In the years immediately preceding and succeeding his arrival, severe criticisms were circulated in Europe by those having first-hand knowledge of the country.[266] Protestant missions were declared a failure. So serious were the accusations that friends of the enterprise felt called upon to issue sturdy rejoinders.[267] Conversions had admittedly not

---

[264] Strong, *The Story of the American Board*, pp. 18ff; *Anecdotes of the Bombay Mission . . . extracted from the Letters and Journals of the Rev. Gordon Hall*, pp. 61ff.

[265] On Duff see George Smith, *The Life of Alexander Duff* (New York, A. C. Armstrong & Son, 2 vols., no date); William Paton, *Alexander Duff, Pioneer of Missionary Education* (New York, George H. Doran Co., no date, pp. 240); Lal Behari Day, *Recollections of Alexander Duff, D.D., LL.D., and of the Mission College which He Founded at Calcutta* (London, T. Nelson and Sons, 1879, pp. 243); and *Memorials of Alexander Duff, D.D., by his son, W. Pirie Duff* (London, James Nisbet & Co., 1890, pp. vii, 118). Duff's own account of the origin of his mission and of his theory of mission methods is in Alexander Duff, *India and Indian Missions* (Edinburgh, John Johnstone, 1839, pp. xxiii, 684) pp. 260-399, 477ff.

[266] A. J. Dubois, *Letters on the State of Christianity in India* (London, Longman, Hurst, Rees, Orme, Brown, and Green, 1823, pp. viii, 222); Nicol-Wisemann, *Unfruchtbarkeit der von den Protestanten zur Berkehrung ungläubiger Völker unternommenen Missionen. Dargethan aus den eigenen Berichten der Missionäre* (Augsburg, Karl Kollman'schen Buchhandlung, 1835, pp. viii, 119. Translated from the Italian original).

[267] Henry Townley, *An Answer to the Abbé Dubois* (London, R. Clay, 1824, pp. viii, 214); James Hough, *A Reply to the Letters of the Abbé Dubois on the State of Christianity in India* (London, L. B. Seeley & Son, 1824, pp. 322); James Hough, *The Protestant Missions Vindicated against the Aspersions of the Rev. N. Wisemen, D.D., involving the Protestant Religion* (London, R. B. Seeley and W. Burnside, 1837, pp. 146). On an earlier attack, which advocated the withdrawal of all missionaries, and the spirited reply, see [L. Richardson], *Considerations on the Practicality, Policy, and Obligation of Communicating to the Natives of India the Knowledge of Christianity, with Observations on the "Prefatory Remarks" to a Pamphlet Published by Major Scott Waring* (London, John Hatchard, 1808, pp. vii, 101).

been numerous and the larger proportion of them had been from members of the lower social strata. During the winning of western Europe the leaders of the various nations had been reached and through them the mass conversions of the peoples had followed. There was little promise of this being the course of Christianity in India.

Duff proposed to alter the prevailing method of approach. He determined to introduce a form of Christian higher education which would both undermine Hinduism and be a safeguard against the religious agnosticism which might follow from a knowledge of Western science which was not closely integrated with Christianity. He believed all truth to be one and held that modern science and Christianity were not antagonistic. He would unite the two in his curriculum. This education he would give, not in an Indian tongue but in English. English, he felt, was better fitted for the transmission of Western science. At the same time, while acquiring it, a language whose concepts and literature had become permeated with Christian ideas, the student, so he held, would be unconsciously or half consciously learning of Christianity. This method, Duff believed, would not arouse the antagonism which a direct attack on Hinduism and the open endeavour to win converts would entail, but would bring about the gradual disintegration of Hinduism and be a preparation for the acceptance of the Christian Gospel. India could best be won, he maintained, through the leadership of its own sons, highly trained to influence the many.

Duff formed a friendship with Ram Mohan Roy, a deeply religious Brahmin much older than himself who had departed from orthodox Hinduism and was the founder of the *Brahmo Samaj*. A reformer, Ram Mohan Roy was too much the intellectual to have a wide popular following, but he influenced some of the higher classes of Hindus who had come in touch with Occidental learning. It was with the assistance of Ram Mohan Roy that Duff opened his first school. This was in Calcutta, the centre of the impact of European culture on India, and where some of the wealthy Hindu families felt it of worldly advantage to their sons to give them as good a training as possible in the civilization of the ruling power. Duff proved to be a great teacher and his school quickly became popular. From time to time opposition arose, especially when some of his pupils became confessed Christians. Always, however, the high character of the institution in providing the desired Western learning brought a resurgence of students. From the converts, men of high caste and able, although they were not numerous, arose some of the outstanding leaders of the emerging Protestant communities.

Duff proved very influential. Arriving in India at a time when the British conscience, in part aroused by the Evangelicals, was awakening to a sense of responsibility for the growing empire and when the British were feeling their way toward an educational system for their Indian domains, Duff showed what could be done with education through the medium of English and probably contributed toward the adoption of that tongue in the schools maintained by the British *raj*. Duff, too, pushed energetically for schools for Indian women, a striking innovation in a land where formal education had traditionally been almost entirely a monopoly of men.

When, in 1843, the Disruption brought about the formation of the Free Church of Scotland, Duff and the missionaries who had reinforced him cast in their lot with the new body. While in the end, through the enlargement of the efforts of the Free Church and the continuation of the labours of the Church of Scotland, the Disruption led to the increase of the enterprises of the Scottish churches in India, for the time being his step brought Duff embarrassment. The Church of Scotland retained his old school and he was compelled to build a new one.

Duff was a man of abounding energy and assisted many enterprises. He joined in founding and later edited the Calcutta *Review*. He helped in the creation of a medical school and of a hospital in Calcutta. He interested himself in the Eurasians (Anglo-Indians). He left his impress upon later developments in the British educational policy and contributed notably to the adoption of the principle of grants of government funds to private schools and to schools on religious foundation. He did much to stimulate support in Scotland for foreign missions. His visit to the United States in 1854 was the occasion for the calling of a union missionary convention which proved a precedent for the growth of interdenominational gatherings for carrying the Christian message to the entire world.

When, in 1863, ill-health compelled him to lay down his work in India, Duff returned to Scotland, but not to inactivity. He encouraged the formation of new missions, raised funds, and almost to the end of his life laboured for the better training of missionaries.

Duff's greatest contribution was to Indian education. More than any other one man he laid the foundations for the use of higher education by Protestants as a means for reaching the youth of India. The results in the permeation of India with Christian ideas were more striking than direct conversions. This was not due entirely to the method. It was, rather, to be attributed to the tenacity of caste. That the schools so established were popular was due not only to the excellence of the instruction offered but also to the demand for the type of education which they gave. It was through that education that employment and advancement in the régime set up by the British were to be obtained. Duff was by no means solely responsible for the method, but he helped to formulate it. Other Scottish missionaries came to Bengal [268] and the enterprise they established was more than a school. Yet Duff's institution and his contribution to education were the outstanding feature of the undertakings both of the Church of Scotland and of the Free Church.

The year in which Duff came to India, 1829, saw the arrival in that country of another great Scottish missionary, John Wilson (1804-1875). [269] Wilson was a son of the Border, the marches between England and Scotland. As a lad he combined promise of marked intellectual attainments with a deeply religious nature which under the influence of the revival spirit then stirring in his native land early ripened into a purpose to enter the ministry and then to become a missionary. He went out under the Scottish Missionary Society, but within a few years he and his colleagues were transferred to the direct supervision of the Church of Scotland. Like Duff, at the time of the Disruption he took his stand with the Free Church of Scotland and remained connected with that body until his death. He and his wife landed in Bombay (1829). He was not the first of his society in that city. Several other appointees had arrived in 1823 and 1824. [270] During the more than four decades of his missionary career, although he made tours, some of them extended, into the adjacent regions, Bombay was the centre of his efforts.

A scholar by temperament, Wilson acquired the tongues of the main communities of the polyglot city of his adoption and established contacts with Hindus, Moslems, and Parsees. He also befriended Jews, Abyssinians, and Negroes. He became a student of the religions about him and made himself familiar with much of Indian literature. He early organized a Presbyterian church, chiefly from converts, and was eager to win others to his faith. He numbered by the hundreds those whom he had been instrumental in attracting to Christianity. His vision ranged to the Jews of Arabia. He was, however, chiefly remembered as an educator and a scholar, for his sympathetic interpreta-

[268] For one of these missionaries, who served in Bengal from 1837 to his death, in 1847, see W. K. Tweedie, *The Life of the Rev. John Macdonald* (Edinburgh, John Johnstone, 1849, pp. xxv, 464). For another who was in India from 1853 into 1857, see Horatius Bonar, *Life of the Rev. John Milne of Perth* (New York, Robert Carter and Brothers, 1870, pp. viii, 488).

[269] The standard biography of Wilson is by his friend, George Smith, *The Life of John Wilson* (London, John Murray, 1879, pp. xiii, 378). Wilson himself wrote the biography of the wife who shared his first years in India in *A Memoir of Mrs. Margaret Wilson* (Edinburgh, John Johnstone, 1838, pp. 636).

[270] On one who arrived in 1827, served for nearly three decades, chiefly in Bombay and Poona, and died in 1855, see J. Murray Mitchell, *Memoir of the Rev. Robert Nesbit, Missionary of the Free Church of Scotland, Bombay* (London, James Nisbet & Co., 1858, pp. viii, 407).

tion to the British rulers of the various races and classes of the country, and for the deep respect with which he was regarded by those drawn from many walks of life.[271] While, like Duff, he would use the English language in higher education, he set greater store by the vernaculars than did the former. These he would employ in primary education. He wished also to make a place for the literature of India in advanced classes. Wilson began many schools, among them an institution which was eventually named for him. He was a sturdy advocate of the education of women. As its first vice-chancellor, he contributed largely to the shaping of the University of Bombay, a government foundation. He had a share in the growth of the Bombay branch of the Royal Asiatic Society, encouraged the assembling of Sanskrit manuscripts, and was a pioneer in the study of some of the ancient rock inscriptions of the land.

The enterprise of the Free Church of Scotland reached inland from Bombay to Poona, on the edge of the Deccan.[272]

Also from Scotland and, like Wilson, the founder of a school which was later to bear his name, was Stephen Hislop (1817-1863).[273] He, too, was a child of the Border and of the religious awakenings which were stirring the Scottish churches in the fore part of the nineteenth century. In 1844 he sailed for India under the youthful Free Church of Scotland. He went to Nagpur, in the Central Provinces, there to inaugurate an enterprise of his church. Protestant Christianity had already been introduced to that city by the influence of the Serampore group and by devout servants of the East India Company. Through one of the latter, Gossner, a German pastor, sent a group of his mission—artisans, farmers, and an apothecary—to the Gonds, a primitive people in the adjacent hills. Through the offer of generous financial support by another of the officials of the East India Company, with John Wilson as intermediary, the Free Church of Scotland sent Hislop to Nagpur. Here and in the vicinity converts were soon made among Tamils, Mahrattas, and Telugus. A college was founded. Tours were undertaken into the surrounding country to broadcast the Christian message. Hislop reached out among the Gonds. He made studies of the geology of the region. He helped to stimulate reforms in the British administration.

In Madras there arose, as in Calcutta and Bombay, the other main centres of British power, a school under the Church of Scotland. It was similar in purpose

[271] The principles on which he conducted his work are incorporated in John Wilson, *The Evangelization of India* (Edinburgh, William White & Co., 1849, pp. xii, 489).

[272] On one who served first in Bombay and later in Poona, see J. Murray Mitchell, *In Western India. Recollections of My Early Missionary Life* (Edinburgh, David Douglas, 1899, pp. xii, 405).

[273] George Smith, *Stephen Hislop, Pioneer Missionary & Naturalist in Central India from 1844 to 1863* (London, John Murray, 1889, pp. xii, 317).

to that organized by Duff and was opened in 1837. Its first head was John Anderson, who had arrived in India that very year. The Madras school, like that in Calcutta, attracted boys from families of high caste. When conversions occurred, followed by baptism, as they did, notably in 1841, the alarm and antagonism aroused among the parents and friends of the pupils threatened to bring the school to an end. However, the demand for the type of Western education represented by the institution was so great that the attendance revived. Other schools were opened, and provision was made for the education of girls. At the time of the Disruption the missionaries took their stand with the Free Church.[274]

The school founded by Anderson, termed the Central Institution, later developed into the Madras Christian College and won an outstanding place in Christian higher education in India. The figure chiefly responsible for this development, if we may anticipate our story slightly, was William Miller (1838-1923). Miller, who was proud of his Viking ancestry, and who had the vigour of body and mind associated with that race, arrived in Madras in 1862, sent for the express purpose of putting the school, then enfeebled, on its feet. At that time the sole agent of the Free Church in Madras, Miller reorganized the mission and made the Institution the centre, not merely, as formerly, an adjunct of his church's enterprise in that area. He gave himself with single-hearted devotion to the school and its pupils, raised funds, some of them the gift of his own brother, Alexander, and of himself, and induced the Church Missionary Society and the Wesleyans to join (1887) in transforming it into the interdenominational Madras Christian College. After various illnesses which sapped his great strength and which necessitated extensive absences from the country, threatened blindness eventually (1907) forced Miller's permanent retirement to Scotland. Yet so well had he done his work that the college continued to thrive.[275]

As in Africa, so in India, it was in education that Scottish Presbyterianism made its most distinctive contributions to the spread of Christianity. This was true of both the Church of Scotland and the Free Church. When, at the Disruption, all the missionaries cast in their lot with the Free Church, the Church of Scotland retained the property, including that of the schools which Duff, Wilson, and Anderson had built up. Although the Free Church was under the

[274] John Braidwood, *True Yoke-Fellows of the Mission Field: the Life and Labours of the Rev. John Anderson and the Rev. Robert Johnston Traced in the Rise and Development of the Madras Free Church Mission* (London, James Nisbet & Co., 1862, pp. vi, 560), *passim.*
[275] See articles by various authors in *The Madras Christian College Magazine*, Oct., 1923, and Jan., 1924.

necessity of erecting new buildings and maintaining its ministry in Scotland, it undertook the support of the missionaries in India and in time made possible new physical plants for the schools in Calcutta, Bombay, and Madras. Those who remained by the Church of Scotland did not have, on the average, as much missionary zeal as those who constituted the Free Church, but the Church of Scotland retained its educational institutions at Calcutta, Bombay, and Madras and in 1855 began a new enterprise in the Punjab.[276]

In 1841 the initial contingent of the Irish Presbyterian Church Mission arrived. A field, in Kathiawar, was chosen on the advice of John Wilson. This was the first independent Indian mission of their church. In the 1840's, at the request of that organization, the Irish Presbyterians took over the enterprise of the London Missionary Society in Surat which, as a glance at the map will show, is across the Gulf of Cambay from Kathiawar.[277]

In the decades between 1813 and the end of the East India Company's rule (1858) still other British societies and agencies began operations in India. In 1821 the first representatives of the New Connexion of General Baptists reached India. (It was the Particular Baptists who supported William Carey and the Baptist Missionary Society.) On arriving in India they sought the advice of the Serampore Trio and at their suggestion selected a field in Orissa. Orissa was already under British rule and the Bible had been translated into its language.[278] Several stations were opened and in 1828 the first baptism, that of a Brahmin, was administered. In the 1830's General Baptists from the United States came to the assistance of their English brethren and sent missionaries who laboured in close fellowship with the others.[279] In 1821 Miss Cooke of the British and Foreign School Society reached Calcutta and began the organization of schools for girls. By the close of the year 1823, twenty-two had come into existence. In 1824 a Ladies' Society for Native Female Education in Calcutta was organized to care for these schools. Assistance in funds and personnel came to it from the Society for Promoting Female Education in the East, which was formed in England in 1834. In 1852 the Calcutta Normal School was brought into being. In 1852, also, a committee which a few years later grew into the Indian Female Normal School and Instruction Society was constituted in London to assist the enterprise. The institution had as its purpose the training of teachers who would give instruction to women and girls in their own

[276] Richter, *Indische Missionsgeschichte*, pp. 210, 211.

[277] Jeffrey, *The Indian Mission of the Irish Presbyterian Church*, pp. 29-42.

[278] Amos Sutton, *A Narrative of the Mission to Orissa* (Boston, David Marks, 1833, pp. viii, 424), *passim*.

[279] Amos Sutton, *Orissa and Its Evangelization* (Derby, Wilkins & Son, 1850, pp. 396), pp. 101 ff.

homes. It proved to be the nucleus from which arose the undenominational Zenana Bible and Medical Mission and, in 1880, the Church of England Zenana Missionary Society, which laboured in close connexion with the Church Missionary Society.[280]

Wesleyan missions in India began as an outgrowth of the enterprise inaugurated in Ceylon in 1814 as a result of the dreams of Thomas Coke. In 1817 James Lynch, of the Ceylon mission, came to Madras. He found there an organized group of Methodists. In 1819 a local Wesleyan Methodist Missionary Society was formed which raised funds among the British residents. Chapels were erected and before long efforts were begun to reach the Tamils of the city. Although centres were opened at a number of places, notably in Madras, Bangalore, and Negapatam, and operations were begun in the native state of Mysore, progress was slow. For years the attention of the small staff was divided between the British soldiers and European residents on the one hand and the Indians on the other. However, reinforcements came, stations were multiplied, and by 1857 in several centres promising beginnings had been made among the Indians.[281]

As early as 1833 there were Plymouth Brethren in India. In that year Anthony Norris Groves began travels through the country in which he met a number of scattered Europeans who, like himself, were of these convictions. He returned to Great Britain, recruited missionaries there and in Europe, and in 1836 landed in Madras with a party of thirteen. Beginnings were made in the Madras Presidency, including an attempt by Groves to make the mission self-supporting by engaging in agriculture.[282]

Until 1840 the Welsh Calvinistic Methodists had expressed their missionary interest through contributions to the London Missionary Society. However, in that year they sent missionaries of their own to India. These arrived in their field in 1841 and undertook to reach the Khasis, an animistic people in the Khasia and Jaintia Hills of Assam, which had recently been pacified by British arms. Carey had been interested in the Khasis and had given them the New Testament in their tongue, but the actual penetration of the region by resident missionaries was first accomplished by these Welsh Presbyterians. Schools were

[280] Stock, *The History of the Church Missionary Society*, Vol. II, p. 162; Barnes, *Behind the Pardah*, pp. 2-9.

[281] Findlay and Holdsworth, *The History of the Wesleyan Methodist Missionary Society*, Vol. V, pp. 176ff.; Alfred Barrett, *Holy Living Exemplified in the Life of Mrs. Mary Cryer* (London, 1849, pp. iv, 326), *passim;* Hoole, *Madras, Mysore, and the South of India*, pp. 38ff.; William Arthur, *A Mission to the Mysore* (London, Partridge and Oakey, 1847, pp. xi, 560), *passim.*

[282] *Memoir of the Late Anthony Norris Groves, Containing Extracts from his Letters and Journals, Compiled by his Widow* (London, James Nisbet & Co., 1856, pp. vi, 544), *passim.*

opened, a fresh translation of the Bible was begun, and eventually converts were won and churches gathered.[283]

In the 1840's some of the British officers and civilians in Simla, when the Church Missionary Society because of lack of funds declined to begin an enterprise in that district, organized the Himalaya Mission. Before long the Church Missionary Society reversed its earlier decision and adopted the undertaking.[284]

More American societies also entered India after 1813. In 1833[285] came Presbyterians, sent by the Western Foreign Missionary Society (in 1837 absorbed into the newly formed Board of Foreign Missions of the Presbyterian Church). Ill health and death took a heavy toll from the first contingent,[286] but a field was staked out in the Punjab, and in what later became the United Provinces, a region chosen because it was more neglected by the Protestant forces than some other parts of the country. Prominent among the reinforcements was Charles W. Forman. Forman arrived in 1848 and spent more than forty years in India. He began a college at Lahore which eventually was given his name.[287]

To the Punjab came from the United States representatives of other members of the family of Reformed and Presbyterian churches. In 1855 there arrived Andrew Gordon and his family, sent by the Associate Presbyterian Synod. When that body joined, in 1858, in constituting the United Presbyterian Church, the Indian enterprise was transferred (1859) to the new denomination. The first converts were from outcaste aborigines, the Chuhras. In later years a mass movement to Christianity was to take place in that group.[288] On their arrival the Gordons found already at work near the Punjab missionaries of the Reformed Presbyterian Church of America.[289]

For a number of years the (Dutch) Reformed Church in America carried on its foreign missions through the American Board. In 1819 there went to Ceylon under that society John Scudder, a physician. In 1836, together with a colleague, he moved to Madras there to inaugurate a mission of the American Board. He had a large family and in 1853 his two eldest sons began an enterprise, still un-

[283] Morris, The Story of Our Foreign Mission (Presbyterian Church of Wales), pp. 9ff.

[284] Stock, The History of the Church Missionary Society, Vol. II, pp. 202, 203.

[285] John C. Lowrie, Two Years in Upper India (New York, Robert Carter and Brothers, 1850, pp. 276). By one of the original contingent.

[286] Brown, One Hundred Years, pp. 560-566. For a biography of one of the pioneers who died soon after reaching India, see E. J. Richards, Memoir of Mrs. Anna Maria Morrison (New York, M. W. Dodd, 1843, pp. 176).

[287] Brown, op. cit., pp. 560-566; Joseph Warren, A Glance Backward at Fifteen Years of Missionary Life in North India (Philadelphia, Presbyterian Board of Publication, 1856, pp. 256), passim.

[288] Gordon, Our India Mission, pp. 17ff.; Anderson and Watson, Far North in India, pp. 177ff.

[289] Gordon, op. cit., p. 42.

der the American Board, at Arcot, south-west of Madras. A number of additional stations were quickly opened. When, in 1857, the Reformed Church in America organized its own board of foreign missions, the Arcot field was transferred to it. There eventually at least three generations of Scudders laboured.[290]

Late in 1835 Nathan Brown and several other missionaries of the American Baptists reached Calcutta. Before long they were on their way into Assam.[291] In 1836 there arrived in Calcutta Samuel S. Day, also of the American Baptists. He inaugurated a mission of his society among the Telugus. In 1840 he established himself at Nellore. For years the enterprise had only a precarious existence. The foreign staff was small, ill health depleted its ranks, and it came to be known by the somewhat cryptic sobriquet "The Lone Star Mission." [292]

In the 1830's and 1840's American Lutherans began missionary efforts in India. In the 1830's funds were sent to Rhenius, a German Lutheran who had long served in South India under the Church Missionary Society, but who, when efforts were made to bring him and his enterprise into conformity with the Church of England, withdrew and maintained an independent mission.[293] When, after the death of Rhenius, his associates returned to the service of the Church Missionary Society, American Lutherans were moved to begin an undertaking of their own. In 1841 the General Synod, an organization of American Lutherans, appointed C. F. Heyer to India and, on the advice of the American Board of Commissioners for Foreign Missions, chose the Telugus as their objective. However, the General Synod's board of missions entered into a plan of co-operation with the American Board. To this Heyer objected and went to India under the missionary society of the Pennsylvania Ministerium, another American Lutheran organization, arriving in 1842. He found his field among the Telugus, making Guntur his headquarters. The General Synod, undiscouraged, in 1843 sent out a representative, Walter Gunn, who also chose a field among the Telugus. Within a few years the enterprises of the two American bodies coalesced, the Foreign Missionary Society of the General Synod bearing the chief financial burden. In 1846 Heyer returned to America and the Guntur project passed entirely under the control of the General Synod. When, in 1848, Heyer again landed in India, his salary was borne by the Pennsylvania Ministerium. Heyer remained in India until 1857.[294]

[290] Chamberlain, *Fifty Years in Foreign Fields*, pp. 24, 25.
[291] *Baptist Missionary Magazine*, Vol. XVI, p. 142.
[292] Clough, *Social Christianity in the Orient*, pp. 61ff.
[293] Drach and Kuder, *The Telugu Mission of the General Council of the Evangelical Lutheran Church in North America*, pp. 4-6.
[294] Drach and Kuder, *op. cit.*, pp. 17-113; L. B. Wolf, *After Fifty Years, or an Historical*

In 1856 the Missionary Society of the Methodist Episcopal Church inaugurated a mission in India. For their pioneer it chose William Butler. William Butler was born in Ireland and had come to the United States as a Methodist clergyman. He offered himself for the new mission and became its first superintendent. Arrived in India, he chose for a field Bareilly, a province in the North-west in which no Protestant body was as yet represented.[295]

By 1858 none of these new American missions had attained large dimensions. However, all had staked out fields which they were later to develop and in which by the year 1914 each was to have a very large growth.

It was to be expected that missionary societies from the continent of Europe, and especially those of German and Scandinavian Protestantism, would seek to send representatives to India. It was the Danish-Halle undertaking, an enterprise in which both Danes and Germans had joined, which had inaugurated the first large-scale Protestant effort to win Indians to the faith.[296] Now that so much of the fruits of that mission had passed into Anglican hands, and now that the modifications of the charter of the East India Company (especially in 1833) had made easier the establishment of non-British missions within British territory, it was but natural that the rising tide of life and of missionary interest in German and Scandinavian Protestantism should seek expression in this former scene of Lutheran missionary achievement.

The Basel Mission, with headquarters in German Switzerland and drawing largely from Germany, was the first of the Continental societies to establish itself in India. This, too, was not surprising. In 1818, two years after the founding of the training institution around which the Basel Mission later centred, two men prepared in the school had gone to India under the Church Missionary Society. Others had followed with that same hospitable support and direction.[297] In 1834, the financial means having been provided by a substantial gift from a generous benefactor of the Basel Mission, Prince Otto Victor of Schönberg-Waldenburg, an initial contingent of three was sent. Of these the best remem-

Sketch of the Guntur Mission of the Evangelical Lutheran Church of the General Synod in the United States of America (Philadelphia, Lutheran Publication Society, 1896, pp. 320), pp. 27ff.

[295] Thirty-Seventh Report of the Missionary Society of the Methodist Episcopal Church (1856), p. 47; Thirty-Ninth Annual Report of the Missionary Society of the Methodist Episcopal Church (1858), pp. 58-60; William Butler, The Founder of Two Missions of the Methodist Episcopal Church, by his Daughter (New York, Eaton & Mains, 1902, pp. 239), passim; Clementina Butler, Mrs. William Butler (Cincinnati, The Methodist Book Concern, 1929, pp. 202), passim; Harper, The Methodist Episcopal Church in India, pp. 1-10. See scattered autobiographical reminiscences of these years in Butler, From Boston to Bareilly and Back.

[296] Vol. III, pp. 278-281.

[297] Schlatter, Geschichte der Basler Mission, Vol. II, pp. 1-3.

bered was Samuel Hebich (1803-1868).[298] The son of a Lutheran pastor, Hebich had as a lad gone into business, in his late teens had had a conversion experience, and in his late twenties had gone to Basel for training as a missionary. Something of an autocrat who found team-work difficult, a celibate, deeply in earnest and forthright, Hebich preached and made personal contacts in crowded streets, at non-Christian religious festivals, and wherever else he could gain a hearing. He gave much attention to the spiritual welfare of Europeans. The group made Mangalore, on the Canara coast, their centre, for that region was as yet practically untouched by Protestant missions.

By 1850 fairly numerous reinforcements, both men and women, had arrived, and additional stations had been opened, mainly in Dharwar, east of Goa, south of Mangalore along the Malabar coast in Cannanore and Tellichery, and in the Nilgiri Hills. The Basel missionaries received substantial assistance from several British officials and planters who were warmly interested in things Christian.[299] Among the outstanding missionaries, in addition to Hebich, were Hermann Gundert[300] and Herrmann Mögling.[301] Gundert, son of a secretary of the Württemberg Bible Society, who through deep spiritual agony in his student days had come into a clear faith, had first come to India with Groves, of the Plymouth Brethren. Approaches were made to several different groups and classes, among them Tamils and British officials and soldiers. Schools were inaugurated and maintained, and outstations were opened. Converts were made and catechists trained. In 1850, at the behest of the committee in Europe, the various stations were co-ordinated under a district conference and a general conference, with Hebich as president and Mögling as secretary.[302] There arose in time a fairly well-integrated enterprise extending over an extensive but not uncompact territory in the South-east. Attempts to establish stations in Central India under Gottlieb Pfander, whom we met in the last chapter, and in Bengal, were not enduring.[303] The Basel Mission, deeming it necessary to assist its converts in making a living, especially since so many of them were by their baptism

[298] See the following biographies of Hebich: [Gundert and Mögling], *The Life of Samuel Hebrich by two of his Fellow-Labourers,* translated from the German by J. G. Halliday (London, Seeley, Jackson, & Halliday, 1876, pp. xvi, 364) ; George N. Thomssen, *Samuel Hebich of India* (Cuttack, Orissa Mission Press, 1905, pp. viii, 351) ; Traugott Schölly, *Samuel Hebich* (Basel, Missionsbuchhandlung, 1911, pp. iv, 262).

[299] Schlatter, *op. cit.,* Vol. II, pp. 4ff.

[300] I. Hesse, *Aus Dr. Hermann Gundert's Leben* (Calw and Stuttgart, Vereinsbuchhandlung, 1894, pp. 368).

[301] H. Gundert, *Herrmann Mögling* (Calw and Stuttgart, Vereinsbuchhandlung, 1882, pp. viii, 390) ; H. Mögling and Th. Weitbrecht, *Das Kurgland und die evangelische Mission in Kurg* (Basel, Missionshaus, 1866, pp. viii, 334).

[302] Schlatter, *op. cit.,* Vol. II, pp. 16ff. For a picture of the mission in 1851 see I. Hesse, *Joseph Josenhans* (Calw and Stuttgart, Vereinsbuchhandlung, 1895, pp. 323), pp. 121ff.

[303] Schlatter, *op. cit.,* Vol. II, pp. 10-15.

cut off from caste groups which were also occupational, undertook agricultural and industrial enterprises to enable the Christians to support themselves. Skilled artisans were sent from Europe to supervise the training of the converts. A printing establishment was maintained which gave employment to some. Others became weavers. Here were arising Christian communities,[304] distinct in their economic as well as in their religious life, within the larger structure of the Indian scene.

The Gossner Mission[305] sent representatives to India. Beginning with 1839, numbers came to the country and laboured in various places.[306] The mission to the Gonds which we mentioned a few pages above was brought to an abrupt end by the death, through cholera, of four of the six who constituted the original staff.[307] In contrast with this tragic history, in the Ganges Valley, in the neighbourhood of Patna and Benares, centres were opened in the 1840's and 1850's which formed the foundations of a continuing enterprise.[308]

The leading Gossner undertaking in India was in Chota Nagpur among the Kols, a folk of primitive culture. The initial contingent reached Ranchi, the capital city of the region, in 1845. The first baptisms were in 1850. In 1857 the Christians numbered about nine hundred, most of them having been won, not by the missionaries but by fellow Kols.[309] Here in the course of the next half century, in spite of losses to the Anglicans and the Jesuits, a Christian community arose which numbered tens of thousands.

The *Frauenverein für Bildung des weiblichen Geschlechts in Morgenlande,* founded in Berlin in 1842, laboured in India in connexion with the Church Missionary Society.[310] From 1842 to 1849 the Berlin Missionary Society maintained a station in India which it discontinued to concentrate on its rapidly growing enterprise in South Africa.[311] In 1843 the North German Missionary Society undertook to reach the Telugus, but in 1850 turned over to American Lutherans what it had begun.[312]

In 1840 the Evangelical Lutheran Mission, which first had headquarters in

---

[304] Schlatter, *op. cit.,* Vol. II, pp. 150-166. For the description of one station, see Christian Irlon, *Malabar und die Missionsstation Talatscheri* (Basel, Missionshaus, 1864, pp. iv, 159).

[305] Vol. IV, p. 91.

[306] Richter, *Indische Missionsgeschichte,* pp. 213, 214. For one of the missionaries, who reached India in 1848 and who died in 1863, see W. Krüger, *Dr. Friedrich Ribbentrop* (Bremen, C. Ed. Müller, 1873, pp. vi, 197).

[307] Notrott, *Die Gossnersche Mission unter den Kohls,* Vol. I, pp. 168, 169.

[308] *Stand und Arbeit der Gossnerschen Mission in Jahre 1905/1906,* p. 10.

[309] Gerhard, *Geschichte und Beschreibung der Mission unter den Kohls in Ostindien,* pp. 5-15; Notrott, *op. cit.,* Vol. I, pp. 169-187.

[310] Richter, *op. cit.,* p. 24.

[311] *Ibid.*

[312] Wischan, *Wilhelm Grönning,* pp. 26, 50.

Dresden and later (1848) transferred them to Leipzig and henceforth bore the name of the latter city, sent a missionary, Heinrich Cordes, to India. Cordes reached Madras late in December, 1840. The purpose of his society in sending him was the renewal of the Lutheran enterprise in South India, for most of that, as we saw a few pages above, had passed to the Anglicans. Some of the Danes were eager to see this revival accomplished and had already made efforts toward that end in Tranquebar, which was still in their possession. Cordes, therefore, went to Tranquebar. The purchase of that Danish foothold by the English (1845) did not end the Lutheran effort. The Dresden-Leipzig society represented strong and distinctively Lutheran convictions and strove to extend Lutheranism in South India. When the Danes retired, the Tranquebar native Lutherans and the property of the Danish Mission passed to the Dresden Mission (1847). Reinforcements were sent. New stations were founded,[313] but Tranquebar remained the chief centre.

Large accessions of membership came to the German Lutheran enterprise. These were in part from non-Christians. They were also in part from the British missions. Several congregations which had originally been gathered by the Danish-Halle missionaries and had later been under British societies returned to their earlier Lutheran allegiance. The motive of the change of affiliation was not entirely one of differences in creed and forms of worship and church government. The Leipzig missionaries dealt more tenderly with caste among the Christians than did the British, and this proved attractive. The large movement of Christians from other bodies to the Lutherans gave rise to much criticism and friction.[314] Internal dissensions plagued the mission. One of these was a phase of the Adiaphoristic Controversy—on the issue of certain usages which were claimed by some to be a perpetuation of what were deemed superstitions inherited from the Roman Catholic Church. Another was over the co-operation of Swedes. Still another had to do with caste.[315] Yet the Leipzig enterprise grew.

It was in connexion with the Leipzig Mission that Swedish Lutherans began assisting in the spread of Christianity in South India. Partly through the influence of Fjellstedt and Lund,[316] Swedes came to india and laboured under the Leipzig society, the first of them, J. B. Glasell, arriving in 1849. Strains de-

---

[313] Karsten, *Die Geschichte der evangelisch-lutherischen Mission in Leipzig*, Vol. I, pp. 66, 67, 109-150; Fleisch, *Hundert Jahre lutherischer Mission*, pp. 27ff.; Handmann, *Die Eangelisch-lutherische Tamulen-Mission in der Zeit ihrer Neubegründung, passim;* Cordes, *Heinrich Cordes, passim.*
[314] Karsten, *op. cit.*, Vol. I, pp. 215ff.
[315] Karsten, *op. cit.*, Vol. I, pp. 365ff.
[316] Vol. IV, p. 150.

veloped between the Swedes and the Germans over several issues, and eventually a distinct Swedish mission arose.[817]

We must here note the beginning of a heroic and persistent Moravian effort to penetrate Tibet from the Indian frontier. Stimulated by Gützlaff, the pioneer German Protestant missionary to China, in the 1850's the Moravians sent representatives to India to seek, by way of that country, to establish a mission in Tibet. Gützlaff's suggestion had been a mission to Mongolia. That proved impracticable, and Tibet, also a Buddhist land in inner Asia, was substituted. After being balked in several efforts to enter Tibet, in 1856, with the advice and financial aid of a British official, the Moravians began a station on a highway leading from the Punjab and Kashmir into Tibet. Other stations were later opened in the endeavour to reach the great closed Buddhist stronghold.[318]

For the first half of the nineteenth century adequate statistics are lacking for Protestant missions in India. Imperfect returns give the following totals. In 1851 there were said to be 91,092 Indian Protestant Christians, of whom more than three-fourths were in the Madras Presidency.[319] Another set of figures reports in South India and Ceylon on January 1, 1852, 94,637 Protestant Christians and adherents among the Indians, and on January 1, 1858, 106,190 in that category. Communicants in these two years in South India and Ceylon were 13,943 and 19,685 respectively. The overwhelming majority were in South India rather than Ceylon.[320] As the British conquest was carried towards completion, Protestant missionaries were increasingly covering the land with stations, notably in many of the chief cities.[321]

The growing multiplicity of societies and denominations represented in India did not make for the confusion which might at first thought have been anticipated. Friction there was, to be sure, sometimes between denominational groups and quite as often within them. However, there were also consultation and co-operation across denominational lines. The rise of the Evangelical Alliance in the Occident in the 1840's had its repercussions in India. In 1855 a conference was held in Calcutta of fifty-five members representing six missions

[817] Karsten, op. cit., Vol. I, pp. 365-413; Sandegren, Svensk Mission och Indisk Kyrka, pp. 15ff.; Bengt Sundkler, Svenska Missionssällskapet 1835-1876. Missionstankens Genombrott och Tidigare Historia i Sverige (Stockholm, Svenska Kyrkans Diakonistyrelses Bokförlag, 1937, pp. xxxvi, 614), pp. 406ff.

[318] Clark, The Punjab and Sindh Missions of the Church Missionary Society, pp. 147, 148; Schulze, 200 Jahre Brüdermission, Vol. II, pp. 538ff.

[319] Richter, Indische Missionsgeschichte, p. 217.

[320] Proceedings of the South India Missionary Conference . . . 1858, table VI.

[321] For a survey of the Protestant occupation of India in the 1830's, still showing large gaps, see William Buyers, Letters from India (London, John Snow, no date, pp. xii, 295), pp. 268ff.

and three of the European churches in Bengal and it was declared that for years the Bengal missionaries had in essence if not in name maintained an Evangelical Alliance.[322] In 1857 there was a gathering at Benares of missionaries from seven societies.[323] In 1858 there assembled at Ootacamund a conference of thirty-two missionaries from eight societies labouring in South India and Ceylon.[324] More than one society, in seeking a field in which to begin its efforts, deliberately avoided duplicating what was being done by another body by entering a region in which no other Protestants were at work. Here and there, notably in the larger centres of British power such as Madras, Bombay, and Calcutta, two or more denominations established themselves. At times competition developed. There was, however, much sense of fellowship and of a common cause.

By the latter part of the 1850's Protestant Christianity was displaying a fairly rapid growth. Societies and missionaries were increasing. Converts were multiplying, and a beginning in training Indian leadership had been made.

Now, in 1857, there came a storm which for the moment threatened British rule with extinction but which was followed by a new era. It was what the English came to remember as the Mutiny. It centred about a rebellion of the sepoys, the troops in the British service staffed by British officers. Although there had been a core of Europeans, the bulk of the armies which had subdued India had been recruited from the country itself. By 1857 the British conquest had been practically completed. At the height of the British success, however, great sections of the Indian forces which were associated with the achievement revolted. Mutinies among the sepoys had broken out in earlier years, but there had been nothing which in extent equalled the uprising of 1857. Not since the contests with the French in the eighteenth century had British rule been so menaced. Only when the twentieth century was well advanced was an equally serious challenge to be given it. Fortunately for the British the rebellion was confined almost entirely to the North—to the Ganges Valley including Bengal and to the Punjab. It was the Bengal army and its offshoots which were the most contumacious. The forces in the Madras Presidency remained loyal and most of the Bombay Presidency was comparatively quiet. After hard fighting the English succeeded in restoring their authority. The crisis was quickly followed (1858) by the transfer of the administration of British India from the East India Company to the Crown. That step had long been advocated by some of the British statesmen. The Mutiny provided the occasion and the

---

[322] *Proceedings of a General Conference of Bengal Protestant Missionaries, Held at Calcutta, September 4-7, 1855* (Calcutta, Baptist Mission Press, 1855, pp. 183), *passim*.
[323] *World Missionary Conference, 1910. Cooperation and the Promotion of Unity*, p. 178.
[324] *Proceedings of the South India Missionary Conference . . . 1858, passim*.

stimulus to bring to an end the anachronism of the rule of a vast empire through a corporation whose original functions had been primarily commercial.

In the decades after the Mutiny British rule in India was consolidated and under British administration and through British initiative much of Western culture penetrated the land. Territorially British India had been built. All of India except the slight enclaves which remained to the French and the Portuguese was either directly or indirectly under the British conquerors. The Indians had submitted. Not for a generation were there serious beginnings of the nationalistic unrest which was to make much of the twentieth century unquiet. The British overlords avowed the purpose of training the Indians in self-government and of increasingly sharing the administration with them. Yet for the time being, except in the native states, the leading governmental posts were in British hands. Under British leadership and largely with British capital, railways were built, irrigation works were constructed, and untilled lands were brought under cultivation. The legal structure of laws and courts was developed with strong infusions of British ideals and practice. Education of a Western type flourished, partly because that was the will of the administration and partly because it was the road to employment in the government and in the various enterprises which the Occidental had introduced. Ambitious Indian students were flocking to the British Isles with the hope of returning to lucrative posts. Occidental civilization was rapidly penetrating the country.

Under these favouring circumstances Protestant missions prospered. The Mutiny had wrought no very great damage to the Christian communities. The large majority of the latter were in the Madras Presidency, the region least affected by the outbreak. To be sure, missionaries and Indian Christians in the North had suffered. The mutineers identified them with the hated European and in more than one place vented their anger on them. About thirty-eight chaplains and missionaries and members of their families perished. Among them both British and American missions were represented. At least twenty Indian catechists, teachers, and wives and children lost their lives.[325] However,

[325] M. A. Sherring, *The Indian Church during the Great Rebellion* (London, James Nisbet and Co., 1859, pp. xii, 355), *passim*. See also J. J. Lucas, *Memoir of Rev. Robert Stewart Fullerton . . . Compiled from his Letters . . . and his Narratives of the trials, faith and constancy of Indian Christians during the Mutiny of 1857* (Allahabad, The Christian Literature Society, U. P. Branch, 1928, pp. 268); Kennedy, *Life and Work in Benares and Kumaon, 1839-1877*, pp. 174-204; Stock, *The History of the Church Missionary Society*, Vol. II, pp. 219-226; Wm. Owen, *Memorials of Christian Martyrs, and Other Sufferers for the Truth, in the Indian Rebellion* (London, Simpkin, Marshall, and Co., 1859, pp. 236); J. Johnston Walsh, *A Memorial of the Futtehgurh Mission and her Martyred Missionaries* (Philadelphia, Joseph M. Wilson, 1859, pp. 338).

of the missionaries in the affected region less than ten per cent. were killed.[326] In the territory most severely affected the majority of the missions were of recent foundation and had had time to build up neither large staffs nor extensive bodies of Christians. The explosion in the North had reverberations throughout the country, but it caused no great damage to the missions or the Indian Christian communities in the South. Since they had not experienced any marked reverse through the Mutiny, Protestant missions were prepared to take advantage of the peace and the progressive penetration of the land by the Occident in the decades which followed. Advance was aided by the rising tide of missionary interest in Protestant circles in the West. From the British Isles, some of the British dominions, the United States, and the continent of Europe great accessions came to the missionary forces. Societies already represented in India were largely reinforced. Many societies entered for the first time.

In early sequence to the Mutiny came a more friendly attitude of the government of India to the propagation of Christianity. Some critics insisted that old fears had been justified and that Christian missionaries, by arousing religious antagonisms, were responsible for the outbreak.[327] However, the trend was in the opposite direction. The Punjab, where the revolt had been severe, was pacified by men of pronounced Christian convictions who wished to see India of their faith.[328] The demand was now made that the government of India abandon its policy of religious neutrality and come out openly for Christianity and actively assist its spread. The proponents of the change declared that the alleged neutrality had in fact been anti-Christian and pro-pagan. In 1858 and again in 1859 they urged their case. British officials prominent in the Punjab advocated the teaching of the Bible in government schools, the withdrawal of recognition of caste in the army and the courts of justice, the restricting or abolishing of Hindu and Moslem religious processions, the end of toleration for certain phases of immorality, and the severing of official connexion with the opium traffic. The debate which ensued centred largely on the issue of placing the Bible on the curriculum of government schools. On this point the friends of missions were defeated. Yet in several ways the attitude of the government became more favourable. In the royal proclamation which announced the assumption by the Crown of the direct administration of India, the Queen,

[326] Richter, *Indische Missionsgeschichte*, p. 221. For some who escaped, see M. A. Sherring, *The Missionary Life and Labours of the Rev. William Smith . . . Benares* (Benares, Medical Hall Press, 1879, pp. vii, 196), pp. 63ff.
[327] Stock, *op. cit.*, Vol. II, p. 223.
[328] Stock, *op. cit.*, Vol. II, p. 218.

while disclaiming any intention of imposing her convictions on any of her subjects, strongly avowed her own Christian faith. Lord Palmerston, as Prime Minister, declared it both the duty and the interest of Great Britain to promote the diffusion in India of the Christian religion. Sympathetic British officials now found themselves much more free to promote the spread of Christianity.[329] The government of India did not give to the propagation of Christianity the same support which had been accorded it by the Spanish and Portuguese governments in their colonial domains in the sixteenth, seventeenth, and eighteenth centuries. Many British officials were distinctly disdainful of missionaries. Yet in general the official attitude was henceforward inclined to be somewhat more friendly than it had previously been, and here and there were officials who were quite open in their assistance.

The Anglican episcopate for India was continued and enlarged. To some degree its growth was in response to the expansion of the Anglican communion in India and was made necessary by the need for adequate episcopal supervision for a growing enterprise. Calcutta retained its position as the metropolitan see. The indomitable Daniel Wilson died, at a great age, about the time the Mutiny was suppressed. He was succeeded by George Edward Lynch Cotton (1813-1866). Cotton came to his post from the headmastership of a school in England, and one of the outstanding features of his episcopate was his contribution to education. He stressed particularly schools for the Anglo-Indians, the neglected children of European and Indian parentage. Like his predecessors, he was required by the duties of his office to travel extensively in a diocese which contained nearly a million square miles. While on tour in Assam he was accidentally drowned.[330] Cotton was followed by Robert Milman (1816-1876), nephew of the famous Dean of St. Paul's Cathedral, London. Milman's preparation in England had been that of a parish priest, part of the time in a living among the underprivileged. He was an enormous worker, a man of prodigious physical energy, generous with money as well as time. He was a notable preacher. He, too, travelled almost incessantly over his huge see. A decade in India under the burdens of a diocese in which his church was rapidly expanding exhausted even Milman's great strength. He died, worn out, while on an official visit to the Punjab.[331] His death precipitated the division

[329] Stock, op. cit., Vol. II, pp. 235-261.
[330] Memoir of George Edward Lynch Cotton . . . with Selections from his Journals and Correspondence. Edited by Mrs. Cotton (London, Longmans, Green, and Co., 1871, pp. xiii, 576).
[331] Frances Maria Milman, Memoir of the Right Rev. Robert Milman . . . with a Selection from his Correspondence and Journals (London, John Murray, 1879, pp. xii, 390).

of the diocese of Calcutta, for it had now become evident that no one man should be asked to carry the load imposed by the growth of the see.[332] In the course of the next few decades at least six new dioceses were created. So populous was the territory which remained to the see of Calcutta and so great was the growth of the Anglican communion within it that the later bishops found the reduced area a sufficient burden.[333]

The first of the new dioceses to be delimited from that of Calcutta after the Mutiny was Lahore, in the Punjab. Anglican enterprise in the Punjab was begun not long after the British conquest of that region. Before the two societies had sent representatives Anglican efforts had begun.[334] In advance of the Mutiny, in 1852, the pioneers of the Church Missionary Society arrived. One of them, Robert Clark (1825-1900), a Cambridge Wrangler, became the leader of the mission. He was in active service for nearly half a century, until 1898.[335] Among other enterprises we hear of a Christian settlement gathered from the Chuhras, one of the underprivileged groups.[336] In 1854 came the two first agents of the Society for the Propagation of the Gospel in Foreign Parts. Several of the foreign staff perished in the Mutiny, but reinforcements soon arrived and expansion followed, with the opening of many new stations.[337]

The diocese of Lahore was founded in memory of Milman, who had so sadly come to his end within its borders. Its initial bishop was the remarkable Thomas Valpy French (1825-1891).[338] The son of an Evangelical clergyman, in his university days at Oxford (where he had a distinguished career as a scholar) French heard the call to India and responded. He went out in 1850 under the Church Missionary Society, arriving early in 1851 and going at once to his field, at Agra. His first assignment was the founding of a college, St. John's, which was designed to do for the central part of the Ganges Valley what Duff's institution was accomplishing in Calcutta. St. John's College became one of the

[332] Allen and McClure, *Two Hundred Years: the History of the Society for Promoting Christian Knowledge, 1698-1898*, pp. 298, 299.
[333] Chatterton, *A History of the Church of England in India*, pp. 333ff.
[334] Stock, *The History of the Church Missionary Society*, Vol. II, pp. 202-205.
[335] Stock, *op. cit.*, Vol. II, pp. 206-213; Henry Martyn Clark, *Robert Clark of the Punjab* (London, Andrew Melrose, 1907, pp. xii, 364). For the life of one who gave more than thirty years to the North-west and was best remembered as an itinerant evangelist, see R. Maconachie, *Rowland Bateman* (London, Church Missionary Society, 1917, pp. x, 208).
[336] Kheroth Mohini Bose, *The Village of Hope, or the History of Asrapur, Punjab* (London, Marshall Brothers, no date, pp. vi, 131).
[337] Pascoe, *Two Hundred Years of the S.P.G.*, pp. 613ff.; *The Story of the Delhi Mission* (Westminster, Society for the Propagation of the Gospel in Foreign Parts, 1908, pp. viii, 171), *passim*.
[338] Eugene Stock, *An Heroic Bishop. The Life Story of French of Lahore* (London, Hodder and Stoughton, 2d ed., 1914, pp. vii, 126); Herbert Birks, *The Life and Correspondence of Thomas Valpy French, First Bishop of Lahore* (London, John Murray, 2 vols., 1895).

most important Christian educational contributions to India. French also preached to whomever would listen, made personal contacts outside college walls, and debated with the Moslems who were so strong in that part of the land. After the Mutiny, in 1861, he helped to inaugurate an enterprise of the Church Missionary Society on the fanatically Moslem borders of Afghanistan. This was begun at the invitation of a warmly Christian British official and at the outset was partly financed from that same generous source. Although a break in health compelled French's retirement from that difficult region, the frontier mission so begun continued.

We must digress long enough to say that physicians were especially prominent in this Afghan undertaking, both in relieving physical suffering and to some degree, however slight, in mollifying the intensely anti-Christian atmosphere. Particularly notable was Theodore Leighton Pennell (1867-1912).[339] Although frail as a child, on reaching maturity Pennell displayed marked vigour and intense vitality which fitted him for his frontier career. Tall of stature and of a commanding personality, he made a deep impression upon the warriors of the border. In 1892 he went to India, his mother accompanying him as a fellow labourer. Through his school and hospital and through tours he served the marches, winning much respect and here and there a convert.

Constrained by the illness which had taken him from the frontier, French spent several years in England. He returned to India in 1869, still under the Church Missionary Society, to head a new divinity college in Lahore for the training of Indian clergy. In 1874 illness again forced him to England, but in 1878 he came out once more, this time as the first Anglican Bishop of Lahore. For a decade he was in this new post which, like the others to which he had given himself, was in the nature of a pioneer undertaking. Although with a strong Evangelical background, he identified himself with no ecclesiastical party and by his saintliness of life commended himself to all. Again infirm health compelled a change of scene, but, as we saw in the preceding chapter, in spite of the handicap which three times had forced him out of India, French ended his days in another quest, even more daring than the others, at Muscat.[340]

French was followed at Lahore by Henry James Mathew, who came to the post from the chaplaincy. He, too, served ten years.[341] He was succeeded by George Alfred Lefroy.[342]

[339] Alice M. Pennell, *Pennell of the Afghan Frontier* (London, Seeley, Service & Co., 1914, pp. xiv, 464).

[340] On a notable convert from Islam, Imad ud Din, a friend and admirer of French, see Andrews, *North India*, pp. 120ff.

[341] Chatterton, *op. cit.*, p. 256.

[342] H. H. Montgomery, *The Life and Letters of George Alfred Lefroy* (London, Longmans, Green and Co., 1920, pp. viii, 265).

The son of a rector and dedicated by his mother before his birth to a missionary career, Lefroy went to India in 1879 as one of the early members of the Cambridge Mission to Delhi. This enterprise had been begun (1877) partly at the suggestion of French and partly on the initiative of Sir Bartle Frere, a distinguished British official in India and an earnest Christian. It was manned, as its name indicates, by graduates of Cambridge. It was engaged both in preaching and in education and was in close connexion with the Society for the Propagation of the Gospel in Foreign Parts. Out of it came St. Stephen's College in Delhi, which by 1900 had achieved a unique place in higher education in the Punjab. It also maintained a high school, boarding and elementary schools, classes for catechists, schoolmasters, readers, bazaar preaching, pastoral care, and itinerating. In association with it the women's Community of St. Stephen conducted medical work and schools for girls.[343] It was in connexion with the Cambridge Mission, beginning in 1904, that C. F. Andrews served his apprenticeship in India.[344] In the post-1914 period, Andrews, by his devotion and his wide-ranging activities, made a marked impression upon many Indians and upon the world-wide Church. For twenty years Lefroy served at Delhi, during most of the time as head of the Cambridge enterprise. He proved to be an earnest preacher, was interested in the Moslems, and combined the abilities of a man of affairs with a deeply religious life. In 1899 he became Bishop of Lahore and held that assignment until 1913, when he was made Bishop of Calcutta and Metropolitan of India.

We must note that in this difficult area in the North-west, where the highly resistant Islam was particularly strong, The Church Missionary Society developed a wide-flung enterprise. By the end of the century substantial beginnings had been made in raising up a native clergy. Church councils were formed of Indian clergy and lay delegates from the various congregations and local church committees were constituted which had an important voice in the

---

[343] Bickersteth, *The Life and Letters of Edward Bickersteth*, pp. 27ff.; Pascoe, *Two Hundred Years of the S.P.G.*, pp. 626-628c. For the life of one who reached India in 1879 and in 1900 became head of the Cambridge Mission, see Cecil H. Martin, *Allnutt of Delhi. A Memoir* (London, Society for Promoting Christian Knowledge, 1922, pp. vi, 168). See also *The S.P.G. and Cambridge Mission to Delhi and the South Punjab. The Thirty-Fifth Report of the Cambridge Committee . . . for 1912* (London, Richard Clay & Sons, 1913, pp. 87); F. F. Monk, *A History of St. Stephen's College, Delhi* (Calcutta, Y.M.C.A. Publishing House, 1935, pp. vi, 262); Lilian F. Henderson, *The Cambridge Mission to Delhi. A Brief History* (London, Offices of the Mission, 1931, pp. 59).

[344] C. F. Andrews, *What I Owe to Christ* (London, Hodder & Stoughton, 1932, pp. 311), pp. 252ff.; F. F. Monk, *A History of St. Stephen's College, Delhi. Compiled for the Cambridge Mission in Commemoration of the Fiftieth Anniversary of the Founding of the College, 1931* (Calcutta, Y.M.C.A. Publishing House, 1935, pp. vi, 262).

management of ecclesiastical affairs and in spreading the Christian message.[345] Not only in the portion of the frontier made memorable by the activities of French and Pennell, but also in other segments of the resolutely Moslem northwest border of India, stations were maintained.[346] There was even occasional penetration into Afghanistan and Baluchistan.[347] In Kashmir, too, a medical mission established a base hospital and from it made tours into the adjacent lofty mountains and the passes reaching toward Central Asia and hostile Buddhist Tibet.[348]

In 1879, not long after the creation of the Anglican diocese of Lahore, the diocese of Travancore and Cochin, embracing the native states of those names, was carved out of that of Madras. The Anglicans in that area were eventually comprised chiefly of converts from the depressed classes and the primitive or semi-primitive hill tribes with a minority of descendants of Syrian Christians.[349]

Slightly earlier, in 1877, two assistant bishops had been consecrated to assist the Bishop of Madras. One of these, Edward Sargent, was to supervise the missions of the Church Missionary Society and the other, Robert Caldwell, was to have jurisdiction over the enterprises of the sister organization, the Society for the Propagation of the Gospel in Foreign Parts. The field of both was in the South, slightly east of Travancore, in Tinnevelly, where Anglican converts were very numerous.[350]

In Tinnevelly, where mass movements had begun before the Mutiny, rapid growth continued. The great famine which devastated much of South and Central India in the 1870's was followed by thousands of accessions to the flocks of both the Anglican societies. The conversions seem to have been due not to

[345] Robert Clark, *The Punjab and Sindh Missions of the Church Missionary Society,* *passim.*
[346] Vernon Harold Starr, *1882-1918 and after* (London, Church Missionary Society, no date, 2d ed., pp. vi, 106); A. R. MacDuff, *The Utmost Bound of the Everlasting Hills, or Memories of Christ's Frontier Force in North-western India* (London, James Nisbet & Co., 1902, pp. ix, 279).
[347] For one who was an itinerant missionary in India and Persia, including especially the Punjab and the frontiers, see Lewis, *George Maxwell Gordon, passim.*
[348] Ernest F. Neve, *A Crusader in Kashmir. Being the Life of Dr. Arthur Neve, with an Account of the Medical Missionary Work of Two Brothers and Its Later Developments down to the Present Day* (London, Seeley, Service & Co., 1928, pp. 218. Partly autobiographical), *passim,* and A. P. Shepherd, *Arthur Neve of Kashmir* (London, Church Missionary Society, 1926, pp. 126), *passim.* For a woman who served in Kashmir under the Church Missionary Society, see Mrs. Ashley Carus-Wilson, *Irene Petrie, Missionary to Kashmir* (London, Hodder and Stoughton, 1901, pp. xxiii, 343). For a physician who had but a few years in Kashmir before his early death, see W. Burns Thomson, *A Memoir of William Jackson Elmslie* (London, James Nisbet & Co., 1881, pp. 294).
[349] Chatterton, *A History of the Church of England in India,* pp. 278, 279; Stock, *The History of the Church Missionary Society,* Vol. III, pp. 183, 184.
[350] Chatterton, *op. cit.,* p. 198; Stock, *op. cit.,* Vol. III, pp. 171, 172.

the lure of physical succour, for relief was administered without discrimination to both Christians and non-Christians, but to the conviction that the old gods had failed in the emergency and that Christianity had more to promise. Many of the neophytes thus gathered lapsed after the emergency had passed.[351] Caldwell, an outstanding Tamil scholar, who spent the greater portion of his long life in a Christian hamlet, was remembered as one of the great missionaries of his church.[352] The Christian communities were organized into pastorate, circle, and district councils, and every village, Hindu or Christian, was made the responsibility of some one parish. The Christians were originally largely from one of the lower branches of the Sudras who made their living by climbing the palmyras. Later converts were largely from the outcastes. In 1896 Tinnevelly was created a separate diocese. In the course of time it became noted for its support of its own clergy and its building of its own churches by local contributions.[353]

Another diocese, that of Chota Nagpur, was erected in 1890. The Anglican mission in that region was an outgrowth of the Gossner enterprise whose beginnings we traced a few pages above. In 1857, when he was in his middle eighties, Gossner wished to transfer the undertaking to the Church Missionary Society. However, the German staff demurred, for it had developed the enterprise on Lutheran principles and depended upon German Lutheran support. After Gossner's death the recruits sent from Germany pursued policies quite different from those of their seniors. Some of the older missionaries thereupon withdrew, carrying many of their converts with them, and were dismissed by the home committee as seceders. In 1869 they were received into the Anglican communion by Bishop Milman. Three of their number and one of their Rajput catechists were given Anglican ordination, and hundreds of the Christians were confirmed. The Society for the Propagation of the Gospel in Foreign Parts sent as superintendent one of their staff, J. C. Whitley, already of tried experience in India. Church buildings were erected. The training of Indian clergy was pursued. Reinforcements came. The mass movement from the aboriginal population continued. In the first ten years the Anglican membership nearly doubled and the number of communicants multiplied more than fivefold—from 900 to 4,670. The presence of the competing enterprises of the

[351] Stock, *op. cit.,* Vol. III, pp. 172-178; Sharrock, *South Indian Missions,* p. 49; Gledstone, *South India,* p. 52.
[352] Sharrock, *op. cit.,* pp. 49-52.
[353] Chatterton, *op. cit.,* pp. 309-311; Gledstone, *op. cit.,* p. 52. For one of the leading representatives of the Church Missionary Society see Amy Wilson Carmichael, *Walker of Tinnevelly* (London, Morgan & Scott, 1916, pp. xiv, 458). For an account of the Ramnad mission see *The Steep Ascent. Ramnad Records and Memorials* (Derby, Bemrose & Sons, no date, pp. xiii, 262).

Lutherans and the Jesuits did not halt the growth. The area was made a separate Anglican see, although technically still a part of the diocese of Calcutta, and in 1890 J. C. Whitley was consecrated bishop. In 1892 there arrived the initial contingent of the Dublin University Mission, with Eyre Chatterton as its head. The mission had arisen out of the desire of several members of Trinity College, Dublin, to serve in connexion with the Society for the Propagation of the Gospel in Foreign Parts. It was, therefore, under that society and received much of its financial support from that source. It was composed of clergymen as full members and of lady associates. Out of the Dublin University Mission came St. Stephen's College, secondary and primary schools, medical work, and efforts through evangelism to reach non-Christians. The converts were largely from the aborigines, as were those of the Lutherans and the Roman Catholics. It was recognized that the motives which attracted these simple folk were usually more secular than religious, but it was hoped that Christian instruction would lead to a better comprehension of the faith.[354]

In 1893 the Anglican diocese of Lucknow was created for the episcopal care of the growing enterprises of the Church Missionary Society and the Society for the Propagation of the Gospel in Foreign Parts in the United Provinces in the central part of the valley of the Ganges.[355] In this area laboured the brothers, George H. and Foss Westcott, sons of a distinguished father. Both brothers were eventually bishops, the one of Lucknow, the other of Calcutta. They constituted a nucleus of an Anglican brotherhood.[356] In this diocese there was developed Christ Church College, founded in 1892, in Cawnpore, to forestall the setting up of a college by the vigorously anti-Christian Arya Samaj and to give leadership in higher education in that city to the Christian forces.[357]

In 1903 still another diocese was created, that of Nagpur. It is not to be confused with that of Chota Nagpur. It bordered on the latter on the west and south, but it was of far greater extent. It embraced the political divisions known as the Central Provinces, Central India, and Rajputana, and included native states as well as portions of British India. As in the case of some of the other dioceses, financial assistance for the support of the bishop came from the government of India as well as private sources. State aid was given on the ground that the bishop would supervise British chaplains who had in their care British

[354] Eyre Chatterton, *The Story of Fifty Years' Mission Work in Chhota Nagpur* (London, Society for Promoting Christian Knowledge, 1901, pp. xii, 210), *passim; Dublin University Mission to Chota Nagpore. Working under the Society for the Propagation of the Gospel in Foreign Parts* (Annual Reports, Dublin, University Press, 1891ff.).

[355] Chatterton, *A History of the Church of England in India*, pp. 308ff.

[356] *The Story of the Cawnpore Mission* (Westminster, The Society for the Propagation of the Gospel in Foreign Parts, 1923, pp. viii, 217).

[357] Pascoe, *Two Hundred Years of the S.P.G.*, pp. 599a, 795.

officials and British troops. Indian Christians who were connected with the Anglican communion numbered only a few thousand, widely scattered. The diocese included a mission to the Gonds, one to a primitive people, the Bhils, one in Chanda of the Scottish Episcopal Church, enterprises in Jubbulpore and Kanti, and two undertakings in Rajputana. The first bishop was Eyre Chatterton, who had come to India as the head of the initial contingent of the Dublin University Mission.[358],

In 1912 an important and significant step was taken in the consecration of V. S. Azariah as the bishop of the new diocese of Dornakal. Azariah was a Tamil, the first Indian to be elevated to the Anglican episcopate. At the outset the diocese was small, but it later was enlarged and became the scene of extensive mass movements to Christianity.[359] Azariah proved extremely able and combined administrative gifts with religious vision and devotion. Thus on the eve of 1914 the leadership of the Anglican communion in India was beginning to pass into indigenous hands. The Church was becoming rooted in the soil.

While new sees were being carved from them, the older Anglican dioceses, in their new contracted territorial forms, continued to display vigour. Their church grew within their borders.

In the area covered by the diocese of Bombay the Anglican communion did not enjoy as great expansion as it experienced in the areas originally covered by its two sister dioceses, Calcutta and Madras. To be sure, the missionary staff showed an increase from two in 1834 to twenty-six in 1868.[360] Yet the Church Missionary Society did not devote as much energy to the region as to some others,[361] and for years such labour as was expended by it yielded few tangible results.[362] Although the Society for the Propagation of the Gospel in Foreign Parts had been responsible for several enterprises in the first half of the nineteenth century and gave attention to Europeans and Anglo-Indians, not until a decade or so after the Mutiny did it embark on a fairly wide extension of its activities.[363] Moreover, the area was not as favourable for the spread of Chris-

---

[358] Eyre Chatterton, *India Through a Bishop's Diary or Memories of an Indian Diocese by its First Bishop* (London, Society for Promoting Christian Knowledge, 1935, pp. 207), *passim.* For the life of one of the clergy who was successively Bishop of Chota Nagpur and Bishop of Nagpur, see Eyre Chatterton, *Alex Wood, Bishop of Nagpur* (London, Society for Promoting Christian Knowledge, 1939, pp. ix, 145). On the Scottish Episcopal mission see Alex Wood, *In and Out of Chanda: Being an Account of the Mission of the Scottish Episcopal Church to the City and District of Chanda.* Edited by E. C. Dawson (Edinburgh, The Foreign Mission Board, 1906, pp. vi, 70).
[359] Chatterton, *A History of the Church of England in India,* pp. 324ff.
[360] Sir Bartle Frere, *Indian Missions* (London, John Murray, 1874, pp. vi, 102), p. 23.
[361] Chatterton, *op. cit.,* pp. 208, 209.
[362] Stock, *The History of the Church Missionary Society,* Vol. III, p. 139.
[363] Chatterton, *op. cit.,* p. 211.

tianty as were some others in India. By 1914, however, the Anglican communion was strongly represented in a number of places. The Church Missionary Society had, among others, a noteworthy enterprise among the Bhils, a primitive hill folk in Rajputana.[364] The Society for the Propagation of the Gospel in Foreign Parts reached out to the east and south, among other centres to the Indian state of Kolhapur, to Poona, to Ahmednagar, and to Hubli, where an outstanding effort was made among a folk whose traditional occupation was thievery.[365] In the Bombay diocese, too, laboured the Fathers of St. John the Evangelist, known more briefly as the Cowley Fathers, and the Wantage Sisters, communities which had arisen out of the Anglo-Catholic revival in the Church of England. The first of their number to reach India arrived in Bombay in 1874. In Bombay and Poona they and their successors served in schools, hostels, boys' homes, medical missions, churches, and, around Poona, in giving the Christian message in the villages. They were striking examples of self-denying living.[366] The founder of the Cowley Fathers, Richard Meux Benson, had himself offered (1859) to go to India as a missionary. That dream was never fulfilled, but he kept in touch with his spiritual sons in that land,[367] notably with one of the original nucleus of the Cowley Fathers, O'Neill, who in Indore lived a life of great asceticism.[368] One of the Indian associates of the Society of St. John the Evangelist was a convert from a Brahmin family, Nehemiah Goreh, a sensitive spirit, scholarly, who had suffered much in becoming a Christian and was an early companion of O'Neill. He was the means of winning some highly educated, deeply religious souls to the Christian faith.[369]

The diocese of Madras enjoyed a striking development under Frederick Gell,

---

[364] Ashley-Brown, *On the Bombay Coast and Deccan*, pp. 211-215; Stock, *op. cit.*, Vol. III, p. 468.

[365] Ashley-Brown, *op. cit.*, pp. 156ff.

[366] *The Missionary Association of SS. Mary & John for the support of the Cowley Fathers (S.S.J.E.) Indian Missions in Bombay and Poona and the Wantage Sisters' (C.S.M.V.) Mission in Poona. Annual Report for 1911 (January, 1912)* (London, W. Knott, 1912, pp. 77), *passim;* Ashley-Brown, *op. cit.*, pp. 217ff.; Elwin, *Thirty-Nine Years in Bombay City, Being the History of the Mission Work of the Society of St. John the Evangelist in that City* (London, A. R. Mowbray & Co., 1913, pp. viii, 130); Elwin, *Thirty-Four Years in Poona City. Being the History of the Panch Howds Poona City Mission, India* (London, A. R. Mowbray & Co., 1911, pp. 109); Edward F. Elwin, *Indian Jottings from Ten Years' Experience in and around Poona City* (London, John Murray, 1907, pp. xi, 314).

[367] *Letters of Richard Meux Benson, Selected and Arranged by G. Congreve and W. H. Longridge* (London, A. R. Mowbray & Co., 1916, pp. xx, 380), pp. 5, 134ff.

[368] *Further Letters of Richard Meux Benson. Edited by W. H. Longridge* (London, A. R. Mowbray & Co., 1920, pp. xxiv, 332), *passim.*

[369] C. E. Gardner, *Life of Father Goreh* (London, Longmans, Green and Co., 1900, pp. xviii, 403); Andrews, *North India*, pp. 61-81.

who was bishop from 1861 to 1899. A graduate of Rugby under Arnold and of Cambridge, Gell came to India at the age of forty. A celibate, he gave himself to his diocese with single-hearted devotion and during his earlier years in India toured his vast see incessantly. During his administration the number of baptized Anglicans increased from 39,938 to 122,371 and the body of Indian clergy from 27 to 154. His successor, who had twenty years as Bishop of Madras, was Henry Whitehead. Whitehead came to the post from the principalship of Bishop's College, Calcutta, and the leadership of the Oxford Mission.[370] Theological education of a high standard was provided by two colleges maintained respectively by the Church Missionary Society and the Society for the Propagation of the Gospel in Foreign Parts.[371] The activity of the diocese embraced European troops through their chaplains, Anglo-Indians, Telugus, and other groups of Indians. The Society for the Propagation of the Gospel in Foreign Parts won a large Telugu following among the lowly Malas and Madigas, especially the Malas. Many came in 1879-1889 after the relief given in the famine of 1876-1877.[372] There was an interesting enterprise for a small tribe, the Todas, in the Nilgiri Hills.[373]

The see of Calcutta, from which several dioceses had been carved, in 1914 still embraced Bengal, with its teeming lower reaches of the valleys of the Ganges and the Brahmaputra, and populous Assam. In addition to its many activities in Calcutta—Bishop's College for preparation in theology and the arts, numbers of other schools of various grades[374] and for Anglo-Indians as well as Indians, and churches—the Anglican communion reached out into the rural districts and into Assam.[375] It was in this diocese, moreover, that the Oxford Mission had its field. The Oxford Mission was begun in part at the suggestion of one of the Cowley Fathers who in 1879 was holding a mission in Calcutta. A contingent of three sailed in 1880 and opened their first house in Calcutta in January, 1881. The Oxford Mission was a brotherhood living under a definite but simple rule. Its original objective was the Bengali students who thronged the city. To this end it maintained student hostels. Moreover, it had

---

[370] Chatterton, *A History of the Church of England in India*, pp. 196-199.

[371] Stock, *op. cit.*, Vol. III, p. 472; A. Westcott, *Our Oldest Indian Mission. A Brief History of the Vepery (Madras) Mission* (Madras, Madras Diocesan Committee of the S.P.C.K., 1897, pp. vi, 108), pp. 53ff.; Pascoe, *Two Hundred Years of the S.P.G.*, p. 510. For the beginning of a college by the Church Missionary Society, see Cecil Edward Barton, *John Barton* (London, Hodder and Stoughton, 1910, pp. xv, 167), pp. 55ff.

[372] Pascoe, *op. cit.*, pp. 563-568.

[373] Stock, *op. cit.*, Vol. IV, p. 240; C. F. Ling, *Dawn in Toda Land* (London, Morgan & Scott, 1909, pp. xi, 90); Catherine F. Ling, *Sunrise in the Nilgiris* (London, The Zenith Press, no date, pp. xi, 60).

[374] Pascoe, *op. cit.*, pp. 474-478.

[375] Chatterton, *op. cit.*, pp. 339-341.

schools of its own, endeavoured to lift the level of the moral life of the professing Christians of the city, and assumed charge of the Christians in villages of the delta of the Ganges south of Calcutta. With it was associated the Sisterhood of the Epiphany.[376]

We must record the fact that in 1863 the Society for the Propagation of the Gospel in Foreign Parts began a mission to European employees of one of the railways. Several chaplains were maintained for the purpose by the government and the Additional Clergy Society.[377]

We must also note the widely flung fields of two women's societies, the Church of England Zenana Missionary Society [378] and the Zenana Bible and Medical Mission.[379] Both co-operated with the Church Missionary Society. The Zenana Bible and Medical Mission also collaborated with other Protestant societies in India. The first was an outgrowth from the second and was constituted (1880) by some who disliked the latter's interdenominational character and wished to work exclusively with the Church of England. The two societies, to avoid overlapping, divided the Indian field between them. The first was represented in the Punjab, Sindh, the Central Provinces, Bengal, the Madras Presidency and South India. The second was chiefly in the Ganges Valley, the

---

[376] George Longridge, *A History of the Oxford Mission to Calcutta . . . revised and abridged for the second edition by W. H. Hutton* (London, A. R. Mowbray & Co., 1910, pp. xxiv, 222) ; *India and Oxford. Fifty Years of the Oxford Mission to Calcutta* (London, Society for Promoting Christian Knowledge, 1933, pp. 79).

[377] Pascoe, *op. cit.*, p. 575.

[378] *The Thirty-Fourth Annual Report of the Church of England Zenana Missionary Society . . . 1914;* Barnes, *Behind the Pardah, passim;* A. D., *Until the Shadows Flee Away: The Story of the C.E.Z.M.S. in India and Ceylon* (London, C.E.Z.M.S., no date, pp. 247). For two of the missionaries of the society see C. E. Tyndale-Biscoe, *Elizabeth Mary Newman, 1855-1932, The Florence Nightingale of Kashmir* (London, Seeley, Service & Co., pp. 18) ; and E. M. Tonge, *Fanny Jane Butler* (London, C.E.Z.M.S., no date, pp. x, 54). For part of the South India story, told in fascinating style, see Amy Wilson Carmichael, *Things as They Are. Mission Work in Southern India* (Chicago, Fleming H. Revell Co., 1904, pp. xvi, 304) ; Amy Wilson Carmichael, *Overweights of Joy* (London, Morgan & Scott, 1907, pp. xiv, 300) ; Amy Wilson Carmichael, *Lotus Buds* (London, Morgan & Scott, 1910, pp. xii, 341) ; Amy Carmichael, *Gold Cord. The Story of a Fellowship* (London, Society for Promoting Christian Knowledge, 1932, pp. viii, 373). Also on South India, see Henrietta S. Streatfield, *Glimpses of Indian Life* (London, Marshall Brothers, 1908, pp. x, 171) ; E. M. Tonge, *Fanny Jane Butler, Pioneer Medical Missionary* (London, Church of England Zenana Missionary Society, no date, pp. x, 54).

[379] *The Annual Report of the Zenana and Medical Mission in Co-operation with the Church Missionary and other Protestant Missionary Societies in India (founded 1852), for the year 1913* (London, 1914). For the lives of two of the missionaries, together with detailed pictures of some of the institutions in connexion with the society, see Ella Luce, *Glimpses of Christian India* (London, Marshall, Morgan & Scott, no date, pp. vii, 216) ; Thomas Carter, *Rose Harvey, Friend of the Leper* (London, The "Z" [Zenana] Press, no date, pp. ix, 159). See also A. R. Cavalier, *In Northern India. A Story of Mission Work in Zenanas, Hospitals, Schools and Villages* (London, S. W. Partridge & Co., no date, pp. xiv, 174).

Punjab, the Bombay Presidency, and the Deccan. Both conducted schools, engaged in medical activities, and visited women in zenanas and villages.

Interesting, too, was the short-lived Brotherhood of the Imitation, a small Anglican celibate community in the Himalayas.[380]

From the Church of England in Canada came a few missionaries. In 1914 it had a field in the Punjab.[381]

No other non-Roman Catholic communion covered so much of India as did the Anglicans. None had nearly so large a missionary staff or so numerous a following among the Indians. Indeed, in no other major area in Asia were the Anglicans as relatively outstanding as in India. This leading position was not surprising. It arose from several closely connected circumstances—the fact that India was a British possession, the presence of numerous Anglican chaplains maintained for Europeans by the government, the provision made by the government for the Anglican episcopate, and the sense of responsibility felt by earnest members of the Church of England for a great land which had been brought under the British flag. By the year 1914 the foundations had been laid for the Church of India, Burma, and Ceylon, which emerged in 1930 as an autonomous member of the Anglican communion.

Although, because of the British connexion, the Presbyterian churches of the British Isles might have been expected to be almost as prominent as the Church of England, they did not loom nearly as large statistically in the propagation of the Christian faith in India as did the latter. They were represented, however, and, as we have suggested a few pages above, made peculiarly important contributions through a few institutions for higher education. The difference may have been due to larger support by the government for the Anglican communion and to the greater size and wealth of England as contrasted with Scotland. It seems also to have arisen in part from the fact that the Scottish Presbyterians concentrated on the cities and that urban centres were more difficult fields than rural villages.[382]

The Scottish churches, especially the body which had by far the largest number of missionaries, the Free Church (later the leading element in the United Free Church of Scotland) placed great emphasis upon secondary schools and colleges.[383] Conversions resulting directly from these were very few

[380] See the constitution under the signature of Samuel E. Stokes in *The East and West*, Vol. VI (1908), pp. 344-346. See also Samuel E. Stokes, *The Love of God* (London, 5th ed., 1912), *passim*.

[381] Beach and St. John, *World Statistics of Christian Missions*, p. 65; *Report of the Missionary Society of the Church of England in Canada*, 1913, pp. 132-142.

[382] *The India Mission of the Free Church of Scotland*, p. 5.

[383] *The India Mission of the Free Church of Scotland*, pp. 8-20.

as compared with the mass movements in some of the Anglican fields, and there is no way of measuring with any degree of accuracy the somewhat intangible permeation of Indian life with Christian ideas which issued from the impact of the colleges upon the educated classes. The colleges founded before the Mutiny continued, some of them with growing resources and student bodies. In Calcutta the college founded by Duff and which, beginning with 1889, bore his name, did not retain the prominent position which it held in the days when it was a pioneer in a new type of education. It remained, however, a substantial institution and among its graduates were a few outstanding Christians who were active in the life of the general community.[384] In 1908 Duff College was combined with the institution founded by Duff and which remained under the Church of Scotland after the Disruption, to form the Scottish Churches College. The merger was followed by substantial growth.[385] In Bombay near the end of the century Wilson College had the largest enrollment of any of the colleges in the presidency.[386] Its growth and influence were in no small degree due to its long-time principal, Dugald MacKichan (1851-1932) who also served four terms as vice-chancellor of the University of Bombay.[387] In Nagpur the high school of the mission became, in the 1880's, Hislop College, affiliated with Calcutta University.[388] The Madras Christian College, which had the Free Church's institution as its nucleus, under the leadership of William Miller experienced a phenomenal growth in student body, buildings, and influence.[389]

The Free Church of Scotland did not confine its educational activities to colleges. It maintained high schools, normal schools, primary schools, and schools for girls as well.[390]

The Free Church of Scotland also reached out beyond its schools in efforts to spread the Christian message and to help raise up Christian communities and churches. Thus one of its more prominent missionaries, Kenneth S. Macdonald, not only taught in Duff College, he also engaged in open-air preaching, undertook literary tasks, and championed various reforms in the community at large—all of them attempts to propagate the Christian faith and to make it

[384] *Our Church's Work in India: Story of Our Bengal Mission*, pp. 29ff.; *The Indian Mission of the Church of Scotland*, pp. 47-50.
[385] *Our Mission in Bengal*, pp. 53, 54.
[386] *Our Church's Work in India: Story of Our Maratha Missions*, pp. 30, 31.
[387] *Forty-Five Years in India. Memoir and Reminiscences of Principal MacKichan*, edited by David Williamson (London, Ivor Nicholson & Watson, 2d ed., 1934, pp. xi, 116).
[388] *Our Church's Work in India. Story of Our Maratha Missions*, pp. 67, 68.
[389] *Our Church's Work in India. The Story of Our Madras Mission*, pp. 49-63.
[390] *The India Mission of the Free Church of Scotland*, passim.

effective.[391] In Bengal the Free Church approached the rural areas. The founder of some of the stations was Duff himself, who took time from his educational activities to go out from Calcutta into smaller cities and towns.[392] There were hospitals and dispensaries.[393] The Free Church also conducted enterprises among the aboriginal peoples who proved such fruitful fields for both Roman Catholics and Protestants. This it did among the Santals, an animistic folk in Bengal. In the 1860's both the Church Missionary Society and the Scandinavians, the latter under the remarkable Boerresen and Skrefsrud, with whom we are to become better acquainted a few pages below, began missions among them. In that same decade, partly at the suggestion of Duff, the Free Church explored the possibilities of an enterprise for them. Early in the 1870's it began a continuing undertaking which in time expanded to several stations with churches, schools, and medical care.[394] In the 1860's, partly at the instance of Hislop, the Gonds, an aboriginal people in Central India, were approached, an outreach from the centre which had been opened in Nagpur. In the 1880's the Gond undertaking was handed over to a Swedish missionary society.[395] We hear, too, of a wild tribe in the Western Ghats and of low caste people east of Bombay who were reached.[396] In the semi-arid Rajputana with its large number of native states the United Free Church of Scotland had an enterprise which came to it through the United Presbyterian Church, one of its constituent bodies. It was largely because of the challenge given by the Mutiny that the United Presbyterians decided to begin a mission in India. The initial contingent reached Bombay in 1859. There John Wilson of the Free Church proved a sage counsellor and accompanied them on their northward trip to their field. Reinforcements came and several centres were occupied. In the severe famine of 1899-1900 the missionaries gave relief and gathered into orphanages some of the children who were made waifs by the disaster. Some of the Bhils, a primitive people, were reached. Women of the mission made

[391] James M. Macphail, *Kenneth S. Macdonald* (Edinburgh, Oliphant, Anderson & Ferrier, 1905, pp. 320). For a description of some phases of the Bengal mission see Mrs. Murray Mitchell, *In India* (London, T. Nelson and Sons, 1876, pp. 319), pp. 20-227. See also *Jubilee of the Rev. Dr. Murray Mitchell* (privately printed, 1889, pp. 56), *passim.*

[392] *Our Mission in Bengal*, pp. 30ff.

[393] For the life of one of the medical missionaries see *Dr. Agnes Henderson of Nagpur. A Story of Medical Pioneer Work* (Edinburgh, United Free Church of Scotland Woman's Foreign Mission, Publication Department, 1927, pp. 64).

[394] *Our Church's Work in India. Santalia, passim;* Hunter, *History of the Missions of the Free Church of Scotland in India and Scotland,* pp. 328-332.

[395] *Our Church's Work in India. Story of Our Maratha Missions,* pp. 66, 67; Hunter, *op. cit.,* pp. 332-336; [J.W.H.], *A. Mackay Ruthquist* (London, Hodder and Stoughton, 1893, pp. viii, 380), *passim.*

[396] *Our Church's Work in India. Story of Our Maratha Missions,* pp. 38-60.

their way into the homes to the women and girls.[397] In connexion with the Foreign Mission Committee of the United Free Church of Scotland there was formed the Scottish Mission Industries Company whose purpose it was to found and develop industries to enable converts, orphans, and other adherents of the mission to become self-supporting.[398] In the Madras Presidency the United Free Church had physicians, gathered and nourished churches, and established several Christian villages on pieces of land where it could direct the entire life of the community and train the Christians in agriculture and simple industries.[399]

In connexion with the enterprises of the Free Church of Scotland the Free Church of Scotland Ladies' Society for Female Education in India and South Africa sent representatives to India.[400]

Although the Church of Scotland's missions in India were dealt a severe blow by the adherence of all the foreign staff to the Free Church at the time of the Disruption, they continued. The property of the missions remained in the hands of the Church of Scotland and in time a staff was recruited to man it. The higher educational institutions in Calcutta, Bombay, and Madras were maintained, but that in Calcutta eventually merged in the Scottish Churches College and that in Madras later joined in the Madras Christian College. There were attempts, not very extensive, to penetrate to the villages, and there was a centre at Poona.[401] In 1856, through a bequest from an army officer who had served in that region, the Punjab became the scene of a new mission of the Church of Scotland. The pioneers lost their lives in the Mutiny, but after the storm subsided reinforcements were sent. In the course of the next several decades Sialkot and a number of cities and towns, mostly within the range of fifty miles from Sialkot, were occupied by central stations. Schools, orphanages, hospitals, and dispensaries were developed, neighbouring villages were penetrated, a college and high school arose, and churches came into being.[402]

[397] Frank Ashcroft, *Story of Our Rajputana Mission* (Edinburgh, Oliphant, Anderson & Ferrier, 1909, pp. 134), *passim;* George Carstairs, *Shepherd of Udaipur and the Land He Loved* (London, Hodder and Stoughton, 1926, pp. xi, 307), *passim.*

[398] Nicol Macnicol, *Tom Dobson, a Champion of the Outcastes* (London, Hodder and Stoughton, 1924, pp. xi, 192), *passim,* but especially pp. 23, 24.

[399] *Our Church's Work in India. Story of Our Madras Mission, passim;* Mrs. Murray Mitchell, *In Southern India. A Visit to some of the chief Mission Stations in the Madras Presidency* (London, The Religious Tract Society, 1885, pp. 383), pp. 33-71; George Pittendrigh and William Meston, *Story of Our Madras Mission* (Edinburgh, Foreign Mission Office, United Free Church, 1907, pp. 128).

[400] Pitman, *Missionary Heroines in Eastern Lands,* pp. 6-46.

[401] *Reports of the Schemes of the Church of Scotland,* 1878, pp. 105-126, 1911, pp. 101-132.

[402] H. F. Lechmere Taylor, *In the Land of the Five Rivers. A Sketch of the Work of the Church of Scotland in the Panjab* (Edinburgh, R. & R. Clark, 1906, pp. xiv, 166), *passim.*

North of Calcutta, in the mountains, with Darjeeling as the best known centre, the Young Men's Guild of the Church of Scotland built up an enterprise. It was begun in 1889. There, in the Himalayas, chiefly among the farmers of the hill peoples, converts were made, catechists were trained, and the beginnings of an indigenous church were seen.[403]

In 1862 an enterprise of the English Presbyterian Church was inaugurated by one of Duff's Indian pupils. In time it had a small foreign staff but it never attained large proportions.[404]

The Welsh Presbyterians (Welsh Calvinistic Methodists) continued the mission which they had begun before the Mutiny in the Khasia and Jaintia Hills of Assam. By 1891 they had 189 churches and preaching places and 2,147 communicants. After 1891 there was an even more rapid advance. In that year a translation of the Bible was completed. In 1895 the single presbytery was expanded to five and an assembly was constituted. Contacts were established with additional aboriginal tribes. The revival which deeply stirred Wales in 1904 spread to India and had profound effects in the Khasia Hills. From the Khasia Hills the Welsh Presbyterians extended their operations to the plains of Sylhet and Chachar to the south, but here their progress was very slow, partly because there they had to deal with peoples of higher caste. In 1892 they reached out into the Lushai Hills, to the east and south of the Khasia and Jaintia fields. There they came in touch with a people of Mongolian strain, not so far along in culture as the folk of the plains, and their advance was rapid. Throughout their missions the Welsh Presbyterians placed much emphasis upon preaching and the development of Indians who could undertake it. It was through the native preachers that many of the gains were made.[405]

The missions which the Irish Presbyterians had begun before the Mutiny in Kathiawar and Gujarat, north of Bombay, partly on the advice of John Wilson, were continued and multiplied. Various groups in the region were touched, both high and low caste. One of the distinctive methods of the Irish Presbyterians was the settlement of many of their converts in farm colonies, Christian communities on pieces of land acquired for that purpose. Christians were thus in part removed from the persecution which would have been their

---

[403] D. G. Manuel, *A Gladdening River. Twenty-Five Years' Guild Influence among the Himalayas* (London, A. & C. Black, 1914, pp. xxiii, 244), *passim;* J. H. Graham, *On the Threshold of Three Closed Lands. The Guild Outpost on the Eastern Himalayas* (Edinburgh, R. & R. Clark, 1897, pp. x, 166), *passim.*

[404] *Minutes of the Synod of the Presbyterian Church of England,* Vol. XII, 1910-1912, pp. 1184, 1185.

[405] Morris, *The Story of Our Foreign Mission (Presbyterian Church of Wales),* pp. 31ff.; W. M. Jenkins, *Life and Work in Khasia* (Newport, W. Jones, no date, pp. 97), *passim.*

lot had they remained domiciled among their non-Christian neighbours and kindred, and were also enabled to break with the contaminating influences of the non-Christian environment in which they would otherwise have been immersed.[406]

Another undertaking arising from the Presbyterianism of the British Isles was the Edinburgh Medical Missionary Society. It assisted medical education in Travancore and a training institution and dispensary in Bombay.[407]

The Baptist Missionary Society which had done so much to inaugurate the new era of Protestant missions in India continued operations in that land. With the coming of an ever-increasing number of societies, relatively it was not as prominent as in the closing years of the eighteenth and the fore part of the nineteenth century. However, it enjoyed a healthy even if unspectacular growth. In 1913 the Christians associated with it totalled 31,473. It concentrated its efforts upon the general area to which Carey had introduced it. Its operations were largely confined to Bengal and the adjoining Bihar and Orissa. Here it maintained schools and student hostels, reached out into villages, and won followings among peoples such as the Garos, the Santals, and the Khonds, who were not far from the primitive stage of culture. It also conducted enterprises in North India in such centres as Agra, Delhi, and Simla, and had sympathetic relations with Baptist churches for Anglo-Indians, including one in Bombay.[408]

It was British Baptists, moreover, although not agents of the Baptist Missionary Society, who in 1893 began an enterprise for the tribesmen in the Lushai Hills, the region and peoples who the year before had become a field for the Welsh Calvinistic Methodists. Within the next twelve or thirteen years this Assam Frontier Pioneer Mission won several hundred converts.[409]

[406] Jeffrey, The Indian Mission of the Irish Presbyterian Church, pp. 131ff.; J. Sinclair Stevenson, Robert Henderson (London, James Clarke & Co., 1922, pp. 160), passim; Pitman, Missionary Heroines in Eastern Lands, pp. 89-147; Mrs. George T. Rea, A Broken Journey. Memoir of Mrs. Beatty, Wife of Rev. William Beatty (London, James Nisbet & Co., 1894, pp. xiv, 184), passim; Margaret Stevenson, Do You Remember Sinclair Stevenson? (Oxford, Basil Blackwell, 1931, pp. xi, 257).

[407] Thomson, Reminiscences of Medical Missionary Work, pp. 144-155.

[408] 121st Annual Report of the Baptist Missionary Society . . . to March 31st, 1913, pp. 23-52; Henry Oakley, "Greatly Beloved." Memories of the Life of the Rev. Arthur Long, Pioneer Missionary to the Khond Tribe, India (London, The Baptist Missionary Society, pp. 48), passim; Isabel M. Angus, Salvage of Souls. A Memorial of the Work of Gertrude Morley Fletcher (London, The Carey Press, no date, pp. 112), passim; Dorothy Angus, The Favour of a Commission. The Life of Isabel Angus, 1858-1939 (London, The Carey Press, no date, pp. 77), passim; G. W. Shaw, Our First Field. British Baptists in India (London, The Baptist Missionary Society, no date, pp. viii, 71); S. Pearce Carey, Dawn in the Kond Hills (London, The Carey Press, 1937, pp. 132).

[409] Herbert Anderson, Among the Lushais (London, The Carey Press, 1914, pp. viii, 43), passim; Grace R. Lewis, The Lushai Hills . . . The Story of the Lushai Pioneer Mission (London, The Baptist Missionary Society, 1907, pp. 80), passim.

Following up the beginnings it had made in the closing years of the eighteenth and the opening years of the nineteenth century, the London Missionary Society developed its enterprises in Bengal, in and around Benares, in the Madras Presidency, and in the native states of Mysore and Travancore.

In what is thought of as North India, the London Missionary Society's fields were in Bengal, chiefly Calcutta, and in and near Benares. In Calcutta the enterprise long centred around an educational institution which maintained a programme reaching into and through the college grades. For many decades this was popular as a medium of the Western learning coveted by those who desired profitable employment in the new order introduced by the British occupation. In later years, as schools for the new learning multiplied under government and non-Christian private auspices, it was not so prominent. There were other schools, among them a notable one for girls. There was preaching to the throngs of Calcutta and in the rural villages. A few miles out of the city a small Christian settlement was developed. Several churches, most of them small, came into being. A hundred miles or so north of Calcutta, still within Bengal, various activities, evangelistic and educational, were carried on. Some of the Santals were reached. Beginning in 1820, the London Missionary Society maintained an enterprise in Benares, the great stronghold of Hinduism. In the region of Benares a few other centres were opened. In 1914 the numerical results of the more than a century in North India were not very striking.[410]

In the Madras Presidency and in the adjacent native state of Mysore the London Missionary Society spread its efforts over a wide area. It had stations from Coimbatore in the south to Bangalore in Mysore, Madras on the coast, and Bellary in the North-west. It sought to reach Tamils, Kanarese, and Telugus. In Bangalore it joined in the Union Theological College which served much of South India and Ceylon. Among the Telugus a mass movement began in the 1860's, chiefly from the Malas, an outcaste group, which in time led to about 250 congregations and about 25,000 Christians. Later some of the Madigas, also outcastes, began coming. In 1898 a mass movement toward Christianity occurred among the Tamils of Erode, south-west of Madras. In 1912 the area had 2,767 church members and 30,882 adherents.[411]

[410] *The Hundred and Nineteenth Report of the London Missionary Society . . . the year 1913,* pp. 74-110; William Bolton, *North India* (London, London Missionary Society, 1909, pp. 112) ; James Kennedy, *Life and Work in Benares and Kumaon, 1839-1877* (New York, Cassell and Co., 1885, pp. xxiii, 392) ; James Kennedy, *Memoir of Margaret Stephen Kennedy* (London, James Nisbet & Co., 1892, pp. xi, 276) ; W. J. Wilkins, *Daily Life and Work in India, City, Rice-Swamp, and Hill* (London, London Missionary Society, 1893, pp. 224) ; Lewis Johnson, *Hilda Johnson, A Memoir* (London, London Missionary Society, 1920, pp. 118).
[411] *The Hundred and Nineteenth Report of the London Missionary Society . . . the*

In Travancore the pioneer of the London Missionary Society was Ringel-taube, who reached the country in 1806. In the course of the century reinforce-ments came, and the society developed a field in the southern portion of the state, from Nagercoil north to Quilon. Here Syrian Christians, so numerous in the northern part of the state, were very few. The London Missionary Society was long the only representative of Protestant Christianity. It drew a large proportion of its converts from the Shanars, a socially depressed group. Later the faith penetrated to those still lower in the social scale. From 1875 to 1877 nearly nine thousand of the poorer classes, fearing that a census then being taken was preliminary to a compulsory transportation of labourers to other lands, enrolled themselves as Christians with the motive of obtaining the pro-tection of the European missionaries. When the excitement subsided, most of these mass converts remained with the churches. Education was developed, and the London Missionary Society became the pioneer of modern schools in the state. At the top of the mission's structure of schools were the Scott Christian College and a theological seminary. In connexion with efforts to reach and provide for women, extensive industries for the manufacture of lace and embroideries were developed which gave employment to many and turned into the treasury a substantial profit which was used for the support and exten-sion of the mission's activities. The London Missionary Society was slow to administer baptism and insisted upon a high standard of character and con-duct as a prerequisite to it. In 1907 it had only 9,764 church members in Travan-core, but counted 72,080 adherents. Usually in a given district there was a central church with a fairly large building and smaller church buildings and organizations in the surrounding villages. By 1914 substantial progress had been made towards creating an Indian clergy and towards undertakings by a local missionary society in hitherto unreached districts.[412]

The Wesleyans of the British Isles greatly expanded the enterprises which they had begun before the Mutiny. They had entered India somewhat later

year 1913, pp. 67, 111-168; William Bolton, The South India Mission (London, London Missionary Society, 1913, pp. 100); Herbert J. Goffin, At Grips. Talks with the Telugus of South India (London, London Missionary Society, 1913, pp. 156).

[412] I. H. Hacker, A Hundred Years in Travancore 1806-1906. A History and Descrip-tion of the Work of the London Missionary Society in Travancore, South India, during the Past Century (London, H. R. Allenson, 1908, pp. 106); William Bolton, Travancore (London, London Missionary Society, 1908, pp. 89); The Hundred and Nineteenth Report of the London Missionary Society . . . the year 1913, pp. 168-183; Samuel Mateer, The Gospel in South India (London, The Religious Tract Society, no date, pp. 255); Rebecca J. Parker, Father of Twenty-Five Thousand, Arthur Parker, Missionary in India (London, Morgan & Scott, no date, pp. 120), pp. 52ff.; J. H. Hacker, Memoirs of Thomas Smith Thomson, L.R.C.P., L.R.C.S., Medical Missionary at Neyoor, Travancore, South India (London, The Religious Tract Society, 1887, pp. 126); Samuel Mateer, "The

than had the other major forms of Christianity of Great Britain and were slower in getting under way. Anglicans, Presbyterians, Baptists, and Congregationalists were much more prominent before the Mutiny than were they. This was in spite of the fact that during the closing years of the eighteenth and the first half of the nineteenth century the Wesleyans were having an extraordinary growth in the British Isles. In the second half of the nineteenth century, however, the Wesleyan enterprises registered a substantial increase. This was through the major branch of the Wesleyans, the Wesleyan Methodists. By 1914 the Wesleyan Methodists had carved out fields which they had divided administratively into seven districts—(1) Madras, (2) Negapatam and Trichinopoly, (3) Mysore, (4) Hyderabad, (5) Bengal, (6) Lucknow and Benares, and (7) Bombay and the Punjab.[413] As was due from their prominence in the British Isles, they had taken their place with the Anglicans, the Presbyterians, the Baptists, and the Congregationalists as numerically among the five leading British communions in India.

In Madras Wesleyan Methodism's first missionary arrived in 1817, but it was not until the 1850's that the period of pioneer uncertainties, small staff, and depletion by illness and death began to give place to encouraging expansion and substantial growth. In the 1860's hymns composed in Indian metres and set to Indian tunes were displacing translations of English hymns set to European tunes and the training of an Indian ministry was begun. The Wesleyans reached out both northward and southward into areas which later were made into distinct districts. In time self-support was achieved in some of the circuits.[414] Among the outstanding missionaries of the Madras district were George Mackenzie Cobban, large-hearted, with a profound knowledge of the Tamils and sympathetic with both the educated and the outcastes, and William Goudie. Goudie was of Shetland Islands stock, devoted and of an iron constitution. It was he who had much to do with reaching the Pariahs and with extending the operations of his mission into Hyderabad. In fifteen years he built up a centre for the outcastes, with chapel, hospital, a lace-making industry, and homes for boys and girls.[415] In the last third of a century before 1914 a marked increase in strength was registered in the Madras district. In 1880 there were

Land of Charity." An Account of Travancore and Its Devil Worship (New York, Dodd and Mead, preface 1870, pp. vi, 370), pp. 25ff.

[413] For a general description of the Wesleyan Methodists' Indian enterprise see Edgar W. Thompson, *The Call of India* (London, The Wesleyan Methodist Missionary Society, 1912, pp. xv, 319).

[414] Findlay and Holdsworth, *The History of the Wesleyan Methodist Missionary Society,* Vol. V, pp. 213-252.

[415] James Lewis, *William Goudie* (London, Wesleyan Methodist Missionary Society, 1923, pp. 176), *passim.*

two Indian ministers and 256 Indian members. In 1913 these had risen to 17 and 2,242 respectively.[416]

In 1885 the southern part of what had been the Madras district of the Wesleyans was created a separate ecclesiastical division under the name of the Negapatam and Trichinopoly district. At that time it had four central stations, each the nucleus of several outstations. Here, too, growth was recorded. At Negapatam a college was developed, bearing in time the name of its founder, Findlay. In contrast with other Wesleyan Methodist districts, numbers of converts were won from social groups above the depressed class level. Many Sudras became Christians and hundreds of Sudra children were in attendance in the Sunday schools. Occasionally a Brahmin asked for baptism, braving ostracism by his friends and family, and that in a region noted for the strength of Hinduism and the proud prominence of the Brahmin caste.[417]

In 1847 a Wesleyan Methodist district was instituted for the state of Mysore. Bangalore, the capital and containing a large British cantonment, became the main centre. As in so many other missions, the great famine of the 1870's led the missionaries to devote themselves to relief and was followed by a substantial influx of converts. The orphanages used for the care of rescued children were the source of many teachers and preachers and were developed into industrial schools. In a division of territory between the Wesleyans and the London Missionary Society, the former were given the region west of Bangalore, about four-fifths of the province. Schools were multiplied, culminating in Hardwicke College, in Bangalore. There were hospitals. In some of the villages group movements towards Christianity occurred. A noteworthy one, which for a time seemed to promise large dimensions, was among a section of Sudras. There was care for the English residents. The main divisions of the Wesleyan enterprise in the South were for the Tamils and the Kanarese.[418]

The state of Hyderabad became the scene of a very prosperous enterprise of the Wesleyan Methodists. The mission owed its inception to a letter from a British sergeant who was stationed at Secunderabad, near to Hyderabad, the capital city, calling attention to the opportunity in the European garrison. In response to the letter two missionaries came (1878) from Madras to view the situation. One of the two, William Burgess, became the pioneer of the Hyderabad Mission. A man of great physical vigour, he was able to endure the rigours entailed by the founding and remarkable growth of the mission and was chairman of the district until his retirement to England, in 1896. The Wesleyans

[416] Findlay and Holdsworth, op. cit., Vol. V, p. 251.
[417] Findlay and Holdsworth, op. cit., Vol. V, pp. 253-261.
[418] Findlay and Holdsworth, op. cit., Vol. V, pp. 262-310.

found their chief field among the Malas, outcaste cultivators and agricultural labourers numerous in Hyderabad. They did not purpose thus to limit themselves, but the fact that so many of this class came repelled other social groups and made of the Wesleyans in Hyderabad primarily a Mala church. In the twentieth century hundreds were won from the Madigas, an outcaste group of scavengers, leather workers, and carrion eaters of an even lower social level than the Malas. In its earlier days the growth of the mission was aided by the friendship of European officials, among them a judge who was a close friend of Burgess. In the years 1896-1900 drought brought two serious famines to Hyderabad. Missionaries administered relief, and from the refugee camps there were many baptisms. In the four years, 1898-1901, they numbered 4,199. Other hundreds were refused the rite, for the missionaries feared their inability to give proper spiritual supervision to additional numbers. Children orphaned by the famine were received into boarding schools and from them eventually came teachers and preachers. Especially remarkable was the development by C. W. Posnett of a centre at Medak. Here the unlettered villagers were taught the Gospel story until they knew it by heart, and here was placed an institution for the training of evangelists. As a result of all the various efforts, by 1910 the Christian community numbered 14,000, a total which had doubled in the preceding decade.[419]

In Bengal the Wesleyan Methodists did not begin a continuous undertaking until 1859. To be sure, in the 1830's there had been an attempt, with resident missionaries, but it was short-lived. When it was resumed, in 1859, it was at first directed to the care of Methodists in the British army. In 1861 a missionary arrived who was assigned to the Indians. Even then the growth was small. At the close of the 1870's there were in all the valley of the Ganges, except for Lucknow, less than 150 members. Late in the 1870's reinforcements were sent which inaugurated more active efforts to reach the Indian population. In the 1880's promising beginnings were made in the training of an Indian leadership. Schools were opened. However, in 1913 there were only 6 Indian ministers, 60 catechists, and 1,494 full members.[420]

In 1879 the region around Lucknow and Benares was made an ecclesiastical district distinct from that of Calcutta. At that time very few Wesleyans were to be found in the area and the division had as its motive administrative

[419] Findlay and Holdsworth, *op. cit.,* Vol. V, pp. 311-347; Frederick Lamb, *The Gospel and the Mala. The Story of the Hyderabad Wesleyan Mission* (Mysore, Wesleyan Mission Press, 1913, pp. 120), *passim;* F. Colyer Sackett, *Vision and Venture. A Record of Fifty Years in Hyderabad, 1879-1929* (London, The Cargate Press, no date, pp. 255). *passim.*
[420] Findlay and Holdsworth, *op. cit.,* Vol. V, pp. 348-362.

efficiency. In spite of earnest effort in various centres growth was not large.[421]
J. A. Elliott, born in India of European parents and, for that reason, possessed
of an amazing command of the language, proved a notable preacher.[422] Several
hundreds of converts came from the Doms, outcaste carrion eaters and professional robbers. The first of their number to ask for baptism had as his motive
escape from the exactions of venal police. The Christian faith and the tutelage
of the missionaries worked marked improvement in the Dom Wesleyans.[423]
Some accessions came from the Chamars, outcastes and leather workers.[424]

The last Wesleyan Methodist district to be created in India was one which
embraced Bombay and the Punjab. This was in 1901. In Bombay the chief
effort was for the Mahrattas. Elsewhere it was among an English-speaking
constituency, largely soldiers. Although the first missionary had been sent to
Bombay as early as 1819, the initial effort did not have a long life. A second
attempt, also in Bombay and of only a few years' duration, was made in the
1850's and 1860's. It was not until the 1880's that a continuing enterprise was
begun in that great port. The numbers in the district were never impressive.[425]

In addition to the Anglicans, Presbyterians, Baptists, Congregationalists, and
Methodists, numerically the principal Protestant denominational groups in the
British Isles, a number of other Protestant bodies from these islands conducted
missions in India.

The Open Brethren, a branch of what are often known as the Plymouth
Brethren, through what they chose to call Christian Missions in Many Lands,
continued the mission which had been inaugurated before the Mutiny. In 1914
their missionary staff numbered well over one hundred and was in several sections of the country, chiefly in different portions of the Madras Presidency.
The communicants, however, totalled only slightly over fifteen hundred.[426]

The Friends' Foreign Mission Association, of British Quakers, was formed
in 1868. Almost at once financial assistance was given to a Quaker who was
serving with the Church Missionary Society in Benares, and by 1874 a separate
field was found in Hoshangabad, in Central India. Later operations were also
begun in the neighbouring native state of Bhopal. In the course of the years
various approaches and forms of service akin to those of other foreign missions

[421] Findlay and Holdsworth, op. cit., Vol. V, pp. 363-374.
[422] A. W. Newboult, editor, Padri Elliott of Faizabad, a Memorial (Chiefly Autobiographical) (London, Charles H. Kelly, 1906, pp. vii, 350), passim.
[423] C. Phillips Cape, Prisoners Released. The Redemption of a Criminal Tribe (London,
Wesleyan Methodist Missionary Society, 1924, pp. 143), passim.
[424] Findlay and Holdsworth, op. cit., Vol. V, p. 370.
[425] Findlay and Holdsworth, op. cit., Vol. V, pp. 363, 375-380.
[426] Jones, The Year Book of Missions in India, Burma and Ceylon, 1912, pp. 596-598;
Beach and St. John, World Statistics of Christian Missions, p. 65.

were undertaken—preaching, literature, schools, medical care, orphanages, and famine relief. Perhaps because their methods of worship were not congenial to the Indians, possibly for other reasons, the Christian communities gathered by the Friends remained small and followed the leadership of the missionaries.[427]

In 1882 the Salvation Army was introduced to India. The inaugurator of its enterprise was the charming, colourful, enthusiastic, devoted, and extraordinarily able Frederick St. George de Latour Tucker.[428] Tucker's grandfather had been a director of the East India Company and his father a member of the Indian Civil Service. Tucker himself was for a time a promising member of that same service. However, while in England preparing for that occupation he had become a convert through Moody. Back in India he was impressed by the reports of the Salvation Army, an organization then in its early youth. He returned to England, joined the Army, and prevailed on its head, William Booth, to extend its work to India. Booth appointed him to lead the new undertaking. A few years later Tucker married a daughter of Booth and became known as Booth-Tucker. The first contingent in India had to meet the prejudice which the Army had aroused in Britain by its novel methods. There were arrests for attempts to hold the Army's type of outdoor meetings, but appeals to the courts eventually brought toleration. Through Tucker's leadership and example the Salvation Army went far in adapting its programme to Indian conditions. A modification of Indian dress was adopted for the Army's uniform. The officers of the Army, including Tucker, lived somewhat like the traditional Indian holy men. They followed a vegetarian diet, went barefooted (later modified by sandals) through the villages preaching, at times carrying a begging bowl, and took Indian names. Because of the failure of his wife's health Tucker returned to England. There he became foreign secretary for the Army. He was next sent to the United States to head the Army in that country in a time of crisis. After his wife's death in a railway accident Tucker went back to London. In 1904 he was again on his way to India to assume command. He was followed by scores of others. In 1914 the Army had a foreign staff of 174, which was among the largest missionary bodies in the country.[429] They were fairly widely distributed. Although the Army made efforts, as had so many other missions, to win converts from the higher castes that through them, supposedly the natural leaders, the lower castes might be reached, like

[427] Joseph Taylor, *The Story of Friends' Foreign Missions. India* (London, Friends' Foreign Mission Association, 1911, pp. 89); Caroline W. Pumphrey, *Samuel Baker of Hoshangabad. A Sketch of Friends' Missions in India* (London, Headley Brothers, 1900, pp. vi, 228), *passim*.

[428] F. A. Mackenzie, *Booth-Tucker, Sadhu and Saint* (London, Hodder and Stoughton, 1930, pp. xv, 295), *passim*.

[429] Beach and St. John, *op. cit.*, p. 65.

the others, its numerical successes in the upper social strata were not marked. Its great contributions, as might have been anticipated from the history of other missions in India and its original objectives in England, were among the underprivileged. It sought to serve convicts. It had a following among the Bhils, a primitive folk in the Bombay Presidency, among the Dhers, weavers of Gujerat, and among professional criminal tribes. Agricultural colonies were developed, notably in the Punjab. Several villages were created for the criminal tribes in which these annoying parasites could be trained in law-abiding ways. In them converts were gathered into Christian communities. Cottage industries were fostered, principally weaving, silk, needlework, and mat making. In furthering the silk industry the Army was assisted by the wealthy Parsee Tata family. An Arbour Day was instituted. Schools were inaugurated and at least one hospital was established. Statistics for 1923 showed 2,370 officers, foreign and Indian, and 4,757 centres. Nearly half the officers and not far from a third of the centres were in the southern area. The smallest number were in the eastern area, made up chiefly of Bengal and Assam.[430]

Other British organizations represented in India included the Missionary Settlement of University Women, in undenominational enterprise in Bombay inspired in part by such undertakings as Toynbee Hall,[431] the Kurku and Central India Hill Mission, primarily for the Kurkus, a tribe of aborigines,[432] the Bethel Santhal Mission,[433] the Central Asian Mission, the Ceylon and India General Mission, the Ludhiana Zenana and Medical Mission, the Regions Beyond Missionary Union, the India Industrial Evangelistic Mission, the Strict Baptists, the United Original Secession Church of Scotland, the Poona and Indian Village Mission, the Lohaghat Tanakpur Medical Mission, the Burning Bush Mission, the Indian Christian Mission,[434] the Children's Special Service Mission, the Pentecostal Missionary Union for Great Britain and Ireland, and the Tehri Medical Mission.[435] There were, as well, the British and Foreign Bible Society, the National Bible Society of Scotland, and the Christian Literature Society for India, a name assumed in 1891 by an interdenominational organization

---

[430] F. Booth Tucker, *Muktifauj, or, Forty Years with the Salvation Army in India and Ceylon* (London, Marshall Brothers, no date, pp. xx, 257), *passim;* Matilda Hatcher, *The Undauntables. Being Thrilling Stories of Salvation Army Pioneering Days in India* (London, Hodder and Stoughton, 1933, pp. 208), *passim.*

[431] Una M. Saunders, *Mary Dobson, Musician, Writer and Missionary* (London, A. & C. Black, 1926, pp. xiv, 191), *passim,* especially pp. 15, 16.

[432] Mrs. M. Baxter, *The Story of the Kurku Mission* (London, Christian Herald Office, 1912, pp. 122), *passim.*

[433] A. Haegert, *The Santhals and the Lord's Work among them* (London, John F. Shaw & Co., 3d ed., no date, pp. 70).

[434] Jones, *op. cit.,* pp. 564-599.

[435] Beach and St. John, *op. cit.,* p. 65.

which had been formed soon after the Mutiny under the title of the Christian Vernacular Education Society for India.[436] The Lakher Pioneer Mission had its field in mountains on the edge of Assam in a region which was almost entirely independent and ruled by its own chiefs.[437] None of these bodies attained such large dimensions as did the ones to which we have addressed ourselves in the preceding paragraphs. Here and there, too, were missionaries unconnected with any society.[438] In the main, British Christianity was propagated in India by denominational societies representing the chief communions of the islands and, except for the Roman Catholic Church, roughly in proportion to their numerical strength in the mother country. No undenominational British mission occupied nearly the place of prominence held in China by the China Inland Mission, to which we are to come later in this volume.

Missions were also planted in India by societies from other parts of the British Empire, notably Australia, New Zealand, and Canada.

In 1914 the Protestant missionaries in India from Australia and New Zealand totalled somewhat less than one hundred. That the number was so large was more remarkable than that it was no larger. Australia and New Zealand had been peopled by white men for only about a century. Indeed, New Zealand and most of Australia had had their initial white settlements considerably less than a century. The churches in these lands had only recently been founded and were not yet entirely emancipated from the assistance from Great Britain which had helped to make their growth possible. The natural mission fields of these churches, moreover, were not in so distant a land as India but among their own aborigines and the adjacent islands of the Pacific. It is, therefore, an indication of the vitality of the Protestant Christianity of Australia and New Zealand that so many missionaries were sent to India. The body with the largest number of representatives in India was the Australian Baptist Missionary Society. It began operations in 1882. Its field was in the lower part of eastern Bengal and among the Garos, a primitive folk in the hills. There were also represented the Presbyterian Church of Australia, the Churches of Christ in Australia, the Presbyterian Church of New Zealand, the Methodist Missionary Society of Australasia, and the Baptists of New Zealand.[439]

---

[436] Henry Morris, *The Life of John Murdoch, LL.D., The Literary Evangelist of India* (London, The Christian Literature Society for India, 1906, pp. 285), *passim,* especially pp. 97-107, 177.

[437] Reginald A. Lorrain, *Five Years in Unknown Jungles for God and Empire* (London, Lakher Pioneer Mission, preface 1912, pp. xii, 274).

[438] For one of these see George Everard, *The Starry Crown. A Sketch of the Life Work of Harriett E. H. Urmston* (London, Hodder and Stoughton, 1898, pp. xii, 254). Mrs. Urmston gave herself chiefly to Europeans.

[439] Jones, *op. cit.,* pp. 563, 564; Beach and St. John, *op. cit.,* p. 65. For an Australian Baptist who served under the Poona and Indian Village Mission, see Mrs. W. H. Hinton,

A larger number of missionaries came from Canada than from Australia and New Zealand. This is not surprising. Canadian Protestantism did not have so extensive a foreign field at its very doors as did the Australians and the New Zealanders in the islands of the South Pacific. While more missionaries went from Canada to China than to India, in 1914 there were more than twice as many Protestant missionaries in India from Canada than from Australia and New Zealand.[440] It was from Baptists and Presbyterians that most of the representatives of Canadian Protestantism came.

Canadian Baptists entered India on the inspiration of their brethren of the United States. In 1866 the Baptists of Ontario organized an auxiliary of the American Baptist Missionary Union. Their first missionaries, A. V. Timpany and his wife, were appointed in 1867 to the Telugus, where the Baptists of the United States already had the Lone Star Mission which we noted a few pages above. In 1869 John McLaurin and his wife followed. In 1873 the Baptists of Ontario and Quebec formed their own Foreign Mission Board and took over an undertaking started independently by a Telugu Christian near the outlet of the Godavari River, about two hundred miles from the nearest station of the American Baptist Missionary Union. The step was taken with the full approval of the latter body. In that area the Canadian Baptists developed an extensive enterprise. They were joined by Baptists from the Maritime Provinces. Earlier than those of Ontario, the Baptists of the Maritime Provinces had sent missionaries in co-operation with those of the United States. Their field had been Burma. Now, as an independent body, they laboured side by side with their brethren from Ontario and Quebec. In 1912 the two organizations—those of Ontario and Quebec and of the Maritime Provinces—united. Together with the Baptists of Australia, the United States, and England, the Canadian Baptists joined in serving a fairly continuous territory nearly a thousand miles long between Calcutta and Madras. The Canadian Baptists, like so many other missions, had their chief gains among the outcastes. By industrial enterprises and education they strove to improve the lot of these unfortunates and to provide them churches with trained leaders.[441]

Ethel Ambrose (London, Marshall, Morgan & Scott, no date, pp. 255). For an account of Australian Baptist effort among the Garos, a primitive folk, see C. D. Baldwin, *God and the Garos* (Sydney, The Australian Baptist Publishing House, 1933, pp. 160), *passim.*

[440] Beach and St. John, *op. cit.,* pp. 64, 65.

[441] M. L. Orchard, *Canadian Baptists at Work in India* (Toronto, Missionary Education Department of the Foreign Mission Board, 1922, pp. 202), *passim;* M. L. Orchard and Miss K. S. McLaurin, *The Enterprise. The Jubilee Story of the Canadian Baptist Mission in India, 1874-1924* (Toronto, The Canadian Baptist Foreign Mission Board, no date, pp. xiv, 348), *passim;* John Craig, Helena Blackadar, and A. A. Scott, *Beacon Lights. A Sketch of the Origin and Development of Our Mission Stations in India*

Beginning as early as the 1850's Canadian Presbyterians began participating in missions to India. For some time, however, they did it in conjunction with Scottish organizations. Two women missionaries sent in 1873 served with the American Presbyterians. One of the earliest acts of the Presbyterian Church in Canada, a body constituted in 1875 by a union of earlier bodies, was to undertake missions to India. The first appointees reached India in 1876 and 1877. A field was found in Central India in the native state of Indore. In the course of the years several stations were opened in Central India, churches were gathered, some of them from the primitive Bhils, schools were developed, culminating in a college in Indore, an Indian clergy was trained, a women's and girls' industrial home was founded, a leper asylum conducted, hospitals built, and a mission press conducted.[442]

During the nineteenth century thousands of Protestant missionaries came to India from the United States. In 1914 the total missionary body from that country serving in India was about five-sixths as numerous as that from the British Isles.[443] This was in spite of the fact that the United States had no political commitments in India and that its commercial interests were not large. It was not through imperialistic contacts or motives that missionaries went to India from the great American republic. Nor, in any but a very few instances, did they come at the call of British societies or as ancillary to related British denominations. For instance, the Protestant Episcopal Church did not undertake a share in the Indian field, although its sister communion, the Church of England, had more missionaries there than any other non-Roman Catholic body. Nor did American Presbyterians come at the behest of Scottish Presbyterians. No nationalistic rivalry existed between American and British societies. There was often co-operation. Yet American missionaries were attracted not by the sense of responsibility accruing from a political connexion, as was true of so much of British effort, but by what appealed to them as the spiritual and physical needs of the Indian people and the door opened to meet these needs by the *pax Britannica*. However, the chief efforts of the American Protestant

(Toronto, Canadian Baptist Foreign Mission Board, 1922, pp. 210), *passim*. For accounts of individual missionaries from the Maritime Provinces, see Grace McLeod Rogers, *Letters from My Home in India* (New York, George H. Doran Co., 1916, pp. 305).

[442] W. A. Wilson, *The Redemption of Malwa. The Central India Canadian Presbyterian Mission* (Toronto, Arbuthnot & MacMillan, 1903, pp. 94), *passim;* J. T. Taylor, *In the Heart of India. The Work of the Canadian Presbyterian Mission* (Toronto, Board of Foreign Missions, Presbyterian Church in Canada, 1916, pp. ix, 225), *passim;* Margaret O'Hara, *Leaf of the Lotus* (Toronto, John M. Poole, 1931, pp. 188), *passim;* Norman Russell, *Village Work in India. Pen Pictures from a Missionary's Experience* (Chicago, Fleming H. Revell Co., 1902, pp. 251), *passim*.

[443] Beach and St. John, *World Statistics of Christian Missions*, pp. 64, 65.

churches abroad were not directed to India. They went, rather, to the geographically nearer lands of the Far East. Denominationally the American missionary body in India was not so closely a cross section of the Protestantism of the United States as was the British missionary body of the Protestantism of the British Isles. Several of the larger American ecclesiastical bodies were entirely unrepresented. For instance, none of the major denominations of the southern states assumed obligations in India.

All but two of the American organizations which were most largely represented in India in 1914 had entered the land before the Mutiny. We will first carry the story of these pre-Mutiny missions down to 1914 and will then speak of the entrance and development of the others.

After the Mutiny the American Board of Commissioners for Foreign Missions expanded the footholds it had acquired before that event. These had been among the Mahrattas, reaching out from Bombay, where the first missionaries had acquired a precarious status, and among the Tamils, mainly from Madura. For a time, as a result of a deputation from the home churches headed by Rufus Anderson, a secretary of the board who combined marked ability with positive convictions as to programme, the organization of churches, self-support, and the training of an Indian ministry were stressed. This was for the purpose of ensuring that as soon as possible Indian Christianity should cease to be dependent. In contrast with the trend to which Duff was giving so great an impetus, Anderson maintained that education should be limited to the children of the Christian community and should be largely in the vernacular.[444] This educational policy was so contrary to the tradition of American Congregationalism and to the prevailing opinions in missionary circles in India that it was not permanently pursued.

The centre of the Mahratta mission of the American Board was at Ahmednagar. A remarkable growth was witnessed in the decades after the Mutiny. In addition to the congregation in that city, churches were founded in many of the villages. Nearly four times as many members were added to the churches in the last quarter of a century before 1914 as in the preceding seventy-five years. While the numbers of missionaries remained about stationary, the Indians giving full time to the churches rapidly increased.[445] Among the missionaries were several members of the Hume family. Literature was prepared, including hymns and the circulation of a translation of the Bible. Schools were

---

[444] Anderson, *History of the Missions of the American Board of Commissioners for Foreign Missions in India*, pp. 241ff.; Strong, *The Story of the American Board*, pp. 166, 167.
[445] *Centennial Report of the American Marathi Mission of the A.B.C.F.M., 1913*, statistical chart before p. 3.

multiplied, from village schools to central boarding schools for boys and girls, a normal school, and a theological seminary. Hospitals were opened. During the famine years 1897-1902 thousands of destitute children were cared for in boarding schools and relief was given in additional ways. In 1912 communicants numbered 7,699 and the total Christian community 13,972.[446] Although the main station was at Ahmednagar, Bombay, where the American Board had gained its first foothold in India, continued to have a strong Indian church.[447] It was at Bombay, moreover, that the major part of the long missionary career of George Bowen was spent. After an unusual spiritual pilgrimage Bowen came to India under the American Board (1847). For a time he severed, amicably, his connexion with that organization, but later resumed it. He wrote extensively for the Bombay *Guardian*, a religious journal, lived with extreme simplicity, and left upon many the impression of Christian saintliness.[448]

The American Board's enterprise at Madura, a stronghold of Hinduism in South India, had been opened in 1835 on the initiative of missionaries of the board in Ceylon. The first church in Madura, composed of missionaries, was organized in 1836 and the first convert was received the following year. By 1851 converts had been won in about 100 villages, 12 churches had been organized, a Christian community of about 2,700 was enumerated, of whom 276 were church members, and more than 1,700 pupils were enrolled in schools.[449] In 1871 the churches totalled 27 and the membership nearly 1,500.[450] Tamil lyrics, composed in the eighteenth century by one of Schwartz's converts, were widely utilized.[451] There were normal, high, and industrial schools as well as primary schools, and in time a college and a theological school were maintained. In 1909 churches numbered 36 and members nearly 7,000.[452]

The mission of the (Dutch) Reformed Church in America in the Arcot

[446] William Hazen in *Centennial Report of the American Marathi Mission of the A.B.C.F.M., 1913*, pp. 70-75; *Memorial Papers of the American Marathi Mission 1813-1881* (Bombay, Education Society's Press, 1882, pp. xi, 147), *passim.* On the biography of one member of the mission, see *Was it Worth While? The Life of Theodore Storrs Lee by Some Friends of His* (New York, Association Press, 1915, pp. xii, 177). On a popular description of a missionary's life, see Isabel Brown Rose, *Our Parish in India* (New York, Fleming H. Revell Co., 1926, pp. 191).

[447] *The Centenary History of the Hume Memorial Church, Byculla, Bombay, 1827-1927* (Bombay's British India Press, 1928, pp. 39), *passim.*

[448] Robert E. Speer, *George Bowen of Bombay* (privately printed, 1938, pp. viii, 366).

[449] Chandler, *Seventy-Five Years in the Madura Mission*, p. 148.

[450] Chandler, *op. cit.*, p. 282.

[451] Chandler, *op. cit.*, pp. 247, 248.

[452] Chandler, *op. cit.*, p. 427. See also, on the Madura mission, *American Madura Mission, Jubilee Volume 1834-1884* (Madras, American Madura Mission, 1886, pp. 83, viii), *passim;* John S. Chandler, *A Madura Missionary, John Eddy Chandler* (Boston, Thomas Todd, no date, pp. 67); and A. J. Saunders, *Dr. Washburn of Madura* (Pasumalai, American Mission Lenox Press, 1928, pp. vii, 171).

region, south-west of Madras, begun in connexion with the American Board of Commissioners for Foreign Missions, but from 1857 under an independent board, continued to prosper. When later the members of the mission looked back upon their history, they thought of the years 1861-1878 as characterized by a village movement, the years 1879-1903 as marked by the development of institutions for the training of the Christians and the service of the general community, and the decade 1904-1913 as a period when union enterprises were being developed in conjunction with other denominations and when leadership and control were devolving more and more upon Indians. There was the usual accompaniment of schools and hospitals. In 1914 there were 9 stations, 200 outstations, 17 organized churches, 3,063 communicant members, and a total baptized community of 11,924.[453] Famous in the life of the mission was the Scudder family.[454] Latterly the most distinguished member was Ida S. Scudder, a physician, who was instrumental in developing not only a hospital but also a medical school for women.[455] Notable also were the Chamberlains, father and son, Jacob and William Isaac.[456]

The enterprises of the (Northern) Presbyterian Church in the United States of America both in foreign staff and in numbers of converts were larger than those of the American Board of Commissioners for Foreign Missions and the Reformed Church in America. The Northern Presbyterians for the most part concentrated their efforts on the regions in which they had begun and where they were at work before the Mutiny, the North-west. Here they developed intensively the areas for which they made themselves responsible. In 1857, on the eve of the Mutiny, they had 16 stations and 294 communicants.[457] Their centres were scattered from Peshawar on the edge of Afghanistan to Allahabad near the middle of the Ganges Valley.[458] The Mutiny cost the Presbyterians the lives of several Indian Christians and of 14 missionaries and their wives and 2 children, and the destruction of some of their property.[459] Reinforcements were sent, but

[453] Eighty-Second Annual Report of the Board of Foreign Missions of the Reformed Church in America, 1914, pp. 46-105.

[454] For the first of the line see Horace E. Scudder, Life and Letters of David Coit Scudder, Missionary in Southern India (New York, Hurd and Houghton, 1864, pp. v, 402).

[455] Mary Pauline Jeffery, Dr. Ida: India. The Life Story of Ida S. Scudder (New York, Fleming H. Revell Co., 1938, p. 212).

[456] See a biographical sketch by Henry Nitchie Cobb in Jacob Chamberlain, The Kingdom in India (Chicago, Fleming H. Revell Co., 1908, pp. 1, 301), pp. xi-l. Books by Jacob Chamberlain are In the Tiger Jungle (Chicago, Fleming H. Revell Co., 1896, pp. 218) and The Cobra's Den (Chicago, Fleming H. Revell Co., 1900, pp. 270), both of them stories of missionary life.

[457] Brown, One Hundred Years, p. 586.

[458] The Twentieth Annual Report of the Board of Foreign Missions of the Presbyterian Church in the U. S. A. (1857), pp. 39-62.

[459] The Twenty-First Annual Report of the Board of Foreign Missions of the Presby-

the communicant body grew slowly. In 1885 it was still only 893.[460] By 1914 through a period of solid growth 26 churches and 4,543 communicants were reported.[461] Outstanding in the achievements in the North was Forman Christian College at Lahore. Named for its first head, it owed its growth chiefly to James C. R. Ewing. Ewing came to India in 1879, but was not appointed principal until 1888. He became one of the outstanding educators of India. For a time he was vice-chancellor of Punjab University. He won the respect and confidence of many different groups, Christian and non-Christian.[462] A further field was developed in the native state of Kolhapur, immediately north of Goa. Here the American Board of Commissioners for Foreign Missions had sent Royal G. Wilder (whose son, Robert P. Wilder, was later to be the chief founder of the Student Volunteer Movement for Foreign Missions).[463] For a time Wilder, having severed his connexion with the American Board over a question of policy, carried on the Kolhapur enterprise as an independent mission. In 1870 it passed into the control of the Board of Foreign Missions of the Presbyterian Church in the United States of America.[464] Additional stations were opened in the region. Particularly notable was the medical centre developed at Miraj by William Wanless. Wanless reached India in 1889. At Miraj in the course of the ensuing decades under his leadership there was built up a hospital, leper asylum, and medical school which became famous throughout India.[465]

The enterprise of the Associate Presbyterian Church whose beginning we noticed a few pages back had a striking development after the Mutiny. Its original centre was at Sialkot, in the Punjab, not far from the southern boundary of Kashmir. The undertaking had barely been inaugurated when the storm of the Mutiny broke upon it. The American staff survived [466] and the first two converts, one an outcaste Chuhra and the other a high caste Hindu, were baptized together in October of 1857, the Mutiny year.[467] When the Associate Pres-

terian Church in the U. S. A. (1858), pp. 47-49; Wherry, Our Missions in India, pp. 92ff.
   [460] Historical Sketches of the India Missions of the Presbyterian Church in the United States of America (Allahabad, Allahabad Mission Press, 1886, pp. iv, 182, iv),·p. 182.
   [461] The Seventy-Seventh Annual Report of the Board of Foreign Missions of the Presbyterian Church in the United States of America (1914), pp. 199-231. For a description of one of the fields in the area, see James F. Holcomb and Helen H. Holcomb, In the Heart of India . . . or Beginnings of Work in Bundela Land (Philadelphia, The Westminster Press, 1905, pp. ix, 251).
   [462] Robert E. Speer, Sir James Ewing (New York, Fleming H. Revell Co., 1928, pp. 307), passim.
   [463] Vol. IV, pp. 96, 97.
   [464] Wherry, op. cit., pp. 199ff.
   [465] William Wanless, An American Doctor at Work in India (New York, Fleming H. Revell Co., 1932, pp. 200), passim.
   [466] Gordon, Our India Mission, pp. 143-164.
   [467] Gordon, op. cit., p. 177.

byterians joined in the formation of the United Presbyterian Church (1858) the Indian mission quickly passed into the control of the new body. Gains were made among the Chuhras and the Megs. The latter, a weaver caste, seem first to have heard the Christian message from a wandering Christian fakir and appear to have made their initial approaches to the missionary stirred by a genuine religious hunger.[468] The 1880's saw a rapid increase in church membership, from 1,373 in 1881 to 8,033 in 1893, an advance registered chiefly among the Chuhras. In the ensuing decades the numerical growth continued and there were also solid developments in schools, including a theological seminary and a college (Gordon Mission College), in hospitals and dispensaries, and in the deepening of the life of the Christian community. The mission confined its efforts to the general area to which it had been introduced by its pioneers. While more centres than Sialkot were opened, they were all in the upper part of the Punjab not far from the southern border of Kashmir.[469] In 1913, out of the 9,374 cities and villages in what the United Presbyterians regarded as their field, 1,524 contained Christians. There were 54 organized congregations, a church membership of 31,631 (which had shown a net growth of 2,106 in 1913), a Christian community of 58,034, an American staff of 83, and a large Indian staff which included 38 ordained clergymen.[470]

In 1914 the American Baptist Foreign Mission Society had connected with the churches which it served in India more baptized Christians than did any other Protestant organization except the Church Missionary Society, the Society for the Propagation of the Gospel in Foreign Parts, and the Methodist Episcopal Church.[471] It was operating in three areas, in South India among the Telugus, in Assam, chiefly among hill tribes, and in Bengal-Orissa.

Of the three fields, in 1914 that in South India contained the largest number of Christians. A few pages back we noted the foundation of this mission and its discouraging beginnings. At Nellore, where Day, the pioneer, established a centre, the first Telugu convert was baptized in 1841 and a church was organized in 1844.[472] Reinforcements came slowly and converts were few. There was

[468] Gordon, op. cit., pp. 173-230.

[469] Anderson and Watson, Far North in India, pp. 227-261. For biographical notices of a missionary who had only a few years in India, see A Memorial of the Life of John Herbert Morton . . . by His Friends and Fellow-Laborers (Printed by order of the Sialkot Mission, no date, pp. 94).

[470] Annual Report of the Board of Foreign Missions of the United Presbyterian Church of North America, 1914, pp. 221, 222.

[471] Beach and St. John, World Statistics of Christian Missions, pp. 64, 65. The tables include the figures for Burma, where the Baptists were very numerous. For the Baptist figures for India alone, see One Hundredth Annual Report of the American Baptist Foreign Mission Society, 1914, pp. 90, 101, 115.

[472] Downie, The Lone Star Mission, p. 29.

talk in the United States of discontinuing the Lone Star Mission. Day's health broke and he returned to America, leaving Lyman Jewett and his wife the only Western missionaries. In 1862 the suggestion was made for the third time— and the last—that the Telugu enterprise be abandoned. Jewett, then on health leave in America, insisted that he would go back, if necessary alone. He was permitted to return and was given a colleague, John E. Clough.[473] Clough reached India in 1865.[474] Assistance, as we saw a few paragraphs above, came in that decade from the Canadian Baptists. That decade, too, witnessed the slow beginnings of what later became a remarkable mass movement of the outcaste Madigas. This came partly as an outgrowth of an indigenous awakening among these people begun by an illiterate religious teacher who was looking for spiritual satisfaction, was seeking it through traditional Indian ways, and had stirred up among some of his fellows a similar longing. In the Christian message, received partly through contacts with Clough, these Madigas found that for which they had been hungering. Soon converts began pouring in by the hundreds, chiefly at Ongole, where Clough had been in charge since 1866. Many of them were immersed in a baptistry built on the site of a pagan shrine.[475] The fact that the Madigas were coming discouraged inquirers from other social groups. The Madigas were of the lowest social level and were despised by all others. A few Malas, also of depressed social status, were baptized, but most of these who became Christians, as we saw a few pages above, joined themselves to the Wesleyans.

Of the Madiga converts Clough demanded as a test of their faith that they observe Sunday, refrain from eating carrion, and abstain from pagan ceremonies. By these three seemingly simple demands he ran athwart the customs of the community and threatened the disintegration of village life. In the village economy the Madigas had by custom a distinct part. They were labourers, and to refuse to work on Sundays inconvenienced their employers. They were scavengers who disposed of the dead cows of their Hindu neighbours and they had traditionally furnished music and dancing for village religious festivals. To renounce either function would threaten the existing order. When, on Clough's insistence, the Madiga Christians met these requirements, they faced persecution. They persevered and by doing so to some degree won their emancipation.[476]

Then came the famine of 1876 which played so large a part in the growth of several of the missions. The Madigas, being chronically poverty-stricken, suf-

[473] Downie, op. cit., p. 47.
[474] Clough, Social Christianity in the Orient, p. 71.
[475] Clough, op. cit., p. 93.
[476] Clough, op. cit., pp. 158ff.

fered acutely. Clough helped to administer aid. As a relief project he supervised the construction of a portion of an irrigation canal which the British authorities were putting through as a means of giving employment and as a safeguard against future dearth. In hiring labourers Clough gave preference to Christians. However, he declined to baptize any applicants for the rite, fearing that those asking it were coming for purely economic reasons. Not until July, 1878, did he begin administering it, and then chiefly because Roman Catholic priests told him that they would do so if he did not. They knew of the many applicants, were themselves baptizing hundreds in other areas, and felt that in the Ongole region those who desired the rite should be given it. Clough besought them not to come in, urging the unfortunate religious division which would be created in the villages if the Christians were in two rival camps—Baptist and Roman Catholic. In three days in July, 1878, he and his assistants baptized 3,536, and in six months 8,691. It must be added that the Roman Catholic missionaries, evidently impressed by Clough's pleading and his prompt action, did not compete.[477] By the close of 1882 the number of Baptist church members in the Ongole area was 20,865.[478]

While the mass movement was most marked in and near Ongole, it was to be found in other places.[479] By the time the American Baptist Telugu Mission celebrated its semi-centennial (1886) it had stations from Madras in the South to the native state of Hyderabad in the North.[480] Mass movements occurred again in later years. In 1890 and 1891 there were thousands of baptisms in Ongole and in Cumbum.[481] However, no later influx was of the spectacular dimensions of that of 1878.

For the multitudes of ignorant and economically and socially depressed who thus came into the Christian Church much remained to be done. Schools were provided, hospitals were developed, Indian clergy were trained, attempts to provide industrial training were made, and first steps were taken on the long hard road toward self-support and autonomy in administration. Progress was inevitably slow and at times met discouraging reverses. Yet it was achieved.[482]

---

[477] Clough, op. cit., pp. 286ff.; Downie, op. cit.; pp. 88-108. For a popularly told account of the movement among the Madigas in and around Ongole, see Emma Rauschenbusch-Clough, While Sewing Sandals. Tales of a Telugu Pariah Tribe (London, Hodder and Stoughton, 1899, pp. xi, 321).

[478] Downie, op. cit., p. 112.

[479] Downie, op. cit., p. 105.

[480] Map in The "Lone Star" Jubilee. Papers and Discussions of the Conference held in Nellore, February 5-10, 1886, to Celebrate the Fiftieth Anniversary of the American Baptist Telugu Mission (Madras, Addison and Co., 1886, pp. iv, 264).

[481] Downie, op. cit., p. 113.

[482] Downie, op. cit., pp. 134ff.; One Hundredth Annual Report of the American Baptist Foreign Mission Society, 1914, pp. 101ff. For the autobiography of one of the able mis-

The mission of the American Baptists in Assam was inaugurated a few months earlier than that among the Telugus, but by 1914 had not attained as large numerical proportions. Not long after the British occupation of Assam, the pioneers made their way up the Brahmaputra (1835), partly at the invitation of a British captain and partly with the hope of effecting an entrance into the then closed land of China. The founder and chief pioneer was Nathan Brown.[483] For the first few decades attention was paid chiefly to the peoples of the plains. Beginning in the 1860's, however, the mission reached out to the hill tribes. Here it was to find a striking response. By 1914 followings had been won among the Garos, the Rabhas (mixed with the Garos), the Nagas, the Abors, and the Miris. Later efforts were also made to give spiritual care to Christians who had come in as labourers in the tea gardens. In 1914 churches numbered 137 and members 13,317. A marked increase was in progress which was to mount rapidly in the next few years. Here, as by other missions, steps were taken to educate the converts so suddenly drawn from animism and primitive society and to provide a trained lay and clerical leadership. At Jorhat a centre of Christian schools was developed.[484]

The entrance of the American Baptist Foreign Mission Society into Bengal and Orissa came through the Free Baptists, who, after their merger with the Northern Baptists, the supporting constituency of the society, turned over to it, in October, 1911, their Indian field.[485] The Free Baptists of the United States had begun their mission in Orissa at the suggestion of the General Baptists of England, who were of kindred theological outlook and who had for several years been at work in the region. The initial contingent of Free Baptists reached Calcutta in 1836 and established themselves in their first permanent station, Balasore, in 1838. Eventually they spread into the southern part of

sionaries, see David Downie, *From the Mill to the Mission Field* (Philadelphia, The Judson Press, 1928, pp. 194). For a biographical sketch see *The Young Missionary. The Story of the Life of Annie Kennard Downie, by her Mother* (Philadelphia, American Baptist Publication Society, 1904, pp. 106).

[483] Sword, *Baptists in Assam*, pp. 41ff.; Bowers, *Under Head-Hunters' Eyes*, pp. 5, 6; *The Whole World Kin: a Pioneer Experience among Remote Tribes and Other Labors of Nathan Brown* (Philadelphia, Hubbard Brothers, 1890, pp. 607).

[484] Sword, *op. cit.*, pp. 83ff.; *The Assam Mission of the American Baptist Missionary Union. Papers and Discussions of the Jubilee Conference held in Nowgong, December 18-29, 1886* (Calcutta, Baptist Mission Press, 1887, pp. xiii, 297); E. Marie Holmes, *Sowing Seed in Assam* (New York, Fleming H. Revell Co., 1925, pp. 195), *passim;* Harriette Bronson Gunn, *In a Far Country* (Philadelphia, American Baptist Publication Society, 1911, pp. 244), *passim;* Mary Mead Clark, *A Corner in India* (Philadelphia, American Baptist Publication Society, 1907, pp. xvi, 168), *passim;* William Carey, *A Garo Jungle Book, or the Mission to the Garos of Assam* (Philadelphia, the Judson Press, 1919, pp. 283), *passim.*

[485] *Ninety-Eighth Report of the American Baptist Foreign Mission Society*, 1912, p. 91.

Bengal. Contacts were formed with more than one social group.[486] In 1914 churches numbered 23 and members 1,623.[487]

What in 1914 was the largest of the enterprises founded by American religious bodies in India was that of the Methodist Episcopal Church. Indeed, in numbers of missionaries and of the Christian community gathered, it ranked next to those of the Roman Catholics and the Anglicans.[488] As we saw a few pages above, the American Methodists were fairly late in entering India. Their pioneer was William Butler. He arrived in 1856 and under his leadership a field was selected in Oudh and Rohilkhand in what later became the United Provinces. Here by 1864, through the assistance of reinforcements, 9 cities had been entered, 10 churches organized, 12 congregations gathered, and 117 members and 92 probationers won. Chapels and school-houses had been built, a press begun, orphanages founded, and a Christian agricultural colony projected. Several of the converts had been gathered from Mazhabi Sikhs, a group of depressed social status with an unsavoury criminal record.[489] In December, 1865, a step was taken towards giving an ecclesiastical structure to the infant church which tended to place it on a par with the mother body. An Annual Conference was constituted and the principle was established that Indian clergy should have equal dignity and responsibility with the clergy sent from the United States.[490] Butler now felt that the mission for which he had been sent was accomplished and, in part constrained by ill health, returned (1865) to America.[491] When, in 1883, he again visited India, it was to see the results of an amazing growth during the intervening eighteen years.[492]

This growth was achieved largely under the leadership of James Mills Thoburn and William Taylor. At the initial meeting of the Annual Conference, at the request of the British commissioner in charge of the area, the decision was made to extend the operations of the mission to Garhwal, a mountainous region

---

[486] Mrs. M. M. Hutchins Hills, *Reminiscences. A Brief History of the Free Baptist India Mission* (Boston, F. B. Printing Establishment, 1886, pp. vi, 335), *passim;* Thomas H. Stacy, *Rev. Otis Robinson Bacheler, M.D., D.D., Fifty-Three Years Missionary to India* (Boston, The Morning Star Publishing House, 1904, pp. 512), *passim;* Dr. J. L. Phillips, *Missionary to the Children of India—by his Widow* (London, The Sunday School Union, 1898, pp. 264), *passim.*

[487] *Hundredth Report of the American Baptist Foreign Mission Society,* 1914, pp. 115.

[488] Beach and St. John, *World Statistics of Christian Missions,* pp. 64, 65.

[489] Thoburn, *India and Malaysia,* pp. 219-232, 263-278; William Butler, *The Land of the Veda: being Personal Reminiscences of India* (New York, Phillips & Hunt, 1871, pp. 557), pp. 506-526. See also scattered references in Butler, *From Boston to Bareilly and Back.*

[490] Harper, *The Methodist Episcopal Church in India,* pp. 28-30; Thoburn, *op. cit.,* p. 277.

[491] Thoburn, *op. cit.,* p. 278.

[492] Butler, *From Boston to Bareilly and Back, passim.*

north of Rohilkhand.[493] With an unconscious prophecy of the future, the assignment of the task of pioneering in this rough territory was given to Thoburn.[494] Thoburn (1836-1922) was born in Ohio, the son of Irish Methodist immigrants.[495] He went to India in 1859. It was after his first term in India, a term made sorrowful by the death of his wife, and after a furlough in the United States that he was given this task of blazing a new trail.[496] Not many years later, in 1870, while district superintendent for his church in Oudh, Thoburn led in an expansion beyond the original field of his mission, crossing the Ganges to hold services in Cawnpore.[497] In that same year, partly through his suggestion, there arrived in India his sister, Isabella Thoburn.[498] She was an appointee of the newly organized Woman's Foreign Missionary Society of her church. The formation of the society had been to some degree stimulated by the desire of Miss Thoburn to go to India under the auspices of a woman's organization of her own church rather than under the interdenominational Woman's Union Missionary Society, as her brother had at first suggested. In India Miss Thoburn gave herself chiefly to the education of her sex. She founded and long headed a school for girls at Lucknow which eventually grew into a college that was given her name and which was a notable pioneer in higher education for the women of India.[499] Incidentally, while in the United States on an extended health leave, Miss Thoburn helped to inaugurate the deaconess movement in her church in Chicago and Cincinnati. The Thoburns were given to leading in new undertakings for the extension and application of their faith. With Miss Thoburn on her first trip to India there came, as the other initial appointee of the Woman's Foreign Missionary Society, a physician, Clara Swain, who as a pioneer in the medical care of the women of India by women was to give many years to the land of her adoption.[500]

An invitation from Thoburn was a contributing factor towards the extended visit to India of William Taylor.[501] We have already met Taylor as a remarkable itinerant Methodist preacher, in California, South America, Australia, and

[493] Scott, History of Fifty Years, pp. 79, 80.
[494] Thoburn, My Missionary Apprenticeship, pp. 123, 143-147.
[495] Oldham, Thoburn—Called of God, is a brief biography by a bishop of his church.
[496] Thoburn, op. cit., pp. 137-197.
[497] Oldham, op. cit., pp. 81-85; Thoburn, India and Malaysia, pp. 291-294.
[498] The standard account of Isabella Thoburn's life is by her brother, J. M. Thoburn, Life of Isabella Thoburn (Cincinnati, Jennings and Pye, 1903, pp. 373).
[499] For one who served for a time as head of the college, see A Girl of an Indian Garden. Letters of Flora Robinson Howells to Her Friends, edited by Ruth E. Robinson (New York, Fleming H. Revell Co., 1928, pp. 91).
[500] Mrs. Robert Hoskins, Clara A. Swain, M.D., First Medical Missionary to the Women of the Orient (Boston, Woman's Foreign Missionary Society, Methodist Episcopal Church, 1912, pp. 31), passim.
[501] Thoburn, My Missionary Apprenticeship, pp. 278-280.

INDIA 171

Africa,[502] who, even more than the great founder of Methodism, made the world his parish. It was after his experiences in California, Australia, New Zealand, and South Africa, but before his famous mission in South America and his African episcopate that Taylor spent four years in India.[503] It was from a second tour of the West Indies, a second visit to Australia, and a series of meetings in Ceylon that Taylor came to India. He arrived in 1870 and went almost at once to Thoburn in Lucknow.[504] After some time in that area he moved on to Bombay, Poona, Calcutta, Madras, Bangalore, and other centres. He preached to Europeans, Anglo-Indians, Parsees, and Indians, in English where possible and, where not, through an interpreter. His methods were those of some of the revivals of the United States and were accompanied by emotional awakenings and moral and spiritual transformations akin to what had been seen in America. Methodist churches were organized in several centres, notably in Bombay and Calcutta. Taylor wished these congregations to be self-maintaining and to assist them to spread the Christian message undertook to call missionaries who would be locally supported.

Thoburn joined his voice to that of Taylor in urging that the Methodist Episcopal Church follow up the efforts thus begun and broaden its field.[505] Thoburn himself went to Calcutta and headed a congregation which was primarily among Europeans and Anglo-Indians but which made contacts with other groups.[506] As in South America, so in India, Taylor's plan of missionaries supported locally did not succeed and it became necessary for the General Conference of the Methodist Episcopal Church to assume responsibility if the enterprises inaugurated with such promise were not to disintegrate. This it was the more constrained to do as the congregations organized by Taylor reached out beyond the English-speaking communities into the vast mass of Indian life.[507] In 1876 the General Conference authorized an Annual Conference bearing the name of South India.[508] In Thoburn's judgment this was tantamount to permission to regard all India as a field for his church.[509] He had been irked by what he deemed the limited vision of his society in planning a mission in only one portion of the country rather than for all India.[510] In 1884, responding to

[502] Vol. IV, p. 191; Vol. V, pp. 118, 119, 121, 136, 330, 385, 400, 451.
[503] For Taylor's own account, see William Taylor, *Four Years' Campaign in India* (London, Hodder and Stoughton, 1876, pp. xvi, 416).
[504] For an account and estimate of Taylor's visit in that area, see Thoburn, *op. cit.*, pp. 278-287.
[505] Badley, *Visions and Victories in Hindustan*, pp. xvii-xx.
[506] Thoburn, *op. cit.*, pp. 323ff.
[507] Badley, *op. cit.*, pp. xix, xx.
[508] Thoburn, *India and Malaysia*, p. 297.
[509] Thoburn, *op. cit.*, p. 298.
[510] Harper, *The Methodist Episcopal Church in India*, p. 23.

pressure from India and following up a preliminary experiment known as the Delegated Conference which first met in 1881, a new organizational device, the Central Conference, was authorized as a means of co-ordinating the activities of the Methodist Episcopal Church in the vast area into which it was moving.[511]

It was partly through Thoburn that American Methodism spread to Burma,[512] to Singapore and the Malay Peninsula,[513] and, eventually, into the Philippines.[514] In this extension Thoburn was a leader, even though not the only leader. His was something of the temperament and vision which more than three centuries before had led Francis Xavier to dream in terms of carrying the Christian Gospel to the entire South and East of Asia. He combined the gifts of a mystic with those of a practical man of affairs. His was a single-hearted devotion which, in 1873, felt it to be his duty to cease drawing a salary from his society and to depend completely upon God for financial support.[515] He was, too, a preacher of singular power in revival services, intent upon winning individuals one by one and in groups. It was fitting that in 1888 the General Conference should elect him its first Missionary Bishop for India and Malaysia. To cover this vast area for a church which was rapidly spreading into various new sections required almost incessant travel and labour. In 1900 his health gave way under the strain and two additional missionary bishops were appointed for the region.[516] Yet he served on into his seventies, not retiring until 1908, and lived until his eighty-seventh year.[517]

Thanks in part to the impulse given by Taylor and to the leadership of Thoburn, by 1914 all India was embraced within the ecclesiastical framework of the Methodist Episcopal Church. Not all the country was effectively occupied, but the six conferences into which it was divided covered between them the entire land, and the large cities in which American Methodism was not represented were comparatively few.[518]

The comprehensive fashion in which the Methodist Episcopal Church sought to deal with India was not without its critics. Repeatedly the complaint was made that the Methodists were disregarding the comity by which various other

[511] Harper, op. cit., pp. 38-41; Thoburn, op. cit., p. 299.
[512] Thoburn, op. cit., pp. 449-451.
[513] Thoburn, op. cit., pp. 520-522.
[514] Oldham, Thoburn—Called of God, pp. 148ff.
[515] Thoburn, My Missionary Apprenticeship, pp. 301ff.
[516] Scott, History of Fifty Years, pp. 273-275. For the biography of one of these first two bishops (who died within a few months of his election), see J. H. Messmore, The Life of Edwin Wallace Parker (New York, Eaton & Mains, pp. 333).
[517] Dictionary of American Biography, Vol. XVIII, p. 419.
[518] Annual Report of the Board of Foreign Missions of the Methodist Episcopal Church for the Year 1914, pp. 13-88.

Protestant denominations, in the hope of preventing competitive overlapping, had endeavoured to divide the land. Yet the Methodists persevered.[519]

Although the Methodist Episcopal Church scattered its efforts over so large a proportion of India, its numerical growth was very unevenly distributed. Its chief gains were in the region in which was its earliest Indian field, in what it called its North India Conference, and in what it termed its North-west Conference. In 1914 more than four-fifths of its members and nearly two-thirds of its probationers were in these two conferences.[520] The increase had been mainly from the depressed classes and by mass movements. These movements began gaining momentum in 1888 [521] and in 1914 were still in progress. They were not confined to the two northern conferences, but were also seen in Gujarat and Hyderabad, in the Bombay and South India Conferences respectively.[522] On at least one occasion the missionaries were embarrassed by the majority decision of representatives of more than a score of villages to become Christians when not a man could be spared to prepare them for baptism.[523] The missionaries encouraged the mass converts to come into the Church through their natural groupings. In at least some instances baptism would be administered to none until all in the village were deemed ready for the rite.[524] Much use was made of the *chaudris,* or village head-men. These, whom the villagers were accustomed to follow, were held responsible for their groups and, that they might be intelligent in their leadership, were given especial training in things Christian.[525]

American Methodists employed many of the methods and built many of the types of institutions which we have found characteristic of other Christian bodies. There were schools, from those of primary grade in the villages, through those of secondary grade, to colleges. Some of the schools were for boys and others for girls. There were orphanages. Hospitals were erected and dispensaries conducted. Provision was made for the recruiting and training of an Indian clergy. The proportion of Indian to American leadership fairly rap-

[519] Harper, *op. cit.,* pp. 83-86.

[520] *Annual Report of the Board of Foreign Missions of the Methodist Episcopal Church for the Year 1914,* pp. 274, 275.

[521] On the early stages of these movements see James M. Thoburn, *Light in the East* (Evanston, Thomas Craven, 1894, pp. 128), pp. 46ff.

[522] Harper, *op. cit.,* pp. 57-68, 107.

[523] *Annual Report of the Board of Foreign Missions of the Methodist Episcopal Church for the Year 1914,* p. 42.

[524] *Annual Report of the Board of Foreign Missions of the Methodist Episcopal Church for the Year 1914,* pp. 39, 40.

[525] *Annual Report of the Board of Foreign Missions of the Methodist Episcopal Church for the Year 1914,* pp. 39, 40, 43; Harper, *op. cit.,* p. 173.

idly increased. Women were reached in their homes by women. Here and there were industrial schools. There were the preparation and publishing of Christian literature. Sunday schools were promoted. We hear of summer conferences, partly for Bible study. There was preaching, much of it through itineration from village to village.[526]

Some features were peculiar to Methodist Episcopal missions, either because of the organization and tradition of that church or because of unique individuals. The system of conferences was one of these. Modifications were made in the structure transported from the United States to render it more useful in the Indian scene. A few paragraphs above we noted the invention of the Central Conference as a means of co-ordinating the activities in Southern Asia. This assumed increasing importance.[527] District Conferences were added to the familiar Annual Conferences. Their purpose was the direction and training of Indian preachers, teachers, and Bible readers of humble origin and mediocre ability who did not seem to have the qualifications for membership in the Annual Conferences.[528] Thanks in part to the precedents established by Taylor and Thoburn, more attention was paid to Europeans and Anglo-Indians than by most denominations.

Famous for her identification of herself with the care of lepers was Mary Reed.[529] Miss Reed went to India in 1884 under the Woman's Foreign Missionary Society of the Methodist Episcopal Church. In 1890, ill with an obscure disease, she returned to America. While in the United States she discovered, partly through her own intuition, an intuition confirmed by expert medical diagnosis, that her malady was leprosy. Telling her secret only to a sister, she set out for India, resolved there to give herself to her fellow lepers. In India she was placed in charge of an asylum in the foothills of the Himalayas maintained by the Mission to Lepers.[530] Before many years the course of her own illness was

[526] Badley, *Visions and Victories in Hindustan, passim; The Year 1901 in Our India Missions, being a report from each Presiding Elder's District, with notes from reports of some Committees, etc., etc.* (no place or date of publication, pp. 87), *passim;* Frederick B. Price, editor, *India Mission Jubilee of the Methodist Episcopal Church in Southern Asia* (Calcutta, Methodist Publishing House, 1907, pp. xxii, 306), *passim.* For accounts of two of the missionaries, see Lewis A. Core, *The Life and Work of William Albert Mansell, Missionary* (Madras, Methodist Publishing House, 1914, pp. xiii, 201), and J. L. Humphrey, *Twenty-One Years in India* (Cincinnati, Jennings and Graham, 1905, pp. 283). For vivid pictures of the itinerant missionary see T. J. Scott, *Missionary Life among the Villages of India* (Cincinnati, Hitchcock and Walden, 1876, pp. 343).
[527] Harper, *op. cit.,* pp. 71-73.
[528] Harper, *op. cit.,* p. 37.
[529] John Jackson, *Mary Reed, Missionary to Lepers* (London, The Mission to Lepers, 11th ed., 1912, pp. 134); Lee S. Huizenga, *Mary Reed of Chandag* (Grand Rapids, Zondervan Publishing Co., 1939, pp. 36); E. Mackerchar, *Miss Mary Reed of Chandag* (London, The Mission to Lepers, 2d ed., no date, pp. 32).
[530] For this society see Vol. IV, p. 101.

arrested—by prayer she profoundly believed—but she remained on, living to an advanced age, ministering to the physical needs of the patients and seeking to transmit to them the faith in the strength of which she laboured.

It was no accident that the two religious bodies of the United States which led numerically in introducing Protestant Christianity to India were the Baptists and Methodists. As we saw in our fourth volume, they were the denominations which were most prominent in spreading the Protestant form of the Christian faith in their homeland among the masses of the population on the westward moving frontier and among the Negroes. They were actively missionary and were experienced in reaching what in the United States was the nearest approach to a proletariat among the older white stock and the Negroes. It is not surprising, therefore, that in India, where the vast majority of converts were from the lower social strata, they were peculiarly successful.

Nor should it be surprising that numerically they were more prominent in India than were the corresponding denominations of the British Isles. In the British Isles Baptists and Wesleyan Methodists drew more from the middle classes than from the proletariat. Perhaps for that reason they were less able to reach the underprivileged masses of India than were the Baptists and Methodists of the United States. It is certain that in 1914 British Baptists and Methodists, although they had been longer in India than American Baptists and Methodists, both in the gross and in proportion to the size of their foreign staffs, had smaller Christian communities than did their American brethren. This was in spite of the fact that the British Wesleyans, like the American Methodists, had large accessions from mass movements among the outcastes.

The remaining religious bodies of the United States which had entered India before the Mutiny were Lutheran—the General Synod and the Ministerium of Pennsylvania. A mission had been established among the Telugus which had passed primarily into the hands of the General Synod. By the time of the Mutiny a promising enterprise was in existence.[531] Then, from 1862 to 1872, a most discouraging decade came upon the mission. The American Civil War and dissensions within the General Synod led to a decrease in interest and financial support. In the ten years no reinforcements arrived and the missionary staff was reduced to a man and his wife.[532] The dissensions led to the severing of the ties between the General Synod and the Ministerium of Philadelphia and the formation, in 1867, at the instance of the latter, of the General Council.[533] In 1869 the General Council took over from the General Synod one of the

[531] Drach and Kuder, *The Telugu Mission of the General Council of the Evangelical Lutheran Church in North America*, pp. 34-106.
[532] Drach and Kuder, *op. cit.*, pp. 106-113, 119-130.
[533] *The Lutheran World Almanac . . . 1921*, p. 73.

latter's stations in India. This it did at the instance of Heyer, the pioneer missionary of the American Lutherans in the India field. Heyer had been away from India for some years, mainly engaged as a home missionary on the Minnesota frontier. He was stirred by the proposed transfer by the General Synod, in its straightened circumstances, to the Church Missionary Society, of a station which had been received from the North German Missionary Society on the condition that it remain Lutheran. This Heyer regarded as a breach of trust. Although seventy-six years of age, he not only roused the General Council to action, but also went back to India to inaugurate the new enterprise. Reinforcements soon came, and the intrepid patriarch, deeming his work completed, once more made his way to the United States.[534]

With the 1870's better days dawned for the American Lutheran undertakings. Not only did the General Council assume responsibilities in India. It also made India its major foreign field.[535] The General Synod rallied from the decline which had all but extinguished its Indian enterprise and sent extensive reinforcements. Mass movements began and increased after the famine of 1876. Subsequent to 1892 the growth of converts was particularly marked.[536] In 1914 the General Synod was maintaining a more numerous staff than the General Council and had connected with it a larger Christian community. In that year it had 49,605 members of whom 17,209 were communicants.[537] In 1912 the General Council reported a membership of 19,377. This represented a gain of 2,797 in two years. The members were scattered among 314 congregations and 577 villages.[538] Both missions, as formerly, were among the Telugus and both had the usual accompaniment of schools, medical relief, and the recruiting and training of Indian catechists, teachers, and clergy. The General Council's mission developed lace making as a means of employment for women.

In the little more than a half century between the Mutiny and 1914 numbers

---

[534] Drach and Kuder, *op. cit.*, pp. 133-155.
[535] Drach and Kuder, *op. cit.*, pp. 162ff. On a German who went to India under the General Council, in a book which gives a first hand account of details of missionary activities, see F. Wischan, *Wilhelm Grönning, Missionar im Telugu-Lande in Indien* (Philadelphia, 1891, pp. 301).
[536] J. Aberly in *The Diamond Jubilee Report 1842-1917 of the American Evangelical Lutheran Mission, Guntur, September 30th, 1917. Published by the Board of Foreign Missions of the General Synod of the Evangelical Lutheran Church in the United States of America*, pp. 11ff.; Magdalen Keith Burger, *Our India Story. An Account of the Work of the Women's Home and Foreign Missionary Society in India* (Baltimore, [1918], pp. 62), *passim;* L. B. Wolf, *After Fifty Years, or an Historical Sketch of the Guntur Mission of the Evangelical Church of the General Synod in the United States of America* (Philadelphia, Lutheran Publication Society, pp. 320), *passim.*
[537] *The Guntur Mission, India. Annual Report 1913-1914.*
[538] *The Board of Foreign Missions of the General Council of the Evangelical Lutheran Church in North America. Biennial Report. 1911-1913,* pp. 15-32.

of additional American societies inaugurated enterprises in India. None of them, however, attained the dimensions of the largest of those which traced their beginnings to the years before the Mutiny. The Lutheran representation was given added diversity by the arrival of the Missouri Synod (1895) and the distribution of its missionaries in south central portions of the Madras Presidency and Travancore.[539] Another of the bodies of German provenance, the Evangelical Synod, in 1869 sent missionaries to the Central Provinces who found their first intensive field among the depressed Chamars.[540] Two branches of still another of the German groups, the Mennonites, established themselves in the Central Provinces in 1899 and 1900 respectively. They grew in part through a mass movement from the Chamars. They first administered famine relief but later developed most of the customary features of Protestant mission effort—orphanages, education, medical service, and the gathering of churches.[541] Still another denomination whose membership was largely from German stock, the Church of the Brethren, began a mission in India, in Bulsar, north of Bombay, in 1884, and in time built a missionary staff which was larger than those of both the Mennonite bodies.[542] In 1882 the Disciples of Christ sent their first missionaries to India. A field was found in the Central Provinces.[543] By 1914 a number of centres had been developed in that area.[544] Out of William Taylor's mission and his appeal to Christians in the United States to send missionaries and from the earnest desire of a British official came the impulses which brought into being a mission in Berar, in the Central Provinces. This in turn became the first station in India of what was eventually the Christian and Missionary Alliance.[545] By 1914 this organization counted a foreign staff of sixty-nine.[546] The Seventh Day Adventists entered India in 1894 or 1895 and by 1914 had nearly a hundred missionaries in various parts of the country.

---

[539] Beach and St. John, *World Statistics of Christian Missions*, p. 64; Jones, *The Year Book of Missions in India, Burma, and Ceylon, 1912*, p. 543.

[540] Beach and St. John, *op. cit.*, p. 65; Martin P. Davis, *Sadhu Hagenstein* (Washington, The Board for Foreign Missions, Evangelical Synod of North America, no date, pp. xv, 310), *passim*.

[541] Beach and St. John, *op. cit.*, p. 65; Jones, *op. cit.*, pp. 541, 542; *Twenty-five Years with God in India* (Berne, Indiana, Mennonite Book Concern, 1929, pp. 250), *passim;* Mary Yoder Burkhard, *Life and Letters of Jacob Burkhard, Missionary to India* (Goshen, Indiana, the author, 1936, pp. xiii, 214), *passim;* Kaufman, *The Development of the Missionary and Philanthropic Interest among the Mennonites of North America*, pp. 152-155, 379-391.

[542] Moyer, *Missions of the Church of the Brethren*, pp. 169-179.

[543] Emma Richardson Wharton, *Life of G. L. Wharton* (Chicago, Fleming H. Revell Co., 1913, pp. 251), pp. 36ff.

[544] *The Missionary Intelligencer*, Nov., 1914, pp. 452-462.

[545] Helen S. Dyer, *A Life for God in India. Memorials of Mrs. Jennie Fuller of Akola and Bombay* (Chicago, Fleming H. Revell Co., no date, pp. 190), *passim*.

[546] Beach and St. John, *op. cit.*, p. 64; Jones, *op. cit.*, pp. 504-556.

By 1914, however, their membership was less than four hundred.[547] It was in the year 1896 that the Pentecostal Bands began their enterprises in India. Through orphanages child sufferers from famine were rescued and reared and some of them trained as preachers. A leper asylum was maintained.[548] Among other American organizations supporting missions in India in 1914 were the Bible Faith Mission, the Associate Reformed Presbyterian Church, the Reformed Episcopal Church, the Churches of God, the Burning Bush Mission, the Brethren in Christ, Ohio Quakers, the Free Methodist Church, the Pentecostal Church of the Nazarene, the Hephzibah Faith Missionary Association, the Calvinistic Methodist Church, the Wesleyan Methodist Connexion, the Peniel Missionary Society, the Scandinavian Alliance Mission of North America, and the Vanguard Faith Mission.[549] Of these the one with the largest foreign staff seems to have been the Scandinavian Alliance Mission, in the Himalayas, with a missionary force of not far from forty.[550] The others were small. The undenominational Woman's Missionary Society of America, founded in 1861, had India as its chief field, and in 1913 had twenty-five missionaries in various centres in the North, chiefly in schools, hospitals, and orphanages, but also among the women in their homes and in the villages.[551] We hear of Mormon missionaries, but they seem not to have attracted an extensive following.[552]

From America came the largest proportion of the secretaries of the Young Men's Christian Association. Others were from the British Isles, and some from Australia, New Zealand, and the continent of Europe. The British secretaries went chiefly to the cities where the associations served mainly the Europeans and Anglo-Indians. One of these was J. H. Oldham, who was later to win distinction as secretary of the International Missionary Council. The American secretaries went mainly to the associations whose membership was predominantly Indian.[553] The first secretary from the United States, David McConaughy, the initial appointee to India of the International Committee

[547] Beach and St. John, op. cit., p. 65; Jones, op. cit., pp. 560, 561; Seventh Day Adventist Conferences, Missions, and Institutions, Fifty-first Annual Statistical Report. Year ending Dec. 31, 1913, p. 10, supplement, p. 2; M. D. Wood, Fruit from the Jungle (Mountain View, Calif., Pacific Press Publishing Ass'n, 1919, pp. 331), passim.

[548] Beach and St. John, op. cit., p. 65; Forrest B. Whisler and Iva C. Whisler, India's Awakening (Indianapolis, Pub. House of the Pentecostal Bands, no date, pp. 101), pp. 65ff.

[549] Beach and St. John, op. cit., pp. 64, 65.

[550] Jones, op. cit., p. 560.

[551] Fifty-third Annual Report of the Woman's Union Missionary Society of America, 1914; Beach and St. John, op. cit., p. 65.

[552] Pascoe, Two Hundred Years of the S. P. G., p. 489.

[553] International Survey of the Young Men's and Young Women's Christian Associations, pp. 319, 320.

of the Young Men's Christian Associations, reached India on January 1, 1890. He organized the Madras Young Men's Christian Association and the movement spread rapidly. Thirty-five associations were reported when the first national convention met in 1891. McConaughy became the first secretary of the national organization. In the 1890's more efforts began to be made to reach non-Christians, including the influential student class.[554] In 1896 there came to India to travel among the students Sherwood Eddy, later to be a flaming preacher of the Christian faith in many lands. His closest Indian friend, whom he drew into the secretaryship of the associations, was Azariah, later the first of his nation to be raised to the Anglican episcopate.[555] For a time Robert P. Wilder was secretary for students in the North and then succeeded McConaughy as national secretary.[556] In 1914 the International Committee of the Young Men's Christian Associations had more than seventy on its missionary staff in India.[557]

The National Board of the Young Women's Christian Associations did not send nearly so many representatives to India as did its brother organization. The service of the Young Women's Christian Associations was confined almost entirely to the Anglo-Indians.[558]

The Christian Endeavour movement reached India in the 1880's through existing American missions. The founder, Francis E. Clark, visited India in 1893 and 1897. At the beginning of 1897 Christian Endeavour societies numbered about 200. In that year a regional organization, the United Society of Christian Endeavour in India, Burma, and Ceylon, was formed. By 1911 there were 849 societies and the membership was approximately 32,000.[559]

In contrast with the Roman Catholics, only a small minority of the Protestant missionaries in India were from the continent of Europe. In 1914 slightly more than one out of ten of the Protestant personnel was from Continental European societies.[560] Of these the three which in 1914 had the largest staffs and together had almost four-fifths of the communicants associated with Continental churches had entered India before the Mutiny.

[554] David McConaughy, *Pioneering with Christ* (New York, Association Press, 1941, pp. 101), pp. 26ff.

[555] Eddy, *A Pilgrimage of Ideas*, pp. 86-110.

[556] Ruth Wilder Braisted, *In this Generation. The Story of Robert P. Wilder* (New York, The Student Volunteer Movement, 1941, pp. xvi, 205), pp. 81-86; Robert P. Wilder, *Christian Service among Educated Bangalese* (no place or publisher, 1895, pp. vi, 76), *passim*.

[557] Beach and St. John, *op. cit.*, p. 64.

[558] *International Survey of the Young Men's and Young Women's Christian Associations*, p. 322.

[559] McGaw in *The Christian Endeavour Manual for India, Burma and Ceylon*, pp. 18-26.

[560] Beach and St. John, *op. cit.*, pp. 64, 65.

The Basel Mission, the first to renew Continental European Protestant enterprise in India, in 1914 had by far the largest missionary body, although it was second to the Gossner Mission in communicants. After the Mutiny it continued to develop its field on the south-west coast. Although it opened new centres, it concentrated its efforts on this general area. Eventually its stations stretched from Coimbatore in the South to North Canara and to the territory west of Goa. It sought to reach several different linguistic and social groups and, unlike some of the missions we have met, was not identified with any particular community. The general outlines of the programme which it pursued through the latter half of the nineteenth century were established under the administration of Josenhans, who was the inspector, or head, of the entire society from 1850 to 1879. Through Josenhans the home committee increased its control over the mission. An ecclesiastical structure was developed with presbyteries and synods. Josenhans feared that the control of the schools of the mission by the government would mean secularization. The schools were maintained primarily for Christians. Josenhans made the theological seminary for the training of pastors the apex of the educational system. In 1870 the mission's schools came within the state system but preserved their liberty of giving religious instruction. The mercantile and industrial undertakings which had been begun before the Mutiny were continued. Independent companies were created to carry on these phases of the enterprise, but the profits were devoted to the mission's work. Few mass movements occurred to swell the ranks of the churches. Yet there was much preaching among the people and solid growth was registered. In the opening years of the twentieth century the nationalistic temper in the country hastened progress toward a larger participation by Indians in the control of the churches.[561]

The Gossner Mission, known officially as the German Evangelical Lutheran Mission, while having enterprises in Assam and in the Ganges Valley in the vicinity of Patna, concentrated chiefly on Chota Nagpur.[562] Here its phenom-

[561] Schlatter, *Geschichte der Basler Mission 1815-1915*, Vol. II, pp. 54ff.; R. Schweizer, *Die Ergebnisse der protestantischen Mission in Vorderindien mit besonderer Berücksichtigung der Leistungen der evangel. Missionsgesellschaft in Basel* (Bern, Karl H. Mann, 1868, pp. viii, 222), *passim;* Richter, *Indische Missionsgeschichte*, pp. 283-288; Richter, *Die deutsche Mission in Südindien*, pp. 14-23, 142-228; K. Hartenstein, editor, *Das Werden einer jungen Kirche im Osten: 100 Jahre Basler Missionsarbeit in Indien* (Stuttgart, Evang. Missionsverlag, 1935, pp. 127), *passim;* Johannes Layer, *Lebensbild und Zeugnisse der Wahrheit* (Basel, Missionsbuchhandlung, 1891, pp. 141).

[562] On the Gossner mission, especially its enterprises in Chota Nagpur, see Notrott, *Die Gossnersche Mission unter den Kols,* Vol. I, pp. 175ff., Vol. II, *passim;* Gerhard, *Geschichte und Beschreibung der Mission unter den Kohls in Ostindien, passim;* Karl Heinrich Christian Platt, *Gossners Mission unter Hindus und Kohls um Neujahr 1878. Reisebriefe* (Berlin, Buchhandlung der Gossnerischen Mission, 1879, pp. viii, 296), *passim;* Karl Heinrich Christian Platt, *Gossners Segenspuren in Nordindien. Eine geschichtliche*

enal gains were mainly from the Kols, animistic folk of primitive culture, village-dwelling cultivators of the soil. Kol, it must be noted, was a collective name for the aborigines. Embraced under that designation were numbers of tribes and more than one language. The first baptism was in 1850. By the time of the Mutiny the Christian community totalled about eight or nine hundred. The first missionaries were in part self-supporting, living communally by farming. During the Mutiny they were forced to flee and the Christians were persecuted. After the Mutiny the enemies of the Christians were punished. In the ensuing decade thousands of Kols became Christians. One of the reasons for the large influx seems to have been the belief that Christians were under the protection of the victorious English and that adherence to the faith would bring support in the struggle for the soil against the zemindars, or landowners.

The course of the Chota Nagpur Mission was stormy. In the late 1860's internal dissensions among the missionaries led, as we saw a few pages above, to the secession (1869) to the Church of England of the older missionaries and many of their followers. The younger men, remaining by the Gossner enterprise, reorganized the mission and its policies. They opened additional stations, set themselves to getting in closer touch with the Kols by learning the vernaculars and reducing them to writing, and established a system of schools to enable them to train an Indian staff. In 1872 for the first time a Kol was ordained. From the beginning the device of having Indian elders had been employed. It seems to have been through these that when the older missionaries went over to Anglicanism (1869) about two-thirds of the Christians held to the younger men.

The land problem and the relation of the Kols to the zemindars continued acute. Agitators, called sardars, arose out of the discontent and fanned it, insisting that Chota Nagpur belonged to the Kols, that the Moslems and Hindus, from whom the oppressive zemindars were largely drawn, should be expelled, and that appeal should be taken direct to the Queen-Empress to protect the rights of her Kol subjects. The missionaries were more and more unhappy over the movement. In 1887 an open break came and the sardars forbade their followers to attend the Lutheran churches or to send their children to the

und missionstheoretische Reisebeschreibung (Berlin, Buchhandlung der Gossnerschen Mission, 1896, pp. 162), *passim;* H. Kausch and F. Hahn, *50 Bilder aus der Gossnerschen Kols-Mission* (Berlin, Buchhandlung der Gossnerschen Mission, no date, 2d ed., pp. 96), *passim;* Ferdinand Hahn, *Einführung in das Gebiet der Kols-Mission* (Gütersloh, C. Bertelsmann, 1907, pp. viii, 158), pp. 130ff.; H. O. Kausch, *Festschrift zum 75 jährigen Bestehen der Gossnerschen Mission* (Berlin, Gossnersche Mission, 1911, pp. 204), pp. 51ff.; Richter, *Nordindische Missionsfahrten,* pp. 1-115; Richter, *Indische Missionsgeschichte,* pp. 305-328; *Stand und Arbeit der Gossnerschen Mission in Jahre 1905/1906* (Berlin, Gossnersche Mission, 1906, pp. 152), *passim.*

Gossner schools. In consequence, hundreds of Christians withdrew from the churches. It was due to the hope of assistance in their economic and social problems that many had accepted the Christian faith. When that help was denied them in the form in which they demanded it, angered and disillusioned, they broke away. In the 1890's a former Christian, Daud Birsa, led a movement which combined religious and social elements and which allied itself to the sardars. It brought together ingredients of Christian, pagan, and Moslem provenance, proclaimed the imminent end of the world, forbade sacrifices to demons, the eating of beef and pork, and (on the ground that Christ had preached in the out-of-doors) religious services in churches and chapels. To the attesting of the truth of the message miracles were alleged. An outbreak against the English and the zemindars ensued. Daud Birsa was arrested, clapped into prison, and there (in 1900) died of cholera.[563] His following and that of the sardars disintegrated. The indigenous disturbances arising from the land problem were complicated for the Gossner Mission by the presence of the Anglicans and the Roman Catholics. The advent of each of these other religious bodies meant initial schisms from Lutheran ranks.

Yet the Gossner enterprise in Chota Nagpur continued and flourished. Reinforcements and funds came from Germany. Church buildings were erected. Schools, for both boys and girls, were multiplied. In the 1890's and after 1900 additional stations were opened, especially in regions in which new mass accessions to Christianity had taken place. The mission in Assam, inaugurated in 1901, was begun to care for the Kols who had gone there as labourers on the tea plantations. Indian pastors, catechists, school-teachers, Bible-women, and colporteurs continued to be trained and utilized. At the end of 1905 the baptized Lutheran Christians numbered 67,321, as against about 15,000 Anglicans and 60,000 Roman Catholics. In 1913 the number of baptized was nearly 84,000. Leper asylums were founded. Orphans and sufferers from famine were cared for. There was medical service. Of the Lutheran Christians, in 1905 about 8,000 could read and scores were finding employment under the government. A literature had been prepared in the vernaculars. The houses of Christians were said to be cleaner than those of their non-Christian neighbours. Polygamy was forbidden and Christians were discouraged from the eating of carrion and the drinking of alcoholic beverages.

The Leipzig Mission which fell heir to much of the earlier Danish-Halle enterprise among the Tamils and which had its chief centre at Tranquebar, in foreign staff and numbers of Indian Christians did not attain to the dimen-

---

[563] On this movement, in addition to references in the preceding footnote, see a Roman Catholic account in Hoffmann, *37 Jahre Missionär in Indien,* pp. 8, 9.

sions of either the Basel or the Gossner undertakings. In 1914, however, in missionary body and communicants it ranked next to these among the Continental European missions.[564] The Leipzig missionaries cherished the tradition of their Danish-Halle predecessors. They held to the liturgy, hymnal, catechism, and translation of the Bible prepared by the latter. After severe controversy which all but disrupted the mission and was carried to the home constituency, the policy was confirmed of maintaining the inherited attitude of leniency with caste differences among Christians. For many years reinforcements were few and the growth of the Christian communities was slow. In 1876 there were only 11 missionaries to supervise 9,200 Christians. Between 1877 and 1885 no new missionaries arrived. The inherited constituency was largely from the Sudras, among the middle and upper social strata of the Tamils. In the course of the years numbers from lower social levels, impelled to some extent by the desire to have their physical needs met, sought Christian instruction. They were cared for in part by Tamil pastors of Sudra background. In 1914, of the nearly 22,000 Christians connected with the Leipzig enterprise, about 8,000 were of Sudra and approximately 14,000 of outcaste provenance. Karl Graul, who as director of the society in its formative years determined the main lines of its subsequent policies, dreamed of creating a Tamil national church. For this an Indian pastorate and independent congregations were necessary. A theological seminary was founded, but some of its products proved disappointments and the progress toward self-supporting, self-governing congregations was not as rapid as had been hoped. Yet advance was registered. Activities for women were undertaken. Schools for girls were developed, with women teachers. There were schools for boys and a mission press. Attempts were made at Christian group agricultural settlements on pieces of land which had been purchased for that purpose. There was some medical work.[565]

Even before the Mutiny Swedes had begun to co-operate with the Leipzig Mission. Originally it was hoped that a society representing the Swedish Lutherans but independent of the state would develop an extensive participation in the Lutheran enterprise of the Leipzig society. This dream, however, was

[564] Beach and St. John, *World Statistics of Christian Missions*, p. 65.
[565] Fleisch, *Hundert Jahre lutherischer Mission, passim;* Richter, *Indische Missionsgeschichte,* pp. 289-301; Richter, *Die deutsche Mission in Südindien,* pp. 32ff.; Karsten, *Die Geschichte der evangelisch-lutherischen Mission in Leipzig,* Vol. I, pp. 166ff., Vol. II, *passim;* Handmann, *Die Evangelisch-lutherische Tamulen-Mission in der Zeit ihrer Neubegründung,* pp. 400ff.; Rautenberg, *Rundschau über die Geschichte der dänisch-sächsischen evangelisch-lutherischen Mission unter den Tamulen* (Leipzig, Buchhandlung des Vereinshauses 1888, pp. iv, 195), pp. 70ff.; Cordes, *Heinrich Cordes, passim;* Alwin Gehring, *Johannes Kabis, ein Vater der Paria* (Leipzig, Verlag der Evangelischen-lutherischen Mission, no date, pp. 78), *passim.*

only feebly fulfilled. In 1874 an official Swedish Church Mission with the Swedish primate as its head came into being and in 1877 succeeded to the share in the Leipzig undertaking previously assumed by an earlier society in Stockholm. The Swedes wished their Indian activities to be independent of the German society. In 1901, after long strain and controversy, a separate diocese was created for the Swedes with Madura as its centre.[566]

The Danish Lutherans not unnaturally desired to continue to have a part in the enterprise through which in the eighteenth century they had helped to initiate Protestant missions in India. In 1847, two years after the cession of Tranquebar to Great Britain had ended the Danish rule in that scene of the beginning of the Danish-Halle undertaking, the Collegium through which the Danes had conducted their mission transferred its interests to the Dresden (from the following year the Leipzig) society.[567] However, the Danish Missionary Society, which had been organized in 1821, eventually wished to assume independent responsibilities in India. It found itself unable to join with the Leipzig Mission, for in contrast with the latter it declined to tolerate caste. After the Mutiny it developed a small enterprise in the South which by 1914 had centres in Madras, Bangalore, and South Arcot.[568] In 1910 it had 22 missionaries, 5 Indian clergy, and 1,263 Christians, and five years later 44 missionaries, 6 Indian clergy, and 2,210 Christians.[569]

It was through a former missionary of the Leipzig society, Mylius, that the Hermannsburg mission entered India. In the years 1847-1851 Mylius had served in India as a Leipzig appointee, then had gone back to Europe and had there been a pastor. He wished to return to India and in 1864 his friend, Louis Harms, the founder of the Hermannsburg mission, sent him out. Mylius found a field among the Telugus in the general vicinity of Nellore. He was welcomed by the American Baptist, Jewett, who declared that there was room for them both. Reinforcements were sent, but the Hermannsburg enterprise was never large.[570]

[566] Fleisch, op. cit., pp. 89, 90, 173-175; Harald Frykholm, Mannen och Missionären. Sjalvbiografiska Antechningar med Tillägg av Hans Maka (Stockholm, Svenska Kyrkans Diakonistyrelses Bokförlag, 1937, pp. 203); Sandegren, Svensk Mission och Indisk Kyrka, passim.
[567] Fleisch, op. cit., pp. 29, 30.
[568] Fleisch, op. cit., pp. 85, 89; T. Løgstrup, Den nyere danske Mission blandt Tamulerne (Copenhagen, Chr. Christiansen, 1885, pp. 240), pp. 89ff.; C. H. Kalkar, editor, Den danske Mission i Ostindien i de seneste Aar. En Samling af Breve (Copenhagen, Grœbes Bogtrykkeri, 1870, pp. xxi, 274), passim; Knud Heiberg, Madras. Lidt om Byen og Missionen (Copenhagen, Det Danske Missionsselskab, 1913, pp. 40), passim.
[569] Niels Bundgaard, Billeder fra D.M.S.s Missionsarbejde i Indien (Der danske Missionsselskab, 1937, pp. 56), 57.
[570] Richter, Indische Missionsgeschichte, pp. 301, 302; Richter, Die deutsche Mission in Südindien, pp. 229ff.; Johann Wörrlein, Die Hermannsburger Mission in Indien (Her-

In 1882 another German Lutheran missionary organization came to the east coast of India. This was the Schleswig-Holstein Evangelical Lutheran Missionary Society at Breklum. On the advice of the American Lutherans of the General Council it found a field somewhat north of most of those of the other Lutheran bodies which we have thus far mentioned. This was on the fringe of the Telugu area, north of the mouth of the Godavari, in and near the Eastern Ghats, some distance south of Chota Nagpur. The first continuing station was in the small city of Salur. Other stations were later developed. Here, among Telugus and various animistic, low caste, and outcaste folk, partly in the native state of Jeypore, the Breklum society gathered and nourished Christian communities which in 1914 numbered over four thousand communicants and over twelve thousand baptized non-communicants.[571]

Other societies from the continent of Europe were the *Evangeliska Fosterlands-Stiftelsen* (Evangelical National Missionary Society) of Sweden, which we met in the preceding chapter in Ethiopia and which, beginning in 1877, developed an enterprise in the Central Provinces;[572] the *Kvinnliga Missions Arbetare;* the Swedish Alliance Mission; and the *Teltmissionen.*[573]

One of the most remarkable of the Continental European enterprises was what was first called the Indian Home Mission to the Santals and eventually the Santal Mission of the Northern Churches. It owed its beginning and most of its growth to a Dane, H. P. Boerresen (1825-1901), and a Norwegian, Lars Olsen Skrefsrud (1840-1910). Boerresen, a mechanical engineer, had a religious awakening while in Berlin and, with his young wife, felt impelled to become a missionary. Skrefsrud came to Berlin with a letter of introduction to Boerresen. Skrefsrud had a mother who was committed to the Haugean revival, but, after her death and while yet in his teens, he had fallen into evil ways and had served a term in prison. Through a girl who later became his wife and who, like his mother, was indebted spiritually to the Haugean movement, he had a remarkable conversion while he was in prison. He resolved to become a missionary, found himself viewed with suspicion by the missionary college in

mannsburg, Missionshandlung, 1899, pp. vii, 236), pp. 24ff.; Johann Wörrlein, *Dreizehn Jahre in Indien* (Hermannsburg, Missionsdruckerei, 2d ed., 1885, pp. vi, 248), *passim;* Johann Wörrlein, *Vierzig Jahre in Indien* (Hermannsburg, Missionshandlung, 1913, pp. 263), *passim.*
  [571] Richter, *Indische Missionsgeschichte,* pp. 302-305; Beach and St. John, *World Statistics of Christian Missions,* p. 65; Gloyer, *Geschichte unserer Missionsstation Kotapad in Jeypur (Vorderindien)* (Breklum, Missionshaus, 1907, pp. 135), *passim;* Bracker, *Die Breklumer Mission in Indien. Ein Reisebericht* (Breklum, Missionshaus, no date [the journey was in 1911-1912], pp. 653), *passim.*
  [572] *Evangeliska Fosterlands-Stiftelsens Årsberättelse för . . . 1913* (Stockholm, pp. 284), pp. 122-138.
  [573] Beach and St. John, *op. cit.,* p. 65.

his native Norway to which he applied for admission, and went to Berlin. In Berlin he was befriended by Boerresen and studied in the Gossner mission school. In 1863 he went to India under the Gossner mission and two years later was followed by the Boerresens. Because of strains with their German colleagues arising from the war between Denmark and Prussia, Boerresen and Skrefsrud left the Gossner mission and in 1867 went to Bengarhia in Bihar and Orissa near the western border of Bengal and began a mission of their own among a primitive folk, the Santals. In the first few years the necessary funds came largely from India, raised by Boerresen. Skrefsrud proved to be an amazing linguist. He compiled a grammar of the Santal tongue which was long standard. He studied Santal customs and laboured to introduce the Christian faith in such fashion as to work as slight a disturbance as possible in native life. He composed hymns and set them to folk tunes. Largely through Boerresen and Skrefsrud, support came from Norway, Denmark, and Scandinavians in the United States. Reinforcements arrived. Conversions multiplied. By the time of Skrefsrud's death the churches connected with his mission had a membership of over fifteen thousand. It was through Skrefsrud, too, that thousands of Santals moved from their somewhat unfruitful habitat to virgin fertile soil in Assam.[574]

We must notice the continuation of that Moravian endeavour to enter Tibet by way of India whose inception in pre-Mutiny days we recorded some pages back. In the nature of the situation the mission could not be expected to attain large dimensions. The Moravians were a small body with commitments in several other parts of the world. In seeking to penetrate Tibet they were confronted by a land which was all but closed to foreigners, was physically difficult of access, and was dominated by a powerful Buddhist hierarchy. It was in 1856 that the first station was begun. By the close of the year 1900 four others had been founded and a missionary had been placed at Simla. A handful of converts had been won. It was a long siege to which the Moravians had settled down and to which patient faith was essential.[575]

[574] Mathew A. Pederson, *In the Land of the Santals* (New York, 1929), *passim;* M. A. Pederson, *Sketches from Santalistan* (Minneapolis, Den Lutherske Missionaer, 1913, pp. 187), *passim,* especially pp. 180-187; W. J. Culshaw in *The International Review of Missions,* Vol. XXXI, pp. 347-353; Scheurer, *Lars Olsen Skrefsrud* (Stuttgart, Evang. Missionsverlag, 1933, pp. 61), *passim;* Ivar Saeter, *Lars Olsen Skrefsrud,* translated by Anna Plieninger and Anna Oehler (Stuttgart, Evang. Missionsverlag, 1930, pp. vi, 204); Ludvig Hertel, *Den nordiske Santhalmission* (Copenhagen, 1884, pp. 344), *passim;* Ludvig Hertel, *Indisk Hjemmemission blandt Santalerne ved H. P. Børresen og L. O. Skrefsrud* (Kolding, Indisk Hjemmemission, 1877, pp. 242), *passim;* N. N. Rønning, *Lars O. Skrefsrud, an Apostle to the Santals* (Minneapolis, The Santal Mission in America, 1940, pp. 93), *passim.*

[575] H. G. Schneider, *Leh in Kaschmir. Eine Missionstation der Brüdergemeine* (Herrn-

In addition to societies which were foreign in origin, there were a number of organizations which arose primarily in India and which shared in the propagation of the Christian faith. Some of these were initiated by Europeans. Others were of Indian inception and leadership. We must not undertake even to catalogue all of them.

Among those of foreign creation were the Christian Literature Society for India, really of British origin as the Christian Literature Society for India and Africa, organized in 1858, and by 1914 with four regional branches in India;[576] the North India Christian Tract and Book Society, begun at Agra in 1848 with a member of the civil service as its first president and in later years with an Indian as secretary for three decades;[577] the Calcutta Tract and Book Society and similar ones in Bangalore, Bombay, Madras, the Punjab, and South Travancore, all but one of them begun before the Mutiny and all assisted by the Religious Tract Society of England;[578] the Board for Tamil Christian Literature, representing a union of twelve missions and societies in the Tamil field and formed in 1905;[579] the Boys' Christian Home Mission, dating from 1900;[580] the Dohnavur Fellowship, organized in 1901;[581] the Highways and Hedges Mission, constituted in 1875;[582] the Railway Mission;[583] the Home Missionary Society of India, founded in 1905 as the Women's Home Missionary Society of India, with the purpose of arousing Anglo-Indians and Eurasians to a sense of responsibility for the conversion of India;[584] the India Sunday School Union, begun in 1876 to aid in promoting Sunday schools in India;[585] and the United Council on Work among Young People in India, formed in 1907 to assist denominational and other agencies in the development of the Christian life of the youth.[586]

Some enterprises with Indian headquarters had Indian leadership, but depended in part on foreign aid. Such were the Mukti Mission, undenomina-

hut, Missionsbuchhandlung, no date, pp. 104) ; G. Th. Reichelt, *Die Himalaya-Mission der Brüdergemeine* (Gutersloh, C. Bertelsmann, 1896, pp. 87) ; H. Schneider, *Ein Missionsfeld aus dem Westlichen Himalaya* (Gnadau, Unitäts-Buchhandlung, 1880, pp. iv, 95).

[576] Strong and Warnshuis, *Directory of Foreign Missions*, p. 205.

[577] J. J. Lucas, *History of the North India Christian Tract and Book Society, Allahabad, 1848-1934* (Allahabad, The North India Christian Tract and Book Society, no date, pp. 116), *passim*.

[578] Strong and Warnshuis, *op. cit.*, p. 208.

[579] Strong and Warnshuis, *op. cit.*, p. 204.

[580] *Ibid.*

[581] Strong and Warnshuis, *op. cit.,* p. 205.

[582] Strong and Warnshuis, *op. cit.*, p. 206.

[583] Inglis, *Protestant Missionary Directory of India for 1912-1913*, p. 91.

[584] Strong and Warnshuis, *op. cit.*, p. 206.

[585] *Ibid.*

[586] Jones, *The Year Book of Missions in India, Burma and Ceylon, 1912*, pp. 422-424.

tional, formed in 1887 to support the enterprises of Pandita Ramabai, of whom we are later to hear more, and in 1913 with a staff of twenty foreigners from England, America, and Australia and a contingent of Indians; [587] and Keskari's Christian Mission at Sholapur, begun in 1899.[588]

Several societies were primarily or entirely Indian in personnel and support and were indications that Protestant Christianity was becoming sufficiently rooted to stir its Indian adherents to undertake the winning of their fellow countrymen to their faith. Notable was the National Missionary Society of India. This was brought into being in Serampore in 1905 and was inter-denominational. It had V. Z. Azariah, later bishop, as its first secretary. A little more than twenty years after its inception it had a staff of ninety-seven working in five different parts of India.[589] Azariah was also active in the formation (1903) of the Indian Missionary Society of Tinnevelly, connected with the Anglican communion. It found a field in the state of Hyderabad among the Telugus out of which grew the diocese of Dornakal over which Azariah in time became bishop.[590] There was, too, the Mar Thoma Syrian Christian Evengelistic Association, representing the effort of the branch of the ancient Syrian communion which had been most affected by the Anglican enter-prise.[591] We hear also of the Travancore and Cochin Church Missionary Asso-ciation, established in 1889; the Home Mission of the Ludhiana Church Council (begun in 1895); the Home Mission of the Khasia and Jaintia Hills, in Assam (commenced in 1901); the Gospel Extension Society of the Madras Church Council of the South India United Church (inaugurated in 1903); the Madura Home Missionary Society (founded 1908); the Home Mission of the Allahabad Presbytery; the Home Mission of the Gujarat and Kathiawar Presbytery; the Home Mission of the Sialkot Presbytery; the Home Mission of the Rajputana Presbytery; the South India Missionary Society; [592] the Indian Baptist Missionary Society, in Bengal (founded in 1899); and the Telugu Baptist Home Mission Society (founded in 1897).[593] Even the mere list of these organizations, with their dates of inception, is significant. They began late in the nineteenth century and were mounting in the first decade of the twentieth century. They are evidence of a rapidly increasing participation by

[587] Jones, op. cit., p. 427; Beach and St. John, op. cit., p. 65.
[588] Jones, op. cit., p. 427.
[589] Philip, Report on a Survey of Indigenous Christian Efforts in India, Burma, and Ceylon, pp. 2-11; Mackenzie, The Christian Task in India, pp. 204-208; Eddy, A Pilgrimage of Ideas, pp. 96, 97.
[590] Eddy, op. cit., p. 96; Mackenzie, op. cit., p. 210; Gledstone, South India, pp. 56, 57.
[591] Mackenzie, op. cit., p. 210; Philip, op. cit., p. 9.
[592] Philip, op. cit., pp. 5-9.
[593] Warneck, Geschichte der protestantischen Missionen, p. 176.

Indian Protestant Christians in the propagation of their faith. As might have been expected, the major part, although by no means all, of this effort by Indian Protestant Christians was from the South, where Protestant Christianity had been longer established and was numerically stronger than in the North. So far as formal societies were concerned, the total amount, in numbers of personnel and of converts won, was less than that of one of the foreign societies of medium size. Organized Indian Christian activity in spreading the faith was rapidy mounting, but it had only begun to get under way.

We need not give much separate space to the methods employed by Protestant missions. In spite of the multiplicity of societies and denominations engaged in propagating the Protestant forms of Christianity, in procedures nearly all bore a striking family likeness. Nearly every society displayed unique features, and emphasis on one or another method varied from organization to organization. Yet through the programmes of most societies ran a common pattern. They also resembled those of nineteenth century Protestant missions in other lands. In the preceding pages we have, in connexion with our accounts of the individual religious bodies, incidentally spoken of the plans which were followed. We can, therefore, cover in a few summary paragraphs the processes by which Protestant Christianity addressed itself to its Indian task.[594]

One method, fairly obvious, was preaching to non-Christians. Part of this was itinerant, from village to village. Much was in the bazaars or market places of the cities and large towns. Some was at popular religious festivals, or melas, which brought together crowds. Part of it was by foreigners. As time passed, more of it was by Indian Christians. Foreigners became absorbed in institutions and the care of churches. While efforts were not lacking to reverse the trend, and some missions were more insistent than others that Westerners participate in this phase of the Christian enterprise, the drift was toward assigning to Indians this portion of the programme.[595]

Protestant missions placed great emphasis upon schools.[596] In these a pre-

---

[594] Some of the books which are devoted to Protestant missionary methods or which include more or less comprehensive pictures of them are Georg Stosch, *Im fernen Indien. Eindrücke und Erfahrungen im Dienst der lutherischen Mission unter den Tamulen* (Berlin, Martin Warneck, 1896, pp. vi, 223); J. P. Jones, *A Volume in Commemoration of the Opening of the Twentieth Century by South India Protestant Missions* (Pasumalai, American Mission Press, 1900, pp. 74); Robert P. Wilder, *Christian Service among Educated Bengalese* (no place or publisher, 1895, pp. vi, 76); Wm. C. Irvine, *Handbook for Indian Christian Workers* (The Literature Committee, "Christian Missions in Many Lands," no date, pp. 89); John Murdoch, *Indian Missionary Manual. Hints to Young Missionaries in India* (London, James Nisbet & Co., 4th ed., 1895, pp. xi, 535).

[595] Richter, *Indische Missionsgeschichte*, pp. 391-395; Jones, *The Year Book of Missions in India, Burma and Ceylon, 1912*, pp. 244ff.; Murdoch, *Indian Missionary Manual*, pp. 133-199.

[596] Jones, *op. cit.*, pp. 270ff.; Richter, *op. cit.*, pp. 419-443; *The Christian College in*

dominately Western type of education was given. In the Occidental forms of education missionaries were pioneers. Until the Mutiny they had a practical monopoly of elementary schools of Western types and about half the enroll-ment in higher schools was in Protestant institutions. Duff and the Scottish Presbyterians were especially prominent in introducing Western higher edu-cation under Christian auspices. Eventually extensive financial assistance in the form of grants-in-aid came from the government. For schools so supported there were government supervision and inspection. Government help was given, not because the schools were Christian but because they were schools. However, it encouraged missions to undertake education rather more exten-sively than they might otherwise have done. For instance, far more colleges were maintained by Protestants in India than in China, although, in 1914 the Protestant missionary staff and the total population in China were larger than in India.

Differences of educational policy existed. Some missions, at least for a time, declined to fit into the government system. Some maintained schools only for Christians. The majority encouraged the enrolment of non-Christians and regarded the schools as a means of winning converts. Duff had thought of Christian higher education as an instrument for gaining accessions for the Church from the higher classes and for destroying much of Indian culture. Another greater Scottish educator, Miller, of the Madras Christian College, conceived the purpose of the Christian college to be, rather, the gradual per-meation of Indian life by Christianity, a preparation for the eventual acceptance by the entire country of the Christian faith.[597]

Special types of schools were maintained—industrial, normal, and theological. Much emphasis was placed upon training leadership for the emerging churches. Protestant missions, too, stressed the education of women.

Protestant efforts for the educated were not confined to Christian schools. Attempts were made to reach students in non-Christian institutions. Some missionaries were set aside for them. Hostels were maintained in which the students could live under Christian influence. A few special lecturers came from the Occident for brief periods to address students.[598]

We must remember that personal contacts counted for much, whether made through preaching, schools, or in other ways.

Attention was paid to the preparation, printing, and distribution of literature which would present the Christian message directly to non-Christians, help to

India, pp. 33-38; Allen and McClure, Two Hundred Years. The History of the Society for Promoting Christian Knowledge, pp. 289-303; Murdoch, op. cit., pp. 380-439.

[597] Braisted, Indian Nationalism and the Christian Colleges, pp. 86-91.

[598] Richter, op. cit., pp. 443-449; Jones, op. cit., pp. 344-355.

instruct and nourish Christians in their faith, or leaven Indian thought with Christian ideals. There were many translations of the Bible,[599] and various societies, including the British and Foreign Bible Society and its several local auxiliaries, the American Bible Society, the National Bible Society of Scotland, the Society for Promoting Christian Knowledge, the Bible Translation Society, and the Tranquebar Tamil Bible Society, aided in translating, printing, and distributing the Scriptures.[600] In 1861 nearly a score [601] and in 1914 more than two score of mission presses published Christian literature.[602] Quantities of literature were issued in English and the vernaculars.[603] In 1914 more than one hundred magazines, newspapers, and periodicals were published, most of them by missions rather than by Indian Christians, either in English or in one of the vernaculars.[604] Book shops and colporteurs assisted in the sale of the literature so produced.[605] J. N. Farquhar as a secretary of the Young Men's Christian Associations inaugurated a new era in the production of Christian literature and helped to bring about a reorientation of the Protestant missions towards non-Christian religions.[606]

As was so largely true of Protestant missions elsewhere in the nineteenth and twentieth centuries, much emphasis was placed upon medical care. This was in part for the purpose of relieving physical suffering and in part as a means of propagating the Christian faith. Hospitals and dispensaries were maintained; and there was training of physicians and nurses. The number of medical missionaries and nurses paralleled the rapid development of medical science in the West in the latter half of the nineteenth century. In 1889 there were said to be 60 medical missionaries in India and on the eve of 1914, 335. In 1912 the number of foreign nurses was 294.[607]

What may be called a special phase of medical missions was care for lepers. It was a foreshadowing of what Protestant missions were to do that Carey opened a leper asylum. In 1915 Protestants had twenty-five such institutions. Of these the majority were assisted by the Mission to Lepers in India, a society

[599] Richter, op. cit., pp. 395-405.
[600] Warneck, Geschichte der protestantischen Missionen, p. 415; Mullens, A Brief Review of Ten Years' Missionary Labour in India, pp. 149-151.
[601] Mullens, op. cit., p. 163.
[602] Jones, op. cit., pp. 356-363; Richter, op. cit., p. 409.
[603] Jones, op. cit., pp. 337-340; Richter, op. cit., pp. 405-419.
An impressive set of lists of Christian literature made up in 1917, 1918, and 1919 by various authors and agencies for different sections and language groups was bound and issued under the back title Surveys and Reports of Christian Literature in India, 1918.
[604] Jones, op. cit., pp. 341-343, 638-648.
[605] Murdoch, op. cit., pp. 448-458.
[606] The Christian College in India, p. 129.
[607] Wanless, An American Doctor in India, passim; Richter, op. cit., pp. 468-478; Jones, op. cit., pp. 364-375.

formed in 1874 and later broadened to include the entire world in its scope.[608]

Again and again we have noted the relief given by missionaries during the famines which were long such a tragically recurring feature of Indian life.[609] As a form of that relief children orphaned in these times of dearth were gathered into homes and reared as Christians.[610]

Partly as an outgrowth of the mass movements of outcastes towards Christianity which were so marked a feature of the spread of Protestantism, were efforts to help improve the physical status of these poverty-stricken converts. Here and there were agricultural colonies formed by settling Christians on land acquired for that purpose.[611] A few experts on agriculture were included in the missionary body. They sought to devise and inculcate improved methods of making the most out of the soil and domestic animals.[612]

Of growing importance were the activities of women for members of their own sex. Some of this was through visiting women in their homes. Some was by schools.[613] Women physicians ministered to women in the name of Christ.[614]

Here and there were missionaries who urged that the immediate purpose of missions should not be the winning of avowed converts and the building of distinct Christian communities, but rather the permeation of all Indian life by Christianity looking towards the eventual conversion of the entire country *en masse.*[615] However, the overwhelming majority of the missionaries sought, whether by preaching, teaching, medical care, or some other form of ministry,

[608] Richter, *op. cit.,* pp. 478-489; W. C. Irvine, *25 Years Mission Work among the Lepers of India* (London, Pickering & Inglis, no date, pp. 144), *passim;* John Jackson, *Lepers. Thirty-Six Years Work among Them. Being the History of the Mission to Lepers in India and the East, 1874-1910* (London, Marshall Brothers, 1910, pp. xvi, 208), *passim;* Wellesley C. Bailey, *A Glimpse at the Indian Mission-Field and Leper Asylums in 1886-87* (London, John F. Shaw and Co., 1888, pp. iv, 188); Wellesley C. Bailey, *The Lepers of Our Indian Empire. A Visit to Them in 1890-91* (Edinburgh, The Darien Press, 1899, pp. viii, 249), *passim.*
[609] As in Pascoe, *Two Hundred Years of the S.P.G.,* p. 599c.
[610] Richter, *op. cit.,* pp. 494ff.
[611] Phillips, *The Outcastes' Hope,* pp. 57-60.
[612] Christlieb, *Indian Neighbours,* pp. 84-94; Hunnicutt and Reid, *The Story of Agricultural Missions,* pp. 17, 27-35.
[613] Richter, *op. cit.,* pp. 449-462; Jones, *op. cit.,* pp. 376-387; Murdoch, *op. cit.,* pp. 459-480.
[614] Margaret I. Balfour and Ruth Young, *The Work of Medical Women in India* (Oxford University Press, 1929, pp. xiv, 201), pp. 75-89. For a few concrete lives see Arley Munson, *Jungle Days. Being the Experiences of an American Woman Doctor in India* (New York, D. Appleton and Co., 1913, pp. viii, 298); Charlotte E. Vines, *In and Out of Hospital. Sketches of Medical Work in an Indian Village Mission* (London, Church of England Zenana Missionary Society, 1905, pp. 192); and Charlotte E. Vines, *Indian Medical Sketches* (London, Church of England Zenana Medical Missionary Society, 1908, pp. viii, 127).
[615] See this view presented in Bernard Lucas, *The Empire of Christ* (London, Macmillan and Co., 1908, pp. vii, 151) and Bernard Lucas, *Our Task in India. Shall We Proselyte Hindus or Evangelize India?* (London, Macmillan and Co., 1914, pp. x, 183).

to lead men and women into the Christian life and to an open profession of their faith, and to bring into existence and nourish Indian churches. To this end converts were baptized, churches were gathered, and catechists and clergy were trained.[616] By the year 1914 notable progress had been registered and Indian Protestant Christian communities were beginning to act on their own initiative in propagating their faith and in associating themselves together for various objectives.[617]

We have said that in the nineteenth century the expansion of Christianity in India was almost entirely through Roman Catholic and Protestant effort. This is true. However, there were accessions, even though slight, to the ancient Syrian bodies. Thus some Brahmins seem to have joined themselves to the Syrian Church, especially because they had been expelled from their caste for what their fellows deemed misdemeanours.[618] In 1888 within the Mar Thoma Syrian Church there was organized, as we saw a few pages above, the Mar Thoma Syrian Christian Evangelistic Association. It found its field chiefly among the depressed classes.[619] By 1912 the Jacobite Syrian Church was maintaining missionaries and had about twenty-five congregations of converts from the depressed classes.[620]

From our narrative of the spread of Roman Catholic and Protestant Christianity in India during the century preceding 1914 and our brief note of the minor part which the Syrian bodies had in that expansion, we must proceed to an attempt to describe and appraise the effects of Christianity in that period.[621]

To those who have had the patience to make their way through the preceding pages of this chapter it must be clear that the influence of Christianity was mounting as the century proceeded. In numbers of professed adherents and in the working of its leaven in many aspects of life, Christianity was having an increasing place in the Indian scene. Many of its effects were the direct result of missions. Others were due to the efforts of British Christians in the gov-

[616] Richter, op. cit., pp. 512-522.
[617] See some instances of this in Jones, op. cit., pp. 209-226, 433-436.
[618] E. A. Varghese in Asia, Vol. XXXII, pp. 121, 122.
[619] Philip, Report on a Survey of Indigenous Christian Efforts in India, Burma, and Ceylon, p. 4.
[620] The Year Book of Missions in India, Burma and Ceylon, 1912, pp. 146, 147.
[621] For an excellent brief although incomplete account of the effect of Christianity on India, see A. I. Mayhew in L. S. S. O'Malley, Modern India and the West. A Study of the Interaction of their Civilizations (Oxford University Press, 1941, pp. xii, 834), pp. 305-337.

ernment in India or working through Parliament and the India Office in Great Britain. Some sprang from the presence of Christianity as an integral element in the culture of the Occident which through the British connexion was permeating and altering the life of India. In many instances it is fairly easy to determine through which of these channels Christianity produced a particular effect. In others Christian influence came by more than one avenue. As in so much of the rest of our study, moreover, it is often impossible to assess accurately the share of Christianity in a particular movement. We may be fairly sure that it had a part but we cannot demonstrate precisely the extent of its responsibility.

We pass first of all to those results of Christianity which were wrought primarily through the activities of missions.

Of these the most obvious were the Christian communities. Earlier in the chapter we noted the numerical strength of Christianity near the year 1914. In 1911, we reported, Roman Catholics were said to number 2,223,546, and Protestants, in the year 1914, not far from 1,000,000. Both Roman Catholics and Protestants were most numerous in the South, below the latitude of Bombay. Here, too, were most of the Syrian Christians. The relative strength of the different branches of Christianity varied greatly from region to region.[622] At the outset of the nineteenth century, Roman Catholics, thanks to earlier missions, had been much more numerous than Protestants. Proportionately, however, the latter increased much more rapidly in that century than did the former. The difference in rate of growth was due in part to the handicap to Roman Catholicism of the prolonged controversy over the Portuguese padroado, in part to the much larger foreign staff sent by Protestants in the course of the century, and, perhaps, although much less tangibly, to the fact that the ruling power, Great Britain, was officially Protestant.

To what degree it was the compulsive winsomeness of Christianity as a religion which drew the converts who were the bases of these totals we cannot surely know. Nor can we be certain of the extent to which the children of converts were shaped by their inherited belief and how far by other factors. Obviously the motives which led converts to accept Christianity were mixed and differed from individual to individual. Clearly, too, many, particularly of the outcastes, were first attracted by the desire for food, for the protection of the foreigner, and for larger social, intellectual, and economic opportunity for themselves and their children. Among other impelling forces were disgust with idolatry, dissatisfaction with popular forms and expressions of religion,

[622] For statistical tables showing these variations and also for tables showing the total strength of each of the major communions, see J. C. Houpert, a Jesuit of Madura, in *Die katholischen Missionen*, Vol. XLI (Feb., 1913), pp. 116, 117.

a sense of sinfulness with a consciousness of moral impotence, the desire for a saviour from sin and its power, the attraction of Christ, a search for inner rest which had failed of satisfaction through the inherited faiths, the desire for service, and the fear of hell and of judgment to come.[623]

The changes wrought in the individual, whether by conversion from a non-Christian religion or by the conscious acceptance and deepening of an inherited Christianity, also varied greatly. That they tended, in general, to progressive conformity to Christian standards is clear.[624]

We must remember that the Christian would hold that the most important results of his faith are on the other side of the grave in an eternal life of adoring love of God. Into this realm the historian cannot expect the arts of his craft to enable him to penetrate. They are beyond history.

Yet there are results within history. Some of these we can record. They can be made vivid by telling of a few individuals.

Here was a professional brigand who, after his baptism, did not rob but helped travellers. Robberies were done in his name, and, when at last he was apprehended by the police, he offered no resistance and was shot and killed.[625]

We read of a non-Christian holy man who through the Gospel according to St. John found in the Christ it portrayed the satisfaction of his own quest, and led many of his former disciples to follow him into his new faith.[626]

One of the most famous of Indian Christian women was Pandita Ramabai (1858-1922).[627] Her father, a learned Brahmin and Hindu saint, taught her Sanskrit and the Hindu sacred writings. He and her mother died in the famine of 1876-1877. She and her brother eventually made their way to Calcutta. Here she was marked out as unusual as a learned woman and unmarried. She longed for the emancipation of her sex and was distressed by the sad lot of the out-castes. Eventually she married a Bengali lawyer, but after nineteen months of happy wedded life cholera took him from her and she was left a widow with a daughter. Increasingly she determined to give herself to the women of her country. She had lost confidence in Hinduism and felt herself desperately in need of a religious faith. In her spiritual pilgrimage she was deeply indebted to the Wantage Sisters and it was partly through them that she was led to

---

[623] Annett, *Conversion in India,* pp. 14-32, 118-136.

[624] See some of these in Annett, *op. cit.,* pp. 33-55, 156-173.

[625] Amy Carmichael, *Raj, the Brigand Chief* (New York, Fleming H. Revell Co., no date, pp. 312), *passim;* Singha and Shepherd, *More Yarns on India,* pp. 7-18.

[626] Stevenson, *Without the Pale,* pp. 75ff.

[627] Helen S. Dyer, *Pandita Ramabai* (Chicago, Fleming H. Revell Co., 1900, pp. 170); Clementina Butler, *Pandita Ramabai Saravasti* (New York, Fleming H. Revell Co., 1922, pp. 96); Nicol Macnicol, *Pandita Ramabai* (London, Student Christian Movement, 1926, pp. vi, 147).

ask for baptism (in 1883, while in England). After studying in Britain and America, she returned to India. There she undertook education, especially in the form of a home for widows. This institution, at first in Bombay, in 1890 was moved to Poona. The famine of 1896 led her to make provision for several hundred girls who were left stranded by it. At Mukti, about thirty miles from Poona, she developed an additional institution, largely for girls of low caste. On this she more and more concentrated her effort. Help in personnel and funds came from Britain, America, Australia, New Zealand, and Sweden. Her own faith grew and many of her girls became Christian, hundreds of them through a highly emotional revival at Mukti in 1901. Clearly her achievements were due both to her Hindu rearing and to Christianity. The latter was increasingly important.

Another woman convert, also a Brahmin, was Chundra Lela. She had been a Hindu devotee, and in her search for spiritual satisfaction was a pilgrim, an ascetic who subjected her body to painful ordeals, and a priestess. Eventually she became disillusioned with her inherited religion, found in Christianity what she had sought, and became its missionary.[628]

Samuel Rahator was the son of Christian parents and entered upon his own transforming experience through the preaching of a British officer who in turn had owed much to a Wesleyan missionary. Rahator gave himself to the Christian ministry and spent most of his working life serving the desperately poor factory labourers in the slums of Bombay.[629]

Sundar Singh was from a wealthy Sikh family and in 1904, while in his middle teens, became a Christian through contacts made in a Christian school. He determined to lead the life of a Christian sadhu, combining the Indian ideal of a holy man with what had come to him through his Christian faith. He was strikingly a mystic and made a marked impression upon many in his generation.[630]

Henry Baber, an Assamese Christian, volunteered to go with a pioneer foreign missionary to one of the bold, raiding hill tribes, a step which required no little courage. After some years there he was recalled to help in the revision of a translation of the New Testament and became a teacher and pastor of Jorhat. On his small salary he managed to give each of his sons a good education.[631]

These instances can scarcely be called typical. They are outstanding and most

[628] Ada Lee, *An Indian Priestess: the Life of Chundra Lela* (London, Morgan & Scott, no date, pp. 121).

[629] Frank Hart, *Rahator of Bombay, the Apostle to the Marathas* (London, The Epworth Press, 1936, pp. 189).

[630] B. H. Streeter and A. J. Appasamy, *The Sadhu* (London, Macmillan and Co., 1921, pp. xv, 264).

[631] Bowers, *Under Head-Hunters Eyes*, pp. 129-133.

of them are not from the social strata from which the overwhelming majority of the Christians were drawn. Yet they illustrate some of the fruits of Christianity in individual lives. Christianity wrought changes, but in an Indian environment which also contributed powerfully to the result.

In many converts the alterations brought by Christianity were by no means so marked. Some Christians were of unworthy character. Some shifted back and forth between the Roman Catholics and Anglicans in hope of greater material aid.[632]

Yet the Christian faith wrought changes even in the rank and file of the mass converts, including those from the depressed classes. The Christian Garos gave up their hereditary head hunting [633] and required that all who joined their churches become total abstainers from alcoholic drinks.[634] In South India the proportion of Christians convicted of crime was less than a fifth of that of the Hindus and less than a third of that of the Moslems.[635] The Anglicans forbade the traditional dances to their converts in Chota Nagpur, for fear of sexual irregularity from them.[636] In general the Malas, a depressed group, poor, dirty, ignorant, addicted to mean and servile vices, as Christians became cleaner in their persons and homes, ceased from their two main crimes, cattle poisoning and grain stealing, abstained from infant marriage and concubinage, no longer ate carrion, and lost some of their servile spirit.[637] These examples are typical and could be duplicated many times. In the large majority of converts an advance, even though at times slight, was registered towards Christian standards.

One of the most striking of the fruits of Christian missions was the growth of the Church, or, perhaps one should say, the churches. The increase in membership we have already noted. In the course of our narrative we have seen something of the ecclesiastical structures which were brought into being. The churches as institutions were the creation of Christian missions.

By the year 1914 an Indian Christian leadership was emerging. No longer were the churches so palpably exotic. They were beginning to take root. The Roman Catholic Church had long been drawing a large proportion of its priests from the natives of India, although these were not always of pure Indian blood. As the nineteenth century passed it made increased provision for the recruiting and training of an Indian clergy. The various Protestant bodies were also making rapid progress in the education of Indian staffs. In both Roman Catholic and Protestant circles foreigners were still dominant, but here and

[632] Pascoe, *Two Hundred Years of the S.P.G.*, pp. 528, 560c, 599c.

[633] Albaugh, *Between Two Centuries*, p. 66.

[634] Bowers, *op. cit.*, pp. 181, 182.

[635] Warneck, *Geschichte der protestantischen Missionen*, p. 403.

[636] E. H. Whitley, in *The East and the West*, Vol. XVI, pp. 295-301.

[637] Pascoe, *op. cit.*, p. 566a; Pickett, *Christian Mass Movements in India*, p. 131.

there an Indian was coming to the fore, both by the wish of the foreigners and because of his own ability and devotion. We have already noted the role which Upadhyaya Brahmabandhav played in the Roman Catholic fold and the prominence of Goreh and Azariah in the Anglican communion. Outstanding among the Presbyterians in the Punjab was Kali Charan Chatterjee.[638] Chatterjee was a Brahmin who became a Christian through the influence of a mission school and for a time was under the influence of Duff. During forty-eight years he was a missionary in the Punjab and, in contrast with the tradition of his Brahmin ancestry, gave much of his time and energy to those of the lower social strata. K. T. Paul, born of Christian parents and educated in Christian schools, was, with Azariah, a leader in organizing the National Missionary Society of India, for a time was its secretary, and eventually became the first Indian national general secretary of the Young Men's Christian Association.[639] Abraham, on whom as a boy Sherwood Eddy urged the claims of the impoverished masses, after studying in the Occident returned to India with a deep desire to awaken his communion, the Mar Thoma Syrian Church, to a responsibility for the outcastes, became a bishop and as such received members of the depressed classes into membership.[640] We hear, too, of an outcaste boy who became pastor of a church and won decorations and recognition from the government of India and various subordinate governments.[641]

On that basic and stubborn Indian social institution, caste, Christianity was making an impression. As we have seen again and again in the preceding pages, neither Roman Catholic nor Protestant Christianity completely eradicated caste distinctions among their adherents. Nor did either speak with united voice against caste. Yet the trend in each was to lessen caste differences, even at the cost of grave personal sacrifices on the part of high caste converts, and to make of the Church a brotherhood in which these would have no place.[642] Moreover, as we have also repeatedly noted, a large proportion of the Christians, both Roman Catholic and Protestant, were drawn from the depressed classes and the tribes of primitive culture. To these underprivileged members of Indian society Christianity opened doors of opportunity to education, improved economic status, self-respecting dignity, and better moral and spiritual life. Largely be-

---

[638] J. C. R. Ewing, *A Prince of the Church. Being a Record of the Life of the Rev. Kali Charan Chatterjee* (Chicago, Fleming H. Revell Co., 1918, pp. 128).
[639] H. A. Popley, *K. T. Paul, Christian Leader* (Calcutta, Y.M.C.A. Publishing House, 1938, pp. xv, 254).
[640] Eddy, *A Pilgrimage of Ideas*, p. 100.
[641] Buck, *India Looks to her Future*, pp. 93-95.
[642] For a few of the references to the attitude of the churches towards caste, see Richter, *Indische Missionsgeschichte*, 179-186; Pascoe, *Two Hundred Years of the S.P.G.*, pp. 504a, 504b, 560, 580-586b, 592, 593, 602; Wanless, *An American Doctor in India*, pp. 120-123.

cause of Christianity, thousands of these folk, long condemned by the accident of birth to poverty, ignorance, vice, and degradation, were on the march towards a better life.[643]

Repeatedly we have seen the large place which schools played in the programmes of Christian missions. As a consequence, although Christians were predominantly from groups which were traditionally illiterate, in the twentieth century the rate of literacy among Christians was between three and four times that in the country as a whole.[644] Christians became leaders in promoting schools in their villages.[645] Numbers entered the professions and government service.[646] Early in the twentieth century about a quarter of those holding the degree of bachelor of arts, although by no means all of them Christians, were from the Christian higher schools.[647]

With education went the preparation of literature. Languages were reduced to writing.[648] The Bible was translated into many of the languages and dialects. Not only in some of the tongues which had previously not had a written form, but also in so widely used a language as Bengali, Christian missionaries were responsible for either the inception of a literature or gave to vernacular literature a marked impetus.

Christian missionaries contributed notably to the introduction and dissemination of Western medicine, of reforms in sanitation, and of public health measures.[649] While this had a part in the enormous increase in population which became one of the most pressing problems of the India of the twentieth century, the Christian felt that in the face of the suffering due to disease which confronted him at every turn he could not but bring to its alleviation all the skill at his command.

The concern of Christians for the relief of physical suffering also showed itself in the part which missionaries took in administering relief in the famines which had long been a recurring feature of Indian life and in the orphanages which they maintained for some of the child victims.

[643] For a few references see Pickett, *Christian Mass Movements in India*, pp. 58-85, 89, 122, 123, 127, 128, 131, 140ff.; Layman's Foreign Missions Inquiry, *Fact-Finders' Reports. India-Burma*, Vol. IV, Supplementary Series, Part 2, pp. 45, 46, 287; Phillips, *The Outcastes Hope*, pp. 79ff.

[644] Richter, *op. cit.*, p. 439; Laymen's Foreign Missions Inquiry, *op. cit.*, Vol. IV, Supplementary Series, Part 2, p. 44.

[645] Pickett, *op. cit.*, p. 74.

[646] Warneck, *Geschichte der protestantischen Missionen*, p. 404.

[647] Warneck, *op. cit.*, p. 414.

[648] Albaugh, *Between Two Centuries*, p. 70.

[649] Wanless, *An American Doctor at Work in India*, p. 67. Yet in Calcutta Christians seemed to have had a larger incidence of tuberculosis than did Hindus.—Pickett, *op. cit.*, p. 152.

Here and there missionaries extended their care even to wounded and sick animals.[650]

Persistent efforts to alter the lot of women were a striking feature of the Christian enterprise. Schools were provided for girls. Numbers of the pioneers among Indian women in furthering education for their sex were Christians.[651] In consequence, in the twentieth century the literacy rate among Christian women was more than ten times that among their non-Christian sisters and was even higher than that among non-Christian men.[652] Missionaries fought the early marriage [653] and the prostitution which bore particularly hard on women. The social purity movement was begun by them.[654] They inaugurated rescue homes for prostitutes.[655] They discouraged polygamy. They permitted the remarriage of widows and cared for the widows to whom Hindu custom forbade remarriage. The advance in the status of Indian womanhood which the twentieth century witnessed was due in part, although not entirely, to the Christian missionary.[656]

Some movements outside Christian circles for social reform can be traced in part to Christian missions, yet were not due entirely or even primarily either to Christian missions or to Christianity. The Servants of India Society was founded in 1905 by a Hindu, G. K. Gokhale, for the purpose of promoting the progress of the country by the devoted service of its members.[657] Its headquarters were at Poona and to some extent it seems to have owed its inception to the contact of Gokhale with the Cowley Fathers in that city.[658] More influential, both politically and in social changes, than the Servants of India Society was Mohandas Karamchand Gandhi. Gandhi was primarily shaped by Hinduism, but he was also indebted to Christianity. He is said to have declared that it was the New Testament, and especially the Sermon on the Mount, which first stirred him to undertake the passive resistance which he employed so successfully in South Africa and then, on a larger scale, in India,[659] that it was through

[650] Carter, Rose Harvey, pp. 53-59.
[651] Sattianadhan in Modak, Directory of Protestant Indian Christians, p. ix.
[652] Laymen's Foreign Missions Inquiry, op. cit., Vol. IV, Supplementary Series, Part 2, p. 44.
[653] Pickett, op. cit., p. 134.
[654] Laymen's Foreign Missions Inquiry, op. cit., Vol. IV, Supplementary Series, Part 2, p. 475.
[655] Laymen's Foreign Missions Inquiry, op. cit., Vol. IV, Supplementary Series, Part 2, p. 476.
[656] Laymen's Foreign Missions Inquiry, op. cit., Vol. IV, Supplementary Series, Part 2, p. 478.
[657] Farquhar, Modern Religious Movements in India, pp. 376-380.
[658] Conversation of a Christian member of the Servants of India Society, S. P. Andrews-Dubé, with the author, Dec. 13, 1938.
[659] Andrews, Mahatma Gandhi's Ideas, p. 191.

Christianity that his fierce hatred of child marriage was awakened, and that the attack of Christians on untouchability reinforced his desire to contend against the continuation of the discrimination which made the lot of the depressed classes so unhappy.[660]

Many of the humanitarian measures adopted by the British Government in India appear to have arisen in some degree from the quickening of conscience brought by the Christian faith in some of the British officials and from the support of a public opinion created by actively Christian elements in Great Britain. Indeed, the marked contrast between the exploitation of India by the East India Company in the seventeenth and eighteenth centuries and the benevolent imperialism of the nineteenth and twentieth centuries appears to have been in part, perhaps in large part, due to the Evangelical and other awakenings which strengthened the religious life of Britain during that period. The precise extent of the influence of Christianity upon these movements would be difficult to determine. It is clear that several of those who led in shaping British policy for India were earnest Evangelicals and sought to govern their actions by their Christian purpose. Charles Grant, a director of the East India Company and three times chairman of its board, was not only an outstanding Evangelical, active in the founding of the Church Missionary Society and the British and Foreign Bible Society and prominent in the campaign against Negro slavery. He also fought famine in Bengal, struggled to purge the East India Company of some of its worst abuses, and insisted that British rule must be for the benefit of India.[661] One of his sons, Charles, later Lord Glenelg, who shared many of his father's religious convictions and activities,[662] as president of the Board of Control from 1830 to 1834 was primarily responsible[663] for the modification of the East India Company's charter[664] in 1833. This revision of the charter, among other measures, provided for the early abolition of slavery in British India and by opening office in India under the company to all regardless of religion, colour, or race, helped to pave the way for Indian participation in government. As president of the Board of Control Charles Grant the younger supported Lord William Bentinck, Governor-General of India from 1827 to 1835, in enacting reforms for which that administration was famous.[665] Among them was the abolishment of suttee, the immolation of the Hindu widow on the funeral pyre

---

[660] *Report of the Commission of Appraisal of the Laymen's Foreign Missions Inquiry* (mimeographed), Chap. II, p. 15.

[661] Stock, *The History of the Church Missionary Society,* Vol. I, pp. 52-55.

[662] Stock, *op. cit.,* Vol. I, pp. 81, 263, 373.

[663] *The Encyclopædia Britannica,* 14th ed., Vol. X, p. 427.

[664] Stock, *op. cit.,* Vol. I, p. 294.

[665] Stock, *op. cit.,* Vol. I, p. 293; Boulger, *Lord William Bentinck,* pp. 68ff.; Wilson, *The Indirect Effect of Christian Missions in India,* p. 30.

of her husband.[666] Other reforms of this period included the stamping out of the thugs, professional assassins, and the prohibition of the murder of aged parents, the exposure of infants, the custom of devotees throwing themselves under the wheels of image-bearing cars, and the practice by religious ascetics of self-torture by hook swinging.[667] The Christian conscience insisted, at length successfully, upon the dissociation of the British administration from the maintenance of pagan shrines and non-Christian religious ceremonies which had been a source of revenue.[668] Other Evangelicals prominent in the government of India were Charles Elliott, one of the original committee of the Church Missionary Society and Lieutenant-Governor of Bengal,[669] and Robert Grant, a son of Charles Grant the elder and Governor of Bengal.[670] John Lawrence, later Governor-General, earlier famous for his military exploits in the Punjab and in the Mutiny, sought to govern all his acts by a transparently genuine Christian faith which led him, among other achievements, to mitigate the lot of peasant tenants in the Punjab and Oudh.[671] Herbert Benjamin Edwardes, famous as a commander in the later stages of the conquest of India and in the Mutiny, believed that the latter event was a judgment of God upon the English for withholding Christian truth from India and declared in a way which carried public weight that all un-Christian principles must be eliminated from the government of India.[672]

We must also note that chaplains and voluntary Christian organizations had something of an influence in safeguarding British soldiers in India from camp vices, notably intemperance, and in rescuing those who had fallen victims to the temptations of their environment.[673] This in itself would modify, even if slightly, the impact of Occidental life upon India.

Upon other religions Christianity had effects. In some instances these were slight. In others they were marked. Much was intangible. Through missions, through the study of English literature in the schools, and through other channels, the thought, life, and even the phraseology of professed adherents of other faiths were altered by Christianity.[674] Although most of those who were willing

[666] Boulger, op. cit., pp. 66, 77-111.
[667] Stock, op. cit., Vol. I, p. 293.
[668] Stock, op. cit., Vol. I, pp. 294-296; Richter, Indische Missionsgeschichte, pp. 199-208.
[669] Stock, op. cit., Vol. I, p. 70.
[670] Stock, op. cit., Vol. I, p. 81.
[671] Aitchison, Lord Lawrence, pp. 114, 148-153.
[672] Aitchison, op. cit., p. 117.
[673] For a very few of many examples, see G. M. Davies, A Chaplain in India (London, Marshall, Morgan & Scott, 1933, pp. xi, 321), passim; Elsie B. Fisk, The Great Sirkar in Quetta for the Souls of Men (London, Marshall, Morgan & Scott, no date, pp. 126), passim.
[674] Macnicol, The Living Religions of the Indian People, p. 287.

to call themselves Christians and ally themselves with the Church were from the depressed classes and the aboriginal tribes and relatively few converts were from the upper classes, thousands of the latter had their views modified by Christianity. Some might be termed "invisible Christians." [675]

The influence of Christianity upon other faiths was particularly discernible in movements, some of them Hindu sects or drawn from Hinduism, a few of them Moslem, and several so syncretistic that it was hard to classify them under an earlier religion. We can take the space to call attention only to the most prominent, and to them we can give only the briefest mention.

One of the most famous and influential was the Brahmo Samaj.[676] The founder, Ram Mohun Roy (1772-1833),[677] a Brahmin, had become an earnest reformer of Hinduism before he had intimate knowledge of Christianity. He organized the Brahmo Samaj in 1828. Several years before doing so he had had close contacts with the Serampore missionaries and had made a careful study of Christianity. He regarded Christ highly but would never call himself a Christian. The Brahmo Samaj was theistic, had strong sympathies with Christian Unitarianism, and was influential among a comparatively few of the highly educated. The next leader, Debendranath Tagore,[678] had been reared in a wealthy Hindu home which was friendly to Ram Mohun Roy, early had a profound religious experience, and in 1841 became the head of the Brahmo Samaj. He reorganized it and brought into it more of worship and religious warmth. He seems not to have been so deeply influenced by Christianity as was his predecessor.[679] His fourth son, Rabindranath Tagore, attained world-wide fame as a poet, philosopher, and educator. The next outstanding leader, Keshub Chandra Sen,[680] who headed what he made an actively missionary branch of the Brahmo Samaj, was more strongly impressed by Christianity and Christ than were either of the previous leaders and introduced much of Chris-

[675] For one of these, Susil Rudra, a pupil of Duff, see Andrews, *What I Owe to Christ*, pp. 158, 159.

[676] Farquhar, *Modern Religious Movements in India*, pp. 29-74; Frank Lillingston, *The Brahmo Samaj & Arya Samaj and their bearing upon Christianity* (London, Macmillan and Co., 1901, pp. xvi, 120), pp. 44-107.

[677] Sophia Dobson Collet, edited by Hem Chandra Sarkar, *Life and Letters of Raja Rammohun Roy* (Calcutta, A. C. Sarkar, 1914, pp. lxxx, 276).

[678] *The Autobiography of Maharshi Devendranath Tagore* (London, Macmillan and Co., 1914, pp. xlii, 295).

[679] Yet his eldest son meditated more and more on the Sermon on the Mount.—Andrews, *What I Owe to Christ*, pp. 225-227.

[680] Farquhar, *op. cit.*, pp. 41-69; P. C. Mozoomdar, *The Faith and Progress of the Brahmo Samaj* (Calcutta, The Calcutta Central Press Co., 1882, pp. xiii, 410), *passim;* P. C. Mozoomdar, *The Oriental Christ* (Boston, Geo. H. Ellis Co., 1883, pp. 193), *passim;* Sophia Dobson Collet, editor, *The Brahmo Year-Book for 1881. Brief Records of Work and Life in the Theistic Churches of India* (London, Williams and Norgate, 1882, pp. 151), *passim,* especially pp. 38-48.

tian terminology and practice. A branch which separated from that of Keshub, the Sadharan Brahmo Samaj, also showed Christian influence.[681]

Out of the stimulus given by John Wilson, the distinguished Scottish missionary educator of Bombay, came the theistic Prarthana Samaj. In its beliefs it was much like the Sadharan Brahmo Samaj, but it was not so actively missionary.[682]

Ramakrishna, intensely religious, had a long spiritual pilgrimage, but seems never to have been much shaped by Christianity.[683] He was, indeed, a defender of Hinduism. Yet his disciple and popularizer, Vivekananda, for a time in his youth a student in a mission school, inspired the organization of the Ramakrishna Mission, on a Christmas Eve, by telling the story of Jesus.[684]

The Arya Samaj owed little or nothing in its inception to Christianity. As an active champion of Hinduism against Islam and Christianity, it may have had its urge to be missionary strengthened by its opposition to the latter.[685]

Led chiefly by Europeans who bore traces of their hereditary Christianity but who were ardent admirers of what they believed they found in Hinduism, was Theosophy. It became a kind of Hindu mission among Occidentals.[686]

In contrast with the actively anti-Christian Arya Samaj, we hear of several Hindu sects, usually small, which based their distinctive teachings upon one or another Christian document.[687]

Coming out of Islam was the Ahmadiya sect, strong in the Punjab, in part a Moslem reaction against Christianity, whose leader claimed to be the Christian Messiah but greater than Christ.[688]

Hinduism and Islam were sapped by the acids of modernity. Many of their adherents who were educated in the Western fashion, while nominally adhering to their ancestral faith, became agnostics or atheists. Yet these major religions of India had sufficient vitality to give rise to new movements. Some of the latter owed much to Christianity and either incorporated elements from it or were aroused to greater activity by a passion to counteract it.

[681] Dwijadas Datta, *Behold the Man or Keshub and the Sadharan Brahmo Samaj* (Calcutta, the author, 1930, pp. xvii, 289), *passim;* Farquhar, *op. cit.*, pp. 70-74.

[682] Farquhar, *op. cit.*, pp. 74-81.

[683] *Life of Sri Ramakrishna, compiled from Various Authentic Sources* (Mayavati Almora, Himalayas, Advaita Ashrama, 1925, pp. vi, 765); Farquhar, *op. cit.*, pp. 188ff.

[684] Buck, *India Looks to Her Future*, p. 129.

[685] Lajput Rai, *The Arya Samaj. An Account of Its Origin, Doctrines, and Activities, with a Biographical Sketch of the Founder* (London, Longmans, Green and Co., 1915, pp. xxvi, 305).

[686] Farquhar, *op. cit.*, pp. 208-291. For the life of one of the leaders, see Theodore Besterman, *Mrs. Annie Besant, a Modern Prophet* (London, Kegan Paul, Trench, Trubner & Co., 1934, pp. xi, 274).

[687] Richter, *Indische Missionsgeschichte*, pp. 357, 358; Farquhar, *op. cit.*, pp. 150-157.

[688] Farquhar, *op. cit.*, pp. 137-148; D. B. Macdonald in *The Encyclopædia of Islam*, Vol. II, p. 525; H. A. Walter, *The Ahmadiya Movement* (Calcutta, Association Press, 1918, pp. 185), *passim*.

Down to the year 1914 the Indian environment had much less effect upon Christianity than Christianity had upon the environment. This was to be expected. Christianity was either largely confined to minority enclaves, such as the Syrian Church and the Portuguese and French possessions, or had been so recently propagated that it was still dependent upon foreign initiative and had only begun to take root in Indian soil. Moreover, the great majority of the nineteenth century converts were from the depressed classes, groups which by tradition had a servile attitude and were disposed to accept passively both foreign leadership and the imported customs. Yet by the year 1914 a few evidences were appearing that India was beginning to place its stamp upon Christianity and, especially, that under the stress of rising Indian nationalism missionaries were seeking to make the Church less Occidental and Indian Christians were endeavouring to put an Indian impress upon the forms of their faith and to assume more and more responsibility for the Church. After 1914 this movement was rapidly to gain momentum. In the closing pages of this chapter we must recount the first steps with their foreshadowings of the future.

It was to be expected that caste, so basic a social institution in India, would affect the Christian communities. In the course of our story we have repeatedly noted the persistence of caste differences within the Church and that in spite of the efforts of large numbers of Roman Catholic and Protestant authorities.[689] Moreover, the churches themselves tended to become castes. The acceptance of baptism cut the Indian off from his former caste—unless others of his caste came with him. The church which he joined therefore seemed to him and to his fellows, both Christian and non-Christian, to be another caste.[690] Here and there a particular communion became all but identified with one caste group. Thus among the Telugus the Wesleyans, quite against the original plan of the missionaries, came to be the church of the Malas and the American Baptists the church of the Madigas. When a church was partly transformed into a caste group it was inclined to be self-contained, as were the Hindu castes, and to cease to reach out for converts, except perhaps to members of the particular social group from which its members had been drawn. Thus the Syrian Christians had long been ingrowing and had been almost entirely non-missionary until some of them were inspired to fresh activity by contact with missionaries from the Occident.[691] Among the Syrian Christians divisions due to doctrinal

[689] See, as a sample of many references, Becker, *Indisches Kastenwesen und Christliche Mission*, pp. 56, 57, 67, 71, 97, 100, 102, 132ff.; Pickett, *Christian Mass Movements in India*, p. 41; Ayyar, *Anthropology of the Syrian Christians*, p. 258.

[690] Pascoe, *Two Hundred Years of the S.P.G.*, p. 485.

[691] In 1888 there was formed, as a missionary society of the Mar Thoma Syrian Church, that body which owed its separate existence to contact with Protestantism, the Mar Thoma Syrian Christian Evangelistic Association. It laboured chiefly among the depressed

differences hardened into caste groups between whose members there was no intermarriage.[692] Tamil Protestants of old Christian stock had little zeal for winning their neighbours.[693] At the dawn of the nineteenth century Roman Catholic Christianity had become to a large extent coterminous with the communities which claimed Portuguese blood. Such progress as it made outside these groups was due to European missionaries, not to those of Indian birth. Some of the later Protestant missionaries were not eager for outright conversions and took a friendly attitude toward the saints of other faiths. They thus partly conformed to the Hindu tradition that each must abide in the religion and the social status in which he was born.[694] Had Christianity in India fully accepted this position it would have sacrificed its basic conviction of universality and would have acceded to a fundamental feature of Hinduism. This the Christian communities longer in India were inclined to do. Fresh infusions of energy from the Occident, however, worked against the trend.

Because of the traditional solidity of the caste group, the movement towards Christianity, as we have repeatedly seen, was often made by that unit. Although many of the religious bodies represented, notably several of the Protestant denominations, theoretically stressed the conversion of individuals and required the narration of a personal religious experience as a prerequisite to church membership, in practice in India, as in so many other parts of the world in the nineteenth century, they spread by groups.[695] At least four-fifths of the Protestant church membership are said to have come in this fashion.[696] This was true not only among the depressed classes but also among the Sudras.[697] It was not peculiar to Christianity. It was in this manner that most of the converts to Islam had been won.[698] Moreover, even a cursory examination of our volumes will show that conversion *en masse* was not confined to India. It was the process by which not only Christianity but also other faiths had spread wherever they became numerically significant. However, because of the caste structure of the country, it was particularly prominent in India.

classes.—Philip, *Report on a Survey of Indigenous Christian Efforts in India, Burma, and Ceylon*, p. 4. On some earlier accessions, presumably not due to active missionary effort, see E. A. Varghese in *Asia*, Vol. XXXII, pp. 121, 122. By 1912 the Jacobite Syrian Church also was maintaining missionaries and had about twenty-five congregations of converts from depressed classes.—*The Year Book of Missions in India, Burma and Ceylon, 1912*, pp. 146, 147.
[692] Ayyar, *op. cit.*, pp. 1, 60, 61.
[693] *The Girl who Learned to See*, p. 22.
[694] As in Andrews, *What I Owe to Christ*, pp. 164, 165.
[695] Pickett, *op. cit.*, p. 28; Macnicol, *The Living Religions of the Indian People*, pp. 21, 23, 288, 289.
[696] Pickett, *op. cit.*, pp. 313-315.
[697] Pickett, *op. cit.*, pp. 27-28.
[698] Pickett, *op. cit.*, p. 36.

As another effect of the environment we must again call attention to a characteristic of Christianity in India—the lowly provenance of the overwhelming majority of the church membership. Here and there a convert came from the Brahmins or from another of the higher castes.[699] The vast body of the Christians, however, were from the depressed classes and the aboriginal tribes. Those who were not from these strata were largely from the Sudras and not from the higher castes. It was chiefly the sufferers from the existing order who sought Christian instruction. Here was at once the opportunity, the glory, and the acute problem of the Church in India.

It is not strange that caste should have been so resistant. The basic assumptions which were used to support caste—metempsychosis and the attendant *karma* by which one's deeds in preceding existences determined one's status in his present incarnation—were so utterly opposed to Christian teaching that those who profited by caste could scarcely be expected to adopt it lightly. It was those who palpably suffered from caste who heard the Christian message gladly.

Moreover, as evidence of the power of caste it must be noted that Islam had drawn the bulk of its converts in India from approximately the same social strata as did Christianity.

Since so many Christians came from the depressed classes, with their hereditary sense of inferiority and dependence, Indian leadership for the churches was somewhat slow in developing. The Christians were inclined to look to the missionary for direction and in other ways displayed the results of their pre-Christian background. They were not easily weaned from practices which were inconsistent with Christian standards. Financial self-support was late in being achieved.[700]

Here and there customs and beliefs from the Indian environment were found in the Christian communities. Some persisted from pre-Christian days. Some were conscious adaptations. For instance, among the Syrian Jacobites early marriage was long common, as it was among their Hindu neighbours. The age for boys was between ten and twelve and for girls six or seven. Only latterly did education and the efforts of ecclesiastical authorities raise the age for boys and girls to sixteen and fourteen respectively.[701] Some Hindu customs were followed in the marriage ceremony.[702] Among the Syrian Christians as

[699] On a maharajah who was baptized and on a rajah who, while not baptized, openly expressed himself as desiring to follow Christ, see Mullens, *A Brief Review of Ten Years' Missionary Labour in India*, pp. 64, 65. On an Indian Christian nobleman in the Punjab, see Modak, *Directory of Protestant Indian Christians*, p. 349. On other prominent Christians see Modak, *op. cit.*, p. vii.

[700] Modak, *op. cit.*, p. xxv. Yet we hear of some self-supporting churches.—Modak, *op. cit.*, p. 325.

[701] Ayyar, *op. cit.*, pp. ix-xvii.

[702] *Ibid.*

among the Hindus the parents usually arranged for the marriage of their daughters without consulting the latter and frequently also similarly provided for the marriage of their sons.[703] It was reported that among the low caste Christians the most resistant customs were those connected with birth, marriage, death, and a belief in spirits.[704] It is said that early in the twentieth century there were Christian shrines in the South at which both Hindus and Christians worshipped, each in their own way.[705] It is also declared that among Roman Catholics of the Portuguese tradition there was much connivance by catechists at what their church deemed superstitions and illegitimate marriages.[706] We hear a Roman Catholic lament that in a number of Roman Catholic communities a Hindu god was honoured at weddings and festivals, that Brahmin astrologists and Hindu priests were called in, that the religious marks of the Hindus were copied, and that the use of pagan charms as a protection against evil spirits and disease was so deeply ingrained that it was necessary to give as substitutes Christian medals, crucifixes, and rosaries.[707] We read that Goanese Roman Catholics preferred passage on boats bearing the name of *Francis Xavier,* believing that this precaution would bring them security.[708] Many of the Roman Catholic missionaries, especially in the South, to avoid offence to Christians of Hindu antecedents refrained from eating beef.[709] We hear that in at least one place Christians, following an ancient custom, came to church in a procession headed by native drums and bringing gifts of fruits and sweets to the clergy.[710] Some Indian evangelists in presenting the Christian message made it not so much one of salvation from sin as deliverance from evil spirits.[711]

One of the phases of conformity to the Indian environment was the development of organizations which would fit into the geographic pattern of the country and tend to erase differences transported from the Occident. This was not particularly difficult for Roman Catholics. As we saw earlier in this chapter, in the 1880's they created a hierarchy for India and Rome was represented by an Apostolic Delegate. A national structure for the country within the fellowship of the Roman communion was in process of emerging.

[703] Ayyar, *op. cit.,* pp. 70-74.
[704] Macnicol, *op. cit.,* p. 292.
[705] G. A. Grierson, in *The Journal of the Royal Asiatic Society of Great Britain and Ireland,* 1907, p. 312.
[706] De Bussierre, *Histoire du Schisme Portugais dans les Indes,* pp. 115ff.
[707] Becker, *Indisches Kastenwesen und christliche Mission,* p. 74.
[708] Capuchin Mission Unit, *India and Its Missions,* p. 217.
[709] Becker, *op. cit.,* p. 87.
[710] Lemerle, *My Diary,* p. 49.
[711] Moody, *The Mind of the Early Converts,* p. 260.

Protestants, with their many divisions, found the problem more resistant, but by 1914 they had made marked advances towards a similar goal. There were efforts to bring together those of the same denominational families. Thus in 1875 there was formed the Presbyterian Alliance of India.[712] This culminated, in 1904, in the constitution of the Presbyterian church in India.[713] Beginning in 1895 the Lutheran missions in the Telugu country began holding conferences which convened about every two years and in 1906 commenced the publication of a joint magazine, The Gospel Witness. In 1908 the All-India Lutheran Conference was organized,[714] and a meeting of this conference in 1911-1912 urged the establishment of a united Lutheran theological seminary at Madras.[715] To avoid competition and duplication of effort, agreements were entered into between representatives of different societies delimiting geographic fields.[716] In 1903 an elaborate Board of Arbitration was set up for India and Ceylon to advise on the occupation of new territory and to adjudicate disputes over fields of labour.[717] Attempts were made to effect unions of churches of denominations of more than one family. In 1908, after preliminary steps going back for several years, bodies in the South connected with the United Free Church of Scotland, the Reformed Church in America, the London Missionary Society, and the American Board of Commissioners for Foreign Missions formed themselves into the South India United Church.[718] Movements towards wider co-ordination and more comprehensive union were also under way, but, quite understandably, were slower in approaching consummation. The gatherings of missionaries of several missions in 1855, 1857, and 1858 which we noted a few pages back were followed by more comprehensive ones and a growing machinery for co-operation. In 1879 there was held a missionary conference of South India and Ceylon [719] and in 1900 one for South India,[720] both in the series which began in 1858, and each larger and representative of more societies than its predecessor. A missionary conference for the Punjab was convened in December, 1862.[721]

[712] Parker, The Development of the United Church of Northern India, pp. 18-25; Badley, Indian Missionary Directory and Memorial Volume, p. 132.
[713] Parker, op. cit., pp. 40ff.
[714] Drach, Our Church Abroad, p. 55.
[715] Drach and Kruder, The Telugu Mission, p. 388.
[716] For one of these which did not prove satisfactory, see Pascoe, Two Hundred Years of the S.P.G., pp. 554, 558, 559.
[717] The Year Book of Missions in India, Burma and Ceylon, 1912, pp. 195ff.
[718] The Year Book of Missions in India, Burma and Ceylon, 1912, pp. 238-243.
[719] The Missionary Conference: South India and Ceylon, 1879 (Madras, Addison & Co., 2 vols., 1880).
[720] Report of the South Indian Missionary Conference, held at Madras, January 2-5, 1900 (Madras, The M. E. Publishing House, 1900, pp. xvi, 108).
[721] Report of the Punjab Missionary Conference held at Lahore in December and January, 1862-63 (Lodiana, American Presbyterian Mission Press, 1863, pp. xix, 398).

Beginning in 1872 at Allahabad [722] decennial missionary conferences for the entire country were held, in Calcutta in 1882,[723] in Bombay in 1892,[724] and in Madras in 1902.[725] At the Punjab missionary conference of 1862-1863 a paper was read on the topic "An Indian Catholic Church" [726] but the time was not ripe for the early attainment of such a goal. As the result of conferences at Jubbulpore in 1909 and 1911 a plan for a federation of Christian churches in India [727] was worked out. The movement in India was caught up in the tide which was flowing elsewhere in the Protestant world. In 1912 as an outgrowth of the World Missionary Conference at Edinburgh in 1910, under the leadership of John R. Mott, chairman of the Continuation Committee of that gathering, there were held in India regional gatherings which culminated in a national gathering. From the latter there issued a plan for provincial representative councils and a national council, with an ad interim committee,[728] which prepared the way for the formation, after 1914, of the National Christian Council. By 1914 the currents were setting strongly towards a greater unity of the Protestant forces of India.

In spite of the fact that so large a proportion of Christians came from the depressed classes and that emancipation from the ensuing dependence on the foreign missionary was retarded, by the year 1914 Indian leadership was rapidly emerging and was making conscious attempts to free Indian Christianity from its Occidental accretions and to give it an Indian dress. The trend was accentuated by the rapidly rising spirit of nationalism. One of the ablest of the Brahmin converts who had laboured faithfully in the Scottish mission towards the end of his life remarked bitterly: "I am just a black Scotchman." [729] K. C. Banerjea, a Bengali Christian lawyer and an earnest Christian, was prominent in the early years of the Indian National Congress. Dissatisfied with the foreign character of the Church, he founded what proved to be a short-lived Christo Samaj.[730] N. V. Tilak, a Brahmin, became a Christian in part because he believed that the rebirth of India to hope would come through submission to

[722] *Report of the General Missionary Conference held at Allahabad, 1872-73* (London, Seeley, Jackson, and Halliday, 1873, pp. xxviii, 548).
[723] *Report of the Second Decennial Missionary Conference held at Calcutta, 1882-83* (Calcutta, Baptist Mission Press, 1883, pp. xxx, 462).
[724] *Report of the Third Decennial Missionary Conference held at Bombay, 1892-93* (Bombay, Education Society's Steam Press, 2 vols., 1893).
[725] *Report of the Fourth Decennial Indian Missionary Conference held in Madras, December 11th-18th, 1902* (London, Christian Literature Society, no date, pp. xxxiv, 367).
[726] *Report of the Punjab Missionary Conference*, pp. 299ff.
[727] *The Year Book of Missions in India, Burma and Ceylon*, pp. 227ff.
[728] *The Continuation Committee Conferences in Asia, 1912-1913*, pp. 15-153.
[729] Macnicol, *India in the Dark Wood*, p. 113.
[730] Macnicol, *op. cit.*, pp. 119, 120.

Christ. He fused the Christian message with the Hindu tradition of *bhakti* and composed Christian songs in his native tongue.[731] In his later years, B. C. Sircar, a Bengali who had been active in the Young Men's Christian Association, sought inward self-culture along the road of *yogi* and founded a Christian shrine at a great centre of Hindu pilgrimage.[732] Now and then a missionary experimented with wearing Indian dress as a means of coming closer to the people.[733] In an effort to acclimatize Christianity, Indians were more and more placed in positions of responsibility in the churches and Christian institutions.[734] Through indigenous effort Indian Christian Associations were being formed. There was an Indian Christian Provident Fund and in 1912 in Madras the Indian clergymen had a conference with monthly meetings.[735] In 1914 the movement towards Indianization was only beginning, but it was in progress.

May we attempt to summarize this long chapter?

In the beginning of the nineteenth century several of the main branches of Christianity were already represented in India. There were Roman Catholics, Syrian Christians in communion with one or more of the Eastern churches, Armenians, and Protestants. They were most numerous in the South but were by no means confined to that region.

In the course of the nineteenth century Christianity experienced a very rapid growth. This was not because of the vigour of the existing Christian communities but was through missionaries from the Occident, expressions of the marked awakenings in the churches of the West. The missionaries took advantage of the conquest of the country by Great Britain. In many ways the British occupation was of assistance to the spread of Christianity. In other ways, however, it was a handicap. For the most part missionaries were not aided by the British Government but came quite independently of it. Indeed, in the fore part of the nineteenth century they faced the suspicion and even the hostility of the East India Company, the instrument through which the British conquest was effected. Missionaries were both Roman Catholic and Protestant. Less than half were from the British Isles. Almost all the Roman Catholic missionaries were from the continent of Europe. Protestant missionaries were from the British Isles, the British Dominions, the United States, and the continent of

---

[731] Macnicol, *op. cit.*, p. 128.

[732] Macnicol, *op. cit.*, p. 131.

[733] As in Culshaw, *A Missionary Looks at his Job*, pp. 54-56.

[734] For instance, in 1906 S. K. Rudra was made Principal of St. Stephen's College, Delhi.—Monk, *A History of St. Stephen's College, Delhi*, pp. 112ff.

[735] *The Year Book of Missions in India, Burma and Ceylon, 1912*, pp. 433-436.

Europe. The Christianity of India was, therefore, varied. Of the Protestant groups the Anglicans were the most wide-spread and numerically the strongest, both in missionary staff and in Indian Christians. The Presbyterian and Reformed, the Methodist, and the Baptist denominational families were also prominent. Protestantism was proportionately growing more rapidly than the Roman Catholic form of the faith. The latter was handicapped by remnants of the Portuguese padroado and its missionary staff did not increase as rapidly as did that of the Protestants.

The Christians, both Roman Catholic and Protestant, were overwhelmingly from the depressed classes and the tribes of primitive or near-primitive culture which had never been fully assimilated to Hindu civilization. In the South, numbers of Christians were from the Sudras, social strata which were midway between the depressed groups and the higher castes. For the most part the natural leaders of the country, the higher castes, were only slightly affected. Through mission schools and other channels of Western education ideas of Christian origin had begun to modify the beliefs and the attitudes of many, but from the upper social levels those who were willing to commit themselves openly to Christianity were comparatively very few. Nor did many converts come from the large Moslem communities.[736]

More than in most lands, especially in Asia in the nineteenth century, conversion was by groups, so-called mass movements.

Of the pre-nineteenth century Christian groups, in the year 1914 the Syrians were divided into three communities—those who acknowledged as their spiritual head the Jacobite Patriarch of Antioch, those who were under the Nestorian Catholicos of the East, and the Mar Thoma Syrian Church which had arisen out of contacts with Protestantism. In addition, thousands of Syrian Christian ancestry were in communion with the Church of Rome and hundreds with the Church of England. The first and third of the groups had undertaken some missionary effort, but increased chiefly through the excess of births over deaths.[737] The Armenians continued, but were content to confine themselves to members of their own nation.[738]

Efforts were made, mainly by Protestants but to some extent by Roman Catholics, to hold to their traditional faith the Europeans who came to India. There were also efforts for the Anglo-Indians, or Eurasians.

---

[736] Hundreds of converts were gathered from Islam by Protestants, especially in the North and the Punjab, but they were in the small minority in the total Christian community. See *The Year Book of Missions in India, Burma and Ceylon, 1912,* pp. 390, 394, 395.

[737] *The Year Book of Missions in India, Burma and Ceylon, 1912,* pp. 136ff.

[738] Seth, *Armenians in India, passim.*

Christianity was influencing India from a number of different angles. Through their schools Christian missions were pioneering in Western education, notably for women and the depressed classes. The Bible had been translated in whole or in part into numbers of the many languages of India. It and other Christian literature were being widely distributed. Missions were aiding in the introduction of Occidental medicine and were assisting in the relief of famine and the care of famine victims, especially orphans. The Christians from the underprivileged groups, sufferers from the traditional pattern of Indian life, were having opened to them doors to a larger life, materially, intellectually, morally, and spiritually. They were making remarkable advances. Hundreds of thousands of individuals were being introduced to the richer life which in all lands and times is the most distinctive fruit of the Christian faith. Entire villages and communities were also examples of the change.

Upon the non-Christian religions Christianity was having some effect. In a few movements of only moderate numerical size this was fairly marked.

In the vast mass of Hinduism and Islam the results of the Christian impact were less tangible and probably as yet were not very great. The core of Indian life had been but slightly affected. This core was to be found in Hinduism and the intimately associated caste structure. Here and there individuals had been torn away from the higher castes. From some of the lower strata, notably the Sudras, thousands had become Christians. A woman's movement owed much to Christianity, but so far this was confined to a small minority. Quite apart from the activities of Christians, the acids of modernity, the science and the material forces of the Occident, were sapping the strength of the religious convictions of thousands of those educated in Western thought. Christianity had placed its stamp on the views of many who remained Hindus. Yet the main body of Hinduism had not been revolutionized or even extensively modified. This was also true of the next larger religious group, the Moslems. It was only among those on the fringes of Hindu culture, the depressed classes and the primitive tribes, that Christian influence was striking. The results here were notable, but Indian life as a whole was all but unchanged.

India was beginning to modify the imported Christianity. Caste made its impress. It persisted in some churches and, in general, in the various regions each communion tended to be confined to a particular caste. Since so many Christians were drawn from the depressed groups, classes which were traditionally without much initiative or freedom, Indian Christianity was inclined to be passive. In general it was willing to submit to foreign direction and to conform to the transmitted patterns. By the year 1914, however, this was changing, in some places in very striking fashion. Indian Christian leadership was appearing in increasing strength and here and there efforts were being made to put Christianity into native dress.

As the century wore on Christianity was a mounting force in Indian life. Not only was it increasing in numerical strength, it was also becoming less alien in leadership and was beginning to be more extensively rooted in the soil. It entered the next period of its history in India on a rising tide. The large majority of Hindus and Moslems and the main structure of Indian life were as yet but little affected. Yet Christianity was rapidly approaching the position from which it might be expected to exert more wide-spread and profound influence.

Chapter IV

SOUTH-EASTERN ASIA. CEYLON: THE LACCADIVE AND MALDIVE ISLANDS: BURMA: THE ANDAMAN AND NICOBAR ISLANDS: MALAYA: SIAM: FRENCH INDO-CHINA

FROM India we turn to the lands in south-eastern Asia. These were Ceylon, the Laccadive and Maldive Islands, Burma, the Andaman and Nicobar Islands, Malaya, Siam, and the region which in 1914 was known as French Indo-China. In all of these except Malaya and the eastern portions of French Indo-China Indian influence had been dominant in the shaping of culture. In 1914 all except Siam were politically under the control of Europeans. All, even Siam, were being penetrated by Occidental civilization. Except in parts of Ceylon and of Malaya the European political conquest was effected in the nineteenth century. In each of these regions except the Laccadives, Maldives, Andamans, and Nicobars Christianity was present at the beginning of the nineteenth century. In all save these four insular groups in the course of that century it enjoyed a large growth. That growth was in conjunction with the presence of the augmented power of the Occident. However, here, as in other parts of the world, it was primarily the result of the active missionary effort of the churches of the West.

Separated physically from India by only a narrow and shallow strait, the island of Ceylon was culturally and racially akin to its huge neighbour. In religion, it was predominantly Buddhist, for here that faith had not so nearly vanished as it had from its native land. There were, however, many Hindus and a smaller but important Moslem community. Caste was present, but, as was natural in a prevailingly Buddhist region, was less prominent than in India.

Ceylon came earlier under European rule than did India. In the sixteenth century large portions of it were governed by the Portuguese. In the seventeenth century the Portuguese were supplanted by the Dutch. They in turn controlled much but not all of the island. During the wars of the French Revolution and Napoleon, while Holland was occupied by the French, the English expelled the

Dutch (1795-1796). The British conquest was effected through the East India Company, but before the end of the century the British portions of the island were transferred from the company to the Crown. Ceylon became and remained a crown colony. The year 1815 which saw the end of the Napoleonic Wars also witnessed the extension of British rule into the interior, over such sections of the island as had heretofore remained independent. Under British administration Ceylon prospered. Both population and wealth increased. Religiously, the British Government was tolerant and neutral. The security which it gave and the facilities it afforded for the penetration of Western culture provided a favourable setting for the spread of Christianity.

At the dawn of the nineteenth century Christianity was strongly represented. As we saw in an earlier volume,[1] in the Portuguese period Roman Catholic Christianity had flourished. The Dutch had striven to suppress it and to inculcate Protestantism. At the time of the British conquest Protestants may have numbered somewhat more than a third of a million.[2] Yet Roman Catholicism persisted and in A.D. 1800 is said to have had more adherents than Protestantism.[3]

The British period witnessed the revival and growth of Roman Catholic Christianity and an initial decline followed by a later growth of Protestantism. At the close of the nineteenth century Protestantism was thriving but was not nearly so strong numerically as Roman Catholicism.

An early effect of the advent of the English was a rapid loss of membership in the Protestant communities which had been built up under the Dutch. Thousands joined the Roman Catholics, to whom they had long been secretly attached, presumably through hereditary affiliation. Other thousands went over to Buddhism and Hinduism. It is said that by the year 1810 Protestants were only half as numerous as in 1801 and that for a time thereafter each year showed them further diminished.[4]

It may have been that in the fore part of the nineteenth century the Roman Catholic Church also suffered a numerical loss. One set of statistics declares that in 1806 the island contained only 66,830 of that faith.[5] If these figures and the ones given in the third paragraph above are correct, they indicate a striking defection from the Roman Catholic fold. It is possible, however, that the earlier total was inflated. Certainly one estimate places the Roman Catholics in 1717 at 70,000.[6] Yet even that may contribute to the evidence of some loss in the first years of British rule.

[1] Vol. III, Chap. 9.
[2] Tennent, *Christianity in Ceylon*, pp. 63, 64, 82.
[3] Tennent, *op. cit.*, pp. 63, 64.
[4] Tennent, *op. cit.*, pp. 83, 84; Harvard, *A Narrative*, pp. lxviii, lix.
[5] *The Jaffna Ecclesiastical Directory*, 1875, p. 14.
[6] *Ibid.*

If Roman Catholics suffered a numerical decline in the initial years of the British regime, they soon began to recoup their strength. By a regulation of the British Government in 1806 Roman Catholics were accorded full liberty of worship,[7] a step which was confirmed in 1829 by the application to Ceylon of the Catholic Emancipation Act passed by Parliament in that year.[8] In charge of the spiritual care of the Roman Catholics were Goanese Oratorians, largely Brahmin in background. Until 1842 they were the only order represented.[9] Down to the mid-1830's Ceylon was under the Bishop of Cochin, but a vicariate apostolic was then created for the island. The first three vicars apostolic were Oratorians of Goa.[10]

The efforts at recovery and advance in the early decades of the nineteenth century led by the Indian priests were troubled by at least two unfortunate factors. One was the low level of spiritual life among the existing Roman Catholics. The young were poorly instructed. Usually the only two sacraments administered after baptism were marriage and extreme unction. Confirmation and the communion were rare.[11] The dissensions over the Portuguese padroado which so troubled the Roman Catholic Church in India extended to Ceylon. As in India, the struggle was precipitated by the creation of vicariates apostolic in the 1830's, but it seems not to have become acute until non-Goanese priests arrived and it appears to have subsided somewhat earlier than on the adjoining continent.[12] However, it again became a live issue late in the century and gave rise to a schism which spread from India and which was not healed until 1902.[13]

One of the first of the European priests to arrive in the new century was an Italian Oratorian, Bettachini, who went to Ceylon in 1842 in response to a request of Roman Catholic Burghers, Eurasians, who had petitioned the Propaganda for European clergy. In 1845 Bettachini was made coadjutor to the vicar apostolic and took up his residence in Jaffna. In the later 1840's Ceylon was divided into two vicariates, Colombo and Jaffna, and Bettachini was assigned to the latter.[14] Even before Jaffna had been made a distinct vicariate, Bettachini had gone to Europe in search of reinforcements. In answer to his plea there

[7] Bonjean, *Marriage Legislation in Ceylon*, p. 7.
[8] Kuruppu, *The Catholic Church in Ceylon*, pp. 11ff.
[9] *Ibid.*
[10] Prakasar, *XXV Years' Catholic Progress*, p. 1; Duchaussois, *Sous les Feux de Ceylan*, pp. 74-76; Huonder, *Der einheimische Klerus in den Heidenländern*, pp. 262-264; Jonquet, *Mgr. Bonjean*, Vol. I, pp. 69-72.
[11] Jonquet, *op. cit.*, Vol. I, p. 68.
[12] Jonquet, *op. cit.*, Vol. I, pp. 236ff.; Vol. II, pp. 132, 141-147; Rommerskirchen, *Die Oblatenmission auf der Insel Ceylon*, pp. 18-21; Kuruppu, *op. cit.*, pp. 12-15; *The Jaffna Ecclesiastical Directory*, 1875, p. 15; Duchaussois, *op. cit.*, pp. 69-73.
[13] Jonquet, *op. cit.*, Vol. II, pp. 141-147; Prakasar, *op. cit.*, pp. 20ff.
[14] Rommerskirchen, *op. cit.*, pp. 18-21.

came (1847) the first contingent of Oblates of Mary Immaculate, one of the new congregations of the nineteenth century. It was led by Stephen Semeria.[15] There also arrived seculars and, from Madura, Jesuits.[16]

In time the vicariate apostolic of Jaffna passed into the hands of the Oblates. Relations between them on the one hand and, on the other, Bettachini and various other European priests became strained.[17] At the outset the clergy were so few that they were engrossed with the care of the Christians and had no leisure to reach out to non-Christians.[18] Semeria became coadjutor to Bettachini and on the latter's death (1857) succeeded him as vicar apostolic.[19] Under his able administration the Christians in the vicariate increased, partly through conversions (many of which occurred through the marriage of non-Christians to Christians) but chiefly by the excess of births over deaths.[20] Schools multiplied and Sisters of the Holy Family, affiliated with the Oblates, arrived to help with them.[21] Semeria was followed (1868) as vicar apostolic by Ernest Christophe Bonjean. During Bonjean's administration accessions from non-Christians multiplied, notably through those who were aided during the famine years of 1877-1878, the period which was so fruitful in conversions in South India.[22] Even in the latter part of the nineteenth century, however, the clergy were too burdened with their ministry to the Christians to have much time for the non-Christians. The numbers of Roman Catholics in the diocese rose from 39,672 in 1896 to 55,062 in 1917.[23] With that growth came also a continued improvement in the religious life—evidenced in part by the great increase of communions and pilgrimages, the growth of various organizations, and an advance in theological education.[24] Such conversions as were witnessed were chiefly from the lower social strata.[25]

Colombo was the centre of the largest Roman Catholic population on the island and the seat of what in A.D. 1800 was the only vicariate apostolic. In 1850 Josef Maria Bravi, an Italian Benedictine of St. Sylvester, became coadjutor to the Goanese Oratorian who held the see.[26] Other Sylvestrians arrived and until 1883 the vicariate remained in their charge. Seculars were also brought in to

[15] Rommerskirchen, *op. cit.*, p. 22.
[16] Piolet, *Les Missions Catholiques Françaises au XIXe Siècle,* Vol. II, p. 135.
[17] Rommerskirchen, *op. cit.*, pp. 30ff.
[18] Rommerskirchen, *op. cit.*, p. 23.
[19] Rommerskirchen, *op. cit.*, pp. 32, 33.
[20] Rommerskirchen, *op. cit.*, p. 99.
[21] Rommerskirchen, *op. cit.*, p. 72.
[22] Rommerskirchen, *op. cit.*, p. 116.
[23] Prakasar, *op. cit.*, pp. 3ff.
[24] Prakasar, *op. cit.*, *passim.*
[25] Prakasar, *op. cit.*, pp. 204, 205.
[26] Piolet, *op. cit.*, Vol. II, p. 135; Rommerskirchen, *op. cit.*, p. 166.

help rear an indigenous clergy. Spanish Benedictines entered. However, a pest wasted the coffee plantations on which the wealth of the region largely depended and so cut down local support. In Italy new laws placed irksome restrictions on the mother congregation. As a result, in 1883 Colombo was handed over to the Oblates, who were better prepared to cope with the large task presented by the area, and a new vicariate, that of Kandy, with fewer Christians, was created for the Sylvestrians.[27] Bonjean was thereupon transferred to Colombo. In 1886, when a hierarchy was created for India, one was also provided for Ceylon. Colombo was made the seat of an archbishop and Bonjean was appointed the first incumbent. In the six years which intervened before his death, Bonjean, in spite of the annoyance of a Goanese schism, saw improvements in the schools and in the care of the poor.[28] Under his successor still further progress was registered, including the formation of the Catholic Union of Ceylon with branches in important centres in the island.[29]

In 1893 the diocese of Trincomalee, on the east coast, was created and entrusted to French Jesuits of the province of Champagne. Under them the Roman Catholic population mounted.[30]

In that same year there was erected, in the South, the diocese of Galle. This was assigned to Belgian Jesuits. In the course of the next twenty-five years the number of Roman Catholics nearly trebled, that of chapels more than quadrupled, schools multiplied nearly tenfold, and communions more than fortyfold.[31]

Under the care of the Goanese and then the European missionaries the Roman Catholics of Ceylon increased in numbers. In 1873 the total in the island was said to be 184,399,[32] in 1901, according to the civil census, 285,018, and in 1911, on that same authority, 339,300 and according to ecclesiastical count 322,163.[33] In 1911 not quite two-thirds of these were Sinhalese of the lowlands, slightly less than a third Tamils, and a few thousands Burghers and Kandyan Sinhalese.[34] Much of the growth was through the natural increase in which the Roman Catholic community shared in that of the island as a whole, but some

---

[27] Piolet, op. cit., Vol. II, pp. 156, 157; Rommerskirchen, op. cit., pp. 163, 167.

[28] For the life of Bonjean see Jonquet, op. cit., passim. See also Schwager, Die katholische Heidenmission der Gegenwart, p. 358.

[29] Schwager, op. cit., p. 359.

[30] Schwager, op. cit., p. 365; Programme des Fêtes Célébrées à l'Occasion du Jubilé Épiscopal de Monseigneur Charles Lavigne de la Compagnie de Jésus, Évêque de Trincomalee (Ceylan) 1887-1912 (Toulouse. Imp. J. Fournier, pp. 9), passim.

[31] La Missione di Galle nell' Isola di Ceylan (India) affidata ai Padri della Provincia di Napoli della Compagnia di Gesù (Naples, Procura delle Missioni, 1925, pp. 36), passim.

[32] The Jaffna Ecclesiastical Directory, 1875, p. 16.

[33] Catholic Directory of India, 1913, p. 435.

[34] Catholic Directory of India, 1913, pp. 440, 441.

was through conversions. In the wave of nationalism evoked by the Japanese victory over Russia in 1905 there were anti-Christian riots, for the Sinhalese Buddhists looked upon the Japanese as co-religionists and regarded their triumph as one of their faith over that of the Christians.[35] Yet at most these disturbances were only a temporary reverse.

Growth in numbers was paralleled by an improvement in the quality of Roman Catholics. Schools multiplied.[36] While still Vicar Apostolic of Jaffna, Bonjean insisted as a prerequisite to baptism that pagans break off all connexion with non-Christian cults, that they be reconciled to their enemies, restore goods taken wrongfully, make good other injuries, and give up polygamy.[37] If any Christian gave cause for public scandal he was, at least in theory and to some extent in practice, required to make reparation publicly and to do public penance.[38] The central theological seminary for India authorized by the Pope in the 1890's also included Ceylon, was placed on that island, and helped to train an indigenous clergy.[39] Although some traces of caste persisted among Christians, the ecclesiastical authorities strove to weaken them.[40] The bishops fought, not unsuccessfully, for state recognition of marriage rites performed in their churches, as a means of strengthening Christian marriage and the Christian home.[41] We hear of an agricultural colony for low caste converts in which Christians were brought together for community life in a village under ecclesiastical oversight.[42] We read of what by the Roman Catholics was counted as an evidence of faith, a centre of pilgrimage, a shrine to Our Lady of Madhu, to which throngs came much as was the custom at Lourdes in France, and the dust of which was declared to be efficacious in curing physical afflictions, notably snake bites.[43] We also are told of the multiplication of confraternities which encouraged retreats and frequent communion.[44]

As two other phases of Roman Catholic activity, Oblates were in charge of the only reformatory for child delinquents on the island [45] and spiritual care

[35] Capuchin Mission Unit, *India and Its Missions*, pp. 164, 166.
[36] *The Jaffna Ecclesiastical Directory, 1875*, pp. 32, 33.
[37] Rommerskirchen, *op. cit.*, p. 114.
[38] Balangero, *Australia e Ceylan*, p. 321.
[39] Capuchin Mission Unit, *op. cit.*, p. 165.
[40] Duchaussois, *op. cit.*, pp. 40-44; Rommerskirchen, *op. cit.*, p. 83.
[41] Ch. Bonjean, *Marriage Legislation in Ceylon* (Trichinopoly, The Scottish Press, 1864, pp. xi, 166), *passim; Documents Regarding the Marriage Legislation in Ceylon* (Mangalore, The Codialbail Press, 1898, pp. 91), *passim*.
[42] *Fides News Service*, May 28, 1938.
[43] Jonquet, *op. cit.*, Vol. I, pp. 236ff.; Léon Hermant, *La Perle des Indes* (Brussells, Éditions de la Revue des Auteurs et des Livres, 1924, pp. 146), pp. 76-81.
[44] Prakasar, *op. cit.*, pp. 21-27.
[45] Duchaussois, *op. cit.*, pp. 239-243.

was given to Irish Roman Catholic soldiers serving in Ceylon with a temperance society and a club with recreational and literary adjuncts.[46]

In spite of the British connexion, in the nineteenth century Protestantism was not as flourishing in Ceylon as was Roman Catholicism. The British rulers sought for a time to halt the disintegration which had been brought about by the collapse of the Dutch regime. The Dutch Reformed faith was regarded as the established religion and it was suggested that the Dutch clergy be reinforced by ministers from the kindred Church of Scotland. For several decades the Dutch Reformed ministers, together with the chaplains of the Church of Scotland and the Church of England who served the British community, were subsidized by the state.[47] Efforts were made to restore the Dutch schools.[48] Mass baptisms of children were common, by clerical functionaries called proponents who had been inherited from the Dutch. In many districts practically all the Sinhalese were baptized. Yet these "Christian Buddhists" or "Government Christians" still maintained their Buddhist rites.[49] It was quickly discovered that under the new regime preference in office holding was no longer accorded Christians. The Dutch Reformed Church rapidly declined and became confined almost entirely to a few hundred of the Burghers, descendants of mixed unions of Dutch and natives.[50]

Within a few years after the dawn of the nineteenth century several Protestant missionary agencies, mostly British but also one American, entered Ceylon. At the outset they were given friendly greeting by the British authorities, and that in spite of the fact that until past the middle of the century the British administration appointed the leading priests in the chief non-Christian temples.[51] Under these societies Protestantism experienced a fresh growth, mainly by conversions from non-Christians.

The London Missionary Society was first in the field. From 1804 through 1818 it had representatives on the island. Two of these, Germans, became ministers of Dutch churches and passed out of the control of the society. Soon after 1818 the undertaking was discontinued.[52]

As was natural because of the wide-ranging vision of Carey and his Serampore associates, the Baptist Missionary Society was the first to begin a continuing

[46] Balangero, op. cit., p. 334.
[47] Tennent, Christianity in Ceylon, pp. 78-80.
[48] Tennent, op. cit., p. 80.
[49] Tennent, op. cit., pp. 87-90.
[50] Tennent, op. cit., pp. 101-103.
[51] Lennox A. Mills, India Under British Rule, 1795-1932 (Oxford University Press, 1933, pp. vi, 311), p. 126.
[52] Lovett, The History of the London Missionary Society, Vol. II, pp. 18-21.

enterprise. In 1812 James Chater of that society, forced out of Burma by war and the illness of his wife, landed in Colombo. Reinforcements came from time to time, notably, in 1830, soon after Chater's death, Ebenezer Daniel. Activities were undertaken at several centres. The number of converts was not large and in 1914 the Baptist community totalled only between 3,000 and 4,000. Yet many of the Christians displayed zeal in bringing their faith to new villages. Fresh work was done in translating and distributing the Bible. An English-speaking congregation in Colombo was nourished through its infancy.[53]

In 1814 came the Wesleyans, in a group which had been led by the devoted Thomas Coke, whom we have met in more than one country as a pioneer of Methodism.[54] It was at the suggestion of the Chief Justice of Ceylon made through Wilberforce that Coke planned the enterprise. On the outward voyage Coke died. His colleagues, undaunted, persevered and inaugurated the mission. Before long schools were opened, preaching was begun, and converts came, some from the Buddhist priesthood.[55] The Wesleyans extended their activities to several different parts of the island. They addressed themselves to the British elements, the Burghers, the Sinhalese, and the Tamils. They developed an unusually able indigenous ministry. Much emphasis was placed on schools, primary, industrial, and higher. A press was conducted.[56] In the year 1914 the Methodists counted 6,266 full members, 2,169 on probation, 8,755 others baptized, and 27,222 pupils in schools.[57] Twelve Sinhalese and Tamil circuits and one English circuit had reached the goal of self-support and self-government.[58]

After the collapse of the Dutch Reformed Church, the Church of England was more strongly represented in Ceylon than any other non-Roman Catholic body. With the British occupation came Anglican chaplains.[59] Until the 1880's subsidies from colonial revenues were paid to them and to the Anglican bishop.[60] Alexander Johnston, the chief justice who had so much to do with the inception

[53] John A. Ewing, Lanka: the Resplendent Isle. The Story of the Baptist Mission in Ceylon (London, The Baptist Missionary Society, preface 1912, pp. ix, 119), pp. 16ff.
[54] Vol. III, p. 235; Vol. IV, pp. 72, 187; Vol. V, pp. 54, 60, 142, 330.
[55] W. M. Harvard, A Narrative of the Establishment and Progress of the Mission to Ceylon and India Founded by the Late Rev. Thomas Coke, LL.D., under the Direction of the Wesleyan-Methodist Conference (London, the author, 1823, pp. lxxii, 404), passim.
[56] Findlay and Holdsworth, The History of the Wesleyan Methodist Missionary Society, Vol. V, pp. 15-115; Thomas Moscrop and Arthur E. Restarick, Ceylon and Its Methodism (London, Robert Culley, no date, pp. 128), passim; Edward Strutt, A Missionary Mosaic from Ceylon (London, Charles H. Kelly, 1913, pp. 251), passim; Samuel Langdon, The Happy Valley: Our New "Mission Garden" in Uva, Ceylon (London, Charles H. Kelly, 1890, pp. 137), passim.
[57] Findlay and Holdsworth, op. cit., Vol. V, pp. 52, 107.
[58] The One Hundredth Report of the Wesleyan Methodist Missionary Society (1914), p. 48.
[59] Pascoe, Two Hundred Years of the S.P.G., p. 660.
[60] Stock, The History of the Church Missionary Society, Vol. III, p. 541.

of the Wesleyan enterprise, urged that Anglicans undertake missions in the island and himself circulated Christian literature.[61] In 1817 the Church Missionary Society sent an initial contingent of four clergymen. They were welcomed by the governor and at his suggestion a centre was opened at Kandy, in the interior, recently subdued by the English.[62] Progress was slow,[63] but the society and its missionaries persevered, conversions were registered, some of them of Buddhist priests, congregations were gathered, schools were conducted, an indigenous clergy was trained, and an unusually vigorous Native Church Council was developed.[64] Assistance and supervision were given to the Tamil Coolie Mission, begun among the Tamil labourers on the coffee plantations and supported in part by non-Anglican planters.[65] Similar, but for the Sinhalese, was the Sinhalese Itinerancy.[66] From 1876 into 1880 a disturbing controversy was carried on over some features of episcopal jurisdiction, but eventually this was amicably settled.[67] The Church of England Zenana Missionary Society was represented, labouring in close conjunction with the Church Missionary Society.[68] The first missionary of the Society for the Propagation of the Gospel in Foreign Parts reached Ceylon in 1840. Others followed and in the course of time several centres were opened.[69] The Society for Promoting Christian Knowledge gave a substantial grant to assist in founding a college at Colombo.[70] In 1845 a separate see was created for Ceylon and bore the name of Colombo.[71] Thus provision was made for local episcopal supervision.

The other British organizations represented were much less prominent than those we have thus far mentioned. Among them were the Ceylon and India General Mission, with the villages as its objective,[72] and the Salvation Army.[73]

In 1815 representatives of the American Board of Commissioners for Foreign

[61] Stock, op. cit., Vol. I, p. 216.

[62] Stock, op. cit., Vol. I, pp. 216, 217.

[63] Stock, op. cit., Vol. I, p. 218; Vol. II, pp. 288-29..

[64] Stock, op. cit., Vol. III, pp. 537-547. For concrete pictures of the early years of the enterprise, see James Selkirk, Recollections of Ceylon, after a Residence of Nearly Thirteen Years; with an Account of the Church Missionary Society's Operations in the Island: and Extracts from a Journal (London, J. Hatchard and Son, 1844, pp. xv, 544), pp. 195ff.

[65] Stock, op. cit., Vol. II, pp. 286, 287; R. P. Butterfield, Padre Rowlands of Ceylon (London, Marshall, Morgan & Scott, no date, pp. viii, 182), pp. 39-58, 92-113.

[66] Stock, op. cit., Vol. IV, p. 263.

[67] Stock, op. cit., Vol. III, pp. 203-215.

[68] Stock, op. cit., Vol. IV, p. 264.

[69] Pascoe, op. cit., pp. 660-681.

[70] Allen and McClure, Two Hundred Years. The History of the Society for Promoting Christian Knowledge, p. 294.

[71] Memorials of James Chapman, D.D., First Bishop of Colombo (London, Skeffington & Son, 1892, pp. x, 236), passim.

[72] Strong and Warnshuis, Directory of Foreign Missions, p. 28.

[73] Year Book of Missions in India, Burma and Ceylon, 1912, p. 523.

Missions arrived. Indeed, one of the original group sent by that board to the East had been in Colombo for a time in 1813. Jaffna was chosen as the main centre of the enterprise. The constituency, therefore, was primarily Tamil. From time to time additional missionaries were sent, and as the years passed schools were developed, culminating in a college, medical work was conducted, churches were gathered, and an indigenous clergy trained.[74]

By the year 1914, thanks to these various organizations, Protestantism had taken firm root in Ceylon. Numerically it was not as strong as in Dutch times, but in vigour it was far ahead of its pre-nineteenth century days. The Christians were much better instructed. They were, moreover, beginning to take responsibility for the propagation of their faith. In 1887, for instance, the Lanka Baptist Mission was formed and in 1913 the undenominational National Missionary Society of Ceylon was constituted.[75]

At the close of the pre-1914 period Christianity in Ceylon, both Roman Catholic and Protestant, was growing fairly steadily and was in a far healthier condition than ever before. Between 1901 and 1911 the numbers of Christians had risen by more than a sixth, or at a faster rate than any other religious group in the island.[76] The increase was due in part to the excess of births over deaths, yet accessions were also coming from non-Christian faiths. Buddhism was paying Christianity the compliment of imitating its methods and terminology. There were Buddhist Sunday schools, catechisms, lay preachers, and hymns and carols adapted from Christian models.[77] In the census of 1911 more than one-tenth of the population were shown to be Christians, a much larger proportion than in India. Christianity was making a growing impression.

The Laccadive Islands, in the nineteenth century brought directly under British sway, and the Maldive Islands, governed by the British under Ceylon, need not long detain us. They were coral archipelagoes with small populations which were Moslem in religion. In 1887 the Propaganda proposed placing both

[74] Helen I. Root, compiler, *A Century in Ceylon. A Brief History of the American Board in Ceylon 1816-1916* (The American Ceylon Mission, 1916, pp. 87), *passim;* James Read Eckard, *A Personal Narration of Residence as a Missionary in Ceylon and Southern Hindoostan* (Philadelphia, American Sunday School Union, 1844, pp. 254); Miron Winslow, *A Memoir of Mrs. Harriet Wadsworth Winslow, Combining a Sketch of the Ceylon Mission* (New York, Leavitt, Lord & Co., 1835, pp. 408); Mary and Margaret Leitch, *Seven Years in Ceylon* (New York, American Tract Society, 1890, pp. viii, 170).
[75] Philip, *Report of a Survey of Indigenous Christian Efforts in India, Burma and Ceylon,* p. 3.
[76] *The One Hundredth Report of the Wesleyan Methodist Missionary Society* (1914), p. 48.
[77] Stock, *op. cit.,* Vol. III, p. 769.

groups in a prefecture apostolic with the southern part of Ceylon. Archbishop Bonjean of Ceylon demurred, declaring that missionaries were not admitted to the islands and that the Laccadives belonged with India rather than with Ceylon.[78] Apparently his advice was taken. Neither Roman Catholic nor Protestant missionaries seem to have established themselves in either group.

Far otherwise was it with Burma. Burma became the scene of very active Christian missions.

Here was a land which in some respects resembled Ceylon. In both the prevailing religion was Buddhism of the Hinayana or southern type. Both had strong cultural connexions with India. Both saw an immigration of Indians, largely labourers, in the nineteenth century. By the close of the nineteenth century both were under British rulers.

Yet marked differences existed. In Burma very much larger groups of folk with primitive or near-primitive cultures were to be found than in Ceylon. The Burmese proper, who were the prevailing people in the fertile valleys, were solidly Buddhist, although their Buddhism had in it non-Buddhist strains, but in the hills which flanked the valleys were other peoples, chief of whom in numbers were the Karens. The Karens were predominantly animistic. Among other animistic peoples were the Chins, Kachins, Lahus, and Was. The Shans, Buddhists, were strong. Burma had much fewer Moslems and a smaller Hindu element than did Ceylon. It was later in being brought under British rule.

The British conquest was effected in three stages. A British-Burmese war in 1824-1826 resulted in the cession to the victors of the coastal provinces of Arakan and Tenasserim. A second war, in 1852, led to the British annexation of the province of Pegu, in Lower Burma. In 1885 a third war was followed by the annexation of Upper Burma (January 1, 1886). Later the British domain was extended into adjacent territory, notably the Shan states and the Chin Hills. Through the accident of history, for the conquest of Burma was accomplished as a corollary of that of India, until after 1914 Burma was administered as part of the latter country. It was not held as a separate crown colony, as was Ceylon.

In several respects Christianity had a course in Burma very different from that in Ceylon. It entered upon the nineteenth century with no such large constituency as in Ceylon. Roman Catholicism had been introduced in the seventeenth century by the Portuguese and in the eighteenth century Barnabites had laboured to make converts.[79] However, at the dawn of the nineteenth cen-

[78] Rommerskirchen, *Die Oblatenmissionen auf der Insel Ceylon,* p. 226.
[79] Vol. III, pp. 293, 294.

tury Roman Catholics were few. Protestantism did not arrive until early in that century. In the nineteenth century it was not, as in Ceylon, the Roman Catholic Church which made the chief gains, but Protestantism. In contrast with Ceylon, where British missions predominated, Protestantism was represented mainly by Americans, chiefly Baptists. As in Ceylon, Christianity tended to follow the advancing frontier of British rule. However, in some places it antedated it and it received much less official British encouragement and support than in Ceylon. In Burma the majority of the accessions to Christianity, whether Roman Catholic or Protestant, were from the Karens and not from the Buddhist Burmese. In 1911 Christians were less than half as numerous in Burma as in Ceylon, but the Protestant body was about twice and the Roman Catholics less than a sixth as strong as in the great island to the south.[80] By the census of 1921 Christians totalled 257,106, or slightly less than 2 per cent. of the population. Of these only 207,760 were from indigenous races, 24,058 were Indians, 8,630 were Europeans, and 16,658 were Anglo-Indians. Of the indigenous Christian community 178,225, or 69.3 per cent. were Karens, or nearly 15 per cent. of that people; only 14,924, or 5.8 per cent., were from the other non-Burmese indigenous folk, approximately .81 per cent. of that section of the population; and only 14,611, or 5.7 per cent., were from the Burmese and the Talaing, or less than .16 per cent. of that majority group. Of the Indians, largely immigrants, 2.6 per cent. were Christians.[81] This, it may be noted, was about twice the percentage which Indian Christians constituted in the portions of their native land that were within the British Empire.

For fully the first half of the nineteenth century the Roman Catholic Church made but little headway. The French Revolution and the wars of Napoleon brought difficulties to the Barnabites, for they led to the expulsion of the latter from France and the despoiling of some of their colleges in Germany and Italy. In 1806 the vicar apostolic went to Europe in search of reinforcements, but was disappointed.[82] In 1825 only two priests were left in the country, one of them a native and the other a Portuguese Indian. In 1827 one of these died. In 1830 the Barnabites formally surrendered the mission and placed it in the hands of the Pope. The Propaganda sent out as vicar apostolic Frederico Cao of the Clerks Regular of the Mother of God. With Cao came two priests, an Italian Tyrolese secular and a Genoese Augustinian. In 1832 these were augmented by a Neopolitan Augustinian and a Swiss Benedictine.[83] In 1841 Roman Catholics in Burma

[80] Government census, reproduced in *Catholic Directory of India, 1913*, pp. 440, 441, and McLeish, *Christian Progress in Burma*, p. 78.
[81] McLeish, *op. cit.*, p. 84.
[82] Gallo, *Storia de Christianesimo nell' Impero Barmano*, Vol. III, pp. 98-106.
[83] Gallo, *op. cit.*, Vol. III, pp. 124-169.

were said to number 4,500.[84] In 1842 the mission was entrusted to Italian Oblates of Mary Immaculate.[85] Between the years 1800 and 1854 thirty-seven Roman Catholic missionaries, most of them Oblates, reached Burma. In 1847 the first sisters arrived. Four more came in 1852.[86] The Italian Barnabites, discouraged by the restrictions being imposed on religious orders in their mother country, asked that Burma be assigned to the Société des Missions Étrangères of Paris, an organization which had long been active in the south-east of Asia. This was done and in 1856 a member of that society was appointed vicar apostolic.[87] At that time the Christian community seems to have been dwindling. It belonged to several races, was scattered widely over the country, and was in dire straits both materially and spiritually.[88] By 1862 the Paris society could count in the country one bishop, eleven missionaries, one native priest, one college, and approximately six thousand Christians.[89] Thirty years later, in 1892, a substantial if not spectacular growth could be recorded. The Paris society now had two vicariates apostolic. In the southern one Roman Catholics numbered 22,000, with 39 missionaries, 10 native priests, 54 catechists, 28 lay brothers, and 57 sisters of two congregations, that of the Good Shepherd and that of St. Joseph of the Vision. There was a seminary, there were 48 other schools with 3,280 pupils, and a printing press was maintained. In the northern vicariate Roman Catholics totalled 4,500, with 27 missionaries, 2 native clergy, 10 catechists, and 8 sisters. There was a seminary and there were 25 schools with 660 pupils.[90] In the meantime, in 1866, the Seminary of Milan had been charged with the care of a vicariate in eastern Burma. Its first priests arrived in 1868. In 1912 Roman Catholics in this vicariate numbered 14,316, those in the southern vicariate 58,423, and those in the northern one 9,800.[91] The larger part of the conversions were from the Karens. From them, too, came several of the indigenous priests. In the year 1914 in the South there were several thousand Indian Roman Catholics and in Rangoon about three thousand Roman Catholics among the Europeans and the Anglo-Indians.[92] Roman Catholics were a growing force.

The propagation of Protestant Christianity in Burma had its inception through the vision and purpose of William Carey and his Serampore colleagues.

[84] *Notizie Statistiche delle Missioni di Tutto il Mondo Dipendenti dalla S.C. de Propaganda Fide,* p. 541.
[85] Hull, *Bombay Mission History,* Vol. I, p. 256.
[86] Gallo, *op. cit.,* Vol. III, pp. 164-169.
[87] Launay, *Histoire Générale de la Société des Missions-Étrangères,* Vol. III, pp. 315, 316.
[88] Launay, *op. cit.,* Vol. III, p. 317.
[89] Launay, *op. cit.,* Vol. III, p. 446.
[90] Launay, *op. cit.,* Vol. III, pp. 550ff.
[91] Streit, *Atlas Hierarchicus,* p. 99.
[92] Schwager, *Die katholische Heidenmission der Gegenwart,* pp. 436-440; Launay in Piolet, *Les Missions Catholiques Françaises au XIXe Siècle,* Vol. II, pp. 313-350.

When, in 1806, the East India Company, alarmed by a mutiny in its Indian troops in Vellore which it believed had arisen from religious antagonism aroused by the activity of missionaries, forbade the landing of reinforcements to the Baptist mission, Carey suggested that one of the new arrivals, Chater, go to Burma. With him he sent his son, Felix Carey. The Serampore group also translated part of the New Testament into Burmese. Before many years Chater left and inaugurated the Baptist enterprise in Ceylon. After the tragic drowning of his wife and some of his children, Felix for a time proved unstable and brought grief to the mission.[93] The English Baptist undertaking did not prosper.

In 1810 two representatives of the London Missionary Society were in Rangoon, but war and the death of one of them led the other to withdraw.[94]

What was probably the greatest contribution of the English Baptists to the Christian cause in Burma was the hospitality given to Adoniram Judson.[95] This led to the beginning of the activities of the American Baptists in Burma and so to the emergence of what in time became the largest body of Christians in that country. It will be recalled [96] that Judson was among the group of students of Andover Theological Seminary whose purpose brought into being the American Board of Commissioners for Foreign Missions and that he was of the first contingent sent abroad by that society. As we also saw, on the voyage Judson and his wife, knowing that in India they would meet the Baptist Carey, studied the issue on which their own communion, the Congregational, chiefly differed from the Baptists, became convinced that the latter were right, and were immersed at Calcutta by William Ward, one of the Serampore Trio. A colleague of the Judsons, Luther Rice, having come to a similar conclusion, returned to the United States to plead with the Baptists of that country to rise to the opportunity so unexpectedly thrust upon them. Excluded from India by the unfriendly East India Company, to escape deportation to Great Britain

[93] Carey, *William Carey*, pp. 257-261, 272-274, 289, 319-322.
[94] Lovett, *The History of the London Missionary Society*, Vol. II, p. 38.
[95] On Judson and his mission the most recent good account is Stacy R. Warburton, *Eastward! The Story of Adoniram Judson* (New York, Round Table Press, 1937, pp. xi, 240). Excellent older accounts are Francis Wayland, *A Memoir of the Life and Labours of the Rev. Adoniram Judson, D.D.* (Boston, Phillips, Samson and Co., 2 vols., 1853) and Edward Judson, *The Life of Adoniram Judson* (New York, Anson D. F. Randolph & Co., 1883, pp. xii, 601). See also, on the women who successively held the place of wife to him, the readable Ethel Daniels Hubbard, *Ann of Ava* (New York, Missionary Education Movement, 1913, pp. 245); Ann H. Judson, *An Account of the American Baptist Mission to the Burman Empire: in a Series of Letters Addressed to a Gentleman in London* (London, J. Butterworth & Son, 1823, pp. xv, 334); Arabella M. Willson, *The Lives of Mrs. Ann H. Judson, Mrs. Sarah B. Judson, and Mrs. Emily C. Judson, Missionaries to Burmah* (New York, Miller, Orton & Mulligan, 1856, pp. 371); Fanny Forester, *Life of Sarah B. Judson* (London, T. Nelson and Sons, 1873, pp. 230); and A. C. Kendrick, *The Life and Letters of Mrs. Emily C. Judson* (New York, Sheldon & Co., 1860, pp. 426).
[96] See Vol. IV, pp. 80-83.

the Judsons went to the Isle of France and from there to Rangoon. Judson had earlier thought of Burma as a field, so the decision was by no means hasty. He and Mrs. Judson landed in Rangoon in July, 1813, and found a home in the English Baptist mission house. There followed years of difficulty and privation. Judson had marked linguistic and scholarly gifts and gave himself early to the task of translation and the preparation of a dictionary. He also engaged in preaching. To approach the Burmese in a way which would not seem to them too alien, he erected a *zayat,* a type of building found in most Burman villages where men gathered, and there taught. Not until 1819 did he baptize his first convert. In 1824, after an earlier preliminary visit, he established himself at the capital, Ava. Within a few months the first Anglo-Burmese War broke out. Judson, as an English-speaking foreigner, was politically suspect and was cast into prison. His wife, heroic Ann Hasseltine Judson, was allowed to remain at liberty, ministered to him, and pled for his release. The weeks were terrible ones, with severe illnesses for them both. Eventually he was freed and they retired to Rangoon. In 1826, however, a fresh disaster overtook Judson. Ann Hasseltine died. She was a woman of unusual ability and strength of character and they had been a devoted couple. Before long Judson transferred his head-quarters to Moulmein. Now followed a period of peculiarly intense self-discipline. He came under the influence of the writings of the French Roman Catholic mystic, the somewhat eccentric and emotionally unstable Madame Guyon (1648-1717). Since a precocious childhood and youth when he had been the centre of an adoring family, Judson had found pride and selfish ambition a temptation. He had charm and for him winning the friendship of the great was easy. All this he now sought to renounce and by stern measures to eradicate. He continued his literary labours and in 1834 completed his translation of the entire Bible into Burmese. He later revised his translation of the Old Testament. He prepared other books in Burmese, including a liturgy and a large life of Christ. He made contacts with non-Christians in some of the larger cities and undertook tours among the Karens. In 1834 he married Sarah Hall Board-man, the widow of a colleague of whom we are to hear more in a moment. This marriage, like his first one, proved singularly happy. Judson returned to the United States only once, in 1845 and 1846, and then because his wife's health demanded it. She died on the westward voyage. In the United States he was married to Emily Chubbuck, an author of promise. In Burma once more, he worked at a dictionary and completed the English-Burmese section. He began the Burmese-English portion, but failing health overtook him and he died (1850) on the voyage which he had undertaken in the hope of recovery. Like another great pioneer, Coke, he was buried at sea.

Before his death Judson had already become the inspiration of a growing mission. His leadership in the first American Protestant mission outside the Western Hemisphere, his dramatic change of denomination, and the story of his imprisonment at Ava and of the devotion of the indomitable Ann Hasseltine made a deep impression in Baptist circles in the United States. Reinforcements came to him [97] and Burma claimed and continued to hold a prior place in the affections of the churches which had rallied to his support.

Among the American Baptists who came to the Burmese mission was George Dana Boardman (1801-1831).[98] He was in the East only a little over five years. Of that time, because the first Anglo-Burmese War interfered, slightly less than four years were spent in Burma itself. Boardman was best remembered as the first American missionary to give himself to the Karens. Some of the Karens were in and near Moulmein, where for a time the Baptist mission had its chief centre. Judson and his colleagues became interested in them,[99] and one of them, Ko Tha Byu, became a Christian.[100] Ko Tha Byu had been a robber and a murderer and had a violent temper, but the Christian faith, patiently taught him by Judson, wrought a change in him. In 1828 a new station was opened at Tavoy, south of Moulmein, and Boardman was placed in charge. With Boardman went Ko Tha Byu. Soon after their arrival at Tavoy Ko Tha Byu was baptized by Boardman and then began preaching in the Karen villages in the mountains and hills of the vicinity. He proved a flaming evangelist and started what before long became a mass movement among his people towards Christianity. The Karens were prepared for what he had to say.[101] They were by no means a primitive folk, but they were nearer to the primitive stage than were their Burmese neighbours. The latter viewed them with contempt. Animism was prominent in their religion, but they also had a belief in a Creator and had a story which resembled the Biblical account of the fall of man by which they accounted for their own unhappy social position. They also cherished an account of a sacred book which their fathers through carelessness had lost. Although illiterate, and without a written form to their language, they longed for the restoration of the vanished volume. They were accordingly not unwilling listeners to the message of Ko Tha Byu and the white missionaries who fol-

[97] On three of these see Colman and Wheelock, or, the Early Called of the Burman Mission (Philadelphia, American Baptist Publication Society, 1853, pp. 132), and Mrs. A. M. Edmond, Memoir of Mrs. Sarah D. Comstock (Philadelphia, American Baptist Publication Society, 1854, pp. 228).

[98] Alonzo King, Memoir of George Dana Boardman (Boston, Lincoln, Edmands & Co., 1834, pp. 320); Joseph Chandler Robbins, Boardman of Burma (Philadelphia, The Judson Press, 1940, pp. 178).

[99] Wylie, The Gospel in Burmah, p. 41.

[100] Francis Mason, The Karen Apostle: or Memoir of Ko Thah-byu (Boston, Gould, Kendall and Lincoln, 1843, p. 153).

[101] Marshall, The Karen People of Burma, pp. 210ff.

lowed him, for from them they heard of the possibility of salvation from their forefathers' sins and of the recovery of the book. Through contacts with those who came to Tavoy to see him and through his travels among their villages, Boardman had begun to witness the ingathering, but his life was cut short (1831) before he could do more than lay foundations.

Before his death (1840) Ko Tha Byu had carried his new faith to the Karens in the vicinity of Rangoon and Bassein. The stirring among the Karens aroused the suspicion of the Burmese authorities and until the annexation of Lower Burma by the British (1853) the Christians were subject to recurring persecutions. However, their faith continued to spread. To the Karen the white man meant relief from the oppression of the Burmese and he was therefore inclined to adopt the white man's faith.[102]

The Karen movement toward Christianity in which Judson, Boardman, and Ko Tha Byu had been pioneers continued. Wade reduced the Karen language to writing.[103] Literature was prepared, including translations of the Bible into the tongues of various branches of the Karens. In 1856, 11,878 church members were reported.[104] In 1914 the total was 47,530 and there were 192 ordained and 541 unordained preachers and 883 teachers.[105] Schools were organized. Clergy were trained.[106] The Karens undertook the financial support of their churches and schools and became more nearly independent of subsidies from the outside than almost any other group of Christians in southern and eastern Asia.[107] They were active in winning non-Christians. Christianity was transforming them and giving them a more prominent place as a people.[108]

In the 1860's a schism occurred, led by Mrs. Mason.[109] From those who fol-

[102] Howard, *Baptists in Burma,* pp. 56, 57.

[103] Wylie, *op. cit.,* pp. 46, 47.

[104] Marshall, *op. cit.,* p. 300. On two of the early missionaries to the Karens, see Calista V. Luther, *The Vintons and the Karens. Memorials of Rev. Justus H. Vinton and Calista H. Vinton* (Boston, W. G. Corthell, 1880, pp. xi, 251). For sketches of a later stage see Alonzo Bunker, *Sketches from the Karen Hills* (Chicago, Fleming H. Revell Co., 1910, pp. 215).

[105] *One Hundredth Annual Report, American Baptist Foreign Mission Society, 1914,* statistical tables.

[106] On two who gave much of their lives to the training of the Karen pastors, see Mrs. J. G. Binney, *Twenty-Six Years in Burmah: Records of the Life and Work of Joseph G. Binney, D.D.* (Philadelphia, American Baptist Publication Society, 1880, pp. 384) and Emma M. Marshall and Harry I. Marshall, *Daniel Appleton White Smith* (no place or date of publication, pp. 62).

[107] *Report of the Commission of Appraisal of the Layman's Foreign Missions Inquiry,* Vol. V, p. 10.

[108] On the Karen mission as a whole see Edward Norman Harris, *A Star in the East. An Account of American Baptist Missions to the Karens in Burma* (New York, Fleming H. Revell Co., 1920, pp. 223), *passim.*

[109] For an account of the earlier stages of her mission, see Mrs. Mason, *Civilizing Mountain Men, or Sketches of Mission Work among the Karens* (London, James Nisbet & Co., 1862, pp. x, 384).

lowed her out of the Baptist fellowship, some became Anglicans, some Roman Catholics, and some reverted to paganism.[110]

The success of their enterprise among the Karens did not lure the American Baptists from those among whom Judson had first laboured, the Burmese proper. Adherents of Buddhism, even though in them that faith overlay animistic strata, the Burmese were resistant to the penetration of Christianity. Especially was progress delayed in areas as yet unsubmissive to the advance of British rule. The British conquest was followed by the cessation of persecution, but conversions were still slow.[111] Yet by 1914 Baptists counted only a few less than four thousand Burmese in the membership of their churches.[112]

The American Baptists also sought to approach the other races of Burma, for they regarded almost all the country as their responsibility. In the 1870's efforts were made to reach the Kachins. Among the first missionaries was a Karen. The initial baptisms took place in 1882.[113] In 1914 there were nearly seven hundred Baptists among the Kachins.[114] The Kachin language had been reduced to writing, the New Testament and part of the Old Testament had been translated into it, other literature had been prepared, and schools had been opened.[115] The Shans, professedly Buddhists, but Buddhists with strong admixtures of other religious beliefs, were approached. In the 1860's Josiah Nelson Cushing travelled among them. It was not until much later that continuous effort through resident stations was begun. Schools and medical work were inaugurated, although slowly.[116] Yet in 1914 over eleven thousand Shans were counted in Baptist churches.[117] Although efforts for the Talaing centred about Moulmein, one of the earliest stations of the mission, and included schools, literature, and a hospital, only a few hundred converts were gathered.[118] It was

[110] Purser, Missions in Burma, pp. 118-120.

[111] Hughes, The Evangel in Burma, pp. 34ff. For the biography of one who gave much time to the Burmese but who reached out also to other peoples, see Willis S. Webb, Incidents and Trials in the Life of Rev. Eugenio Kincaid, D.D., the "Hero" Missionary to Burma, 1830-1865 (Fort Scott, Kansas, Monitor Publishing House, 1890, pp. 284) and Alfred S. Patton, The Hero Missionary, or a History of the Labors of the Rev. Eugenio Kincaid (New York, H. Dayton, 1858, pp. 312). See also Henry Park Cochrane, Among the Burmans, A Record of Fifteen Years and its Fruitage (Chicago, Fleming H. Revell Co., 1904, pp. 281), pp. 167ff.

[112] One Hundredth Annual Report, American Baptist Foreign Mission Society, 1914, statistical tables.

[113] Howard, op. cit., pp. 79-84.

[114] One Hundredth Annual Report, American Baptist Foreign Mission Society, 1914, statistical tables.

[115] Hughes, op. cit., pp. 106, 107.

[116] Hughes, op. cit., pp. 87ff.; Wallace St. John, Josiah Nelson Cushing (Rangoon, American Baptist Mission Press, 1912, pp. 208), pp. 35ff.

[117] One Hundredth Annual Report, American Baptist Foreign Mission Society, 1914, statistical tables.

[118] Hughes, op. cit., p. 99.

late in the 1880's that Arthur E. Carson reached Burma with the express assignment to the Chins. He was assisted by Karens. He reduced the language to writing. The first station was opened in 1888 and a new one, in the Chin Hills among a tribe which had not previously been touched, in 1899. Carson died in 1908, but reinforcements had come.[119] By 1914 over twelve hundred Chins were church members.[120] Efforts were made for the Telugus, Tamils, and Chinese.[121] The schools founded by the Baptists were crowned by a college in Rangoon, which later (1919) was given the name of Judson.[122] There were the usual accompaniments of a mission press and hospitals. A succession of women who served as missionaries opened and maintained schools for girls, including high and normal schools, gave medical care to women, and made provision for orphans.[123]

By 1914, only a hundred and one years after the Judsons had landed, somewhat forlornly, in Rangoon, their dream had been more than realized in an enterprise which was touching all the principal peoples of the land and which had given rise to growing Christian communities.

To the assistance of the Baptists of the United States came personnel from Canadian Baptists.[124]

The Church of England was early represented by chaplains in the British army. Some of these accompanied the British forces in 1825.[125] In 1852-1853, when the second Anglo-Burmese War led to the annexation of Lower Burma, chaplains began raising a Burma mission fund for the spread of the faith among the Burmese. In 1859 the Society for the Propagation of the Gospel in Foreign Parts placed a missionary, a Eurasian, in Moulmein. In 1859, too, there came to Burma under the society J. E. Marks, of Jewish extraction, who was to have four decades in the country in a notable missionary career.[126] Late in the 1860's and early in the 1870's a school and church were erected in Mandalay at the expense of the King of Burma. Rangoon also became a centre with a school for girls and St. John's College.[127] In the 1870's an enterprise was begun among

---

[119] Laura Hardin Carson, *Pioneer Trails, Trials and Triumphs* (New York, Baptist Board of Education, 1927, pp. 255), pp. 94ff.; Hughes, *op. cit.*, pp. 112ff.

[120] *One Hundredth Annual Report, American Baptist Foreign Mission Society, 1914,* statistical tables.

[121] Hughes, *op. cit.*, pp. 118-124, 129.

[122] Hughes, *op. cit.*, p. 153.

[123] Howard, *op. cit.*, pp. 92, 93.

[124] D. A. Steele, *Our Pioneer. Impressions Regarding Mrs. H. M. N. Armstrong* (no place or date of publication, pp. 35).

[125] Purser, *Christian Missions in Burma*, p. 107.

[126] Purser, *op. cit.*, pp. 109-118. *Forty Years in Burma, by Dr. Marks,* edited by W. C. B. Purser (London, Hutchinson & Co., 1917, pp. x, 307).

[127] Purser, *Christian Missions in Burma*, pp. 111-118. On an early missionary in Mandalay see James Alfred Colbeck, *Letters from Mandalay* (Knaresborough, Alfred W. Lowe, 1892, pp. v, 113, ii).

the Karens. It was commenced in part at the invitation of Mrs. Mason but chiefly to keep those Karen Christians who had followed her out of their Baptist allegiance from slipping back into paganism or going over to the Roman Catholics. As with the Roman Catholics and the Baptists, the Karen branch of the Anglican enterprise throve, while that among the Burmese made only slow headway.[128]

Somewhat akin to indigenous movements which we have found in many other peoples in the nineteenth century were two among the Karens which for a time embarrassed the Anglicans. One was devised in the 1860's by Ko Pai San, a wealthy Karen merchant who sought to combine Buddhism and Christianity in a faith which attracted large numbers of his fellows and which continued into the twentieth century.[129] The other, known as Kleeboism, begun by a Karen priest of the Anglican communion, Thomas Pellako, in the 1890's, also proved popular and culminated in the assumption by its leader of the designation "King of the Karens," until the refusal of his followers to pay taxes, and the arrest of the self-styled monarch by the British authorities (1910).[130]

Anglican enterprises were carried on for the Chins,[131] among the Tamil and Chinese immigrants,[132] and among the Eurasians and the Europeans. For the English residents, where they were numerous enough to justify it, the government maintained chaplains.[133] There were several schools and orphanages.[134] A notable school for the blind was built up, chiefly after 1914, by William Henry Jackson, himself blind from his early childhood and in spite of that handicap a graduate of Oxford.[135] Assistance was given to the Anglican undertakings from the diocese of Winchester, in England, by what was at first called the Winchester Mission and later the Winchester Brotherhood.[136] For the supervision of the Anglicans a bishopric was created, the first incumbent of which was consecrated in 1877.[137]

To Burma, from India, came the American Methodists. This was in 1879. Some whom the Methodists had touched in Calcutta went to Rangoon. Thoburn, with his comprehensive vision and his zeal for pioneering, felt it im-

[128] Pascoe, *Two Hundred Years of the S.P.G.*, pp. 642-647.
[129] Purser, *op. cit.*, p. 128.
[130] Purser, *op. cit.*, p. 130.
[131] Purser, *op. cit.*, pp. 179-183.
[132] Purser, *op. cit.*, pp. 190-195.
[133] Purser, *op. cit.*, pp. 138-155.
[134] Purser, *op. cit.*, pp. 238, 239.
[135] Mary C. Purser, *An Ambassador in Bonds. The Story of Willian Henry Jackson, Priest, of the Mission to the Blind of Burma* (Westminster, The Society for the Propagation of the Gospel in Foreign Parts, 1933, pp. 83).
[136] Purser, *Christian Missions in Burma*, pp. 196ff.
[137] Pascoe, *op. cit.*, p. 630.

portant to follow them. This he did in person and through a man especially appointed for the new enterprise. A church was quickly organized among the European and Eurasian community. Later other centres were occupied. Efforts were chiefly for the Europeans, the Eurasians, the Burmese, the Chinese, and the immigrants from India—Tamils, Telugus, Punjabis, and Hindustanis.[138]

English Wesleyans saw in the British annexation of Upper Burma (1886) a challenge which was in the nature of an obligation. At that time there was a dearth of other Protestant enterprise in that region. Only Lower Burma could be thought of as fairly effectively covered. In 1887 the first appointees landed. One became a chaplain in the British forces, one was assigned to the Burmese, and an experienced Sinhalese came from Ceylon. Reinforcements followed. Mandalay was the chief but not the only centre. The Burmese rather than the other peoples of the land were the main objectives. Progress among them was slow, as it had been for the other Christian bodies. Yet by 1914 several hundred members had been gathered. Schools were organized and a leper asylum conducted.[139]

Late in 1892 the Churches of Christ in Great Britain established a mission in Burma at Ye, in the south-east, among the Talaing.[140]

By 1914, the Seventh Day Adventists, too, had entered Burma but had not as yet made much headway.[141]

The Andaman and Nicobar Islands need not long detain us. They are the major groups of a chain of islands, summits of a submerged mountain range stretching southward from one of the mountain systems of Burma to the island of Sumatra. In 1914 their native population seems to have been less than ten thousand. The Andamanese were a primitive, negroid people, of a very backward culture. The Nicobarese were quite distinct from the Andamanese and were perhaps akin to the Karens or to some of the people of the Malay Peninsula and were animists. In the latter part of the eighteenth century the British

---

[138] Badley, *Visions and Victories in Hindustan*, pp. 431ff.; Thoburn, *India and Malaysia*, pp. 443-454; *Annual Report of the Board of Foreign Missions of the Methodist Episcopal Church for the year 1914*, pp. 89-91; Julius Smith, *Ten Years in Burma* (Chicago, Student Missionary Campaign Library, 1902, pp. 326), pp. 216ff.

[139] Findlay and Holdsworth, *The History of the Wesleyan Methodist Missionary Society*, Vol. V pp. 381-391; F. Deaville Walker, *The Land of the Gold Pagoda. The Story of the Burma Mission of the Methodist Missionary Society* (London, The Cargate Press, no date, pp. 152), pp. 48ff.; W. R. Winston, *Four Years in Upper Burma* (London, C. H. Kelly, 1892, pp. xii, 266).

[140] *Forty-eighth Annual Meeting held at Birmingham, August . . . 1893*, pp. 22-25.

[141] *Annual Report of the Board of Foreign Missions of the Methodist Episcopal Church for the year 1914*, p. 89.

authorities had planned to use the Andaman Islands as the site for a penal colony for criminals from India, but it was not until the third quarter of the nineteenth century that both island groups were brought under British administration.

In the second half of the eighteenth century the Moravians made an heroic if futile attempt, very costly in life, to plant a continuing mission on the Nicobars.[142] Another effort is said to have been made in 1851.[143] In the second half of the nineteenth century the Moravians declined invitations to return to the Nicobar Islands and to inaugurate a mission on the Andamans.[144] In the 1830's and again in the 1840's Roman Catholic missionaries essayed, vainly, to found a mission on the Nicobars.[145] In 1885 the (Anglican) Society for the Propagation of the Gospel in Foreign Parts appointed a missionary to the Andamans. An orphanage was begun for boys from the Andamans and the Nicobars. The following year the missionary was transferred to Rangoon, but a government chaplain remained and a Tamil catechist, V. Solomon, continued the orphanage. In 1896 Solomon changed his field to the Nicobars, there built an orphanage, reduced the language to writing, translated into it the liturgy, one of the Gospels, and a catechism, won several scores of converts, and taught them methods of agriculture and handicrafts.[146]

In the course of the nineteenth century the English, intent upon obtaining possession of strategic positions along the main trade routes of the earth, gained control of the southern portion of the Malay Peninsula and its closely adjacent islands. There, in 1914, they had the crown colony called the Straits Settlements, which was made up of Singapore, a city of their construction, of Malacca, formerly Portuguese and latterly Dutch, and of the island of Penang with an adjacent strip of the mainland. They also controlled the Federated Malay States and had under their protection and supervision the non-federated states. In 1914 the population was extremely varied. It was said to total about two millions. Of these about one hundred thousand were aborigines of at least three strains, about eight hundred thousand were Malays, Moslem by religion, about eight hundred and fifty thousand were Chinese, perhaps one hundred thousand were Tamils and other Indians, and there were small

[142] H. Römer, *Geschichte der Brüdermission auf den Nikobaren und des "Brüdergartens" bei Trankebar* (Herrnhut, Missionsbuchhandlung, 1921, pp. 80).
[143] Purser, *Christian Missions in Burma*, p. 183.
[144] Hutton, *A History of Moravian Missions*, pp. 489, 490.
[145] Launay, *Histoire Générale de la Société des Missions-Étrangères*, Vol. III, pp. 110-112.
[146] Purser, *op. cit.*, pp. 184-187; Pascoe, *Two Hundred Years of the S.P.G.*, pp. 654, 655.

minorities of Europeans and Eurasians.[147] Both racially and religiously the Malay Peninsula was more akin to the Malay Archipelago, which we covered in our last volume, than to Asia. However, geographically it was part of Asia and, unlike the East Indies, in the nineteenth century it was in the hands of the English.

British rule brought augmented prosperity. Tin, which for centuries had attracted foreign merchants, was further developed. Coffee and sugar were important exports, and not far from the beginning of the twentieth century the rise of motor transportation in the West led to the rapid multiplication of rubber plantations. Indians, mostly Tamils, flocked in, chiefly as labourers, and Chinese immigrants increased. Roads and railways were built and schools of a modern Occidental type were introduced. The region was being permeated with nineteenth century Western culture, here, as elsewhere in most of the world, by the year 1914 a rapidly mounting tide.

So far as we know, Christianity first entered the region through the Portuguese, in the sixteenth century. When the Dutch supplanted the Portuguese at Malacca some of the church buildings were transferred to the Protestants.[148] At the dawn of the nineteenth century the bishopric of Malacca, which had been created in 1557, had long been vacant.[149] The papal brief *multa praeclare* of 1838 which dealt with ecclesiastical jurisdiction in India erased the see of Malacca and placed the area provisionally under Cao, Vicar Apostolic of Ava and Pegu. Cao had no clergy to spare and asked that the region be assigned to some other mission. In 1840, therefore, Rome handed it over to the Société des Missions Étrangères of Paris, long active in Siam and Indo-China and already maintaining a seminary on Penang. In 1841 a new vicariate apostolic was created to include the British possessions in Malaya.[150] At the outset Roman Catholics were few, claimed Portuguese blood, and had been served by Goanese priests.[151] The controversy over the Portuguese padroado troubled the infant undertaking, but the French missionaries baptized several non-Christians, apparently chiefly or entirely Chinese.[152] In 1844 there were said to be 500 Roman Catholics in Singapore and 2,110 on Penang.[153] In the 1840's a few converts were made from the primitive folk near Malacca.[154] By 1855 the total of Roman

[147] *The Encyclopædia Britannica*, 11th ed., Vol. XVII, pp. 472, 473.
[148] Vol. III, pp. 294, 295.
[149] Launay, *Histoire Générale de la Société des Missions-Étrangères*, Vol. III, p. 107.
[150] Launay, *op. cit.*, Vol. III, p. 108.
[151] Launay, *op. cit.*, Vol. III, p. 109; Hull, *Bombay Mission History*, Vol. I, p. 256.
[152] Launay, *op. cit.*, Vol. III, pp. 109, 110.
[153] *Notizie Statisiche delle Missioni di Tutto il Mondo Dipendenti dalla S.C. de Propaganda Fide*, pp. 544, 545.
[154] Laurence E. Browne, *Christianity and the Malays* (London, S.P.G., 1936, pp. 78), pp. 48-50.

Catholics in the vicariate apostolic stood at about 7,000.[155] In 1888 the vicariate apostolic became the bishopric of Malacca, but the bishop resided at Singapore. The Paris society remained in charge.[156] Early in the 1890's there was a Roman Catholic population of 17,511, served by a bishop and 27 missionaries.[157] About 1912 Roman Catholics were reported to number 32,582, priests 42, lay brothers 52, and sisters 118.[158] The Christians were declared to be largely Chinese and Indians.[159]

We hear of Armenian Christians in Singapore in the first half of the nineteenth century who contributed to the erection of a Roman Catholic church.[160]

Protestantism was first represented by the Dutch. The arrival of the British brought a new era in the Protestant history of the region. With the English came the Church of England and clergymen of that communion. The clergymen were chaplains for the British community. A Dutch church at Malacca was used and church buildings were early erected at Penang and Singapore.[161] When, in 1867, the Straits Settlements were transferred from the jurisdiction of the government of India to the position of a crown colony, the chaplains, heretofore on brief tenure, were made permanent incumbents. In 1869 they were removed from the supervision of the Bishop of Calcutta and were placed under the jurisdiction of the Bishop of Labuan.[162] It seems not to have been until shortly after the middle of the nineteenth century that the Anglicans reached out to non-Europeans. In the 1850's a congregation in Singapore established a mission for the Chinese in that city.[163] In the 1860's the Society for the Propagation of the Gospel in Foreign Parts began sending missionaries, primarily for non-Europeans. In the course of time its agents laboured among Chinese of several dialects, Tamils, Sinhalese, and the Malays. The Society for Promoting Christian Knowledge gave financial assistance. Schools and Sunday schools were conducted and congregations were gathered. Tamil and Chinese as well as British clergymen served in the area.[164]

In the days before China was opened to Christian missions, when Protestant effort in that empire was possible only at Canton and Macao, and then under severe restrictions, the London Missionary Society, the pioneer Protestant agency in China, addressed itself to the Chinese in the British possessions in Malaya. At

[155] Launay, *op. cit.*, Vol. III, p. 446.
[156] Launay, *op. cit.*, Vol. III, p. 534.
[157] Launay, *op. cit.*, Vol. III, p. 551.
[158] Streit, *Atlas Hierarchicus*, p. 99.
[159] Schmidlin, *Katholische Missionsgeschichte*, p. 460.
[160] Launay, *op. cit.*, Vol. III, p. 109.
[161] Ferguson-Davie, *In Rubber Lands*, p. 37.
[162] Pascoe, *Two Hundred Years of the S.P.G.*, p. 695.
[163] Pascoe, *op. cit.*, p. 696.
[164] Pascoe, *op. cit.*, pp. 695-702; Ferguson-Davie, *op. cit.*, pp. 31ff.

Malacca William Milne opened a school and, at the instance of Robert Morrison, the first Protestant missionary to China, the Anglo-Chinese College was launched (1818), an institution whose broad purpose it was to acquaint Chinese with Christianity and Western civilization and Westerners with the Chinese language and culture.[165] At Malacca, too, a press was maintained and a periodical issued.[166] Missionaries were stationed at Penang and Singapore. There was a school for Malays which had a few converts.[167] When the Anglo-Chinese treaty for 1842 brought enlarged opportunity in China itself, the London Missionary Society transferred its staff to that country.[168]

To Singapore, in 1843, came Miss Grant, a representative of the Society for Promoting Female Education in the East, a British organization which owed its origin to the suggestion of David Abeel, a pioneer American Protestant missionary to the Chinese.[169] She took over a school for Chinese girls which had been begun under the London Missionary Society. As her successor, in 1853, there arrived Sophia Cooke, who except for infrequent leaves in England remained in Singapore until her death, in 1895. Some of the graduates of her school went as missionaries to China.[170] In 1900 the school was taken over by the Church of England Zenana Missionary Society.[171]

In 1856 an appointee of the foreign board of the Presbyterian Church of England reached Singapore. This church had a mission in South China, in and around Swatow and Amoy. From these regions many Chinese, including some Christians, came to Malaya, and the English Presbyterians entered the door thus opened to them. In 1907 they had eleven stations with several churches and schools.[172]

We hear also of the Plymouth Brethren in Singapore,[173] of Seventh Day Adventists, of the Young Men's and Young Women's Christian Associations, and of the British and Foreign Bible Society.[174]

Along with that of the Anglicans, the strongest non-Roman Catholic mission

[165] Milne, A Retrospect, pp. 17ff., 136-183; The Chinese Repository, Vol. III, p. 128, Vol. IV, pp. 98, 99.
[166] The Chinese Repository, Vol. I, pp. 316, 325.
[167] Memoir of the Life and Public Services of Sir Thomas Stamford Raffles, Vol. II, p. 260.
[168] Lovett, The History of the London Missionary Society, Vol. II, pp. 437-438.
[169] Female Agency among the Heathen, as Recorded in the History and Correspondence of the Society for Promoting Female Education in the East (London, Edward Suter, 1850, pp. viii, 292), pp. iii, 209ff.
[170] E. A. Walker, Sophia Cooke (London, Elliot Stock, 1899, pp. 91), passim.
[171] The Twenty-First Annual Report of the Church of England Zenana Missionary Society, 1901, p. 85.
[172] Dale, Our Missions in the Far East, pp. 59-62.
[173] Dale, op. cit., p. 59.
[174] Beach and St. John, World Statistics of Christian Missions, p. 64.

in British Malaya was maintained by the (American) Methodist Episcopal Church. It took its inception from the vision of that leading builder of Methodism in southern Asia, James M. Thoburn. In 1884 Thoburn called for two young men for Singapore. William F. Oldham was appointed and reached the city in 1885. A Methodist church was soon organized among the English-speaking population. Reinforcements came. The mission expanded its efforts to Chinese and Tamils, to Penang, Malacca, and several points on the mainland. Schools proved popular. A press was conducted. Plans were laid for reaching the Moslems as well as the non-Moslem elements of the population.[175]

By the year 1914 the portions of Malaya under British control were the scene of a rapid expansion of Christianity, both Roman Catholic and Protestant. There were churches for the European population and there were thousands of Christians among non-Europeans, chiefly the immigrant groups, Chinese and Indian, who, removed from the traditional patterns of their native land, presumably were somewhat favourably disposed towards a faith which seemed to them to be that of the dominant race and to be identified with the culture to which they were in part conforming.

One wishes that it were feasible to determine the effects of Christianity through the British rulers, but this seems difficult and perhaps impossible. The chief creator of British power, Raffles, was apparently a man of devout Christian faith,[176] but it is not clear that his vigour in suppressing gambling and abolishing slavery in Singapore[177] was due to his religious convictions. Nor do we know precisely how far the partial permeation of British life by Christianity was accountable for other colonial policies. Trade and British power in the Far East were obviously primary. Yet exploitation was modified by humanitarian considerations. It is not clear to what extent these arose from Christianity.

Siam was the only country in south-eastern Asia which in the nineteenth century succeeded in maintaining fully its political independence of the aggressive Western powers. This it was able to do partly because the two great rivals

[175] W. F. Oldham, *India, Malaysia, and the Philippines. A Practical Study in Missions* (New York, Eaton & Mains, pp. viii, 299), pp. 224-248; Thoburn, *India and Malaysia*, pp. 443-454; Nathalie Tom Means, *Malaysia Mosaic. A Story of Fifty Years of Methodism* (Singapore, The Methodist Book Room, 1935, pp. 142), pp. 15ff.
[176] *Memoir of the Life and Public Services of Sir Thomas Stamford Raffles*, Vol. I, pp. 7, 8.
[177] *Memoir of the Life and Public Services of Sir Thomas Stamford Raffles*, Vol. II, pp. 169, 273, 275.

in the region, Great Britain and France, would neither of them consent to its control by the other and allowed it to continue as a buffer state between their respective holdings. Each took part of its territory, Great Britain sections of the Malay Peninsula and France portions contiguous to her possessions on the east. The entrance of Western cultural influences was furthered by two monarchs, Mongkut and Chulalongkorn, who reigned successively from 1851 to 1910 and who promoted the introduction of some Occidental devices, including Western forms of education. Foreign commerce reinforced the infiltration of Western ways.

The land presented a mosaic, both linguistically and racially. The Thai were dominant, but with them had mingled the Khmers, earlier on the scene, and there were other peoples. Population was centred chiefly in the fertile valleys, notably in the alluvial plain of the Menam and in and around the capital, Bangkok. That city had risen to prominence after the destruction of the former capital, Ayuthia, in the third quarter of the eighteenth century. The prevailing religion was Buddhism, of a Hinayana type. Here, even more than in Ceylon and Burma, it offered effective opposition to the rapid spread of Christianity. From infancy the Siamese were nourished in Buddhist terminology and beliefs. The Buddhist priesthood was numerous, well organized, and alert. The head of the hierarchy was dependent on the monarch.[178] Hinduism, or Brahminism, also exerted an influence on the prevailing Buddhism and numbered a few communities which held to it as their primary faith.

In proportion to the population, in 1914 Christians were fewer in Siam than in any other of the major political divisions covered in this chapter—whether Ceylon, Burma, British Malaya, or French Indo-China. The difference was probably due mainly to four factors—the prevalence of Buddhism (although that religion was also potent in Ceylon and Burma), the absence of such strong animistic enclaves as in Burma provided the chief source of conversions to Christianity, the comparatively small nineteenth century immigration from South India which in Ceylon, Burma, and British Malaya constituted a field for Christian missions, and the fact that the rulers were not European and were Buddhist rather than technically Christian.

Roman Catholic Christianity had been in Siam since the sixteenth century. Since the seventeenth century it had been represented chiefly by the Société des Missions Étrangères of Paris.[179] At the end of the eighteenth century Roman Catholic Christianity was at a low ebb. The upheavals in Europe combined with

[178] K. E. Wells in *The International Review of Missions*, Vol. XXXI, pp. 199-204.
[179] Vol. III, pp. 295, 296.

the invasion of Siam by the Burmese to work ill to the mission. There were said to be only a thousand or twelve hundred Christians.[180] In 1825 Roman Catholic Christianity was but little if any better off.[181] The division in 1841 of the huge vicariate apostolic which had borne the name of Siam seems to have worked to the advantage of the Roman Catholic cause, for the Malay Peninsula and its adjacent British possessions which had previously been included were now a distinct vicariate apostolic and the vicariate apostolic of Siam was centred upon that country.[182] The first Vicar Apostolic of Siam under the new arrangement, Pallegoix, was a man of ability and a notable scholar in things Siamese, the author of a Siamese-French-Latin-English dictionary and of a two volume work on the country. He was a friend of King Mongkut. Before his accession to the throne, the latter had studied with Pallegoix and for a time contemplated the inauguration of a new religion which would be a compound of Buddhism and Christianity. Pallegoix also sent a missionary to introduce Christianity into Chiengmai, in the northern part of Siam. Efforts were begun to reach the Chinese who were numerous in Bangkok and other portions of the delta of the Menam.[183] In 1849 the missionaries were ordered out of the country, ostensibly because they had forbidden Christians to join in offerings which the state had ordered to check an epidemic of cholera. When, in 1851, Mongkut came to the throne, he invited the missionaries to return, showed Pallegoix marked favour, and later sent a letter to Pope Pius IX assuring the latter that he was giving the Christians special protection.[184] The treaty of 1856 between Siam and France guaranteed to French missionaries the right to preach and teach their faith, to build churches, seminaries, schools, and hospitals, and to travel anywhere in the kingdom.[185] In the 1870's missionaries reached north into Laos, a region on both sides of the Mekong.[186] In the 1890's friction between the French and the Siamese over the former's territorial aggressions at the expense of the latter led to some persecution of the Roman Catholics, because of their French connexion.[187] However, this period passed, King Chulalongkorn was, on the whole, friendly, the mission had able leadership under the scholarly Vey, and the Roman Catholic communities grew. Under French extraterritorial protection, mission lands were largely independ-

---

[180] Launay, *Histoire Générale de la Société des Missions-Étrangères*, Vol. II, pp. 147, 148.
[181] Launay, *op. cit.*, Vol. II, p. 495.
[182] Launay, *op. cit.*, Vol. III, p. 108.
[183] Launay, *op. cit.*, Vol. III, pp. 115-122.
[184] Launay, *op. cit.*, Vol. III, pp. 244-247.
[185] Launay, *op. cit.*, Vol. III, pp. 338, 339.
[186] Launay in Piolet, *Les Missions Catholiques Françaises au XIXe Siècle*, Vol. II, pp. 371-373.
[187] Launay in Piolet, *op. cit.*, Vol. II, p. 374.

ent of Siamese jurisdiction and attracted some who were appealed to by a possible exemption from taxation and military service. The Christian communities tended to become distinct enclaves, under the supervision of the Church. In these were included Annamite and Cambodian refugees from persecution in lands to the west. The Franco-Siamese treaty of 1907 somewhat altered this situation.[188] Yet most of the Roman Catholic Christians were said to be Chinese or fisher folk.[189] In 1880 what is declared to have been the first full-blooded Siamese to be ordained in the Roman Catholic Church was raised to the priesthood.[190] In 1898 there was a staff of one bishop, 53 priests, 18 native priests, 81 catechists, 90 sisters of 3 congregations (of whom the majority were natives), 29,200 Roman Catholics, a seminary, a college, 52 schools with over 3,000 pupils about equally divided between boys and girls, 19 orphanages, and a hospital for Europeans.[191] In 1912 the number of Christians had risen to about 36,000.[192]

The first attempts to propagate Protestantism in Siam seem to have been in the fore part of the nineteenth century. Ann Hasseltine Judson came in touch with Siamese captives in Rangoon, studied their language, and prepared in it a translation of a catechism which was published by the Baptist press at Serampore and a translation of one of the Gospels.[193] In 1828 Gützlaff, of the Netherlands Missionary Society, and Jacob Tomlin, of the London Missionary Society, arrived in Bangkok. The latter was there less than a year, but Gützlaff did not permanently leave until the death of his wife and infant daughter and his own ill health compelled him to do so, in 1831. In the interval he and his wife performed the prodigious feat of translating the Bible into Siamese and portions of the Bible into the Lao and Cambodian tongues, and prepared a grammar and dictionary of Siamese and Cambodian. He baptized one convert, a Chinese.[194] The London Missionary Society did not long pursue its project for a Siamese mission.[195] Beginning in 1831, at the instance of David Abeel, the American Board of Commissioners for Foreign Missions maintained an enterprise in Siam until the close of 1849. On its staff, among others, were a physician, Dan Beach Bradley, who won the favour of the royal family and sought to stem smallpox by inoculation, and Jesse Caswell, who became a tutor to the future King Mongkut.[196] The American Board transferred its mission to

[188] Thompson, *Thailand*, pp. 652-655.
[189] Schmidlin, *Katholische Missionsgeschichte*, p. 460.
[190] Huonder, *Der einheimische Klerus in den Heidenländern*, p. 155.
[191] Launay in Piolet, *op. cit.*, Vol. II, pp. 379, 380.
[192] Streit, *Atlas Hierarchicus*, p. 99.
[193] McFarland, *Historical Sketch of Protestant Missions in Siam, 1828-1928*, p. 1.
[194] McFarland, *op. cit.*, pp. 1-5.
[195] Lovett, *The History of the London Missionary Society*, Vol. II, p. 439.
[196] Strong, *The Story of the American Board*, pp. 114-116; McFarland, *op. cit.*, pp. 6-22.

the American Missionary Association. The latter did not develop an extensive programme, but Bradley, although largely self-supporting, continued on its staff, and he and his family gave prolonged service and made notable contributions.[197] In 1832 came American Baptists in response to a call for help from Tomlin and Gützlaff. They hoped that Siam would be a way-station to the penetration of the then closed China. The first Baptist converts were Chinese and in 1834 a missionary, William Dean, was appointed especially for the Chinese. In 1837 Dean organized, in Bangkok, the first Protestant church in the land. In 1861 a Baptist church was inaugurated for the Siamese. In the latter part of the century, however, the American Baptists did not press their enterprise. After 1914 they discontinued it, but left a strong Chinese church as a tangible witness to their endeavour.[198]

What became the leading Protestant enterprise in Siam, that of the American Presbyterians, was begun in 1840, at the suggestion of a representative who had visited the country in 1838. Because of the illness of the wife of the first missionary, it was suspended from 1844 to 1847. Stephen Mattoon, his wife, and a physician, Samuel R. House, then renewed it.[199] The Congregational and Baptist missionaries gave them a cordial welcome and Bangkok was chosen as a centre. King Mongkut, who ascended the throne in 1851, proved friendly.[200] A mission press was begun (1861) [201] and schools were opened.[202] Together with women of other Protestant missions, Mrs. Mattoon gave instruction in the English language to the princesses of the palace.[203] Converts were slow in coming, but one of the earliest of them, after training in medicine in the United States, became head of the first government hospital run in a Western manner.[204] In the 1860's, thanks chiefly to the initiative of Daniel McGilvary, a centre was established in the North at Chiengmai among the Lao. McGilvary, not a physician, won favour through his use of medicines. After an initial brief persecution, the mission became popular among the Lao for its works of mercy and its extensive schools. New stations were opened, converts were gathered, churches organized, and a theological seminary was established. Several of the tribes of the North were touched and tours were undertaken into Chinese, Burmese, and French territory.[205] It was in the North that the Presbyterians had their largest

[197] McFarland, op. cit., pp. 22-26; Beard, A Crusade of Brotherhood, pp. 55-60.
[198] McFarland, op. cit., pp. 27-34; Dean, The China Mission, pp. 233-240, 279-282.
[199] McFarland, op. cit., pp. 35-40; George Haws Feltus, Samuel Reynolds House of Siam (New York, Fleming H. Revell Co., 1924, pp. 256), passim.
[200] McFarland, op. cit., pp. 44, 45.
[201] McFarland, op. cit., p. 52.
[202] McFarland, op. cit., p. 60.
[203] McFarland, op. cit., p. 45.
[204] McFarland, op. cit., pp. 56, 57.
[205] Daniel McGilvary, A Half Century among the Siamese and the Lao: an Autobi-

Christian communities. Between 1884 and 1894 the enrolment in the Lao churches rose from 152 to 1,841.[206] Then followed a pause in the growth and the placing of more responsibility upon the Lao churches. By the end of the century increase had been resumed and the spread of the faith was largely through the efforts of the Lao Christians.[207] Progress continued in the South. In 1878 King Chulalongkorn appointed a member of the mission, Samuel G. McFarland, superintendent of public instruction and head of the royal college in Bangkok. George B. McFarland, a son of Samuel, became superintendent of the government hospital and dean of the royal medical college.[208] The Bangkok Christian College was founded and on the eve of 1914 a theological college was inaugurated in Bangkok. Yet in 1914 the South had only 13 churches and 662 communicants as against 26 churches and 6,299 communicants in the Laos Mission.[209] The difference is probably to be attributed to the fact that the Lao were nearer to the primitive stages of culture than were the Siamese and therefore less resistant to the advent of another religion. They were nominally Buddhist, but Buddhism sat more lightly upon them than upon the Siamese proper.

Anglican Christianity entered Siam first through English residents. For them a church and a chaplain were maintained in Bangkok. In 1903 the chaplain, William Greenstock, who before coming to Siam had long been a missionary in South Africa, resigned his post to serve under the Society for the Propagation of the Gospel in Foreign Parts as a missionary to the Siamese. In 1914, however, the enterprise was still of small dimensions.[210]

In 1903 the Churches of Christ in Great Britain entered Siam by way of their Burma undertaking.[211] We hear, too, of Mormon missionaries, but they seem not to have founded a continuing mission.[212]

Numerically Christianity, whether Roman Catholic or Protestant, had made somewhat slower progress in Siam than in the other major lands of south-eastern Asia. Yet that progress had been substantial and in 1914, as in so much of the rest of the world, was rapidly mounting. In pioneering in the introduction of

---

ography (New York, Fleming H. Revell Co., 1912, pp. 429), *passim; Siam and Laos as Seen by Our American Missionaries* (Philadelphia, Presbyterian Board of Publication, 1884, pp. 552), pp. 479ff.

[206] Freeman, *An Oriental Land of the Free*, p. 163.

[207] Freeman, *op. cit.*, pp. 165-167.

[208] Arthur Judson Brown, *The Expectation of Siam* (New York, The Board of Foreign Missions of the Presbyterian Church in the U. S. A., 1925), p. 118.

[209] *The Seventy-Seventh Annual Report of the Board of Foreign Missions of the Presbyterian Church in the United States of America*, 1914, pp. 369-396.

[210] McFarland, *op. cit.*, pp. 257, 258.

[211] McFarland, *op. cit.*, pp. 261-266.

[212] Thompson, *Thailand*, p. 660.

various phases of Occidental culture, notably in education and medicine, Christianity was proving much more influential than the size of its communities would have led one to expect.

French Indo-China was appropriately named. In 1914 it was under the political control of France. The first steps towards that control had been taken late in the eighteenth century (1787) when France acquired territorial footholds in the extreme South. Until past the middle of the nineteenth century the French advance paused. Then, in a series of steps which roughly paralleled the expansion of European domination in that period in several other parts of the globe, France extended her dominion over the entire realm. From 1858 to 1862 came a war, undertaken jointly by France and Spain because of the persecution of Roman Catholic missionaries of these nations, which ended with the cession to France of three provinces of Cochin-China and the reluctant granting of other privileges. In 1863 Cambodia became a French protectorate. In 1867 three additional provinces of Cochin-China were annexed. In the 1860's French penetration of Tongking was in progress and in 1874 Annam, which ruled Cochin-China and Tongking, formally recognized the annexation of 1867, renounced the right to enter into alliances with states other than France, and opened to trade several ports and the Red River. In 1882 the French began the conquest of Tongking. This was followed, in 1884 and 1885, by war with China, which claimed overlordship. France was victorious and confirmed and strengthened her authority in Tongking and Annam. In the last decade of the nineteenth and the first decade of the twentieth century France pushed her frontiers westward at the expense of Siam. French control took the form of a colonial status for Cochin-China and of protectorates over other major divisions.

Long before the beginning of the French advance both India and China had placed their impress upon the land. Indian influence had been established in part through rulers and merchant settlers in the early centuries of the Christian era. It was strongest in the south-west and was evidenced in the nineteenth century by the presence of Buddhism in most of the land and remnants of Hinduism. Over long periods beginning before the time of Christ much of the eastern portion of the region had intermittently been governed by China. The most numerous of the peoples of the land, the Annamese, were akin to the Chinese in language and possibly in blood. Much of Chinese culture permeated the region, particularly to the east of the great mountain range which, thrusting down from the massif of south-west China, formed a formidable but not insuperable barrier between the south-western and the eastern portions of the land. The educated studied the Chinese classics. Confucianism was a factor in ethical and religious practices and reinforced or tolerated the reverence for ancestors and the animism which were religiously basic.

The chief peoples were the Cambodians, presumably of Khmer stock and of Indian culture, the Chams, the Lao, the Annamese, and the Chinese. There were numbers of primitive peoples, divided into many tribes and chiefly in the northern mountains and in the recesses of the Annamite range. They were, however, only a small proportion of the population.

In the nineteenth century the course of Christianity in French Indo-China was intimately associated with the advance of French rule. Christianity was represented almost solely by the Roman Catholic Church. It had been introduced and propagated before the nineteenth century by Italian, Spanish, and French missionaries [213] and at the outset of the nineteenth century was dependent chiefly on Spanish Dominicans of the Province of the Holy Rosary with headquarters at Manila and on the Société des Missions Étrangères of Paris. There were also a few Franciscans. In the year 1800 there were in the area later covered by French Indo-China the vicariates apostolic of Cochin-China, western Tongking, and eastern Tongking, in which were reported 15 missionaries, 119 native priests, and 310,000 Roman Catholics.[214] In the closing years of the eighteenth century there had been persecutions in both upper Cochin-China and Tongking, with martyrdoms.[215]

The new century opened fairly peacefully. On the throne of Cochin-China and of Annam was a monarch known as Gia-long who owed his accession in part to French assistance procured through the good offices of a vicar apostolic, Pigneau de Behaine. He seems to have been grateful to Pigneau. At least he gave him (1799) a magnificent funeral.[216] Yet he could not be persuaded to endorse Christianity and at times countenanced persecution.[217] In 1804, indeed, he issued an edict which, while encouraging the construction of Buddist shrines, denounced the Christian faith and forbade the repair of church buildings.[218] However, he forbore many active anti-Christian measures. Under his reign some existing churches were rebuilt and several new ones were erected.[219] Christians were also often exempted from contributions to community non-

[213] Vol. III, pp. 296-299.
[214] Baudrillart in Descamps, *Histoire Générale Comparée des Missions,* p. 547.
[215] Louvet, *La Cochinchine Religieuse,* Vol. I, pp. 463-474.
[216] Louvet, *op. cit.,* Vol. I, pp. 474-481.
[217] Louvet, *op. cit.,* Vol. I, pp. 455-474.
[218] Louvet, *op. cit.,* Vol. II, pp. 18, 19.
[219] Louvet, *op. cit.,* Vol. II, p. 21. For a picture of the state of Christianity from 1799 to 1823 see Adrien Launay, *Histoire de la Mission de Cochinchine, 1658-1823. Documents Historiques, III, 1771-1823.* (Paris, P. Téqui, 1925, pp. 538), pp. 397ff.

Christian observances, which had been a bone of contention.[220] Although between 1800 and 1830 the numbers of Christians appear to have been about stationary, the quality of the Christian communities seems to have improved.[221] The death of Gia-long (1820) did not immediately alter the situation. However, beginning in the 1830's a period of severe persecution came upon the Christians and their pastors. This had been foreshadowed in 1825 or 1826 by a decree which denounced Christianity as destructive to native customs and which forbade the entrance of missionaries.[222] Although there were some arrests,[223] the edict was not vigorously enforced and new missionaries succeeded in making their way into the country.[224] In 1833 a more drastic decree was issued. It renewed the denunciation of Christianity as perverting the *mores* of the land, ordered all Christians, whether officials or common people, to renounce their faith and trample on the cross, and commanded the destruction of all church buildings.[225] Both documents bore resemblances to anti-Christian laws and actions in the great empire on the north, whose culture was influential in Annam, but there seems to be no proof that they were suggested by them. The decree of 1833 brought consternation among the Christians and for some months the missionaries were constrained to keep out of sight. In October a missionary was executed.[226] In 1834 an Italian Franciscan was martyred, the last of his order to serve in the region.[227] Still another missionary was apprehended, tortured, and killed (1835).[228] In 1836 a fresh edict was issued commanding greater thoroughness in eradicating the foreign faith.[229] In 1837 a European priest and a native catechist were executed.[230] In 1838 the enforcement of the decrees became more insistent. An additional anti-Christian royal order was promulgated.[231] Numbers of priests, foreign and native, and of catechists were put to death.[232] In July, 1840, a vicar apostolic, Dumoulin Borie, was executed, along with two native priests.[233] Many humbler Christians, probably hun-

[220] Louvet, *op. cit.*, Vol. II, p. 21.
[221] Louvet, *op. cit.*, Vol. II, p. 13.
[222] Shortland, *The Persecutions of Annam*, pp. 154, 155.
[223] Launay, *Histoire Générale de la Société des Missions-Étrangères*, Vol. II, pp. 530-544.
[224] Shortland, *op. cit.*, pp. 155-157.
[225] Shortland, *op. cit.*, pp. 157, 158; Launay, *op. cit.*, Vol. II, pp. 544-546.
[226] Louvet, *La Cochinchine Religieuse*, Vol. II, pp. 63-69.
[227] Lemmens, *Geschichte der Franziskanermissionen*, pp. 117, 118.
[228] Shortland, *op. cit.*, pp. 158-162.
[229] Louvet, *op. cit.*, Vol. II, pp. 86-94.
[230] Louvet, *op. cit.*, Vol. II, pp. 100, 101; Shortland, *op. cit.*, pp. 163-173.
[231] Louvet, *op. cit.*, Vol. II, p. 109.
[232] Louvet, *op. cit.*, Vol. II, pp. 173ff.; *Memorias de las Misiones Catolicas en el Tonkin*, pp. 63ff.
[233] *Vie du Vénérable Serviteur de Dieu Pierre-Rose-Ursule Dumoulin Borie . . . par un Prêtre du Diocèse de Tulle* (Paris, Jacques Lecoffre Fils et Cie, 3d ed., 1875, pp. 350), pp. 266ff.

dreds, all told, paid for their faith with their lives.[234] Yet by 1840 and 1844 Christians and their clergy showed an increase as against the dawn of the century. In 1840 there were said to have been 3 vicars apostolic, 2 coadjutors, 24 missionaries, 144 native priests, and 420,000 Roman Catholics.[235] In 1843 Roman Catholics are reported to have totalled 411,800.[236]

The death of the persecuting monarch (January 20, 1841) brought something of a respite. The new ruler was no lover of the Christians, but he was less energetic than his predecessor. The missionaries, while still preserving caution, enjoyed comparative peace and even reached out into a new area among mountain-dwelling aborigines.[237] A new vicariate, that of western Cochin-China, was created (1844).[238] Yet there were imprisonments and martyrdoms.[239]

The accession of the next monarch (1847) was marked by a general amnesty which brought deliverance to the imprisoned Christians. Moreover, in spite of an anti-Christian edict issued early in the reign (1848), for a time the ruler was too engrossed with other matters to push the execution of the laws against the foreign faith and its adherents.[240] However, new anti-Christian laws were promulgated in 1851 and 1855 and some degree of enforcement followed.[241]

In 1857 the storm broke out afresh and with accentuated intensity. The occasion seems to have been the visit of a French man-of-war which sought to cultivate friendly relations.[242] It may have been, moreover, that the authorities were alarmed by the war which Great Britain and France were then waging against China, the overlord of Annam, and feared Christians and missionaries as presumptive supporters of the potential enemy.

In 1858 Pellerin, the Vicar Apostolic of northern Cochin-China, went to France to ask protection of Napoleon III. That emperor, nothing loth, sent a naval expedition. In this Spain joined, for Spanish Dominicans and their flocks were also sufferers.[243] It is not surprising that the course of the war was marked by fresh anti-Christian edicts and intensified persecution, more martyrdoms, and the dispersal of some of the Christian communities. It is interesting, as an

[234] Louvet, op. cit., Vol. II, pp. 75, 84, 85.
[235] Baudrillart in Descamps, Histoire Générale Comparée des Missions, p. 548.
[236] Notizie statistiche delle Missioni di Tutto il Mondo Dipendenti dalla S. C. de Propaganda Fide (1844), pp. 547-553. For statistics for the Dominican mission in Eastern Tongking in 1844 see Memorias de la Misiones Catolicas en el Tonkin, pp. 310, 311.
[237] Louvet, op. cit., Vol. II, pp. 119-130, 147, 149. For the history of the mission to the aborigines see Dourisboure, Les Sauvages Ba-Hnars (Cochinchine Orientale, Souvenirs d'un Missionnaire (Paris, E. De Soye, 1873, pp. 449).
[238] Louvet, op. cit., Vol. II, p. 154.
[239] Louvet, op. cit., Vol. II, pp. 130-147, 164-168.
[240] Louvet, op. cit., Vol. II, pp. 171-174; Shortland, op. cit., pp. 268-276.
[241] Louvet, op. cit., Vol. II, pp. 182-207; Olichon, Le Baron de Phat-Diem, p. 35.
[242] Louvet, op. cit., Vol. II, p. 219; Shortland, op. cit., p. 288; Olichon, op. cit., p. 51.
[243] Louvet, op. cit., Vol. II, pp. 223, 224.

indication of the penetration of the faith into some of the higher circles, that one decree was directed specifically against officials who were Christians.[244] It is said that in the years 1857-1862 five thousand Christians were killed and forty thousand were reduced to want.[245] Among those executed in these years were Théophane Venard, whose career and tragic fate were to attract much attention in Roman Catholic circles in the West,[246] and Jeronimo Hermosilla.[247] In the treaty which concluded the hostilities (1862) the King of Annam undertook to permit his subjects to embrace Christianity and, in consequence, in July, 1862, promulgated a grudging edict of partial toleration.[248]

It was not to be expected that concessions thus wrung from an unwilling monarch would be fully respected. Missionaries returned to their posts, but in 1862 and 1863 restrictions were placed on the religious liberty of the Christians.[249]

However, in 1874, under French pressure,[250] another treaty was obtained from the King of Annam in which there was incorporated a much stronger section promising freedom for the Christian faith. Christians were no longer to have discriminatory taxes levied against them, missionaries and Annamite priests were to be free to exercise their functions, to travel in the realm, and to preach their faith, and the purchase of land and the erection of churches, schools, hospitals, and orphanages were permitted.[251] Under these favourable conditions the missions revived, Christians multiplied, schools were conducted, and many churches were built.[252] In 1875 Sisters of Providence of Portieux arrived and began developing the institutions and works of charity usually associated with the congregations of women.[253] A mission was begun among the Lao.[254] Attracted by the prestige of missionaries under the powerful French support, whole villages became Christian.[255]

This period of prosperity was interrupted in the 1880's by internal disorders

---

[244] Louvet, op. cit., Vol. II, pp. 247-287; Olichon, op. cit., pp. 54, 57.

[245] Berg, Die katholische Heidenmission als Kulturträger, Vol. I, p. 226.

[246] Trochu, Théophane Venard, passim.

[247] Galarreta, Vida del Martir Ilmo. Fr. Jerónimo Hermosilla, Obispo del Orden de Predicadores, Vicario Apostolico del Tonquin (Barcelona, Tip. Ariza, 1906, pp. 336), passim.

[248] Louvet, op. cit., Vol. II, pp. 310, 311.

[249] Louvet, op. cit., Vol. II, pp. 397-418.

[250] On the part of a vicar apostolic in invoking this pressure, see C. d'Allenjoye, Un Apotre Français au Tonkin, Mgr. Puginier (Paris, Tequi, 1896, pp. 218), pp. 87ff.

[251] Louvet, op. cit., Vol. II, pp. 432, 433.

[252] Louvet, op. cit., Vol. II, pp. 441-473; Teysseyre, Monseigneur Galibert, p. 175.

[253] J. C. Bouchert, Un Cinquantenaire, 1876-1926. Les Soeurs de la Providence de Portieux dans la Mission de Phnôm-Penh Indochine (Paris, S. A. Gravure et Impressions, 1926, pp. 71), passim.

[254] J-B. DeGeorge, A la Conquête du Chau-Laos (Hongkong, Imprimerie de la Société des Missions-Étrangères, 1926, pp. xiii, 232), pp. 16ff.

[255] Thompson, French Indo-China, p. 273.

and foreign complications which culminated in another war with France. Again the Christians and their pastors suffered. This time the persecution was peculiarly severe. That was not surprising in view of the French connexion of many of the missionaries and the protection accorded to the Christians by the French. Numbers of missionaries and tens of thousands of Christians were massacred.[256] Hundreds of churches, chapels, and schools were sacked and burned.[257]

The return of peace and the firm establishment of French administration brought a cessation of official persecution. To be sure, the growing spirit of anti-clericalism under the Third Republic made for friction between French colonial officers and missionaries. The missionaries had great influence with the Christians and through their schools and printing presses exercised a power which the anti-clericals found annoying and had no hesitation in denouncing. Anti-clerical French functionaries sought to curb the Church.[258] Moreover, when two princes of the blood royal became Christians (1891) they were banished and their goods were confiscated.[259] Yet there was no such extensive open persecution as there had been under the uncurbed native rulers.

The numbers of Christians continued to increase. The great devotion of the missionaries could not but win the respect of many of the Annamese. Converts were attracted by the economic advantages which accrued to Christians. Missionaries sought to obtain for them lighter taxes. They introduced new crops and improved arts, crafts, and methods of agriculture. The villages of Christians were usually more prosperous than those of their non-Christian neighbours.[260] For example, under the skilful leadership of the native priest in one parish great reaches of fertile delta land were reclaimed from the sea and the numbers of Christians and settlers rose from about eight thousand to approximately fifteen thousand.[261] Missionaries produced a Christian literature.[262] On the eve of 1914 there were twelve vicariates apostolic, of which ten were in the hands of the Société des Missions Étrangères of Paris and two in the charge of the Spanish Dominicans. Christians numbered slightly less than a million, or about five per cent. of the population.[263]

[256] Launay, Histoire Générale de la Société des Missions-Étrangères, Vol. III, pp. 518-532.
[257] Teysseyre, op. cit., p. 305; Hubert Hansen, Ein Missionsberuf. Leben des P. Alois Nempon (Steyl, Missionsdruckerei, 1907, pp. 341), p. 306.
[258] Thompson, op. cit., pp. 272-275.
[259] Berg, Die katholische Heidenmission als Kulturträger, Vol. I, p. 226.
[260] Thompson, op. cit., pp. 138, 273.
[261] Huonder, Der einheimische Klerus in der Heidenländern, p. 151; Olichon, Le Baron de Phat-Diém, passim.
[262] Trochu, Théophane Venard, pp. 359, 360.
[263] Streit, Atlas Hierarchicus, p. 99.

As was to be anticipated from the history of the country and the French connexion, Protestant Christianity was scarcely represented in French Indo-China. In the 1890's the Christian and Missionary Alliance made efforts to enter the land, but it was not until 1911 that it established its first continuing station.[264] The only other Protestants at work in 1914 seem to have been the Plymouth Brethren.[265]

Through Roman Catholic missions Christianity had a marked effect upon French Indo-China. To it was in part due the coming of French political control. Missionaries had not only built up a large Christian constituency. They had also been pioneers in introducing Western forms of education and medicine, in improving economic conditions, and in the relief of the poor and the orphans. The Roman Catholic Church was still administered by European bishops, but a large body of native clergy had been trained and in a later period the transition to a native episcopate was fairly readily made.

In the various islands and lands of south-east Asia, as in much of the rest of the world, Christianity came to the year 1914 on a rising tide. It had more than recouped the losses that it had suffered in the closing years of the eighteenth and the beginning of the nineteenth century. It had made its way to peoples which it had not previously touched. In Ceylon, among the Karens, and in French Indo-China Christians constituted an appreciable proportion of the population. Christian missionaries had been pioneers in Western types of education and in some instances had reduced languages to writing. A large quantity of Christian literature, including translations of the Bible, had been prepared and were being distributed. Trained indigenous clergy were emerging. Here and there, notably among the Karens, Christianity was starting an entire people upon a fresh course of conscious cultural advance. The churches were still predominantly under the leadership of Occidentals, but now and again the native Christians were displaying initiative and in a few places the era of foreign tutelage was palpably waning. Christianity was not only being carried into new areas, it was also beginning to take root in the soil.

[264] E. F. Irwin, *With Christ in Indo-China. The Story of Alliance Missions in French Indo-China and Eastern Siam* (Harrisburg, Christian Publications, 1937, pp. 164), pp. 25ff.
[265] Beach and Fahs, *World Missionary Atlas*, p. 83.

Chapter V

THE CHINESE EMPIRE (CHINA PROPER: MANCHURIA: MONGOLIA: SINKIANG: TIBET). ROMAN CATHOLICS: RUSSIAN ORTHODOX: PROTESTANTS: EFFECT ON THE ENVIRONMENT: EFFECT OF THE ENVIRONMENT

WE MUST now pass on to the Chinese Empire. As we do so, we almost instinctively contrast it with India, the only other political and cultural entity in Asia which compared with it in population. Like India, China was a great centre of civilization. Also like India, its culture was largely but not entirely indigenous and had profoundly influenced its neighbours. More than the Indians, the Chinese, proud of their civilization, at the dawn of the nineteenth century regarded other peoples as barbarians and disdained to learn from them. The Chinese were even more numerous than the Indians. No accurate census was taken, but it was generally estimated that throughout most of the nineteenth century the population of China remained about stationary at a total of not far from four hundred millions, while in 1901 that of India, after the initial increases brought by the *pax Britannica,* was somewhat less than three-fourths of that figure. India was in the main a cultural entity, although exhibiting great diversity, but had never, not even under British rule, all been brought under one political administration. China proper was much more a cultural whole. It displayed far fewer and less striking variations of race and customs. It had no caste. Aboriginal peoples of primitive culture were less numerous and prominent than in India. There were no masses of hereditarily depressed as in the latter. To be sure, in some respects the literati of China, the haughty exponents and guardians of the dominant school, Confucianism, resembled the Brahmins of India, who were closely wedded by interest to Hinduism. Both were resistant to any change which would unseat them. Yet the former were more fluid and much less hereditary than the latter. Through most of the Christian era China had been ruled as a unit. It was an empire in a sense in which India had never been. Throughout the nineteenth century it was governed by a dynasty which had been set up in the seventeenth century by the Manchus, foreign conquerors who had accepted Chinese culture and ruled according to traditions and through an administrative machinery which

253

the Chinese had gradually evolved during the course of more than two millen-
niums.

As a kind of shield on the marches, but together embracing more square
miles than China proper, were several outlying dependencies. They were
sparsely settled. In all of them the Chinese were immigrants and, except in
Manchuria, in the minority. They had been conquered by the Manchus and
were governed as part of the empire. They were Manchuria, Mongolia, Sinkiang
(or Chinese Turkestan), and Tibet. In Mongolia and Tibet Buddhism was
dominant. In Sinkiang Islam prevailed.

The Manchu dynasty had reached the apex of its power in the eighteenth
century and during the nineteenth century was declining. It did not surrender
its authority until 1912, but for two generations or more it had been palpably
decadent.

So strong a cultural and political unit as China was much more resistant
to the aggressive Occident than India. It was, moreover, farther removed from
Europe. During most of the nineteenth century it strove to hold the West at
arm's length. It endeavoured to preserve both its political and its cultural
independence. Eventually the collapse of the old structure of life was more
striking and thoroughgoing in China than in India, but the disintegration
began much later. It did not become marked until the opening years of the
twentieth century and in 1914 was only beginning to get well under way.
Politically China was never as fully subject to an Occidental power as was
India to Great Britain.

Under these circumstances, in the nineteenth century the Chinese Empire
was more nearly impervious to Christianity than was India. There were no
depressed classes to welcome that faith as a way of escape from their hereditary
bondage. Animistic tribes who had not been assimilated to the dominant culture were not so large or so widely scattered a part of the population in China as
in India. Confucianism presented an even more solid front than did Hinduism.
The government and the ruling class, based upon Confucianism and thoroughly
committed to it, viewed Christianity with mingled scorn and fear. In the
peripheral regions (except Manchuria) Buddhism and Islam were so firmly
entrenched that Christianity found the road even more difficult than in China
proper.

It is not surprising, therefore, that the course of Christianity in China differed decidedly from that in India. At the outset of the nineteenth century
Christianity was not nearly so strong in the former as in the latter land. It
had come to China in continuing form several centuries later than it had to
India. In the Middle Kingdom it seems first to have been introduced in the

seventh century,[1] whereas in India it had been present from at least as early as the fifth century and possibly much earlier.[2] Twice Christianity was planted in China proper only to die out.[3] Not until late in the sixteenth century was it reintroduced in such fashion that it persisted into the nineteenth century.[4] In the year 1800 Christianity was not so varied in China as in India. In the latter country it was represented by the Syrian communities, the Armenians, Roman Catholicism, and Protestantism. In China in that year there were only Roman Catholicism and a very small contingent of Russian Orthodox. Christianity's numerical strength was then probably between two hundred thousand and two hundred and fifty thousand,[5] or only about a fourth or a fifth of that in India. There were no such solidly Christian enclaves as existed in India in the Portuguese possessions and in the communities of the Syrian churches. The nearest approach to them was the small Portuguese foothold at Macao and the even more minute Russian community in Peking. As in India, so in China, for the Roman Catholics the eighteenth century was one of retarded growth and even of decline. Some of the same factors contributed in both countries to produce this result. In each land the decay of Portuguese power, the suspension of the Society of Jesus (1773), and the European wars which punctuated the century and which culminated in the struggles of the French Revolution and Napoleon dealt serious blows to the progress of Christianity. However, in China there were added persecutions more severe and nation-wide than those known in India and the prolonged controversy over the rites was probably even more weakening than was that in India over the padroado.[6] In China the padroado brought embarrassment, although much less markedly than in India.

In the nineteenth century the slower penetration of China by European culture was paralleled by a more delayed growth of Christianity than in India. In India in the fore part of the century the progress of the Roman Catholic Church was slowed by the prolonged difficulties over the padroado and that of Protestantism was for a time handicapped by the antipathy of the East India Company. The first of these obstacles was not fully overcome before 1914 but by early in the second half of the century had ceased to give much trouble except in limited areas. By the close of the second quarter of the century the second was no longer of great consequence. In China until the third quarter of the century the open propagation of Christianity was impossible except in only

---

[1] Vol. II, p. 277.
[2] Vol. I, pp. 107, 108, 231-233.
[3] Vol. II, pp. 277-280, 330-333, 339.
[4] Vol. III, pp. 338ff.
[5] Latourette, *A History of Christian Missions in China*, pp. 182, 183.
[6] Vol. III, pp. 349-358; Latourette, *op. cit.*, pp. 130-184.

about a half dozen port cities. Throughout the remainder of the century it met with popular persecution and officials offered as much resistance as they dared. In 1914, in spite of rapid growth in the preceding two or three decades, Christians were not so numerous in China as in India and Roman Catholics were proportionately farther ahead of the Protestants than in the latter land. In 1914 Christians in India totalled not far from three and a half millions while in China the corresponding figure was only about half that, and this in spite of the fact that the population of China was then probably a fifth larger than that of India and foreign missionaries probably slightly more numerous than in the latter country. In India in 1914 Protestants were about half as many as Roman Catholics, but in China were only between a third and a fourth as numerous. In 1914 Protestants in China were about a third or half those in India, while their missionary body was a little larger. In India the overwhelming majority of the accessions to Christianity were from the primitive and near-primitive tribes and the depressed classes. In China they were from all ranks of society and by 1914 Christianity, and especially Protestant Christianity, was, partly through its schools, bringing into being a leadership for the nation which was influential out of all proportion to the size of the Christian community. The large part taken by Christians in engineering the political, intellectual, and social revolution of China seems to have been due to the moral and spiritual dynamic of their faith and to the fact that much more than in India Christian missionaries were pioneers in introducing the intellectual, medical, and philanthropic aspects of Western culture. In India the British Government, to some degree impelled by the Christian faith professed by the British nation, took much of the initiative in bringing in the education and the philanthropic features of Occidental civilization. In China until almost the close of the nineteenth century the government did little to encourage—and even discouraged—the importation of Western culture, except, rather grudgingly, military equipment and methods. Save for what seeped in through commerce and the foreign-dominated maritime customs service, which was not inconsiderable, it was left to Christian missionaries and to Chinese Christians, mostly Protestants, to assume the initiative in bringing in Western culture. This they did, for what they deemed the best interests of China. The fruits began to be apparent before 1914 but did not fully ripen until after that year.

Political and international developments in China, as in India, with the attendant penetration of the land by Western culture, markedly affected the spread of Christianity. By successive steps the aggressive Occident battered down the barriers which China presented and the old structure of the empire weakened and then collapsed. This is not the place to describe these stages in detail. We must, however, make room for their main outline, for it was in that framework that the progress of Christianity was achieved.

Until 1842 China endeavoured with marked success to hold the West at arm's length. A handful of Russians, a commercial-ecclesiastical-diplomatic mission, were tolerated at Peking. There were a few European Roman Catholic priests and bishops scattered through the empire. In 1810 they were said to number thirty-one.[7] Macao, a small peninsula on an island not far from Canton, was a Portuguese leasehold. Foreign merchants were permitted to reside in a closely restricted district on the water-front at Canton. Here, in the "Thirteen Factories," the Westerners lived during the trading season a life closely regulated by the Chinese authorities.[8] Christianity was officially proscribed. Under these conditions only the most limited attempts could be made to propagate the Christian faith.

An Anglo-Chinese war from 1839 to 1842 effected a partial but still very limited opening of China to the Occident. British merchants were restive under the restraints imposed on their trade and their persons and under the refusal of China to open diplomatic relations with their government on the basis of equality. The attempt of the Chinese Government to stop the influx of opium, the major British import, precipitated hostilities. China was defeated and constrained to enter into treaty relations (1842) with Great Britain. Treaties with other Western powers followed, notably with the United States (1844) and France (1844). In consequence, Hongkong was ceded to Great Britain, five ports (Canton, Amoy, Foochow, Ningpo, and Shanghai) were opened to the residence and commerce of Occidentals, foreigners were permitted to study the Chinese language, extraterritorial status was accorded the citizens of the treaty powers, aliens were allowed to build houses, hospitals, schools, and places of worship in the open ports, intercourse between Chinese and foreign officials was placed on the basis of equality, and most favoured nation clauses promised to all whatever was granted to one. Several other provisions were included which did not particularly affect the spread of Christianity.[9] In 1844, at the request of the French envoy, the Chinese Government granted toleration to Roman Catholic Christianity but, in accordance with the treaty prohibition of travel by foreigners outside the five ports, expressly forbade its propagation by

---

[7] Marchini's map of Roman Catholic missions quoted in *The Chinese Repository*, Vol. I, p. 443.

[8] See an excellent description by an American who lived at Canton in this period in [William C. Hunter], *The 'Fan Kwae' at Canton before Treaty Days. By an Old Resident* (Shanghai, Kelly and Walsh, 1911, pp. vi, 157). See also Morse, *The International Relations of the Chinese Empire*, Vol. I, pp. 63-88.

[9] See texts in Mayers, *Treaties between the Empire of China and Foreign Powers*, pp. 1-6, 49-58, 76-83. See also Morse, *op. cit.*, Vol. I, pp. 298-332.

missionaries beyond these cities.[10] However, an oral promise is said to have been made that if the missionaries were prudent the officials would close their eyes to their presence outside these bounds.[11] In 1845 the appropriate Chinese official made it clear that the toleration was intended for all branches of Christianity and for missionaries of all Western states.[12] In 1846 an imperial decree was published which commanded the restoration to the Roman Catholics of such of their houses of worship as were erected in the reign of K'ang Hsi and had since been confiscated, except those which had been converted into temples and dwelling-houses.[13]

From 1856 to 1860 there came a new foreign war, at first Anglo-Chinese, but in which France soon joined on the side of the English. From the Chinese standpoint the treaties of the 1840's had conceded too much. From the British and French viewpoint they had not granted enough. Recurring friction led to the resumption of hostilities. The French found an occasion for entering the struggle in the torture and execution by the Chinese authorities of Auguste Chapdelaine, a missionary of the Société des Missions Étrangères of Paris who was apprehended in the disturbed province of Kwangsi.[14] Again the Chinese were defeated and again concessions were wrung from them. By the ensuing treaties, of 1858, supplemented by the conventions of 1860 and paralleled by treaties with powers which had not formally participated in the war, including particularly Russia and the United States, relations between China and the Occident were placed on a footing which permitted the progressive penetration of China by Western culture and which until after 1914 remained a chief basis for official intercourse between China and most of the chief Occidental powers.[15] The terms of these treaties which most affected the further spread of Christianity were the opening of additional ports to foreign residence—ports which reached from Newchwang in Manchuria to T'aisan and Tamsui in Formosa, Kiungchow in Hainan, and Kiukiang and Hankow on the Yangtze River; the privilege accorded to foreigners of travel in the interior; the right to place diplomatic officers in the capital, Peking; the exaction of indemnities, of which a small proportion went to missions as compensation for property destroyed;[16] and the

[10] Williams, The Middle Kingdom, Vol. II, pp. 355-358.
[11] Servière, Histoire de la Mission du Kiang-nan, Vol. I, p. 133.
[12] Williams, op. cit., Vol. II, p. 357.
[13] Williams, op. cit., Vol. II, p. 358.
[14] Morse, op. cit., Vol. I, pp. 480-484.
[15] Morse, op. cit., Vol. I, pp. 557ff. For the texts of the chief treaties see Mayers, op. cit., pp. 11-31, 59-75, 84-92, 100-117.
[16] Great Britain, Accounts and Papers. State Papers, 1871, Vol. LXX, China. Return Relative to Claims for Indemnity under the Convention of Peking, 1860; United States, Executive Documents, 3d session, 40th Congress, Vol. XIV, pp. 156ff.

guarantee of the toleration of Christianity with a promise of protection in the exercise of their faith both to missionaries and to Chinese Christians. The last of these provisions was particularly important, for it implied authorization to foreign governments to see that Chinese Christians were accorded the promised liberty and so placed the latter under foreign protection. This clause seems first to have been suggested by the Russians.[17] Missionaries serving as interpreters obtained its inclusion in the American document.[18] The French convention of 1860 secured the formal confirmation of the imperial edict of 1846 which promised the restoration of Roman Catholic property confiscated in the years of persecution.[19] The Chinese text of this convention also contained a clause which permitted French missionaries to rent and purchase land in all the provinces and to erect on them churches and houses.[20] Since the French treaty of 1858 had declared the French text to be authoritative,[21] the Chinese later challenged this concession.[22] However, in 1865 it was virtually confirmed by a further convention.[23] The governments of the United States and Great Britain would not support the efforts of Protestant missionaries to obtain the extension of this privilege to their citizens under the most favoured nation clauses,[24] but local Chinese officials sometimes permitted American and British missionaries to acquire land outside the treaty ports. American and British officials often supported their respective nationals in their title to lands thus purchased.[25] The treaties and conventions of 1858 and 1860, therefore, gave legal basis for the extensive permeation of China by Christianity.

We must add that in a later treaty with the United States, that of 1903, formal permission was granted to American missionary societies "to rent and to lease in perpetuity, as the property of such societies, buildings or lands in all parts of the Empire for missionary purposes." As an outgrowth of the experience in the years subsequent to the toleration clause in the treaty of 1858 provisions were included to guard against a Chinese seeking entrance to the Church to escape the consequences of a crime or to avoid taxes (except those for religious customs contrary to the Christian faith) and to prevent missionaries from inter-

---

[17] Williams, *Life and Letters of Samuel Wells Williams*, p. 270.
[18] Williams, *op. cit.*, pp. 270-282.
[19] See the French text in Mayers, *op. cit.*, p. 73.
[20] See the Chinese text in Tobar, *Kiao-ou Ki-lio*, pp. 50, 51.
[21] Mayers, *op. cit.*, p. 60.
[22] Latourette, *A History of Christian Missions in China*, p. 309.
[23] See text in Tobar, *op. cit.*, p. 73.
[24] See, for example, *House Executive Documents*, 2d session, 43d Congress, Vol. I (*Foreign Relations*), pp. 232-246.
[25] United States, *Foreign Relations*, 1st session, 44th Congress, Vol. I, p. 332.

fering with the exercise by Chinese officials of their authority over Chinese subjects.[26]

Under the terms of the treaties of 1842-1844 and 1858-1860, and under the growing pressure of an expanding Occident and the mounting missionary interest which marked the closing decades of the nineteenth century, the penetration of China by Western culture and Christianity proceeded. However, the resistant structure of Chinese life seemed to be but slightly affected.

Then, in the 1890's, began a chain of events which precipitated the rapid crumbling of the inherited Chinese culture. There commenced a revolution which was without precedent in China's history and which eventually transformed every phase of the civilization of the land. The first severe blow to Chinese isolation was delivered by Japan. That nation, which had derived its earlier culture from China, in the latter half of the century had adopted the tools of the West. Utilizing these, in 1894-1895 it defeated China. Many Chinese, including some in high position, their pride stung by the disaster, believed that if it were to avoid further humiliation the empire must take over those processes of the Occident by which their diminutive neighbour had subdued it. Still more indignities were suffered before China had accomplished the needed reorganization. Ambitious European powers, made vividly aware by the Japanese feat of the weakness of China, began what threatened to be the partition of the empire. From 1895 through 1899 several of them acquired special concessions in the form of territory, leaseholds, spheres of influence, mining privileges, and liens on railways under construction or about to be built. Roused by the aggression, Chinese conservatives blindly hit back and sought to expel the foreigner and all his works. The reaction culminated in what was known as the Boxer uprising (1899-1900). The "Boxers" trusted in magic to reinforce their arms aganst the alien. They were endorsed by some elements in the imperial court. The powers mishandled the situation and China stumbled into war against the world. Numbers of foreigners, including missionaries, were killed, and thousands of Chinese Christians as "secondary foreign devils," accused of treason to their country and its culture, fell victims to the Boxers' rage. The foreign diplomatic corps, together with many missionaries and Chinese Christians, stood siege in the legation quarter in Peking. Some Roman Catholic missionaries with their flock were beleagured at the same time in one of their churches in the capital. The destruction was chiefly confined to the North. Troops of several nations joined in rescuing the legations and in suppressing the Boxers. A treaty, the Boxer Protocol, was imposed on China (1901), which

[26] See text in MacMurray, *Treaties and Agreements with and concerning China*, Vol. I, pp. 430, 431.

included a large indemnity and the stationing of foreign armed forces at Tient-sin and Peking to prevent a recurrence of the disaster.[27] Under the pretext of restoring order and protecting her nationals, Russia moved into Manchuria and sought to checkmate Japan in Korea. There followed (1904-1905) a war be-tween Russia and Japan which, to the chagrin of informed Chinese, was fought largely on Chinese soil. In consequence, Japan replaced Russia in southern Manchuria.

Her political independence and territorial integrity imminently threatened by this bewildering succession of disasters, China set about adopting many phases of Western culture as the only escape from the impending doom. Intel-lectual, political, economic, social, and religious revolution followed. The ancient system of civil service examinations, the basis of the all-powerful civil bureauc-racy, was abolished (1905) and schools of Western types were encouraged. A rev-olution (1911) inaugurated what professed to be a republic and ended (1912) the monarchy whose beginnings went back before the time of Christ. Modern fac-tories, railways, and steamship lines were developed, albeit slowly. Changes in social customs, in relations between the sexes, and even in the basic family system were under way. Confucianism, on which the structure of the state, education, morals, and society had been based for eighteen centuries, was de-moted from its position as a state cult. Chinese culture was fluid as it had not been since before the advent of Christ. The time was most favourable for the spread of Christianity. To a greater degree than in any other era and in any other major civilized land there was the opportunity to build Christianity into the warp and woof of the emerging civilization, the China which was to be.

We must now turn to the story of the expansion of Christianity in China between 1800 and 1914. We shall watch the difficult propagation in the days before the treaties, the slow penetration between 1842 and 1895, and the rapid growth after 1895, interrupted by the brief test of the Boxer conflagration. We shall see how the growing opportunity in China was matched by the rising tide of missionary enthusiasm in the Occident. We will first turn to Roman Catholi-cism, as the form of Christianity most strongly represented at the beginning of the nineteenth century. We will next describe briefly the small enterprise of the Russian church, the other form of the faith present in 1800. Then we will sketch the introduction and progress of Protestant Christianity. Finally we will

[27] Of the voluminous literature on the Boxer outbreak the following are among the important titles: George Nye Steiger, *China and the Occident. The Origin and Develop-ment of the Boxer Movement* (Yale University Press, 1927, pp. xix, 348); B. L. Putnam Weale [B. L. Simpson], *Indiscreet Letters from Peking* (New York, Dodd, Mead and Co., 1910, pp. vii, 447); and Arthur H. Smith, *China in Convulsion* (Chicago, Fleming H. Revell Co., 2 vols., 1901).

deal with the familiar topics of the effect of Christianity on its environment and of the environment on Christianity.

In the history of the Roman Catholic Church in China A.D. 1800 is not a natural dividing date. Conditions before that year had been progressively adverse. For a time after 1800 they continued to be so. Periodical persecutions beset such Roman Catholic communities as existed. The decay of the Manchu dynasty was beginning and was marked by unrest and local rebellions. In these the Christians suffered, partly through the general disorder and partly because, compelled to meet semi-secretly, Christians were suspected by imperial officials of potential or actual sedition. In 1805 a persecution broke out in Peking, precipitated by the seizure of a map which was being sent to Rome to elucidate a dispute between priests over ecclesiastical jurisdiction but which aroused the fear that a foreign invasion of China was being planned.[28] In 1811 came a fresh imperial anti-Christian edict, apparently excited by the apprehension of a Chinese priest which gave evidence of Christian activity. Further restrictions were placed upon the dwindling scientific mission long tolerated in Peking and now in the hands of six Lazarists and one aged ex-Jesuit.[29] From time to time European priests were caught and expelled from the empire.[30] In 1814 a school in West China for the training of clergy, although hidden in the mountains, was discovered and destroyed.[31] In that same year Dufresse, Vicar Apostolic in West China, was beheaded.[32] In 1816 a Franciscan was executed in Changsha, in the province of Hunan.[33] In 1817, 1818, and 1821 there were executions of Chinese priests.[34] In 1819 a Lazarist, François-Régis Clet, was strangled at Wuchang.[35] The imperial authorities had been somewhat loth to resort to such violent measures. Often the presence of missionaries and Chinese Christians was winked at. Yet the laws of the realm were clear. Christians, by being

[28] Nouvelles Lettres Édifiantes, Vol. IV, pp. 135-162, 207-211, 219-224.
[29] Nouvelles Lettres Édifiantes, Vol. IV, pp. 551ff., Vol. V, pp. 3-14.
[30] Nouvelles Lettres Édifiantes, Vol. IV, p. 292.
[31] Nouvelles Lettres Édifiantes, Vol. IV, pp. 132-161.
[32] Nouvelles Lettres Édifiantes, Vol. V, pp. 108-131, 162-171, 175-180; Annales de la Propagation de la Foi, No. 4, p. 44.
[33] Nouvelles Lettres Édifiantes, Vol. V, pp. 181-207; Antoine du Lys, Un Vrai Frère Mineur. Vie et Martyre du Bienheureux Jean de Triora, Béatifié le 27 Mai 1900 (Paris), passim.
[34] Nouvelles Lettres Édifiantes, Vol. V, pp. 208-245; Launay, Histoire Générale de la Société des Missions-Étrangères, Vol. II, p. 490.
[35] Annales de la Propagation de la Foi, No. 6, pp. 23, 24; Demimuid, Vie du Bienheureux François-Régis Clet (Paris, 1900); Montgesty and Gilmore, Two Vincentian Martyrs, p. 94.

Christians, were violating them, and the normal Chinese official would feel that in enforcing them he was but fulfilling his duty.

Yet in the year 1800 Roman Catholic Christianity had by no means disappeared. In 1810 thirty-one European missionaries and eighty Chinese priests were reported.[36] Several centres were maintained for the training of priests.[37] In 1800, as we said a few paragraphs above, the number of Roman Catholics was probably between two hundred thousand and two hundred and fifty thousand.[38] Apparently they were in all the eighteen provinces of China proper, with the possible exception of Kansu, in Formosa, and in Mongolia and Sinkiang. They were most numerous in the great far-western province, Szechwan.[39]

Soon after 1815, with the return of peace in Europe and the beginning of the revival in the Roman Catholic Church, reinforcements began to trickle into China in slightly larger numbers than in the years of the Napoleonic Wars. From 1820 to 1838 twelve missionaries reached Szechwan.[40] In 1831 two Lazarists made their way into China and seven others embarked for that country.[41] We hear of three other missionaries entering the empire in 1829.[42] In the three years 1838-1840 five new vicariates apostolic were created,[43] an indication that the Roman Catholic enterprise was once more expanding. The Society of Jesus, revived a few years before, in 1841 and 1842 renewed its mission in China, in the lower part of the Yangtze Valley.[44] In 1834 the Comte de Besi, a Jesuit and an intimate of Pope Gregory XVI, sought to reintroduce his society to the Middle Kingdom. After various vicissitudes he was made administrator of the diocese of Nanking. It seems to have been chiefly through him that the Jesuits were substituted for the Lazarists in that region.[45]

Yet adversities continued. In 1840 the Lazarist Perboyre was executed in Wuchang.[46] In 1842 a member of the imperial family died in prison for his

[36] Marchini's map of Catholic missions, quoted in *The Chinese Repository*, Vol. I, p. 443.
[37] *Annales de la Propagation de la Foi*, Vol. III, p. 239, Vol. V, pp. 659, 660, Vol. IX, pp. 222, 223; Montgesty and Gilmore, *op. cit.*, pp. 52, 148; *T'oung Pao*, Vol. XX, p. 121; Moidrey, *La Hiérarchie Catholique en Chine, en Corée et au Japon*, pp. 190, 191.
[38] Medhurst, *China*, pp. 244, 245; Montgesty and Gilmore, *op. cit.*, p. 150.
[39] Medhurst, *op. cit.*, p. 245; *Annales de la Propagation de la Foi*, Vol. VII, p. 348, Vol. IX, p. 58, Vol. XII, p. 333.
[40] Launay, *op. cit.*, Vol. III, p. 58.
[41] *Annales de la Propagation de la Foi*, Vol. V, p. 560.
[42] *Annales de la Propagation de la Foi*, Vol. IV, p. 422.
[43] Moidrey, *op. cit.*, pp. 62, 85, 114, 117, 135, 153.
[44] Moidrey, *op. cit.*, p. 188; Broullion, *Memoire sur l'État Actuel de la Mission du Kiang-nan 1842-1855*, p. 47.
[45] Thomas, *Histoire de la Mission de Pékin depuis l'Arrivée des Lazarists jusqu'a la Revolte das Boxeurs*, pp. 142-145.
[46] Montgesty and Gilmore, *op. cit.*, pp. 174, 175.

faith.[47] From 1836 to 1840 there was persecution in Fukien.[48] The renewed severity may have been due to the Anglo-Chinese hostilities.

The treaties of 1842-1844 and especially the imperial edict of toleration of 1844 gave to the Roman Catholic Church an enlarged, even though a still restricted opportunity. In the later 1840's representatives of European sisterhoods reached China,[49] apparently the first to labour in that land. In the 1850's two Chinese sisterhoods were organized.[50] The renewed Society of Jesus rapidly developed the mission which had been assigned to it at the mouth and on the lower reaches of the Yangtze. From 1843 to 1857 inclusive fifty-eight, mostly Europeans, joined its staff.[51] Headquarters were established on the outskirts of Shanghai, at Zikawei, the ancestral village of Hsü Kuang-ch'i, a distinguished convert of the Ming dynasty.[52] Notable educators that they were, the Jesuits inaugurated schools and by 1853 had one hundred and seventy-four (of which thirty were run by sisters) with over twelve hundred pupils.[53] In the first nine months of 1855 nearly two thousand adults were baptized in the Jesuit area.[54] In 1854 the Jesuits were assigned a new vicariate in the North, with headquarters at Hsien Hsien, in south-eastern Chihli.[55] Among the early arrivals was Joseph Gonnet, who reached Shanghai in 1844 and was to have slightly more than a half century in China, part of it as superior of his mission in the Yangtze Valley and part of it as superior in the North. He did much to put the mission in Chihli on a sound financial basis and to develop the schools and other institutions.[56] The Lazarists who in the difficult years of the preceding century had courageously come to the rescue when the Society of Jesus had been dissolved also had a growing staff. From 1846 to 1859 inclusive fifty-two priests, Chinese and foreign, were added to them.[57] The outstanding leader of the Lazarists was Joseph Martial Mouly. He reached China in the 1830's, spent his introductory years in the small Christian settlement of Hsi-wan-tzŭ, in Mongolia, and there brought new life to the group, building a church, founding

---

[47] Launay, Le Cinquante-deux Vénérables Serviteurs de Dieu, pp. 388-390.
[48] Gentili, Memoire di un Missionario Dominicano nella Cina, Vol. II, pp. 413-415.
[49] The International Review of Missions, Vol. IV, p. 467; Manna, The Conversion of the Pagan World, p. 167.
[50] Arens, Handbuch der Katholischen Missionen, p. 144.
[51] Catalogus Patrum ac Fratrum e Societate Jesu qui . . . in Sinis Adlaboraverunt, pp. 50ff.
[52] Servière, Histoire de la Mission du Kiangnan, Vol. I, pp. 112-114.
[53] Broullion, op. cit., p. 224.
[54] Annales de la Propagation de la Foi, Vol. XXVIII, p. 210.
[55] Leroy, En Chine au Tché-ly S. E., p. 191.
[56] Becker, Joseph Gonnet, passim.
[57] Catalogue des Prêtres, Clercs et Frères de la Congrégation de la Mission qui ont Travaillé en Chine depuis 1697.

schools, and inaugurating retreats.[58] In 1841 he was made the first Vicar Apostolic of Mongolia.[59] It was while holding this post that he sent two Lazarists, Joseph Gabet and Regis-Evariste Huc, on a journey which eventually took the two to Lhasa, in Tibet, and, through Huc's lively but not always reliable narrative, brought them fame.[60] Later Mouly became administrator of the diocese of Peking.[61] In 1856 he was made the first incumbent of the new Vicariate Apostolic. of Northern Chihli,[62] which included the city of Peking. In Fukien between 1844 and 1859 the Dominicans built thirteen churches.[63] In 1846 the Société des Missions Étrangères of Paris, in addition to the large territories for which it was responsible in China proper, was assigned the difficult and distant Tibet.[64] Heroic attempts to penetrate that great closed land followed, some of them through Assam and the valley of the Brahmaputra, in one instance with death for two priests as the consequence.[65] In 1838 the Paris society was given the newly created Vicariate Apostolic of Manchuria, which was adjacent to Korea, a field in which it was already interested.[66]

In China as in India the Portuguese attempted to exert control under the padroado.[67] In China, however, no such extensive bodies of Christians claiming Portuguese descent existed as in India, and Rome had much less difficulty in asserting its authority. In 1856 it suppressed the dioceses of Nanking and Peking to which the Portuguese claimed the right to name the bishops.[68]

The Roman Catholic Church was registering distinct progress. In 1851 an unofficial synod of vicars apostolic was held in Shanghai. It recommended the institution of a hierarchy similar to those in Europe, with bishops and archbishops. Either foreigners or Chinese were to be eligible for these posts and both Chinese and foreign clergy were to join in electing the incumbents.[69] Ap-

[58] Thomas, op. cit., pp. 150-165.
[59] Thomas, op. cit., pp. 178ff.
[60] A standard edition is E. Huc, Souvenirs d'un Voyage dans la Tartarie et le Thibet pendant les Années 1844, 1845 et 1846, edited by J.-M. Planchet (Peking, Imprimerie des Lazaristes, 2 vols., 1924). See also the standard English translation edited, with an important introduction, by Paul Pelliot (London, George Routledge and Sons, 2 vols., 1928), and S. Camman, New Light on Huc and Gabet, in The Far Eastern Quarterly, Vol. I, pp. 348-363.
[61] Thomas, op. cit., pp. 244-265.
[62] Moidrey, La Hiérarchie Catholique en Chine, en Corée et au Japon, p. 140.
[63] André-Marie, Missions Dominicaines dans l'Extrême-Orient, Vol. I, pp. 237-254.
[64] Launay, Histoire Générale de la Société des Missions-Étrangères, Vol. III, p. 290.
[65] Annals of the Propagation of the Faith, Vol. XXVI, pp. 356ff.; Becker, Im Stromtal des Brahmaputra, pp. 109-166.
[66] Launay, op. cit., Vol. III, pp. 104, 105; Thomas, op. cit., pp. 166, 167.
[67] Servière, op. cit., Vol. I, pp. 48ff., 93ff.; Moidrey, op. cit., p. 33.
[68] Moidrey, op. cit., pp. 34, 40.
[69] Servière, op. cit., Vol. I, pp. 189-195.

parently, however, Rome deemed the step too drastic and did not approve it. The gradual penetration of China by Western influences in the years between the war of 1856-1860, with its resultant treaties, and the upheavals which followed the Sino-Japanese War of 1894-1895 was effected in part through the growth of Roman Catholic missions.

One of the results of the treaties of 1844 and 1858 and of the conventions of 1860 was that Roman Catholics and their activities were placed under the protection of France. The French Government took over this role from no particular zeal for the faith. Indeed, during much of the time after the establishment of the Third Republic (1871), in its own territories, domestic and colonial, the French administration was anti-clerical. However, French commerce with China was much less important than that of Great Britain and in the diplomatic support of Roman Catholic missions of whatever nationality France found a means of asserting herself. It was through French pressure that the toleration of Roman Catholic missions was obtained. It was French treaties which gave to Roman Catholics the chief legal basis for their activities and their expansion. It was at the instance of the French Chargé d'Affaires that in 1869 and 1870 the provincial authorities of Kiangnan, Hukuang, and Szechwan took measures favourable to Christianity.[70] It was through pressure from the French legation that a section was added (1870) to the Chinese imperial code suppressing existing prohibitions of Roman Catholicism and assuring toleration for that faith.[71] French diplomatic officers gave effective support to the efforts of Roman Catholic missionaries to obtain the restoration of sequestered church property which had been promised in the Sino-French convention of 1860.[72] France issued passports, not only to French missionaries but also to Roman Catholic missionaries of other nationalities.[73] In the 1880's Italy was thwarted in her endeavour to substitute for Italian missionaries her passports for those of France.[74] In the 1880's, however, the head of the German missionaries in Shantung decided to accept German rather than French protection.[75] It is significant evidence of the waning power of Portugal in the Far East that Lisbon, while insisting stoutly on its claims under the padroado in India, seems to have registered no opposition to the substitution of France for itself as the guardian of Roman Catholic interests in China. It clung to Macao. In the 1840's and 1850's

[70] Servière, op. cit., Vol. II, pp. 168-171.
[71] Tobar, Kiao-ou Ki-lio, p. 57.
[72] See instances of this in Servière, op. cit., Vol. II, pp. 32-34; Annals of the Propagation of the Faith, Vol. XXII, pp. 136-140.
[73] Cordier, Histoire des Relations de la Chine avec les Puissances Occidentales, Vol. II, pp. 637-41; Koo, The Status of Aliens in China, pp. 298, 299.
[74] Cordier, op. cit., Vol. III, pp. 77-79; Grentrup, Jus Missionarium, pp. 400-402.
[75] Grentrup, op. cit., pp. 399, 400.

it brought some embarrassment to the Holy See. But after the 1850's it appears to have placed no obstacles in the way of either the French protectorate or the exercise of papal authority in China outside Macao.[76] Nor does France seem to have employed her favoured position to attempt to name the bishops for China. That may have been for the reason that after the abolishment of the dioceses of Nanking and Peking episcopal administration, except for Macao, was by vicars apostolic who by the nature of their office were more directly.under the Holy See than were bishops who ruled in their own name. The vicars apostolic, it will be remembered, were usually titular bishops named to extinct sees who exercised their authority in the name of the Pope. In India and the Far East they had been in part a device to avoid the complications brought by the Portuguese padroado. Clearly the French Government, even if it had been so disposed, would have found it difficult to gain a voice in their selection.

A corollary of the French protectorate was the use made of it by some Roman Catholic missionaries to gain converts. China was a land of conflicts between groups and between individuals. Many of these went to the courts and lawsuits were common. If in these contests one participant could obtain the support of the foreigner he might gain the advantage over his adversary. Since the victories of the Western powers officialdom was inclined, although with much inward unwillingness and sense of outrage, to seek to avoid trouble with the truculent Occidental. If there were unpleasantness involving the treaties, the consul or the minister of the aggrieved nation might bring the issue to the attention of the higher provincial or national dignitaries. They, in turn, would hold responsible the unfortunate magistrate within whose jurisdiction the incident had occurred. A litigant, therefore, might represent his case to a missionary as being one of persecution for an inclination towards Christianity and as falling within the scope of the toleration clauses of the treaties of 1858. Or he might offer to become a Christian if the missionary would speak on his behalf to the magistrate. Or a Chinese catechist or priest, wishing to make a good showing in numbers of converts with his ecclesiastical superior and employer, might promise to exert his influence with the missionary in behalf of those who enrolled as catechumens and then interpret a lawsuit or possible lawsuit as persecution. At times the mere hint that the missionary might intervene would be sufficient to intimidate the magistrate.[77] The treaties gave opportunity for these inducements to Protestants as well as Roman Catholics, but the governments of the United States and Great Britain, from whose countries a majority of Protestant missionaries came to China, were reluctant to accord support in

[76] Beckmann, *Die Katholische Missionsmethode in China*, pp. 26, 27.
[77] Gibson, *Mission Problems and Mission Methods in South China*, pp. 293-298.

such cases, and in general, while not all of them were innocent in such matters, Protestant missionaries avoided interference in lawsuits.[78] However, the French Government, as a means of augmenting its prestige, was disposed to support such Roman Catholic missionaries as were willing to use pressure in litigation as a means of obtaining adherents.

How far Roman Catholic missionaries took advantage of the situation to increase their flocks is not clear. One Roman Catholic writer declared that a very large proportion of the catechumens were attracted by the hope of obtaining the protection of the missionary in difficulties with their neighbours and the courts.[79] Yet that same writer reported that some missionaries refused to go to court.[80] Beginning at least as early as the 1880's, various synods endeavoured to discourage Christians from feeling that they enjoyed any special privileges, sought to regulate the methods of using lawsuits, and forbade catechists to go to the magistrate without the consent of the missionary.[81] One Roman Catholic appraisal declared the situation to be deplorable. It held that the mixing of missionaries and their subordinates in lawsuits had made for ill-feeling among officials and non-Christians, that attempts to regulate it had been far from successful, and that as a mission method it was to be condemned.[82]

Roman Catholic missionaries, even French citizens, were not all of one opinion as to the desirability of the French protectorate. Some of the French were critical. Others favoured it. Some of the non-French believed it of advantage.[83]

Beginning early in the twentieth century, the French protectorate waned. In France there was criticism of it.[84] In 1899 a Chinese imperial rescript was issued which sought to regulate the approach of Roman Catholic missionaries to officials.[85] This seems to have augmented the friction, for it had the effect of appearing to sanction what had in part already been the practice of the

[78] Latourette, *A History of Christian Missions in China*, p. 280; Gibson, *op. cit.*, pp. 299-312; *The Chinese Recorder*, Vol. XXXIX, pp. 657-675.

[79] Becker, *Joseph Gonnet*, pp. 245-247.

[80] Becker, *op. cit.*, p. 247.

[81] Beckmann, *op. cit.*, pp. 160, 161.

[82] Beckmann, *op. cit.*, pp. 163-165. On one regrettable incident in which some Christians had falsified the seal of an official to obtain privileges not belonging to them, a case whose solution greatly puzzled the missionary, see Habig, *Pioneering in China*, p. 137.

[83] Beckmann, *op. cit.*, pp. 20-23.

[84] See one vigorous attack, unfriendly to the protectorate and critical of missions, in Paul Boell, *Le Protectorat des Missions Catholiques en Chine et la Politique de la France en Extrême-Orient* (Paris, Institut Scientifique de la Libre-Pensée, 1899, pp. vii, 71).

[85] MacMurray, *Treaties and Agreements with and Concerning China*, Vol. I, p. 718. See on this an important article by G. Nye Steiger, *China's Attempt to Aborbe* [sic] *Christianity. The Decree of March 15, 1899* (*T'oung Pao*, Vol. XXIV, pp. 215-246).

Roman Catholic priests and vicars apostolic of assuming official insignia and exercising a certain degree of civil jurisdiction over their flocks.[86] In 1908 the rescript of 1899 was revoked.[87] The separation of Church and state in France in 1905 was followed (January, 1906) by the notification of the Chinese Government by the French Minister that henceforth the French legation would concern itself only with cases affecting French missionaries.[88] In 1903 and 1905 the Italian Government assumed the protectorate of Italian missionaries.[89]

Partly assisted by the French protectorate, after 1860 the Roman Catholic missionary force was largely augmented and reached out actively for new converts. Until the 1860's Roman Catholic missionaries had for many years contented themselves chiefly with the care of existing Christians and their children. If catechumens came from the non-Christians they regarded their instruction more as a duty than a joy.[90] This was probably because the long decades of persecution had placed the missionaries on the defensive and forced them to labour quietly. It was possibly also of a piece with the attitude in India at the close of the eighteenth and the beginning of the nineteenth century when few missionaries exerted themselves to win converts. After the treaties of 1858-1860 a more aggressive policy was pursued.

From 1860 onward Roman Catholic organizations already in China added to their staffs.

The Jesuits, who in the sixteenth century had been responsible for the reintroduction of Christianity to the empire after its extinction in an earlier period of the Ming dynasty, and who during the seventeenth and much of the eighteenth century had carried the main burden of the propagation of the faith, did not become relatively as prominent as formerly. However, in the 1840's and 1850's they had been assigned two portions of the large fields which had once been theirs and these they developed. The larger and more strategic was that of Kiangnan, in the provinces of Kiangsu and Anhui. It was in the populous and wealthy lower reaches of the valley of the Yangtze and included what was to become the chief port of China, Shanghai. In 1866-1867 the Jesuit staff in Kiangnan embraced 42 European and 14 Chinese priests. In 1878-1879 these numbers had grown to 55 and 26 respectively,[91] and in 1912 to 129 and 66.[92]

[86] Gilbert Reid, *The Sources of the Anti-Foreign Disturbances in China* (Shanghai, 1903), pp. 76-104; Wen Ching, *The Chinese Crisis from Within* (London, 1901), p. 303.
[87] MacMurray, *op. cit.*, Vol. I, p. 718.
[88] Koo, *The Status of Aliens in China*, p. 309.
[89] Beckmann, *op. cit.*, p. 26.
[90] Beckmann, *op. cit.*, p. 3.
[91] Servière, *Histoire de la Mission du Kiangnan*, Vol. II, p. 321.
[92] Streit, *Atlas Hierarchicus*, p. 100.

In the same period Roman Catholics had risen from 73,847 in 1866-1867 to 94,310 in 1878-1879 [93] and to 208,164 in 1912.[94] In both numbers of priests and of Roman Catholics these figures were larger by far than the corresponding ones in any other of the ecclesiastical divisions of China. It must be said, however, that the population was also much larger than that of any of the other vicariates apostolic and, since Kiangnan was on the coast and contained the main centre of the foreign commercial penetration of China, the growth in the Christian community could be expected to be marked. In 1912 the proportion of Christians to the population of Kiangnan was exceeded in several other vicariates, including that of the Jesuits themselves in south-eastern Chihli, that of the Lazarists in the section of Chihli which included Peking, that of the Congregation of the Immaculate Heart of Mary on the southern edges of Mongolia, and that of the Milan Seminary in Hongkong.[95] In at least two of the cities on the Yangtze, it may be noted, the initial footing was obtained through the very tangible support of a French gunboat.[96]

The growth of Jesuit enterprise in the much smaller south-eastern Chihli was, as we hinted two sentences above, proportionately even more striking. In 1854, when the Jesuits were placed in charge, the Roman Catholics may have numbered 9,000. In 1870 they were said to total about 19,000, in 1896, 43,736,[97] and in 1912, 83,088.[98]

The Jesuits were not content merely with adding to the numbers of Christians and giving spiritual care to them. They also developed institutions which were designed mainly to educate Chinese who would assist in the nurture and growth of the Church. In Kiangnan, notably at Zikawei, there were seminaries, a college, a printing press, and a great orphanage.[99] In south-eastern Chihli there were schools for boys and girls, schools for preparing both men and women catechists, a theological seminary, and dispensaries for European medicines.[100]

The Lazarists, who had so manfully stepped into the breach made by the dissolution of the Society of Jesus in the second half of the eighteenth century, had heroically kept the light of the Christian faith burning in a large part of China during the dark days of the persecutions and the low ebb of support from Europe. In the course of the nineteenth century some of the territory which they had served was turned over to other orders. However, on the eve of 1914

[93] Servière, op. cit., Vol. II, p. 321.
[94] Streit, op. cit., p. 100.
[95] Ibid.
[96] Servière, op. cit., Vol. II, pp. 135-138.
[97] Leroy, En Chine au Tché-ly S.-E., p. 188.
[98] Streit, op. cit., p. 100.
[99] Servière, op. cit., Vol. II, pp. 259ff.
[100] Leroy, op. cit., pp. 224-230.

they were still in charge of most of the metropolitan province of Chihli,[101] including Peking and the great port city, Tientsin (except for some Jesuit footholds), and of the important provinces of Kiangsi and Chekiang.[102] In these territories they had more Christians under their care than did any other of the orders or societies, whether Roman Catholic or Protestant, then labouring in China.[103] From 1860 to 1899 inclusive, 235 priests, foreign and Chinese, were added to the Lazarist ranks,[104] and in 1912 their foreign priests totalled 193 and their Chinese priests 170.[105] In accordance with the treaties and through the good offices of the French, the sites of the four principal seventeenth and eighteenth century churches in Peking were restored to the Lazarists.[106] One of the churches had never been destroyed, and by the early part of 1867 worship was re-established at the other three centres.[107] The funds which made possible the reconstruction were in part from the indemnities collected by France through the treaty of 1858 and the convention of 1860.[108] Napoleon III also sent (1862) 7 missionaries and 14 Sisters of Charity to reinforce the Lazarist mission in Chihli.[109] In 1897 the popular and energetic Alphonse-Marie Favier (1837-1906) became coadjutor to the Vicar Apostolic of northern Chihli (which included Peking) and in 1899 succeeded to the post of vicar apostolic. He served through the stormy Boxer period.[110]

In point of area and population the regions administered in 1914 by the Société des Missions Étrangères of Paris far exceeded those assigned to any other organization. They embraced some which the society had served during the long period of adversity and others which were added in the nineteenth century. They included most of the coastal province of Kwangtung, with the important city of Canton, the provinces of Kwangsi, Kweichow, Yünnan, and Szechwan, Tibet, which bordered on this area, and the much more distant Manchuria.[111] Manchuria in turn bordered on Korea, which in 1914 was a field of the Paris society. Korea was not far from Japan, the larger part of which was

[101] For the history of a section in this area, see J. M. Planchet, *Les Lazaristes à Suanhoafou 1783-1927* (Peking, Imprimerie des Lazaristes, 1927, pp. 182).

[102] Streit, *op. cit.*, p. 100. For the life of a vicar apostolic of South Kiangsi, see *Notice sur Monseigneur François-Adrien Rouger* (Paris, Retaux-Bray, no date, pp. 209).

[103] Streit, *op. cit.*, p. 100.

[104] *Catalogue des Prêtres, Clercs et Frères de la Congrégation de la Mission qui ont Travaillé en Chine, passim.*

[105] Streit, *op. cit.*, p. 100.

[106] Cordier, *Histoire des Relations de la Chine avec les Puissances Occidentales*, Vol. I, pp. 54-56.

[107] *Annales de la Propagation de la Foi*, Vol. XLI, p. 246.

[108] Favier, *Peking*, Vol. II, p. 229.

[109] *Ibid.*

[110] Moidrey, *La Hiérarchie Catholique en Chine, en Corée et au Japon*, p. 141.

[111] Streit, *op. cit.*, p. 100. On the society's operations in Kwangsi, see Joseph Cuenot, *Kwangsi, Land of the Black Banners*. Translated by George F. Wiseman (St. Louis, B. Herder Book Co., 1942, pp. xvii, 279).

then also in the ecclesiastical domain of the society. It was a prodigious responsibility which the Missions Etrangères of Paris carried, but unlike most of the orders and societies represented in China, particularly the older ones, the Paris fathers had concentrated their efforts entirely on the Far East. In 1914 the numbers of Christians cared for by the society in the Chinese Empire were not as great as the extent of territory might have led one to expect. This was not from any dereliction of duty. It was, rather, because of the nature of the field. Much of the vast area was sparsely populated, notably Tibet and Manchuria. Most of it was remote from the coast and from immediate contact with Occidental commerce and culture. In it, therefore, were few who were affected by the new age which was pressing so aggressively on the coastal fringes of the empire. Indeed, far from being remiss, in 1912 the Paris society had more than twice as many foreign priests, an even four hundred, in China, including twenty-five in Tibet and fifty-nine in Manchuria, than did any other Roman Catholic organization.[112] In spite of the fact that one of the foremost original purposes of the society had been the creation of an indigenous secular clergy, in proportion to foreign priests the number of Chinese priests in 1912 connected with the Paris society was not nearly as large as that of the Lazarists and slightly less than that of the Jesuits. However, the total was one hundred and ninety-seven, which was greater than that of any other organization, and in the areas, in Szechwan, where in the eighteenth and the fore part of the nineteenth century the society had had its main Christian communities, in 1912 the Chinese priests almost equalled the total of the foreign priests. It was in more difficult areas, such as Kwangsi and Tibet, that the disparity was the most striking.[113] In 1912 the largest number of Roman Catholics in the care of the Paris society in any one province was 113,285, in Szechwan, but in proportion to the population Roman Catholics were most numerous in mountainous Kweichow.[114] There the 1860's saw a very rapid growth, apparently due to the power of France made evident in curbing persecution in the 1850's and the first years of the 1860's.[115] Of all the regions assigned to the Paris fathers Tibet was the most difficult. Persistent efforts were made to enter the country by way of both China and India,[116] but resident stations could be established merely on the frontier of the great closed land[117] and in 1912 there were only slightly more than seven thousand Roman Catholics on the Tibetan marches.[118]

Franciscans had long been in China. It was they who in the thirteenth and

[112] Streit, op. cit., p. 100.
[113] Ibid.
[114] Ibid.
[115] Latourette, A History of Christian Missions in China, pp. 310, 326.
[116] On attempts from India see Becker, Im Stromtal des Brahmaputra, pp. 173, 174.
[117] Latourette, op. cit., p. 328.
[118] Streit, op. cit., p. 100.

fourteenth centuries first propagated Roman Catholic Christianity in the empire. Although in the fourteenth century they disappeared from China, they reappeared in the sixteenth century. In the seventeenth century they began continuing enterprises in a number of centres. In 1912 they were still to be found in some of the sections where they had established themselves in pre-nineteenth century days.[119] They were in Shantung, Shansi, Shensi, Hupeh, and Hunan.[120] They were of several nationalities, but Italians were numerous among them.[121] By 1914 part of Shansi was entrusted specifically to the Dutch Brothers Minor, part of Hupeh to the Belgians, part of Shantung to the French, part of Shensi to the Spaniards, and a portion of Shantung was passing from Italian to German personnel. However, the general of the order reserved the right to send missionaries wherever they were needed, regardless of their nationality.[122] It seems to have been Franciscans who were the first Roman Catholic missionaries to come to China from the United States. They reached China in the 1880's and one of them later became a bishop.[123] In 1912-1913 the Franciscans were reported to have in China 10 bishops, 218 foreign priests, 128 Chinese priests, and 192,200 Christians.[124]

Spanish Dominicans of the province which embraced the Philippines and Indo-China had long been in Fukien. In the eighteenth century their field had also included Chekiang and Kiangsi, but they had gradually withdrawn from these provinces and in 1838 were glad to see them transferred to the Lazarists.[125] They concentrated their efforts on Fukien and the neighbouring island of Formosa. Gradually they reinforced their staff and erected churches.[126] In 1859 they re-entered Formosa.[127] In 1883 an additional vicariate apostolic was created

---

[119] For a chronological summary see Ioannes Ricci, *Chronologia Missionum Fratrum Minorum in Sinis Finitimisque Regnis* (Ad Claras Aquas, Typis Collegii S. Bonaventurae, 1925, pp. 149).

[120] For Franciscans in their various provinces see Marie-Pacifique Chardin, *Les Missions Franciscaines en Chine. Notes Geographiques et Historiques* (Paris, Auguste Picard, 1915, pp. x, 254), *passim.*

For a Franciscan in Hupeh see Rembert Wegener, *P. Viktorin Delbrouck* (Trier, Paulinus Druckerei, 1911, pp. 98).

For the Franciscan history in Hunan see Giovanni Ricci and Ercolano Porta, *Storia della Missione Franciscane e del Vicariato Apostolico del Hunan Meridionale dalle sue Origini ai Giorno Nostri* (Bologna, Stabilimenti Poligrafici Riuniti, 1925, pp. 222), pp. 33ff.

[121] Moidrey, *La Hiérarchie Catholique en Chine, en Corée et au Japon*, pp. 65-68, 91-93, 182. For the life of a Catalan Franciscan in Shensi in the fore part of the twentieth century, see Francesc Pons, *Episodis de la Vida Missionera. Notes Biografiques del P. Francesc Bernat* (Vich, Editorial Serafica, 1927, pp. 125).

[122] Moidrey, *op. cit.*, p. 183.

[123] Habig, *Pioneering in China. The Story of the Rev. Francis Xavier Engbring, O. F. M., the First American Priest in China, 1857-1895, passim.*

[124] Moidrey, *op cit.*, p. 183.

[125] Moidrey, *op. cit.*, p. 185.

[126] *Los Dominicos en el Extremo Oriente*, pp. 110ff.

[127] *Los Dominicos en el Extremo Oriente*, p. 159.

with Amoy as its centre, but this was left in the hands of the Dominicans.[128] In 1912 the Dominicans had two vicars apostolic, forty-eight European priests, twenty-eight Chinese priests, and nearly fifty-seven thousand Christians.[129]

Several additional orders, congregations, and societies entered China in the slightly more than half a century between 1860 and 1914. One of the first of these to send representatives was the Congregation of the Immaculate Heart of Mary, a Belgian enterprise with headquarters at Scheutveld. The congregation had come into being through the initiative of a young priest, Theophile Verbist (1823-1868). While in charge of raising funds for the Association of the Holy Childhood [130] in the archdiocese of Malines, Verbist had become interested in China and had been impressed by the dearth of missionaries in that vast land. Since the recent treaties of 1858 and 1860 had opened the empire to the Christian Gospel, why should not Belgian Roman Catholics, he thought, have a more active share in taking advantage of the opportunity? He gathered together a small group of friends whom he infected with his enthusiasm. Two of them petitioned (1861) the endorsement of the bishops of Belgium and promptly received it. Money came quickly from the benevolent, but missionary candidates were slow to offer themselves. However, in 1862 the young congregation was given the provisional approval of the Archbishop of Malines and in 1863 that of the Propaganda. September 1, 1864, the Propaganda assigned Mongolia to the Scheutveld Fathers, and a few weeks later Verbist and his companions took their formal vows of poverty, chastity, and obedience. In August, 1865, Verbist and three others sailed for China.[131] Mongolia seems to have been the choice of Verbist. The selection had the approval, at first with hesitation, of Mouly, the energetic Lazarist who was then Vicar Apostolic of Mongolia.[132] Although in theory the territory entrusted to Verbist and his confreres was all of the vast region known as Mongolia, for the most part the Belgians concentrated their efforts on Inner Mongolia. This was the border area between China proper and Mongolia. In it were both Chinese and Mongols. It was a frontier region, in which Mongol herdsmen of nomadic antecedents and habits and Chinese farmers and town dwellers were both present. The Chinese were attempting to press forward the boundaries of cultivation against a desert whose southern margins fluctuated with the variations in the rainfall. In Inner Mongolia were already some Christians with a centre at Hsi-wan-tzŭ. It was at Hsi-wan-tzŭ that the Belgians first established headquarters. In February, 1868, Verbist died,

[128] Los Dominicos en el Extremo Oriente, p. 119.
[129] Streit, Atlas Hierarchicus, p. 100.
[130] See above, Vol. IV, p. 57.
[131] Rutten, Les Missionnaires de Scheut et leur Fondateur, pp. 1-23.
[132] Rutten, op. cit., pp. 25-31.

presumably of typhus, in a poverty-stricken village, his last hours attended by a faithful Chinese priest.[133] The early loss of the founder was a severe blow, but, undismayed, the survivors continued. The enterprise grew rapidly. Recruits came from all the dioceses of Belgium and from several dioceses of Holland.[134] Outposts were rapidly established westward into Kansu. By the year 1913 the Scheutveld Fathers serving in China numbered one hundred and sixty-nine and Chinese priests associated with them forty-five. The vast territory assigned to the congregation included not only Mongolia but also Kansu and Sinkiang. Compared with China proper, the population was sparse, but in 1912 the Roman Catholics totalled about eighty thousand.[135] A method extensively employed was the gathering of Christian settlements on lands owned by the mission.[136] In a region of uncertain and scanty rainfall and peculiarly subject to drought these colonies proved attractive. Much attention was also given to famine relief and the care of orphans.[137]

Slightly earlier than the Scheutvelders came representatives of the Seminary of Foreign Missions of Milan. It was founded in 1850 by Ramazzotti, then Bishop of Pavia, and in 1858 representatives from it reached Hongkong and the prefecture apostolic which bore that name became their field. In 1874 the prefecture apostolic was made a vicariate apostolic. The area included not only the island of Hongkong but also part of the neighbouring mainland. In 1869 the Milan Seminary was also assigned the province of Honan, formerly served by the Lazarists. Not far from the year 1913 it had in Hongkong a bishop, seventeen European and twelve Chinese priests, and about seventeen thousand Roman Catholics, and in Honan, by that time divided into two vicariates apostolic, two bishops, thirty-five European priests, thirteen Chinese priests, and about twenty-seven thousand Christians.[138]

In 1885 the youthful Seminary of St. Peter and St. Paul, of Rome, sent six priests to Shensi. In 1887 the southern part of the province was made a vicariate apostolic and was entrusted to it. In 1891 Canossian Sisters came to assist in reaching the women. In 1911 there were fifteen Italian and five Chinese priests, thirteen Canossian Sisters, and twelve Chinese tertiates. Christians numbered more than thirteen thousand.[139]

We have already met the Society of the Divine Word in South America,

[133] Rutten, op. cit., p. 160.
[134] Rutten, op. cit., p. 196.
[135] Streit, op. cit., p. 100.
[136] Beckmann, Die katholische Missionsmethode in China, p. 148.
[137] Beckmann, op. cit., p. 115.
[138] Moidrey, La Hiérarchie Catholique en Chine, en Corée et au Japon, pp. 201-210.
[139] Moidrey, op. cit., pp. 208-210.

New Guinea, the Philippines, and Africa.[140] It was organized in 1875 to enlist German Roman Catholics in the spread of the faith. The moving spirit was Arnold Janssen. Headquarters were established, not in Germany itself, but in Steyl, just across the Dutch boundary. The endorsement was obtained of Dutch, German, and Austrian bishops. The first Steyler missionaries were sent to China, where, in the southern part of Shantung, a field had been assigned them in 1882. The leader of the initial group was Johannes Baptist Anzer.[141] Near the close of the nineteenth century a German leasehold was obtained and a German sphere of influence was established in that region. Indeed, the German Government took the occasion of the murder of two of the Steyl Fathers to seize these advantages.[142] It may have been association with the powerful German support which accounts in part for the growth of the Christians in the area. In 1912 Roman Catholics numbered about seventy thousand. They were cared for by a bishop, sixty-five European and twelve Chinese priests, twelve lay brothers, and thirty-seven foreign and two Chinese sisters.[143]

In 1904 there arrived in Honan, a province where Italians of the Milan Seminary were already at work, missionaries, also Italian, from the newly founded Seminary of St. Francis Xavier for Foreign Missions, the headquarters of which were at Parma. In 1906 their region in the southern part of Honan was made a prefecture apostolic and in 1911 a vicariate apostolic. In 1913 the Parma enterprise had a bishop, eleven missionaries, and about forty-six hundred Christians.[144]

Spanish Augustinians had been active in China in the sixteenth, seventeenth, and eighteenth centuries,[145] but were late in re-establishing themselves. In 1879 a section in the northern part of Hunan was assigned to Augustinians of the province of the Philippines and in 1896 this was made a vicariate apostolic. In 1913 the vicariate contained about five thousand Roman Catholics, but it was said that only two-thirds of the twenty-seven missionaries spoke the language and that progress was slow.[146]

In 1902 the Salesians of John Bosco opened an orphanage in Macao. Later they were driven out by a revolution in Portugal, but returned in 1912.[147]

[140] Vol. V, pp. 73, 96, 97, 245, 273, 295, 401, 445.
[141] H. Fischer, *Arnold Janssen, Gründer des Steyler Missionswerkes. Ein Lebensbild* (Steyl, Missionsdruckerei, 1919, pp. v, 493), pp. 81, 82, 101ff., 286ff. Aug. Henninghaus, *P. Jos. Freinademetz. Sein Leben und Wirken* (Yenchowfu, Druck und Verlag der Katholischen Mission, 2d ed., 1926, pp. vi, 653), is an account of a member of the mission.
[142] Morse, *The International Relations of the Chinese Empire*, Vol. III, pp. 106, 107.
[143] Moidrey, *op. cit.*, p. 213.
[144] Moidrey, *op. cit.*, p. 214.
[145] Latourette, *A History of Christian Missions in China*, pp. 89, 90, 118, 128.
[146] Moidrey, *op. cit.*, p. 180.
[147] Planchet, *Les Missions de Chine et du Japon, 1916*, p. 33.

In the 1880's a new departure was made in missions in China. A Trappist (Cistercian) community was founded in the mountains several days' journey west of Peking. In 1886 it became a priory and in 1891 an abbey. In 1916 the abbey counted a membership of ninety, of whom twelve were Europeans and seventy-eight were Chinese.[148]

A few contingents of teaching brotherhoods, such as the Marist brothers, conducted schools,[149] but they did not loom prominently.

In addition to the men's organizations represented in China and to which sections of the empire were assigned, there were also sisterhoods. The nineteenth century was one of growing participation of women in the spread of Christianity, whether Roman Catholic or Protestant. Women made up an increasing proportion of the missionary staffs of these two wings of the Church. By 1913 there were slightly more than half as many foreign sisters in China as there were foreign priests (743 of the one as against 1,365 of the other) and Chinese sisters far outnumbered the Chinese priests and lay brothers (1,429 of the one as against 807 of the other).[150] The most widely spread of the women's congregations were the Franciscan Missionaries of Mary. They were in many provinces and vicariates and in connexion with several of the men's orders and societies.[151] The Daughters of Charity had entered earlier, the first group of them having sailed in 1847. They established themselves at Macao, but left four years later because of conflict between Portugal and the Holy See. They then went to Ningpo.[152] Eventually we hear of them in Chihli,[153] Kiangsi,[154] Shanghai,[155] and Chekiang.[156] The Canossian Sisters were also present.[157] We read of the Sisters of St. Vincent de Paul;[158] of the Société des Auxiliatrices des Ames du Purgatoire, which, founded in 1856, sent a contingent to China in 1867;[159] the Carmelites of St. Joseph;[160] the Little Sisters of the Poor, who cared for indigent

[148] Planchet, op. cit., pp. 51, 52.
[149] Planchet, op. cit., pp. 71, 151, 206.
[150] Streit, Atlas Hierarchicus, p. 100.
[151] Planchet, op. cit., p. 37. For the life of one of the sisters who went to China early in the twentieth century, see Karl Salotti, Schwester Maria Assunta Pallotta (Vienna, Franziskanerinnen Missionärinnen Mariens, 1926, pp. 371), passim.
[152] Planchet, op. cit., pp. 34-36.
[153] Planchet, op. cit., pp. 57, 64. For the life of one of these in Chihli see Henry Mazeau, The Heroine of the Pe-tang Hélène de Jaurias, Sister of Charity (1824-1900), translated from the French (London, Burns, Oates & Washbourne, 1928, pp. xiii, 252).
[154] Planchet, op. cit., p. 186.
[155] Planchet, op. cit., p. 203.
[156] Planchet, op. cit., p. 218.
[157] Planchet, op. cit., p. 162.
[158] Servière, Histoire de la Mission du Kiang-nan, Vol. II, p. 151.
[159] Servière, op. cit., Vol. II, pp. 153-156.
[160] Planchet, op. cit., p. 205.

aged in Shanghai; [161] the Third Order of St. Dominic; [162] and the Sisters of St. Paul of Chartres.[163] There were, too, several purely Chinese sisterhoods, among them the Sisters of the Holy Family,[164] the Sisters of St. Joseph,[165] and the Sisters of Purgatory.[166]

As we come to consider the methods employed by Roman Catholic missionaries in the nineteenth and the first decade and a half of the twentieth century it is important to remember that most of the territory of China was served by orders and societies which had been there in the several generations of persecution which the Church suffered in the eighteenth and the fore part of the nineteenth century. Traditions formed in those difficult days tended to carry over into the new age, especially since, in spite of the treaties, persecutions, as we are to see a few pages below, continued into the twentieth century. To be sure, innovations were seen, even in the fields of the old orders. The new congregations and orders, especially the women's congregations, were able in part to blaze untried paths. Yet there was much of conservatism in methods of approach, particularly away from the treaty ports.

It may be that to this conservatism can be attributed the slowness in achieving an empire-wide organization and a Chinese episcopate. Whatever the reason, it was not until after 1914 that either came into being. India was given a national ecclesiastical structure in the 1880's, approximately a generation before one was worked out for China. It was not until the period which we reach in the next volume that Rome departed from the long tradition, broken only in the case of Gregory Lopez, in the seventeenth century,[167] and raised a Chinese to the episcopate. For this delay various reasons were given. It was argued that since a foreign bishop enjoyed extraterritorial status he was independent of the jurisdiction of Chinese officials, but that a Chinese bishop, as a Chinese subject, would be under the authority of even the meanest Chinese official and would therefore suffer in dignity. It was also said that a European bishop would have better standing than a Chinese with European naval, military, and diplomatic officers.[168]

Nor did Roman Catholic missionaries reach out as ambitiously in an effort to touch the nation through the imperial court, the bureaucracy, and the literati

[161] Ibid.
[162] Planchet, op. cit., p. 235.
[163] Planchet, op. cit., pp. 235, 296, 301.
[164] Planchet, op. cit., p. 144.
[165] Planchet, op. cit., p. 192.
[166] Planchet, op. cit., p. 223.
[167] Vol. III, p. 346.
[168] Kervyn, Méthode de l'Apostolat Moderne en Chine, pp. 592, 593; Servière in The Chinese Recorder, Vol. XLIV, pp. 623, 624.

as they had in the seventeenth and much of the eighteenth century through the precedent established by Ricci.[169] That outstanding Lazarist, Mouly, advocated the renewal at Peking [170] of the scholarly mission which had been maintained by the Society of Jesus and then by the Congregation of the Mission as a means of gaining the esteem of high officials and of winning the masses through the ruling classes. There was also a suggestion that the scientific mission of French Jesuits established in the days of K'ang Hsi [171] be revived. However, a leading Jesuit argued against the step and it was not taken.[172] To be sure, a Lazarist, Jean Pierre Armand David, achieved an enviable reputation for scientific work and assembled in Peking a notable museum of natural history.[173] At Zikawei the Jesuits developed a centre of scholarship famous for its meteorological observatory. Yet the day had gone when the kind of undertaking personified in Ricci, Schall, and Verbiest could be effective. None of the decadent Manchus ruling in Peking had the vigour and the active intellectual curiosity of K'ang Hsi. Until the early years of the twentieth century the civil bureaucracy and the literati preserved most of their former prestige and influence, but their supremacy was passing. Although few if any in the nineteenth century foresaw the sudden collapse of their position witnessed in the twentieth century, from the vantage of a later time it is obvious that their hours were numbered.

The China of the new age was to be governed by new men. Some of these were scions of families which had come to power under the old literary traditions, but even they were trained in Occidental learning. Increasingly it was those educated after the Western pattern who were preparing the way for the new China. When, in the twentieth century, that China emerged, they were its leaders. The kind of enterprise once maintained at Peking was probably not the device best adapted to share in the creation of the new rulers. These could be best produced in schools of Western types, particularly secondary and higher schools. Upon the development of such schools would depend very largely the obtaining of the kind of influence with the leaders of the nation of the twentieth century which Ricci had dreamed of winning in the seventeenth century. In this respect Protestants were far ahead. By the year 1914 here and there a higher school was being conducted by Roman Catholics.[174] There was talk of establish-

[169] Vol. III, pp. 340-342, 344, 345.

[170] Thomas, *Histoire de la Mission de Pékin depuis l'Arrivée des Lazaristes jusqu'a la Révolte des Boxeurs*, pp. 491-511.

[171] Vol. III, p. 345.

[172] Servière, *Histoire de la Mission du Kiangnan*, Vol. II, pp. 35-42.

[173] Thomas, *op. cit.*, pp. 491-511.

[174] Desmet in Blakeslee, *Recent Developments in China*, p. 38; *Catholic Missions*, Vol. II, p. 5, Vol. XIII, p. 90; *Missions en Chine, au Congo, et au Philippines*, 1908, pp. 241-245.

ing a university at Peking.[175] In general, however, Roman Catholics were much slower in attempting to reach the more influential classes in the country, either actual or potential, than the great Jesuits of the sixteenth and seventeenth centuries had been. The rank and file of their members were confessedly from the lower ranks of society—boatmen, fishermen, and peasants.[176] These, of course, were in the majority in the population as a whole. Yet the Roman Catholic Church had almost none of the scholar class. Indeed, in view of the prohibition by Rome, dating from the days of the controversy over the rites,[177] of the participation by Christians in the ceremonies in honour of Confucius— ceremonies which were compulsory for civil officials and the literati—none from that important class could well become consistent Roman Catholics.

In attracting converts the Roman Catholics employed a number of methods. A few non-Christians were reached through schools. There were preaching halls to which pagans were welcome. Here and there the missionary undertook medical care, usually incidentally, for he was seldom a trained physician. Refuges were established for the cure of the opium addicts who were so numerous in the nineteenth and twentieth centuries, and some of the patients became Christians.[178]

To many the first appeal of Christianity came through relief given to the poor, very largely during famines.[179] For instance, during a great famine in the North in the 1870's assistance was accorded on the condition that the recipients would renounce their pagan practices, undertake provisionally Christian observances, and study the Christian faith.[180] In Chihli a Jesuit in time of famine gave aid to non-Christians on the condition that they would place themselves under the instruction of a catechist. He also took a mortgage on the lands of those assisted. As the loans were repaid he not only cancelled part of the principal but also reinvested the proceeds locally as an endowment for the Christian community.[181] A very large proportion of the catechumens were attracted by the hope of obtaining protection against their neigbours and the courts.[182] In Chihli, the Lazarists maintained catechumenates, usually during the winter months when the absence of work in the fields permitted the farmers to come. In these they paid the expenses of those who attended. The Paris

[175] Zeitschrift für Missionswissenschaft, Vol. IV, p. 138.
[176] Servière in The Chinese Recorder, Vol. XLIV, p. 614.
[177] Vol. III, pp. 349-355.
[178] Becker, Joseph Gonnet, pp. 238-244.
[179] Becker, op. cit., pp. 244, 245.
[180] Becker, op. cit., p. 126.
[181] Chine, Ceylan, Madagascar, March, 1910, pp. 486, 487.
[182] Becker, op. cit., pp. 245, 246.

society also employed this method.[183] Many missionaries spent much of their time travelling through the district assigned to them. Chapels had guest rooms attached to them. Here the itinerant priest could meet non-Christians. The latter were invited, if interested, to attend the various services and feasts of the church. The opening of a new mission station also provided an opportunity of explaining the Christian faith to non-Christians, for, partly out of curiosity and partly because of what the customs of the country encouraged, the people of the vicinity would call, be shown hospitality, be conducted through the chapel, and be given a description of the use of the building.[184]

As a rule, isolated individuals were not encouraged to become Christians. The effort was made, rather, to win at least a family. When there were no other Christians in the neighbourhood the aim was to reach several families at a time. It was felt that an individual would have difficulty in maintaining his faith and that if the natural social group, the family, joined, particularly in conjunction with other families, Christianity would have a greater chance of surviving and spreading.[185] In Chihli, land from which families were moving because of flood was purchased and other families were placed on it on the condition that they become Christians. Rents were used to maintain catechists, virgins in the service of the Church, and schools.[186] In Mongolia especially, thanks in part to the policy pursued by Vicar Apostolic Bax of the Scheutveld Fathers, there were numbers of Christian settlements, a succession of mission stations around which catechumens were colonized and built into Christian communities.[187] In Manchuria, too, the Paris society had compact groups of Christians. It was remarked, however, that in Manchuria these Christian enclaves made no effort to reach the non-Christians about them but, rather, regarded them with disdain.[188]

One of the chief means of winning converts was the provision of orphanages. In a sense these were the outgrowth of a method which had been extensively employed before the nineteenth century, the baptism of infants in danger of death. In crowded China poverty was chronic and infant mortality high. Many infants were abandoned. In time of drought or flood the mortality rate mounted. Since in Roman Catholic belief the baptism of a dying infant ensured the immediate entrance into heaven of one who had never been guilty of conscious sin, it became an act of Christian mercy to administer the sacrament to as many

[183] Schmidlin in Zeitschrift für Missionswissenschaft, Vol. V, p. 22.
[184] Beckmann, Die katholische Missionsmethode in China, pp. 45-48.
[185] Kervyn, Méthode de l'Apostolat Moderne en Chine, p. 377; Servière, in The Chinese Recorder, Vol. XLIV, p. 619.
[186] Becker, op. cit., pp. 128, 129.
[187] Beckmann, op. cit., pp. 148, 149.
[188] Beckmann, op. cit., p. 149.

as possible of the moribund innocents. Much of this was done. Christian charity also enjoined the saving of the physical lives of as many as possible. Waifs were, accordingly, gathered into orphanages and reared as Christians. Under the nineteenth century treaties this was possible as it had not been, or at least not to so great an extent, in the decades when Christianity was proscribed. Many of the sisters who entered the empire in increasing numbers devoted themselves to orphanages. Boys were taught handicrafts. Often matches were made between the boys and girls who had been reared in orphanages and thus additional Christian families were created. Girls nurtured in orphanages might be married into the families of new converts and help to familiarize the neophytes with the prayers and practices of the Church.[189] In 1912 more than a hundred thousand infants in danger of death were baptized and there were nearly thirty thousand children in nearly four hundred orphanages.[190] The large number of Roman Catholics who were recruited in this fashion increased the lowly elements in the Christian community, but in this the missionaries gloried even when they recognized it as a problem.

Less important numerically than orphanages, but also a means of expressing Christian charity and of winning converts, were homes for the aged. In a society which placed as much emphasis as did China upon the family and the duty of children to care for their parents, only unusual disaster would cast the aged adrift. Yet some of these there were. They were generally illiterate and diseased. For a few of them Roman Catholics made provision. They gave physical care without constraining the beneficiaries to accept their faith. On admission, the majority of the inmates were pagans. However, many asked for religious instruction and became converts. The first of the homes was said to have been founded in Shanghai in the 1860's. In succeeding years additional ones were opened in various other vicariates.[191]

Among a people who held the written word in as high regard as did the Chinese, at least some use of the printed page would be made. As we shall see a little later in this chapter, Protestants utilized it extensively. It was through books and pamphlets that they did much of their proclamation of the Christian message. The great Jesuits in the sixteenth and seventeenth century hey-day of their mission had also stressed literature and its publication. Perhaps it was because persecution had so long restricted Roman Catholics to the poorer and less literate elements of the empire, but whatever the reason nineteenth century

[180] Becker, op. cit., p. 126.
[190] Streit, Atlas Hierarchicus, p. 100.
[191] Beckmann, op. cit., p. 123.

Roman Catholics employed the press less than they did several other means of spreading their faith. Many missionaries recognized in principle the value of literature as an approach to non-Christians. In 1883 the Propaganda called to the attention of the vicars apostolic the importance of having a printing press in each vicariate. There existed a fairly considerable body of literature which included translations from the Bible, lives of the saints, apologetic works, and school books. Some presses were maintained and by 1914 a number of periodicals were being issued. Yet the fact remained that even in the fore part of the twentieth century literature was still given a place subordinate to some other methods of presenting the Christian faith and nourishing the Christian community.[192]

A few paragraphs above we noted that less emphasis was placed upon schools by Roman Catholics than by Protestants. However, Roman Catholics were not without these institutions. In China, schools, like the written and printed page, were held in high honour. In theory and to a large extent in practice the land was governed by scholars. Roman Catholic missionaries, therefore, would have been blind to one of the most obvious of opportunities if they had not employed schools. Presumably they could not hope to prepare pupils as effectively for the civil service examinations, based as these were upon traditional Chinese literature, as could the non-Christian schools. Yet as the old learning passed and, especially after 1895 and 1900, the demand for Western education mounted, Occidental missionaries were in a peculiarly favourable position to meet a growing demand. Roman Catholics then began to increase the hitherto slight emphasis placed upon secondary and higher schools for others than candidates for the priesthood. For years primary schools had been conducted. These, however, were chiefly for the children of Christians. The Propaganda placed restrictions upon the admission to them of children of non-Christians.[193] Moreover, the primary schools were mainly for the purpose of teaching the rudiments of the Christian faith, including the catechism, and presumably would not attract many non-Christians. Children of Christians were discouraged from going to non-Christian schools. Apparently the Roman Catholic authorities were endeavouring to rear Christians as little contaminated as possible by the non-Christian environment. Until towards the close of the period few schools were designed to reach non-Christians or to influence Chinese society as a whole.

[192] Henninghaus in *Zeitschrift für Missionswissenschaft*, Vol. I, pp. 201ff.; Beckmann, *op. cit.*, pp. 144-148.
[193] *Collectanea S. Congregationis de Propaganda Fide*, Vol. II, pp. 193, 194; Caubrière, *Synthesis Decretalium Sinarum*, p. 266; Kervyn, *Méthode de l'Apostolat Moderne en Chine*, p. 419.

In this they were in sharp contrast with the developing purpose of Protestant schools. In 1874 there were said to be 946 schools with about 10,000 pupils.[194] In 1912 Roman Catholic elementary schools totalled 6,974 with about 130,000 pupils and the higher schools 157 with about 4,500 pupils.[195]

One of the distinctive purposes of Roman Catholic schools, and especially those of secondary and higher grade, was the preparation of leadership, particularly of priests, for the Church. The number of Chinese priests rose from 135 in 1848 to about 239 in 1866, 371 in 1890, 445 in 1900,[196] and 721 in 1912.[197] This growth of the Chinese priesthood sprang from a conscious and persistently followed policy. Again and again the Propaganda from Rome and synods in China declared that an indigenous clergy must be reared if the Christian faith were to obtain a firm footing in the land.[198] Candidates for the priesthood were given a long preparation which began in their early youth. In 1851 the vicars apostolic discussed the wisdom of ordaining old men and widowers after a short training but decided against it.[199] Boys could not be enrolled as candidates before the age of ten and generally not after the age of fourteen. They had to be without physical defect and of blameless character.[200] They were usually admitted only from families which had long been Christian. Eldest sons, sons of widows, and sons of the poor were discouraged from applying. This was because of the strong possibility that boys in these categories would have pressure brought on them by their relatives to abandon their vocation.[201] In spite of these precautions, obstacles were often found in betrothals which, in accord with Chinese custom, had been made for the boys in childhood by their elders.[202] The course of preparation was long. It embraced a thorough preparation in Chinese literature, that the priest might command respect as a scholar as measured by the exacting Chinese standards. It included much Latin, for it was only through this language that direct access could be had to the thought of the Church so essential to a priest. It had in it a firm grounding in philosophy and theology. After 1900, because of the popularity of Western learning, it also made room for a smattering of Occidental science.[203] Ordination was usually

[194] Beckmann, *Die katholische Missionsmethode in China*, p. 133.
[195] Streit, *Atlas Hierarchicus*, p. 100.
[196] Huonder, *Der einheimische Klerus in den Heidenländern*, p. 186.
[197] Streit, *op. cit.*, p. 100.
[198] Beckmann, *op. cit.*, p. 52.
[199] Beckmann, *op. cit.*, p. 53.
[200] Beckmann, *op. cit.*, p. 54.
[201] *Catholic Missions*, Vol. VIII, pp. 153-155.
[202] *Ibid.*
[203] Servière in *The Chinese Recorder*, Vol. XLIV, pp. 621, 622; Huonder, *op. cit.*, pp. 188-191; Kervyn, *op. cit.*, pp. 579, 580.

not administered before the age of twenty-five or thirty.[204] A large proportion of those who began this prolonged and arduous course did not complete it. Many either dropped by the wayside or were content with becoming catechists, lay brothers, or teachers.[205]

Nearly every mission had a preparatory or "little" seminary.[206] There were numbers of more advanced seminaries in which the course could be completed. In 1912 the number of seminaries was given as fifty-four and the total of students in them as over sixteen hundred.[207] There was talk of a central seminary for the empire, somewhat like that which was created at Kandy in the 1890's for India and Ceylon. However, here as in some other respects the Roman Catholic Church was slower to advance in China than in India and the seminary did not materialize.[208] There existed among the missionaries much opposition to giving theological training to Chinese in Europe,[209] and but few seminarists were sent there. In some of the missions the long course was broken by a period of practical service in the field under the supervision of a European priest.[210]

Even after ordination the Chinese priests were often assigned a status below that of their European confreres.[211] Numbers of them were admitted to the orders and congregations which maintained missions, but others remained seculars.[212] Difference of opinion existed as to the character of the indigenous clergy. That may have reflected an actual variation in quality between individuals. It may also have arisen from the contempt with which many Europeans in the East, including some missionaries, viewed the peoples among whom they laboured and their unwillingness to accord them any other position but that of subordinates. We read of indigenous clergy who were said to be more successful in winning converts than the European missionaries and of some of exemplary lives.[213] On the other hand we hear laments of the pride, the ingratitude, the avarice, the tendency to falsehood, the nepotism, and the lack of the spirit of sacrifice of the Chinese clergy. In some instances Chinese clergy set themselves against their European colleagues.[214] There was a conviction on the part of at least part of the European clergy that it would be a tragic mistake

[204] Servière in *The Chinese Recorder*, Vol. XLIV, pp. 622, 623.
[205] *Ibid.*
[206] *Zeitschrift für Missionswissenschaft*, Vol. II, p. 216.
[207] Streit, *op. cit.*, p. 100.
[208] Beckmann, *op. cit.*, pp. 56, 57.
[209] Beckmann, *op. cit.*, p. 58.
[210] Beckmann, *op. cit.*, pp. 65, 66.
[211] Kervyn, *op. cit.*, pp. 586ff.
[212] Huonder, *op. cit.*, pp. 200, 201.
[213] Beckmann, *op. cit.*, p. 70.
[214] Kervyn, *op. cit.*, pp. 586ff.; Beckmann, *op. cit.*, pp. 71, 72.

to entrust any territory exclusively to Chinese priests.[215] Yet we are to see in the next volume the rapid progress made after 1914 in transferring entire ecclesiastical districts to the Chinese and the satisfaction with which the outcome was heralded.

Much use was made of catechists. In 1912 these numbered more than seven thousand, of whom over a third were women.[216] Some were used as heads of the local Christian communities, taking the place of the missionary in his absence. Others were servants and companions of the missionaries, accompanying the latter in their itineraries. Still others were precursors of the missionaries, those who made the initial contacts with the non-Christians. As the Church was organized in China they were essential to it, both in winning converts and in nourishing the religious life of the Christians. Many were trained in schools set up especially for that purpose. The Propaganda made the suggestion that they be brought together, for reciprocal reinforcement, in societies, but an attempt to give this effect, in Kiangnan, in 1865, proved disappointing. Yet various methods were employed to assemble the catechists in different areas for conference and prayer.[217]

Chinese virgins, who might be called women catechists, were as important as male catechists. The precedents established before the nineteenth century largely persisted into the new age. Some of the virgins lived in small communities. Others remained under the parental roof. Through them contacts were made with non-Christians and in many instances the initial steps towards conversion taken. At least one vicar apostolic declared them to be so successful that no need existed for European sisters. However, some of the vicars apostolic regarded them as nuisances. These critics averred that many of the virgins chose the unmarried state to avoid the duties of wifehood and motherhood. They complained that they were proud, contentious, disobedient to their superiors, and neglectful of prayer. Apparently their usefulness outweighed their defects, for in the second half of the nineteenth century schools were organized to train them and their numbers increased.[218]

In an empire in which indigenous leadership in the church was kept as subordinate to Europeans as it was in China before the year 1914, much depended upon the foreign clergy. As to the average character of the European priests we have no certain information. That heroism and devotion were required seems clear. Most of the missionaries came out for life. Some, apparently mostly

[215] Beckmann, *op. cit.*, p. 73.
[216] Streit, *op. cit.*, p. 100.
[217] Beckmann, *Die katholische Missionsmethode in China*, pp. 77-84.
[218] Beckmann, *op. cit.*, pp. 84-87.

Italians, became discouraged and returned home.[219] The majority, however, remained by their posts without furloughs and until death. Many of them were much on the road from chapel to chapel and from Christian community to Christian community. Their life was one of physical hardship. It also tended to intellectual narrowness, for their horizon was often limited to the province or district in which they laboured. There were complaints that many of them knew Chinese imperfectly, whether for speaking, reading, or writing, and that they excused themselves on the ground that their contacts were chiefly with the lower and usually scarcely literate social strata.[220] The Roman Catholic missionary body of the nineteenth and the fore part of the twentieth century, although far more numerous, included no such outstanding scholars in the Chinese language and literature as had that of the seventeenth and eighteenth centuries. Yet both Rome and synods in China stressed the importance of becoming expert in the language.[221] Even though many remained inadept in their use of Chinese, numbers of the missionaries conformed so far as they consistently could do so to Chinese garb and customs. They dressed in Chinese style, although they were enjoined to avoid luxurious and costly clothing.[222] However, other missionaries deliberately accentuated the contrast between their European manners and those of the Chinese and held Chinese culture and manners in contempt.[223] They remained by choice French, German, or Italian. In contrast with his predecessor of the eighteenth century, the average European in China in the nineteenth and much of the twentieth century regarded the Middle Kingdom, its populace, and its civilization with high disdain. To this the missionary body showed exceptions, but it also contained many who conformed.

Almost all the missionaries came from the continent of Europe. The largest number were from France, that land which led in Roman Catholic missions in the nineteenth century.

From time to time there were attempts to bring about an inclusive co-ordination of Roman Catholic activities in China. In 1870 the Vatican Council brought together the vicars apostolic of China. There they took the opportunity to discuss their common problems. They planned to divide the empire into five regional synods. Yet they opposed the erection in Peking of an apostolic delegation as an unnecessary curb on their freedom.[224] Not until 1879 did the

[219] Little, *Intimate China*, p. 236.
[220] Beckmann, *op. cit.*, pp. 33, 34.
[221] Beckmann, *op. cit.*, p. 35.
[222] Beckmann, *op. cit.*, p. 39.
[223] Beckmann, *op. cit.*, pp. 41-43.
[224] Servière, *Histoire de la Mission du Kiangnan*, Vol. II, pp. 183, 184.

Propaganda implement the regional plan. The five regional synods were then ordered convened once every five years. They met for the first time in 1880 and fairly regularly thereafter.[225]

The financial support of the Roman Catholic enterprise came partly in the form of contributions from abroad, chiefly from Europe, through private gifts to the various orders and congregations and through grants from the Society for the Propagation of the Faith and the Association of the Holy Childhood. There were extensive investments in China itself, largely, in the fashion of the country, in land. Much of this land was in the ports. It had been acquired in a variety of ways. Some of it was obtained in exchange for church property confiscated in the eighteenth or the fore part of the nineteenth century and ordered restored by the treaties and imperial command of the mid-nineteenth century.[226] In the early days of the foreign settlements in Shanghai the business agencies of various missions purchased land when it was inexpensive. Later, as the city grew, the tracts so bought became extremely valuable. Buildings were erected on the various plots and yielded handsome rentals.[227] In Peking real estate was purchased, partly with funds from the Boxer indemnity, and greatly appreciated in value.[228] We hear of more and more farm land bought and the revenues from it increasing.[229] Some of the missions were much less supplied with funds than were others. In Eastern Mongolia, for instance, only $6,000 came from abroad for 48 priests, 15 residences, 66 schools, and a number of catechists.[230]

Most of the energy of the foreign and Chinese priests and their lay assistants was devoted to winning converts and nourishing the life of the Christian communities. Effort was centred upon building the Church. For the strengthening of the Church and the religious and moral life of its members numbers of methods were employed. In Mongolia missionaries endeavoured to visit every Christian community three times a year, on each occasion remaining from four days to three weeks, saying mass, hearing confessions, administering the sacraments, holding services, and preaching.[231] It was a frequent policy to gather the Christians into villages apart from non-Christians where their entire life could be supervised and where there would be a minimum of con-

[225] Caubrière, *Synthesis Decretalium Sinarum,* pp. 41-43; *Zeitschrift für Missionswissenschaft,* pp. 85-87.

[226] Servière, *op. cit.,* Vol. II, pp. 138, 139.

[227] Hagspiel, *Along the Mission Trail,* Vol. IV, p. 23.

[228] Walsh, *Observations in the Orient,* pp. 118, 119.

[229] Little, *Gleanings from Fifty Years in China,* p. 294.

[230] Desmet in Blakeslee, *Recent Developments in China,* p. 384.

[231] Desmet in *op. cit.,* p. 381; Kervyn, *Méthode de l'Apostolat Moderne en Chine,* pp. 496-504.

taminating contact with pagans. Each of these communities normally had as its head a man chosen by his fellows and approved by the vicar apostolic and the director of the district. He presided at public prayers, weddings, and funerals. In the absence of a priest he administered baptism. He cared for the sick and dying.[232] Much was made of the festivals of the Church. Pilgrimages were promoted with Christian shrines as their objectives.[233] In 1912 there was inaugurated, after the fashion of what was to be found in many other countries, the Union of Chinese Catholic Action. Its "propagators" were each to agree to attempt the conversion of a minimum of three families a year, and to encourage their fellow Christians to win at least one non-Christian every twelvemonth. The union had a journal and a general conference.[234]

We hear of a number of organizations of Chinese Christians, some for women and some for men. Among them were the Oblates of the Holy Family, of women, the Companions of Our Lady of Good Counsel, the Sisters of Purgatory, the Institute of the Immaculate Conception, the Daughters of Christian Doctrines, the Society of the Holy Heart of Mary, the Sisters of the Precious Blood, the Servants of the Holy Ghost (for women),[235] the Brothers of St. Paul, the Mariales, the Josephines, the Daughters of the Sacred Heart, the Servants of the Sacred Heart, the Tertiates (Franciscan) of the Holy Infancy, the Brothers of the Sacred Heart,[236] the Xaverian Society, whose members agreed to pray for the conversion of their neighbours,[237] the Sisters of the Presentation, the Daughters of St. Anne, the Congregation of the Mother of God, the Virgins of Our Lady of Good Counsel, and the Servants of the Sacred Heart.[238]

Since Roman Catholic missionaries concentrated their efforts on building and nourishing the Church, relatively little attempt was made to influence the nation as a whole. There were works of mercy, such as hospitals, orphanages, and famine relief, and there were schools, but wherever possible these were ancillary to the main objective. As a result, Roman Catholics, while much more numerous, had less effect upon the empire than did the Protestants.

It is not surprising that even after the treaties and the edicts of toleration the progress of the Roman Catholic forces in China was punctuated by persecutions. Here was a disturbing element in Chinese life. Christians were departing from the time-honoured *mores* of the community. Their church forbade

---

[232] Caubrière, *op. cit.*, pp. 69-80.
[233] *Correspondence du Père J. B. Aubrey*, p. 156; Ricci, *Barbarie e Trionfi*, pp. 134-139.
[234] *Annals of the Propagation of the Faith*, Vol. LXXVI, p. 83.
[235] Arens, *Handbuch der katholische Missionen*, pp. 150, 161-164.
[236] *The Christian Occupation of China*, pp. 460, 461.
[237] *Annals of the Propagation of the Faith*, Vol. LXXIV, pp. 135-139.
[238] *The Christian Occupation of China*, pp. 460, 461.

them to participate in the ceremonies in honour of the ancestors and Confucius which were integral to Chinese culture. Some of their practices gave rise to ugly rumours. The eagerness to baptize children in danger of death was incomprehensible to the average Chinese and was given most sinister interpretations. Since, to avoid attracting attention, the sacrament was administered unostentatiously and even surreptitiously, and since it was so often followed by the death of the child, rumour declared that the object had been the acquisition of the eyes or some other part of the body for the purpose of concocting the strange drugs which foreigners were known to employ. The death of children in orphanages, where—because of the pauper provenance of those admitted—the mortality rate might be high, tended to confirm the suspicion. The protection accorded Christians under the treaties and the fashion in which a profession of Christianity complicated many lawsuits aggravated the animosity. Extreme unction was reported to be a means of obtaining photographic materials. Priests were accused of sexual irregularities and, as in the first centuries of the faith in the Roman Empire, Christian services were declared to be marked by promiscuous relations between men and women.[239] Moreover, the 1850's and 1860's witnessed extensive and devastating rebellions and banditry, and Christians, along with other peaceful Chinese, suffered severely.[240]

We can take the space to mention only the more spectacular of the attacks from which Roman Catholics suffered, for even a bare catalogue of the deaths by violence of Chinese Christians and European missionaries would prolong these pages unduly.[241]

The most outstanding incident between 1858 and the closing years of the century was at Tientsin in 1870. Tientsin and the vicinity had been the scene of much of the fighting in the Anglo-French War against China (1856-1860). In the subsequent occupation of the city by the allied forces the French troops established a bitter record. Moreover, on the site of an imperial temple the French erected a church, calling it, with tactless arrogance, *Notre Dame des Victoires*. The building was consecrated in 1869 in the presence of Chinese officials, who must have been unwilling spectators of this symbol of Chinese humiliation. Under these circumstances the populace was predisposed to believe the reports which declared that French sisters were kidnapping children to employ their vital organs for charms and medicines. An epidemic in the sisters' orphanage with its resulting deaths fed fuel to the flames. Local Chinese authori-

---

[239] Kervyn, *Méthode de l'Apostolat Moderne en Chine*, pp. 274-277.
[240] For instances see Latourette, *A History of Christian Missions in China*, pp. 347, 348.
[241] For an incomplete list, with footnote references to the sources, see Latourette, *op. cit.*, pp. 348, 349, 353-356, 544-547.

ties formally laid before their superiors the charge against the nuns. An official investigation was made and the accusation disproved. However, a mob gathered and was soon out of control. It was precipitated, so the Chinese later declared, by the actions of the French consul in losing his temper and firing on the officials. The orphanage was plundered and destroyed, and the church and mission premises were set on fire. Several Frenchmen and Frenchwomen were killed, including the offending consul, ten of the nuns, and two priests. Three luckless Russians also shared their fate. Repercussions followed in various parts of the empire, with threats to foreigners and some destruction of chapels. Western powers, especially France, took vigorous action. The Chinese Government executed a few of the populace who were accused of participating in the riot, an indemnity was paid, and a mission of apology was sent to France.[242] The handling of the incident emphasized the might of the Westerner but did nothing to allay the sullen resentment against the alien and the alien missionaries.

The other major explosion was even more violent and was much more widespread. It was the Boxer outbreak. Roman Catholics were the chief victims of the Boxers. This was largely because they were numerous in the regions which were most affected by the hostilities. The Boxer operations were mainly in the North, especially in Manchuria and in the provinces of Chihli and Shansi. Here Roman Catholics were present and in Shansi and Chihli they had strong Christian communities whose origins went back before the nineteenth century. In February and March, 1900, preliminary mutterings of the impending storm were heard in the looting of several villages in Chihli and the killing of seventy Roman Catholics.[243] The tempest rapidly became more intense. Both missionaries and Chinese Christians were subjected to its full force. Missionaries were obviously foreign—"foreign devils" as all foreigners had long been dubbed by the Chinese—and Chinese Christians were associated with them as "secondary devils." In Peking in June, 1900, three of the churches were destroyed and numbers of Christians slain. Surviving Roman Catholics and their pastors took refuge either in the legation quarter, where the majority of the foreigners stood siege, or in the Pei T'ang, the leading Roman Catholic church in the city. In the Pei T'ang , its compound, and the adjoining house of the Daughters of Charity the vicar apostolic, Bishop Favier, gathered missionaries and Chinese Christians— perhaps thirty-four hundred in all—and with the aid of a small contingent of French marines held the enemy at bay until the middle of August, when the

---

[242] For a good summary see Morse, *The International Relations of the Chinese Empire,* Vol. II, pp. 239-261.
[243] Smith, *China in Convulsion,* Vol. I, p. 206.

allied armed forces succeeded in fighting their way to the capital and broke the siege.[244] Outside the city the Christians suffered severely. The ancient cemetery not far from the walls, where were the graves of the great Jesuit missionaries of the seventeenth and eighteenth centuries, was desecrated. The walls of a memorial chapel later erected on the site bore the names of six or seven thousand martyrs in that one vicariate.[245] Bishop Favier estimated the deaths in his flock at between fifteen and twenty thousand and declared that three-fourths of the existing chapels had been destroyed.[246] In Shansi the governor, Yü Hsien, was notoriously anti-foreign and pro-Boxer. There two bishops, several priests and sisters, and a number of seminarians and servants were haled before the governor's tribunal and killed. The governor himself dealt one of the bishops the first blow. In the entire province about two thousand Roman Catholics perished.[247] In Mongolia, Bishop Hamer, Vicar Apostolic in the Ordos, was captured, mutilated, and taken from village to village until death brought him release. Several priests and many Chinese Christians were killed. In a few centres Christians fortified their places of refuge and fended off attack until the storm blew over. However, it is said that in Mongolia three thousand Chinese Christians and nine missionaries were killed and that many others perished from privation.[248] In Manchuria fourteen or fifteen hundred Christians are said to have been massacred. In Mukden the vicar apostolic, two priests, two sisters, and hundreds of Christians were burned in a church by order of the authorities.[249] Here and there outside the North there were sporadic riots and destruction. In Hunan especially, a stubbornly anti-foreign province, there were many deaths, including that of a bishop, and no little destruction of property.[250] We also hear of devastation in Hupeh, Kiangsi, and Chekiang.[251] From the standpoint of the loss of life the Boxer outbreak was the most severe blow, with the possible exception of Indo-China and Korea, which the Roman Catholic Church

---

[244] Favier, The Heart of Pekin. Bishop A. Favier's Diary of the Siege, May-August, 1900. Edited by J. Freri (Boston, 1901), passim; J. M. Planchet, Documents sur les Martyrs de Pekin pendant la Persécution des Boxeurs (Peking, 2 vols., 1922), passim.

[245] J. M. Planchet, Le Cimetière et les Oeuvres Catholiques de Chala 1610-1927 (Peking, Imprimerie des Lazaristes, 1928, pp. vii, 287), pp. 102ff.

[246] Favier in Annals of the Propagation of the Faith, Vol. LXIV, pp. 18, 19.

[247] Ricci, Barbarie e Trionfi, passim.

[248] Missions en Chine et au Congo, 1901, pp. 1-6, 13-19, 33ff., 38-41, 60-62, 67-71, 73-89, 97-108, 121-131, 145-157, 176-181, 202-208; 1902, p. 31; 1906, pp. 92-95; Annals of the Propagation of the Faith, Vol. LXVIII, pp. 61, 62.

[249] Morse, The International Relations of the Chinese Empire, Vol. III, p. 242; Annals of the Propagation of the Faith, Vol. LXVIII, pp. 83-98, 393-403.

[250] Ricci and Porta, Storia della Missione Francescana e del Vicariato Apostolico del Hunan Meridionale dalle sue Origini ai Giorni Nostri, pp. 105-119.

[251] L'Œuvre de la Propagation de la Foi. Dix Années d'Apostolat Catholiques dans les Missions, 1898-1907, pp. 52, 53.

suffered anywhere in the world in the century between the years 1815 and 1914. In spite of the many obstacles, the Roman Catholic Church registered a very substantial growth in the nineteenth and the fore part of the twentieth century. That growth was particularly rapid after 1900. By 1844 the number of Roman Catholics seems to have stood at not far from 240,000.[252] If this estimate is correct, the total had not greatly increased since the beginning of the century. Another set of figures, however, declares that in the first half of the century the total had risen about 60 per cent., or from 202,000 to 330,000.[253] This same authority gives the number of Roman Catholics in 1870 as not far from 383,000 and in 1890 as 576,440.[254] Another set of figures for 1870 places the total in that year as 404,530.[255] An official set of statistics declares the total in the mid-1890's to have been 581,575.[256] In 1901 it was reported to have risen to 720,540.[527] In 1906 it was said to be 888,131.[258] In 1910 it was asserted to be 1,364,618[259] and in 1912, 1,431,258.[260] Presumably the increase was both from an excess of births over deaths in the Christian community and from conversions of adults. The latter are said to have totalled more than 61,000 in the year 1911-1912.[261] The distribution was uneven. In 1912 about a fourth of the Roman Catholics were in Chihli, about a tenth in Shantung, about a sixth were in Kiangnan, a little more than a twentieth were in Chekiang and Fukien, and about a twentieth in Hongkong and Kwangtung.[262] In other words, not far from two-thirds were in the coastal provinces, where the impact of Western culture was most pronounced. In the twentieth century the increase in the country as a whole was proportionately a little more rapid than that in the number of missionaries.[263] The augmented rate of growth after the year 1890 was presumably associated with the accelerated permeation of the country by Western culture and the beginning of the disintegration of inherited Chinese institutions. As the old structure of Chinese life weakened and Occidental ways began to be adopted, Christianity, coming in connexion with the Occident, found it easier to make headway.

[252] *Notizie Statistiche delle Missioni di Tutto il Mondo Dipendenti dalla S.C. de Propaganda Fide* (1844), pp. 557-572.
[253] Louvet, *Les Missions Catholiques au XIXe Siècle*, p. 234.
[254] Louvet, *op. cit.*, pp. 218-234.
[255] *Bulletin des Missions Catholiques*, cited in *The Chinese Recorder*, Vol. IX, p. 118.
[256] *Missiones Catholicae Cura S. Congregationis de Propaganda Fide*, 1895, p. 311.
[257] *Missiones Catholicae Cura S. Congregationis de Propaganda Fide*, 1907, table 44.
[258] *Missiones Catholicae Cura S. Congregationis de Propaganda Fide*, 1907, table 38.
[259] *Catholic Missions*, Vol. VI, p. 76.
[260] *Zeitschrift für Missionswissenschaft*, Vol. IV, p. 42.
[261] Streit, *Atlas Hierarchicus*, p. 100.
[262] *Ibid.*
[263] These were 1,375 in 1901 (*Missiones Catholicae Cura S. Congregationis de Propaganda Fide*, 1907, table 44) and 2,086 in 1912 (Streit, *op. cit.*, p. 100).

The only other form of Christianity represented in China at the dawn of the nineteenth century (except for the few Protestant merchants at Canton who made no effort to propagate their faith) was the Russian Orthodox. Since the latter part of the seventeenth century it had been present in a small Christian community in Peking, descendants of prisoners taken at Albazin. To this had been added, in the first half of the eighteenth century, an official diplomatic-commercial-ecclesiastical mission.[264] In 1860 there were less than two hundred in the Russian Orthodox enclave.[265] Until that time the chief purpose of the mission had been to give spiritual care to the descendants of the Albazinians, who continued to centre in the north-eastern section of Peking, and to prepare interpreters for such slight official and commercial intercourse as existed. The expenses were borne by the Russian Government. That government discouraged and at times forbade any effort to make converts from among non-Christian Chinese.[266] A few scholars were developed. The most notable of these was Piotre Ivanovitch Kafarof, usually better known as Palladius (1817-1878), who had an enormous literary output and whose chief contribution was a Chinese-Russian dictionary.[267]

The changes brought by the Russo-Chinese treaty of 1858 with its toleration clause and the greater freedom for foreign residence and travel were followed by a partial separation of the ecclesiastical and diplomatic functions of the mission and attempts to propagate the faith. However, in spite of the fact that a station was opened at Urga, efforts to win converts were not very vigorous and the staff was small. Schools opened in Peking were only for the children of Christians. In 1870 from ten to forty converts were being made each year in Peking. In 1906 the Russian Orthodox community numbered only about five hundred.[268]

Then followed the Boxer outbreak. The mission suffered the destruction of most of its buildings and its library and the death of approximately two hundred of its Christians.[269] Proportionately to its numerical strength its losses were greater than those of either the Roman Catholics or the Protestants.

Following the Boxer tragedy the mission became much more active. This was associated with the enhanced Russian political activity. Indeed, in 1898 when the Russians were building the Chinese Eastern Railway, the railroad began to erect Russian Orthodox churches. Numbers of new centres were opened, many

---

[264] Vol. III, p. 359.
[265] Bishop Innocent in The Chinese Recorder, Vol. XLVII, p. 680.
[266] Bishop Innocent in The Chinese Recorder, Vol. XLVII, pp. 678, 679.
[267] Couling, The Encyclopaedia Sinica, pp. 420, 421; Bishop Innocent in The Chinese Recorder, Vol. XLVII, pp. 681, 682.
[268] The Chinese Recorder, Vol. IV, pp. 186-191, Vol. XLVII, pp. 682, 683.
[269] The Chinese Recorder, Vol. XLVII, pp. 683-685.

of them in the province of Chihli and some in the Russian sphere of influence in Manchuria and in such marts of foreign commerce as Hankow and Shanghai. A vigorous leader, Innocent (Figourovsky), who had come to China not long before 1900 as archimandrite, returned in 1902 as bishop. Indemnity paid for the Boxer losses gave funds for rebuilding and fresh construction. The Russo-Japanese War (1904-1905) witnessed some reverses, notably in Manchuria, but seems not seriously to have retarded the growth of the mission.[270] In 1910 the staff included the bishop, ten priests, of whom three were Chinese, and six deacons, of whom two were Chinese.[271] At the end of the year 1914 the mission was reported to have, in addition to the bishop, three archimandrites, ten priests, three deacons, two subdeacons, one psalm reader, eight monks, and five nuns. It had convents in Peking and Manchuria, sixteen churches, several additional centres, mainly in the provinces of Chihli and Hupeh, a number of schools, a printing press, some industries, and about five thousand Chinese in its membership, in addition to the Russians who were affiliated with it. In the year 1914 nearly eight hundred adults and infants were baptized from paganism.[272] It is clear that the Russian church had had a striking growth in the opening years of the twentieth century. However, when compared with the Roman Catholics and Protestants it remained distinctly a minority enterprise.

In 1800 Protestantism was not actively represented in China. The few merchants of that faith in Canton made no effort to propagate it and had they tried to do so would have been balked by the Chinese authorities. Indeed, in 1793 the Emperor in his reply to the King of England through Lord Macartney expressly forbade the propagation of the "English religion" in his domains.[273] Not until 1819 does a chaplain seem to have arrived for the (British) East India Company's factory.[274] The Dutch mission in Formosa in the seventeenth century [275] had long since come to an end and presumably no Christian communities survived to witness to its existence.

Not far from the turn of the century the mounting missionary interest in Great Britain began to be attracted by China. In its first report, dated May, 1801, the Church Missionary Society announced the offer of financial assistance

[270] Ibid.; Contemporary Manchuria, Vol. II, p. 85.
[271] The China Mission Year Book, 1910, pp. 425ff.
[272] The China Mission Year Book, 1915, pp. 583, 584.
[273] Morse, The Chronicles of the East India Company Trading to China, 1635-1834, Vol. II, pp. 227, 251.
[274] Morse, op. cit., Vol. III, p. 364. See also for mention of a chaplain, Morse, op. cit., Vol. IV, pp. 164, 187, 346.
[275] Vol. III, pp. 359, 360.

for printing a manuscript translation into Chinese of a part of the New Testament, presumably made by Roman Catholics, and then in the British Museum, and opened a separate fund for that purpose.[276] In its first report, the British and Foreign Bible Society also called attention to that manuscript, but decided against publishing it.[277] In 1806 Marshman, of the Serampore group, began the study of Chinese and fifteen or more years later completed a translation of the Bible.[278]

In spite of this interest in China, Protestants were much later in inaugurating missions in China than they were in India. The Danish-Halle Mission in the latter country was paralleled by no contemporary Protestant effort in the Middle Kingdom. Carey's arrival in India antedated that of the first British Protestant missionary in China by fourteen years and chaplains of the East India Company were in India generations before they were resident in China. The restrictions placed by the Chinese Government on foreigners within its doors were so severe that until past the middle of the nineteenth century Protestant effort was much more difficult than in India. It is no wonder that Protestantism was so much slower in getting under way in China and that in 1914 it was numerically far behind Protestantism in India.

The honour of sending the first Protestant missionary to effect a residence on the mainland of China belongs to the London Missionary Society. In 1804 that body, then less than ten years old and already embarked upon enterprises in Tahiti, South Africa, and India, appointed Robert Morrison to China.[279] Robert Morrison (1782-1834) was born in Northumberland, of a Scottish father who at one time was an agricultural labourer and was later an artisan in Newcastle.[280] Young Morrison was reared in the Presbyterian church in Newcastle in which his father was an elder and in his middle teens had the experience of conversion and became a communicant. He was a serious-minded lad, seemingly almost devoid of a sense of humour. He was studious and managed to do a large amount of reading in spite of long hours spent at physical labour as an apprentice in his father's workshop. At the age of twenty-one he went to Lon-

[276] *Proceedings of the Church Missionary Society for Africa and the East,* Vol. I, pp. 84-86, 95-102.

[277] *Reports of the British and Foreign Bible Society,* Vol. I, pp. 18, 19.

[278] Marshman, *The Life and Times of Carey, Marshman, and Ward,* Vol. I, pp. 244, 245, Vol. II, p. 63.

[279] Lovett, *The History of the London Missionary Society,* Vol. I, p. 104.

[280] On Morrison see *Memoirs of the Life and Labours of Robert Morrison . . . by his Widow* (London, Longman, Orme, Brown. Green, and Longmans, 2 vols., 1839) ; Marshall Broomhall, *Robert Morrison, a Master-Builder* (London, Church Missionary Society, 1924, pp. xvi, 238) ; and Milne, *A Retrospect of the First Ten Years of the Protestant Mission to China* (Malacca, The Anglo-Chinese Press, 1820, pp. viii, 376).

don to prepare at Hoxton Academy for the ministry. There an earlier attraction to a missionary career was heightened and upon his application the London Missionary Society gave him an appointment.

In preparation for his assignment Morrison studied medicine, astronomy, and Chinese. The latter he obtained through the aid of a Chinese then living in London and by transcribing the British Museum's copy of the Chinese translation of portions of the New Testament and a manuscript Latin-Chinese dictionary. In this he was deeply indebted to a dissenting clergyman, William Moseley, who had been pressing various societies and men of prominence to translate and distribute the Bible in Chinese.

In 1807 Morrison sailed for Canton. Because of the unwillingness of the East India Company, then in possession of a monopoly of the British trade with China, to permit passage on its ships to missionaries, he was compelled to to go by way of the United States. There an American ship bound for Canton accepted him. It was later recalled that the ship's owner said, with a sardonic smile, as he arranged the business details, "And so, Mr. Morrison, you really expect to make an impression on the idolatry of the great Chinese Empire." To which sally it is reported that Morrison replied, somewhat sternly, "No, sir, I expect God will."

Morrison had need of all of his resolute sense of duty and mission. When, in September, 1807, he reached Canton, he found himself sharply restricted. In addition to the cramped conditions under which foreign trade with China was carried on, he experienced great difficulty in obtaining, in face of the official prohibition of such pursuits, Chinese to teach him the language. The high cost of living distressed his frugal soul. He feared that the Chinese might forbid his residence in Canton and that the Portuguese, moved by the animosity of the Roman Catholic clergy towards a Protestant missionary, might deny him refuge in Macao.

Yet Morrison managed to remain and to acquire the language. With the aid of Chinese Roman Catholics he studied the local vernacular, the standard mandarin or Pekingese, and the written language. He worked at the compilation of a dictionary. Such good use did he make of his time that in less than eighteen months after his arrival the East India Company appointed him Chinese translator. The position provided him with an ample income and made him secure against deportation. His official duties were heavy but did not deter him from the labours to which he had given himself as a Christian missionary. For a time, indeed, the directors of the East India Company ordered his dismissal from their service on the ground that by publishing Christian literature in Chinese he was jeopardizing British trade in China. However, the

Canton representatives of the East India Company delayed putting the order into effect until further word could be received.

In spite of the arduous duties entailed by his position with the East India Company, Morrison found time to perform an amazing amount of work on behalf of the enterprise which had first brought him to the empire. Because of the imperial edicts against Christianity and the extremely limited contacts between Chinese and Westerners, Morrison was compelled to restrict himself largely to the preparation of literature. To this he devoted himself with undeviating diligence. In 1819 he completed the translation of the entire Bible, a project the foundations for which had been laid in the Roman Catholic version which he had studied while still in England. He also translated the shorter catechism of the Church of Scotland and part of the Book of Common Prayer of the Church of England. He prepared pamphlets on the Christian faith and compiled a Chinese-English dictionary and a grammar. He had few formal converts. The first was not baptized until 1814, when he had been in China nearly seven years. Yet he dreamed of ampler days to come. It was largely through him that reinforcements were sent and that efforts were made to reach the Chinese who were accessible to Westerners outside the empire. He was the leader in what came to be known as the Ultra-Ganges Mission, which sought to approach the empire through these emigrants. He projected and contributed generously to the Anglo-Chinese College of which we spoke in the last chapter and which was the child of his brain. His plans embraced Japan, at that time even more sealed against the outside world than China. He conceived the task of the Christian missionary to China as being not only the propagation of his faith in that land, but also the spread in the Occident of an appreciative understanding of the Middle Kingdom and its culture.

In time honours began to come to this doughty pioneer. During his one visit in Great Britain, in 1824-1826, he was fêted by the great and was made a fellow of the Royal Society. He spent the time, characteristically, in seeking to arouse an interest in missions to China and in the study of the Chinese language and culture. He urged, in vain, the establishment of chairs of Chinese at Cambridge and Oxford and offered to present to the nation his Chinese library. His pleading for more support for missions to the Chinese aroused something of a response, although still in limited circles.

Once more in Canton, Morrison found himself caught in the growing friction between foreigners and Chinese which eventually culminated in the first Anglo-Chinese War. As translator for the East India Company he was forced to become a negotiator between the conflicting interests.

It is not strange that a life lived so earnestly and with such unremitting toil in an enervating climate amid many strains should end early. Death came in 1834, in Morrison's early fifties, to a body which had long been showing the effects of the adverse conditions but which the resolute will of its master had kept going until almost the very last.

Morrison had the satisfaction of seeing reinforcements come in response to his appeals. In 1813, after six years without a colleague, he had the joy of welcoming William Milne.[281] Milne was of Scottish birth and rearing. In his teens he, like Morrison, had the experience of conversion. He had fellowship with one of the dissenting groups of Scotland and through it acquired an interest in missions. This led him to China. Since permission could not be obtained to reside in Macao and since Canton seemed similarly out of the question, after a few months spent in Canton at the study of the language Milne went on a tour of the Chinese settlements in the East Indies and eventually settled at Malacca. There under British protection he established a mission to the Chinese in that port and the neighbouring regions. Still others came from Britain to strengthen the staff. Prominent among these was William Henry Medhurst, a printer.[282] Missions were begun at Penang, Singapore,[283] and Batavia[284] at which efforts were made to reach the Chinese who were resident in these centres of European power.

A few converts were made in these introductory years of the pioneer Protestant enterprise to China. Of these the best remembered was known as Liang A-fa.[285] Born of a humble village family, it was as an apprentice to an engraver of wooden blocks for printing purposes that Liang was first brought into contact with Christianity. He was won to the faith by Milne, who took him to Malacca as a printer. He was enrolled in the Anglo-Chinese College, later studied with Morrison, and, becoming a preacher, remained faithful to his calling.

From the North the London Missionary Society made another approach to the Chinese Empire. In 1817 a mission was begun for the Buriats, a Mongol tribe. It was not until 1819, however, that a residence was established among them east of Lake Baikal. The enterprise was chiefly and perhaps entirely in Russian territory, but the Buriats ranged over a region of which a large pro-

---

[281] Milne, *A Retrospect of the First Ten Years of the Protestant Mission to China*, pp. 100ff.; Robert Philip, *The Life and Opinions of the Rev. William Milne, D.D., Missionary to China* (Philadelphia, Herman Hooker, 1840, pp. 435), *passim*.

[282] Wylie, *Memorials of Protestant Missionaries to the Chinese*, pp. 25-40; Medhurst, *China. Its State and Prospects*, pp. 311, 331.

[283] Medhurst, *op. cit.*, pp. 325-328.

[284] Medhurst, *op. cit.*, pp. 329ff.

[285] George Hunter McNeur, *China's First Preacher; Liang A-fa, 1789-1855* (Shanghai, Kwang Hsueh Publishing House, 1934, pp. 128), *passim*.

portion was within the Chinese Empire. The Old Testament was translated into Mongolian and a revision was made of a translation of the New Testament published by the Russian Bible Society. A few converts were won. Not far from the year 1841, however, the mission was discontinued by order of the Russian Holy Synod and the Emperor.[286]

In the last chapter we became acquainted with the name of Gützlaff. Karl Friedrich August Gützlaff (1803-1851) had an important role in inaugurating missions to China from the Protestantism of Continental Europe.[287] Gützlaff was born in Prussian Pomerania, the son of a tailor. In his middle teens, through contact with what the school at Basel was doing, he formed a desire to become a missionary. He prepared at Jänicke's school in Berlin, received appointment from the Netherlands Missionary Society, and reached Batavia in January, 1827. He proved to be an unusually adept linguist. After the period in Bangkok which we noted and the untimely death of his wife, in the 1830's, he made voyages along the coast of China, going as far north as Tientsin and Manchuria and touching at Korea and Formosa. He even attempted to make his way into Japan. On these trips he distributed Christian literature. A few paragraphs below we shall meet him again as an enthusiastic furtherer in Britain and Europe of an interest in China and the organizer of an enterprise which, in spite of ill-judged features, led to solid continuing missions.

To the nascent Protestant efforts in China there came contributions from the United States which in some degree forecast the varied and extensive share which the citizens of that republic were to have in the spread of Christianity in China and especially of Protestant Christianity. In 1828 the American Board of Commissioners for Foreign Missions reported that a message had come from Morrison asking that it begin an enterprise in China.[288] Within the next year it had appointed Elijah Coleman Bridgman.[289] Passage and support for one year in Canton had been assured by D. W. C. Olyphant, a deeply religious American engaged in the China trade. With Bridgman went David Abeel (1804-1846)[290] as a representative of the American Seaman's Friend Society to serve the many American sailors who frequented Canton. His coming was also made possible by Olyphant. The two reached Canton in 1830. At the end of the year, by prearrangement, Abeel was transferred to the staff of the American Board of Commissioners for Foreign Missions. Abeel seems never to have been

[286] Lovett, *The History of the London Missionary Society*, Vol. II, pp. 585-600.
[287] Kesson, *The Cross and the Dragon*, pp. 221-231.
[288] *Report of the American Board of Commissioners for Foreign Missions*, 1828, p. 111.
[289] *Report of the American Board of Commissioners for Foreign Missions*, 1829, pp. 92-96.
[290] G. R. Williamson, *Memoir of the Rev. David Abeel, D.D., Late Missionary to China* (New York, Robert Carter, 1848, pp. 315), *passim*.

robust and his career was punctuated by periods of illness. Yet he toured the East Indies, spent time in Siam and Singapore, and, when forced by sickness to leave the East (1833), he travelled in Europe and Great Britain arousing interest in missions. Back in the United States, he traversed much of the country, stimulating support for foreign missions, especially in his own denomination, the Dutch Reformed Church. Repeated ill health delayed his return to China, but in 1839 he was again in that land. He inaugurated the mission of the Dutch Reformed Church at Amoy, an enterprise which was to have a continuing life. In 1845 waning strength once more forced him to America and he did not long survive his return.

Bridgman (1801-1861) had a much longer career in China.[291] He devoted himself to the language, opened a small school for boys, and in 1832 commenced the publication of *The Chinese Repository,* a periodical in English which attained distinction as a medium of information to foreigners, not only as a source of news on the progress of Christian missions, but also for its information on the history and culture of China and the changing political and commercial scene. With but one brief furlough in America, and that forced by ill health, he spent the remainder of his life in China and lived on into the new age brought by the treaties of the 1840's and the 1850's.

Accessions came to the mission of the American Board. The most noted were Samuel Wells Williams (1812-1884) [292] and Peter Parker (1804-1888).[293] Williams was appointed as printer and reached China in 1893. He helped in the editing of *The Chinese Repository* and became outstanding as a sinologist. His best known works were *The Middle Kingdom,* for more than a generation the standard general book in English on China, and a Chinese-English dictionary. His later years in China were spent in the diplomatic service of his country, but he remained a missionary in faith and purpose. Peter Parker was the first Protestant medical missionary to China. He arrived in Canton in 1834 and the following year opened the Ophthalmic Hospital, an institution which did much to allay the prejudice of the Chinese against missionaries.[294] He, too, eventually entered the diplomatic service of the United States. For a time he was the American Minister to China.

[291] Eliza J. Gillett Bridgman, editor, *The Life and Labors of Elijah Coleman Bridgman* (New York, Anson D. F. Randolph, 1864, pp. xi, 296), *passim.*

[292] Frederick Wells Williams, *The Life and Letters of Samuel Wells Williams, LL.D., Missionary, Diplomatist, Sinologue* (New York, G. P. Putnam's Sons, 1889, pp. vi, 490), *passim.*

[293] George B. Stevens, *The Life, Letters, and Journals of the Rev. and Hon. Peter Parker, M.D.* (Boston, Congregational Sunday School and Publishing Society, 1896, pp. 362), *passim.*

[294] On the hospital in Parker's years, see Cadbury, *At the Point of a Lancet,* pp. 1-75.

In the 1830's the American Baptists sent missionaries to the Chinese. William Dean, the first appointed specifically for that purpose, sailed in 1834 and went to Bangkok to study the language. Two or three Chinese had already been baptized there by J. Taylor Jones, a Baptist whose especial charge was the Siamese. In December, 1835, Dean baptized three and organized them into what he believed to be the first Protestant church composed of Chinese. The church prospered and reinforcements arrived.[295] In 1835 J. Lewis Shuck and his wife, Henrietta, sailed for China. Going to Macao, they became the first Baptist missionaries in China proper. In 1842 they moved to Hongkong.[296]

In 1835 two representatives of the Domestic and Foreign Missionary Society of the Protestant Episcopal Church reached Canton. They soon went to Singapore to study Chinese and then were persuaded by Medhurst to begin a centre among the Chinese at Batavia. In 1837 they were joined by William J. Boone, who became the real founder of the mission of his church in China.[297]

The Presbyterian Board of Foreign Missions, representing the Old School branch of that denomination, appointed two couples to China in 1837. They stopped at Singapore, there to labour among the Chinese until such time as the empire should be open. However, death and sickness soon terminated their undertaking. The next couple sent were also constrained by ill health to return to America. Yet the board persevered and about the time that the first group of treaties partially opened the borders it had representatives on hand to take advantage of the opportunity.[298]

In 1835 several friends of the pioneer missionary formed, in his memory, the Morrison Education Society to conduct schools which would teach the learning of the Occident and the Christian faith.[299] As a teacher for this society there arrived, in 1839, Samuel R. Brown (1810-1880), who was to be a pioneer missionary in both China and Japan. That very year a house was procured for him in Macao and he began the study of Chinese and the teaching of English.[300] His school, later removed to Hongkong, was to have striking fruits in the introduction of Western learning to China.

In 1838 the Medical Missionary Society was constituted, with the support of

[295] Dean, *The China Mission*, pp. 95-101, 115.
[296] Dean, *op. cit.*, pp. 119, 120; J. B. Jeter, *A Memoir of Mrs. Henrietta Shuck* (Boston, Gould, Kendall & Lincoln, 1846, pp. xii, 251), *passim;* Thomas S. Dunaway, *Pioneering for Jesus. The Story of Henrietta Hall Shuck* (Nashville, Sunday School Board of the Southern Baptist Convention, 1930, pp. 160).
[297] *Proceedings of the Board of Missions of the Domestic and Foreign Missionary Society of the Protestant Episcopal Church in the United States of America,* 1836, p. 94, 1837, p. 94, 1838, p. 76.
[298] Brown, *One Hundred Years*, pp. 274, 275.
[299] *The Chinese Repository*, Vol. V, pp. 373-381.
[300] Griffis, *A Maker of the New Orient*, pp. 57-73.

Peter Parker's hospital as an immediate objective. Funds came partly from Great Britain and America through the efforts of Parker. Parker's plea contributed to the organization of the Edinburgh Medical Missionary Society, but that body also assisted hospitals in other countries.[301]

The first Anglo-Chinese War and the treaties which followed it pushed the door ajar for Protestant missions. The five ports which were opened and the island of Hongkong, together with the promised toleration of Christianity within these centres, gave to Protestant missions a greater opportunity than they had yet known. In the interval before the next Anglo-Chinese conflict the growing missionary interest in Protestant circles in Europe and America sought to take advantage of the openings thus afforded. Protestant missionaries quickly moved into the newly available cities. For the most part the staffs which had been waiting on the fringes of the empire, seeking to reach the Chinese emigrants under British, Dutch, and Siamese rule, were transferred to China proper. Reinforcements were sent by societies already represented and several additional organizations entered the country.

The London Missionary Society, the pioneer Protestant society in China, by 1856 had established itself in four of the six centres—Canton, Hongkong, Amoy, and Shanghai.[302] In Hongkong its chief representative was James Legge. James Legge (1815-1897) [303] was of Scottish birth, the son of a prosperous business man who was active in an Independent chapel in which missionary interest was vigorous. The young Legge gave great promise as a linguist and on graduating from the university was informally assured succession to a professorship if he would enter the Church of Scotland. That he felt would be disloyalty to the paternal tradition. Instead, a few years later (1839) he went to the Far East under the London Missionary Society. For a time he was head of the Anglo-Chinese College while that institution was in Malacca. Then, in 1843, after the British had begun to develop their new possession, Hongkong, Legge and the college moved to that island. There Legge became an important figure. He was largely responsible for the founding and programme of the educational system of the colony. He was a devoted missionary. Out of a conviction that missionaries to China should make themselves familiar with the literature and learning of a people who held scholarship in such high esteem as did the Chinese, he turned his linguistic gifts to the study of the books which were regarded as the classics of the dominant Confucian school and translated a number of them into

[301] Lockhart, *The Medical Missionary in China*, pp. 139, 144-146; Williams, *The Middle Kingdom*, Vol. II, pp. 335-337.
[302] *The Report of the Directors to the . . . London Missionary Society*, 1856, pp. 63-68.
[303] Helen Edith Legge, *James Legge, Missionary and Scholar* (London, The Religious Tract Society, 1905, pp. viii, 248), *passim*.

English. In his late fifties he retired to Great Britain and there, a few years later, became the first incumbent of a chair of Chinese at Oxford which was made possible by the gifts of some of the British merchants engaged in the China trade. Thus part of the dream of Robert Morrison was fulfilled, and in the person of a member of the mission which he had inaugurated.

In 1856 the largest staff which the London Missionary Society had at any one point in China was at Shanghai, for that city was rightly deemed strategic. On it were several whose names became household words in Protestant missionary circles—Joseph Edkins (1823-1905),[304] a notable philologist and expert in Chinese religion; Alexander Williamson (1829-1890),[305] founder of the Book and Tract Society for China, which grew later into the Society for the Diffusion of Christian and General Knowledge among the Chinese, eventually called the Christian Literature Society, an organization with a notable record as a pioneer in acquainting China with Western thought; William Lockhart (1811-1896),[306] famous as a medical missionary; Walter Henry Medhurst (1796-1857),[307] the author of several scores of books in Chinese, Malay, and English; William Muirhead (1822-1900),[308] who had a long life in China and itinerated widely out of Shanghai, preaching; Griffith John (1831–1912),[309] who left a lasting impression upon Central China as a Protestant pioneer; and Alexander Wylie (1815-1887),[310] printer, as agent of the British and Foreign Bible Society travelling widely in China, and a distinguished and careful scholar in Chinese literature. In this group of unusual men, as well as in Robert Morrison and James Legge, the London Missionary Society made outstanding contributions to the planting and nourishing of the Christian Church in China and the interpretation of China to the Occident.

Gützlaff, the pioneer Protestant missionary to China from the continent of Europe, was a man of widely ranging imagination who was impatient to bring the Christian Gospel to all China. More than any other Protestant missionary of pre-treaty days he had travelled up and down the coast, seeking entrance and distributing literature.[311] He helped as interpreter in the negotiations of the

[304] Couling, The Encyclopaedia Sinica, p. 153; The Chinese Recorder, Vol. XXXVI, pp. 282-289. See also Jane R. Edkins, Chinese Scenes and People (London, James Nisbet and Co., 1863, pp. vi, 307).
[305] Couling, op. cit., p. 602; The Chinese Recorder, Vol. XXI, pp. 461-468.
[306] Couling, op. cit., p. 313; Lockhart, The Medical Missionary in China, passim.
[307] Couling, op. cit., p. 344.
[308] Couling, op. cit., p. 384; Griffith John in The Chinese Recorder, Vol. XXXII, pp. 1-9.
[309] R. Wardlaw Thompson, Griffith John: The Story of Fifty Years in China (London, The Religious Tract Society, 2d ed., revised, 1908, pp. xvi, 552).
[310] Couling, op. cit., p. 610; The Chinese Recorder, Vol. XVIII, pp. 199-203.
[311] Charles Gützlaff, Journal of Three Voyages along the Coast of China in 1831, 1832, & 1833 with Notices of Siam, Corea, and the Loo-Choo Islands (London, Frederick Westley and A. H. Davis, 1834, pp. xciii, 450), passim.

Anglo-Chinese treaty of 1842. With the coming of the new order inaugurated by that document he made his home in Hongkong. From that vantage point he sought to penetrate with the Christian message every province of the empire. This he planned to do by means of Chinese. By 1850 he had gathered about him a Chinese staff of preachers and colporteurs who professed to be distributing the Bible and bringing into being Christian groups in each of the eighteen provinces except Kansu. He wrote extensively to Germany, describing his enterprise and urging support. Help came to him from several organizations, including the Rhenish Missionary Society, the Basel Missionary Society, a Berlin association, and the Berlin Women's Missionary Society for China. In 1849 and 1850 Gützlaff was in Europe, preaching and organizing societies among which he divided responsibility for the various provinces of the empire. However, while he was in Europe those who had come from Germany to assist him became suspicious of the character of the Chinese staff. Soon a sorry story was disclosed. While some of the agents were sincere, many were thoroughly dishonest. They had fabricated the reports of their travels, had spent their time and Gützlaff's money in low dives, and had sold to the printers the literature which they were supposed to be distributing. The printers had then resold it to the over-trustful Gützlaff. On returning to Hongkong Gützlaff was confronted with the facts. He planned a more adequate supervision by Westerners but died (1851) before he could complete the reorganization. Yet he was by no means a failure. The Rhenish and Basel societies, the Berlin Missionary Society for China (later succeeded by the Berlin Missionary Society), and the Berlin Women's Missionary Society for China continued. Their agents, undaunted by the initial disillusionment, laid foundations for substantial and enduring enterprises in South China.[312] Moreover, Gützlaff must be credited with directing the attention of the Moravians to Mongolia and so of stimulating the inauguration of the mission of that body to Tibet (since Mongolia proved inaccessible) which we noted in the

---

[312] There is as yet no adequate biography of Gützlaff. The bibliography relating to him is fairly extensive. There are a number of books and pamphlets by him. Several arose from his trip to Europe in 1849 and 1850. These include C. Gützlaff, *Die Mission in China, Zweiter Vortrag, Dritter Vortrag, Vierter Vortrag, Fünfter Vortrag,* and *Sechster Vortrag* (Berlin, 1850, pp. 18, 17, 14, 16, 18), and his *Abschiedswort an alle Chinesischen Vereine Europa's* (Stargard, 1850, pp. 16). See also *Jahresbericht des Pommerschen Haupt-Vereins für Evangelisirung China's* (Stettin, 1851ff.); *Mittheilungen aus China. Herausgegeben vom Pommerschen Hauptverein für Evangelisirung China's* (Stettin, 1858ff.); and *Geschichte der Missionen in China von den ältesten Zeiten bis auf Gützlaff* (Stettin, R. Grassmann, 1850, pp. 76), pp. 30ff. For one of the initial agents of the Basel society, see W. Schlatter, *Rudolf Lechler. Ein Lebensbild aus der Basler Mission in China* (Basel, Missionsbuchhandlung, 1911, pp. 203), *passim.* See also L. von Rohden, *Geschichte der Rheinischen Missionsgesellschaft* (Barmen, J. F. Steinhaus, 1856, pp. 232), pp. 214ff.; Schlatter, *Geschichte der Basler Mission,* Vol. II, pp. 271ff.; Richter, *Das Werden der christlichen Kirche in China,* pp. 324-329.

chapter before the last.[313] He had, too, a share in bringing into being the Chinese Evangelization Society. It was under the auspices of that ephemeral organization that Hudson Taylor first came to China. Through him, therefore, Gützlaff was one of the sources of the China Inland Mission, which by the year 1914 was to have in China a larger and more widely distributed foreign staff than any other Christian society whether Roman Catholic or Protestant.

The China missionaries of the American Board of Commissioners for Foreign Missions, like those of its sister organization, the London Missionary Society, wished to enter all of the six ports made available by the Anglo-Chinese treaty of 1842.[314] However, in 1857 representatives of the American Board were to be found only in Canton, Foochow, Shanghai, and Amoy.[315] The Amoy Mission was staffed by members of the Dutch Reformed Church. When, in 1857, the latter denomination formed its own board the Amoy enterprise was transferred to it.[316]

The American Baptist missionaries also were eager to be in Hongkong and each of the five treaty ports. In 1843 they appealed to their American constituency to send a missionary family to each of the six cities. This their home board found its funds too restricted to undertake.[317] Moreover, in 1845 the Baptists of the southern states formed their own convention and the forces in China were divided.[318] In 1843 a Baptist church was organized on the island of Hongkong.[319] By 1856 Southern Baptists were in Canton and Shanghai. Prominent in Shanghai was Matthew T. Yates.[320] He was long to be the outstanding figure of his denomination in that city. The Northern Baptists were in Hongkong, from which, in 1860, they moved to Swatow.[321] They also established a centre in Ningpo.[322]

Boone, the only missionary of the Protestant Episcopal Church who was in the Far East at the time of the Anglo-Chinese treaty of 1842, in 1843 and 1844

[313] Schulze, 200 Jahre Brüdermission, pp. 538, 539.

[314] Bridgman, July 31, 1843, in The Missionary Herald, Vol. XL, p. 32.

[315] Report of the American Board of Commissioners for Foreign Missions, 1857, pp. 118-128.

[316] Pitcher, Fifty Years in Amoy, p. 18.

[317] Baptist Missionary Magazine, Vol. XXIII, p. 316.

[318] Ashmore, Historical Sketch of the South China Mission, pp. 7, 8.

[319] Ashmore, op. cit., p. 6.

[320] Charles E. Taylor, The Story of Yates, the Missionary, as Told in His Reminiscences (Nashville, Sunday School Board Southern Baptist Convention, 1898, pp. 304), passim.

[321] Dean, The China Mission, pp. 121-129; Ashmore, op. cit., p. 22.

[322] Dean, op. cit., pp. 134-136.

was in the United States seeking to quicken the interest in the China mission. To such good effect did be labour that his board appointed six new missionaries.[323] In 1844 Boone was consecrated Missionary Bishop for China.[324] On returning to China he decided to fix the centre of the mission at Shanghai.[325] In 1851 a Chinese was ordained as deacon and two Chinese candidates for holy orders were reported.[326] With this beginning, it was natural that the lower part of the Yangtze Valley should become the chief field of the American Episcopalians.

The American Presbyterians pursued the beginnings which they had made before 1842. By 1856 they had established themselves in Canton, Ningpo, and Shanghai.[327] They were to continue in all of these cities. By that year, moreover, their staff had been reinforced by a number of remarkable men, some of whom were to have long and distinguished careers in the Far East. In Canton J. G. Kerr was in charge of the Opthalmic Hospital founded by Peter Parker and was later to achieve distinction as the outstanding pioneer in the scientific care of the insane of China.[328] In Canton there was also Andrew D. Happer, the first president of what was known successively as the Christian College in China, Canton Christian College, and Lingnan University, the leading Christian institution for higher education in South China.[329] In Ningpo there had been for a short time Walter M. Lowrie, whose promising career was cut short by drowning at the hands of pirates.[330] To Ningpo came, in 1844, as its first resident Protestant missionary, D. B. McCartee, a physician.[331] After nearly thirty years in Ningpo be became a teacher in Japan, for a time was in the consular service of the United States, for another period was adviser to the Chinese legation in Japan, and eventually returned to the staff of the Presbyterian Board, but in Japan. In 1850 there arrived in Ningpo two brothers, Martin by name. The

---

[323] The Spirit of Missions, Vol. IX, pp. 334, 502.

[324] The Spirit of Missions, Vol. X, p. 250.

[325] The Spirit of Missions, Vol. XI, p. 85.

[326] The Spirit of Missions, Vol. XVII, pp. 405-407.

[327] The Twentieth Annual Report of the Board of Foreign Missions of the Presbyterian Church in the United States of America, pp. 65-76.

[328] Cadbury, At the Point of a Lancet, pp. 101ff.; The China Mission Year Book, 1915, pp. 544-549.

[329] H. Clay Trumbull, Old Time Student Volunteers. My Memories of Missionaries (Chicago, Fleming H. Revell Co., 1902, pp. 281), pp. 164-168.

[330] Memoirs of the Rev. Walter M. Lowrie, Missionary to China, edited by his Father (New York, Board of Foreign Missions of the Presbyterian Church, 1850, pp. viii, 500), passim.

[331] Robert E. Speer, A Missionary Pioneer in the Far East. A Memorial of Divie Bethune McCartee (New York, Fleming H. Revell Co., 1922, pp. 224. Largely the autobiography of McCartee), passim.

more famous was William Alexander Parsons Martin (1827-1916).[332] He early
wrote a book on Christian evidences which over many years had an enormous
circulation in China and Japan. He was an interpreter in the negotiation of the
American treaty of 1858 with China. By translating into Chinese a Western
treatise on international law he assisted in introducing the Chinese to the practices of Occidental nations in their relations with one another and so helped
them in the adjustment to the international society into which they had been
so rudely thrust by the Western powers. He was also president and teacher of
international law in the T'ung Wên Kuan, an institution organized under the
Tsungli Yamen, or foreign office of China, in the attempt to acquaint prospective Chinese officials with the ways of the West. Later he was the first
president of the Imperial University in Peking. He had, therefore, a prominent
part in aiding the Chinese in the acquisition of the learning of the Occident so
essential to the new world in which they found themselves. He was given
official position by the Chinese Government. In his later years he returned to
the staff of the Presbyterian Board, but without salary, and lived to a great age.
There arrived in Ningpo in 1856 John L. Nevius (1829-1893).[333] Nevius later
served not only in the Yangtze Valley but also and chiefly in Shantung. He
became a formulator and warm advocate of a method of encouraging the self-
support of young Chinese churches from their very beginning. The method,
which was known by his name, became particularly influential in the Presbyterian enterprise in Korea.

The school maintained at Hongkong by the Morrison Education Society was
discontinued in 1849 or 1850. Support had failed because some of the original pa-
trons were no longer in China and the merchant community at Canton had been
scattered with the opening of other ports.[334] Samuel R. Brown, the outstanding
teacher in the school, had earlier (January, 1847) been forced by his wife's
health to leave for America.[335] Three of his pupils accompanied him to take up
study in the United States. One of these had later to go back to China because
of illness.[336] Another, Wang-fun, assisted by the foreign merchants in China
who had borne the support of the three lads, went to Edinburgh for medical

[332] W. A. P. Martin, *A Cycle of Cathay or China, South and North, with Personal Reminiscences* (Chicago, Fleming H. Revell Co., 1896, pp. 464), *passim; The Chinese Recorder*, Vol. XLVIII, pp. 116-123.
[333] Helen S. Coan Nevius, *The Life of John Livingstone Nevius* (Chicago, Fleming H. Revell Co., 1895, pp. 476), *passim;* Helen S. C. Nevius, *Our Life in China* (New York, Robert Carter and Brothers, 1876, pp. 504), *passim.*
[334] Williams, *The Middle Kingdom*, Vol. II, p. 344; Griffis, *A Maker of the New Orient*, pp. 102-104; Yung Wing, *My Life in China and America*, p. 17.
[335] Griffis, *op. cit.*, p. 202.
[336] Yung Wing, *op. cit.*, p. 31.

training, graduated with honours, returned to China under the London Missionary Society, and practised his profession in Canton with distinction until his death (1878 or 1879).[337] The third, Yung Wing, graduated from Yale, the first Chinese to take a degree in the United States. In China once more, he sought to enlist the support of influential officials in adopting phases of Western civilization which he felt would be useful to the empire. His most memorable achievement was his important share in the sending of Chinese youths to the United States for study in the 1870's and 1880's, forerunners of the later extensive student migration from China to America.[338]

Another organization which arose out of the intimate foreign community of pre-treaty days, the Medical Missionary Society of China, did not, like the Morrison Education Society, perish with the passing of that era. It continued and aided hospitals not only in Canton but also in other ports.[339]

In addition to organizations represented before the first treaties, other Protestant bodies entered the country between the two wars.

Prominent among these was the Church Missionary Society. The news of the Treaty of Nanking stimulated friends of the society to begin a fund for a China enterprise.[340] In 1844 two men were sent, one of them George Smith, to survey the field. Smith returned in 1846 with a report.[341] Additional recruits were obtained, and in 1849 Smith was consecrated Bishop of Victoria, Victoria being the name of the chief British settlement on the island of Hongkong. The Society for the Propagation of the Gospel in Foreign Parts contributed to the endowment of the bishopric.[342] Urged by Smith, the Church Missionary Society determined to send a contingent to Foochow. It accompanied Smith when he sailed for China after his consecration.[343] By 1850 centres had also been established at Ningpo and Shanghai.[344]

The British and Foreign Bible Society, which had aided with financial subsidies the preparation and distribution of the Bible before the first treaties, now

---

[337] Yung Wing, op. cit., pp. 32, 33; Lockhart, The Medical Missionary in China, p. 142; Williams, op. cit., Vol. II, p. 345.

[338] Yung Wing, op. cit., pp. 34ff.

[339] Lockhart, op. cit., pp. 139ff.

[340] Stock, The History of the Church Missionary Society, Vol. I, pp. 471, 472.

[341] George Smith, A Narrative of an Exploratory Visit to Each of the Consular Cities of China and to the Islands of Hong Kong and Chusan in behalf of the Church Missionary Society in the Years 1844, 1845, 1846 (New York, Harper & Brothers, 1847, pp. xv, 467), passim.

[342] Stock, op. cit., Vol. I, pp. 472, 473.

[343] Stock, op. cit., Vol. I, pp. 473, 474.

[344] Stock, op. cit., Vol. I, pp. 472, 473, Vol. II, p. 293.

assisted both in a revision of the Scriptures—the so-called Delegates' Version—and in the circulation of the completed work.[345]

When the Treaty of Nanking opened five ports and Hongkong to Protestant missionaries, the Wesleyan Missionary Society was burdened with debt and felt itself so committed to fields already entered that it did not at first deem it feasible to take advantage of the newly opened door. However, funds kept coming for the purpose. Moreover, George Piercy, an unordained Yorkshire lad, a local preacher, determined to go at his own expense and sailed for Hongkong in 1850. In Hongkong he was welcomed by Legge and organized a Methodist society among the soldiers of the garrison. Late in 1851, after some months of studying the language, he went to Canton. In 1853 the Wesleyan Missionary Society sent two men to China, one of them being Josiah Cox, who later planted his denomination in the very heart of the empire, in Hankow. They carried with them to Piercy appointment to the service of the society and what was equivalent to letters of ordination. Wesleyan Methodism had been introduced to China.[346]

The British Wesleyans were not the first of the Methodist fellowship to inaugurate an enterprise in the Middle Kingdom. In 1847 two couples were sent to Foochow by the (American) Methodist Episcopal Church.[347] In 1844 the Methodists of the southern states formed their own church. They soon began planning a mission to China. It was not until 1848, however, that their initial representatives reached Shanghai.[348]

It was in 1847 that the first appointee of the English Presbyterians sailed for China. The English Presbyterians had been recently (1844) organized into a national body. Since both the Free Church and the Church of Scotland were troubled by the disruption which brought the former body into existence and had missionary responsibilities elsewhere, when the five ports and Hongkong were opened, the English Presbyterians saw in the new opportunity an inescapable challenge.[349] William C. Burns (1815-1868) went as their pathfinder.[350] Burns was a son of a manse of the Church of Scotland. In 1839 he had been accepted as a missionary to India of the Church of Scotland. Then, before he could sail, he became a leader in a remarkable religious revival which broke

[345] Canton, *A History of the British and Foreign Bible Society*, Vol. II, pp. 389-403.

[346] Findlay and Holdsworth, *The History of the Wesleyan Methodist Missionary Society*, Vol. V, pp. 431ff.

[347] Reid, *Missions and Missionary Society of the Methodist Episcopal Church*, Vol. I, pp. 321ff.

[348] Cannon, *A History of Southern Methodist Missions*, pp. 95, 96.

[349] Johnston, *China and Formosa*, pp. 1-6.

[350] Islay Burns, *Memoir of the Rev. Wm. C. Burns* (London, James Nisbet & Co., new edition, 1885, pp. x, 372), *passim*.

out under his preaching in his father's parish. He thereupon became a preacher of the awakening in Scotland, Ireland, England, and Canada. Incidentally the tides of new life profoundly affected Andrew Murray and his brother, then boys in Scotland, and through them later had marked repercussions in South Africa.[351] For a number of years this itinerant ministry delayed the fulfilment of Burns's foreign missionary purpose. In 1846 he offered himself to the Free Church of Scotland for India but found no vacancy. The English Presbyterians then asked him to go to China. He accepted. He felt that his assignment in China should be that of an evangelist, not unlike that in which he had been engaged for the past several years. He, therefore, toured widely over such of China as was accessible to him. He arrived in China in 1847 and for a time served a small Scottish congregation in Hongkong. A colleague who was soon sent him found a continuing centre for the mission at Amoy, a place which the home committee had deemed advisable and where a sister member of the Presbyterian family, the (Dutch) Reformed Church of America, was also at work. For a time Burns, too, lived in Amoy. Possessed of considerable linguistic gifts, he did translating, including a widely used Chinese version of *The Pilgrim's Progress*. For more than six years Burns was without a convert. This must have been a sore trial to one whose preaching in the Occident had been attended by throngs and remarkable religious movements. Then accessions began to come in a market town not far from Amoy. Burns felt that his was not the task to organize the converts and to become their pastor. That he left to others while he moved on. Colleagues of his mission followed him and out of his itineracy came continuing congregations. He was also the pioneer of his society in Swatow and prepared the way for an enduring enterprise in and near that city. He touched at others of the ports of China and by his transparent devotion and saintliness made a profound impression on many. Through friendship and close association he contributed to the growth of Hudson Taylor, of whom we are to hear much a few paragraphs below. In 1855 there came to Amoy Carstairs Douglas, one of the most distinguished missionaries of his day, noted for sound judgement, perseverance, zeal, and accurate Chinese scholarship.[352] The English Presbyterians were gaining footholds.[353]

Other societies came to China between 1842 and 1856. Only one of them persevered. Yet some contributed to enterprises which persisted. The one which

---

[351] Vol. V, pp. 324ff.

[352] John M. Douglas, *Memorials of the Rev. Carstairs Douglas* (London, Waterlow and Sons, 1878, pp. 76), *passim*.

[353] For a member of the staff whose career was early cut short, see Andrew A. Bonar, *Memoir of the Life and Brief Ministry of the Rev. David Sandeman* (London, James Nisbet & Co., 1862, pp. 313), *passim*.

continued was the Seventh Day Baptist Missionary Society, an American organization. It entered China, at Shanghai, in 1845, but it was never to have either a large staff or many converts.[354] The British General Baptists sent two missionaries to Ningpo, but before many years turned over to the English Methodists what they had began. In 1859 the (English) Baptist Missionary Society commenced a continuing effort in Chefoo, but not until 1875 did this present a vigorous life.[355] In 1849 and 1850 a Swedish society sent two representatives. One was killed and the other terribly injured, and the enterprise was not reinforced.[356] The Cassel Missionary Society entered China in the 1850's but seems to have sent out only one man.[357] The Netherlands Chinese Evangelization Society appears to have had a very similar record.[358] The Chinese Evangelization Society also sent representatives to China in the 1850's but did not long persist. However, it was the channel through which Hudson Taylor first came to the Middle Kingdom and through him it had an extraordinary fruitage.[359]

The multiplicity of societies and the small number of centres opened to them would seem to have called for co-operation. Some of that there was. Often missionaries of different denominations aided one another. In Amoy the London Missionary Society, the Dutch Reformed, and the English Presbyterians so collaborated that the Chinese Christians did not know that denominational differences existed between them.[360] However, the only fairly comprehensive co-operation was in translating the Bible. Since Protestants stressed the Bible, joint effort in giving it a suitable Chinese dress seemed the obvious course. This was particularly true of the version in the literary form of the language. The literary language could be read by the educated anywhere in the empire, whereas the vernaculars differed widely, especially in those areas first opened to Protestant missionaries. In 1843 a meeting was held in Hongkong in which missionaries of several societies were present. A plan was devised for collaboration in the translation into the literary style. However, differences arose, some of which gave rise to acrimonious debate. The Baptists wished a word for baptism which would connote immersion, but to that the others could not assent. The term to be used for God provoked dissent. This, it will be recalled, was part of the issue in the rites controversy which disturbed the Roman Catholics in the seventeenth and eighteenth centuries.[361] No Chinese term could be quite the equiva-

---

[354] MacGillivray, *A Century of Protestant Missions in China*, p. 344.
[355] MacGillivray, *op. cit.*, p. 69.
[356] MacGillivray, *op. cit.*, p. 645.
[357] *Ibid.*
[358] *Ibid.*
[359] *Ibid.*
[360] Johnston, *China and Formosa*, pp. 85, 86, 106.
[361] Vol. III, pp. 349, 352.

lent of what to the Christian was connoted by the word God, and division over the nearest approach to it was inevitable. The Protestants did not use *T'ien*, as had Ricci, or *T'ien Chu*, as did the contemporary Roman Catholics. Instead, some favoured *Shang Ti* and others *Shên*. In general the British missionaries stood for the former and the Americans for the latter. The American Bible Society supported an edition with the latter and the British and Foreign Bible Society one with the former term. In the case of the Old Testament some advocated a style which would appeal to the Chinese who prized literary form and others wished one which was simpler and nearer to the original texts. Accordingly, no single translation was produced and the Delegates' Version did not represent the entire Protestant missionary body.[362]

In the fourteen years between the two Anglo-Chinese wars the future Protestant ecclesiastical map of the coast of China from Shanghai southward began to take shape. Various denominational bodies entered the five ports and Hong-kong and began to develop enterprises which they were to continue in the ensuing decades. When the next group of treaties made that possible, they were to expand into the *hinterland* back of each of these ports. Here and there a few shifts occurred, but in the main the outlines of the future denominational alignment on the south coast were beginning to become apparent.

By the year 1856 Protestant Christianity had not made nearly the progress in China that it had in India. In the latter country it was much older, it was represented by more societies, and a much larger proportion of the country had been entered. The Mutiny almost exactly coincided with the second Anglo-Chinese War. It caused more havoc to Protestant missions than did the latter struggle. In both lands after these hostilities a great expansion of Protestant missions was witnessed. Between the coming of peace in 1860 and the period of rapid change which began with the defeat of China by Japan in 1895 Protestant missions penetrated all of the eighteen provinces of China proper and Manchuria, but that penetration was accompanied by much unrest and some riots and was in the face of the resistance of a culture whose solid front was as yet all but unbroken.

It will be remembered that the treaties of 1858 and 1860 theoretically made all the empire accessible to the efforts of Protestant missionaries. Numbers of new ports were opened to foreign residence, including several from Shanghai north to Manchuria and up the Yangtze as far as Hankow. Toleration was granted for the preaching and teaching of the Christian faith and Chinese were allowed to become converts. Foreigners might travel anywhere in the empire.

[362] Williams, *The Middle Kingdom*, Vol. II, pp. 363, 364; Canton, *A History of the British and Foreign Bible Society*, Vol. II, pp. 396-399.

In practice, although not by formal treaty provision, Protestant missionaries were permitted to acquire land outside the treaty ports. Under these circumstances, in spite of local opposition, Protestant missionaries now made their way through most of the interior and established residences at many points.

For Protestant missions the period between 1860 and 1895 was still one of pioneering. Emphasis was placed upon the proclamation of the Christian Gospel by spoken word, printed page, and personal friendship. Converts were being won and churches organized. The Protestant ecclesiastical map of the empire was being further elaborated, not so much by joint planning as by the opportunistic endeavours of individual missions and missionaries. New centres were chosen and stations developed. These in turn became the bases of continuing enterprises. Here and there, as in Szechwan, a fairly comprehensive plan was devised by two or more denominations or societies for an entire region, but this was the exception. Usually a society or an individual in choosing a new field sought to find one where no others were represented. That was especially the policy of the China Inland Mission. By 1895 a beginning had been made of a co-operative programme embracing all of Protestantism and of China. Yet it was only a beginning. Moreover, foreigners were still dominant in the nascent churches. Efforts were being made to train a Chinese leadership, but the Christian communities were too young and too small to stand by themselves. The period was one in which the incipient Protestant movement, if such uncoordinated undertakings could be called by that collective name, was in its foreign and missionary stage. The Protestant missionaries were often great individuals, with the characteristics of pioneers—sturdy, with a kind of confidence in the finality of their convictions which was born of a sense of direct commission and continued guidance by God combined with the necessity of blazing new trails in the face of a resistant and apparently unyielding culture. Sometimes they did not find it easy to work with others and were domineering, both over the Chinese and their younger colleagues. But they were persevering and dauntless. Some of them were men and women of large vision and dreamed in terms of all of China and the far as well as the near future. Institutions such as schools and hospitals were in their infancy. To most Chinese they were still unwelcome, for they were representative of the civilization of the foreign "barbarians." The day of their popularity had not yet dawned. The schools were attended chiefly by those who hoped to find a livelihood in connexion either with the missions or with foreign firms and consulates. The hospitals were often a last resort, either by the very poor or by those who had sought but failed to find healing at the hands of the practitioners of the traditional therapies. The majority of Protestant missionaries were British. The British prominence in Protestant missions paralleled the British dominance in sea-borne commerce and in diplomatic relations. It was the British who had blasted open the doors of China and who were profiting by their victories. It was natural that Christian missions arising out of the abounding life of the British churches should see in the situation both an opportunity and an obligation. Yet the Protestantism which was being introduced was varied, both nationally and denominationally. A substantial minority of the missionaries were from the United States and a number were from the continent of Europe. All the chief kinds of Protestantism were represented. The future Christianity of China would be the heir, as was that of India, of most of the historic strains of the faith. Presumably, therefore, it would be the richer for the numerous forms in which the Christian heritage had come to it, even though for the moment the cynical could glibly characterize the Protestant missionary enterprise as leading China "from Confucius to confusion."

Most of the societies represented in China before 1856 expanded their fields of operation in the ensuing forty years.

The London Missionary Society reached out into both Central and North China. In 1861 Griffith John and a colleague inaugurated the first continuing mission in Hankow. Under John's vision and energetic initiative his society reached into the neighbouring Wuchang and Hanyang and other portions of Hupeh, westward into Szechwan (residence was established in Chungking in that province in 1888), and southward into Hunan. In the latter province, bitterly anti-foreign, it was possible only to make infrequent visits, and no station could be founded.[363] In the North, in 1861, centres were established in Tientsin and Peking in the wake of the occupying British armies, in the former by Edkins [364] and in the latter by Lockhart.[365] From these cities enterprises were developed in the surrounding country.[366] The effort to win the Mongols, begun a generation before by way of Siberia but later, because of the Russian Government, allowed to lapse, was renewed through North China in 1870 by James Gilmour (1843-1891).[367] For approximately two decades, until his death, Gilmour, although reared in a home of affluence, lived a life of physical hardship

[363] Griffith John, *A Voice from China* (London, James Clarke & Co., 1907, pp. 271), pp. 187ff.; *Sowing and Reaping. Letters from the Rev. Griffith John, D.D.* (London, The London Missionary Society, 1897, pp. 63), *passim; The China Mission Hand-book*, Part II, pp. 15-18. See also on a distinguished member of the mission, *Arnold Foster, Memoir, Selected Writings*, etc. (London, London Missionary Society, 1921, pp. 188), *passim*.

[364] *The China Mission Hand-book*, Part II, pp. 18, 19.

[365] *Ibid*.

[366] *Ibid*.

[367] Richard Lovett, editor, *James Gilmour of Mongolia, his Diaries, Letters, and Reports* (London, The Religious Tract Society, 1892, pp. 336); Richard Lovett, *James Gilmour and his Boys* (London, The Religious Tract Society, 1894, pp. 288); James Gilmour, *Among the Mongols* (London, The Religious Tract Society, no date, pp. 383); James Gilmour, *More about the Mongols, Selected and Arranged from the Diaries and Papers of James Gilmour by Richard Lovett* (London, The Religious Tract Society, 1893, pp. 320).

and privation, labouring heroically among the nomads, chiefly in the parts of Mongolia which bordered on China proper, and that in spite of the discouragement of seeing only a few converts and finding some of these undependable.

Until after 1895 the four German societies which had been introduced to China by the sanguine Gützlaff and which we noted a few pages above as continuing their undertakings in spite of the disillusionment which came with the discovery of the perfidy of many of the Chinese agents, did not reach outside of Hongkong and Kwangtung, the region to which Gützlaff had introduced them. Within that territory, however, they developed substantial enterprises. The Basel Mission expanded from Hongkong onto the mainland and established stations there.[368] The Berlin Missionary Society took over from the Rhenish society the undertaking among the Hakkas which had been begun by the Berlin Missionary Society for China, but no large growth was witnessed until after 1895.[369] The Rhenish Missionary Society was also in Kwangtung and among its distinguished missionaries numbered F. Genähr and the sinologue E. Faber.[370] The Berlin Women's Missionary Society for China slowly enlarged the home for girls which it maintained in Hongkong.[371]

The American Board of Commissioners for Foreign Missions did not seek to occupy quite as much territory as did its sister organization, the London Missionary Society. In 1866 it withdrew from Canton,[372] but in the 1880's it renewed its efforts in Kwangtung, using Hongkong as a base. This was for the purpose of following up the Chinese whom the Congregationalists were reaching in the United States and who, returning to China, would naturally be a starting point for new churches in the empire.[373] The enterprise begun at Foochow was extended into other parts of Fukien.[374] In the 1860's the station at Shanghai was discontinued, largely because so many of its staff had gone to the newly opened North. In that decade centres were opened in Tientsin, Peking, T'ungchow (just outside of Peking), and Kalgan. In the following two decades the American Board also extended its efforts into Shantung and Shansi.[375] The enterprise in Shansi was at the outset staffed by graduates of Oberlin. Several members of the classes in church history in 1879-1880 in that institution under the instruction of Judson Smith, later a secretary of the American

[368] MacGillivray, *A Century of Protestant Missions in China,* pp. 474-483.
[369] MacGillivray, *op. cit.,* pp. 484-487.
[370] MacGillivray, *op. cit.,* pp. 492-497.
[371] MacGillivray, *op. cit.,* pp. 490, 491.
[372] Strong, *The Story of the American Board,* p. 257.
[373] Smith, *Congregational Missions in the Heavenly Kingdom,* pp. 37-41.
[374] Blodget and Baldwin, *Sketches of the Missions of the American Board in China,* pp. 43 ff.
[375] Blodget and Baldwin, *op. cit.,* pp. 13 ff.

Board, asked him to head them in establishing a mission in China after the fashion of the Irish monks in western Europe centuries before. Smith did not go, but some of the group did. A man and his wife went in 1881 and three others followed in 1882.[376]

The American Baptists also expanded. Representatives of the Northern Convention continued at Ningpo and in 1860 moved from Hongkong to Swatow and later extended their operations into the region back of that port. Their going to Swatow was determined by the fact that in Siam the pioneers had learned from emigrants the dialect of the region.[377] The most distinguished Baptist missionary in the Swatow mission was William Ashmore.[378] The Baptists also made their way to the Hakkas, back of Swatow.[379] Early in 1890 the Northern Baptists entered the great western province of Szechwan, then a pioneer Protestant field,[380] and in the early 1890's opened a station at Hanyang, in Central China.[381]

In spite of the disruption and hardships entailed for the churches of the Southern Baptist Convention by the Civil War which broke out in 1861 and by the almost equally difficult years of reconstruction which followed, the Baptists of that fellowship developed their missions in and near Canton.[382] In several of the cities of Kiangsu, after a long period in which activity had been confined to Shanghai, stations were opened.[383] In 1860, before the Civil War had inaugurated the lean years, the Southern Baptists established themselves in Shantung.[384] Not far from the year 1892 several of the American staff formed the separate Gospel Baptist Mission. This they did partly to encourage self-support on the part of the Chinese churches by keeping foreign money out of view and partly to maintain more direct contact with individual churches in the United States than seemed possible through a board representing a convention. They sought to enter territory as yet untouched by the Christian message.[385]

The history of the Seventh Day Baptists was one of difficulties. In the United

[376] Smith, op. cit., pp. 32, 33.
[377] Ashmore, The South China Mission of the American Baptist Foreign Mission Society, pp. 6, 8, 15.
[378] Ashmore, op. cit., pp. 9, 12-15, 24.
[379] Ashmore, op. cit., pp. 76ff.
[380] MacGillivray, op. cit., p. 340.
[381] MacGillivray, op. cit., p. 339.
[382] MacGillivray, op. cit., pp. 313ff.; The China Mission Hand-book, Part II, pp. 341-345.
[383] MacGillivray, op. cit., pp. 317-321. For a prominent figure in the Kiangsu mission, see F. Catherine Bryan, His Golden Cycle. The Life Story of Robert Thomas Bryan (Richmond, Rice Press, 1938, pp. xiii, 297).
[384] MacGillivray, op. cit., p. 322.
[385] MacGillivray, op. cit., p. 330; The China Mission Hand-book, Part II, pp. 255, 256; L. S. Foster, Fifty Years in China. An Eventful Memoir of Tarleton Perry Crawford, D.D. (Nashville, Bayless, Pullen Co., 1909, pp. 361).

States their constituency was not large. The Civil War cut off support from the enterprise which had been begun in Shanghai. For all but about eight months during the sixteen years between 1864 and 1880 the little church which had been gathered was left without a foreign pastor. Beginning with the 1880's reinforcements began to come.[386]

It was in 1859, as we saw a few paragraphs above, that the organization which owed so much to Carey, the (English) Baptist Missionary Society, had its first representatives in China. The real founder of the English Baptist enterprise in the empire and its most widely known and most influential missionary was Timothy Richard (1845-1919).[387] Richard was the son of a devout Welsh farmer and in his youth came into a warm Christian life through a revival. He reached China in 1870, but it was not until 1875 that he boldly moved the centre of the mission from the treaty port, Chefoo, into the interior of Shantung. At that time death and illness had deprived him of his colleagues and he was left the sole representative of his society. His were an optimistic spirit, a daring and creative imagination, and a dauntless courage which led him to think and act in large terms. He addressed himself to the men of good repute in the community for character and devoutness. Some of these were active in the existing faiths, notably in small groups, often syncretistic, whose members were not satisfied with the conventional religion around them but were seeking something better. In the 1870's he obtained and distributed relief for a famine which was devastating Shantung. In 1877 he administered relief in Shansi, then prostrate before the same severe famine.[388] Following up this experience he inaugurated a mission in Shansi. In the capital, T'aiyüanfu, he especially sought out the scholars. He wished to introduce Western science, for he felt that this would bring enlightenment, would help to avert the recurrence of famine, and would raise the standard of living of the masses above the chronic grinding poverty. By 1886 he was proving more appreciative in his attitude towards the non-Christian faiths than were his younger colleagues. Because of the ensuing strain he left the mission which he had founded. He proposed to the London committee that the best way to win China as a whole would be to found a college in the capital of each of the eighteen provinces, beginning with those of the coast and especially with Shantung. Thus the literati would be reached for the Christian faith and through them the empire. His daring seemed to his

[386] MacGillivray, *op. cit.*, pp. 344-346.
[387] William E. Soothill, *Timothy Richard of China* (London, Seeley, Service & Co., 1924, pp. 330) ; Timothy Richard, *Forty-Five Years in China. Reminiscences* (New York, Frederick A. Stokes Co., 1916, pp. 384) ; D. MacGillivray, *Timothy Richard of China* (Shanghai, The Christian Literature Society, 1920, pp. 21).
[388] On the Shansi mission see Burt, *Fifty Years in China*, pp. 79ff.

British supporters beyond their resources. He, therefore, resigned from the society (1889) of which he had been the outstanding leader in China. He made contacts with some of China's most influential officials and suggested to them plans for introducing Western education on a scale which was also beyond their faith but which did not cost him their confidence. In 1891, after the death of Williamson, he became secretary of the Society for the Diffusion of Christian and General Knowledge, later the Christian Literature Society for China. He used the post as a means of producing in Chinese a wide variety of literature, not only the strictly religious, but also distributed over much of the wide range of Occidental knowledge. Through it he strove to introduce the Chinese to the best features of Western civilization. He did this at a most opportune time. The Chinese were beginning to grope eagerly and somewhat blindly towards an understanding and appropriation of the culture which was impinging so forcefully upon them both directly from the Occident and through the doughty Japanese. After 1895 some of his works had an enormous circulation. Richard, like the earlier Ricci, dreamed of the conversion of the empire through its educated leaders. Because of the fortunate juncture with a period when the Chinese were seeking help he was more successful than was the great Jesuit. He resembled, too, Alexander Duff of India, who was even more influential in shaping the policy of Protestant missions and in effecting the impact of Western culture upon a great people in a critical age.

In 1890, in response to an invitation from Christians from Shantung who had made their homes in Shensi, the English Baptists began a mission in the latter province. Eventually it grew to fairly large proportions.[389]

The Protestant Episcopal Church concentrated its effort upon the Yangtze Valley east of the Gorges. For a time it made tentative approaches to Chefoo and Peking, but it soon limited its field to the lower reaches of the Yangtze. Its chief centre was Shanghai, but in 1868 it established itself in Wuchang and Hankow.[390] The outstanding figure in the mission during the second half of the century was Samuel Isaac Joseph Schereschewsky (1831-1906).[391] Schereschewsky was born in Russian Lithuania, the son of Jewish parents. He was reared in the Jewish faith and given an excellent education. Gradually he became convinced of the truth of the Christian position, but was not baptized until after coming to the United States. In America he obtained a theological education

---

[389] MacGillivray, *A Century of Protestant Missions in China*, p. 83; Burt, *op. cit.*, pp. 104, 105.

[390] MacGillivray, *op. cit.*, p. 297; Huntington, *Along the Great River*, pp. 39-46.

[391] James Arthur Muller, *Apostle of China. Samuel Isaac Joseph Schereschewsky, 1831-1906* (New York, Morehouse Publishing Co., 1937, pp. 279), *passim; Dictionary of American Biography*, Vol. XVI, pp. 428, 429.

and formed the purpose of going to China to translate the Bible into the language of that empire. Late in 1859 he arrived in Shanghai under Bishop Boone, who had recruited him, among others, to take advantage of the opportunity afforded by the new treaties. Schereschewsky proved a remarkable linguist. For a number of years he was in Peking, devoting himself chiefly to the task to which he had felt himself called. He assisted in the translation of the New Testament into mandarin, the vernacular of the capital and, in one variety or another, of most of China, put the entire Old Testament into that form of the language, and aided in giving a mandarin form to the Book of Common Prayer. In 1875, while in America on furlough, he was chosen bishop of his church for China. At first he declined, but, after great hesitation, he accepted a renewal of the election and was consecrated in 1877. Returning to China, he had as one of the chief objects of his episcopate the founding of a college in which Chinese could study both the Christian faith and modern science. He would thus, as would Timothy Richard and Alexander Duff, reach the youth of the East, the future leaders of their peoples, with the Christian faith. Out of this purpose came St. John's, later to bear the name of university, on the outskirts of Shanghai, for years a pioneer in Christian higher education in China. In 1881, while in Wuchang, he was stricken with an acute illness which left him a paralytic invalid, but with unimpaired mind. When it became clear that full recovery could not be expected, he resigned his episcopate (1883). Cripple though he now was, he set himself afresh to the fulfilment of the dream which had first taken him to China. Working on a typewriter with the finger of one hand, he accomplished the prodigious task of translating the Bible and the Book of Common Prayer into a form of the literary language called easy *Wênli*, and of revising his mandarin translation of the Old Testament and his easy *Wênli* translation of the Bible. For this purpose he returned to China and then, because of the greater facilities there for printing, resided in Tokyo. It was in Tokyo that he died.

The Church Missionary Society, the only other organization of the Anglican communion which before 1856 had been seeking to penetrate China, developed enterprises from the four centres where it had established itself before that year. From Hongkong it reached out into Kwangtung, and, just before and after 1900, into Kwangsi and Hunan.[392] From Foochow it developed stations in various towns and cities of Fukien. From Foochow the Chinese Christians sent two of their number to Korea in 1885 to inaugurate a mission in that hermit land, but recently opened to Protestants, but after several years withdrew. To assist the Church Missionary Society there came, beginning in 1895, personnel

[392] MacGillivray, *A Century of Protestant Missions in China*, pp. 38-44.

from Canada.[393] In 1883 there arrived a representative of the Church of England Zenana Missionary Society, followed in later years by others.[394] In 1888 there came the first contingent of the Dublin University Fukien Mission.[395] It was in Fukien that the Church Missionary Society had its most extensive development in China in this period. The Church Missionary Society continued in Shanghai, but because so many other Protestant organizations were in that city it did not greatly reinforce its enterprise there.[396] However, using Ningpo as a base, its missionaries travelled extensively in Chekiang and in time established a number of centres in that province. Hangchow was made a continuing station in 1864 and in that and succeeding decades other cities were occupied.[397] Prominent in this "Mid-China Mission" were the brothers George and Arthur Evans Moule, sons of a clergyman. The elder, George, eventually became bishop and the younger, Arthur Evans (1836-1918), who declined the bishopric that his brother might have it, archdeacon.[398] Famous was the Scottish physician, Duncan Main (1856-1934), who, a warm Evangelical and possessed of humour, sympathy, and enthusiastic devotion, came to China in 1881 and in the course of the following generation developed in Hangchow a noted medical centre.[399] In 1891 the Church Missionary Society ventured boldly away from the coast provinces into Szechwan.[400] In 1895 W. W. Cassels was consecrated bishop for that area.[401] Widely though it was beginning to extend its enterprises, in 1895 the Church Missionary Society was not as prominent in China, either relatively or actually, as in India.

[393] MacGillivray, op. cit., pp. 32-36; Stock, The History of the Church Missionary Society, Vol. III, pp. 217-224, 562-569; Eugene Stock, The Story of the Fuh-kien Mission of the Church Missionary Society (London, Seeley, Jackson, & Halliday, 1890, pp. 326).

[394] MacGillivray, op. cit., pp. 51-53.

[395] A History of the Dublin University Fuh-Kien Mission, 1887-1911 (Dublin, Hodges, Figgis & Co., no date, pp. 40), passim.

[396] Stock, The History of the Church Missionary Society, Vol. III, pp. 569, 570.

[397] Stock, op. cit., Vol. III, pp. 570-573; MacGillivray, op. cit., pp. 23-26; Arthur E. Moule, The Story of the Cheh-kiang Mission of the Church Missionary Society (London, Church Missionary Society, 1891, pp. vi, 190), passim.

[398] Arthur Evans Moule, Half a Century in China. Recollections and Observations (London, Hodder and Stoughton, 1911, pp. xii, 343); Arthur Evans Moule, Missionary to the Chinese. A Memoir by his Six Sons (London, The Religious Tract Society, 1921, pp. 112).

[399] Alexander Gammie, Duncan Main of Hangchow (London, Pickering & Inglis, no date, pp. 159); Kingston De Gruché, Dr. D. Duncan Main of Hangchow, who is known in China as Dr. Apricot of Heaven Below (London, Marshall, Morgan & Scott, no date, pp. 242).

[400] MacGillivray, op. cit., pp. 44-49. There was an initial exploration in 1888.—Stewart, Forward in Western China, pp. 5-8.

[401] Marshall Broomhall, W. W. Cassels, First Bishop in Western China (London, The China Inland Mission, 1926, pp. xxiii, 378).

The Presbyterian Church in the United States of America greatly expanded its operations in the three and a half decades between 1860 and 1895. From Canton it spread westward into Kwangsi, northward into southern Hunan,[402] and southward into the island of Hainan.[403] From Ningpo and Shanghai it stretched out into the provinces of Chekiang and Kiangsu, not only in the countryside but also into Hangchow, Soochow, and Nanking.[404] In the North it had strong centres in Peking and Paotingfu.[405] It also established itself in several of the leading cities of Shantung and from these covered numbers of the rural districts.[406] Prominent in Shantung were Nevius, whom we mentioned a few paragraphs above, and two scions of the sturdy Scotch-Irish stock of Pennsylvania who came to China in 1863, Hunter Corbett (1835-1920), who spent most of a long life in Chefoo,[407] and Calvin Wilson Mateer (1836-1908), who was remembered as the chief builder of a college and as a scholar who did much literary work. Mateer's bulky *Course of Mandarin Lessons* was long a standard introduction to the study of the colloquial language.[408]

In and around Amoy the Dutch Reformed (American) and the English Presbyterians continued in close co-operation. In 1862 the Chinese churches associated with the two bodies organized a presbytery. In 1863 two Chinese were ordained and their support was fully undertaken by the congregations of which they were pastors. By the year 1895 there were ten self-supporting churches in connexion with the Dutch Reformed mission and eight associated with the English Presbyterians. In the 1880's the Amoy presbytery undertook, without foreign aid, a mission to the Hakkas near the Fukien-Kwangtung border.[409] The English Presbyterians continued as well the enterprise inaugurated by Burns in Swatow. In 1870 the Swatow missionaries began a station among the Hakkas in a group of villages north-west of that port.[410] In 1865 the English Presbyterians extended their field to the island of Formosa. Here were Chinese speaking the Amoy dialect, a natural field for a mission already

[402] MacGillivray, *op. cit.*, pp. 384, 387.
[403] *The Isle of Palms. Sketches of Hainan. The American Presbyterian Mission, Island of Hainan South China* (Shanghai, The Commercial Press, 1919, pp. 153), pp. 51ff.
[404] *Jubilee Papers of the Central China Presbyterian Mission, 1844-1894* (Shanghai, The American Presbyterian Mission Press, 1895, pp. 116), *passim*.
[405] MacGillivray, *op. cit.*, pp. 388, 389.
[406] MacGillivray, *op. cit.*, pp. 389-391; Heeren, *On the Shantung Front*, pp. 47-103.
[407] James R. E. Craighead, *Hunter Corbett: Fifty-Six Years Missionary in China* (New York, The Revell Press, 1921, pp. 224).
[408] Daniel W. Fisher, *Calvin Wilson Mateer, Forty-Five Years a Missionary in Shantung, China* (London, T. French Downie, 1911, pp. 342); Robert McCheyne Mateer, *Character-Building in China. The Life-Story of Julia Brown Mateer* (Chicago, Fleming R. Revell Co., 1912, pp. 184).
[409] *The China Mission Hand-book*, Part II, pp. 258, 259.
[410] *The China Mission Hand-book*, Part II, pp. 52-68.

acclimatized to that city. A centre was opened in the capital of the island.[411]

The Methodist Episcopal Church (North), true to the expansive policies which were so characteristic of its genius, by 1896 was represented in several different parts of the empire. At Foochow, its first station in China, it developed a strong centre. Chinese clergy were early trained and ordained, and in 1881 an Anglo-Chinese college was opened. Through the efforts of a Chinese who, a native of a pirate district, had been notorious for his rough ways and had been converted in Foochow in 1862, the Methodists spread to Hinghwa, on the coast north of Amoy.[412] In 1867, after the opening of the Yangtze to foreigners, a centre was inaugurated at Kiukiang, a treaty port. Here one of the pioneers was Virgil C. Hart (1840-1904).[413] Under the leadership of Hart, who in 1869 was made superintendent of what was termed the Central China Mission, Methodism was planted widely. Hart himself travelled almost incessantly, establishing stations, dealing with unwilling officials, and meeting hostile mobs. He it was who took the initiative in gaining extrance for Methodism to Nanchang, the capital of Kiangsi, and to Nanking, the ancient imperial city on the Yangtze. When, in 1886, the recently (1882) opened Methodist mission in Chungking, in West China, was destroyed by a mob, Hart was appointed to direct its re-establishment. Later, while invalided in America, he directed the attention of the Canadian Methodists to Szechwan. He then headed (1891) the initial party which went to China to begin the new undertaking. In 1889 the Methodists founded the institution to which they gave the ambitious name of Nanking University.[414] In 1869 they entered the North. There within the next third of a century centres were developed in Peking and Tientsin, other stations were opened, Peking University was begun, and a woman physician had treated successfully the wife of Li Hung-chang, one of the outstanding Chinese officials of the day.[415]

The Methodist Episcopal Church, South, which had sent its first representative to China only a year after the first contingent of the Northern Methodists, did not attain in the empire the dimensions that its larger neighbour of the northern states achieved. It concentrated its efforts in the provinces of Kiangsu

[411] On the Formosan mission see William Campbell, *Handbook of the English Presbyterian Mission in South Formosa* (Hastings, F. J. Parsons, 1910, pp. xxx, 405), W. Campbell, *Sketches from Formosa* (London Marshall Brothers, preface 1915, pp. 394), and Edward Band, *Barclay of Formosa* (Tokyo, Christian Literature Society, 1936, pp. 212).

[412] MacGillivray, *A Century of Protestant Missions in China*, pp. 429-440. For a prominent member of the Foochow mission see S. Moore Sites, *Nathan Sites* (Chicago, Fleming H. Revell Co., 1912, pp. 256).

[413] E. I. Hart, *Virgil C. Hart: Missionary Statesman* (New York, George H. Doran Co., 1917, pp. 344), *passim*.

[414] MacGillivray, *op. cit.*, p. 443.

[415] MacGillivray, *op. cit.*, pp. 447-450.

and Chekiang. Here, in such important cities as Shanghai, Soochow, Huchow, Changchow, and Wusih, and in adjoining towns and villages, it built up a fairly compact enterprise. The American Civil War shut off reinforcements for fifteen years, from 1860 to 1875, but the ordeal was survived and substantial growth later came to reward the faith of those who had persevered through the dark years.[416] The outstanding pioneer and long the most prominent figure was Young J. Allen (1836-1907).[417] With the exception of furloughs, he was in China from 1860 to 1897. During most of his early years in the empire, because of the devastation wrought in his home constituency by Civil War and Reconstruction, he found it necessary to support himself and his family. Yet he seems never to have wavered and found time for much missionary effort. He gave much of his energy to education and writing. He laid the foundations for the McTyeire Home and School for Girls, an institution in Shanghai designed for the daughters of the well-to-do. He wished, as did so many other far-sighted missionaries, to reach the empire through educated leaders.

Among the Chinese associated with the Southern Methodist enterprise in these years was Charles Jones Soon, or, in the more accustomed spelling, Soong (the Chinese form was Soong Chiao-shun. Originally his family name had been Han, which was changed to Soong on his adoption). Soong later became famous as the father and father-in-law of men and women who were to be outstanding in the creation of a new China.[418] He was born in Hainan and was adopted by a childless uncle. While serving that uncle in the latter's tea and silk shop in Boston he became possessed of an ambition for an education. In 1880 he ran away, stowing himself on a coastal steamer. The master of the vessel befriended him and placed him in the home of a Methodist clergyman in North Carolina. There he was baptized. He obtained his desired education in Trinity College (later Duke University), a Methodist institution in North Carolina, and in Vanderbilt University in Tennessee. He returned to China in 1885 (he arrived early in 1886) in the service of the Southern Methodists. There he was assigned a circuit. He married a descendant of Hsü Kuang-ch'i, the famous scholar-official Jesuit convert of the Ming dynasty.[419] She proved a loyal Methodist and a very able helpmeet. Before many years he left the employ of the mission, dissatisfied with the subordinate position and salary assigned him in comparison with Americans no better trained than he. However, he and his

[416] MacGillivray, op. cit., pp. 411-425.

[417] Warren A. Candler, Young J. Allen (Nashville, Cokesbury Press, 1931, pp. 245), passim.

[418] Burke, My Father in China, pp. 3, 6-12, 32-38, 51-54, 225-243, 261-265. This book, incidentally, is the vividly written biography of William Burke, long a Southern Methodist missionary in China and a friend of Soong since their student days.

[419] Vol. III, pp. 341, 342.

wife remained devoted Christians and reared their children in that faith. The Soong home in Shanghai became a refuge for Sun Yat-sen. One of the daughters married him. Another married H. H. Kung (K'ung Hsiang-hsi), a pronounced Christian and later prominent in the national government. Later still another daughter married Chiang Kai-shek. Of this we are to hear more in our final volume.

The Wesleyan Methodist Missionary Society expanded the enterprise in Kwangtung which it had begun before 1856.[420] In Kwangtung it sought to reach not only those of Cantonese speech but also the Hakkas.[421] In 1862 Josiah Cox introduced the Wesleyan Methodists to Hankow. From there they spread into various centres in Central China, including the long resolutely anti-foreign province of Hunan.[422] In Central China the outstanding representative of the Wesleyans was David Hill (1840-1896).[423] David Hill was a man of singular devotion and quiet charm. Through his father's generosity he had an ample income. He did not marry and gave much of his income and some of his principal to the work of the mission and to the suffering, the destitute, and the blind. He lived simply, at times almost ascetically, spending as little as possible on himself. It was characteristic of him that when the news of the great Shansi famine of the 1870's reached him, he left his field for the time being and went North to give such help as was within his power. He there won to the faith Pastor Hsi, one of the most famous of the Chinese Protestant Christians of the third quarter of the century. By his appeals and his saintliness he attracted a number of recruits for the Central China Mission. It was in keeping with the rest of his career that he should come to his death through typhus, probably contracted while distributing among famine refugees in Wuchang relief made possible by funds entrusted him for that purpose by Chinese officials.

Not only did the societies which had been in China before 1856 take advantage of the opportunities brought by the treaties of 1858 and 1860. Numbers of additional Protestant organizations now entered China for the first time. The enlarged openings in China synchronized with the growing missionary interest in Protestant circles in the Occident. Although still resistant, the walls

[420] MacGillivray, op. cit., pp. 99-102; Findlay and Holdsworth, The History of the Wesleyan Methodist Missionary Society, Vol. V, pp. 438-446.

[421] Findlay and Holdsworth, op. cit., Vol. V, pp. 446, 447.

[422] Findlay and Holdsworth, op. cit., Vol. V, pp. 460-486. For prominent figures in the Central China enterprise see Coulson Kernahan, Cornaby of Hanyang (London, The Epworth Press, 1923, pp. 156), and William N. Warren, Gilbert Warren of Hunan (London, The Epworth Press, 1929, pp. 160).

[423] W. T. A. Barber, David Hill, Missionary and Saint (London, Charles H. Kelly, 2d ed., 1898, pp. 337); J. E. Hellier, Life of David Hill (London, Morgan and Scott, no date, pp. xiv, 276).

of China had been breached by the West. Group after group and denomination after denomination responded to the challenge thus presented.

What from the very outset was the most ambitious of the organizations now making their way to China was the China Inland Mission.[424] In some ways the China Inland Mission was unique in the entire history of the expansion of Christianity. It had the backing of no denomination or powerful ecclesiastical body. In this it was like many of what were termed "faith" missions of the nineteenth and twentieth centuries. However, it was by far the largest of them. It arose out of the devotion and daring of one man, James Hudson Taylor, usually better known merely as Hudson Taylor (1832-1905).[425] At the outset Taylor was without influential or wealthy friends. Never physically robust, during part of his mature life he was an invalid or semi-invalid. Yet no other one organization, Roman Catholic or Protestant, sent so many missionaries to China or was found in so many provinces. In no other land of so large an area and population was there ever a single society which planned so comprehensively to cover the whole and came so near to fulfilling its dream. Several Roman Catholic orders and congregations and more than one Protestant denomination sent out more representatives than did the China Inland Mission. However, these had more than one land in their purview. The China Inland Mission concentrated on the one empire. The achievement would have been impossible had there not been within Protestantism, particularly in the British Isles, thousands who shared the religious convictions of Taylor. These were the beliefs which were common to most of the Protestant revivals of the eighteenth and nineteenth centuries and were not confined to any one denomination. However, they were not elsewhere similarly evoked to the achievement of a great task on so extensive a scale as they were by the China Inland Mission. It was a combination of circumstances which gave rise to the exceptional dimensions of the

---

[424] For the China Inland Mission there are three comprehensive, well-written semi-official histories, prepared at different stages in the development of the enterprise: M. Geraldine Guinness, *The Story of the China Inland Mission* (London, Morgan and Scott, 2 vols., 3d ed., 1894); F. Howard Taylor, *These Forty Years. A Short History of the China Inland Mission* (Philadelphia, China Inland Mission, 1903, pp. 435); and Marshall Broomhall, *The Jubilee Story of the China Inland Mission* (London, Morgan and Scott, 1915, pp. xvi, 386). It is upon these, unless otherwise specified, that the following summary is based.

[425] On Taylor's life the following are important: J. Hudson Taylor, *A Retrospect* (Philadelphia, China Inland Mission, no date, 3d ed., pp. 136); Dr. and Mrs. Howard Taylor, *Hudson Taylor in Early Years. The Growth of a Soul* (Philadelphia, China Inland Mission, 1912, pp. xxi, 488); Dr. and Mrs. Howard Taylor, *Hudson Taylor and the China Inland Mission. The Growth of a Work of God* (London, China Inland Mission, 1919, pp. xi, 640); Marshall Broomhall, *Hudson Taylor* (London, The China Inland Mission, 1929, pp. xii, 244); Marshall Broomhall, *Hudson Taylor's Legacy. A Series of Meditations* (London, The China Inland Mission, 1931, pp. xiv, 166).

China Inland Mission. This was in part the size of the Chinese Empire, the fashion in which it became accessible to the Christian message in the second half of the nineteenth and the fore part of the twentieth century, the remarkable religious awakenings within Protestantism, chiefly in Great Britian, the British Dominions, and the United States, which usually are given the name Evangelical, and the ability and faith of Hudson Taylor.

Hudson Taylor was born in Yorkshire of parents who had a strong strain of Methodism in their immediate ancestry and who were themselves active in the local Wesleyan chapel. Before his birth they had, in accordance with an Old Testament injunction, dedicated him, as their first-born son, to God. In young childhood he purposed being a missionary to China. From infancy he was sensitive and physically delicate. At seventeen, after a period of inward distress, he entered into the experience which in the Evangelical circles in which he had been reared was regarded as evidence that he had been found of God and that by faith in the atoning work of Christ he had entered into the Christian life.

Not many months thereafter Taylor had the conviction come to him that he must go to China as a missionary. This was in 1850, when only the five ports and Hongkong were open. He seems early to have planned to go into the interior, although that was not yet legally accessible. The Wesleyans had not begun to send representatives to China. However, the Chinese Evangelization Society, which shared Gützlaff's dream of reaching all China and which was undenominational, was in existence and through this he planned to go. He prepared himself in medicine. While doing so he visited the poor to give them the Christian message and disciplined himself to live as frugally as possible and to trust God completely for his physical as well as his spiritual needs.

In 1853, at the age of twenty-one, Taylor sailed for China, an appointee of the Chinese Evangelization Society. He landed in Shanghai. After acquiring something of the language he began tours outside the city, telling the Gospel story where it had not been heard. For a time, dressing in Chinese garb, he lived in the interior. For a number of months he had W. C. Burns, the Presbyterian itinerant, as a companion and each found in the other a kindred spirit. In 1856 he established a residence in Ningpo. Since the Chinese Evangelization Society was repeatedly in debt, a procedure which to him seemed contrary to the express command "owe no man anything" and to imply a lack of faith in God, he resigned from that organization. He depended on God alone for his needs, and two Old Testament phrases which were later to mean much to the China Inland Mission became his watchwords—*Jehovah Jireh,* "the Lord will provide," and *Ebenezer,* with its suggestion of the assurance "hitherto hath the Lord helped us." Money came from friends in England, he married, a small church was gathered, and a hospital established. Then ill health forced him home to England, in 1860, and it looked as though his apparently mad venture in China had ended.

Not so to the faith of Taylor. In England he completed his professional course and took his medical degree (1862). He also engaged in the revision of the translation of the New Testament into the Ningpo dialect. He prayed that additional missionaries might be found for that province, Chekiang, and had the joy of seeing several sail. More and more he felt the burden of all China with its untold millions who were without the opportunity of hearing of the Christian way of salvation. He had no doubt that if he prayed in faith the missionaries needed to carry the message into the interior would be granted, but he knew that much of the responsibility for so large an enterprise would fall on him and he hesitated to assume it. Finally, after much agony of soul, he felt that he must undertake the heavy load, but in surrendering himself to what he believed to be the divine will, he told God that the responsibility must be His. Not far from this time he, with his wife's help, wrote a small book, *China's Spiritual Need and Claims,* which had an effect not unlike Carey's *Inquiry* written more than seventy years before.

There soon followed, in 1865, the organization of the China Inland Mission. The plan was to use Ningpo as a base and from there to press inland.

In the course of the next few years policies were evolved which became characteristic of the enterprise. Several of these arose out of the background and early experience of Hudson Taylor. An outstanding feature was the undenominational nature of the mission. Members of any Protestant denomination were accepted if they gave promise of being "willing, skilful workers." They were appointed only if they conformed to the theological pattern which in the circles that Taylor knew best was termed Evangelical. Eventually the appointees were grouped by denominations. For instance, in Szechwan the members of the mission were Anglicans. As time passed, the China Inland Mission was not only undenominational, it was also international. It drew financial support from sympathetic circles in a number of Occidental lands. Especially did help come from the United States, Canada, and Australia. With it, too, were associated several societies of similar convictions and programme. Among these were a Swedish mission to China, the Swedish Holiness Union, the Scandinavian Alliance Mission, the German China Alliance, the Liebenzell Mission, the St. Chrischona branch of the China Inland Mission, a mission of the Free Church of Sweden, and the Bible Christian Methodist Mission. Most or all of these chose fields at Taylor's suggestion. In accordance with Taylor's profound conviction, the China Inland Mission was never to go into debt. Its agents were not guaranteed a fixed salary but were to trust God to supply their needs. Taylor believed that if they were doing God's will and had confidence in Him, He would see that they had whatever was necessary. Faith in God went hand in hand with efficient business methods. Taylor was an excellent administrator and the money which came to the mission he regarded as a divine trust to be used carefully. No personal solicitation of funds was made and no collections were taken at meetings. This was partly to avoid competition with other missionary agencies. It also arose from the conviction that Christians must be urged first to give themselves fully to God and that if they took that decisive step, they would contribute of their means to what God's Spirit directed them. Friends of the enterprise were urged to pray for a certain number of missionaries and for the funds needed for outfit, passage, and initial support, but no direct appeal was made for money. The direction of the mission was in China and not in the Occident. For nearly four decades Taylor was the head and in time a council of senior missionaries was developed to advise him and superintend specific districts. Members of the mission were to conform as nearly as possible to the social and living conditions of the Chinese and until well after 1900 for the most part wore Chinese garb.

The main purpose of the China Inland Mission was not to win converts or to build a Chinese church, but to spread a knowledge of the Christian Gospel throughout the empire as quickly as might be. To this end, when a province was entered, stations were opened in the prefectural cities and, later, in subordinate ones. Preliminary exploration would, as a rule, precede these steps. The purpose was to cover the entire empire, so far as that was untouched by other Protestant agencies. Once the Christian message had been proclaimed, the fruits in conversions might be gathered by others. The aim was the presentation of the Christian message throughout the empire in the shortest possible time, not the immediate winning of the largest possible number of converts. In accord with this programme, the China Inland Mission did not seek primarily to build churches, although these were gathered. Nor, although Chinese assistants were employed, did it stress the recruiting and training of a Chinese ministry.

It it a temptation to pursue in detail the progress towards the attainment of this comprehensive ideal. That, however, would require a substantial volume. We can pause in our rapid survey only to mention a few outstanding developments. Taylor's initial prayer on the memorable Sunday in 1865 when he made the momentous decision which issued in the China Inland Mission was for twenty-four recruits, two for each of the eleven provinces then without a Protestant missionary and two for Mongolia. By the close of the year 1865 three had already sailed, in addition to the six who had gone earlier.[426] In 1866 there embarked on one ship Taylor, his wife, four children, and sixteen adults. Soon after arrival they were placed in various centres in Chekiang, the province in which Taylor's missionary apprenticeship had chiefly been served. Early in 1870 the enterprise had so grown that the members of the mission numbered thirty-three in thirteen stations and eight out-stations in four provinces. Inevitably adversities were encountered. Some representatives of other societies were critical. Several of Taylor's colleagues became disaffected and left the mission. Opposition was encountered in gaining footholds in inland cities. Taylor, never robust and upon whom the burden of the mission mainly fell, had repeated illnesses and at one time suffered from a spinal injury which threatened to cripple him for life. His wife and one of his children died. Yet he persevered. From time to time he prayed for reinforcements, always in terms of concrete numbers and of enlarging totals. In 1875 he asked for eighteen, in 1881 for seventy, and in 1886 for one hundred. Invariably the quotas were filled and the necessary financial support was obtained. In 1884, as one immediate result of a visit to Cambridge by Dwight L. Moody, several members of that university, among them two prominent athletes, offered themselves to the China Inland Mission.[427] Soon the Cambridge band numbered seven. Of these one, W. W. Cassels,[428] eventually became the Anglican bishop in western China, another, D. E. Hoste, later became general directer of the mission, and still another, C. T. Studd,[429] after several years in China and a period in India, organized and led the Heart of African Mission. By the close of the year 1893 stations had been opened in the capital cities of eleven provinces and much of the remaining portions of the empire, including parts of Manchuria, Mongolia, Sinkiang, and Tibet had been traversed.[430] In 1895 the China Inland Mission counted 641 missionaries, 462 Chinese helpers, 260 stations and out-stations, and

[426] For the life of one of the three see Marshall Broomhall, *John W. Stevenson* (London, Morgan and Scott, 1919, pp. xiii, 95).

[427] Benjamin Broomhall, *A Missionary Band. A Record and an Appeal* (London, Morgan and Scott, no date, pp. xiv, 152), pp. 1-54.

[428] Marshall Broomhall, *W. W. Cassels, First Bishop in Western China* (London, The China Inland Mission, 1926, pp. xxiii, 378), pp. 177ff.

[429] Thomas B. Walters, *Charles T. Studd, Cricketeer and Missionary* (London, The Epworth Press, 1930, pp. 126), *passim*.

[430] *The China Mission Hand-book*, Part II, p. 112. On one of the pioneers in Shansi see A. T. Schofield, *Memorials of R. Harold A. Schofield* (London, Hodder and Stoughton, 1898, pp. xiii, 257). For a pioneer among the Tibetans see Annie W. Marston, *With the King. Pages from the Life of Mrs. Cecil Polhill* (London, Marshall Brothers, pp. v, 223). On one of Moody's converts, a man of wealth, who gave up business to go to China under the China Inland Mission, see Marshall Broomhall, *Archibald Orr Ewing* (London, China Inland Mission, 1930, pp. xi, 150). See also Mildred Cable and Francesca French, *A Woman Who Laughed. Henrietta Soltau Who Laughed at Impossibilities and Cried 'It Shall be Done'* (London, The China Inland Mission, 1934, pp. 240).

5,211 communicants.[431] It was fitting that Taylor should die, in 1905, in Changsha, the capital of Hunan, which had been the most resistant of the provinces to the entrance of Protestant missionaries and where only four years before the mission had succeeded in establishing a centre. The story was by no means to end there. As we shall see in later pages, the China Inland Mission continued to grow.

We must hasten over the list of the other Protestant organizations which between the years 1856 and 1895 for the first time entered China. In 1859 the Methodist New Connexion Missionary Society, of British constituency, appointed two missionary couples to China. They went to Tientsin in 1860 and there inaugurated an enterprise which expanded into other centres in the North.[432] Its outstanding leader was one of its pioneers, John Innocent.[433] In 1863 there arrived the two initial representatives in China of the Society for the Propagation of the Gospel in Foreign Parts. In the following year the new undertaking was suspended and it was not until 1874 that a continuing mission was begun. This was in Chefoo. In 1880 one of the two who comprised the original Chefoo staff, Charles Perry Scott, was consecrated bishop. The Church Missionary Society soon transferred to its sister organization its station in Peking. Other centres were developed, including Tientsin and some in Shantung, but not until after 1895 was their growth rapid.[434] The National Bible Society of Scotland, formed in 1860, appointed as its first agent in China Alexander Williamson, who had previously served under the London Missionary Society. He reached China in 1863 to assume his new post.[435] The English Methodist Free Church Mission, supported by the United Methodist Free Churches, was begun in 1864 at Ningpo. In 1878 another centre was established at Wenchow, farther south on the Chekiang coast.[436] To this station came W. E. Soothill, who was to have a distinguished career, first there, later in other parts of China as educator and author, and eventually as professor of Chinese in Oxford in the chair once held by Legge.[437]

Additional Presbyterian bodies entered the empire. The mission of the (Southern) Presbyterian church in the United States was begun in 1867, only

[431] *China's Millions*, 1906, p. 124.

[432] *The China Mission Hand-book*, Part II, pp. 104, 105.

[433] G. T. Candlin, *John Innocent: a Story of Mission Work in North China* (London, The United Methodist Publishing House, 1909, pp. xvi, 306).

[434] Pascoe, *Two Hundred Years of the S.P.G.*, Vol. II, pp. 705-711.

[435] *The China Mission Hand-book*, Part II, p. 300.

[436] *The China Mission Hand-book,* Part II, p. 107.

[437] See a description of that mission in W. E. Soothill. *A Typical Mission in China* (Chicago, Fleming H. Revell Co., c. 1906, pp. xi, 293). For an account by Mrs. Soothill of her life in Wenchow see Lucy Soothill, *A Passport to China* (London, Hodder and Stoughton, 1931, pp. xi, 339).

two years after the close of the Civil War which had devastated much of the section upon which that church depended. The first main centre was in Hangchow. A field was developed extending about five hundred miles northward along the Grand Canal in Chekiang and Kiangsu.[438] To follow up the labour and dreams of William C. Burns, who had died in 1868 in Newchwang, the one open port in Manchuria, in 1869 the Irish Presbyterians appointed two men to that area. By the year 1895 stations had been established in Newchwang, Chinchow, Mukden, Kwançh'engtze (eventually Hsinching), and Kirin, all in Manchuria.[439] To Manchuria there also came the United Presbyterians, later amalgamated with the Free Church to form the United Free Church of Scotland. In 1872 their pioneer, John Ross, reached Newchwang. In 1875 a foothold was acquired in Mukden. In 1882 Dugald Christie inaugurated a medical mission in that city which was to develop into a notable medical school. Various other strategic cities and towns were entered in an attempt at systematically reaching the region. In 1891 the Irish and the Scottish missions joined in forming a united presbytery as the basis and symbol of joint effort.[440] In 1877 or 1878 the Church of Scotland began a mission at Ichang, on the Yangtze above Hankow. Reinforcements came slowly and the undertaking did not attain large dimensions.[441] To Formosa there came in 1871 the remarkable G. L. Mackay as the pioneer of the Canadian Presbyterians. There, at times without a foreign colleague, he laid the foundations of a strong church and trained for it indigenous leaders. Converts were made among the Chinese and among the aborigines who had been partially assimilated to Chinese culture.[442] In the 1880's the Canadian Presbyterians opened an additional mission, in Honan. Among the

[438] The China Mission Hand-book, Part II, pp. 213-215; Samuel Isett Woodbridge, Fifty Years in China (Richmond, Presbyterian Committee of Publication, 1919, pp. 231). For the biographies of two members of the mission, A. Sydenstricker and his wife, by their daughter, see Pearl S. Buck, Fighting Angel (New York, Reynal & Hitchcock, 1936, pp. 302), and Pearl S. Buck, The Exile (Reynal & Hitchcock, 1936, pp. 315).

[439] The China Mission Hand-book, Part II, pp. 86, 87. For a member of the mission see Margaret Weir, Andrew Weir of Manchuria (London, James Clarke & Co., no date, pp. 255).

[440] The China Mission Hand-book, Part II, pp. 80-82; Thirty Years in the Manchu Capital in and around Moukden in Peace and War: being the Recollections of Dugald Christie (New York, McBride, Nast & Co., 1914, pp. xiv, 303); Dugald Christie of Manchuria . . . by his wife (London, James Clarke & Co., no date, pp. 232); John Ross, Mission Methods in Manchuria (New York, Fleming H. Revell Co., no date, pp. 251), pp. 119ff.

[441] MacGillivray, A Century of Protestant Missions in China, p. 201; The China Mission Hand-book, Part II, pp. 90, 91.

[442] George Leslie Mackay, From Far Formosa (New York, Fleming H. Revell Co., 1896, pp. 346); Marian Keith, The Black Bearded Barbarian. The Life of George Leslie Mackay of Formosa (New York, Missionary Education Movement, 1912, pp. x, 307).

pioneers were Jonathan Goforth, later notable as a leader of revivals, and D. MacGillivray, eventually prominent for his literary labours.[443]

In 1860 there was formed in New York City, partly through an impulse stemming from the saintly David Abeel, the Women's Union Missionary Society of America. The following year it began financial subventions to various enterprises in China and in 1868 sent three representatives to Peking to assist in a school for girls. Later the school was transferred to Shanghai. In that great port city a hospital was developed and a Bible school was begun.[444]

In 1884 Chinese Christians in San Francisco organized the China Congregational Society and eventually had a small enterprise among their fellow provincials in Kwangtung which was conducted in close co-operation with the agents of the American Board of Commissioners for Foreign Missions.[445]

It was partly through Hudson Taylor that the English Friends sent a representative to China (1884). In 1889 a foothold was obtained in Szechwan which issued in a continuing mission.[446] In 1887 the Ohio Yearly Meeting of Friends sent a missionary to Nanking. Reinforcements followed slowly.[447]

In the 1880's the Disciples of Christ inaugurated a mission in Nanking, where their pioneer, W. E. Macklin, a physician, was to establish a hospital and was long to be a prominent figure.[448]

In 1888 the first representative of the Evangelical Missionary Alliance (soon the International Missionary Alliance) reached China. In 1897 the latter organization was amalgamated with the Christian Alliance to constitute the Christian and Missionary Alliance. It was warmly evangelistic and arose largely out of the inspiration of A. B. Simpson (1845-1919) who conducted a Gospel Tabernacle in New York City.[449] Before many decades the Christian and Missionary Alliance had agents not only in a number of sections of China but also

[443] The China Mission Hand-book, Part II, p. 289; MacGillivray, op. cit., pp. 242-245; Rosalind Goforth, Goforth of China (Grand Rapids, Zondervan Publishing House, 1937, pp. 364), passim.
[444] MacGillivray, op. cit., pp. 468, 469.
[445] The China Mission Year Book, 1910, p. 117.
[446] MacGillivray, op. cit., pp. 164, 165; Robert J. Davidson and Isaac Mason, Life in West China (London, Headley Brothers, 1905, pp. xvi, 248), pp. 161ff.
[447] Walter Rollin Williams, Ohio Friends in the Land of Sinim (Mt. Gilead, Ohio, Friends Foreign Missionary Board of Ohio Yearly Meeting, no date, pp. 229), pp. 23ff.; Walter Rollin Williams, These Fifty Years with Ohio Friends in China (Damascus, Ohio, Friends Foreign Missionary Society of Ohio Yearly Meeting, 1940, pp. 315), pp. 35ff.
[448] Laura Delany Garst, In the Shadow of the Drum Tower (Cincinnati, Foreign Christian Missionary Society, 1911, pp. 136), pp. 57ff.; Edith Eberle, Macklin of Nanking (St. Louis, The Bethany Press, pp. 169), passim.
[449] The New York Times, Oct. 30, 1919, p. 13; Ekvall, After Fifty Years, pp. 18-21.

in other parts of the world. By 1895, however, it was only beginning to get under way in China.[450]

A few paragraphs above we called attention to the inauguration by Canadian Methodists of an enterprise in West China. The initial party left Canada in 1891, led by Virgil C. Hart. It established its first station at Chengtu, the capital of Szechwan, and in 1894 began a second at Kiating.[451]

The Young Men's Christian Association seems not to have made itself felt directly in China until the 1880's. In 1885 two student associations were organized, one in Foochow and one in T'ungchow, just outside of Peking.[452] In 1890 Luther D. Wishard in a world tour for the (North American) International Committee, told the general conference of Protestant missionaries which was meeting in Shanghai that his organization was prepared to send representatives to reside in China if the missionaries in one or more of China's large cities requested it. Appeals soon came from a number of cities and in 1895 a secretary, D. Willard Lyon, was sent, the first of what later became a large and influential company.[453]

The Christian Endeavour movement also entered from North America. It was in 1895 and in Foochow that the first society in China was constituted. It was not until 1903 that a national organization for China came into being.[454]

In 1889, as an outgrowth of a mission for Chinese in Portland, Oregon, an enterprise of the United Brethren in Christ was begun. Canton was made the centre.[455]

Those often known as the Plymouth Brethren had no central organization either in the Occident or in China. The missionaries who came were more or less connected with communities in the West, chiefly in the British Isles. The first seem to have reached China in the 1880's. By the year 1895 there were Brethren in Shantung and Kiangsi.[456]

There were a number of Protestant missionaries unsupported by any denomination or society. We hear of one such at Ningpo begun in 1893.[457]

---

[450] Robert Glover, *Ebenezer, or Divine Deliverances in China* (New York, Alliance Press Co., pp. 120), pp. 12ff.; Ekvall, *op. cit.,* pp. 150ff. For an account of beginnings and also of a life connected with the expansion after 1895, see Wilmoth Alexander Farmer, *Ada Beeson Farmer, a Missionary Heroine in Kuang Si, South China* (Atlanta, Foote & Davies Co., 1912, pp. 325).
[451] *Our West China Mission,* pp. 29-33.
[452] Information given the author by Harlan P. Beach, who organized the Association in T'ungchow.
[453] MacGillivray, *A Century of Protestant Missions in China,* pp. 597, 598.
[454] MacGillivray, *op. cit.,* p. 610.
[455] MacGillivray, *op. cit.,* p. 530.
[456] Couling, *The Encyclopaedia Sinica,* p. 442.
[457] MacGillivray, *op. cit.,* p. 541.

From the United States came representatives of the nineteenth century Protestant immigration from the continent of Europe. In 1888 the American Swedish Free Mission Society began operations in Canton.[458] In the 1890's a society made up of members of Hauge's Synod, of Norwegian stock, inaugurated a station in Hupeh, on the Han River north of Hankow.[459] It was also in this same centre in Hupeh that the Swedish Evangelical Covenant of America opened a station in 1892.[460]

It was in Central China that several Scandinavian organizations found fields. By 1895 the Swedish Mission in China had stations in Shansi, Shensi, and Honan.[461] Beginning in 1890 representatives of the *Svenska Missionsförbundet* (Swedish Missionary Society) obtained footholds in Wuchang and Ichang.[462] Beginning early in the 1890's *Det Norske Lutherske Kina Misjions Forbund* (Norwegian Lutheran China Mission Association) began developing a chain of stations northward from Hankow in the valley of the Han.[463]

A few other Continental European societies entered China. The *Allgemeiner Evangelisch-Protestantischer Missionsverein,* designed largely for a literary approach to the educated, inaugurated an enterprise in Shanghai in 1885 when Ernst Faber, an able scholar in Chinese, formerly in the service of the Rhenish Missionary Society, came onto its staff. Later P. Kranz joined him.[464] In the 1890's the Swedish Baptists, a small body, chose a field in Shantung.[465]

We must also notice that the *Svenska Missionsförbundets* inaugurated a mission in distant and difficult Sinkiang, in Kashgar.[466]

The great increase in the number of Protestant organizations represented in China might well have led to confusion and the lack of any comprehensive plan for covering the empire. To a certain extent this was true. Yet to a surprising degree there were systematic efforts to reach the entire country, an absence of overlapping (so far as the Protestant forces were concerned), and joint thinking. Not only did the China Inland Mission and its associated bodies proceed with a programme for covering the portions of the empire untouched by other Protestant bodies. Various other organizations also sought out "un-

[458] MacGillivray, *op. cit.,* p. 527.
[459] MacGillivray, *op. cit.,* p. 508.
[460] MacGillivray, *op. cit.,* p. 524.
[461] MacGillivray, *op. cit.,* pp. 521, 522.
[462] MacGillivray, *op. cit.,* p. 519.
[463] MacGillivray, *op. cit.,* p. 512. On one of the pioneers, later the home secretary. and an account of the early days of the enterprise, see P. S. Eikrem, *Johannes Brandtzæg. hans Liv og Virke* (Oslo, Det Norsk Lutherske Kinamisjonsforbund, 1934, pp. 285).
[464] MacGillivray, *op. cit.,* p. 498; Richter, *Das Werden der christlichen Kirche in China,* p. 330.
[465] MacGillivray, *op. cit.,* p. 515.
[466] *Svenska Missionsförbundets Årsberattelse,* 1894, p. 102; 1895, p. 103; 1913, p. 51.

evangelized" areas and followed systematic procedures for giving them the Christian message. That, for instance, was true of the Presbyterians in Manchuria.[467] Timothy Richard, as we noticed a few paragraphs above, addressed himself to the leaders of particular regions and of the empire as a whole. The varied policies of the different societies and prominent leaders tended towards inclusiveness. Hudson Taylor and men like him endeavoured to communicate to every Chinese as quickly as possible a knowledge of the Christian faith Others, of whom Timothy Richard was an outstanding example, endeavoured not so much to present directly the Christian Gospel to all the millions of individual Chinese as to mould the life of the entire empire through the introduction of Western learning in connexion with the teaching of Christianity and to effect this through the noblest and most influential of the exponents of China's existing cultures and religions. Usually in this period missionary societies in seeking entrance or in opening new fields deliberately chose regions or towns in which no other Protestants were at work. As between Protestants and Roman Catholics there was much territorial overlapping. Neither would recognize the other as having the true Christian message. Sometimes there was open conflict.[468] More often the one ignored the presence of the other.

Among the many Protestant bodies there was much community of aim and faith. Whatever the denomination, the large majority of the supporting constituencies and the missionaries were from those elements which had been most affected by the Evangelical awakening and kindred revivals of the eighteenth and nineteenth centuries. This common set of convictions and experiences facilitated conferences in which missionaries from various societies and many different sections of the empire were represented. The first of these was held in Shanghai in 1877[469] and the second, also in Shanghai, in 1890.[470] The attendance at the first was one hundred and forty-two and at the second four hundred and forty-five representing thirty-seven societies. In both gatherings the problems confronting the Protestant missionary enterprise were faced fairly comprehensively (although the first eschewed the still controversial issue of the Chinese term to be employed for God). The second sent an appeal "to all Protestant churches of Christian lands . . . to send to China . . . one thousand men within five years from this time"[471] and the women of the gathering called on

[467] Ross, *Mission Methods in Manchuria*, p. 32.
[468] As in Burke, *My Father in China*, pp. 133-143.
[469] *Records of the General Conference of the Protestant Missionaries of China, held at Shanghai, May 10-24, 1877* (Shanghai, Presbyterian Mission Press, 1878, pp. iii, 492).
[470] *Records of the General Conference of the Protestant Missionaries of China held at Shanghai, May 7-20, 1890* (Shanghai, Presbyterian Mission Press, 1890, pp. lxviii, 744).
[471] *Records of the General Conference of the Protestant Missionaries of China . . . 1890*, p. lix.

their sisters at home to undertake work for their sex in China.[472] The second also appointed a number of continuing committees. Progress was being made towards empire-wide co-operation.

By the year 1895 all the Protestant bodies which in 1914 were most largely represented by foreign staffs and indigenous Christians had begun operations in the empire. For the most part they had roughly staked out the fields in which they were later to operate. After 1895 a number of new societies entered the country, but by the year 1914 none of them had attained the dimensions of the major pioneer bodies. A few of the latter expanded into fresh sections. In general, however, the great extension after 1895 was in centres in which stations had already been established or in territories contiguous to these centres.

In 1895 the actual number of Protestant Chinese Christians was inconsiderable. In 1893 communicants were said to total 55,093.[473] In proportion to the population or even to the Roman Catholic body in that year this was very small. However, it represented rapid growth. One set of statistics [474] gave the number of Protestant communicants in 1842 as 6, in 1853 as 350, in 1865 as 2,000, in 1876 as 13,035, in 1886 as 28,000, and in 1889 as 37,287. Clearly Protestants were multiplying. The foreign staff was also growing. In 1889 it was 1,296.[475] About the year 1895 it was said to be 1,324.[476]

The years following 1895 witnessed a still more spectacular increase of Chinese Protestant Christianity. The crumbling of the structure of Chinese culture which took on an accelerated pace after the defeat by Japan and the ensuing encroachments of Western powers was accompanied by a lessening resistance to Western culture and in some quarters by a mounting desire to acquire those features of Occidental civilization which would enable China to defend herself against alien aggression. Coming as it did in association with the West, Christianity had somewhat less difficult access. Particularly did Protestant Christianity profit by the altered situation. The growing missionary interest in the churches of Europe and America saw in the changing China a challenge. The missionary staff was augmented. The schools and hospitals of a Western type which Protestants had created became popular as channels of the desired Western culture. Christian literature had a wider circulation and the spoken message a larger hearing. The growing open-mindedness of China and the increased

[472] Records of the General Conference of the Protestant Missionaries of China . . . 1890, pp. lvii-lix.
[473] The China Mission Hand-book, Part II, p. 325.
[474] Records of the General Conference of the Protestant Missionaries of China . . . 1890, p. 735.
[475] Ibid.
[476] The China Mission Hand-book, Part II, p. 325.

attention of the Western churches was in part evidenced by the rise in the number of Protestants. In 1898 communicants totalled 80,682,[477] in 1904, 131,-404,[478] and in 1914 over 253,210.[479] In 1914 the foreign staff numbered 5,409.[480]

To this mounting Protestant Christian movement the anti-foreign reaction which culminated in the Boxer outbreak in 1900 seemed for a brief while to have dealt a fatal blow. Since Protestantism had existed in China for a much shorter time than had Roman Catholicism and since it was an even more recent arrival in the north-east, where the disturbances were the most violent, many fewer Protestant than Roman Catholic Chinese perished. Yet the number was very considerable. One estimate placed it at 1,912.[481] The Christians connected with the London Missionary Society, the American Board, the Presbyterians in Manchuria, the American Methodists, and the Northern Presbyterians were the chief sufferers. The number of foreign missionaries who lost their lives is uncertain. One count declares the total to have been 134 adults and 52 children, a total of 186. Of these more were from the China Inland Mission and the Christian and Missionary Alliance than from any other society.[482] The blow was by far the most severe that had thus far been dealt to Protestant missions not only in China but also in any other non-European land. In its initial days in Europe Protestantism had a much longer list of martyrs, but never outside of Europe had it had so many who suffered violent death for their faith.

We must not take the time to go into many of the details of the tragic year. A few examples may give some idea of the whole. In Paotingfu on the last day of June and the first day of July the missions of the American Board and of the Northern Presbyterians were destroyed and a number of missionaries and Chinese Christians were killed.[483] One of the foreigners who then perished was Horace Tracy Pitkin. In his last message to his wife Pitkin expressed the hope that when their son, then an infant, should be twenty-five years of age he would come to China to take his father's place.[484] Pastor Mêng of Paotingfu, the first Chinese ordained by the American Board in the North, on learning of the danger to the missionaries, hurried to the city, declined to flee when he might have escaped, commanded his eldest son to make his way to safety to carry on

---

[477] The Chinese Recorder, Vol. XXX, p. 145.
[478] H. P. Beach in China's Millions, 1905, p. 145.
[479] The China Mission Year Book, 1915, p. vii.
[480] The China Mission Year Book, 1915, p. xv.
[481] The Chinese Recorder, Vol. XXXVIII, p. 611.
[482] The Chinese Recorder, Vol. XXXII, p. 150.
[483] Isaac C. Ketler, The Tragedy of Paotingfu (Chicago, Fleming H. Revell Co., 1902, pp. 400), passim.
[484] Robert E. Speer, A Memorial of Horace Tracy Pitkin (Chicago, Fleming H. Revell Co., 1903, pp. 310), p. 293.

his work after he should be gone, and was then tortured and killed.[485] In Mongolia the Christian and Missionary Alliance lost twenty-one of the thirty-eight missionaries which it had in the empire, in addition to fourteen children of missionaries.[486] In Manchuria about three hundred Chinese Protestants were slaughtered, some with great cruelty. One preacher, upon his refusal to recant, had his eyebrows, ears, and lips cut off and his heart torn out and exhibited in a theatre.[487] In Shansi for Protestants as for Roman Catholics the year was particularly disastrous. The truculent Governor Yü Hsien had mercy on neither group. On July 9 thirty-four men, women, and children of the Protestant missionary community were executed by his orders in the capital, T'aiyüanfu.[488] At Hsinchow, about forty-five miles north of T'aiyüanfu, the members of the English Baptist mission hid in a cave, were discovered and imprisoned, on August 9 were taken out, ostensibly for the purpose of being escorted to the coast, were met at the city gates by Boxers, and were there stripped and murdered.[489] The Shansi Mission of the American Board lost every one of its foreign members then on the field—five men, five women, and five children—and nearly half of its Chinese Christians.[490] Two young men connected with the American Board in Shansi, Fei Ch'i-hao and K'ung Hsiang-hsi, refused to apostatize and escaped after great perils.[491] K'ung, a descendant of Confucius, later graduated from Oberlin College, became head of the school maintained in Shansi in the name of Oberlin, eventually married a daughter of the Soong family which we mentioned a few pages above, and was prominent in the national government under the republic. Under pressure some of the Chinese Christians denied their faith, but the stories of fidelity, heroism, and suffering could be multiplied.[492]

[485] Miner, China's Book of Martyrs, pp. 99-101.
[486] Forsyth, The China Martyrs of 1900, p. 82.
[487] J. Miller Graham, East of the Barrier, or Side Lights on the Manchuria Mission (New York, Fleming H. Revell Co., 1902, pp. 237), pp. 179, 180, 300.
[488] Forsyth, op. cit., p. 39
[489] Forsyth, op. cit., pp. 43-46.
[490] The Ninety-First Annual Report of the American Board of Commissioners for Foreign Missions, 1901, pp. 108-112.
[491] Luella Miner, Two Heroes of Cathay. An Autobiography and a Sketch (Chicago, Fleming H. Revell Co., 1903, pp. 238), passim.
[492] For additional accounts see Archibald E. Glover, A Thousand Miles of Miracle in China. A Personal Record of God's Delivering Power from the Hands of the Imperial Boxers of Shan-si (London, Hodder and Stoughton, 1904, pp. xx, 372); E. H. Edwards, Fire and Sword in Shansi (New York, Fleming H. Revell Co., no date, pp. 325); Marshall Broomhall, editor, Martyred Missionaries of the China Inland Mission (Toronto, China Inland Mission, 1901, pp. xxvi, 328); Marshall Broomhall, Last Letters and Further Records of Martyred Missionaries of the China Inland Mission (London, Morgan and Scott, pp. 105); Mrs. A. H. Mateer, Siege Days. Personal Experiences of American Women and Children during the Peking Siege (New York, Fleming H. Revell Co., 1903, pp. 411);

When the news of the Boxer disorders reached the Occident, many declared that the Protestant enterprise in China was ended. Yet the disaster served only to spur it on. The suppression of the Boxers was followed by greater opportunities than ever and many new recruits came to fill the gaps left by the martyrs.

In the settlement which followed the Boxer uprising, indemnities were paid to both Roman Catholics and Protestants. Some of these were from the general fund levied collectively upon the empire. Others were from local and provincial officials or directly from non-Christians. For the most part the missionaries declined compensation for life (although some was collected for the heirs of executed missionaries) and took it only to restore destroyed property.[493] The China Inland Mission, in spite of the fact that its foreign staff had suffered more than that of any other Protestant organization, for the purpose of showing to the Chinese "the meekness and gentleness of Christ" adopted the settled policy of not accepting compensation even if offered.[494] At the suggestion of Timothy Richard, who was called upon by the provincial authorities in Shansi to assist in the post-Boxer settlement, half a million taels were set aside to found in T'aiyüanfu a provincial university in which Western learning should be taught. This was in partial fulfilment of a dream long cherished by Richard for conveying the best of Western culture to that province. The curriculum, the choice of the faculty, and the administration of the funds were placed in his hands for ten years.[495]

In general the accession to Protestant strength after 1895 was more from the United States than from the British Isles and the continent of Europe. In 1895 nearly two-thirds of the missionary body were British, approximately one-third from the United States, and about two or three per cent. from the continent of Europe.[496] In 1914 about half were from the United States, about two-fifths were British, and not far from one-tenth were from the continent of Europe.[497] The mounting wealth and population of the United States and the increasing interest in foreign missions displayed by the Protestant churches of that land were making themselves felt. That missionary interest was being directed largely

---

J. A. Rinell and John H. Swordson, *Boxare-Upproret och Förföljelserna mot de Kristna i Kina 1900-1901* (Stockholm, Baptistmissionens Förlagsexpedition, 1902, pp. 307); James Hudson Roberts, *A Flight for Life* (Boston, The Pilgrim Press, 1903, pp. 402); Walter A. Sellew, *Clara Leffingwell* (Chicago, The Free Methodist Publishing House, 1907, pp. xv, 320), pp. 128-179.
[493] For a summary account, with the appropriate footnote references, see Latourette, *A History of Christian Missions in China*, pp. 519-525.
[494] Broomhall, *The Jubilee Story of the China Inland Mission*, p. 257.
[495] Richard, *Forty-Five Years in China*, p. 299.
[496] *The China Mission Hand-book*, Part II, p. 325.
[497] Beach and St. John, *World Statistics of Christian Missions*, pp. 63, 64.

westward towards eastern Asia. Missionaries from the United States were from the beginning overwhelmingly in the majority in the Protestant enterprise in Japan, Korea, and the Philippines. It is not strange that they should now be of growing relative prominence in China.

We need not take the time to sketch in detail the growth between 1895 and 1914 of the Protestant organizations represented in China before the former year. In 1914 they had more than four-fifths of the foreign missionary body and more than nine-tenths of the communicant members.[498] The China Inland Mission still had a larger foreign staff than any other of the societies and had nearly doubled it in the two decades.[499] However, that was now only about fifteen per cent. of the total missionary body [500] as against forty per cent. in 1895.[501] Whereas, in 1895, next to the China Inland Mission the Church Missionary Society and its associated organizations was the largest, with the American Northern Presbyterians and the American Northern Methodists in second and third place,[502] by 1914 it had slipped to third place and the two American societies had outstripped it, with the Presbyterians leading.[503] In both years Anglicans were less prominent in China, both in missionaries and in communicants, than in India, and Presbyterians of various countries and churches much more so than in the latter country.

The Young Men's Christian Association enjoyed an especially rapid growth. As we saw a few pages back, the initial Young Men's Christian Associations in China were not organized until 1885 and it was only in 1895 that the first foreign secretary came. In 1914 the foreign staff was said to number one hundred and thirty-five.[504] These secretaries were largely from the United States and Canada. They brought to China the enthusiasm and flexibility of a comparatively new movement. It was in the United States that the Young Men's Christian Associations had their largest development. They had become an agency of the Protestant forces for certain types of effort—athletic, social, educational, and religious—for young men in the great cities. They were erecting large buildings for these purposes. They were warmly evangelistic. Dwight L. Moody, for instance, had spent some of his earlier years as a secretary of the Young Men's

---

[498] Ibid.

[499] On an able, wealthy, cultured, and devoted young American who had planned to go to the Chinese Moslems under the China Inland Mission but died in Cairo while studying Arabic in preparation for that enterprise, see Mrs. Howard Taylor, Borden of Yale '09 (London, The China Inland Mission, 1926, pp. xv, 286).

[500] Beach and St. John, op. cit., pp. 63, 64.

[501] The China Mission Hand-book, Part II, p. 325.

[502] Ibid.

[503] Beach and St. John, op. cit., pp. 63, 64.

[504] Beach and St. John, op. cit., p. 64. This must have been inclusive of wives. See the itemized list in The China Mission Year Book, 1915, pp. 86-88.

Christian Association in Chicago. During the closing decades of the nineteenth and the opening years of the twentieth century they had developed a strong organization in the colleges and universities. They had almost a monopoly of the voluntary religious activities in the higher educational institutions in the United States and Canada. From this student constituency they attracted men of outstanding ability. There interdenominational character and the freshness of their approach drew to them those who were eager to pioneer in new lands and new methods. During part of this time the chief figure in both the student and the foreign programme of the Young Men's Christian Associations was John R. Mott, one of the striking figures in the expansion of Christianity in the 1890's and in the first four or more decades of the twentieth century. These American Young Men's Christian Associations found their major foreign field in eastern Asia, particularly in China. The staff which they sent introduced new missionary methods partly by bringing in those developed in North America and partly by devising new ones to meet the situation in China.[505] From the beginning they stressed Chinese leadership to a degree not yet attained by the bodies longer represented. They attracted to the secretariat able young Chinese. There served as officers or secretaries such men as H. H. K'ung, Fei Ch'i-hao, and C. T. Wang. By 1914 Wang was already prominent in the officialdom of the new republic and K'ung was later to become so. Buildings of the American type were being erected in some of the major cities. Special lecturers were brought to further the spread of Western science and of public health. Emphasis was placed on efforts for students. By the end of 1914 there were one hundred and twenty-six student associations as against twenty-nine city associations. For the students summer conferences were held, in a kind of succession to the one at Mount Hermon in 1886 which had been memorable for the beginning of the Student Volunteer Movement for Foreign Missions.[506] Three times before 1915 special meetings in several centres were conducted by Sherwood Eddy.[507] In 1896 and again in 1905-1906 and 1913 John R. Mott held meetings in a number of cities.[508] In these meetings the purpose was to present the Christian message to the new student class, especially to those in government schools. Bible study was prominent, both for those who had become interested through Eddy and Mott and for those reached in other ways. Much was being done to reach the thousands of Chinese students who were going abroad to acquire

[505] The autobiography of one of the early outstanding secretaries is Fletcher S. Brockman, *I Discover the Orient* (New York, Harper & Brothers, 1935, pp. xii, 211).
[506] Vol. IV, pp. 95, 96.
[507] Eddy, *A Pilgrimage of Ideas*, pp. 113ff.
[508] Mathews, *John R. Mott*, pp. 114, 180, 181, 200.

Western learning. Strategy was a word frequently in the mouths of the heads of the Young Men's Christian Associations. It was, therefore, deemed of first-class importance that the students, the presumptive future leaders of China, be reached by the Christian faith and that in this, her day of transition, China should be assisted to build a wholesome national life and the Christian faith be woven into the warp and woof of the newly emerging culture.[509]

A few scattered notes concerning the extension after 1895 of the operations of other organizations which were in China before that year will give some indication of the growth which most of them were experiencing. After the acquisition by Germany of the leasehold at Kiaochow and a sphere of influence in Shantung, some of the German societies previously in China began operations in that area. Both the Berlin Missionary Society and the *Allgemeiner Evangelisch-Protestantischer Missionsverein* moved in.[510] The German occupation was also followed by the strengthening of the American (Northern) Presbyterian effort in the interior of Shantung and the opening of new stations, including one in Tsingtao. The demand for Western education led the Presbyterians to augment their college.[511] The Protestant Episcopal Church (American) further developed the area in the Yangtze Valley in which it had begun operations. For its better administration two new bishoprics were added, one centring in Hankow, in 1901,[512] and one given the name of Wuhu (1910).[513] The American Board of Commissioners for Foreign Missions restored the enterprise in Shansi so nearly wiped out by the Boxer disturbances. In memory of the foreign victims, graduates of Oberlin, from which the martyrs had come, formed the Shansi Memorial Association and sent representatives, most of them engaged in education.[514] The Church Missionary Society brought about the creation of a diocese for Fukien (1906) [515] and, moving northward from its fields in the South, established itself in Hunan, with a new diocese (1909) for that province and Kwangsi.[516] In Manchuria the Presbyterians witnessed, beginning in 1908, a kind of mass movement with public confessions of sin, extreme emo-

---

[509] Much of the preceding account has been gathered from *The Foreign Mail Annual,* 1914, pp. 27-51; *The China Mission Year Book,* 1915, pp. 337-342; and MacGillivray, *A Century of Protestant Missions in China,* pp. 597-608.
[510] Richter, *Das Werden der christlichen Kirche in China,* p. 398.
[511] Heeren, *On the Shantung Front,* pp. 104-147.
[512] W. H. Jefferys, *James Addison Ingle* (New York, Domestic and Foreign Missionary Society, 1913, pp. viii, 286), pp. 197ff.
[513] Huntington, *Along the Great River,* p. 91.
[514] Strong, *The Story of the American Board,* pp. 380, 381.
[515] Stock, *The History of the Church Missionary Society,* Vol. IV, p. 293.
[516] Stock, *op. cit.,* Vol. IV, p. 304.

tional and physical phenomena, moral transformations,[517] and about thirteen thousand baptisms in the years 1908-1912 inclusive.[518] The Foreign Christian Missionary Society added to the field which it developed in and near Nanking around its pioneer, Macklin, a new region on the Tibetan border of Szechwan.[519]

A number of societies entered China after 1895. It was natural that the Young Women's Christian Associations should emerge as a counterpart to the Young Men's Christian Associations. What is said to have been the first was formed in 1890, but a second did not appear until 1899. In that year steps were taken towards a national organization and in 1903 the first secretary was appointed by the World's Committee. In 1905 a national secretary was sent from the United States.[520] By 1914 several city associations and a number of student associations had been constituted and summer conferences had been inaugurated.[521] However, the numerical dimensions of the brother movement were not attained. In 1907 the Church of England in Canada, which for a number of years had been appointing missionaries to Fukien in connexion with the Church Missionary Society, in response to an appeal from the Anglican communion in China undertook responsibility for a new diocese. The initial contingent arrived in 1910 in Kaifeng, the centre of the bishopric.[522] In 1901 the Presbyterians of New Zealand pursued contacts made with Chinese in that land by sending a missionary to Canton to labour through the returned emigrants.[523] In 1913 three Koreans were commissioned by the general assembly of their Presbyterian church to go to Shantung to co-operate with Chinese and American Presbyterians in that province.[524] In 1905 the Free Methodists of North America, stimulated by one of their number who had served under the China Inland Mission, sent several representatives who found a field in Honan.[525] In 1904 there arrived the first appointees to China of the Evangelical Association of North America. They established themselves in Hunan, then being ex-

[517] James Webster, *Times of Blessing in Manchuria. Letters from Moukden to the Church at Home, February 17—June 10, 1908* (Shanghai, Methodist Publishing House, 4th ed., 1909, pp. iv, 92), *passim;* James Webster, transcribed from his letters by John Ross, *The Marvellous Story of the Revival in Manchuria* (Edinburgh, Oliphant, Anderson & Ferrier, no date, pp. 64), *passim; The China Mission Year Book*, 1915, pp. 45-48.
[518] *The Chinese Recorder*, Vol. XLVI, p. 102.
[519] Flora Beal Shelton, *Shelton of Tibet* (New York, George H. Doran Co., 1923, pp. 319), *passim.*
[520] MacGillivray, *A Century of Protestant Missions in China*, p. 609.
[521] *The China Mission Year Book*, 1915, pp. 370-376.
[522] *The China Mission Year Book*, 1912, pp. 208, 209.
[523] MacGillivray, *op. cit.,* p. 249.
[524] *The China Mission Year Book*, 1915, p. 48.
[525] Walter A. Sellew, *Clara Leffingwell* (Chicago, The Free Methodist Publishing House, 1907, pp. xv, 320), pp. 217ff

tensively penetrated by Protestant missions, and in the adjoining Kweichow.[526]
A number of the new missions were Lutheran. Most of them chose areas in
Central China—in Honan, Hupeh, and Hunan. Lutheranism in China had
first been almost exclusively German and in Kwangtung, an outgrowth of
what had been started by Gützlaff. Beginning in the 1890's there developed in
Central China strong bodies of Lutherans which were founded and nourished
chiefly by Scandinavians and Germans, either directly from Europe or from
the emigration to the United States. Some of these, as we saw a few pages
above, came before 1896. Others came after that year. In 1901 the Norwegian
Missionary Society (*Det Norske Missionsselskab*) sent pioneers who went
(1902) to Hunan. Eventually it became strong there and in Hupeh.[527] In 1905
the Augustana Synod, Swedish Lutherans from the United States, found a
field in Honan.[528] In 1913 members of the Missouri Synod, of German background, arrived and began developing an area from Hankow westward up
the Yangtze.[529] In 1901 the first missionaries of the Finnish Missionary Society
arrived. The following year they were in Hunan.[530] We hear also of the American Brethren Mission in Hupeh.[531]

Distant from this group of Lutheran bodies in Central China were the Danish Lutherans, in Manchuria. Port Arthur, entered in 1906, was the first base.
Other centres in South Manchuria were opened in quick succession.[532]

It was in 1902 that the Seventh Day Adventists began to enter China in force.
Since 1888 a representative had been in Hongkong, chiefly among English-
speaking members of that community. Late in 1902 a mission was begun in
Canton. By the end of 1905 there were centres also in Honan and Amoy.[533] By
the close of 1914 several other stations had been started, among them Hankow,
Changsha, Shanghai, Chungking, and Mukden.[534]

Other bodies, most of them small and from the United States, inaugurated
enterprises in China in the two decades between 1895 and the close of 1914.
Simply to list them is to give some indication of their variety. We hear
of Mennonites, Methodist Protestants, United Evangelicals, American Re-

---

[526] MacGillivray, *op. cit.*, p. 541.
[527] J. A. O. Gotteberg, *Ti aar i Hunan* (Stavanger, Det norske missionsselskabs bogtrykkeri, 1912, pp. 52), pp. 17ff.
[528] *The Lutheran Companion*, Vol. XXIII, May 29, 1915, pp. 3, 10, 11; *The China Mission Year Book*, 1915, *Directory According to Missions*, p. 29.
[529] L. Fuerbringer, editor, *Men and Missions. IV. Our China Mission* (St. Louis, Con-
cordia Publishing House, 1926, pp. 48), p. 5.
[530] MacGillivray, *op. cit.*, pp. 502, 503.
[531] *The China Mission Year Book*, 1915. *Directory According to Missions*, p. 29.
[532] MacGillivray, *op. cit.*, p. 526.
[533] MacGillivray, *op. cit.*, pp. 538, 539.
[534] *The China Mission Year Book*, 1915. *Directory According to Missions*, pp. 83, 84.

formed Presbyterians, the (German) Reformed Church in the United States, the Assemblies of God, the Boat Mission (in Canton), the Canadian Holiness Movement Mission, the Church of God, the Ebenezer Mission, the Grace Evangelical Mission, the National Holiness Mission, the South Chihli Mission,[535b] and the Church of the Brethren.[536]

The Yale Foreign Missionary Society was the largest and most ambitious of a number of enterprises begun by the graduates of American universities. Its first representative arrived in 1902. It soon decided upon Changsha as its seat and there in time developed a hospital, medical school, school of nursing, middle school, and college.[537] As a rule the other college and university missions sent out their contingents in connexion with some existing society or institution.[538]

A unique venture was the Mission among the Higher Classes of China, with Gilbert Reid as its moving spirit and the International Institute in Shanghai as its centre. Reid had come to China under the (Northern) Presbyterian Church in the United States of America. In this new undertaking, dating back to the 1890's, but not formally incorporated until 1905, he sought to cultivate friendly understanding between Christians and non-Christians, Chinese and foreigners, and directed his efforts especially to leading Chinese merchants and officials and to outstanding members of the foreign community of Shanghai.[539]

The Door of Hope, founded in Shanghai in 1900 by Cornelia Bonnell as a home for such prostitutes as wished to escape their unhappy lot, was an attempt on the part of herself and other women missionaries to do something to relieve the misery which was one of the dark spots in this great port where the West impinged upon China and the worst elements from the two cultures seemed to flourish.[540]

A mission begun in Shanghai by George Matheson sought to minister to the physical and spiritual needs of the ricksha pullers.[541]

The multiplication of organizations was paralleled by rapidly increasing co-

[535] For the list see *The China Mission Year Book*, 1915. *Directory According to Missions, passim.*
[536] Moyer, *Missions of the Church of the Brethren*, pp. 179-190.
[537] Henry B. Wright, *A Life with a Purpose. A Memorial of John Lawrence Thurston. First Missionary of the Yale Mission* (New York, Fleming H. Revell Co., 1908, pp. 317), *passim; The Vision of a Short Life. A Memorial of Warren Bartlett Seabury*, by his Father (Cambridge, The Riverside Press, 1909, pp. xii, 192), *passim.*
[538] Latourette, *A History of Christian Missions in China*, p. 604.
[539] MacGillivray, *op. cit.*, p. 550; Gilbert Reid, *The International Institute. Annual Reports of the Mission among the Higher Classes in China* (Shanghai, 1901ff.).
[540] *The Door of Hope. Annual Reports.* Shanghai, 1901ff.; *The China Mission Year Book*, 1913, pp. 391-402.
[541] *The Chinese Recorder*, Vol. XLV, p. 525.

operation across denominational lines. The China Inland Mission brought together like-minded people from numbers of denominations and from several countries. As in several other parts of the world, by comity arrangements, either formal or informal, the effort was made, usually with success, to prevent the representation of the Christian faith in a particular area by more than one Protestant denomination. It was chiefly in the larger cites that two or more denominations were found. Thus early in their operations there the denominations divided the great western province of Szechwan among themselves.[542] Representatives of the societies of the Anglican communion united in bringing into being the *Chung Hua Shêng Kung Hui,* or Holy Catholic Church of China, a national body in full communion with the other Anglican churches. This grew out of conferences which began in 1897 and culminated in the first meeting of the General Synod in 1912.[543] Before 1914 steps had been taken towards the formation of one Presbyterian body for China in which the churches which were the children of the various Presbyterian societies would associate themselves in a national structure.[544] In Kwangtung the Basel, Rhenish, and Berlin socities achieved a form of federation.[545]

A comprehensive, nation-wide organization of the Protestant forces was also in process of formation. In 1907 there assembled in Shanghai what was known as the China Centenary Missionary Conference, so designated in memory of the arrival of Robert Morrison and the inauguration of Protestant missions.[546] Like its predecessors of 1877 and 1890, it was made up almost entirely of foreigners. Going beyond these earlier gatherings, it recommended "the formation of a Federal Union under the title, the Christian Federation of China." [547] It suggested the organization of provincial councils composed of delegates, Chinese and foreign, representing all the missions in the area. By 1913 councils had been formed in eleven provinces and in addition there was a West China Advisory Council federating the missions in Szechwan, Kweichow, and Yünnan.[548] A further stage came, as in India, in consequence of the World Missionary Conference held in Edinburgh in 1910. From conferences convened in China in 1913 by John R. Mott under the Continuation Committee of the Edinburgh Conference there was formed the China Continuation Com-

[542] *World Missionary Conference, 1910,* Vol. VIII, p. 24.
[543] *World Missionary Conference, 1910,* Vol. VIII, pp. 98, 99; *The Chinese Recorder,* Vol. XLIII, p. 378; *The China Mission Year Book,* 1914, pp. 396, 397.
[544] *The Chinese Recorder,* Vol. XXXII, p. 553; Vol. XXXIV, pp. 10-15; Vol. XLII, pp. 682-688; Vol. XLV, p. 588; *World Missionary Conference, 1910,* Vol. VIII, pp. 91-93.
[545] *The China Mission Year Book,* 1910, p. 196.
[546] *China Centenary Missionary Conference Records, passim.*
[547] *China Centenary Missionary Conference Records,* pp. 719-721.
[548] *The China Mission Year Book,* 1914, pp. 218, 219.

mittee with an even more far-reaching programme for the union of churches of similar ecclesiastical order, the federation of all the churches, uniform terms for use in the churches, a common hymn book, and the development of the indigenous character of the churches under a trained Chinese leadership.[549] Out of this came, after 1914, as in India, a National Christian Council.

Interdenominational co-operation was rapidly increasing in several other ways. A number of union educational institutions were coming into being, the staff and financial support contributed by two or more denominations. Among these were at least five theological schools. Here and there was a union hospital. There were national organizations which brought together missionaries of specialized interests from numbers of denominations. Among these were the Educational Association of China, the Medical Association of China, and the Evangelistic Association of China. Other similar bodies included the tract societies, the Christian Literature Society, and the Sunday School Union.[550] In cities where more than one denomination was represented union church services in English for foreigners were common. The summer resorts which were developing in the mountains and on the sea-coast usually drew missionaries from several denominations and made possible fellowship, conferences, and worship across confessional lines.

Co-operation was more than keeping pace with the multiplication of denominational agencies.

The approach of the Protestant missionaries to China was varied. Some societies confined themselves to particular functions or to specialized objectives. Of the larger groups this was notably true of the China Inland Mission, the Young Men's and Young Women's Christian Associations, and the various women's societies. Among the denominational societies, especially those from the British Isles and North America, the programmes followed were very similar. Moreover, with modifications due to the differences in environment, they resembled those of the same societies in other countries.

These programmes embraced the preparation and distribution of literature, including the translation of the Bible; the proclamation of the Christian Gospel by word and through the printed page; the creation and nourishing of churches through winning and instructing converts and recruiting and training Chinese clergy; the founding and development of schools from primary through college and university status; medical care, with the building of hospitals, the education of Chinese physicians and nurses, and latterly, public health education; and other works of mercy, among them famine relief, the care of orphans,

---

[549] *The Continuation Committee Conferences in Asia, 1912-1913*, pp. 321ff.
[550] *The China Mission Year Book*, 1914, pp. 200ff.

and provision for the blind, the insane, and other underprivileged members of society.

The activities of Protestant missionaries were more diverse than were those of Roman Catholics. The latter were intent primarily upon building the Church and the cure of souls. To these goals all else was ancillary. Protestants also sought the salvation of souls and the growth of the Church. However, they divided their energies between this objective, the remoulding of the empire and its culture as a whole, and meeting what seemed to them to be human need regardless of whether it led to formal conversion to the Christian faith. Roman Catholics, having had their policy in part shaped during decades of persecution, tended to confine their efforts to building a constituency which for the present must content itself with being a more or less self-contained minority. Protestants, entering China in force at a time when the land was being penetrated and transformed by a conquering, aggressive Occident, dreamed in terms of giving to all Chinese a knowledge of the Christian Gospel, of serving all the empire, and of contributing in a Christian fashion to the reshaping of the entire structure of the empire's life. Not all Protestant missionaries planned in these terms, but some of the ablest and many of the rank and file did so.

All the main branches of the Protestant programme were to be found, at least in embryo, in the pre-treaty third of a century in which Protestant missions were knocking at the still closed door of China and in the decade and a half or so between the first and the second group of treaties. However, partly under the exigencies of the situation, different phases of the programme were stressed in the various periods of the Protestant penetration of China.

In pre-treaty days the chief emphasis was upon the acquisition of the language, the preparation of tools for its study, the translation of the Bible, and the creation of other Christian literature. This was partly because of the importance of the Bible in Protestant eyes but chiefly because it was only through the printed page that there was then any opportunity of bringing the Christian message as Protestants understood it to the masses of the Chinese. Protestant churches were as yet practically non-existent. A few schools were begun, attended as a rule only by the sons of the poor who valued the education given as a preparation for the lucrative service of the Western merchant. A little medical work, notably that of Peter Parker, was undertaken.

The brief period between 1842 and 1858 was one mainly of gaining footholds in the six centres opened to Protestant activity and trying to penetrate, somewhat tentatively, the territory in the near vicinity of these cities. The translation of the Bible was being continued in creating new editions. Here and there churches were organized, schools begun, and hospitals founded.

The generation between the treaties of 1858 and 1860 and the era of rapid change which followed the Sino-Japanese War of 1894-1895 was for Protestants one primarily of penetrating the empire, by word of mouth and through the distribution of literature broadcasting the Christian message to as many as possible, establishing stations, gathering nuclei of churches, and laying the foundations of colleges and hospitals. It was still the day of the pioneer missionary when the burden was carried almost exclusively by the foreigner. There was much of itineration.[551] Most of this was by men, but some of it was by single women.[552] The mission station often had a preaching hall, open to the street, in which the Chinese could stop and rest at will, possibly visiting with one another or smoking while they listened to what the foreigner or his Chinese assistant had to say.[553] Somewhere near the street chapel would be the missionary's residence. There might also be a church building distinct from the street chapel. Services were customarily held each night in the week in addition to Sundays. The hymns were generally translations sung to Western tunes. Usually there were also connected with the mission station a school and a dispensary or hospital. Some missionaries maintained that no foreign money should be paid to a Chinese for preaching the Gospel and that from the very first a local church should be self-supporting.[554] Others subsidized the Chinese rather freely.[555] Some Christians spread the faith with the encouragement but without the assistance of the foreigner. There were beginnings of home mission societies.[556] From the first missionaries recognized that China could not be won to the Christian faith by foreigners and that Chinese leadership was necessary.[557] However, it was not an easy matter to bring into existence a Chinese body of clergy. The pastorate is a unique calling peculiar to Christianity. No precedent for it existed in China. What seemed the nearest parallels were the Buddhist monks and the Taoist priests, and these were not held in high esteem by the Chinese. Teachers, of whom the missions had need, were honoured by Chinese tradition. Higher salaries were paid to them than to unordained preachers and even than to some ordained pastors.[558] Yet theological

[551] The Chinese Recorder, Vol. VI, pp. 241-247; John, Sowing and Reaping, passim.
[552] Davies, Among the Hills and Valleys of Western China, pp. 135-141.
[553] Hampden C. DuBose, Preaching in Sinim: or the Gospel to the Gentiles, with Hints and Helps for Addressing a Heathen Audience (Richmond, Presbyterian Committee of Publication, 1893, pp. 241), pp. 49-61; Burke, My Father in China, pp. 69, 70; Nevius, China and the Chinese, pp. 326-328.
[554] Records of the General Conference of the Protestant Missionaries of China . . . 1877, p. 295; The China Mission Hand-book, Part II, p. 44.
[555] Gibson, Mission Problems and Mission Methods in South China, p. 195.
[556] The Chinese Recorder, Vol. XXXIV, pp. 170-174; MacGillivray, A Century of Protestant Missions in China, p. 8.
[557] Doolittle, Social Life of the Chinese, Vol. II, p. 404.
[558] The China Mission Hand-book, Part II, p. 154.

schools were begun.[559] As early as 1876 twenty were reported, with two hundred and thirty-one students.[560] Most of them, presumably, were of elementary grade. Numbers of "Bible women" were used to reach members of their own sex. There were also men who served as colporteurs and travelling "evangelists."[561]

In the years between 1858 and 1895 attention continued to be given to the preparation and distribution of literature. Revisions and new translations of all or parts of the Bible were prepared.[562] Some of these were in one or another of the vernaculars which abounded in the coast provinces south of the Yangtze.[563] For use by the illiterate or relatively illiterate in Chinese some of these were printed in Roman letters rather than in Chinese characters.[564] Much other Christian literature was produced. Some of it was for the purpose of presenting the Christian faith to non-Christians and some for the instruction and use of Christians. The latter included catechisms, prayer-books, and hymnals.[565] For the printing of this literature nine presses were in existence in 1895.[566] The British and Foreign Bible Society, the American Bible Society, and the National Bible Society of Scotland were active in printing and circulating the Bible.[567] There were also several tract societies, most of them regional.[568] A number of periodicals were issued.[569]

More and more emphasis was being placed upon schools. Most of these were elementary, but here and there were those of secondary grade and foundations were being laid for a few colleges beyond secondary standards. In general schools had some Western subjects on their curricula. The question of whether English should be taught and, if it were taught, whether it should be the medium of instruction, was a matter of warm debate, but in secondary and higher schools English was gradually increasing. At the outset the schools were not popular. Their graduates were not prepared to compete in the civil service examinations which were the goal of the traditional Chinese education and the road to the

---

[559] MacGillivray, *op. cit.*, p. 35. A good summary is C. Stanley Smith, *The Development of Protestant Theological Education in China* (Shanghai, Kelly and Walsh, 1941, pp. viii, 171).

[560] *Records of the General Conference of the Protestant Missionaries of China . . . 1877*, p. 486.

[561] Gibson, *op. cit.*, pp. 178, 256.

[562] See a list in Stauffer, *The Christian Occupation of China*, p. 452.

[563] *Ibid.*

[564] *Records of the General Conference of the Protestant Missionaries of China . . . 1890*, pp. 73-75.

[565] *Ibid.*

[566] *The China Mission Hand-book*, Part II, pp. 315-324.

[567] *The China Mission Hand-book*, Part II, pp. 296-301.

[568] *The China Mission Hand-book*, Part II, pp. 303-306.

[569] *Ibid.* See also some mention in Britton, *The Chinese Periodical Press*, pp. 51-61.

coveted literary degrees and official posts. The chief outlet for the students was in the employment of the missions or of foreign business firms and the customs service. Some missionaries were sceptical about the value of secondary and higher education for any but prospective pastors. Yet in a day when the government clung to the old system Protestant missions were pioneering in education of Western types. They were also beginning the startling innovation of schools for girls.[570]

Medical missionaries were increasing. In the Occident medical science was making enormous strides. In China Protestants were utilizing the advances to relieve human suffering. In 1895 Protestant medical missionaries numbered 143—96 of them men and 47 of them women. There were 71 hospitals and 111 dispensaries. Special attention was being paid to opium addicts. For them 36 refuges were maintained and in 1893, 1,088 opium smokers were admitted to them.[571] A beginning was made in training Chinese in Western medicine. In 1893, 151 men and 28 women were reported as medical students.[572]

By 1895 Protestant missionaries were attacking a variety of evils. Devices were worked out to enable the blind to read. Schools for the blind were maintained.[573] The deaf were educated.[574] Foot-binding was fought.[575] Anti-opium societies were organized.[576] As we saw a few pages above, efforts were made at famine relief. There were orphanages, but no such prominence was given them as by the Roman Catholics.

In the years which followed 1895, when China was in a state of rapid transition, the emphasis of Protestant missions changed. The attempt to reach all the Chinese as individuals with the Christian message was not surrendered. However, increasingly Protestant missionaries saw in the cultural revolution a challenge to influence China as a whole. Timothy Richard believed that through the penetration of China by Christian ideas the conversion of the entire land would come suddenly.[577] Although only a few agreed with Richard's prognosis, it was to the exertion of this influence upon the nation that the efforts of Protestant missions were more and more directed.

The fact that in the years when the empire had been attempting to retain its cultural integrity Protestant missions, chiefly through schools, medical service,

[570] For a summary with appropriate references to the sources, see Latourette, *A History of Christian Missions in China*, pp. 441-451.
[571] *The China Mission Hand-book*, Part II, p. 327.
[572] *Ibid.*
[573] Couling, *The Encyclopaedia Sinica*, pp. 51, 52.
[574] *The Chinese Recorder*, Vol. XXI, pp. 245, 246.
[575] *The China Mission Hand-book*, Part II, p. 11.
[576] *Records of the General Conference of the Protestant Missionaries of China . . . 1890*, pp. li, lxi, 355, 356.
[577] *The Chinese Recorder*, Vol. XXXII, pp. 124, 125.

and literature, had become the chief representatives of these phases of Occidental culture gave them a unique opportunity. Now that the Chinese were hungry for Western learning Protestant missions were in a peculiarly favourable position to supply the demand. In the closing years of the nineteenth and the opening years of the twentieth century most of the best secondary and higher schools in China in which Western learning could be acquired and a large majority of the hospitals and medical schools of an Occidental type were maintained by Protestant missionaries. These institutions were, therefore, strengthened and multiplied.

Not far from 1914, 543 Protestant secondary schools were reported, with more than 33,000 pupils, of whom approximately two-thirds were boys and a third girls.[578] At the same time 33 colleges and universities were listed, with an enrollment of more than 2,000, of whom more than four-fifths were men and slightly less than one-fifth women.[579] Prominent among the colleges and universities were Canton Christian College, later Lingnan University; [580] St. John's University, in 1914 probably the outstanding Protestant higher school in China, maintained by the American Episcopalians at Shanghai; [581] The University of Nanking, in which, in 1909, three denominations united; [582] the Shantung Christian University, in which two denominations joined; [583] Peking University, originally of the American Methodists, but in which the American Presbyterians (Northern) and the American Board were co-operating,[584] and which was later to be merged in a still more inclusive union, Yenching University; and West China Union University, of Chengtu.[585] An ambitious proposal, which failed of ultimate realization, was the United Universities project. It contemplated a great undenominational Christian university at the Wuhan centre (Wuchang, Hankow, and Hanyang). It was led by the English, but American assistance was hoped for.[586] In 1913 the foundations were laid for a union Christian college for women in Nanking, to bear an old name for that city, Ginling.[587] This is by no means a complete list, but it indicates the fashion in which Protestants had placed the strongest of their colleges and universities at leading cities where

[578] Beach and St. John, *World Statistics of Christian Missions*, p. 78.
[579] *Ibid.*
[580] *The China Mission Year Book*, 1913, p. 264.
[581] Cochrane, *Survey of the Missionary Occupation of China*, p. 92.
[582] *The China Mission Year Book*, 1913, p. 259.
[583] *The China Mission Year Book*, 1913, pp. 262-264.
[584] *The China Mission Year Book*, 1915, p. 401.
[585] *The China Mission Year Book*, 1915, pp. 193-197.
[586] William Gasgoyne-Cecil, *Changing China* (New York, D. Appleton & Co., 1910, pp. xvi, 342), pp. vii, 305ff.; *The China Mission Year Book*, 1911, pp. 22, 139.
[587] *Ginling College, The Union College for Women in the Yangtze Valley* (Shanghai, Presbyterian Mission Press, 1915, pp. 11), *passim*.

they were in strategic positions to influence the life of the nation. Several medical schools were maintained, one of which, in Peking, after 1914 was to become the nucleus of the unique Peking Union Medical College, the leading medical school in China. Two of the medical schools were exclusively for women.[588] From the desire to help prevent famines, there was organized at the University of Nanking a department of agriculture and forestry [589] which was to have an outstanding role in the introduction of research in these important branches of economy.

While schools were thus emphasized, they by no means monopolized the attention of Protestants to the exclusion of other methods of approach. Medicine and hospitals were more and more stressed. A medical journal, said to be the first issued in Chinese, was begun in 1912.[590] The Nurses Association of China was organized in 1909.[591] On the eve of 1914, of the foreign Protestant staff 328 were men physicians, 92 women physicians, and 127 nurses.[592] This was a nearly three-fold increase over the figures for 1895. Hospitals now numbered 265 and dispensaries 386,[593] totals about three and a half times those of two decades before. Patients were over a million,[594] more than four times the number of twenty years earlier. Various other channels for relieving suffering or improving crippling customs were tried. Famine relief was administered.[595] Orphanages were maintained, although still on a small scale as compared with the Roman Catholics.[596] A union or standard Braille system was devised for mandarin-speaking blind and a number of schools and institutions for these unfortunates were conducted.[597] We hear of one missionary who in his city induced

[588] The China Mission Year Book, 1913, pp. 293-297; 1914, pp. 331-338.
[589] The China Mission Year Book, 1915, pp. 402-404.
[590] The China Mission Year Book, 1914, p. 335.
[591] The China Mission Year Book, 1914, p. 338.
[592] Beach and St. John, World Statistics of Christian Missions, p. 95. For biographies of some of the medical missionaries of this period see J. C. Keyte, Andrew Young of Shensi (London, The Carey Press, preface 1924, pp. xiii, 313); Alfred J. Costain, The Life of Dr. Arthur Jackson of Manchuria (London, Hodder and Stoughton, 1911, pp. 182); F. W. S. O'Neill, editor, Dr. Isabel Mitchell of Manchuria (London, Clarke & Co., 2d ed., 1918, pp. 222); F. B. Meyer, Memorials of Cecil Robertson of Sianfu (London, The Carey Press, 1913, pp. viii, 168); J. Peill, editor, The Beloved Physician of Tsang Chou. Lifework and Letters of Dr. Arthur D. Peill (London, Headley Brothers, no date, pp. xvii, 293); W. Arthur Tatchell, Booth of Hankow (London, Charles H. Kelly, 1915, pp. 125); See also W. Arthur Tatchell, Medical Missions in China in Connexion with the Wesleyan Methodist Church (London, Robert Culley, introduction 1904, pp. 351).
[593] Beach and St. John, op. cit., p. 95.
[594] Ibid.
[595] The China Mission Year Book, 1911, pp. 66-69.
[596] In 1914 there were 32 Protestant orphanages with 1,353 inmates (Beach and St. John, op. cit., p. 95) as compared with 392 Roman Catholic orphanages with 29,198 inmates in about the year 1912 (Streit, Atlas Hierarchicus, p. 100).
[597] The China Mission Year Book, 1914, pp. 313-330.

the Chinese to set aside a plot of land as a public park and playground and to begin the cleaning of the streets.[598]

The presentation of the Christian message to individuals was augmented. Missionaries continued to reach out toward new areas. A striking example of this was Watts O. Pye, of the American Board. Pye sought to cover systematically an area in Shansi and Shensi.[599] Churches increased in numbers and membership. Although in 1914, because of the growing commitment of the government and private individuals to Occidental culture, Protestant publishing agencies did not hold the prominent place which had been theirs in the later 1890's in introducing Western knowledge to China, specifically religious literature was circulated. The sales of the Bible notably increased. Those by the three great Bible societies rose from 2,519,758 (portions and entire Bibles) in 1905 [600] to 6,148,546 in 1914.[601]

In 1914 the Chinese were ceasing to be as subordinate to the foreigner in the churches as they had been in the initial days of Protestantism in China and were beginning to display independent initiative. Here and there, usually in the chief ports, where Protestantism had been longest represented, congregations developed which were quite independent of foreign control or even of organized relationship with denominations of foreign origin.[602] In 1910 there began the Chinese Student Volunteer Movement for the Ministry. Its outstanding leader, Ting Li-mei, a pastor in Shantung, went about the country presenting to students the claims of that calling.[603] The Young Men's Christian Association, by its lay character and its policy of encouraging Chinese to assume control, attracted to its staff a number of Chinese of marked ability. In 1914 Protestant Christianity, like Roman Catholic Christianity, was still predominantly foreign in its forms and leadership. However, it was giving indications of taking root in Chinese soil. After 1914, for Protestants as for Roman Catholics, the increase of Chinese participation and direction was to be very rapid.

As we approach the question of the effect of Christianity upon China in the period between A.D. 1800 and A.D. 1914 we must remember that until the middle of the nineteenth century Roman Catholics, Russian Orthodox, and Protestants constituted insignificant minorities in a large population. To be sure,

[598] The China Mission Year Book, 1914, pp. 293-299.
[599] Dictionary of American Biography, Vol. XV, pp. 286, 287.
[600] MacGillivray, A Century of Protestant Missions in China, pp. 565, 573, 580.
[601] Stauffer, The Christian Occupation of China, p. 453.
[602] The China Mission Year Book, 1912, pp. 216-223; 1913, pp. 182-191.
[603] The China Mission Year Book, 1914, pp. 170-177.

Roman Catholicism and Russian Orthodoxy had been present in the empire for several generations. However, in the nineteenth century rapid growth did not begin for any branch of Christianity until that era was half gone. As in so many other parts of the world, Christianity reached A.D. 1914 on a mounting tide, and in China much more than in India its effects had only commenced to be seen by that year. Yet even before 1914 Christianity was beginning to make itself felt and in several significant ways.

In the preceding pages some of the consequences of Christianity have been recorded. Although here and there it will be necessary to bring forward data not previously mentioned, for the most part what is now needed is summary and interpretation.

One of the most obvious effects of Christianity was in the rapidly rising number of professed Christians. In the earlier pages of this chapter we have noted that record. We have seen that in 1844 Roman Catholics may have totalled 240,000,[604] that in 1901 the figure was said to be 720,540,[605] and that in 1912 it was reported as 1,431,258.[606] In 1914 Russian Orthodox Chinese numbered about 5,000.[607] Protestant communicants are reported to have increased from 350 in 1853 to 37,287 in 1889,[608] and to over 250,000 in 1914.[609] To make the Protestant data comparable with those for Roman Catholics and Russian Orthodox it would be necessary to know the total of baptized, which would be considerably larger than that of communicants. Incomplete figures for 1914 place it at approximately a third of a million.[610] In 1914, then, baptized Christians in China totalled somewhat more than one and three-quarters millions, or slightly less than one-half of one per cent. of the population. This was little more than half the total in India in that year and about half the percentage that Christians formed of the population of India. As in India, so in China, the Christians seem for the most part to have come from the humbler ranks of society. Here and there were literati, but the majority of that dominant class viewed Christianity with dislike and disdain.

More important but much more difficult to determine is the effect which Christianity had upon the lives of the individual Christians. As was to be expected, the evidence indicates a mixture of results.

[604] *Notizie Statistiche delle Missioni di Tutto il Mondo Dipendenti dalla S.C. de Propaganda Fide*, 1844, pp. 557-572.
[605] *Missiones Catholicae Cura S. Congregationis de Propaganda Fide*, 1907, table 44.
[606] *Zeitschrift für Missionswissenschaft*, Vol. IV, p. 42.
[607] *The China Mission Year Book*, 1915, pp. 583, 584.
[608] *Records of the General Conference of the Protestant Missionaries of China . . . 1890*, p. 735.
[609] *The China Mission Year Book*, 1915, p. vii.
[610] Beach and St. John, *World Statistics of Christian Missions*, p. 63.

In a rather critical report by a Roman Catholic we are informed that the "old" Christians, namely those from families which had been Roman Catholic for two or more generations, had much of formalism, an inclination to conform unthinkingly to tradition, a dearth of moral conviction, and a willingness to compromise, and that real piety among them was rare.[611] We hear the complaint that Roman Catholics reared in orphanages or in Christian schools were lacking in self-reliance.[612] Yet we are also told that Roman Catholic Christians were encouraged to eschew such prevalent customs in non-Christian society as gambling, the smoking of opium, and attendance at theatres.[613] We also read that the "old" Roman Catholics in Kiangnan were characterized by "deep faith, strict observance of traditional customs, and a lavish spirit of charity," yet were inclined to keep themselves so aloof from their non-Christian neighbours that there were few conversions from the latter.[614] A Protestant missionary reported of Roman Catholics whom he knew in Manchuria that they were well-behaved, clean, and industrious,[615] and a Protestant consul said that he had often been impressed by the quiet and respectability in Roman Catholic communities in contrast with the surrounding non-Christians.[616]

As to Protestants, a sympathetic Presbyterian missionary who had served among the Chinese in Formosa and had not allowed his affection to deprive him of objectivity, reported [617] that the Christians were slow to comprehend the Bible and to understand the deeper aspects of the faith, but that they were zealous in winning converts, and that non-Christian Chinese declared that Christians did not smoke opium, gamble, or indulge in vice or filthy language, and that they behaved with meekness and good temper. Here and there were Christians who stood out for their character and service and for whom the community was clearly the better. Such a one was he who became known as Pastor Hsi.[618] Born into a family of scholars and himself in his early maturity a scholar of promise and a man of means, Hsi had fruitlessly sought an answer to the

[611] Kervyn, *Methode de l'Apostolat Moderne en Chine*, pp. 790ff.

[612] *Annals of the Propagation of the Faith*, Vol. LXXX, pp. 232-239.

[613] Beckmann, *Die katholische Missionsmethode in China in Neuesterzeit*, pp. 87ff.

[614] Servière in *The Chinese Recorder*, Vol. XLIV, p. 615.

[615] Christie, *Thirty Years in the Manchu Capital*, p. 19.

[616] W. H. Medhurst, *The Foreigner in Far Cathay* (London, Edward Stanford, 1872, pp. 192), p. 34.

[617] Campbell N. Moody, *The Heathen Heart. An Account of the Reception of the Gospel among the Chinese of Formosa* (Edinburgh, Oliphant, Anderson & Ferrier, 1907, pp. 253); Campbell N. Moody, *The Saints of Formosa. Life and Worship in a Chinese Church* (Edinburgh, Oliphant, Anderson & Ferrier, 1912, pp. 251).

[618] Mrs. Howard Taylor, *One of China's Scholars. The Early Life and Conversion of Pastor Hsi* (London, Morgan and Scott, 10th impression, 1909, pp. ix, 196); Mrs. Howard Taylor, *Pastor Hsi (of North China). One of China's Christians* (London, Morgan and Scott, 12th ed., 1908, pp. xxii, 398).

riddle of life in the faiths with which he was familiar. Discouraged, he took to opium and largely lost his grip on himself. He then came in touch with the Wesleyan missionary saint, David Hill. Hill had come to Shansi, Hsi's native province, to help fight the famine of the 1870's. Through contact with Hill, Hsi became a Christian, was freed by his faith from the opium habit, became reconciled to his estranged brothers, brought back the stepmother whom he had driven away, and by his simple trust in prayer saw his wife healed from the strange malady described as' demon possession. He laboured to win others to his new faith, developed refuges in which opium addicts could be freed from their slavery to the drug, and wrote hymns which were long used. He and his wife denied themselves all but the bare necessities of life that the work to which he had given himself might go on. We hear of a Chinese who before his conversion had been a pugilist and had made many enemies, but who, after he became a Christian, refused to complain to the magistrate when he was attacked and later won some of his foemen to the Christian faith.[619] We read of the head of a community of Buddhist monks who became a Christian through reading one of the Gospels, won freedom from opium, and became a successful pastor.[620] There is the story of a woman who when past seventy years of age found in the Christian faith the inward peace which she had been seeking for forty years through asceticism and religious practices.[621] In Kiukiang was a Christian hospital in which the physicians were two Chinese women, Ida Kahn, adopted as a child by a missionary and educated in America, and Mary Stone, daughter of a Methodist pastor, and also educated in the United States.[622] Theirs were lives of devoted service. These instances could be multiplied.[623] It was not in every professed Christian that the faith had such striking fruits, but enough were of that quality to demonstrate that Christianity was having in China its characteristic results in individual lives.

An obvious effect of Christianity was the planting and the growth of churches. In 1914 they were still for the most part alien enclaves. To be sure, they were

[619] Goforth, By My Spirit, pp. 110, 111.
[620] Marshall Broomhall, In Quest of God. The Life Story of Pastors Chang and Ch'u, Buddhist Priest and Chinese Scholar (London, The China Inland Mission, preface 1921, pp. ix, 190).
[621] Taylor, Guinness of Honan, p. 218.
[622] Margaret E. Burton, Notable Women of Modern China (Chicago, Fleming H. Revell Co., 1912, pp. 271), pp. 115ff.
[623] See a few of them in Burton, op. cit., pp. 15ff.; A Tamarisk Garden Blessed with Rain, or The Autobiography of Pastor Ren translated and edited by Herbert Hudson Taylor and Marshall Broomhall (London, China Inland Mission, 1930, pp. xvii, 228); Gibson, Mission Problems and Mission Methods in South China, pp. 251ff.; Soothill, A Passport to China, pp. 182-189; Taylor, Guinness of Honan, p. 257; and Henry Moule, A Narrative of the Conversion of a Chinese Physician (London, James Nisbet and Co., 2d ed., 1868, pp. x, 101).

made up predominantly of Chinese, but they were largely staffed and almost entirely directed by Westerners, financially they were to a great extent dependent upon the churches of the Occident, and in their organization, methods, architecture, and forms of worship they were in the main reproductions of what missionaries had known in their own homes. However, by 1914 there were indications that they were beginning to take root in Chinese soil. Chinese leadership was being trained by both Roman Catholics and Protestants. Here and there in Protestant circles it was coming to the fore. Numbers of Protestant congregations were becoming self-supporting. After 1914 in both Roman Catholic and Protestant folds the transfer of direction to Chinese and the adaptation to the Chinese environment were to be very rapid. These developments were made possible by the foundation-laying of the pre-1914 years.

Upon the non-Christian religions of China Christianity had very slight effect. That was partly because the most widely spread of these faiths were too nearly moribund to send forth new movements in response to Christian competition. On the eve of 1914 Confucianism was being dealt severe blows. The cancellation of the civil service examinations carried with it the demise of the time-honoured educational system which had prepared candidates for these tests and so removed the chief formal agency for the perpetuation of Confucianism. The coming of the republic in 1911-1912 brought to an end the political structure with which Confucianism had been intimately associated. After 1912 an attempt was made to revive Confucianism as a state and private cult,[624] but that was short-lived. The ideas, ethics, and social structure of the land still bore the impress of the Confucian mould and presumably would do so for generations, but Confucianism as an organized system was dying almost without a struggle. Buddhism had been in recession since the T'ang Dynasty, or approximately for a thousand years, and Taoism was in even worse case. Animism and a popular syncretic polytheism were still flourishing but had little prospect of continuing vigour when once the acids of Western materialism and science became strong. Islam persisted, but only among a minority. No such new movements as yet had come out of the ancient religions in response to Christianity and the impact of the West as had emerged in India. Not far from 1914, but in most instances after rather than before that year, there were fresh stirrings of life in Buddhism, a little quickening in Taoism, and the emergence of syncretistic cults. In some of these Christianity was clearly a factor.[625] Yet in the cultural revolution which was ever more accelerated after 1914, the disintegration of the old faiths, except possibly Islam, proceeded apace. The syncretistic cults flour-

[624] *The China Mission Year Book,* 1914, pp. 61-72.
[625] Hodous in Stauffer, *The Christian Occupation of China,* pp. 27-31.

ished for a brief day and waned. Only Christianity more than held its own and grew in numbers and strength.

Upon the phases of Chinese life which were not, in the formal sense of that word, primarily religious, Christianity was making an impress. In some this was very marked. In others it was slight. The influence of Christianity was in part due to the fact that Christian missionaries were pioneers in such important aspects of Western culture as education and medicine. Indeed, until after 1895 they were almost the only ones who were introducing them to China. Through them, and especially through education, Christian missions affected not only schools but also the economic and particularly the political life of China. It does not necessarily follow that Christianity permeated with its ideals these facets of Chinese life. It means primarily that it was largely through Christian mission-aries that many ideas and processes of Western provenance first obtained cur-rency in China. To a certain extent Christian ideals accompanied them, but this was often very slight.

In the mediation of Western culture to China Protestants were much more prominent than Roman Catholics. This was in accord with the record of the missions of these two great branches of Christianity among most non-European peoples in the nineteenth century.

We must note that Christian missions were by no means the only channel through which Western civilization came to China. The foreign merchant, shipping, and banking communities in the ports were also important. It was they who created much of the demand for the education which the missionary gave, for in the foreign firms many of the graduates of the mission schools could find lucrative employment. Through them, too, came the products of Occidental factories and Western business methods. The fact that in the nine-teenth century British commercial interests were dominant gave particular value to the English language and so reinforced Protestant education. Yet in some features of Western culture Christian and especially Protestant missions were long the most prominent pioneers, even after 1895.

Some of the outstanding contributions of Christian missions have become apparent in the narratives of the preceding pages. The new medical profession of China which employed Western procedures was almost entirely the creation of Christian and especially of Protestant missions. It was missionaries who built and maintained the first hospitals and dispensaries of an Occidental type and who founded the first medical schools. Through missionaries came the nursing profession which, as we have seen,[626] was so deeply indebted in its Western beginnings to Christianity. Missionaries were forerunners in public health edu-

[626] Vol. IV, p. 153.

cation.[627] It was Christian missionaries who were the chief pioneers in schools of Western form, both for boys and for girls. By stressing the education of girls through schools in a fashion unknown to the old China they prepared the way, not only for the later widespread use of schools for girls, but also for a women's movement. Missionaries, too, by example pointed the way to teaching the blind to read and to institutional care of the insane and of lepers. They reinforced Chinese effort to curb the use of opium and to free opium addicts of their habit. They aided in administering famine relief and, notably in the case of Roman Catholics, in the care of orphans. By their translations missionaries helped to introduce Chinese to various aspects of Western literature.

In addition to the contributions which have previously been recorded, Christianity had other effects. Periodicals published by missionaries not only acquainted the educated Chinese with much of the spirit of Western civilization. They also provided models which influenced Chinese magazines when these began to appear.[628] A former student in the school maintained by the Morrison Education Society and taught by Samuel R. Brown, Tong Chik (better known as Tong King-sing), formed the China Merchants Steam Navigation Company, the first Chinese venture in a steam shipping corporation, and is said to have inspired the construction of China's first native-built railroad and her first modern coal mines.[629] Yung Wing, another student of that school, after graduating from Yale, brought about the inauguration of the Educational Mission through which the Chinese Government sent over a hundred youths to school in the United States.[630] When these lads returned to China they were for a time looked at askance by the conservative and were discriminated against. Eventually, however, from among them were those who were prominent as officers of China's first modern navy and who as engineers built railways and telegraph lines and developed mines. Some of them became politically influential in the later years of the empire and the first years of the Republic.[631]

The political effects of the influences which came through Christian missionaries were spectacular and wide-reaching.

Of these one proved tragic. It was what is usually designated as the T'ai P'ing Rebellion.[632] It had as its central figure Hung Hsiu-ch'üan. Hung was

[627] For instance, the Honan Public Health Association was founded largely at the instance of Whitfield Guinness of the China Inland Mission.—Taylor, *Guinness of Honan*, p. 225.
[628] Britton, *The Chinese Periodical Press*, p. 61.
[629] La Fargue, *China's First Hundred*, pp. 19, 20; Morse, *The International Relations of the Chinese Empire*, Vol. II, p. 315.
[630] La Fargue, *op. cit.*, pp. 23ff.; Yung Wing, *My Life in China and America*, pp. 173ff.
[631] La Fargue, *op. cit.*, pp. 67ff.
[632] The best account of the T'ai P'ing movement is William James Hail, *Tsêng Kuo-fan*

a Hakka, from a village in Kwangtung not far from Canton. He was one of thousands of ambitious but unsuccessful scholar aspirants for honours and office through the civil service examinations. He was brought in touch with Christianity in the 1830's through pamphlets written by Liang A-fa, one of the earliest Protestant converts. In an illness there came to him visions which he interpreted in the light of these books and which he believed were a divine commission to win the Chinese from idolatry to the worship of the Christian God.[633] Out of his preaching and that of his earliest converts there arose, at first chiefly in mountainous Kwangsi, a new religious movement. In the original membership Hakka peasants and Miao (a non-Chinese tribal folk) predominated. In the 1840's Hung had personal contacts with Protestant missionaries and from them obtained additional instruction in Christianity. In the 1840's, by steps which are now somewhat obscure, the religious movement took on a political complexion. It was organized into an army which sought to unseat the Manchus and to set up a new dynasty which was to be known by the name of T'ai P'ing, or "Great Peace." Hung was to be Emperor. The title proved a ghastly misnomer. The T'ai P'ing army came into conflict with the imperial authorities. It moved northward in a victorious course to the Yangtze, and in 1852 and 1853 captured the strategic Wu-han cities (Hanyang, Hankow, and Wuchang). Thence it turned eastward down the river, taking the main ports as it went and establishing its capital at Nanking. The T'ai P'ing forces attempted to win control over the North and fought their way across the Yellow River. However, they seem never seriously to have threatened Peking. For some years they were devastating masters of much of the valley of the lower Yangtze. It was not until 1864 that the imperial armies were able to take Nanking and break the back of the rebellion. Hung committed suicide a few days before the fall of the city. In the meantime hundreds of thousands, probably millions, had perished, many of them in battle, and more from marauders, famine, and disease. To the end the T'ai P'ing regime displayed some outward aspects of the Christian elements which had entered into its birth and growth.

and the Taiping Rebellion (Yale University Press, 1927, pp. xvii, 422). See also Wilhelm Oehler, *Die Taiping-Bewegung* (Gütersloh, C. Bertelsmann, 1923, pp. 174), Thomas Taylor Meadows, *The Chinese and Their Rebellions* (London, Smith, Elder & Co., 1856, pp. 137ff.), [A. F. Lindley], Lin-le, *Ti-ping Tien-kwoh; the History of the Ti-ping Revolution* (London, Day & Son, 2 vols., 1866), Lindesey Brine, *The Taeping Rebellion in China* (London, John Murray, 1862, pp. xv, 394), H. B. Morse, *In the Days of the Taipings. Being the Recollections of Ting Kienchang, otherwise Meisun, sometime Scoutmaster and Captain in the Ever-Victorious Army* (Salem, The Essex Institute, 1927, pp. xii, 434).

[633] The nearest approach to a first hand account of the earliest stages of Hung's religious experience is in Theodore Hamberg, *The Visions of Hung-Siu-Tshuen* (Hongkong, 1854). Another and somewhat different account is in W. E. Soothill, *China and the West* (Oxford University Press, 1925, pp. viii, 216), pp. 139, 140.

Indeed, for a time several Protestant missionaries had high hopes that it would be the beginning of the mass conversion of the empire.[634] One of the outstanding leaders of the rebellion had been employed as an evangelist under the London Missionary Society.[635] Several of the missionaries visited Nanking or other T'ai P'ing centres for longer or shorter periods. All, however, returned disillusioned.[636] The T'ai P'ing Rebellion was one in a long succession of movements in China which combined economic and social unrest with religious features and political aspirations. Unlike its predecessors, it contained Christian elements. Presumably but for contacts with Christian missionaries it would not have come into being. Yet among its ingredients those of Christian provenance were in the minority. Here was one of those social-political-religious movements which we have found in various lands in the nineteenth century on the fringes of the expansion of Christianity and which were in part indebted to that faith but were chiefly made up of other constituents.[637] It was the most extensive of these movements, but it was by no means isolated.

The second political movement in China which can be traced in part to Christianity was that which led to the attempt to reorganize the government in 1898 and which had the young Emperor Kuang Hsü as its leader. A chief adviser to Kuang Hsü was K'ang Yu-wei. K'ang Yu-wei was not a Christian, but he declared that he owed his conversion to reform chiefly to the writings of two missionaries, Timothy Richard and Young J. Allen.[638]

More lasting and far-reaching was the inauguration of the republic in 1911 and 1912 with Sun Yat-sen as the chief figure. Through Sun Yat-sen and his warm friend and supporter Charles Jones Soong, together with some less prominent leaders, Christianity contributed largely to the political reshaping of China. Most of the fruitage did not appear until after 1914 and we must, accordingly, revert to it in our final volume. However, it began on the eve of 1914 and we must here note the early contributions of Christianity. Sun Yat-sen had greater influence upon China during the first half of the twentieth century than any other of his fellow-countrymen.[639] He was born in 1866, the son of a farmer, in a village about thirty miles north of Macao. In his boyhood he was

[634] Findlay and Holdsworth, *The History of the Wesleyan Methodist Missionary Society*, Vol. V, pp. 460, 461; Legge, *James Legge*, pp. 93, 94, 97.

[635] Legge, *op. cit.*, pp. 91ff.

[636] Findlay and Holdsworth, *op. cit.*, Vol. V, pp. 461, 462.

[637] As in Vol. IV, p. 322, Vol. V, pp. 128, 183, 268, 361. See also in Vol. VI, Chap. 3, the movement of Daud Birsa in Chota Nagpur.

[638] Peake, *Nationalism and Education in Modern China*, p. 15.

[639] The best account in English of Sun Yat-sen's life is Lyon Sharman, *Sun Yat-sen* (New York, The John Day Co., 1934, pp. xvii, 418). It is from this that much of the paragraph is taken.

taken to Honolulu by an older brother and placed in a school maintained by the Anglicans.[640] There he came in contact with Christianity and wished to be baptized. His brother forbade that step, but the young Sun Yat-sen carried with him to China an English Bible. Back in his native village he came in touch with another Chinese youth who had been away, in this case to Shanghai, and had there become a Christian. The two were imbued with new ideas and Sun Yat-sen, possessed by scorn for the use of idols, defaced an image in the village temple. He went to Hongkong and for a time was in the diocesan school maintained by the Anglicans. He also studied in Queen's College in Hongkong. While in Hongkong he was baptized by a representative of the American Board of Commissioners for Foreign Missions. He was active in spreading his new faith. In 1886-1887 he studied medicine with Kerr in the school attached to that Canton Hospital which had been founded by Peter Parker. He prepared further for the medical profession in Hongkong in a school connected with a hospital of the London Missionary Society [641] and was graduated in 1892. For a time he practised in Macao, but he was more concerned with reshaping China and soon devoted his energies fully to revolutionary propaganda. It was this course which brought him, late in 1911, to the presidency of the provisional Chinese Republic and later made him the patron saint of the new political order. How far he was impelled and sustained by his Christian faith and how far his ideals were moulded by Christian standards it would be impossible to determine. However, his hunger for Western learning was aroused and nourished in schools all but one of which were maintained by the Christian churches and it was in them that his formal education was acquired. His home in Shanghai was that of Charles Jones Soong, an even more earnest Christian.[642] Soong was the financial head of the revolutionary movement.[643] That Christianity not only provided the means by which these men obtained their education but also contributed to the shaping of their purposes and helped sustain them in their struggles seems clear. Through them it was an important factor in remaking China politically.

We have thus far spoken of the effect of Christianity upon China by way of its missions. How far did Christianity make itself felt through the mercantile and diplomatic communities from the Occident? At first sight it would seem that these were more of a hindrance than a help to Christianity. "East of Suez" the morals nurtured in Westerners by an environment in which Christianity

[640] On the Hawaiian years see Henry Bond Restarick, *Sun Yat-sen* (Yale University Press, 1931, pp. xvii, 167), pp. 1-54.

[641] Neil Cantlie and George Seaver, *Sir James Cantlie* (London, John Murray, 1939, pp. xxviii, 279), pp. 96-118; James Cantlie and C. Sheridan Jones, *Sun Yat Sen and the Awakening of China* (Chicago, Fleming H. Revell Co., 3d ed., 1912, pp. 252), pp. 27-35.

[642] Burke, *My Father in China*, pp. 261-265.

[643] Brockman, *I Discover the Orient*, p. 31.

was an important constituent seemed to disintegrate. Yet on more careful examination it becomes clear that many Western merchants and diplomats preserved their Christian faith and tried to give expression to it in their intercourse with the Chinese. We hear, for example, of an American who went to China in connexion with a mercantile house with the express purpose of giving his spare time to religious activities. For a period he was in charge of the American consulate in Shanghai and in that post refused to condone the traffic in coolies.[644] He was an exception but by no means the only one. D. Matheson, once a partner in Jardine, Matheson and Company, one of the prominent British firms in the China trade, resigned from the company because it was engaged in the opium traffic. Later he was chairman of the executive committee of the Society for the Suppression of the Opium Trade and was a member of the Committee on Foreign Missions of the English Presbyterian Church.[645] D. W. C. Olyphant, a prominent American merchant in pre-treaty days, was a devout Christian active in many good works on behalf of China.[646] Anson Burlingame, reared in an earnest Methodist home, as Minister from the United States to China so won the esteem of the officials of the empire for his fairness and freedom from race prejudice that he was asked to head the first diplomatic mission from Peking to Western powers. In that capacity he pled for generous treatment of that realm.[647] The list might be greatly extended.

The Chinese environment was beginning to have its effect upon Christianity. As yet this was not notable in the organization, creeds, or forms of worship of the churches. To be sure, in theory recognition was given to the desirability of freeing Christianity from its foreign trappings. Hudson Taylor, for instance, wished to see Chinese churches under their own pastors, "worshipping in edifices of a thoroughly Chinese style of architecture." [648] By 1914 the active adaptation had not proceeded very far beyond the stage of discussion,[649] but in more subtle and perhaps more important and wide reaching ways the environment was already laying its impress upon the imported faith. Roman Catholics and some Protestants were adopting a Chinese method of maintaining religious

[644] F. Booth Tucker, *Freeman of Shanghai* (London, Marshall Brothers, 1928, pp. 224), *passim.*
[645] *State Papers of Great Britain, China,* No. 3, 1868-9, p. 24; *First Report of the Royal Commission on Opium,* London, 1894, pp. 57-59, 164.
[646] *Dictionary of American Biography,* Vol. XIV, p. 34.
[647] Frederick Wells Williams, *Anson Burlingame and the First Chinese Mission to Foreign Powers* (New York, Charles Scribner's Sons, 1912, pp. x, 370), *passim,* especially pp. 4, 5.
[648] Broomhall, *Hudson Taylor's Legacy,* p. 16.
[649] *The Chinese Recorder,* Vol. XXXIII, pp. 587ff., Vol. XXXVII, pp. 295ff., Vol. XL, pp. 195ff.

establishments by building up endowments in land. Some missionaries were having their inherited beliefs modified by their contacts with Chinese. Impressed with the fine character of many non-Christian Chinese and by admirable features in Chinese ethics, they came to the conviction which was to them a soul-shaking discovery, that God had been in China before they arrived.[650] The fact, too, that Christianity had such marked effects upon the political and educational life of China may be' associated with the conviction long engrained in Chinese life that a religion or philosophy was to be judged by its ability to produce a better society here and now and with the high premium placed by Chinese upon education. It may be significant that in India, with its traditional prizing of mysticism and other-worldliness, Christianity gave rise to Sadhu Sundar Singh and that in China, as in no other non-Occidental land, it contributed to political and social movements which affected the entire nation. The fact that both Roman Catholics and Protestants were slow to place Chinese in positions of leadership in the Church and to develop deliberate adaptations to Chinese traditions appears to be associated with the temper of the Western imperialism which was prominent in China in political and economic realms. The age was one in which Occidentals were aggressive and triumphant and viewed non-Occidentals, including the Chinese, with disdain. Usually only half consciously but no less strikingly this attitude was reflected in the relations of missionaries with Chinese, in the position of the foreigner in the Church, and in the views taken by missionaries of Chinese culture and customs. It may be, moreover, that the prominence of Presbyterians in China was partly to be attributed to the congeniality of the Chinese village and family structure to the Presbyterian type of organization. It is clear that in 1914 Presbyterians of various branches had ,more missionaries and communicants in China than any other confessional group of Protestants. Only the undenominational China Inland Mission exceeded them in numbers of missionaries. Even it did not begin to equal them in Chinese membership. Baptists and Methodists, prominent in India through mass movements from the depressed classes and aborigines, in China were proportionately not so outstanding. This may have been in part because in China no such extensive submerged proletariat existed as in India. However, these less tangible influences of environment must of necessity be in large degree conjectural and beyond accurate measurement.

At the dawn of the nineteenth century the outlook for Christianity in the Chinese Empire was decidedly unpromising. Here was a vast area with the

650 Brockman, *I Discover the Orient, passim.*

largest single block of population in the globe of its day. Its core was China proper, where the overwhelming majority lived, the largest fairly homogeneous group of mankind which the world had thus far seen. Around China proper, on the land side, like great buffer areas warding against contamination from without, were Tibet, Sinkiang, Mongolia, and Manchuria, sparsely populated, mainly by non-Chinese, but under the supervision of Peking. China proper was knit together into a political, social, and ideological structure based upon Confucianism which was seemingly impervious to a foreign faith. To be sure, Buddhism and Islam, foreign importations, were present, and Taoism, a native faith, had survived. But Buddhism had achieved its position over a thousand years before when Confucianism had not been so strong and in an era when the realm was divided politically. Moreover, it had been waning for nearly a millennium and was moribund. Taoism was even more feeble. Islam was represented by small minorities, largely descendants of immigrants of that faith and those in close contact with them. Thrice Christianity had entered China. On the first occasion it had been present for centuries but had been unable to make headway and had disappeared. The second time it had existed in the empire for at least a century but had vanished. The third time it had been propagated, beginning in the sixteenth century, by earnest Roman Catholic missionaries, but, after a few decades of prosperity, had suffered reverses and in A.D. 1800 apparently was on the way to slow extinction. It was persecuted, and reinforcements to the missionary staff found it extraordinarily difficult to make their way into the country. At Peking there were a few Russian Orthodox Christians, connected with the empire of the Czars by a small trickle of trade and diplomatic intercourse. Westerners who came by sea were restricted to Canton and Macao and at Canton residence and commerce were closely circumscribed. The hypothetical traveller from Mars, if he had noticed Christianity at all, would probably have predicted for it a lingering but quite uninfluential demise.

The situation was late in becoming more favourable for Christianity. The impact of the expanding Occident which was making itself felt elsewhere in the world did not become particularly potent until about the middle of the century and not until almost the end of the century did the solid structure of Chinese culture begin to show many signs of yielding. In 1839-1842 an attack by the major commercial and colonial power of the century, Great Britain, forced the doors slightly ajar. A second war with Great Britain, in 1856-1860, in which France joined hands with that ancient rival in the effort to gain additional favourable provisions for the foreigner, made possible more of residence and travel, ushered the reluctant China into a partial membership in the family of nations, and wrung from her a grudging promise of toleration for the Christian missionary and his converts. In 1895, following a war between China and Japan in which the latter won an easy victory, the solid fabric of Chinese culture at last began to disintegrate. Further humiliating experiences with foreign powers accelerated the debacle. China had the misfortune to be in the hands of a decadent semi-alien dynasty. With incompetent leadership at the top it stumbled into a revolution more extensive and thoroughgoing than it had ever before known. In the course of the next few years every phase of its traditional life began to crumble. The old educational system which had sustained its intellectual, social, moral, and political structure was abolished. The ancient imperial form of government was swept aside and an attempt at an Occidental device, a republic, was made. Confucianism was ceasing to be the established philosophy. The family and the economic order yielded more slowly but were clearly weakening.

This crumbling China became a field for a rapidly growing Christian missionary enterprise from the West. The rising tide of missionary devotion in the churches of the Occident which the nineteenth century witnessed found in China a challenging outlet. Roman Catholics, Russian Orthodox, and Protestants came. The Russian Orthodox were numerically unimportant. The chief gains were by Roman Catholics and Protestants. Roman Catholics were mainly from the continent of Europe and chiefly from France. For much of the century they were under the protection of the French Government. They placed their chief emphasis upon winning converts and nourishing a church. Protestants were mostly from the British Isles and the United States, with the latter forging to the fore near the end of the century. There were also representatives of Continental European Protestant forces and a few from Canada, Australia, and New Zealand. Protestants were from all the major and some of the minor denominational families. Through the great China Inland Mission a type of Evangelicalism very strong in Anglo-Saxon lands in the nineteenth century was prominently represented. Protestant efforts were directed through a number of channels and for a group of objectives. The Bible was translated again and again and was widely distributed. Other Christian literature was produced. Converts were won and churches assembled and nourished. Protestants were pioneers in Western medicine and public health and in Occidental types of education. They sought to reach every Chinese with the Christian message. Many of the Protestants also endeavoured to help reshape all of Chinese life wholesomely and to build Christianity into the fabric of the new China which was so painfully emerging.

As a result of these conditions and these efforts Christianity enjoyed the most striking growth which it had had at any time in China's history. Part of this was numerical. In A.D. 1914 Christians totalled not far from two millions, of whom about five-sixths were Roman Catholics and approximately one-sixth were Protestants. The vast majority were in China proper. There were substantial minorities in Manchuria and the parts of Mongolia which bordered on China proper, but only an inappreciable few in Sinkiang and Tibet and still fewer, if any, in Outer Mongolia.

Upon the life of the country as a whole Protestantism, while numerically much smaller, was making a much greater impression than was Roman Catholicism. It was contributing notably to the emergence of a new educational and intellectual life, it was creating a medical and nursing profession, was potent politically, and was inaugurating fresh ways of helping with public health, agriculture, and the care of the blind, the deaf, and the insane. Christianity, both Roman Catholic and Protestant, was fighting famine and opium.

In A.D. 1914 the effect of China on Christianity was as yet not particularly obvious. The churches still were under foreign leadership and preserved their Western forms of organization, programmes, means of financial support, and worship. Roman Catholic orders and congregations from the Occident and Protestant denominations of Western origin projected themselves into the Chinese scene. Protestants were beginning to come together in local and nation-wide co-operation. Both Roman Catholics and Protestants were training Chinese leadership. In the pronounced effects of Protestant Christianity in the realms of education, philanthropic and medical service, and in politics, the currents of Christian influence were being directed into channels congenial to Confucian ideals. Yet Christianity was still largely alien. Not until the post-1914 years was it to become in part acclimatized and deeply rooted in Chinese life.

Already, in A.D. 1914, in spite of its late revival and reinforcement, Christianity was becoming prominent in China. In a land whose ancient culture was rapidly disintegrating and where sensitive and thoughtful souls were dismayed and bewildered by the disappearance of the familiar and the presence of growing chaos, Christianity was bringing elements of hope. It was acquainting China with some of the more constructive features of Western life. It was also helping individuals to victory over their weaker selves and the chronic problems attendant upon individual existence and to unselfish, hopeful effort for the building of a new China. China was in the throes of a great revolution. They might be either the death struggle of a noble civilization or the birth pangs of a new and better order. Christianity was contributing to the death of the old. It was also, and even more significantly, introducing creative impulses which could help to make that death the precursor to a higher life.

Chapter VI

JAPAN. INTRODUCTORY: ROMAN CATHOLIC CHRISTIANITY: THE RUSSIAN ORTHODOX CHURCH: PROTESTANTISM: EFFECT ON THE ENVIRONMENT: EFFECT OF THE ENVIRONMENT: SUMMARY

IN JAPAN in A.D. 1800 the outlook for Christianity was even more grim than in China. In China Christianity, while persecuted, was nurtured by European priests and thus was kept in touch, although tenuously, with the main body of Christians in the West. Moreover, there were Chinese clergy and young men were being trained to fill their ranks. In Japan, in contrast, Christianity, while still in existence, had long since been driven underground and for generations had been without the service of clergy, either foreign or indigenous.[1] In both countries Christianity was illegal, but in Japan anti-Christian measures were much more vigorously and persistently carried out than in China. Edict boards denouncing the faith were widely posted. Moreover, Japan was more nearly sealed against the Westerner than was China. In the latter country Macao constituted an Occidental enclave and merchants of all lands were permitted to carry on commerce, although under irksome restrictions and through only one port, Canton. A small Russian mission was tolerated in Peking. In Japan no alien territorial foothold was allowed. Only one Western people, the Dutch, were admitted to trade, and they merely at one port, Nagasaki, and under more galling and confining regulations than were Westerners at Canton. Hundreds of Chinese went abroad and in ports under European control were accessible to Christianity. Japan's rulers did not consent to any of their subjects' going abroad. If by evil accident, as happened on occasion, fishermen were driven by adverse winds to foreign lands, their return was prohibited. It was from the desire to exclude Christianity that the house which controlled Japan through the Shogunate, the Tokugawa, had sealed the country against the Occident. The Tokugawa had come to view the faith as a threat to Japan's unity and independence. In what they deemed the interest of the nation and of their

[1] Vol. III, pp. 333, 334.

own power they had taken every possible precaution to see that it did not again enter.[2]

The nineteenth century Christian missionary movement was much later in making itself felt than it was in China. In China reinforcements began coming to the diminished Roman Catholic staffs not long after the end of the Napoleonic Wars. Indeed, during that conflict some succeeded in entering. In the first decade of the century Protestant missions gained a foothold. By the middle of the century six centres open to foreign trade had in them substantial groups of missionaries, both Roman Catholic and Protestant, who were reaching out into the surrounding areas. The Bible had been translated and was being circulated. Hospitals and schools had been opened. Already, in a variety of ways, notably in the tragic T'ai P'ing movement, Christianity was having an effect upon the land. In Japan Christian missionaries did not gain an entrance until shortly past the middle of the century. China, under duress, made her first treaties with Western powers in the 1840's. Japan did not grant her first treaties until the following decade.

When Japan once opened her doors she adopted Western culture more quickly than did China. During the second half of the century, while China was endeavouring to hold the Westerner at arm's length, Japan was feverishly acquiring much of Occidental civilization. To a certain extent this made for a rapid acceptance of Christianity by some of those most affected by the new day.

However, while outwardly taking over much from the West, the main fabric of Japan's political and social institutions and of her ideals remained substantially intact. The West was not without its effect, but it was long in working a basic revolution. Indeed, in some respects resistance to Christianity was accentuated by the transformation. The traditional religions of Japan, Buddhism and Shinto, persisted. Shinto, which deified national heroes, the Emperor, and Japan itself, was revived and greatly strengthened. A form of it had the active support of the state. It was inculcated through formal and informal education. Confucianism suffered, but the family system which owed so much to it went on. Nationalism, already vigorous, was reinforced by contact with the nineteenth century Occident. It centred about the Emperor. For a time and among some groups patriotic pride, in an effort to obtain the respect of the West and in an uncritical attempt at making Japan Occidental, facilitated the spread of Christianity, for it regarded that faith as an integral part of European and American life. Usually, however, Shinto, ethnocentrism, and the special veneration for the Emperor proved an obstacle to the acceptance of Christianity. Since by its nature it is supranational and demands primary and supreme al-

[2] Vol. III, pp. 331-333.

legiance to God as revealed in Jesus Christ, Christianity seemed derogatory to the Japanese super-patriots. To them the Japanese were a peculiarly superior people and they would brook no rival to their Emperor.

In contrast, in China after 1895 the cultural revolution proceeded apace. All phases of Chinese life crumbled. This meant lessened resistance to the Christian faith.

In the Middle Kingdom, moreover, Christian missions were long the pioneers of features of Western civilization which the Chinese eventually avidly adopted. As such, they contributed markedly and over a number of decades to the shaping of the new culture. Many of the outstanding leaders of twentieth century China were, accordingly, Christian. In Japan, while in some aspects of life Christian missionaries were the tutors in Western ways, the state early took the initiative in introducing Occidental methods and the period of Christian pioneering was briefer.

For these several reasons by A.D. 1914 Christianity had made much less progress in Japan than in China.

Yet in the nineteenth century Japan's Christians were recruited for the most part from influential circles. To a large extent they came from those groups which had felt most profoundly the changes brought by the West. Numbers of the converts were *samurai,* of the ranks of the military class which enjoyed especial privilege under the feudal regime on which the power of the Tokugawa was based. Among the youths from the *samurai* were those who were attracted by the West and eagerly sought Occidental learning. Many of them acquired that learning through missionaries as the most accessible source. In doing so some became Christians. Moreover, with the abolishment of feudalism in the 1870's the structure which supported the *samurai* crumbled. Members of that class were, accordingly, cast adrift. With the familiar patterns of life and the customary sources of income gone, the *samurai* were more open to the Christian message than they would otherwise have been. From the new professions which sprang up from contact with the West thousands became Christians. These professions included teachers, physicians, engineers, some business men, and their families. They were peculiarly susceptible to influences from the Occident, for it was to them that they owed the demand for their training and of necessity their education was largely of an Occidental type. Some among them obtained their preparation through Christian missionaries. It was presumably for these reasons that Christians, and notably Protestant Christians, were found largely in the cities and from the middle and upper middle classes.

In the nineteenth century Christianity came to Japan in three major forms. Roman Catholic Christianity was reintroduced. This was almost exclusively by missionaries from the continent of Europe and chiefly by the French, who were the most active of the predominantly Roman Catholic peoples both in the building of an overseas empire and in spreading the Christian faith. Russian Orthodox Christianity was propagated, partly through the zeal of a remarkable missionary and partly in association with Russian imperial expansion in the Far East. Several varieties of Protestant Christianity entered. A few were from the continent of Europe and some were from the British Isles, but the large majority were from the United States. It was through representatives of the government of the United States that Japan was induced to come out of her seclusion and to negotiate her first treaties with Westerners. It was in the 1840's that the United States was first bringing its borders effectively to the Pacific. A little later, in 1867 in the purchase of Alaska and in 1898 in the acquisition of the Philippines, Guam, and Hawaii, territorially the United States was moving into the western Pacific. Americans were, therefore, particularly interested in Japan, which of all the great Asiatic nations was nearest to their country. For years they took a peculiar pride in having introduced her to the family of nations and many of them had a feeling of opportunity and responsibility for bringing Christianity to her. Chiefly under the impulse given by missionaries from the United States, Protestantism became more important numerically and more influential in the life of Japan than did either of the other two types of Christianity.

As their missions revived after the Napoleonic Wars, Roman Catholics viewed longingly the land where such striking successes had been witnessed in the sixteenth century and where the seventeenth century had brought such a galaxy of martyrs. In 1832 the Holy See, when creating a vicariate apostolic for Korea, expressed 'the desire to see the mission to Japan resumed. However, since the appointee to the new post was unable to make his way even into Korea, all thought of Japan had for the moment to be postponed.[3] Not far from 1830 twenty Japanese shipwrecked on the Philippines were said to have Christian medals whose use they did not know. Seventeen of the twenty were given Christian instruction and baptized.[4] After the first Anglo-Chinese War brought an increase of Occidental power in the Far East, the Société des Missions Étrangères of Paris looked hopefully towards Japan. In 1844 one of its missionaries, Théodore Augustin Forcade, with a Chinese catechist, took advantage of the presence of a French man-of-war to gain access to the Ryu Kyu (or Liu

[3] Marnas, La "Religion de Jesus" (Iaso Ja-kyō) Ressuscitée au Japon, Vol. I, p. 78.
[4] Annales de la Propagation de la Foi, Vol. IX, pp. 280, 281.

Ch'iu) Islands, which had connexions with both China and Japan but were not fully under the control of either.[5] In 1846 Rome created a vicariate apostolic for Japan and placed Forcade at its head.[6] That year Forcade accompanied a French naval expedition which went to Nagasaki in an attempt to enter Japan. However, rebuffed by the Japanese, the ships, with Forcade, retired without achieving their purpose. Forcade went to France in an effort to obtain more effective support. For a time he administered the Vicariate Apostolic of Hongkong.[7] The mission on the Ryu Kyu Islands proved discouraging and with the death of the lone missionary (1848) was suspended.[8] Two missionaries of the Société des Missions Étrangères of Paris who in 1848 reached Hongkong with Japan as their destination were constrained to wait for seven years before attaining their objective.[9] Before that interval had elapsed, Forcade, ill, found it necessary to return to Europe.[10] His successor, Charles Emile Colin, also of the Paris society, but with the title of prefect apostolic rather than vicar apostolic, died (1854) before he could leave Manchuria, where he had been a missionary.[11] In 1855 three missionaries who had been preparing for service in Japan went to the Ryu Kyu Islands. There they encountered great restrictions and their first convert disappeared soon after his baptism, presumably killed by the enemies of Christianity.[12]

In 1858 a somewhat better day dawned. In that year a treaty of commerce between Japan and France was signed which among other provisions opened three ports, Hakodate, Nagasaki, and Kanagawa, to French residence, permitted to the French the free exercise in these ports of their religion, including the erection of churches and chapels, and declared that the Japanese Government had abolished in the realm all practices injurious to Christianity.[13] This treaty was in part made possible by the success of the French and British arms against China and the fear that if concessions were not made voluntarily to the foreigner they would be exacted at the cannon's mouth. It followed the treaties of 1857 and 1858 obtained by Townsend Harris for the United States. The French treaty pried the door ajar, even if imperfectly, to the Roman Catholic faith. Prudence Séraphin Barthélemy Girard, of the Missions Étrangères of Paris, was named superior of the mission and a few years later was made prefect

[5] Marnas, op. cit., Vol. I, pp. 95ff.
[6] Launay, Histoire Générale de la Société des Missions-Étrangères, Vol. III, p. 206.
[7] Marnas, op. cit., Vol. I, pp. 140-168.
[8] Marnas, op. cit., Vol. I, pp. 169-188.
[9] Marnas, op. cit., Vol. I, p. 191.
[10] Marnas, op. cit., Vol. I, pp 215-232.
[11] Marnas, op. cit., Vol. I, pp. 247, 248.
[12] Marnas, op. cit., Vol. I, pp. 253-263, 279-283.
[13] Marnas, op. cit., Vol. I, pp. 320-326.

apostolic.[14] In 1859 Girard reached Yedo, the later Tokyo, obtaining entrance as interpreter to the French consul general.[15] That same year one of the staff who had acquired a knowledge of the language while in the Ryu Kyu Islands established himself in Hakodate. Before long he was at work on a French-English-Japanese dictionary, had opened a school, and had laid the foundations for a hospital.[16] Girard purchased land at Yokohama (which had early been substituted for Kanagawa as a place for foreign residence) as a site for a chapel and opened a French school in Yedo.[17] However, when a church was erected at Yokohama, the Japanese Government arrested some of its subjects who visited it.[18]

Before many years a startling discovery was made. In Nagasaki, the centre of the strength of the Christianity of the sixteenth and seventeenth centuries, in the fore part of the 1860's the "Church of the Twenty-Six Martyrs" was erected.[19] In March, 1865, not long after the formal dedication of this building, several Japanese presented themselves and declared that they were Christians, descendants of the converts of the earlier centuries. They displayed a knowledge of the names of God, Jesus, the Virgin Mary, and of Joseph, of Christmas and Lent, and of some of the prayers of the Church. They had continued baptism, and the missionaries were able to establish contact with one who made the administration of that sacrament his charge and who a few years before had suffered imprisonment for his faith. The baptismal formula had been per-petuated essentially unaltered. In the mountains back of Nagasaki several Christian villages were disclosed. Usually each village was found to have two leaders, one who presided at the Sunday prayers and brought consolation to the dying, and one who administered baptism. Some Christian books and religious objects had been preserved. Because of the danger of the renewal of persecution, great discretion was observed in visits by the missionaries to the Christians. Yet the visits were made and the Christians, applying to the foreigners the tests of the acknowledgment of the supremacy of the Holy See, the celibacy of the clergy, and the veneration of the Virgin Mary, recognized them as the spiritual suc-cessors to their ancient pastors.[20] As time passed, Christian communities were found in other places, including the Goto Islands, west and north of Nagasaki. Great variety existed in the form of baptism. Sometimes the formula had been said over water which was then sent for distant use and, on occasion, given the

[14] Moidry, *La Hiérarchie Catholique en Chine, en Corée, et au Japon*, p. 165.
[15] Marnas, *op. cit.*, Vol. I, pp. 342, 343.
[16] Marnas, *op. cit.*, Vol. I, pp. 348-352, 379-384.
[17] Marnas, *op. cit.*, Vol. I, pp. 373-377.
[18] Marnas, *op. cit.*, Vol. I, pp. 392-399.
[19] Marnas, *op. cit.*, Vol. I, pp. 475, 479, 483.
[20] Marnas, *op. cit.*, Vol. I, pp. 487ff.

infant to drink. From the Roman Catholic standpoint, many of the marriages were irregular. Non-Christian rites were employed at burials. Numbers of the hereditary Christians submitted to the authority of the French missionaries.[21] A secret Hall of the Immaculate Conception was prepared in Nagasaki .in which Christian rites could be observed. In it a number were given "conditional" baptism, in case their previous baptism had been invalid, and were admitted to communion.[22] On the other hand, not all the Christians were willing to submit to the French priests. Those who conformed to the Roman Catholic faith were said to number about ten thousand. Possibly ten or eleven times as many, while preserving some Christian practices, including Latin and Japanese prayers, remained aloof from the European agents of the Church.[23]

It was not long before persecution broke over the heads of the Christians. The existence of the adherents of the proscribed faith had now been revealed and the laws of the realm were still against them. The first step seems to have been taken in 1867. Christians were arrested, imprisoned, and tortured. The action was protested by diplomatic representatives of the Western powers. Both the American and British Governments had earlier tried to have toleration of Christianity written into the treaties with Japan as it had been in the treaties of 1858 with China. In this they had been unsuccessful. The Shogun, through whom the foreign governments had their relations with Japan, might have been willing, but the Western *daimyo,* who were taking the occasion to make difficulty for the Tokugawa, would have raised such objections that the position of that house would have been made still more precarious.[24] In 1868 the Japanese Imperial Government issued a vigorous edict ordering about four thousand Christians be torn from their homes and distributed in groups of from thirty to two hundred and fifty each among the Western *daimyo.* The latter were directed to induce them to abandon their faith and to punish them if they proved recalcitrant. The number actually deported was much smaller than these totals, but many were imprisoned and several of those incarcerated died. The representatives of the Occidental powers again protested.[25] The Japanese central authorities promised to bring the persecution to an end, but it continued.[26] Indeed, it went on until 1873. Several thousands were put in jail or sent to other parts of the empire. The ministers of the powers continued to

[21] Marnas, *op. cit.,* Vol. I, pp. 531-536.
[22] Marnas, *op. cit.,* Vol. I, pp. 556, 557.
[23] Marnas, *op. cit.,* Vol. II, pp. 234, 235.
[24] Treat, *Diplomatic Relations between the United States and Japan, 1853-1895,* Vol. I, pp. 294-297.
[25] Marnas, *op cit.,* Vol. II, pp. 128-135; Treat, *op. cit.,* Vol. I, pp. 322-325.
[26] Marnas, *op. cit.,* Vol. II, pp. 136ff.

lodge complaints.[27] Finally, in 1873, the Japanese Government commanded that the persecutions be stopped and that the exiles be returned to their homes.[28] One motive seems to have been the desire to obtain the revision of the treaties on terms more favourable to Japan.[29]

The persecutions had not succeeded in stamping out Christianity. To be sure, some Christians apostatized and others, by heredity of that faith, feared openly to identify themselves with the Church. However, Roman Catholic Christianity was gaining in strength. In 1866 Bernard Thaddée Petitjean, who had led in the mission in Nagasaki, was made Vicar Apostolic of Japan.[30] Reinforcements came from the seminary in Paris.[31] Here and there non-Christians were asking Christian instruction.[32] The heroism and fidelity of the Christians under persecution had so impressed some of their captors and others who had seen them, that conversions, including some to Protestantism, could later be traced to this source.[33] On November 1, 1873, Roman Catholics counted in Japan 15,000 of the faithful, 3 churches, 27 oratories, 2 seminaries with 70 students, 7 schools, 2 orphanages, 2 bishops, 29 missionaries, 6 sisters, 227 catechists, and 250 baptizers, and reported during the year the baptism of 120 adult pagans and of 197 children of pagans.[34] The Roman Catholic Church had reclaimed thousands of those who were the descendants of the converts of the sixteenth and seventeenth centuries and in them was obtaining a firm basis for renewed life.

In the years which followed the new leniency of the Japanese Government the Roman Catholic Church enjoyed a fairly steady but not a spectacular growth. In 1876 Japan was divided into two vicariates apostolic.[35] By the end of 1879 there were churches in Tokyo, Osaka, Kobe, Nagasaki, and Yokohama.[36] In the 1870's there arrived nuns of three different congregations—of St. Maur, of the Holy Infant Jesus of Chauffailles, and of St. Paul of Chartres.[37] In 1878

[27] Marnas, op. cit., Vol. II, pp. 172ff.; Treat, op. cit., Vol. I, p. 355; Cary, A History of Christianity in Japan, Vol. I, pp. 308-331.

[28] Marnas, op. cit., Vol. II, pp. 258ff.

[29] Cary, op. cit., Vol. I, p. 330; Marnas, op. cit., Vol. II, pp. 217ff.

[30] Moidry, op. cit., p. 167. For a life of Petitjean see J. B. Chaillet, Mgr Petitjean 1829-1884 et la Résurrection Catholique au Japon au XIXe Siècle (Montceaules-mines, M. Ph. Chaillet, 1919, pp. 446).

[31] Marnas, op. cit., Vol. II, p. 272. For the reminiscences of one who sailed for Japan in 1866 and which covered much of the course of the revived Roman Catholic Christianity in that country, see A. Villion, Cinquante Ans d'Apostolat au Japon (Hongkong, Imprimerie de la Société des Missions Étrangères, 1923, pp. 489, iii).

[32] Marnas, op. cit., Vol. II, p. 273.

[33] Cary, op. cit., Vol. I, pp. 333, 334.

[34] Marnas, op. cit., Vol. II, pp. 273, 274.

[35] Marnas, op. cit., Vol. II, p. 359.

[36] Marnas, op. cit., Vol. II, p. 365.

[37] Marnas, op. cit., Vol. II, pp. 366ff.

the Japanese Government allowed foreigners more freedom to travel outside the ports and Roman Catholics took advantage of the increased leniency to add to the number of their stations.[38] In 1884 the northern vicariate had 5,574 Christians,[39] and the southern vicariate 24,656 Christians.[40] In 1895 Japan was said to contain 50,302 Roman Catholic Christians.[41] In 1891 Rome created a hierarchy for Japan, with an archbishopric for Tokyo and suffragan sees in Nagasaki, Osaka, and Hakodate.[42] Various orders came to share the field with the Société des Missions Étrangères of Paris. In 1904 the Spanish Dominicans of the Province of the Holy Rosary were given a prefecture apostolic on the Island of Shikoku.[43] In 1907 Thuringian Franciscans took over Sapporo, and the Society of the Divine Word Niigata.[44] Trappists came in 1896.[45] Jesuits also arrived, to renew the enterprise in which their predecessors had led in the sixteenth and seventeenth centuries.[46] In 1912 Roman Catholics totalled 66,134, foreign priests 152, native priests 33, lay brothers 133, nuns 232, and catechists at least 165.[47] Roman Catholic Christians, while including a few former *samurai,* appear to have been drawn chiefly from the humbler walks of life.[48]

French Marists, a teaching congregation of priests and lay brothers, were long at the head of the Roman Catholic system of schools. Three of these schools, in Tokyo, Nagasaki, and Osaka, had state recognition. In 1912 the Jesuits purchased a site near the centre of Tokyo on which to erect a university. Government permission for the institution was received in 1913. There were schools for lower grades maintained by some of the other societies and orders. Schools for girls maintained by the various sisterhoods were largely attended.[49] There were also orphanages and at least two leper asylums.[50]

Under the pressure of Japanese nationalism, which in the 1890's was on a rising tide, in 1890 a Roman Catholic council which met at Nagasaki decided to permit Christians to participate in patriotic rites at the Shinto shrines, emblems of the intensified patriotism.[51]

During the Russo-Japanese War (1904-1905) Roman Catholicism seems to

[38] Marnas, *op. cit.,* Vol. II, p. 380.
[39] Marnas, *op. cit.,* Vol. II, p. 411.
[40] Marnas, *op. cit.,* Vol. II, p. 476.
[41] Marnas, *op. cit.,* Vol. II, p. 542.
[42] Marnas, *op. cit.,* Vol. II, p. 538.
[43] *Los Dominicos en el Extremo Oriente,* p. 167.
[44] Schmidlin-Braun, *Catholic Mission History,* p. 632.
[45] Cary, *op. cit.,* Vol. I, p. 363.
[46] Schmidlin-Braun, *op. cit.,* p. 632; Cary, *op. cit.,* Vol. I, p. 363.
[47] Streit, *Atlas Hierarchicus,* p. 100.
[48] *The Christian Movement . . . in Japan,* 1904, p. 197.
[49] Berg, *Die katholische Heidenmission als Kulturträger,* Vol. I, pp. 370-372.
[50] *The Christian Movement . . . in Japan,* 1904, pp. 195, 196.
[51] *Fides News Service,* July 4, 1936.

have suffered. This was because France, although neutral, was known to be bound to Russia by an alliance, and because most of the missionaries were from France. The Japanese, moreover, resented the protectorate which the French Government exercised over Roman Catholic missions. In 1905 Rome took advantage of the reciprocal friendship between Japan and the United States, then very strong, to send an American bishop to Japan as a special envoy.[52] However, the preponderance of missionaries long continued to come from France.

Very unique was the Russian Orthodox mission in Japan. In connexion with it a larger body of converts arose than was won anywhere else by Russian Christianity from among non-Christians outside the domains of the Tsar. This growth was due in part to the eastward expansion of Russia and in an even larger degree to the ability and devotion of a great missionary, Ivan Kasatkin, who was best known under the name Nicolai which he bore as a priest. Nicolai came to Hakodate in 1861 as chaplain to the Russian consulate. He was then in his mid-twenties, a young man of deep piety who had become interested in Japan and had gone to that country partly at the advice of Veniaminoff, whom we have already met[53] as an outstanding missionary in Alaska. There inquirers gradually began to come to him and in 1868 three were baptized, secretly because of the imminent danger of persecution. One of these, Sawabe, was a *samurai* who had originally come to Nicolai with such hatred of Christianity as a supposed tool for enslaving his country that he had determined to slay him if he proved invincible in argument. Nicolai won his respect and then his confidence. Sawabe became an earnest missionary of his new faith and in time was ordained priest. A Christian community arose at Sendai around a nucleus of samurai who, as supporters of the Tokugawa, were greatly disturbed by the abolition of the Shogunate and that family's loss of power. In 1872 Nicolai transferred the headquarters of the mission to Tokyo and acquired ground on a prominent hill. There he taught the Russian language and with it Christianity. Before long several converts were made and baptized.[54]

In the 1870's converts rapidly multiplied. Nicolai obtained extensive financial aid from Russia, but he believed that Christianity must be spread by Japanese and not by Russians. He wished the Church to have a Japanese rather than a Russian aspect. The service books were early translated into Japanese. By 1878

[52] William O'Connell, *Recollections of Seventy Years* (Boston, Houghton Mifflin Co., 1934, pp. ix, 395), p. 247.
[53] Vol. IV, pp. 311, 312.
[54] Cary, *A History of Christianity in Japan*, Vol. I, pp. 377-404; Lübeck, *Die russischen Missionen*, pp. 16ff.

the Christians connected with the mission were said to number about five thousand. In 1885 the total was not far from ten thousand, and in 1890 slightly over seventeen thousand. The 1880's were a time of undiscriminating popularity of things Western and saw a marked expansion of Christianity. The 1890's were years of criticism of much that was foreign and Christianity spread more slowly. In 1897 the Christians were declared to be slightly less than twenty-four thousand and in 1902 a little over twenty-seven thousand. Many of these Christians were in the Hokkaido and the northern portion of the Main Island.[55]

The Russo-Japanese War inevitably proved embarrassing to the Orthodox mission. However, in accordance with the tradition of the Orthodox Church, with its close fellowship with the state, Nicolai, while abstaining from participation in the public services, instructed the Christians to be loyal to Japan, to pray for the success of her arms, and to give thanks for her successes. Saying, however, that the Church could know no difference in nationality, he remained with his flock. In consequence, the number of Christians increased slightly during the war and continued to do so in the years immediately after the conflict.[56]

Nicolai lived until 1912, and so witnessed the celebration of the first half century of the mission of his church in Japan. In the course of the years he had been made bishop and then archbishop. He had seen the enterprise grow from nothing to a body of more than thirty thousand scattered from the Japanese portion of Sakhalin and the Hokkaido on the north to Formosa on the south. He had been given a suffragan bishop, Sergius, who travelled widely, supervising the Christian communities and encouraging the spread of the faith in new localities. In spite of the fact that many of the early converts were from the *samurai,* eventually the great majority of the Christians were drawn from the humbler ranks of society.[57] As late as 1910 the major part of the expenses of the mission seem to have been met from Russia.[58] In 1903 there were thirty-eight Japanese priests, eight Japanese deacons, and one hundred and forty-four evangelists.[59] Schools were few. The Russian staff was very small and in 1914 was limited to one man, Bishop Sergius.[60]

By 1914 the rate of growth of the Russian Orthodox Church had slowed down. In 1912 the total strength was only about thirty-two thousand,[61] or an increase of approximately five thousand in a decade, in contrast with a gain of about ten

[55] Cary, *op. cit.,* Vol. I, pp. 336-361; Lübeck, *op. cit.,* pp. 16-23.
[56] Cary, *op. cit.,* Vol. I, pp. 414-423; Lübeck, *op. cit.,* pp. 16-23.
[57] *Ibid.; The Christian Movement in Japan,* 1911, pp. 289-292, 1913, pp. 417, 418.
[58] *The Christian Movement in Japan,* 1911, p. 290.
[59] *The Christian Movement . . . in Japan,* 1903, p. 104.
[60] *The Christian Movement in Japan,* 1914, p. 122.
[61] *The Christian Movement in Japan,* 1914, statistical table.

thousand in the twelve years before 1902, which included the difficult 1890's. Indeed, the days of marked increase were over. In 1940 the membership was only about forty-one thousand.[62] The period of turmoil and decline ushered in for the mother church by the political upheavals in Russia which followed the World War of 1914-1918 had their discouraging repercussions in the daughter mission.

Although Roman Catholic Christianity began the new era with the advantage of the large body of hidden Christians, fruitage of its labours in the sixteenth and seventeenth centuries, and although for a time the Russian Orthodox Church had a phenomenal expansion, most of the growth of Christianity in the years between the reopening of Japan and 1914 was through Protestantism. Protestants sent a much larger staff of missionaries into the country than did either of the other two major branches of the faith. In 1914 slightly more than three-fourths of the Protestant missionaries were from the United States and Canada. Less than two per cent. were from the continent of Europe, and only about a seventh were from the British Isles.[63] Protestant Christianity in Japan was drawn overwhelmingly from North America and chiefly from the United States.

Even before Japan was opened to the residence of other Westerners than the Dutch, Protestants were seeking to introduce their faith to the land and made converts from Japanese who were outside the empire. In 1818 an American ship which touched at the Bay of Yedo gave to its Japanese visitors two Testaments and some Christian tracts.[64] In 1828 Medhurst, missionary to the Chinese, asked of the Dutch passage to Nagasaki but was refused.[65] In 1828 funds began to come from various sources to the American Board of Commissioners for Foreign Missions for the purpose of opening an enterprise in Japan.[66] In 1832 Gützlaff, the energetic, linguistically gifted, and much travelled German missionary pioneer, touched at the Ryu Kyu Islands and distributed Chinese Christian books.[67] In 1837 the American ship *Morrison* made a voyage to Japan from Canton with the purpose of repatriating seven shipwrecked Japanese and of introducing Western civilization and Christianity. With it went two American missionaries, Peter Parker and Samuel Wells Williams. Gützlaff joined the vessel later. The ship attempted a landing in the Bay of Yedo and at Kago-

[62] *The Japan Christian Year Book*, 1941, p. 231.
[63] Beach and St. John, *World Statistics of Christian Missions*, p. 62.
[64] Cary, *A History of Christianity in Japan*, Vol. II, p. 12.
[65] *Ibid.*
[66] Cary, *op. cit.*, Vol. II, p. 13.
[67] Gützlaff, *Journal of Three Voyages along the Coast of China*, pp. 357-369.

shima but was driven off from both places and was unable to land its expatriates. The latter, deeply disappointed, died in exile. However, Williams and Gützlaff befriended them and at least two of them became Christians.[68] In 1842 a Japanese came in touch with a life of Christ in Dutch and had it translated. While copying the translation he was arrested. He thereupon committed suicide.[69] In 1845 officers of the British navy formed the Loochoo Naval Mission which in 1845 sent as a missionary to the Ryu Kyu group B. J. Bettelheim, a converted Jew and a physician. Bettelheim established a residence on the islands, but, like the Roman Catholics, met much opposition.[70] He baptized four converts, but withdrew about the year 1853. His successor left in 1855.[71]

With the Perry expedition of 1853-1854 which obtained the first treaty of Japan with Western powers, there went, as a marine, Jonathan Goble, who enlisted with the purpose of gaining a knowledge of Japan which would enable him later to become a missionary to that country,[72] and, as an interpreter, Samuel Wells Williams.[73] The expedition also had a chaplain and a burial was conducted on shore according to Christian rites.[74]

Townsend Harris, the first consul and diplomatic representative of the United States in Japan, was deeply religious and, with the knowledge of Japanese officials, held Christian services in his residence in Yedo and in the temple assigned him in the port of Shimoda. At the latter there were said to be six Christian Japanese in attendance.[75] Through the exertions of Harris, in the treaty of 1858 between the United States and Japan Americans were assured the free exercise of their religion and the right to erect suitable buildings for worship. The Japanese also stated that they had abolished the practice of trampling on religious emblems, a clause meant to halt the traditional test in Nagasaki of causing the inhabitants to tread on a cross as a safeguard against Christianity.[76]

Although neither this treaty nor other treaties of the time with Western powers gave permission for Christians to propagate their faith, efforts of that nature were soon begun and before long missionaries established themselves in

[68] Williams, The Life and Letters of Samuel Wells Williams, pp. 94-100; Samuel Wells Williams in The Chinese Recorder, Vol. VII, pp. 391-396.

[69] Herbert H. Gowen, A Precursor of Perry, or the Story of Takano Nagahide (Seattle, University of Washington Chapbooks, 1928, pp. 45), passim.

[70] Cary, op. cit., Vol. II, pp. 18-27.

[71] Cary, op. cit., Vol. II, pp. 34, 35.

[72] Cary, op. cit., Vol. II, p. 29.

[73] S. Wells Williams, A Journal of the Perry Expedition to Japan (1853-1854), edited by F. W. Williams (Transactions of the Asiatic Society of Japan, Vol. XXXVII, Part II, 1910, pp. ix, 259), passim.

[74] Cary, op. cit., Vol. II, pp. 32, 33.

[75] Cary, op. cit., Vol. II, pp. 37, 38.

[76] Cary, op. cit., Vol. II, p. 38; Treat, Diplomatic Relations between the United States and Japan, Vol. I, p. 59.

the open ports. We have already seen how Roman Catholics and Russian Orthodox took advantage of the altered situation. Protestants were also prompt to avail themselves of the opportunity. A chaplain of one of the early ships of the American navy to visit the country instructed several of the eager Japanese youths in things Western, including Christianity.[77] In 1859 there arrived representatives of three American denominations.

Two came from the Protestant Episcopal Church.[78] One of these, C. M. Williams, baptized his first convert in 1866. In that year he became Bishop of China and Japan. This assignment took him temporarily out of the country, but in 1869 he became a resident of Osaka, and, beginning in 1873, of Tokyo. In 1874 he was relieved of the supervision of the China enterprise of his church and, as Bishop of Yedo, devoted his entire time to Japan.[79]

In 1859 J. C. Hepburn (1815-1911), of the Presbyterian Church in the United States of America, reached Japan. Of the sturdy Scotch-Irish stock which contributed notably to the life of the United States and to the Presbyterianism of that country, he was to have a long and notable career.[80] He prepared in medicine and for a time in the 1840's served in Singapore and Amoy under the American Board of Commissioners for Foreign Missions. He was forced back to America by ill health, but in 1859 was once more in the Far East, this time in Japan and under the Presbyterian Board. He first fixed his residence in Kanagawa and then in the neighbouring Yokohama. He was a pioneer in compiling an English-Japanese dictionary and did most of the preparation of an early translation of the Bible into Japanese. He and his wife were also active in making available the Western education which the young Japanese were avidly seeking. Mrs. Hepburn began a school for girls which is said to have been the first of an Occidental type for that sex in Japan. She also taught young men, some of whom were later to be prominent in national affairs. In addition to his medical and surgical practice, Hepburn founded and headed a school in Tokyo and taught medicine. When, in 1892, in his late seventies, he retired to America, it was with the affection and esteem of hundreds of Japanese, many of them his former pupils and some of them in high position.

The (Dutch) Reformed Church in America also had representatives who reached Japan in 1859. One of these was Samuel R. Brown (1810-1880), whom we met in the last chapter as one of the earliest Protestant educators in China.[81]

[77] Cary, op. cit., Vol. II, pp. 41, 42.
[78] Tucker, The History of the Protestant Episcopal Church in Japan, p. 75.
[79] Tucker, op. cit., pp. 75-94.
[80] William Elliot Griffis, Hepburn of Japan (Philadelphia, The Westminster Press, 1913, pp. ix, 238), passim.
[81] Griffis, A Maker of the New Orient, pp. 137ff.

While in the United States in the interval between his two residences in the Far East Brown had been both teacher and pastor and had shared in the foundation of one of the first colleges for women. He was to have about twenty years in Japan, for the most part at Kanagawa and Yokohama. There he was again a pioneer in introducing Western education. Several of his students became prominent in the life of their country. He assisted, too, in the translation of the New Testament.

Another of the initial appointees of the Reformed Church in America, Guido Herman Fridolin Verbeck (1830-1898), became even more distinguished.[82] He was born in Holland and spent his boyhood there, part of it under Moravian influence. As a youth he acquired the languages which were the usual accomplishments of educated Dutchmen—English, German, and French. In 1852 he went to the United States. There, during a serious illness, he determined to become a missionary. To the Reformed Church he seemed peculiarly fitted to lead in the new enterprise in Japan, for his nativity and rearing were of advantage in a land which for long had had its only contact with the West through the Dutch at Nagasaki and his American experience had identified him with the country which had been most influential in opening Japan. He established a residence at Nagasaki, but not until 1866 did he baptize his first converts. These came by chance contact with a copy of the New Testament which had been found in the water of the harbour of Nagasaki. From the study of that book so strangely acquired they had sought from Verbeck instruction in the Christian faith. In Nagasaki Verbeck had a school, teaching through the medium of the Bible the English language then so ardently desired by many. Before many years the government placed him in charge of a school for interpreters. With the revolution which overthrew the Shogunate some of his former pupils became influential in the new regime. Through them came an invitation to go to Yedo. There he headed the school which later grew into the Imperial University. He became the trusted counsellor of officials. It was partly on his advice that the Japanese sent their first modern diplomatic embassy to the Western powers. By him or under his supervision there were translated into Japanese the Code Napoleon, numbers of Occidental legal documents, treatises on law, and constitutions. He also taught Bible classes and preached. Like Hepburn, he was decorated by the Emperor. Unassuming and straightforward, he won the respect of high and low and, probably even more than Hepburn and Brown, helped to mould Japan in the years of its transition.

[82] William Elliot Griffis, *Verbeck of Japan* (New York, Fleming H. Revell Co., 1900, pp. 376), *passim.*

In 1860, the year after the coming of the first three American societies, Jonathan Goble, who had been a member of the Perry expedition, returned to Japan. He came as a representative of the Free Baptists and brought with him a shipwrecked Japanese who had been rescued through Americans and while in the United States had been baptized.[83] This enterprise was short-lived.

For ten years these four were the only Protestant societies in Japan,[84] although in 1860 the Southern Baptist Convention made what was a futile effort to inaugurate a mission.[85]

In the stormy decade which followed the treaties of 1858 with their grudging incomplete opening of Japan and when Japan was still fiercely divided over the admission of the foreigner, Protestant Christianity was seemingly making but slight headway. For Protestants there was no body of hidden Christians to be discovered such as thrilled the Roman Catholics and issued in the rapid revival of that communion. Only a very few converts were won. Yet missionaries were establishing themselves in the ports and to them were coming Japanese youths intent upon acquiring a knowledge of the Occident and the English language. Since it was the United States which had led the way in opening the country and since British commerce and naval power were dominant in Far Eastern waters, the desire for English was especially strong. Protestant missionaries had, accordingly, a unique opportunity. Numbers of those whom they taught became leaders in the reshaping of Japan. Not many of them became Christians, but through them Protestant Christianity facilitated the adjustment of the nation to the new world into which it had been so reluctantly introduced. Beginnings were made, too, in the translation of the Bible[86] and in the preparation of linguistic tools which would be of advantage in the later stages of the introduction of Protestant Christianity to Japan.

As a result of efforts in this decade, Protestant missionaries had gained the confidence of many Japanese, Christianity was viewed with less horror than before, a few Japanese sought to know more of it, Bibles and other Christian literature in Chinese had been distributed, for educated Japanese could read books in the literary form of Chinese, some missionaries had sufficiently mastered Japanese to use it for teaching and preaching, literature had been prepared, schools had been begun, medical care had been given through dispen-

[83] Verbeck in *Proceedings of the General Conference of the Protestant Missionaries of Japan . . . 1883*, p. 26.
[84] *Ibid.*
[85] Cary, *A History of Christianity in Japan*, Vol. II, p. 52; Dozier, *A Golden Milestone in Japan*, pp. 46, 47.
[86] Verbeck in *Proceedings of the General Conference of the Protestant Missionaries of Japan . . . 1883*, pp. 41-44.

saries, and the foreign communities had been provided with churches, Sunday schools, and regular religious services.[87] Up to 1872, however, only ten Japanese had been baptized by Protestants.[88] Merely the bare beginnings had been made of a Japanese Protestant Christianity.

In the years immediately after 1867, with their revolutionary changes in government, and especially in the decade following the removal of the anti-Christian edict boards (1873) with the implied tacit if partial toleration of Christianity, Protestant missions had a substantial growth, converts rapidly increased, and the main outlines of the future Protestant Christianity of Japan began to take form.

Commencing in 1869, after a lull of nearly a decade, additional societies entered the country. In that year came the first representatives of the Church Missionary Society. By the close of 1875 centres had been begun in five cities.[89] In 1859 the Society for the Propagation of the Gospel in Foreign Parts had reserved a fund to inaugurate an enterprise in Japan, but it was not until 1873 that the first appointees of the society actually arrived.[90]

It was in 1869 that the American Board of Commissioners for Foreign Missions inaugurated an enterprise in Japan. This it did partly at the instance of a remarkable Japanese, Neesima.[91] Neesima was of *samurai* parentage and attached to one of the aristocratic establishments in Yedo.[92] As a lad he was stirred by the Western ideas which were beginning to gain entrance and developed a great hunger to learn more. Through a book by Bridgman, the pioneer of the American Board in China, he gained some notion of the United States. He studied Dutch and English. He began a surreptitious reading of the Bible. In 1864, impelled by a passion for a Western education, he left the country, and that in spite of the fact that the laws still made it dangerous to do so. Through the kindness of ship captains he reached America. In Boston Alpheus Hardy, the owner of the vessel on which he had come from China, befriended him and arranged for the education for which the youth had ventured so much and so far. Neesima attended successively Phillips Academy, Andover, Amherst College, and Andover Theological Seminary. Through his contact with the Bible while still in Japan he had taken the first steps towards a Christian faith. In the United States he was increasingly a devoted Christian. As we shall

[87] Verbeck in *op. cit.*, pp. 39-46.
[88] Verbeck in *op. cit.*, pp. 51, 52.
[89] Stock, *Japan and the Japan Mission of the Church Missionary Society*, pp. 111, 112.
[90] Moore, *The Christian Faith in Japan*, p. 59.
[91] Pettee, *A Chapter in Modern Mission History in Modern Japan*, p. 6.
[92] On his life see J. D. Davis, *A Sketch of the Life of Rev. Joseph Hardy Neesima* (2d ed., Chicago, Fleming H. Revell Co., 1894, pp. 156), and Arthur Sherburne Hardy, *Life and Letters of Joseph Hardy Neesima, passim.*

see in a moment, eventually (1874) he returned to Japan in connexion with the American Board.

However, the first missionary of the American Board in Japan was not Neesima but Daniel Crosby Greene (1843-1913).[93] Both Greene's father and maternal grandfather had served on the secretariat of the American Board. Through his mother's brother, William M. Evarts, lawyer, Attorney General, Secretary of State, and Senator of the United States, Greene had important political connexions. He lived first at Kobe, where he shared in the organization, in 1874, of the initial Congregational or *Kumiai* church of Japan. For several years his home was in Yokohama, where he was active in the joint enterprise for the translation of the Bible. Then he was stationed in Kyoto. In Kyoto he taught in the Doshisha, an institution inaugurated by Neesima.

Before returning to Japan Neesima had conceived the purpose of founding in his native land a Christian school which by giving a broad education would contribute to the successful spread of Christianity. He wished the school to become a university, a goal which was eventually attained. For this school he obtained land in Kyoto, the ancient capital of the empire and a centre of conservatism. Title to the property was vested in the Doshisha Company, composed wholly of Japanese. The American Board provided several missionary teachers and substantial contributions to the budget came from the United States. By heroic effort Neesima also raised funds in Japan.[94] So closely associated with Neesima from the beginning as to be a co-founder of the Doshisha was Jerome Dean Davis (1838-1910),[95] a missionary of the American Board who came to Japan in 1871. Neesima died in 1890, in middle life, but the Doshisha continued, the strongest of the Christian universities of the empire. Neesima, it must also be added, was the means of beginning a group of churches in his ancestral district in the interior of the country and was active in other ways in promoting the growth of the faith.[96]

Still others came under the American Board. Prominent among them were John Thomas Gulick, from a missionary family in Hawaii.[97] Early in the 1860's he had gone to Japan, had supported himself by photography and teaching, and had urged the American Board to inaugurate an enterprise there. Because of the American Civil War no funds were available and instead he was appointed to China. Forced out of that country by ill health, in 1876 he went to the land

[93] Greene, *A New-Englander in Japan. Daniel Crosby Greene, passim.*
[94] Hardy, *op. cit.,* pp. 194, 231, 233, 290, 291, 301, 304, 305.
[95] Davis, *Davis, Soldier, Missionary, passim.*
[96] Hardy, *op. cit.,* pp. 188-194, 218, 232, 234, 327.
[97] Addison Gulick, *Evolutionist and Missionary. John Thomas Gulick* (The University of Chicago Press, 1932, pp. xvi, 556).

of his first choice and served until 1899. He became noted for his studies in evolution. John C. Berry arrived in 1872 and was a pioneer in Western medicine. He left Japan in 1893, but in the intervening years he had taught medical subjects at the Doshisha, had been in charge of the hospital there, and was director of a training school for nurses.[98] Notable as a pioneer preacher, organizer, and educator was John Hyde De Forest, who landed in 1874.[99]

In 1872 the American Baptist Missionary Union entered Japan in the persons of two men, one of them that Jonathan Goble who had been in Yokohama for a time in the 1860's.[100]

The following year, 1873, saw the coming of the first representatives of the Methodist Episcopal Church, a body which was to have a much larger growth in Japan than were the Baptists. Yokohama, Tokyo, and Hakodate were early chosen as centres, Hakodate because at that time it contained no Protestant mission. Reinforcements were slow in being sent, for a financial depression in the United States greatly handicapped the Methodist foreign missionary enterprise.[101]

The year 1873 also witnessed the first of the Canadian Methodists.[102] In 1871 the Woman's Union Missionary Society began operations.[103] The year 1875 is given as the date for the introduction of the National Bible Society of Scotland, 1876 for that of the American Bible Society, and 1881 for that of the British and Foreign Bible Society.[104] These are the years of the coming of employed agents of these three organizations.[105] In 1874 the initial missionaries of the United Presbyterian Church of Scotland arrived.[106] The year 1877 was marked by the advent of Cumberland Presbyterians.[107] In 1876 or 1877 came the Evangelical Association, and in 1880 the Methodist Protestants [108] and the (German) Reformed Church in the United States.[109]

[98] Katherine Fiske Berry, *A Pioneer Doctor in Old Japan. The Story of John C. Berry, M.D.* (New York, Fleming H. Revell Co., 1940, pp. 247).
[99] Charlotte B. De Forest, *The Evolution of a Missionary. A Biography of John Hyde De Forest* (Chicago, Fleming H. Revell Co., 1914, pp. 299).
[100] *American Baptist Missionary Union. Fifty-Ninth Annual Report*, 1873, pp. 88, 89.
[101] Harris, *Christianity in Japan*, pp. 44-46.
[102] Cary, *A History of Christianity in Japan*, Vol. II, p. 104.
[103] Cary, *op. cit.*, Vol. II, p. 358.
[104] Cary, *op. cit.*, Vol. II, p. 357.
[105] Canton, *A History of the British and Foreign Bible Society*, Vol. III, pp. 460ff.; Dwight, *The Centennial History of the American Bible Society*, Vol. II, p. 401.
[106] Verbeck in *Proceedings of the General Conference of the Protestant Missionaries of Japan . . . 1883*, p. 71.
[107] Cary, *op. cit.*, Vol. II, pp. 136, 137.
[108] Cary, *op. cit.*, Vol. II, p. 357.
[109] Miller, *History of the Japan Mission of the Reformed Church in the United States, 1879-1904*, p. 7.

In the greater freedom which followed the removal of the anti-Christian edict boards, the three denominations which had entered the land in 1859 expanded their staffs and their operations. The Protestant Episcopalians sent reinforcements, but not enough to take advantage of all the invitations from towns and villages to present the Christian message. Schools were developed, including two for girls and one for the preparation of Japanese clergy. The translation of the Service of the Holy Communion was undertaken in co-operation with the Anglicans from the British Isles.[110] The Presbyterian Church in the United States of America had a more marked growth. It sent numbers of new missionaries. In 1873 it added to a church in Yokohama one in Tokyo, the first Protestant church in the capital. Late in that year a presbytery was organized.[111] Additional churches were gathered.[112] Several Japanese were ordained, and a home missionary society was formed.[113] The (Dutch) Reformed Church in America also appointed additional missionaries. It reached out from Nagasaki, Yokohama, and Tokyo into the adjacent territories to establish new centres for the faith.[114]

In these years when Japan was going to school to the Occident, Christianity spread, not only through missionaries sent by the churches of America and Great Britain, but also through teachers employed by the government and by local and private agencies.[115] Especially notable for their influence were W. S. Clark and L. L. Janes. Clark was president of the Massachusetts Agricultural College and in 1876 went to Sapporo, in the Hokkaido, to assist in the organization of a similiar institution in that frontier region. He was active in teaching his Christian faith to his students and although he was in Japan for only a year he left behind him a strong nucleus of converts. They formed themselves into a church some of whose members rose to prominence.[116] In 1871 Janes was put in charge of a private school at the inland town of Kumamoto, where anti-Christian feeling was high. As soon as feasible he began to give instruction in the Christian faith. A number of his pupils became Christians and early in 1876 bound themselves by a solemn pledge into a Christian society. They faced persecution, but several went to the Doshisha to prepare themselves for service in the Church and were there known as the Kumamoto Band. From

[110] Tucker, *The History of the Episcopal Church in Japan,* pp. 94-98.
[111] Verbeck in *op. cit.,* pp. 58-60.
[112] Verbeck in *op. cit.,* pp. 99, 105.
[113] Verbeck in *op. cit.,* pp. 135, 136.
[114] Verbeck in *op. cit.,* pp. 68, 72, 77, 137-140.
[115] On two of these see Cary, *op. cit.,* Vol. II, p. 74.
[116] Ritter, *A History of Protestant Missions in Japan,* p. 97; Kawai, *My Lantern,* pp. 42, 43.

among them came outstanding leaders of the churches. Two were presidents of the Doshisha.[117]

In 1882 Protestants counted 93 churches (of which 13 were self-supporting), 4,987 adult members, and 145 missionaries. They had 7 theological schools with 71 pupils, 63 other schools with 2,514 pupils, and 49 ordained clergy.[118] These totals compared with 25,633 Roman Catholics in 1881, with a staff of 46 Europeans, and with 7,611 members of the Russian Orthodox Church in 1882.[119]

In the 1880's Protestant Christianity experienced a remarkable growth. This was partly because of the foundations laid by faithful and able pioneers. It was also because of the popularity of things Western and the somewhat uncritical adoption of much of Occidental culture. Sensitive to the attitudes of the powerful Occident and eager to win the respect of the West and to be admitted to the society of that world on the basis of full equality, many Japanese strove to have their country adopt European institutions and manners. In this purpose they were stimulated by the desire to free the empire from the extraterritorial status of aliens and the restraints on tariff autonomy which had been incorporated in the treaties of the late 1850's and which to them had the stigma of inferiority. It was a symptom of the temper of the day that Fukuzawa Yukichi, one of the most influential leaders of thought in the new Japan, founder of a newspaper and a university, who as late as 1881 was advocating restraint on the progress of Christianity,[120] in 1884 and 1885 urged that to obtain admission to Christendom, the international society of Europe and America, Japan should officially become a Christian country and that gradually baptism should be introduced among the upper and middle classes. As a private individual Fukuzawa declared that he had little or no interest in religion, but he argued that regardless of what they might actually believe Japanese should profess to be Christians and so outwardly conform to the Occident.[121] This did not mean that opposition to Christianity had ceased. Local persecutions by officials, Buddhist priests, and the populace still occurred. In the name of Shinto, the ancient faith which the government was reviving, hotheads threatened missionaries with death.[122] Yet the tide was running strongly towards Western

[117] Ritter, op. cit., pp. 69-71; Hardy, Life and Letters of Joseph Hardy Neesima, pp. 208-211; Kozaki, Reminiscences of Seventy Years, pp. 34-38.
[118] Proceedings of the General Conference of Protestant Missionaries of Japan . . . 1883, statistical table opposite p. 184.
[119] Proceedings of the General Conference of Protestant Missionaries of Japan . . . 1883, p. 185.
[120] See quotations from Fukuzawa's writings in Cary, A History of Christianity in Japan, Vol. II, pp. 156, 157.
[121] See quotations from Fukuzawa's writings in Cary, op. cit., Vol. II, pp. 172-174.
[122] Cary, op. cit., Vol. II, pp. 177-179; Ritter, op. cit., pp. 132-139.

ways and towards Christianity as, supposedly, an integral part of Occidental civilization.

Parallel with the pro-Christian trend in some non-Christians there was a quickening of life in existing Protestant churches. In 1883 a nation-wide inter-denominational meeting of Protestant missionaries was held. Preceding and after it there were religious awakenings in several congregations, akin to what in the United States were known as "revivals." One of the most striking was in the Doshisha. Among Christians there was emotion, with confession of sins, followed by a sense of forgiveness. There were many conversions.[123]

Non-Christians were more open than before to the Christian message. Calls came from numbers of cities for the presentation of the Christian faith and thousands crowded the largest available theatres to hear the missionaries.[124] There was preaching by Japanese in the streets of Tokyo, where twenty years before a Japanese would not have ventured openly to call himself a Christian.[125]

The augmented desire for Western ways was accompanied by an increased demand for the study of the English language and for Occidental education. Mission schools were crowded, new schools were started, some of them by Japanese Christians, and missionaries were urged to help with the teaching and to open additional institutions.[126]

Near the close of 1888 Protestants had 249 churches (of which 92 were self-supporting), 25,514 members, 451 missionaries, 14 theological seminaries with 287 students, and 101 other schools with 9,672 pupils. There were 142 ordained Japanese ministers. In the past year there had been nearly 7,000 baptisms of adults.[127] When these figures are compared with those of 1882, given a few paragraphs above, the growth is very striking. Much of the increase was among the intellectuals. Numbers of students in government schools and of officials were to be found in the churches.[128] It is not strange that missionaries and their supporters were optimistic and urged that the time was opportune to reach all Japan.[129] The country was declared to be "embracing Christianity with

[123] Cary, op. cit., Vol. II, pp. 165-172, 189, 190; Ritter, op. cit., pp. 107-120.

[124] Seventy-Eighth Annual Report of the American Board of Commissioners for Foreign Missions, 1888, pp. 90, 91.

[125] Sixty-ninth Annual Report of the Missionary Society of the Methodist Episcopal Church for the year 1887, pp. 270, 271.

[126] Cary, op. cit., Vol. II, pp. 185-188, 203; Seventy-Seventh Annual Report of the American Board of Commissioners for Foreign Missions, 1887, pp. 119, 121.

[127] Cary, op. cit., Vol. II, p. 209.

[128] Cary, op. cit., Vol. II, p. 210.

[129] See appeal by missionaries in Japan in the Seventy-Ninth Annual Report of the American Board of Commissioners for Foreign Missions, 1889, pp. lxvi-lxviii. "The advance of Christianity in Japan continues to be one of the marvels of history."— American Baptist Missionary Union. Seventy-Fifth Annual Report, 1889, p. 286.

a rapidity unexampled since the days of Constantine."[130] It was even predicted that by the beginning of the twentieth century Japan would have become "no longer a foreign mission field, but predominantly Christian."[131]

In these days of opportunity a number of new societies entered the country, most of them from the United States. In 1883 came the Disciples of Christ.[132] In 1885 there arrived the first representatives of American Friends,[133] of the (Southern) Presbyterian Church in the United States,[134] and of the *Allgemeiner Evangelisch-Protestantische Missionsverein,* later called the *Ostasien-Mission,* an exponent of German theological liberalism.[135] In 1886 the Southern Methodists were added. In 1887 the Christian Churches, also from the United States, inaugurated an enterprise.[136] In 1887 came the first agent of the American Unitarians. He preferred not to be called a missionary, but sought friendly relations with the non-Christian religions, especially Buddhism.[137] In 1888 the Wycliffe College Mission, Anglican, from Toronto, Canada, which worked in co-operation with the Church Missionary Society,[138] and the Berkeley Temple Mission, from Boston, later assimilated to the mission of the American Board of Commissioners for Foreign Missions,[139] augmented the list of Protestant bodies. In 1889 the Southern Baptist Convention, whose first appointees to Japan sailed in 1860 but were lost at sea, renewed its effort and began a continuing undertaking.[140] That same year saw the coming of the Christian Alliance.[141] None of these new missions achieved the proportions attained by some of the earlier ones.

Several American types of organizations were introduced and developed. The Woman's Christian Temperance Union, then in its youthful heyday in the United States, stimulated the formation of temperance societies in Japan.[142] The Young Men's Christian Association came in, first for foreigners resident in Tokyo. Then, in 1880, an association was organized in that city by Japanese

[130] *The Spirit of Missions,* Vol. LIII (September, 1888), p. 353.
[131] Editorial in *The Independent* (New York, 1848-1928), Vol. XXXV, p. 1136 (September 6, 1883, p. 16).
[132] *Survey of Service, Disciples of Christ,* pp. 334ff.
[133] Ritter, *A History of Protestant Missions in Japan,* p. 150.
[134] Erickson, *The White Fields of Japan,* p. 71.
[135] Richter, *Die evangelische Mission in Fern- und Südost-Asien, Australien, Amerika,* p. 26.
[136] Ritter, *op. cit.,* p. 150.
[137] Cary, *op. cit.,* Vol. II, pp. 199-201.
[138] Stock, *The History of the Church Missionary Society,* Vol. III, p. 676.
[139] Ritter, *op. cit.,* p. 150.
[140] Dozier, *A Golden Milestone in Japan,* pp. 48, 49.
[141] Ritter, *op. cit.,* p. 150.
[142] Cary, *A History of Christianity in Japan,* Vol. II, p. 188.

and was modelled after what had been seen in the United States.[143] In the 1880's numbers of other associations were inaugurated and before long an American secretary arrived.[144]

Under the pressure of the opportunity the societies already represented sought to expand their staffs and their programmes. The American Episcopalians reached out from Osaka and Tokyo, to which their efforts had chiefly been confined, to neighbouring towns and districts.[145] In 1883 A. W. Poole, who had served in India under the Church Missionary Society, was consecrated as the first English bishop in Japan. After less than a year's residence he was invalided home.[146] As his successor there was consecrated, in 1886, Edward Bickersteth, who had been a member of the Cambridge Mission to Delhi but because of his health had been forced to return to England.[147] In Japan he had over a decade. From the beginning he set before himself the vision of a national church, rooted in the soil of Japan, as was the Church of England in England, and in communion with the other members of the Anglican fellowship.[148] His initiative brought about, in 1887, the formation of the *Nippon Sei Ko Kwai* (the Holy Catholic Church of Japan), which the missions of the Church of England and the Protestant Episcopal Church in the United States were to assist and which grew out of the enterprises of the various societies of these churches.[149] Among other extensions of Anglican operations was one by the Church Missionary Society among the Ainu, primitive folk in the Hokkaido. The enterprise was begun in the 1870's, but it was in the 1880's that the one most responsible for its development, John Batchelor, laid firm foundations for it.[150] The Northern Presbyterians expanded their efforts and among other new undertakings also entered the Hokkaido.[151] In 1877 the *Nippon Kirisuto Itchi Kyokwai*, the United Church of Christ in Japan (later the *Nippon Kirisuto Kyokwai*, the Church of Christ in Japan), was constituted by the congregations which owed their origin to the Northern Presbyterians, the Dutch Reformed,

---

[143] Kozaki, *Reminiscences of Seventy Years*, pp. 61, 62.
[144] Cary, *op. cit.*, Vol. II, p. 223.
[145] Tucker, *The History of the Episcopal Church in Japan*, pp. 132-134.
[146] Moore, *The Christian Faith in Japan*, p. 82.
[147] Samuel Bickersteth, *Life and Letters of Edward Bickersteth*, pp. 141ff.; [Mrs. Marion Forsyth Bickersteth], *Edward Bickersteth, Missionary Bishop in Japan* (Tokyo, Kyo Bun Kwan, 1914, pp. x, 187, iii).
[148] Samuel Bickersteth, *op. cit.*, p. 301.
[149] Samuel Bickersteth, *op. cit.*, pp. 301ff.
[150] John Batchelor, *Sea-Girt Yezo. Glimpses of Missionary Work in North Japan* (London, Church Missionary Society, 1902, pp. vii, 120), pp. 59ff.; Stock, *Japan and the Japan Mission of the Church Missionary Society*, pp. 260ff.
[151] Brown, *One Hundred Years*, p. 704.

and the United Presbyterian Church of Scotland.[152] In the 1880's the missions of the Southern Presbyterians, the Cumberland Presbyterians, and the (German) Reformed Church in the United States connected themselves with it. Presbyterians, like the Anglicans, were presenting a united front.[153] It was this body which in 1888 had the largest membership of any of the Protestant bodies, or approximately one-third of the whole. It also had by far the largest foreign staff labouring in connexion with it, a little less than a third of all Protestant missionaries in Japan.[154]

Prominent in the *Nippon Kirisuto Kyokwai* was Masahisa Uemura.[155] Of *samurai* stock, he was ordained in 1879, was a pastor in Tokyo, and into the twentieth century was outstanding in his denomination.

Next to the *Nippon Kirisuto Kyokwai* in membership in 1888, with more than a fourth of the entire Protestant body in that year, were the churches with which the American Board of Commissioners for Foreign Missions collaborated. Indeed, in 1891 and apparently throughout that decade they outnumbered any other of the Protestant bodies in Japan. This was in spite of the fact that all through the 1890's the foreign missionary staff of the American Board was only about half that of the Presbyterian bodies and was considerably smaller than that of Anglicans[156] and that the American Board had arrived in Japan a decade after the first of the Presbyterians and the Anglicans. It was also a very much smaller staff than that of the Methodists, yet during the 1890's the membership of the churches with which the American Board co-operated was about twice that of the Methodist bodies.[157] This was exceptional for the Congregational fellowship. In a few parts of the world it had been predominant among Protestants, but that was where, as in New England, it had led in the settlement of the country, or where, as in some of the Pacific islands, including Samoa and Hawaii, and in Asia Minor and Armenia, it was the pioneer and had the major portion of the missionary body. In Japan it was not the first to arrive and its missionaries were always in the minority. Its unusual position in the empire was due in part to the impatience of many Japanese Christians with imported denominational differences, the fruit of a sturdy nationalism

[152] Cary, *op. cit.*, Vol. II, pp. 129, 130.
[153] Ryder, *A Historical Sourcebook of the Japan Mission of the Reformed Church in America*, p. 55.
[154] *Proceedings of the General Conference of Protestant Missionaries in Japan . . . 1900*, pp. 987, 989.
[155] Katsuhisa Aoyoshi, *Dr. Masahisa Uemura, a Christian Leader* (Tokyo, Maruzen & Co., no date, pp. 271).
[156] *Proceedings of the General Conference of Protestant Missionaries in Japan . . . 1900*, pp. 987, 989.
[157] *Ibid.*

which wished Japan to place its own stamp on Christianity and not to be subservient to the Occidental forms of the faith.[158] The first Protestant church organized in Japan sought to avoid a denominational label and called itself simply the Church of Christ in Japan.[159] The Kumamoto Band, whose members became very important in the growth of Protestantism, had imbibed from their teacher, Janes, a distrust of denominationalism.[160] When a name was at last adopted by the fellowship of churches with which the American Board co-operated, it was only because denominational appellations were being employed by other bodies. The designation chosen (1886) was *Kumiai,* which meant association, rather than *Kwaishu,* the Japanese equivalent for congregation.[161] In the 1880's there was much talk of union with the *Nippon Kirisuto Itchi Kyokwai,* but the project failed of consummation, largely because the *Kumiai* pastors preferred the greater freedom of the congregational type of organization and feared as a possible curtailment the more closely knit Presbyterian polity.[162] In this attitude may have been another reason for the growth of the *Kumiai* fellowship. Then, too, the fact that Neesima, the most prominent of the early Japanese Protestants, had, through his spiritual and physical pilgrimage, an affiliation with Congregationalists must have carried weight. Next to Neesima in influence in the formative days of the *Kumiai* churches was Paul Sawayama.[163] Of *samurai* stock, Sawayama studied English in Kobe with Greene of the American Board, went to the United States to school and there joined a Congregational church. In 1876 he fulfilled his purpose to go back to his native land as a missionary and soon became pastor of a small church in Osaka. He wished to see Japanese Christianity self-supporting. His church, therefore, received no foreign funds. His devotion, personal magnetism, saintliness, and zeal in spreading his faith made a wide impression. During the 1880's and 1890's the *Kumiai* churches grew with marked rapidity.

Not far from 1890 it became clear that the rapid growth of the past few years was not to continue, at least not at so breath-taking a pace. No longer was the current setting so markedly in the direction of Christianity.[164] The 1890's saw numerical advance in the Protestant forces. In 1891 the foreign staff

---

[158] Kozaki, *Reminiscences of Seventy Years,* p. 80.

[159] Verbeck in *Proceedings of the General Conference of Protestant Missionaries of Japan . . . 1883,* p. 53.

[160] Kozaki, *op. cit.,* p. 81.

[161] Kozaki, *op. cit.,* pp. 79, 80.

[162] Greene, *A New-Englander in Japan,* pp. 209-213.

[163] Jinzo Naruse, *A Modern Paul in Japan. An Account of the Life and Work of the Rev. Paul Sawayama* (Boston, Congregational Sunday-School and Publishing Society, 1893, pp. 178), *passim.*

[164] *American Baptist Missionary Union, Seventy-Sixth Annual Report,* 1890, p. 126.

was 583. In 1900 it was 723. In 1891 organized Protestant churches totalled 297. In 1900 they had expanded to 416. In 1891 the membership was 32,334. In 1900 it had risen to 43,273. Full members in these two years were 31,360 and 37,068 respectively.[165] Both proportionately and in gross figures this advance was substantial. In both respects it was also very much less than that of the preceding decade. In 1900 Japan was far from being the Christian country which some of the optimists of the halcyon 1880's had predicted.

Moreover, the 1890's were for the Protestant churches a time of storm and stress. There was restiveness under missionary control[166] and talk of acclimatizing Christianity in Japan much as Buddhism and Confucianism, both imported systems, had been modified to suit the Japanese environment.[167] Materialistic and radical literature had a wide vogue. Many church leaders were attracted by novel trends in Occidental theology. Some Japanese pastors left the ministry and turned against the faith which they had preached. Several others who remained by the churches sounded notes of doubt. Christianity was stigmatized as foreign and missionaries were accused of teaching obsolete doctrines. Japanese were urged to get at the roots of the faith for themselves. In the Doshisha, the leading pioneer in Christian higher education, an acute and prolonged battle was waged to keep the institution from abandoning its avowed Christian purpose. The struggle ended successfully for the pronounced Christians, but during its continuation it could not but be disturbing.[168] In the theological seminaries the number of students declined from 316 in 1891 to 98 in 1900.[169]

For this reaction against the striking popularity of Christianity and for these dissensions in the Protestant fold several factors were accountable. There was a rebound from the uncritical acceptance of things Western to a reemphasis upon 'distinctively Japanese culture. Japanese nationalism, always strong, was now taking the form of stressing the values of the inherited civilization rather than the desire to win the respect of the West by conforming to Occidental *mores*. The delay in the revision of the treaties in the direction of the elimination of extraterritoriality and the conventional tariff made for irritation. While the revision was obtained in the mid-1890's, the reluctance of Wes-

[165] *Proceedings of the General Conference of Protestant Missionaries in Japan* . . . *1900*, pp. 987-991.
[166] Cary, *A History of Christianity in Japan*, Vol. II, pp. 240, 241.
[167] Richter, *Die evangelische Mission in Fern- und Südost-Asien, Australien, Amerika*, pp. 33, 34.
[168] Davis, *Davis. Soldier, Missionary*, pp. 216ff.
[169] *Proceedings of the General Conference of Protestant Missionaries in Japan* . . . *1900*, p. 997.

tern powers to concede it had fostered ill will. Since Christianity came as the religion of the West, the cooling of admiration for things Occidental was reflected in the attitude toward Christianity.[170] The Imperial Rescript on Education, issued in 1890 and read periodically and ceremoniously in the schools, was held in veneration as the basis of Japan's educational programme. It emphasized some phases of traditional Japanese ethics and many declared it to be directed against Christianity.[171] Not far from this time the custom of bowing to the picture of the Emperor in the schools began to reinforce the ancient sanctity of the ruler. This, too, reacted against Christianity.[172] The expansion of commerce and industry absorbed the attention of many and augmented a trend toward materialism.[173]

Yet, as we have suggested, the record of the 1890's was by no means one of loss. Advance continued, even though less rapidly than in the 1880's. The constitution granted by the Emperor and promulgated in 1889 granted religious liberty. This made for freedom for Christianity. Many missionaries had publicly advocated the speedy revision of the treaties in the direction of Japanese desires.[174] This must have worked some mollification of the Japanese attitude towards them. In the first lower house of the Imperial Diet thirteen out of the three hundred members were Christians, nearly nine times the proportion of Christians in the population of the country at large, and that in spite of the fact that their faith cost them many votes.[175] During the Sino-Japanese War of 1894-1895 Christian soldiers by their bravery disproved the charge that adherents of that faith were lacking in patriotism. Japanese clergymen went as chaplains and missionaries distributed Bibles and other Christian literature among the troops.[176] When, in 1899, extraterritoriality came to an end, aliens were permitted to travel and reside in the interior. Missionaries, as foreigners, shared in this privilege and toured the country more freely than had heretofore been possible.[177] New methods were inaugurated by some of the societies. Among them was the dedication of a ship (1899) by the American Baptist

[170] Cary, op. cit., Vol. II, pp. 212-216; Anesaki, History of Japanese Religion, pp. 358, 359.

[171] Cary, op. cit., Vol. II, pp. 226, 227, 271, 272; Holtom, Modern Japan and Shinto Nationalism, p. 80; Kozaki, Reminiscences of Seventy Years, p. 95.

[172] Cary, op. cit., Vol. II, p. 227.

[173] Cary, op. cit., Vol. II, pp. 253, 254.

[174] Treat, Diplomatic Relations between the United States and Japan, Vol. II, pp. 225, 343.

[175] Cary, op. cit., Vol. II, pp. 228, 229.

[176] Cary, op. cit., Vol. II, pp. 249, 250; Pascoe, Two Hundred Years of the S.P.G., p. 724c.

[177] Cary, op. cit., Vol. II, p. 253.

Missionary Union for the purpose of giving the Christian message to the inhabitants of the many islands which dotted the Inland Sea.[178] A few organizations inaugurated enterprises in Japan. In 1891 came the Scandinavian Alliance Mission of North America[179] and the Universalists, both from the United States.[180] The following year saw the arrival of American Lutherans, representatives of the United Synod of the Evangelical Lutheran Church in the South.[181] 1895 witnessed the coming of the Christian and Missionary Alliance,[182] the Salvation Army,[183] and the United Brethren.[184] In 1896 the initial appointee of the Seventh Day Adventists landed.[185] We hear, too, of the inauguration (1892) of the Postal and Telegraph Mission in Japan, a branch of the International postal and Telegraph Christian Association, an organization with London headquarters and with postmen and postal officials as its objective.[186] The Hepzibah Faith Mission, undenominational, was begun.[187] In 1891 Protestant missions were reopened in the Ryu Kyu Islands, where they had not been present for four decades.[188] When, as a result of the Sino-Japanese War, Formosa became a part of the empire, at least three of the missions and churches of Japan proper reached southward to the new possession.[189]

The twentieth century and the years in it before 1914 saw a decided growth in Protestant Christianity. It was not as spectacular as in the 1880's. The optimistic predictions of the early conversion of the empire were no longer in evidence. Yet Protestantism had a substantial increase and in numbers outstripped Roman Catholicism. In 1913 the total Protestant communicant membership was 89,347.[190] It had more than doubled since 1900, a much larger rate of

[178] Charles Kendall Harrington, *Captain Bickel of the Inland Sea* (New York, Fleming H. Revell Co., 1919, pp. 301), p. 84.
[179] *Proceedings of the General Conference of Protestant Missionaries in Japan* . . . *1900*, p. 929.
[180] *Proceedings of the General Conference of Protestant Missionaries in Japan* . . . *1900*, p. 942.
[181] *Proceedings of the General Conference of Protestant Missionaries in Japan* . . . *1900*, p. 921.
[182] *Ibid.*
[183] *Proceedings of the General Conference of Protestant Missionaries in Japan* . . . *1900*, p. 928.
[184] Drury, *History of the Church of the United Brethren in Christ*, p. 605.
[185] *Proceedings of the General Conference of Protestant Missionaries in Japan* . . . *1900*, p. 931.
[186] *Proceedings of the General Conference of Protestant Missionaries in Japan* . . . *1900*, p. 925.
[187] *Proceedings of the General Conference of Protestant Missionaries in Japan* . . . *1900*, p. 924.
[188] *Proceedings of the General Conference of Protestant Missionaries in Japan* . . . *1900*, p. 189.
[189] Kozaki, *Reminiscences of Seventy Years*, p. 213.
[190] *The Christian Movement in Japan*, 1914, statistical table.

increase than the difficult 1890's had seen. The total membership was 102,790,[191] or half again as large as that of the Roman Catholics. The total foreign missionary staff in 1914 or 1915 had grown to 1,123,[192] which was more than half again the size of that of 1900. Organized churches totalled 877,[193] which was more than twice that of the dawn of the century.

No single set of causes seems to account for the improvement. Several factors appear to have contributed. The reaction had spent its force. With the revision of the treaties, the Anglo-Japanese Alliance (1902, renewed in 1905 and 1911), and the victories over China in 1894-1895 and Russia in 1904-1905, Japan was being recognized, even if still somewhat superciliously, as one of the powers. As a conscious member of the family of nations she was less inclined to resist the growth of the foreign faith.

In some quarters in Japan there was an attempt to represent the Russo-Japanese War as a struggle between Christianity and Buddhism. The Treaty of Portsmouth, which concluded the war, was intensely unpopular with many. When the news that it was signed reached the country, riots broke out in Tokyo and several Christian chapels and churches were destroyed.[194] Yet the Japanese Government was friendly, for it was in alliance with Great Britain and needed and received the goodwill of the United States. It permitted the Young Men's Christian Association to serve the soldiers. To assist the association the Emperor and Empress made a substantial gift.[195] The American Bible Society obtained access to the navy and tens of thousands of portions of the New Testament were distributed among the troops.[196]

The chief growth was by the denominations longest in Japan. These were the *Nippon Sei Ko Kwai,* the *Nippon Kirisuto Kyokwai,* the *Kumiai,* and the Methodists. On the eve of 1914 these four bodies had together more than three-fourths of the Protestant membership.[197]

A few new missions entered the country between 1900 and 1914. Among these were the Lutheran Gospel Association of Finland, the Japan Evangelistic Band, the Nazarene Christian Church, the Young Women's Christian Association,[198] and the Oriental Missionary Society.[199] A unique enterprise was

[191] *Ibid.*
[192] Beach and St. John, *World Statistics of Christian Missions,* p. 62.
[193] *Ibid.*
[194] Kozaki, *Reminiscences of Seventy Years,* pp. 183-186.
[195] Cary, *A History of Christianity in Japan,* Vol. II, pp. 316-321.
[196] Dwight, *The Centennial History of the American Bible Society,* Vol. II, p. 487.
[197] *The Christian Movement in Japan,* 1914, statistical table.
[198] *Ibid.*
[199] E. A. Kilbourne, *The Story of a Mission in Japan* (Tokyo, Cowman and Kilbourne, no date, pp. 81), *passim;* Lettie B. Cowman, *Charles E. Cowman, Missionary Warrior* (Los Angeles, The Oriental Missionary Society, 1928, pp. 411), *passim.*

the Omi Mission. It centred around William Merrill Vories, who came to Japan in 1905 as a teacher in a government school. It took as its field the inland province of Omi, was undenominational, specialized on reaching rural districts hitherto untouched by Protestants and on the underprivileged, and made much of close fellowship between the Japanese and foreign staffs.[200] The International Christian Police Association, which originated in England, extended its operations to Japan, with policemen and their families as its objective.[201]

As in so many other lands, the methods of Protestantism in Japan showed variety. The features which were prominent in other major countries were all present. There were also special adaptations to fit conditions in Japan. There were efforts to reach non-Christians, with the gathering of churches and the recruiting and training of a Japanese ministry. In the twentieth century, especially, large public meetings were held for the proclamation of the Christian message. In 1901, John R. Mott addressed meetings in a number of centres, with the result that about fifteen hundred young men, of whom over one thousand were students, decided to become disciples of Christ.[202] In 1914 a national evangelistic campaign was conducted with the purpose of covering the country in a comprehensive fashion.[203] The fact that Japan was largely and increasingly urban facilitated programmes of this kind, for masses could be reached in the great cities. The missions conducted schools, from kindergartens through universities. For a brief time they had, as in China, almost a monopoly of the Western type of education. Much more quickly than in China the government developed a comprehensive educational system on Western models. As a result, in most branches Christian schools early lost their outstanding position. As a rule, students sought first to enter the state schools. If they failed of admission, they would go to a Christian school as a second choice. Because of the great demand for secondary and higher education, however, and the intense competition for available places, the Christian schools were usually full. They continued to have a leading place in some forms of higher education for women.[204] As was natural among a people predominantly literate, much use was made of the printed page. The Bible was translated and widely distributed. In 1913 over half a million copies of portions or all of the Christian Scriptures were circulated by the British and Foreign Bible Society and its American colleague.[205] In 1914

[200] William Merrill Vories, *A Mustard-Seed in Japan* (Omi-Hachiman, Omi Mission, 4th ed., 1922, pp. 147, vi, iv), *passim*.
[201] *The Christian Movement in Japan*, 1913, p. 427.
[202] Mathews, *John R. Mott*, p. 183.
[203] S. H. Wainright, *Campaigning for Christ in Japan* (Nashville, Publishing House of the M. E. Church, South, 1915, pp. 170), *passim*.
[204] *The Christian Movement in Japan*, 1914, p. 251.
[205] *The Christian Movement in Japan*, 1914, p. 205.

the Christian Literature Society of Japan and the Japan Book and Tract Society were in operation.[206] A variety of Christian literature was published.[207] A channel by which much of Protestant Christianity entered Japan, but largely apart from missionary effort, was the reading of English literature in middle schools and universities. Since English was the Western language chiefly desired, Dickens, Scott, Lamb, Carlyle, Tennyson, and Browning were the daily food of Japanese students. Through these writers many Christian ideas entered Japanese thought.[208] By what was known as newspaper evangelism a plan was developed for inserting in the secular daily papers, at advertising rates, passages from the Bible and brief articles on the Christian faith and for keeping in touch by post and personal contact with those who expressed interest.[209] Christian hostels were maintained for students in government and private schools.[210] Efforts were made, chiefly by the Young Men's Christian Association, to reach the thousands of Chinese and Korean students in the country.[211] There were orphanages, leper asylums, and care for discharged prisoners.[212] We read of a religious movement in one of the prisons in which amid weeping and confessions of sin more than half the inmates decided to become Christians.[213] The Japanese Government early took vigorously in hand the training of a modern medical profession. Protestant missionaries, therefore, did not place as much emphasis upon hospitals and dispensaries as in some other lands. However, some medical care was given. Outstanding was St. Luke's Hospital, later St. Luke's International Medical Centre, in Tokyo, in association with the mission of the Protestant Episcopal Church. Its creator was Rudolf Bolling Teusler, who came to Japan in 1900 and by his charm, devotion, ability, and transparent selflessness made a profound impression.[214] The temperance movement directed against alcoholic beverages was largely of Christian origin.[215] In Tokyo a Florence Crittenden home provided a refuge for the rescue of prostitutes and wayward girls.[216] For non-missionary Westerners there were churches in some of the chief ports.[217]

[206] *The Christian Movement in Japan*, 1914, pp. 201-204, 213-230.
[207] *The Christian Movement in Japan*, 1913, pp. 103ff.
[208] Missionaries of the United Church of Canada in Japan, *Fruits of Christian Missions in Japan*, pp. 170, 171.
[209] *The Christian Movement in Japan*, 1913, pp. 510ff.
[210] *The Christian Movement in Japan*, 1914, pp. 172ff.
[211] *The Christian Movement in Japan*, 1911, pp. 305ff.
[212] *The Christian Movement in Japan*, 1914, pp. 130ff.
[213] Pierson, *Forty Happy Years in Japan*, pp. 80-99.
[214] Howard Chandler Robbins and George K. MacNaught, *Dr. Rudolf Bolling Teusler. An Adventure in Christianity* (New York, Charles Scribner's Sons, 1942, pp. xv, 221), *passim*.
[215] *The Christian Movement in Japan*, 1914, p. 164.
[216] *The Japan Evangelist*, Vol. XX, p. 116.
[217] *The Christian Movement in Japan*, 1911, pp. 282, 283.

It was a varied impact which Protestant Christianity was making on the life of Japan.

The effects of Christianity upon Japan were diverse. It was in a number of ways that Christianity made itself felt in the life of the empire.

Numerically Christians, while growing in strength, in 1914 remained a small minority. They totalled only about two hundred thousand. This was less than one-half of one per cent. of the population. It was possibly a smaller aggregate and was certainly a smaller percentage than at the beginning of the seventeenth century. Of this two hundred thousand Protestants constituted slightly more than half and were increasing more rapidly than either Roman Catholics or Russian Orthodox.

The reasons which induced Japanese to become Christians were varied. One girl accepted the faith because she liked the teachers in the Christian school which she attended.[218] Another became a Christian because she found in the faith an answer to her question as to how the universe came to be, because, in contrast with Buddhism, it brought joyousness, and because it meant a more abounding life for her sex, with greater freedom and less useless self-sacrifice.[219] For many, the intellectual conviction of the truth of the Christian position was a large element. Others were constrained by an emotional experience or by the example of their fellows. Some were impressed by the forbearance and courtesy of Christians under persecution. Others were won by the moral changes wrought among their acquaintances by the Christian faith. In some instances personal sorrow, business adversity, or illness sent the individual upon a religious quest which led to the entrance upon the Christian faith.[220] In these reasons one also has a clue to the fruits which issued from belief. For instance, one who was later an officer of the Salvation Army had been reared in extreme poverty, had been attracted by Confucian ethics and had, in the main, lived an upright life. However, he had become greatly disheartened by the depressing surroundings in which he was constrained to live, when acquaintance with the Christian Gospel brought him joy and moral power and set him to work for those about him.[221]

In its effects upon the country as a whole Protestantism was relatively more

[218] Mishima, *My Narrow Isle*, pp. 17, 18.
[219] Etsu Inagaki Sugitomo, *A Daughter of the Samurai* (New York, Doubleday, Page & Co., 1927, pp. xv, 314), pp. 137-147.
[220] Katsuji Kato, *The Psychology of Oriental Religious Experience. A Study of Some Typical Experiences of Japanese Converts to Christianity* (Menasha, Wis., The Collegiate Press, 1915, pp. 102), pp. 1-52.
[221] See his autobiography in *The Japan Evangelist*, Vol. XIX, pp. 592-595.

prominent than were either of the other major branches of the Christian faith. This was partly because of the multiform programme of the Protestants. It was also because Protestantism drew more largely from the former *samurai* than did the others. It may also have been in part because Protestant missionaries were mainly from the United States and Great Britain, the lands of the Occident which had the greatest influence in shaping the new Japan. By teaching English, the chief Western language studied, Protestant missionaries made contacts with thousands of Japanese, some of whom later became prominent in the life of the empire.

Christianity was less influential in Japan than in China. At first sight this seems surprising. To a much larger extent than in China Christians, and especially Protestant Christians, were recruited from the upper and upper middle classes. It would be a natural assumption that through them Japan would be more moulded by Christianity than was the Middle Kingdom. In Japan, moreover, in 1914, although Christians constituted a slightly smaller percentage of the population than they did in China in that year, Protestants, who in both empires made a greater impact upon culture as a whole than did the other branches of Christianity, were in proportion to the entire population more than twice as strong in Japan as in China. The contrast seems to have been due to the fact that by 1914 the basic structure of the inherited civilization had crumbled to a much greater degree in China than in Japan and by doing so had left the country more open to alien influences, and to the equally important fact that since the government of China delayed longer than did that of Japan in rebuilding its education and its medical profession according to Western models, missionaries, and particularly Protestant missionaries, had for a time a monopoly of these phases of the coming culture. Christians, as leaders in shaping the civilization of the future, and especially the political structure, were, accordingly, much more outstanding in China than in Japan.

In the methods employed by missions, one has a clue to the effects of Christianity upon Japanese life.

One of the most striking of the results was the rise of the various Christian churches. Although small minorities, they were growing and were winning recognition, both by the government and by the general public.

Another contribution was in the field of education. This was seen not only in the existence of Christian schools, but also in the beginnings of other institutions. Verbeck organized the school which developed into the Imperial University of Tokyo.[222] Miss Tsuda, a Christian, denied herself much of what social

---

[222] Cary, *A History of Christianity in Japan*, Vol. II, p. 351.

position and wealth might have given her to devote herself to creating a school for girls.[223]

In the field of efforts for the amelioration of society Christianity was potent. It initiated a number of movements. Some of these spread to non-Christian circles and eventually received from them their chief support. Others continued to depend primarily upon Christians. For instance, John C. Berry, of the American Board of Commissioners for Foreign Missions, was a pioneer in the training of women as nurses.[224] He became interested in prison reform and his recommendations contributed to the later penal system of the empire. Some convicts under his influence changed their ways and became leaders in social service.[225] In the Hokkaido there was a remarkable movement for prisoners which issued in many remade lives.[226] We hear, too, of an instance in which the Christian faith led to the reconciliation of two men who by the ancient customs of the land would have been in blood feud.[227] A Japanese Christian woman opened a rescue home for members of her sex and through it saved from despair and death hundreds who were on the verge of suicide.[228] Another Japanese Christian conducted a home for sailors.[229] Still another, while a medical student, began to care for neglected children and then gave up his proposed profession to conduct an orphanage for them.[230] What is said to have been the first social settlement, an institution bearing the name of Kingsley Hall, was founded by a Japanese Christian, as was also what was declared to be the first society to give financial aid to sufferers from tuberculosis.[231] We hear of a school for the deaf and blind and of another school for blind begun by missionaries.[232] There was care of lepers.[233] The struggle against licensed prostitution and alcoholic beverages and the movements for international peace and greater privileges for women all were indebted to Christianity.[234] Forms of socialism intermixed with Christian teachings came in through Japanese Christians and Western missionaries.[235] A Japanese non-Christian scholar gave it as his con-

[223] Mishima, op. cit., pp. 59-74.
[224] Berry, A Pioneer Doctor in Old Japan, pp. 148ff.
[225] Berry, op. cit., pp. 54-58; Cary, op. cit., Vol. II, pp. 134.
[226] The Japan Evangelist, Vol. I, pp. 195-198.
[227] Carey, op. cit., Vol. II, p. 69.
[228] Missionaries of the United Church of Canada in Japan, Fruits of Christian Missions in Japan, p. 78.
[229] Ibid.
[230] Missionaries of the United Church of Canada in Japan, op. cit., p. 98.
[231] Missionaries of the United Church of Canada in Japan, op. cit., p. 100.
[232] Missionaries of the United Church of Canada in Japan, op. cit., p. 96.
[233] France, Japan, pp. 56, 57.
[234] Missionaries of the United Church of Canada in Japan, op. cit., pp. 101, 102; Saito, A Study of the Influence of Christianity upon Japanese Culture, pp. 12-15.
[235] Asari in Nitobe, Western Influences in Modern Japan, pp. 309, 312; Contemporary Japan, Vol. I, pp. 321-323.

viction that the idea of personality, its dignity and meaning in social life, and the practice of monogamy in aristocratic families were from Occidental influence which, in turn, was indirectly due to Christianity.[236] A Japanese legal expert reported that Christianity had ameliorated the rigour of ultra-nationalistic jurisprudence and had humanized the administration of justice.[237] It has been declared that early Protestant missionary activity was one of the main forces making for parliamentary government in Japan.[238] Beginning in 1876 the government made Sunday an official day of rest. This was not done from a religious motive, but to conform to Western practice. However, it showed Christian influence.[239] Although in Japan Protestant Christianity was primarily urban, it stimulated a few efforts to improve the hard lot of the farmers. A Christian layman organized in the Hokkaido a federation of dairy co-operatives.[240] In the Hokkaido a former member of the Imperial Diet, also a Christian layman, took up a large tract of land on which he founded a colony on Christian principles.[241] Goble, the first Baptist missionary in Japan, appears to have been the inventor of the jinricksha, the two-wheeled man-drawn vehicle which spread widely through Japan and China.[242] Christianity was by no means completely transforming the country, but it was having effects upon the social, political, and economic life of the empire.

Christianity seems to have left its impress upon the music of Japan. Christian missionaries are said to have introduced Western music into the empire. By their congregational singing, Protestants encouraged the people to song. The choir of the Russian Orthodox Church was much admired.[243] Through Christianity many excellent musicians were trained, organ music was developed, choruses came into being, and polyphonic music was introduced. Christian hymnals had a wide sale and in unexpected places one could hear selections from them on the voices of non-Christians.[244]

Results were seen in literature. Early in the twentieth century two or three of the Tokyo daily papers were owned and edited by active Christians. The moral tone of the Japanese press seems to have benefited from Christianity.[245]

[236] Anesaki in Nitobe, op. cit., p. 114.
[237] Takayanagi in Saito, op. cit., pp. 31-34.
[238] Laymen's Foreign Missions Inquiry. Fact Finders Reports, Japan, Vol. VI, Supplementary Series, Part 2, p. 119.
[239] Cary, op. cit., Vol. II, pp. 122, 123.
[240] Laymen's Foreign Missions Inquiry. Regional Reports of the Commission of Appraisal, Japan. Supplementary Series, Part I, Vol. III, pp. 11, 14.
[241] Pierson, Forty Happy Years in Japan, p. 78.
[242] Cary, op. cit., Vol. II, p. 52.
[243] The Japan Mission Year Book, 1929, pp. 225-232.
[244] Laymen's Foreign Missions Inquiry. Fact Finders Reports, Japan, Vol. VI. Supplementary Series, Part 2, p. 7.
[245] Faust, Christianity as a Social Factor in Modern Japan, p. 42.

Certain words increasingly were given a Christian meaning—such as those for love, self-sacrifice, and personality.[246]

Non-Christian religions and religious movements were affected by Christianity. Some of the Buddhist schools, or, as they are often called, sects, took over methods from Christians and especially from Protestant Christians. Among these methods were public preaching, youth associations, tract distribution, orphanages, social settlements, schools for the blind and the dumb, houses for the poor, day nurseries, free dispensaries, visiting nurses' associations, homes for women, Young Men's Buddhist Associations, summer schools, schools for boys and girls, and work for prisoners. To be sure, not all of these were directly copied from Christian missions. Some of them were inspired by what was seen in visits of Buddhist leaders to the Occident. Yet in them Christianity was obviously potent.[247] It is said that in one Buddhist temple the figure of Christ was worshipped under the title of Christ the God of Mercy, and that in several Buddhist temples Christmas was observed.[248] Buddhists organized Sunday schools in which the hymns were taken over bodily from Christian sources with slight alterations in the words.[249] Some of the sects of Shinto, as distinct from state Shinto, seem to have owed a little to Christianity. In most of them non-Christian elements were dominant.[250] Yet at least one of them sought to combine Shinto and Christianity.[251] Here and there were syncretistic movements into which Christianity entered prominently as an ingredient. Such was that which had the name of Ittoen, led by Tenko Nishida, who as a lad had been in touch with Davis of the Doshisha.[252] Masanao Keiu Nakamura (1832-1891), one of the most widely revered men of his day, a member of the faculty of the Imperial University of Tokyo, combined in his teaching Confucianism and Christianity.[253] Soon after the Russo-Japanese War several men who had once been Christians arose and professed to be prophets and saviours of the world.[254] The leader of another movement professed to be a successor to the Old Testament prophets.[255] An ethical society was constituted

[246] Faust, op. cit., pp. 44, 45.
[247] J. T. Addison in The International Review of Missions, Vol. XV, pp. 706ff.; Cary, op. cit., Vol. II, pp. 262, 263.
[248] Kagawa, Christ and Japan, p. 73.
[249] Arthur J. Brown, Japan in the World of To-day (New York, Fleming H. Revell Co., 1928, pp. 322), pp. 256-258.
[250] Clemen, Der Einfluss des Christentums auf andere Religionen, pp. 112-116; The International Review of Missions, Vol. XXIII, p. 548; Kagawa, op. cit., pp. 84, 85.
[251] Kagawa, op. cit., p. 96.
[252] E. V. Yoshida in conversation with the author, September 29, 1935.
[253] Anesaki, History of Japanese Religion, pp. 352, 353.
[254] Anesaki, op. cit., p. 386.
[255] Pascoe, Two Hundred Years of the S.P.G., p. 724e.

by Buddhists and Christian liberals with a former pupil of Neesima as a guiding spirit.[256]

In a land where nationalism ran as high as it did in Japan, the environment was certain to place a deep impression upon Christianity. It was to preserve the independence of Japan that Christianity had been excluded by the Tokugawa. When Christianity was once more admitted, it was in part because Japanese wished to win the respect of the Occident. Some of the Japanese who became Christians, notably among the *samurai,* did so because they believed that their new faith would be of assistance to the country in promoting its spiritual resurrection.[257]

Under these circumstances it is not strange that some Japanese sought to give to Christianity a peculiarly Japanese dress, to divorce it from dependence on the churches of the West, and to erase the denominational differences which had arisen in the Occident and through which Christianity had come to Japan. Here and there were congregations quite independent of any close foreign tie or imported denomination.[258] An outstanding teacher of Christianity who did not associate himself or his adherents with any church was Kanso Uchimura (1861-1930).[259] Uchimura became a Christian while at the agricultural college at Sapporo where during his brief term of service W. S. Clark had such remarkable influence. By lecturing, teaching the Bible, a monthly periodical on Bible study, and other writing Uchimura obtained a wide hearing.[260] The movement toward church union began early. The first Japanese Protestant church, formed in Yokohama in 1872, bore, apparently at the instance of the members rather than the missionaries, simply the name the "Church of Christ in Japan." [261] It was, therefore, without a denominational label. Not long afterward Japanese Christians in Tokyo and Yokohama appealed to the missionaries to rise above their divisions in bringing the Christian message to the land.[262] The augury given by the initial Protestant church of Japan and this appeal was not immediately fulfilled. Indeed, as the preceding pages have disclosed, the large majority of Japanese who became Protestant Christians were

[256] Anesaki, *op. cit.,* p. 368.

[257] Anesaki, *op. cit.,* p. 338.

[258] Kozaki, *Reminiscences of Seventy Years,* pp. 70-72.

[259] Kanzo Uchimura, *The Diary of a Japanese Convert* (Chicago, Fleming H. Revell Co., 1895, pp. 212), *passim.*

[260] Richter, *Die evangelische Mission in Fern- und Süd-ost Asien, Australien, Amerika,* p. 43; *Missionary Yearbook of the Methodist Episcopal Church, South,* 1929, p. 278.

[261] Verbeck in *Proceedings of the General Conference of Protestant Missionaries in Japan . . . 1888,* p. 53.

[262] Greene, *A New-Englander in Japan,* p. 135.

in denominational families which were the projections of those in the West. It was not until after 1914 that the vision of a united church was realized in practice. However, as in India and China, the missionaries themselves tended to co-operate across denominational lines. Out of a meeting of Presbyterian, Dutch Reformed, and Congregational missionaries at Yokohama in 1872 came joint committees on literature and the translation of the Bible.[263] General conferences of Protestant missionaries were held in 1883 and 1900.[264] From the 1900 conference arose the Standing Committee of Co-operating Christian Missions [265] which in time became the Conference of Federated Missions. The World Missionary Conference at Edinburgh was followed by conferences of missionaries and Japanese Christians.[266] In 1911 from the side of the Japanese Christians there sprang the League for the Promotion of the Union of the Christian Churches [267] and the Federation of Churches.[268] In 1914 the *Nippon Kirisuto Kyokwai* and the *Kumiai* organization had long been predominantly Japanese. The Russo-Japanese War (1904-1905) with the emergence of Japan into a more prominent international position gave an impetus to the Japanese churches to achieve a greater independence of foreign funds and foreign control. In 1905 further steps in this direction were taken by the *Kumiai* body and the *Nippon Kirisuto Kyokwai*.[269] In 1907 the churches associated with the three leading Methodist missionary societies united to form a single autonomous church.[270]

Occasionally nationalism ran high in the churches. It did so in the 1890's. At the time of the Russo-Japanese War at least one Japanese pastor declared in a sermon that as in the fifth century before Christ Greece had saved Europe from Persian despotism, so now Japan would free all Asia from the crushing exploitation and blighting control of the West.[271]

The fact that Japanese Protestantism was so largely urban and recruited from the professional and middle classes seems to have been due to at least two factors. One was the circumstance that the first missions and those which, with

[263] Greene, *op. cit.*, pp. 133, 134.
[264] *Proceedings of the General Conference of Protestant Missionaries of Japan . . . 1883, passim; Proceedings of the General Conference of Protestant Missionaries in Japan . . . 1900, passim.*
[265] *Proceedings of the General Conference of Protestant Missionaries in Japan . . . 1900*, pp. 960-962.
[266] *The Continuation Committee Conferences in Asia, 1912-1913*, pp. 409ff.
[267] *The Japan Evangelist*, Vol. XVIII, pp. 227-230.
[268] *The Christian Movement in Japan*, 1912, p. 468.
[269] *The Christian Movement in Japan*, 1906, pp. 193ff.
[270] *The Christian Movement in Japan*, 1907, pp. 266-275.
[271] Sidney L. Gulick, *Toward Understanding Japan* (New York, The Macmillan Co., 1935, pp. ix, 270), pp. 7, 8.

the exception of the Methodists, remained the strongest numerically were of the Presbyterian, Anglican, and Congregational families. These were groups which in the United States, the land whence the earliest and the majority of Protestant missionaries came, appealed primarily to the educated and those from the upper income levels. A discerning Japanese Christian later remarked that as introduced to Japan, Protestantism was strongly intellectualized and that this resulted in a gap between Christianity and the uneducated masses.[272] The second factor, closely related to the first, was the large proportion of *samurai* stock among the Protestant leadership. The prominence of the *samurai* was due in part to an idealism which responded to Christianity, in part to access, through the ability to read Chinese, to the Christian literature in that language, in part because in the dislocation of many of their class by the defeat of the Tokugawa and the abolishment of feudalism the *samurai* were uprooted and unhappy, in part because the school of Confucianism which some of them followed—that of Oyomei (Wang Yang-ming)—seemed to have kinship with Christianity,[273] and in part because many of the younger *samurai* were eager for Western learning and so came in contact with the missionaries who were among its earliest purveyors to the Japanese. Since educated *samurai* were prominent in the churches, they tended to recruit from their own kind and from the other intellectuals and better social classes. It is significant that the two bodies which led numerically in 1914 were the *Nippon Kirisuto Kyokwai* and the *Kumiai,* neither of them by transmitted genius proletarian, that Methodists, the only numerous body in Japan which could be called proletarian in the land from which the missionaries came, was third, and that the Anglicans, far from that social level in the West, were a close fourth. The Baptists and other traditionally proletarian bodies were in the small minority.[274] In striking contrast with India and China, in Japan in 1914 the numerically largest branch of Christianity was not Roman Catholicism but Protestantism, and, also in contradistinction with India and China, Protestantism in Japan was from the middle and the upper middle classes.

The Christianity which re-entered Japan after that land had again, in the second half of the nineteenth century, opened its doors to the West, was Roman Catholic, Russian Orthodox, and Protestant. By 1914 both Protestant missionaries and Japanese Protestant Christians were more numerous than were mis-

[272] Kagawa, *Christ and Japan,* p. 96.
[273] Kagawa in *The Japan Mission Year Book,* 1929, pp. 196ff.
[274] *The Christian Movement in Japan,* 1914, statistical tables.

sionaries and Christians of the other two great wings of the faith. Roman Catholic missionaries were overwhelmingly French. The large majority of Protestant missionaries were from the United States: almost all the others were from the British Isles and Canada.

Christianity spread in spite of the centuries in which it had been vigorously denounced and stringently prohibited. Thousands came to light who had conserved the faith handed down to them from their Roman Catholic ancestors. A substantial proportion of these accepted the ministrations of the Roman Catholic missionaries and constituted the main nucleus of the later Roman Catholic body in Japan. Thanks to a large degree to the zeal of the initiator of its mission in Japan, the Russian Orthodox Church gained a more extensive following in Japan than it won elsewhere in the nineteenth century from among non-Christians outside of Russia. The growth of Protestantism must in great degree be ascribed to the numbers and devotion of its missionary staff and to the circumstance that through these missionaries many Japanese obtained the instruction in the Western culture which they were eagerly seeking. The Roman Catholics and the Russian Orthodox recruited their adherents chiefly from the lower social strata, the Protestants predominantly from the urban middle and upper middle classes.

In proportion to the population, in 1914 Christians were not as numerous as in India and China. This was in part because until well along in the nineteenth century the opposition to Christianity was more consistent and better enforced than in either of these other two lands. It was also because, in contrast with both China and India, the nineteenth century started with a larger number of Christians in these lands than in Japan. In India Christianity was chiefly recruited from the enclaves under Portuguese control and from the underprivileged in the vast areas dominated by the English. In Japan neither of these favouring conditions existed. In China by 1914 the traditional structure of life had crumbled to a degree to which it had not in Japan. By 1914 China was, therefore, less resistant to Christianity than was the latter empire.

Moreover, proportionately to the population there were probably fewer professed Christians in Japan in 1914 than there had been in 1600, and that in spite of the fact that approximately the same length of time had elapsed between the renewal of Christianity in Japan in 1859 and 1914 as between the coming of Francis Xavier with the initial introduction of Christianity (1549) and the beginning of the persecutions (1612) which drove Christianity into hiding. The disparity in the growth in the two periods may have been due to the fact that in the interval Japan had been thoroughly regimented by the Tokugawa and so was less susceptible to a foreign faith and also to the fact that in the nineteenth century the basic structure of Japan did not disintegrate under the impact of the Occident. Japan was more united politically and ideologically than when Xavier arrived. Indeed, in the second half of the nineteenth century the spiritual unity of Japan had been reinforced by the fresh exaltation of the Emperor and the revival of Shinto as the religious foundation of Japanese solidarity. It seems to be significant that after 1859 Christianity made its numerical gains chiefly among the intellectuals who were most affected by Western culture.

Yet, in spite of its numerical weakness, in 1914 Christianity was becoming increasingly a part of Japanese life. The churches were growing and were in touch with the main currents of the Christianity of the Occident. Christians were bearing the characteristic fruits of that faith. They were displaying the hope, the victory over despair and moral weakness, the sense of fellowship with God, the selfless devotion to the unfortunate, and the courage in initiating and maintaining reform movements which were to be expected of their Christian profession. Neither Christianity nor the Occident was working a thoroughgoing revolution in the culture of the land. Yet Christianity was modifying some aspects of Japanese life. It was doing this to an extent quite out of proportion to its numerical strength. It was an increasing and not a waning feature of the Japanese scene. When account is taken of the short time in which it had been renewed—for only fifty-five years had elapsed between its reintroduction and the year 1914 and only slightly more than forty years between the removal of the anti-Christian edict boards and the year which marked the end of an era—and when it is remembered under what handicaps Christianity suffered from the long education against it and from the strengthening of Japanese nationalism and Shinto under the new order, the gains become very remarkable. In 1914 in Japan, as in so much of the rest of the world, Christianity was on an incoming tide.

Chapter VII

KOREA

KOREA had a tragic history which determined in part the course of Christianity within its borders. It had the misfortune to be at once a peninsula in a strategic position between great empires and too small to defend itself effectively. It was, therefore, repeatedly invaded by its more powerful neighbours and was a helpless pawn in the international game of power politics. On one side was China. From time to time, beginning not far from the inception of the Christian era, strong Chinese dynasties extended their authority over portions of the peninsula. Korea, like pre-nineteenth century Japan, was within the Chinese cultural zone. From China it derived the mode of writing most frequently in use, the major part of its literature, Confucianism, and a model for its political organization. At the dawn of the nineteenth century Korea was a tributary state to the Manchu rulers of the Chinese Empire. From early historic times Japanese also invaded Korea. Over long periods southern portions of the peninsula were under Japanese rule. In the closing decade of the sixteenth century the Japanese, directed by Hideyoshi, overran the country with the purpose of using it as a highway towards the conquest of China. From the devastation of these unhappy years Korea was very slow in recovering. It long bore a tributary relationship to Japan as well as to China. In A.D. 1800 it was in the hands of a decadent dynasty and was in poor condition to meet the international intrigues which accompanied the penetration of the Far East by the Occident. Fearful of the complications which might ensue from the coming of Western peoples and later in being subjected to armed pressure by them, the Korean rulers were much more tardy in admitting the Occidentals and entering into treaty relations with them than was either China or Japan. In 1876 Japan wrung a treaty from Korea. In 1882 the United States obtained a commercial treaty. In the 1880's similar treaties were granted to Great Britain, Germany, Italy, Russia, and France. Japan, now emerged from the Tokugawa seclusion and eager again to play a role on the continent, saw in Korea her most tempting opportunity. Competition followed between herself and China. Japan espoused those in Korea who would adjust themselves to Western ways.

China gave support to the conservatives. In 1894 war broke out between China and Japan with Korea as the helpless bone of contention. The Japanese victory had as a consequence the expulsion of Chinese political influence. Russia, then expanding in the Far East, succeeded China as Japan's chief rival in Korea. War was the result (1904-1905). Russia was defeated. Japan thereupon brought Korea into her empire. At first (1905) she obtained control of Korean foreign relations and soon (1910) forced the surrender of the Crown and formally annexed the country. Thereafter, in spite of feeble resistance and abortive plots by Korean nationalists, the Japanese were dominant. It was under the somnolent and conservative years of the close of the eighteenth and the fore part of the nineteenth century that Christianity first entered the country and it was under the turbulent decades immediately preceding 1914 that it had a fairly extensive growth.

Religiously Korea was a mixture. The scene was compounded of animism, a crude polytheism, a decadent Buddhism, Confucianism, and, strongly supported by Confucianism, the ancestral cult. It was this last which, in the earliest stages of the introduction of Christianity, offered the strongest opposition.

Christianity's was a tragic record in this tragic land. The faith was later in gaining a continuing foothold in Korea than in either China or Japan. When once it had won an entrance its course was long punctuated by persecution. Not until the next to the last decade of the nineteenth century was it really tolerated. Both before and after persecution was allayed its growth was irregular. At times it was very rapid. At other times it was slow and even suffered reverses. Christianity first came to Korea in its Roman Catholic form. Beginning in the 1880's Protestantism was added. At the end of the century the Russian Orthodox Church appeared on the scene.

Christianity seems first to have been brought to Korea by a conquering army. The Japanese forces which Hideyoshi sent to the peninsula in the 1590's contained many Christians, fruits of the successful Jesuit mission of that century. In 1593, at the request of some of the Christian officers of the invaders, a European Jesuit and a Japanese lay brother were assigned to minister to the troops. They spent the winter on the island of Tsushima in the straits between the main Japanese island and Korea and early in 1594 reached the peninsula itself. The priest confirmed the faith of the Christians and baptized several of the soldiers. However, the accusation that he was fomenting sedition led to his early recall to Japan.[1] In the 1590's a number of Korean slaves in Nagasaki,

[1] Dallet, *Histoire de l'Église de Corée,* Vol. I, p. 2.

the chief centre of sixteenth century Japanese Christianity, were baptized.[2] When, later in the 1590's, the Japanese armies were withdrawn from Korea, no traces of Christianity seem to have survived in the peninsula, for the faith appears not to have spread to the inhabitants.[3] However, numbers of the Koreans who had become Christians in Japan shared in the persecutions which overtook the faith in that land in the seventeenth century and paid for their fidelity with their lives.[4] The Japanese officials testified to the constancy of the Korean Christians, especially of the women.[5]

The next contacts of Koreans with Christianity were through the Jesuits in China. Members of the periodical embassies sent to Peking met some of the missionaries in that city. At least one of Ricci's treatises on Christianity became known in Korea. Not far from 1770 a Korean from an official family gave himself to the study of Christian books in Chinese which, because of the familiarity with that language possessed by all the educated of his nation, he was able to read. He devoted himself to the practice of the religion which he found in them but seems never to have been baptized.[6]

It appears not to have been until 1784, or on the eve of the nineteenth century, that Christianity began a continuing life in Korea. This came about, like the abortive entrance in the preceding decade, through contacts with Peking. In 1777 a group of scholars were studying together books prepared by Roman Catholic missionaries and obtained through the embassies.[7] One of this group asked a member of the embassy which went to Peking late in 1783 to obtain further information about the strange faith. In consequence, the son of one of the two envoys became so impressed that he asked baptism of the missionaries and was given it. On his return to Korea in the spring of 1784 this convert, Peter Ri (or Ni), carried with him a large number of books, crucifixes, images, and other religious objects. He baptized the friend who had started him on the quest and before long a number of additional converts were won, largely from the official and scholar class.[8] The Christians organized themselves with a bishop and priests from their own number who preached, heard confessions, administered confirmation, and celebrated mass. However, further study of the Christian books aroused doubts as to the validity of this procedure and inquiry

[2] Dallet, op. cit., Vol. I, p. 3.
[3] Dallet, op. cit., Vol. I, p. 4.
[4] Dallet, op. cit., Vol. I, pp. 5-10.
[5] Kirishito-ki und Sayo-yoruku. Japanische Dokumente zur Missionsgeschichte des 17 Jahrhunderts in deutsche übertragen von Gustav Voss, S.J. und Hubert Cieslik, S.J. (Tokyo, Sophia University, 1940), p. 61.
[6] Dallet, op. cit., Vol. I, pp. 11, 12.
[7] Dallet, op. cit., Vol. I, pp. 14, 15.
[8] Dallet, op. cit., Vol. I, pp. 17-25.

concerning it was made of the Bishop of Peking. That dignitary explained that the Korean Christians had gone beyond their proper functions but encouraged them to continue to win converts. The Bishop of Peking also instructed them not to participate in the traditional ceremonies in honour of their ancestors.[9] This, it will be remembered, was in accordance with the decision of Rome in connexion with the famous Rites Controversy.[10]

Persecution by the state was the lot of the Christians almost from the first. An important cause of the opposition was the refusal of the converts to take part in the ancestral cult, for this, as in China, appeared to strike at the very basis of morality and society. There was also the fear that the Christian groups, meeting clandestinely, might, like secret societies, be nuclei of sedition and rebellion. Probably, too, the proscription of Christianity by both Korea's great neighbours, and particularly by China, contributed to the official attitude. Before the end of the century there were a number of martyrdoms.[11]

To the young and sorely beset Christian communities clergy were slow in coming. In 1791 a Portuguese secular from Macao was appointed by the Bishop of Peking but did not succeed in crossing the border.[12] As a successor a Chinese priest was chosen who reached Korea late in 1793. He showed great zeal and by dint of extreme care in keeping away from the police maintained his ministry until 1801. He was then apprehended and executed. By that time the Christians are said to have numbered several thousand. Among them were persons of education and consequence. The persecution associated with the death of the Chinese missionary is reported to have cost the lives of hundreds of Christians. There were also many apostasies. Anti-Christian edicts branded the faith as denying the authority of both parents and king and declared that the Christians were planning to bring in European troops to conquer the country. Since many of the Christians were from prominent families, factional strife aggravated the situation. Enemies of the Christians took the occasion to be rid of their rivals. When, in 1802, the storm subsided, most of the Christians of any social or political importance were dead or in exile and the Church seemed on the way to extinction.[13]

Now ensued difficult years. The Christian remnants attempted to obtain aid from the Bishop of Peking and the Pope. However, the mission in Peking was being persecuted and was at a low ebb. Beginning in 1808 there was no resi-

---

[9] Dallet, op. cit., Vol. I, pp. 25-35.

[10] Vol. III, pp. 349-355.

[11] Dallet, op. cit., Vol. I, pp. 37-127.

[12] Dallet, op. cit., Vol. I, p. 69.

[13] Dallet, op. cit., Vol. I, pp. 70-242, Vol. II, p. 239. See a brief summary in The Catholic Church in Korea, pp. 20, 21.

dent bishop in the city. The Napoleonic Wars were reducing the already diminished aid from Europe to the harassed Christians of China and the Sovereign Pontiff himself was hard bested. Now and again some from the remaining Christians in Korea were arrested and executed.[14]

When the Roman Catholic Church in Europe was beginning to recover from the blows dealt it by the French Revolution and the wars of Napoleon and its missions were once more being reinforced, a letter reached Rome (1827) from the Korean Christians beseeching assistance.[15] This time Rome was able to respond. The Société des Missions Étrangères of Paris which had borne so large a part of the responsibility in the Far East for keeping the faith alive and extending it was asked (1827) to add Korea to its fields. This it did. To the leadership of the difficult undertaking there was appointed, at his own request, Barthélemy Bruguière, who had been designated as coadjutor to the Vicar Apostolic of Siam. In 1831 Bruguière was named Vicar Apostolic of Korea and the following year set out for his post.[16] As a companion he had Pierre Philibert Maubant. In the face of the difficulties besetting European travellers in China he made his way across that country, a task of more than two years, to the Roman Catholic centre at Hsi-wan-tzŭ in Inner Mongolia. In 1835, while on the road to Korea from Hsi-wan-tzŭ, Bruguière suddenly died.[17] Maubant persevered, and early in 1836 reached Korea. He went to Seoul, the capital, and, remaining so far as possible in hiding, began ministering to the Christians.[18] Slightly earlier, in 1834, a Chinese priest trained in the College of the Propaganda at Rome and also designated to assist Bruguière had succeeded in entering the country. He, however, proved a hindrance and had to be sent back to China.[19] Laurent Joseph Marie Imbert, who had served for a number of years in Szechwan, was appointed vicar apostolic. He was consecrated in 1837 and that same year arrived at his post.[20]

In 1839, before the foreign clergy had become fully established in the country, a fresh persecution arose. Indeed, it seems to have been precipitated by the increased activity of the Christians which followed the coming of the missionaries. Bishop Imbert and his two foreign colleagues surrendered themselves to the authorities, hoping that by so doing they might avert some of the official

[14] Dallet, *op. cit.*, Vol. I, pp. 243-380.
[15] Dallet, *op. cit.*, Vol. II, pp. 3-5.
[16] Launay, *Histoire Générale de la Société des Missions-Étrangères*, Vol. II, pp. 575-578, 582, 583.
[17] Launay, *op. cit.*, Vol. II, pp. 583-585.
[18] Launay, *op. cit.*, Vol. II, pp. 586, 587.
[19] *The Catholic Church in Korea*, pp. 23-25.
[20] Moidry, *La Hiérarchie Catholique en Chine, en Corée et au Japon*, p. 160; Launay, *op. cit.*, Vol. III, pp. 62-71.

wrath from the faithful. The three were tortured and executed. Numbers of the Korean Christians, men and women, were also killed. Others were imprisoned or exiled. In contrast with the persecution of 1801-1802, when many of the martyrs were from prominent families and jealousies among the ruling groups entered into the issue, in the storm of 1839 most of the victims were from the humble. The total of the Korean Christians decapitated is said to have been seventy, and of those who were strangled, or beaten to death, or who died of their wounds, sixty. Numbers at first apostatized, but several of these later reaffirmed their faith and testified to their sincerity by their death. While most of the Christian communities were broken up, that was only for a time, and the publicity given to the Church by the measures against it served to familiarize many of the non-Christians with its existence and with some of its tenets.[21]

To the Korean Christians, thus cut off from clerical ministrations, assistance from the outside was slow in coming. Jean Joseph Férreol, who was on his way to Korea in the year of the persecutions, and who was created vicar apostolic, several times essayed to enter the country, but it was not until 1845 that he was successful. In the meantime contact was established between the Christians and their co-religionists in the outer world by an intrepid Korean student for the priesthood, Andrew Kim, who went back and forth between the Christian groups and his ecclesiastical superiors. In 1845 he received ordination, the first of his nation to do so. In 1846 he paid for his daring with his life, a victim of the anti-Christian policy of his government. His execution was precipitated by a letter to the Korean authorities from a French admiral threatening reprisals for the three missionaries who had been killed in 1839.[22]

How many Christians there were in Korea when Bishop Férreol finally made contact with them we do not know. The figure given by the Propaganda, twenty thousand, can obviously be only a rough estimate.[23] Persecuted as they were and deprived of clerical ministrations, it is not surprising that most of them participated to a greater or less extent in non-Christian religious ceremonies. The marvel is that any of them persevered in the faith and that converts were still being won.[24]

In the decade which followed the arrival of Férreol Christianity made

[21] Launay, op. cit., Vol. III, pp. 67-77; Mission de Seoul. Documents Relatifs aux Martyrs de Corée de 1839 et 1846, pp. 1-73; Dallet, op. cit., Vol. II, pp. 186-241; Launay, Martyrs Français et Coréens, 1838-1846, pp. 32-205.
[22] Launay, Martyrs Français et Coréens, 1838-1846, pp. 206ff.; Mission de Seoul. Documents Relatifs aux Martyrs de Corée de 1839 et 1846, pp. 73ff.; Huonder, Der einheimische Klerus in den Heidenländern, pp. 206-210.
[23] Notizie Statistiche delle Missioni di Tutto il Mondo Dipendenti dalla S.C. de Propaganda Fide, 1844, p. 574.
[24] Dallet, Histoire de l'Élgise de Corée, Vol. II, pp. 302, 303.

progress. Although access to the land was still far from easy, other missionaries joined the staff.[25] The fact that China was now partly open facilitated the sending of reinforcements. In 1857 the vicar apostolic reported that Christians numbered slightly over fifteen thousand and that five hundred and eighteen adults had been baptized in the past year.[26] The success of the British and French arms against China in 1856-1860, and especially the capture of Peking in the latter year, created a profound impression in Seoul and may have given occasion for an increase in the rate of growth of the Christian communities.[27]

In 1866 another violent persecution broke out which again threatened the Church with extinction. Why it came is not entirely clear. It followed the death of the King and was associated with the coming to power of a regent who proved to be implacably anti-Christian. It seems to have arisen in part from the fear of foreign aggression. Russia was reaching southward and was making demands on Korea. Some of the Christians, presumably hoping that thus they might obtain powerful foreign protection, suggested to the Regent that he seek French and British help against the northern foe.[28] The persecution appears also to have sprung from conservative opposition to any compromise with Western culture. Whatever the cause, it included the execution of two bishops and seven other missionaries. Three missionaries escaped, but only by fleeing the country. By September, 1868, two thousand of the Christians are said to have perished. A futile attempt of a French admiral to come to the rescue was interpreted by the Koreans as weakness and a confirmation of the suspicion that Christians menaced the independence of the country.[29]

The Société des Missions Étrangères of Paris was undiscouraged and was far from abandoning its perilous field. Attempts were again and again made to place missionaries in the hostile kingdom. In 1876 two French priests were conducted into the country by Korean guides.[30] In 1877 a new vicar apostolic, Felix Clair Ridel, who was among those who had escaped by flight from the persecution of 1866, re-entered the land. He was soon arrested, but pressure from the French upon Peking and by the Japanese obtained his release.[31] Although a fresh

[25] Dallet, op. cit., Vol. II, pp. 322ff.
[26] Dallet, op. cit., Vol. II, p. 434.
[27] Dallett, op. cit., Vol. II, pp. 451ff.
[28] Launay, Histoire Générale de la Société des Missions Étrangères, Vol. III, pp. 464, 465.
[29] Launay, op. cit., Vol. III, pp. 465-477; Dallet, op. cit., Vol. II, pp. 521ff.; Mission de Seoul. Documents Relatifs aux Martyrs de Corée de 1868 (Hongkong, Imprimerie de Nazareth, 1925, pp. 167), passim; C. Appert, adapted from the French by Florence Gilmore, For the Faith. Life of Just de Bretenières, Martyred in Korea March 8, 1866 (Maryknoll, Catholic Foreign Mission Society, 1918, pp. 179), passim.
[30] The Catholic Church in Korea, pp. 55, 56.
[31] The Catholic Church in Korea, pp. 56, 57.

anti-Christian edict was issued in 1881, it was not seriously enforced.[32] In the 1880's Korea was entering into treaty relations with Western nations and the authorities felt it expedient not to aggravate the powers by openly anti-Christian acts.

Now began a time of fairly steady and relatively quiet growth. In 1890 the number of Roman Catholics was reported as 17,577.[33] In the early 1890's the disturbances associated with a religious movement, that of the Tonghaks, were in part directed against the Christians but were only temporary. Churches were erected, including one in Seoul itself. The Regent's wife was baptized.[34] In 1900 Roman Catholics totalled forty-two thousand and in 1911 seventy-seven thousand.[35] In 1911 missionaries and Christians had so far increased that a second vicariate was created. Like the first, it was entrusted to the Paris Society.[36] In 1909 Bavarian Benedictines established a monastery in Seoul. Their purpose was the training of teachers for the Christian schools which were arising in the provinces.[37] Korean Christians were followed as they migrated into Manchuria and by 1908 Chientao, the region where most of them settled, had several thousand Roman Catholics.[38] Candidates were trained for the priesthood. Sisters entered. The coming of Japanese rule did not immediately bring serious embarrassment. Indeed, with the exception of some restrictions on education, it meant toleration and increased opportunity. Lack of financial means and of personnel prevented the Paris missionaries from taking full advantage of the new day,[39] but advance was being made.

The nineteenth century was still early in its second quarter when Protestants had their first contact with Korea. In 1832 the zealous and widely travelled Gützlaff touched at points along the coast and its adjacent islands.[40] However, no enduring enterprise was begun.

It was not until past the middle of the century that other Protestant missionaries reached the country. In 1865 R. J. Thomas, who was serving in China under the London Missionary Society, went to Korea as an agent of the National

[32] *The Catholic Church in Korea*, p. 59.
[33] *The Catholic Church in Korea*, pp. 61.
[34] *The Catholic Church in Korea*, pp. 62, 63.
[35] *The Catholic Church in Korea*, p. 68.
[36] *The Catholic Church in Korea*, p. 71.
[37] *The Catholic Church in Korea*, p. 89.
[38] *The Catholic Church in Korea*, pp. 65, 66.
[39] Schmidlin-Braun, *Catholic Mission History*, p. 626.
[40] Gützlaff, *Journal of Three Voyages along the Coast of China*, pp. 316-356.

Bible Society of Scotland. He did this in company with Roman Catholic Koreans who had been in Shantung and were returning to their native land. He was on the Korean coast for two and a half months and distributed a number of Chinese Bibles.[41] The subsequent year he was back on an American ship, the ill-fated *General Sherman,* which, grounding in an attempt to push its way up a river, was burned. Thomas and all the crew perished.[42] In 1867 Alexander Williamson, the China agent of the National Bible Society of Scotland, was on the Manchurian border of Korea and sold to Koreans a number of Christian books.[43] In 1873 John Ross, who had come to Manchuria the previous year under the United Presbyterian Church of Scotland and who was to have many years in that region, penetrated to the Korean marches. In 1874 he was again on the border and made contacts which enabled him to obtain a Korean teacher. With this assistance he and one of his colleagues translated the New Testament into Korean. In the process at least three Koreans became Christians. Later Korean colporteurs were sent from Mukden to their native land. Conversions followed and when the first Presbyterian church in Seoul was organized, among its original members were those who had come into the faith through these channels.[44] In 1881 and 1884 Ross also baptized Koreans in Manchuria.[45]

It was not until after the first treaties between Korea and Western nations that Protestant missionaries were able to begin residence in the kingdom. As in Japan, it was not British but American societies which were chiefly responsible for the planting and development of Protestantism. Because of the part which Japan had played in the opening of their country, a number of Koreans went to that empire either as political refugees or as students. There Protestant missionaries won a few converts from among them.[46] Almost simultaneously American (Northern) Presbyterians, American (Northern) Methodists, and Anglicans began enterprises in Korea. Representatives of all three denominations reached Korea in 1884.

In September, 1884, Horace Newton Allen arrived for the Presbyterians. He was a physician and gave medical care to the various foreign legations in Seoul. He also saved the life of one of the princes of the royal house and was made court physician. At his suggestion a government hospital was opened in

---

[41] *Annual Report of the National Bible Society of Scotland,* 1865, pp. 35, 36, 1866, p. 41.
[42] *Annual Report of the National Bible Society of Scotland,* 1866, p. 42; *The Seventy-Third Report of the London Missionary Society . . . 1867,* pp. 27, 80.
[43] *Annual Report of the National Bible Society of Scotland,* 1868, pp. 43, 44.
[44] J. Ross in *The Missionary Review of the World,* N. S., Vol. III (1890), pp. 241-248; Paik, *The History of Protestant Missions in Korea,* pp. 46-48.
[45] Clark, *Digest of the Presbyterian Church of Korea,* p. 2.
[46] Paik, *op. cit.,* pp. 69, 71.

1885 and he was placed in charge.[47] Allen did not long remain in the service of the mission but in 1887 became secretary to the Korean legation in Washington and in 1890, after another brief term with the mission, secretary of the American legation in Seoul. Later he became the American Minister to Korea.[48] In 1884 there arrived a second Presbyterian missionary, Horace Grant Underwood (1859-1916).[49] Underwood continued with the mission and in time became not only its Nestor but also outstanding in his achievements as educator, translator of the Bible and of other Christian literature, lexicographer, evangelist, organizer, and unofficial adviser to the King.[50]

R. S. Maclay, who in the 1880's was superintendent of the Japan mission of the Methodist Episcopal Church, had long been interested in Korea. In 1847 he had met Koreans in Foochow. As early as 1872 he had urged the missionary society of his denomination to establish a mission in Korea. In 1884, at the behest of the secretary, he visited that land to pave the way for the continuing undertaking which had been decided upon the preceding year. He obtained royal permission for Protestant missions.[51] In 1885 two missionary families, composed of a physician and the superintendent of the proposed new mission, H. G. Appenzeller, reached Japan. Palace disorders between the conservatives and the progressives delayed the beginning of the new mission, but only for a brief time. In 1885 a foothold had been acquired from which ensued a growing enterprise.[52]

In 1869 the new Bishop of Victoria (Hongkong) proposed a society which would have as its field the Far East, including Korea.[53] After the first Anglo-Korean treaty (1883), three English bishops in China appealed to the Church of England to begin a mission in Korea. In 1884 one of the Church Missionary Society's representatives in Fukien paid a visit to the newly opened land and on his return to Foochow gave so enthusiastic an account of the opportunity that Chinese Christians decided to take advantage of it. Some of them went

---

[47] *The Forty-Eighth Annual Report of the Board of Foreign Missions of the Presbyterian Church in the United States of America*, 1885, p. 130.

[48] Paik, *op. cit.*, pp. 77, 78.

[49] *The Forty-Ninth Annual Report of the Board of Foreign Missions of the Presbyterian Church in the United States of America*, 1886, p. 148.

[50] Lilias H. Underwood, *Underwood of Korea* (Chicago, Fleming H. Revell Co., 1918, pp. 350), *passim*. For reminiscences by Mrs. Underwood, see L. H. Underwood, *Fifteen Years among the Top-Knots, or Life in Korea* (New York, American Tract Society, 1904, pp. xviii, 271).

[51] Maclay in *The Missionary Review of the World*, N. S. Vol. IX, pp. 287-290; *Sixty-Sixth Annual Report of the Missionary Society of the Methodist Episcopal Church*, 1884, pp. 204, 205.

[52] *Sixty-Seventh Annual Report of the Missionary Society of the Methodist Episcopal Church*, 1885, pp. 234, 239.

[53] Stock, *The History of the Church Missionary Society*, Vol. II, p. 588.

to Korea and for a time seemed to be making progress. However, they did not persevere. It was through the Society for the Propagation of the Gospel in Foreign Parts that the Anglicans were chiefly represented.[54]

It was the American Presbyterians and the American Methodists who continued to bear the main brunt of the planting and development of Protestant Christianity in Korea.

To the (Northern) Presbyterian Church in the United States of America was added, in 1892, the (Southern) Presbyterian Church in the United States. This was largely through the appeal of Underwood which aroused students to ask to be sent out and was stimulated by substantial gifts from Underwood and his brother John, who was beginning to accumulate a fortune through the manufacture of typewriters. It was in 1892 that the first group of Southern Presbyterians reached Seoul. The following year a council of all Presbyterian missionaries in Korea assigned them provinces in the south-west.[55] We must note that Presbyterians from Australia had already (1889) entered the country. The pioneers were J. H. Davies and his sister. Davies had been a missionary in India, but ill health had forced him out of that country. He had only about half a year in Korea before death claimed him, but his sacrifice stirred up added support in Australia for the enterprise to which he had given his life, and reinforcements soon came.[56] Still later, in 1898, in part because of the interest aroused by the early death of an independent missionary who was of that communion,[57] came Canadian Presbyterians. In 1914, thanks to the activities of these four churches, Presbyterians had more than half the total Protestant missionary body in Korea and nearly three-fourths of the Protestant communicants. The Northern Presbyterians were by far the most important numerically.[58] The Northern Presbyterians extended their activities northward. In this Samuel Addison Moffett was a pioneer. A centre was established in the important city of Pyeng Yang. At first hostile, after the battle fought there between China and Japan in 1894 Pyeng Yang became more open-minded, for the bewildered populace found that they could trust the missionaries. Later the churches had a striking growth in the region.[59]

The (Northern) Methodist Episcopal Church reinforced its staff. To it, as to the Northern Presbyterians, there was added the southern branch of its communion. The Methodist Episcopal Church, South, came to Korea primarily

[54] Stock, op. cit., Vol. III, p. 565.
[55] Nisbet, Day In and Day Out in Korea, pp. 17-20.
[56] Clark, Digest of the Presbyterian Church in Korea, p. 3; Paik, The History of Protestant Missions in Korea, pp. 175-177.
[57] Underwood, The Call of Korea, p. 141; Paik, op. cit., pp. 265, 266.
[58] Beach and St. John, World Statistics of Christian Missions, p. 62.
[59] Underwood, op. cit., pp. 144, 145; Paik, op. cit., pp. 171, 172.

because of the initiative of a prominent official, T. H. Yun (Yun Chi Ho). As a lad in his teens, Yun, who had connexions at court, studied in Japan and then in the Anglo-Chinese College in Shanghai, of which the distinguished Southern Methodist missionary, Young J. Allen, was the head. Yun was baptized while in Shanghai, and later attended Southern Methodist schools in the United States. He returned to Shanghai and taught in the Anglo-Chinese College until a shift in the political situation following the war between China and Japan made it possible for him to go back to his native land. Once more in Seoul, Yun quickly rose to prominence and became the chief leader in the struggle for constitutional government. He urged upon the Southern Methodists the inauguration of a mission in Korea. In 1895 a bishop of the church and C. F. Reid from the China mission visited the country. In 1896 Reid took up his residence as the first "Presiding Elder of the Korea Conference of the Korea District of the China Mission Conference."[60] The Northern Methodists continued to be larger both in staff and in numbers of Christians than did the Southern Methodists. In 1914 the two together had a little over a fourth of the total Protestant missionary body and between a fifth and a fourth of the Protestant communicants.[61]

The entrance of the Church of England through the Society for the Propagation of the Gospel in Foreign Parts came directly in response to an appeal to the Archbishop of Canterbury by the English bishops in North China and Japan. The decision was reached to appoint a bishop to inaugurate the enterprise. For this post C. J. Corfe, long a chaplain in the British navy, was chosen and consecrated. Bishop Corfe arrived in 1890. Centres were established at Seoul and its port, Chemulpo.[62] In 1892 there came Sisters of the Community of St. Peter (Kilburn) who gave themselves at first to nursing and later added other occupations.[63] Contacts were made with Japanese as well as Koreans and operations were extended into some other parts of the country. The first baptisms took place in 1897. The five years between the Russo-Japanese War and the formal annexation of Korea by Japan witnessed, as in the Presbyterian and Methodist ranks, a very rapid growth. This seems to have been associated with the disintegration of the old order which was occurring in these years.[64] The year 1914 found the Anglican mission in charge of its third bishop, Mark

[60] Ryang, *Southern Methodism in Korea*, pp. 14-17; Wasson, *Church Growth in Korea*, pp. 10-13.
[61] Beach and St. John, *op. cit.*, p. 62.
[62] Pascoe, *Two Hundred Years of the S.P.G.*, pp. 713, 714; *The English Church Mission in Corea: Its Faith and Practice* (London, A. R. Mowbray & Co., 1917, pp. 80); Trollope, *The Church in Corea*, pp. 28-40.
[63] Trollope, *op. cit.*, p. 41.
[64] Trollope, *op. cit.*, pp. 72-84.

Napier Trollope,[65] one of the original pioneers. It then had slightly less than six thousand baptized members.[66]

To these larger bodies a few smaller missions were added. In 1889 the Toronto University Young Men's Christian Association sent a representative.[67] In 1895 the Ellen Thing Memorial Mission was founded by a wealthy layman of Massachusetts in memory of his only daughter.[68] Early in the first decade of the twentieth century the International Committee of the Young Men's Christian Association appointed a secretary for Korea and in 1903 an association was organized in Seoul. For this a building after the American pattern was erected in 1908.[69] In that same decade the Seventh Day Adventists came, but by 1914 they had gathered only about five hundred members.[70] There also were the Oriental Missionary Society, which we noted in Japan,[71] and the British Evangelistic Mission, in Seoul.[72] Out of the work of an independent missionary arose the Korean Itinerant Mission.[73] In 1908 the Salvation Army arrived and quickly attracted large numbers.[74]

In many of its features the programme of Protestant missions in Korea was not unlike that in other lands in the nineteenth century. The Bible was translated and distributed.[75] In 1913 the circulation of the American Bible Society and the British and Foreign Bible Society was over half a million, most of it of portions, not the entire Bible.[76] In 1888 the Korean Tract Society was organized and for a time received financial assistance from the Religious Tract Society of London and the American Tract Society.[77] Periodicals were maintained in the vernacular.[78] Schools incorporating Western methods and subjects were developed, from those of primary grade through secondary schools to colleges.

[65] Constance Trollope, *Mark Napier Trollope, Bishop in Corea, 1911-1930* (London, Society for Promoting Christian Knowledge, 1936, pp. xiii, 187), *passim*.
[66] Beach and St. John, *op. cit.,* p. 63.
[67] Paik, *The History of Protestant Missions in Korea*, pp. 179, 180.
[68] Richter, *Die evangelische Mission in Fern- und Südost-Asien, Australien, Amerika,* p. 95.
[69] Paik, *op. cit.,* pp. 326, 327; Underwood, *The Call of Korea*, p. 119; *The Christian Movement in Japan*, 1914, pp. 502ff.; Brockman, *I Discover the Orient*, pp. 99-104.
[70] Beach and St. John, *op. cit.,* p. 62.
[71] *The Christian Movement in Japan*, 1914, pp. 397ff.
[72] Jean Perry, *Twenty Years a Korea Missionary* (London, S. W. Partridge & Co., no date, pp. 72).
[73] Paik, *op. cit.,* pp. 180, 181, 431-433; Malcolm C. Fenwick, *The Church of Christ in Corea* (New York, George H. Doran Co., 1911, pp. vi, 134), *passim*.
[74] Paik, *op. cit.,* p. 396; *The Christian Movement in Japan*, 1914, pp. 495-498.
[75] Paik, *op. cit.,* pp. 398, 399; Soltau, *Korea*, pp. 79ff.
[76] *The Christian Movement in Japan*, 1914, pp. 442, 445.
[77] *The Christian Movement in Japan*, 1914, pp. 446-448; Underwood, *The Call of Korea,* pp. 114, 115.
[78] Underwood, *op. cit.,* p. 115.

There were schools for each of the sexes.[79] The Northern Methodists, through Mrs. Mary F. Scranton, founded an institution, Ehwa, which gave education to women through the college grades.[80] Increasingly the six major missions coordinated their educational programmes.[81] In 1906 the Union Christian College was instituted at Pyeng Yang.[82] In 1915 the Chosen Christian College was begun in Seoul.[83] Theological training was developed.[84] There was education for the blind and deaf.[85] Protestant missions for a time led the way in the introduction of Western medicine. Several hospitals were founded.[86] The government hospital in Seoul which had been in charge of missionaries became in time purely a Christian institution. In connexion with it the Severance Union Medical College was instituted with the very able A. O. Avison, of the Northern Presbyterians, as the head.[87] In religious education, Sunday schools were highly developed.[88]

A striking feature of the methods employed by Protestant missions was the emphasis upon the participation of Koreans in the spread of the Christian message and upon the financial self-support of the churches from the very beginning. In 1890, when the Protestant enterprise in Korea was still in its early infancy, John L. Nevius, a Presbyterian missionary in China who strongly advocated methods of self-support, visited Seoul and described the principles which he was advocating. Partly in consequence, the main features of his programme were adopted. These called for each Christian to seek to win his neighbours, supporting himself by his trade; for developing ecclesiastical organization only as the Korean Christians were able themselves to manage it; for setting aside some Christians, as the churches were prepared to support them, for spreading the faith; and for church buildings in the local architecture and constructed only when the Koreans could pay for them.[89] In connexion with this plan much emphasis was placed upon training classes in the Bible for lay members. Some foreign funds were employed, but the trend was towards more rather than less self-support.[90]

[79] Underwood, op. cit., pp. 112-114, 117, 118; The Christian Movement in Japan, 1914, pp. 455-470.

[80] The Christian Movement in the Japanese Empire, 1915, pp. 476, 477.

[81] The Christian Movement in Japan, 1914, pp. 451-455.

[82] The Christian Movement in the Japanese Empire, 1915, p. 491.

[83] The Christian Movement in the Japanese Empire, 1918, p. 379.

[84] The Christian Movement in Japan, 1914, pp. 471-473.

[85] The Christian Movement in the Japanese Empire, 1915, pp. 471, 472.

[86] The Christian Movement in the Japanese Empire, 1915, pp. 499ff.

[87] Paik, The History of Protestant Missions in Korea, pp. 321, 322; The Christian Movement in the Japanese Empire, 1915, pp. 506-511.

[88] Clark, The Korean Church and the Nevius Methods, p. 169.

[89] Underwood, op. cit., pp. 109, 110; Clark, op. cit., pp. 16-35, 73, 74.

[90] Clark, op. cit., pp. 75-83.

For the first few years the growth of the Protestant church membership was slow. In 1894 there were said to be only 236 baptized Protestant Christians in the entire country.[91] They then began to multiply rapidly. In the years between the Russo-Japanese War (1904-1905) and the annexation of the country by Japan (1910) there was an especially marked rise. Between 1897 and 1909 the total of Protestant communicants sprang from 530 to 26,057.[92] In 1906 a movement towards Christianity began, with striking emotional manifestations, repentance of sin, and moral reform. Eager to take advantage of the incoming tide, the various denominations united in 1910 in a Million Souls Movement, which had as its goal the presentation of the Christian message to every individual in the country and a million new converts. By that time the impulse had largely spent its force and the objective was not attained.[93] To be sure, church membership continued to rise. In 1914 the number of Protestant communicants was not far from eighty-five thousand and of baptized, including communicants, approximately ninety-six thousand.[94] However, the percentage rate of growth had fallen off.

The reasons for the rapid advance after 1895 and especially between 1906 and 1910 appear to have been mixed. They seem to have been associated with an accession of zeal on the part of the missionaries, with the inspiration of the news of religious revivals in other lands, with the movement away from conservatism and towards Westernization, with the eagerness for Western education and the leadership of the Protestant missions in providing that type of education, with the sense of urgency in the achievement of reorganization after Occidental patterns if annexation by Japan were to be avoided, with the leadership of Christians and those sympathetic with Christianity in the movement for Westernization and reform, with the hope that Christianity might be a means of saving the nation, and with the bewilderment of many because of the changes and the desire for security and direction that the Christian faith and the churches seemed to provide.[95]

Similarly the retardation of growth which followed the striking advance ap-

[91] Clark, op. cit., p. 73.

[92] Clark, op. cit., p. 151.

[93] Clark, op. cit., p. 155; George Heber Jones and W. Arthur Noble, The Korean Revival. An Account of the Revival in the Korean Churches in 1907 (New York, The Board of Foreign Missions of the Methodist Episcopal Church, 1910, pp. 45), passim; George T. B. Davis, Korea for Christ (New York, Fleming H. Revell Co., 1910, pp. 68), passim; William Newton Blair, The Korea Pentecost (New York, The Board of Foreign Missions of the Presbyterian Church in the U. S. A., no date, pp. 51), passim; Wasson, Church Growth in Korea, pp. 51ff.

[94] Beach and St. John, World Statistics of Christian Missions, p. 62.

[95] Clark, op. cit., pp. 228-244; Wasson, op. cit., pp. 46-50, 62ff.

pears to have arisen from varied factors. Among them were the discouragement to liberal nationalists brought by the Japanese annexation, the cramping effect of Japanese regulations and censorship, the rapid growth of government schools under Japanese administration with the declining relative prominence of Christian schools, and conflicts with the Japanese administration. It was felt that Christianity had not saved the nation from its fate and that the churches, far from being safe havens, were under especial pressure from the Japanese.[96]

It is not strange that the Japanese authorities looked askance at Protestants, both Koreans and missionaries, or that suspicion flared up into acute friction. The fact that some Korean Christians were seeking to save their country's independence made them obnoxious to the Japanese. Many Protestant missionaries, and particularly those from the United States, were very critical of Japan. Homer B. Hulbert, who for a time had been a missionary, was prominent in seeking international intervention and action by the United States to prevent Japanese annexation.[97] Beginning at least as early as 1910 Japanese gendarmes were harsh with Korean Christians. In 1911 and 1912 many Christians, among them the distinguished T. H. Yun, were arrested. Several scores of them were accused of conspiring against the life of the Japanese governor-general. Numbers were convicted, but an appeal to a higher court brought the acquittal of all but five, and these, including Yun, were eventually pardoned.[98] The missionaries were clear that the accused were innocent, but the action of the state probably slowed the growth of the churches.

It was to be anticipated that the Russian Orthodox Church would enter Korea. Russian territorial expansion and Russian political ambitions in the East of Asia could be expected to be accompanied by efforts to extend Russian influence through the church which through Russian political absolutism had so long been employed as a tool by the state. In 1899 or 1900, at a time when Russia was seeking to strengthen its power in Korea, a mission of the Russian Orthodox Church was inaugurated in Seoul.[99] Not far from 1901 Koreans who had

[96] Wasson, op. cit., pp. 88-97.
[97] Homer B. Hulbert in Korea Review (Philadelphia), Vol. I, No. 7 (September, 1919), pp. 2, 3.
[98] Wasson, op. cit., pp. 89, 90; Arthur Judson Brown, The Korean Conspiracy Case (Northfield, Northfield Press, p. 27), passim; The Korean Conspiracy Trial. Full Report of the Proceedings by the Special Correspondent of the "Japan Chronicle" (Kobe, Japan Chronicle, 1912, pp. 136), passim.
[99] Homer B. Hulbert, The History of Korea, Vol. II, p. 235; Lübeck, Die russischen Missionen. p. 14.

become Russian subjects and who purported to be agents of the Russian Church were said to be touring the southern provinces extracting money from the populace by intimidation.[100] Missions were also founded among Korean immigrants in Russian territory near the Korean border. These seem to have been as much for the purpose of Russification as for the spread of Christianity. They were supported by the Russian Government. Up to 1904 they had won between eight and nine thousand converts.[101] In spite of the defeat of Russia by Japan, the Russian mission in Korea continued. In 1914 it had about thirty-five hundred converts in nine stations.[102]

Some of the effects of Christianity upon Korea can be gleaned from the preceding pages. Obviously one was the emergence of Christian churches. In 1914 the number of Christians in all churches was not far from 185,000. This was approximately one per cent. of the population, a much larger proportion than in either China or Japan and about that in India, and that in spite of the fact that Christianity was much younger in Korea than in any of these other lands.

As elsewhere, it is not always easy to know what distinctive fruits Christianity bore in the life of the average communicant. Some of the moral standards inculcated, such as honouring parents, abstaining from irregular sexual relations, diligence in business, and the shunning of flagrant sins, were not unlike those of the traditional Confucianism and Buddhism.[103] To these others were added, such as the observance of Sunday and abstention from the worship of ancestors.[104] We hear of a Christian teacher who in front of his desk had mottoes which enjoined the love of God, doing unto others as one would have them do to him, refraining from unkind judgments of others, and secret prayer and meditation.[105] Larger opportunities were opened to women for education and for social activities than were to be found in the existing order.[106] Missionaries, especially Protestant missionaries, were pioneers in introducing schools of Western types, in public health and hygiene, and in Occidental medicine and medical education. A new and vigorous moral and spiritual dynamic had entered through Christianity which was having striking results in the lives of thousands. There was sufficient vitality in the Presbyterian groups to give rise to

[100] Hulbert, op. cit., Vol. II, p. 331.
[101] Raeder in Allgemeine Missions-Zeitschrift, Vol. XXXII, p. 522.
[102] Lübeck, op. cit., p. 14.
[103] Clark, The Korean Church and the Nevius Methods, pp. 97, 98.
[104] Ibid.
[105] Noble, Victorious Lives of Early Christians in Korea, p. 172.
[106] Noble, op. cit., pp. 12-24.

foreign missionary effort, both among Chinese in Shantung and among Koreans in Siberia.[107]

Here and there Christianity was entering as a stimulating factor into indigenous religious movements. This was notably the case in the Chuntokyo cult, more generally known as Tonghak. It was founded by one who had had contact with Roman Catholic Christianity. It was eclectic, combining elements from Confucianism, Buddhism, animism, and Christianity. The designation, Tonghak, or Eastern learning, was in contradistinction to Suhak, or Western learning, a name given to Roman Catholicism. The founder was executed in the 1860's on the charge of being a Christian. Yet the cult continued, acquired political aspects, and in the 1890's gave rise to a serious rebellion. It persisted as a religion and not far from 1912 it began to take on some of the aspects of Protestant Christianity, with Sunday observance, the erection of halls which resembled Protestant churches, the assertion that the founder had died for Korea as Christ had died for foreigners, and young men's and young women's associations.[108]

The Korean environment had not, by 1914, worked any very great change in the imported organization and forms of Christianity. The flow and ebb in the numerical growth of the Church reflected in part the internal and external political situation. Most of the leading Protestant missions, namely, the four Presbyterian and the two Methodist ones, co-operated in nation-wide planning which was encouraged by the apparent advisability of bringing into being a united church for the entire country. The six bodies divided the land among them, to avoid overlapping and duplication of effort, in 1905 constituted a General Evangelical Council, and in 1912 joined in forming a Federal Council of Missions.[109] As with other peoples, an important but intangible effect of the environment was in the mixing of pre-Christian and Christian conceptions in the thinking and purpose of individuals. In ideas of God, of morals, of worship, and of the purpose of religion the inheritance from Korea's past inevitably mingled with what had come through the missionary. Yet the records are so imperfect and the Christians themselves were often so unconscious of what was taking place within themselves that the two strains could scarcely be untangled.

[107] Soltau, *Korea*, pp. 29, 30.
[108] Charles Allen Clark, *Religions of Old Korea* (New York, Fleming H. Revell Co., 1932, pp. 295), pp. 144-172; Paik, *The History of Protestant Missions in Korea*, pp. 161, 162.
[109] Soltau, *op. cit.*, pp. 58ff.

Christianity was late in arriving in Korea. Aside from transient contacts late in the sixteenth and early in the seventeenth century, it did not enter until the last decade of the eighteenth century. It then came in the Roman Catholic form. Until the last quarter of the nineteenth century it faced chronic opposition by the state and organized society which from time to time blazed out in severe persecutions. In the 1880's Protestantism was added and about the turn of the century the Russian Orthodox Church entered.

Christianity spread for a variety of reasons. These were to be found in the zeal of the missionaries, in the nature of Christianity and its appeal to members of all races, cultures, and nations, in the weakness of rival religious systems, in the spiritual hunger and sense of frustration brought about by Korea's political helplessness in the closing years of the nineteenth and the opening decades of the twentieth century, in the hope of patriots that Christianity might be a means of saving the country from its foreign and domestic foes, and in the breakdown of the old culture and the longing for something better and more stable. Russian Christianity was almost negligible and associated closely with Russian political ambitions. In spite of the fact that it entered nearly a century after the other, Protestantism had a more rapid growth than did Roman Catholicism. This was because of the larger number of Protestant missionaries, the fact that Protestants placed greater emphasis upon schools and medical care, the friendly acquiescence of Roman Catholic missionaries in Japanese rule and the tendency of Protestant missionaries to be critical (a difference which attracted ardent nationalists to the latter), and, probably, to the basic contrasts between the two branches of the faith.

When one recalls the long persecutions that beset its early course, the small size of the missionary staff, and the thinly veiled hostility of the Japanese in the decade before 1914, Christianity is seen to have had an amazing growth and a striking effect. In 1914 its adherents were only about one per cent. of the population. This, however, was more than in Japan or China. As in these other two countries, and especially as in China, Christianity, and particularly Protestant Christianity, pioneered in introducing Western methods of education and medicine. Until the Japanese occupation made that impossible, it became an inspiration of efforts at remaking the land and giving it a strong, uncorrupt national life. Annexation by Japan brought growing restrictions, but these were not sufficient to prevent a continued increase in both numbers and influence. As in so many other lands, Christianity was growing rapidly when one age gave way to another.

Chapter VIII

RUSSIA IN ASIA

IN ASIA a vast area was under Russian control. It stretched from Persia and Afghanistan to the Arctic Ocean and from the Ural Mountains, the Ural River, and the Caspian Sea to the Sea of Okhotsk and the Bering Sea. It embraced in general the territory to the west and north of the series of mountains which runs diagonally north-eastward from Persia and Afghanistan to the north-eastern corner of the continent. In the north-east it included some lands to the east of this barrier. Much of the region was desert or semi-desert. Much, too, lay north of the Arctic Circle. Its natural resources, in some places extensive, were but slightly developed. Its population was sparse, in 1914 probably not much in excess of twenty millions. The Russian advance had begun long before the nineteenth century and by 1800 had already reached the Pacific. In the course of the nineteenth century additional territories were acquired, notably east of the Caspian and, in the Far East, north of the Amur River and east of the Ussuri.

The spread of Christianity in the nineteenth century was in part by immigration and in part by missions among non-Christians. As was to be expected, it was mainly through the Russian Orthodox Church. The immigration from European Russia was chiefly in Siberia. There seems to be some uncertainty as to its dimensions. It was most marked in the last quarter of the nineteenth century and the opening years of the twentieth century, when it was facilitated by railways, particularly the Trans-Siberian. Much of it was by penal exile. More of it was voluntary. One estimate declares that in the years 1886-1896 eight hundred thousand peasants settled in Siberia, and that during 1893-1905 four millions were added.[1] Another estimate has it that between 1890 and 1905 the number of free immigrants was a million and a half and that from 1880 to 1890 on an average of twenty thousand exiles a year were sent to Siberia.[2] Of the exiles some were religious dissenters from the official Orthodox Church who were thus punished for nonconformity. Among the free immigrants there were also dissenters.[3] Presumably the vast majority of the others had at least a nominal

[1] *The Encyclopædia Britannica*, 11th ed., Vol. XXIII, p. 873.
[2] *The Encyclopædia Britannica*, 11th ed., Vol. XXV, p. 15.
[3] Lansdell, *Through Siberia*, pp. 527-530.

connexion with the state church. For them church buildings were erected and clergy installed. Late in the 1870's Siberia was said to be divided into six dioceses with over fifteen hundred churches, about the same number of clergy, fourteen monasteries, and four nunneries. Parishes were often very large and could be only inadequately covered by the limited body of clergy.[4] Some religious care was given to the convicts.[5] A traveller on the Trans-Siberian Railway on the eve of 1914 saw in the villages and cities along his route the towers and domes of Orthodox churches rising above the low roofs of the houses. How effective as compared with European Russia the church was in retaining the allegiance of its nominal adherents it would be difficult to determine. In the Trans-Caspian region the immigrants included a few Protestants. These were from the Mennonite colonies in Russia. In the 1880's a few scores of families, some of them led by a strange prophet of their number who expected the early second coming of Christ, journeyed eastward and established themselves in areas under Russian control or near the Russian border.[6] Among the Finnish colonists there were Protestants.[7] The immigrants from Europe to Siberia included many more Roman Catholics than Protestants. Since Lithuania and part of Poland were under Russian rule, and since the Roman Catholic Church was strong in these two countries, several thousand Roman Catholic Poles and Lithuanians were to be found in Siberia. In the larger cities parishes were organized for them. They were supervised by an archbishop who had his residence in St. Petersburg and were closely watched by the Holy Synod.[8]

Efforts by the Russian Orthodox to win the non-Christian peoples had been in progress long before the nineteenth century.[9] They were continued after 1800. In the second half of the eighteenth century, in common with most missions in the world at large, they suffered a decline.[10] However, some of them persisted, notably in Alaska and the Aleutians. In 1799 the Archpriest Gregor Sleptsoff began a mission in a region in the north-east of Siberia north of the Sea of Okhotsk and in 1815 spoke of having won several thousand to the faith. After his retirement in that year to a monastery other priests continued. One of them, who had fifty-five years in the area, is said to have baptized three thousand pagans.[11] In 1834 an archpriest took over the once flourishing Kamchatka

[4] Lansdell, op. cit., p. 163.
[5] Benjamin Howard, Prisoners of Russia. A Personal Study of Convict Life in Sakhalin and Siberia (New York, D. Appleton and Co., 1902, pp. xxix, 389), pp. 92ff., 224ff.
[6] C. Henry Smith, The Story of the Mennonites (Berne, Ind., Mennonite Book Concern, 1941, pp. 823), pp. 454-462.
[7] Lansdell, op. cit., pp. 130, 131.
[8] Zeitschrift für Missionswissenschaft, Vol. XI, pp. 50, 51.
[9] Vol. III, pp. 368, 369.
[10] Smirnoff, Russian Orthodox Missions, p. 15.
[11] Lübeck, Die Christianisierung Russlands, p. 72.

Mission. By that time it had scarcely three thousand Christians. In 1840 Kamchatka, the Aleutians, and the Kuriles were erected into a separate diocese. The very able John Veniaminoff, who had had a distinguished missionary career in Alaska and was later Metropolitan of Moscow, was appointed the first bishop.[12] When, in the 1850's, the Russian boundary was pushed south to the Amur River and up the right bank of the Ussuri, the Russian mission was extended to that territory. Gabriel Veniaminoff, a son of the bishop, laboured there and his father made preaching tours through the region.[13]

Early in the second quarter of the nineteenth century, the energetic Eugenius Kasantseff, as Archbishop of Tobolsk (1826-1831), set about learning the vernaculars of his diocese and inaugurated the Altai mission, in a mountainous country not far from the borders of Mongolia about half-way between the Urals and Lake Baikal. This enterprise had as its outstanding pioneer Archimandrite Macarius (before becoming a monk known as Michael Glucareff). Macarius studied the local tongues, prepared a dictionary, and translated parts of the Bible and the liturgy. He had high standards for neophytes and admitted none to baptism without careful instruction. In fourteen years he administered the rite to less than seven hundred. He gathered his converts into Christian villages with churches and schools. He taught them agriculture and handicrafts. He trained missionary sisters to reach the women. He was followed by others who built on his foundations. In 1880 a bishop was appointed to the mission.[14] Moreover, the labours of Macarius contributed to the formation of the Orthodox Missionary Society.[15] At the beginning of the twentieth century the Altai enterprise was said to be the best organized of all the Siberian missions. Out of a population of forty-five thousand, twenty-five thousand were reported to be Christians. They lived apart from non-Christians in not far from two hundred villages. They had schools, churches, and an institution for training teachers. The non-Christians were also affected and had built themselves houses, taken to agriculture, and established schools in which, at their request, Christianity was taught their children.[16] In the second quarter of the nineteenth century missions were also conducted among tribes north of Tobolsk.[17]

In the fifth chapter of the present volume we saw that the London Missionary Society for a time had a mission among the Buriats which it reached by way of Siberia, and that the enterprise was given up in 1841 at the command of the

[12] Lübeck, op. cit., p. 66.
[13] Lübeck, op. cit., p. 71.
[14] Raeder in Allgemeine Missions-Zeitschrift, Vol. XXXIII, pp. 464-468; Smirnoff, op. cit., pp. 17-20; Lübeck, op. cit., pp. 75-82.
[15] Raeder in op. cit., Vol. XXXIII, pp. 468, 469.
[16] Smirnoff, op. cit., pp. 20, 21.
[17] Raeder in op. cit., Vol. XXXIII, p. 471.

Holy Synod reinforced by an imperial decree.[18] Even before the London Missionary Society withdrew, the Russian Orthodox Church began operations among the Buriats. In the succeeding years a number of stations were established in the Trans-Baikal area and in six years in the seventh decade nearly two thousand Buriats were baptized.[19]

There were other regions in Siberia in which missions were conducted. In that which centred at Irkutsk nearly forty-six thousand were baptized in the last three decades of the nineteenth century.[20] There was an enterprise among the Kirgis, south of Tobolsk. Since the Kirgis were Moslems, the numerical success among them was slight.[21]

For the financial assistance of the Siberian missions there was founded, in 1894, at the instance of the Tsar Alexander III, the Alexander Institute. It received aid from the imperial purse. Much of the financial support of the missions came directly from the state.[22]

The remarkable institution for the training of missionaries and for literary and linguistic labours developed at Kazan in the nineteenth century, largely through the initiative of Ilminski,[23] served the Siberian as well as the European missions of the Russian Orthodox Church.[24]

In the last thirty years of the nineteenth century not far from ninety thousand were baptized in Siberia among previously non-Christian peoples.[25] Most of these seem to have been from animists and shamanists. Lamaistic Buddhism and Islam offered more sturdy resistance than did these more nearly primitive faiths. The animistic folk were mainly in the vast, sparsely settled reaches of the North. For some of them conversion simply meant adding the Christian God to their other beliefs.[26] Few if any gains were made among the Moslems in the Trans-Caspian area or among the Moslems and the Buddhists of the steppes. While often conducted with devotion and religious zeal, the missions were largely supported by the government, presumably primarily as means of assimilating the populations to Russian rule and culture. They were often accompanied by schools and by improved economic as well as better moral and spiritual conditions.

[18] Lovett, The History of the London Missionary Society, Vol. II, pp. 585-599.
[19] Raeder in op. cit., p. 473. See a description of the mission in Lansdell, op. cit., pp. 375, 376.
[20] Smirnoff, op. cit., p. 60.
[21] Lübeck, op. cit., pp. 62, 63, 102.
[22] Lübeck, op. cit., p. 92.
[23] Vol. IV, pp. 121, 122.
[24] Smirnoff, op. cit., p. 48.
[25] Smirnoff, op. cit., p. 60.
[26] Fridtjof Nansen, Through Siberia (translated by Arthur C. Chater. New York, Frederick A. Stokes Co., 1914, pp. xvi, 478), pp. 102, 126.

Chapter IX

CHRISTIANITY IN NINETEENTH CENTURY NORTHERN AFRICA AND ASIA IN RETROSPECT

A S IN retrospect one surveys the course of Christianity in northern Africa and in Asia during the years between A.D. 1800 and A.D. 1914, several characteristics emerge. To the patient but discerning reader who has made his toilsome way through the preceding chapters, the generalizations are inescapable.

As in so much of the earlier volumes which deal with what we have termed "the Great Century," the impression is gained of the near approach to ubiquity of the Christian missionary. Never in the preceding eighteen centuries of its history had the Christian message been so widely proclaimed by word and life in the continent of its origin. Never, indeed, had any religion been so extensively propagated in Asia. Some areas were not reached or were touched but slightly. These, however, were in the interior and for the most part were of an inhospitable geography and a sparse population. Conspicuous among them were Afghanistan, Tibet, Russian portions of Central Asia, Sinkiang, and Outer Mongolia. Yet not even these territories were entirely without some contact with earnest Christians. Never in the periods of the widest expansion of Nestorian Christianity or at the apex of the pre-nineteenth century Roman Catholic efforts had Christianity been so extensively represented in Asia. Not since the Arab conquest had Christians been so active in presenting their faith to the peoples of the northern shores of Africa and of western Asia. Never had they been so widely distributed or so numerous in India, eastern and southeastern Asia, and the northern quarter of the continent.

This wide and rapid propagation of Christianity was due to a combination of factors. It was connected with the expansion of Occidental peoples. By 1914 much of the continent was subject politically to Europeans, and almost all had been penetrated by Western commerce. The impact of the Occident had inaugurated a revolution in the cultures of northern Africa and Asia. The revolution had not proceeded as far as in the primitive and less numerous non-European peoples of the Americas, the Pacific, and Africa. Yet it had begun. It was accompanied by a demand for the type of education and some of the material equipment which seemed to give to European peoples their power and wealth. The incipient revolution rendered some of the peoples of Asia more nearly open-minded to what the Christian missionary, coming as he did from the Occident, had to say. A certain degree of prestige accrued to Christianity because it was the supposed religion of the West. That prestige might obscure the true genius of Christianity, but in some groups it facilitated formal conversion. Yet the Occidental associations of Christianity also proved a handicap. Western domination was resented and attempts to spread Christianity encountered an opposition heightened by this antagonism. The Asiatic origin of Christianity was forgotten or minimized and Christians, whether native or foreign, were regarded as connected with Western imperialism and culture. Christianity spread partly because its missions were often pioneers in making accessible the Western types of education desired by those who wished to profit by the new age brought by the irruption of the Occident. Yet Christian missions did not owe their existence to a desire to assist Western imperialism. They came into being and were maintained through the amazing new surge of life in the churches, both Roman Catholic and Protestant.

The kinds of Christianity which spread were primarily Roman Catholic and Protestant. Proportionately, Protestantism enjoyed a more rapid extension than did Roman Catholicism. This was, in general, characteristic of Christianity in the nineteenth century. Russian Orthodox Christianity here and there had missions—in western Asia, China, Japan, and Korea, and particularly, as was to be expected, in Siberia. Compared with the other two major branches of the faith, however, its growth at the expense of non-Christian faiths was slight.

Numerically, the results of the expansion of Christianity on the northern shores of Africa and in Asia were not very impressive. The entire gain in the nineteenth century, except for the Russian migration into Siberia, was less than ten millions. Even if the migration from European to Asiatic Russia is included, in 1914 the Christians in all North Africa and Asia were probably not much more than ten millions beyond the total of A.D. 1800. They were, moreover, largely from limited groups, usually minorities oppressed by the existing order who found in Christianity a door of escape to an ampler life. In northern Africa and in western Asia few converts were won from the Jews and the Moslems: the gains of Roman Catholics, Protestants, and Russian Orthodox were almost entirely by immigration or from the Eastern churches which had survived the centuries-long attrition of Islam. In India the converts were chiefly from the depressed classes who were held down by the traditional caste structure or from the primitive tribes of the hills who had not been incorporated into Hinduism. Comparatively few came from the castes. In Burma the majority of the Christians were Karens, the largest racial minority in the country but, until Christianity reached them, much behind the Burmese in civilization. In the Malay Peninsula the converts were mostly among Chinese and Indians, immigrants who were uprooted from their native habitat and hence more susceptible to new currents of thought and life. In French Indo-China, where in 1914 Christians numbered not far from a million, accessions had been drawn markedly from backward portions of the population. In China the converts were largely from the lowly. Few of the traditional ruling scholar class became Christians. In Japan Protestants, the most numerous of the Christian communities, were mainly from the urban middle and upper middle classes, professional and business people who had been much affected by Western learning. Many of them were of *samurai* stock who had been uprooted by the changes following the reopening of the country to the Occident. Moreover, many of the Christian minorities in northern Africa and Asia were dependent upon the Occident for leadership and for financial assistance for their schools, churches, and hospitals. In a certain sense they were enclaves of what might be termed Occidental ecclesiastical imperialism. Asia presented to Christianity the high religions which had been most resistant to its course. It had many times more avowed non-Christians than did all the rest of the world. Yet in proportion to the population, in 1914 Christianity, while widely spread, was weaker numerically in Asia than in any other continent. Such converts as the great nineteenth century missionary effort had won were mainly from underprivileged minorities and not from the controlling majorities.

Missionaries, and especially Protestant missionaries, had hopefully tried various approaches which might issue in larger accessions. Some dreamed in terms of the conversion of entire peoples. Many attempted to reach the natural leaders, with the expectation that these would bring the nation with them. Thus Alexander Duff sought through Christian education to gain the higher caste Indians. Others in India endeavoured through colleges to leaven the Indian lump with Christian ideals as a preparation for the Gospel. In China Timothy Richard approached those in the community most respected for their character that through them the others might be won. He outlined a plan of Christian colleges for rearing the future leaders of the empire and dreamed of conversion by the million. In Japan Protestant missionaries addressed themselves primarily to the students, and for a time in the 1880's some believed the conversion of the entire country to be imminent. Similarly, in the first decade of the twentieth century several of the more optimistic of the Protestant missionaries in Korea expected the early mass conversion of the country. None of these dreams were realized.

However, although their faith had foreshortened history, the missionaries were not so fantastic in their aspirations as the numerical account of their achievements in organized churches and baptized Christians might lead one to suppose. When one remembers the brevity of the time in which they had been at work and the nature of the resistance, the results become very striking. It was not until after the middle of the nineteenth century that the numbers of missionaries were impressive. Not even in 1914 did they reach the total of thirty thousand—small when one considers the size of the populations and the dimensions of the area over which they were spread. In India the renewed Roman Catholic enterprise was long handicapped by the Portuguese padroado. Through most of the nineteenth century Christians in Indo-China were visited with periodic persecutions. It was only after 1860 that missionaries, and particularly Protestant missionaries, could move about fairly freely in the interior of China. Even then they were not welcome and in 1900 the Boxer storm wrought havoc among missionary bodies and Chinese churches. Missionaries were not permitted in Japan until the late 1850's and it was 1873 before the edict boards against Christianity were removed. As late as 1866 in Korea Christianity was overtaken by a devastating persecution. In some countries, notably in the Near East, the main structure of society did not weaken in such fashion as to permit of mass movements or even of many individual conversions to Christianity. In India the basic social institution of caste, with its firm resistance to any secessions to Christianity, remained adamant throughout the period. In China the inherited culture did not begin to crumble until the 1890's and in 1914 the disintegration was only commencing to get under way. In Japan, although superficial changes were extensive, the basic institutions were but little altered. In spite of the shortness of the time that the revived Christianity of the nineteenth century had been operating and of the stout resistance to it, Christians were to be found in every land. The churches were growing rapidly in size and in inner strength. The smallness of the number of converts was due in part to the high standards maintained for baptism and communicant membership. Practice varied, but in general both Roman Catholics and Protestants required fairly long probation and careful instruction before admitting catechumens to the Church. This was a far stricter requirement than had usually obtained in the previous history of the spread of Christianity. It limited the number of professed Christians but presumably it led to a better quality of life. Indigenous leadership was arising. Even in India, where so large a proportion of the Christians were from groups which had traditionally been treated as inferiors and had learned to regard themselves as such, native leaders were beginning to emerge, although mostly from the few converts from the upper classes. In China and particularly in Japan the churches were making rapid strides towards independence of the Westerner.

In the larger countries many forms of Christianity, particularly of the congenitally variegated Protestantism, were represented. At first thought this may seem to have made for confusion and weakness. However, it was the means of bringing to these lands the full richness of the historic Christian heritage. As increasingly the peoples of Asia made the faith consciously theirs, presumably they would erase many of the imported divisions but would profit by the multiplicity of interpretation and expression.

We must recall that in the larger lands Christianity was having an influence quite out of proportion to the numerical strength of its adherents. In Egypt and western Asia the permeation of Moslem society by ideals of Christian origin was extending far beyond the churches. In India the dominant Hinduism was showing the effect of Christianity. In many countries, but nowhere more notably than in the most numerous of Asiatic peoples, the Chinese, the Christian forces were pioneers in Western education and medicine. In China, moreover, the political effects were beginning to be striking.

Everywhere that Christianity went it was bearing its characteristic fruits in individual lives and in social change. Thousands of individuals were finding moral and spiritual power. The oppressed and backward were being given glimpses of intellectual and spiritual emancipation. Orphans were being rescued and nurtured. Women were having education opened to them. Lepers were gathered into homes. The blind were taught to read and trained to self-respecting livelihood. Here and there were movements for the remaking of convicts. The Bible was being translated and distributed. Gigantic evils such as opium and famine were being bravely attacked.

In almost every country in northern Africa and Asia as the year 1914 ushered out one era and inaugurated another, Christianity was rapidly gaining in strength and influence and was becoming better rooted in the soil. It is not surprising that in the third of a century after 1914 the numbers of Christians doubled in some of the major countries and that in most of them the effect of Christianity mounted. The year 1914 saw Christianity on a rising tide.

Chapter X

THE GREAT CENTURY. BY WAY OF SUMMARY AND ANTICIPATION

THE period to which we have devoted three volumes requires a summary. In the nineteenth century the geographic stream of Christianity so broadened that we have been compelled to allot as much space to its expansion as we did to its course in all the preceding eighteen centuries. This has required us to traverse practically all of the land surface of the globe. It has involved us in many countries and peoples. In spite of the fact that we have ruthlessly compressed the story, so multiform were the activities of Christianity and so wide its extension that we have been constrained to record great numbers of movements and names. To some readers these must have seemed very confusing. At times the chief trends may have appeared to be obscured by the many details. Before we move on to the fateful years which followed 1914 we must, therefore, pause for a moment for retrospect and for an attempt to disentangle from the masses of facts which we have poured upon our pages the main strands which have run through the decades. We shall then be in a position to view with a little more understanding the stormy era ushered in by the events of 1914 and be better prepared to cast our eyes back over the course of Christianity from the beginning. It is these two tasks which we have reserved for our final volume. As a preparation for that undertaking we must endeavour to see the period from A.D. 1800 to A.D. 1914 as a whole.

The nineteenth century confronted Christianity with problems which for variety and magnitude were unprecedented in the history of that faith. Again, as more than once before in its experience, Christianity faced the disintegration of a culture with which it had become intimately associated. In its first five centuries it had won the professed allegiance of the Græco-Roman world. The achievement had not been completed when that world fell to pieces. The decay had begun long before Christianity became prominent, but that faith proved powerless to arrest it. Moreover, the rise of the Crescent not only tore away much of the Mediterranean from the Cross but also handicapped the latter's spread in the East. Yet Christianity survived the collapse of the Roman Empire and provided the vehicle through which much of the civilization of the region governed by that realm was transmitted to future ages and to other peoples. Christianity entered potently into the creation of the culture of medieval Europe. Indeed, it helped to mould more phases of the Europe of the Middle Ages than it had of the Græco-Roman era. In spite of the obstacles presented by Islam, it expanded, although in minority enclaves, across the entire breadth of Asia. Then the structure of medieval Europe gave place to a new and different one which arose from it. The Crescent, borne by the Ottoman Turks, rose over the Cross in Asia Minor, Constantinople, and the Balkans. The Christian communities scattered across central and eastern Asia disappeared. In its chief remaining stronghold, western Europe, Christianity suffered from internal divisions and corrupt leadership. While Christianity was still at low ebb, European peoples began voyages, conquests, and settlements which carried them over much of the surface of the globe. Then great revivals in the form of Protestantism and the Catholic Reformation brought fresh access of life to the Christianity of western Europe. New movements made that Christianity more vigorous than it had yet been. So potent was it that missionaries accompanied or followed the explorers and settlers and in great areas preceded them and even went where they did not. Christianity was planted more widely than it had ever been and ameliorated the impact of European upon non-European peoples. In the second half of the eighteenth century Christianity was again threatened. The nations through which it had chiefly spread in the preceding three centuries, Spain and Portugal, were in decline. Rationalistic scepticism made sterile the faith of many. The French Revolution, in part anti-Christian, shook Europe. Western peoples were torn by wars, some of them world-wide in their dimensions. These changes were but a prelude to others which profoundly altered the entire life and thought of Western peoples. The scientific method was developed and applied to man and his physical environment. The Industrial Revolution came. Vast shifts and great increases of population were witnessed. Huge cities arose. Man's mental horizons expanded. Old political forms and social institutions disappeared or were altered almost beyond recognition. Many Western Europeans openly disowned Christianity and in several countries the Church was disestablished and ceased to be the official faith of the nation. European peoples poured into sparsely settled portions of the globe and gave rise to new nations. They mastered all the Americas, the islands of the Pacific, and Africa. They dominated most of Asia. Could Christianity persist in this new age? Would it not be at the most a more or less slowly vanishing remnant of an outgrown and discredited order? There were many, among them some of the most intelligent and vocal spokesmen of the fresh movements, who were certain that this would be its fate. Indeed, they declared that the mortal illness had set in and that the death throes could already be discerned.

Once again Christianity proved its capacity to survive the demise of a culture which it had helped to shape and of which it appeared to be an integral part. Not only did it continue but, as in western Europe after the fall of the Roman Empire, it went on to enhanced power. Although its significance was not then appreciated, the revival had commenced in the fore part of the eighteenth century, before the break-down óf the old order had more than begun. It gathered momentum as the decades passed. Through it Christianity accompanied and here and there pioneered in the expansion of European peoples. Never had the faith won adherents among so many peoples and in so many countries. Never had it exerted so wide an influence upon the human race. Measured by geographic extent and the effect upon mankind as a whole, the nineteenth century was the greatest century thus far in the history of Christianity. That extension and .that effect mounted as the century wore on. They were growing when, in 1914, world-shattering events ushered in a new period.

Some features of the nineteenth century favoured the spread of Christianity. The era was one of comparative peace. No wars of the magnitude of those which preceded 1815 and of those which began in 1914 disturbed mankind. Western peoples were accumulating wealth and were multiplying in numbers and in power. Technically they were still embraced within Christendom and their faith came to non-European peoples with the prestige of their dazzling might. Some of their wealth, although only a small fraction of it, was devoted to the financing of Christian missions. Improved means of communication facilitated the travel of missionaries and contacts between the younger churches and the parent churches of the Occident. The disintegration of non-European cultures under, the impact of the Occident lessened resistance to Christianity. In some instances the collapse of the old orders made for a wistful and even eager acceptance of the Christian faith as a source of certainty and guidance in a crumbling world.

Although several exterior circumstances facilitated it, the nineteenth century expansion of Christianity would not have occurred had the faith not displayed striking inward vitality. That vitality expressed itself in part through the revivals which began in the eighteenth and in part through others which came in the nineteenth century.

These were in both Roman Catholicism and what for lack of a better name is called collectively, although inaccurately, Protestantism. They were particularly marked in Protestantism. Indeed, in some respects the nineteenth century was pre-eminently the Protestant century. In both numbers and influence

Protestantism grew relatively much more rapidly than did any other major division of Christianity. The main current of the Christian stream seemed now to be flowing through it.

The reasons for the forging to the fore of Protestantism were not simple nor were all of them clear. They were associated with the leadership of the predominantly Protestant Great Britain in the industrial revolution and with the outstanding place of the British Isles and the United States, both more Protestant than Roman Catholic, in the expansion of European peoples in the nineteenth century Just as between the fifteenth and the nineteenth century the expansion of Europe and of Christianity had been chiefly through Spain and Portugal, Roman Catholic by faith, so now it was powers in which Protestantism was the characteristic religion which were in the ascendant. How far the Portuguese and the Spaniards on the one hand, and the Anglo-Saxons, British and American, on the other, owed their leadership to the particular form of Christianity which they espoused is not clear. That in each instance their faith had some share in their hegemony appears probable. That in the earlier period Roman Catholicism and in the latter period Protestantism profited by the association is certain. Both the vigour and the power of these peoples contributed to the extension of the forms of the faith with which they were so intimately bound.

In several ways the spread of Christianity in the nineteenth century was by processes which differed strikingly from those of any previous period. In spite of the intimate connexion with the expansion of European, ostensibly Christian peoples, there was less direction and active assistance from the state than in any era since the beginning of the fourth century. The extension was chiefly by voluntary organizations supported by the gifts of private individuals. More of these bodies came into being than in any previous century. Never before had Christianity or any other religion had so many individuals giving full time to the propagation of their faith. Never had so many hundreds of thousands contributed voluntarily of their means to assist the spread of Christianity or of any other religion. In general, higher standards were maintained by both Protestants and Roman Catholics for the instruction and baptism of converts from non-Christian religions than had been customary since the first three centuries. To this generalization there were many exceptions, but the trend was decidedly in that direction. This was partly because of a similar tendency in Europe and America. By tradition, Christianity had been the group religion of western and northern European peoples. It had been accepted through mass movements, as have been most religions, and it continued as part of the group heritage. Yet this was not in full accord with the initial genius of Christianity. While it had social implications, the life into which the Christian Gospel led could be entered upon only by individual decision and faith. In the nineteenth century the climate of opinion was increasingly against the automatic identity of membership in the community and the Church. This was partly from revolt against the Church and partly from the greater emphasis by the churches upon the standards for membership. Since the higher requirements were insisted upon by the more earnest elements in the churches, and since it was from these elements that the missionaries and their supporters were chiefly drawn, it was to be expected that the prerequisites for baptism of non-Christians would be fairly exacting.

Thanks to the several favouring circumstances, in the course of the nineteenth century Christianity was diffused across most of the land surface of the globe.

In eastern Europe the Greek Orthodox Church made advances at the expense of paganism and Islam. Here and there in many countries of Europe there were conversions from the Jews. Yet there occurred no mass movement of Jews towards Christianity. In the vast shifts of population in western Europe which accompanied the rise of industrialism and the growth of great cities, thousands lost the close touch with the Church which had traditionally been that of their ancestors. A large proportion of the labourers in the factories drifted away from their hereditary faith. However, in many areas the churches followed the migrations to the cities. New parishes were created and church buildings erected. Fresh methods were devised to meet the novel conditions. In England particularly the labour movement and the co-operatives for the purchase and sale of the necessities of life for the labourers and the middle classes had much of their impulse from the Christian faith, especially through the nonconformist bodies.

In the United States the period opened with less than one-tenth of the population counted as members of churches. During the century Christianity was confronted with a vast westward migration of population, with an almost equally great influx from Europe, with the Indians and the Negroes, exploited non-Christian minorities, and with the progressive industrialization of the land. It met these problems with a high degree of success. The church membership rose from less than one-tenth to more than two-fifths of the total population. The gains were all along the line. Progress was registered in the older settled portions of the country, in winning an increasing proportion of the westward moving population, in holding to their hereditary faith very large sections of the immigration from Europe, and in bringing to baptism about the same proportion of Negroes and Indians as of the whites.

In Canada an even higher proportion of the population acknowledged a relationship with the churches than in the United States, and that in the face of settlement in the West, of fresh immigration from across the Atlantic, of widely scattered Indian tribes, and of Eskimos. Practically all the sparse population of Greenland became Christians. In the West Indies great advances were made among the Negroes who constituted the large majority of the inhabitants of most of the islands under British, Danish, and Dutch rule.

In Latin America the fore part of the nineteenth century witnessed discouraging reverses. During the throes of the struggle for independence and in the subsequent political developments, the Church suffered severely. The successful struggle of the American-born whites to free themselves from the domination of the European-born cost it a large proportion of its higher clergy and its missionaries. The efforts of the new governments to obtain the kind of control over the Church which had been exercised by the Spanish and Portuguese crowns and the reluctance of Spain to acknowledge the new political status brought Rome much embarrassment and retarded the adjustment to the new order. The suspicion and enmity of anti-clericals in high office wrought restrictions on the Church. As a survivor of the colonial era, the Church seemed to many of the progressives obscurantist and the last bulwark of an outmoded and oppressive régime. Many of the missions to the non-Christian Indians fell into ruin and in some sections the quality of the clergy declined. However, the actual numerical losses were slight. In the latter part of the century here and there the morale of the Church began to show improvement. Moreover, Protestantism entered, partly by immigration and partly by active missions to non-Protestants. It made some gains among non-Christian Indians, but its converts were mostly from nominal Roman Catholics. The Eastern churches were represented by small groups of immigrants.

In Australia and New Zealand new nations, predominantly of British stock, came into being. In them the churches were strong and held the professed allegiance of the overwhelming majority of the population. In the islands of the Pacific, very numerous but most of them small, Christianity made rapid progress. In some of them practically the entire population became Christian. In the larger islands conversion was retarded. As in Australia and New Zealand, the Christianity thus planted was chiefly Protestant and secondarily Roman Catholic.

In the great congeries of islands known as the East Indies, the larger part of them brought under Dutch rule, Christianity achieved striking gains, but among the animistic rather than the Moslem or Hindu population. Until 1914 the advance was made mainly by Protestant rather than Roman Catholic agencies.

The Philippines, since the sixteenth century the major outpost of Christianity in the western Pacific, continued to be overwhelmingly Roman Catholic. In the nineteenth century that branch of the faith gained slowly among the animistic folk in the mountains but was unable to make an impression upon the Moros, Moslem Malays in the southern islands. After the American occupation, in 1898, Protestantism entered and won adherents, chiefly from the Roman Catholics. A large nationalistic schism tore away hundreds of thousands from the Roman Catholics into an independent church. The Roman Catholics began a reorganization of their forces.

In Madagascar notable accessions came to Christianity, both Protestant and Roman Catholic, chiefly from the dominant Hòva but also from some of the other tribes. In several of the island groups between Madagascar and India or which fringed Africa Christianity was either planted for the first time or was reinforced.

In South Africa a new nation arose, governed by a British and Dutch minority, within the British Empire. The white population was, for the most part, professedly Christian. Active missions, mostly Protestant, won large numbers of the blacks. In all the other political entities into which Africa south of the Sahara was carved by European states before 1914, Christianity, both Roman Catholic and Protestant, had a rapid spread, particularly in the generation immediately preceding 1914.

Roman Catholic and Protestant missionaries were numerous and active on the northern shores of Africa and in western Asia. Since, however, the region was overwhelmingly Moslem, few converts were made. On the northern coast of Africa, chiefly in Algeria and Tunisia, Christian communities arose, but by immigration from Europe. Elsewhere in the traditional strongholds of Islam Christian missionaries found their fields predominantly among the Christian minorities which persisted from pre-Moslem days.

In India a striking growth of Christianity was witnessed. It was facilitated by the British conquest, but it came primarily in consequence of the revivals in the Christianity of the Occident. The majority of the missionaries were not British. Roman Catholic missionaries were mostly from the continent of Europe and a large proportion of the Protestant emissaries were from that continent and the United States. Yet the British led in the Protestant enterprise and had a part, even though small, in the Roman Catholic undertaking. In 1914 Christianity was strong, as it had been in 1800, in the Portuguese enclaves and the South. It had also made extensive gains in other parts of the land, notably in the South. The ancient communities of Syrian or St. Thomas Christians persisted, but in so far as they increased they did so almost entirely by an excess of births over deaths. They gained very few converts. The great advances were made by the

Roman Catholics and the Protestants. These were mainly from among the depressed classes and the primitive hill tribes.

In 1914 Ceylon had a larger percentage of Christians than did any other land in Asia except Siberia, some portions of western Asia, and, if they be included in the Asiatic world, the Philippines. The Christians of Ceylon were chiefly the fruits of the Portuguese occupation. To them were added some by nineteenth century Roman Catholic and Protestant missions. In Burma the gains were mainly among the Karens and somewhat more by Protestants than by Roman Catholics. In Siam, because of the nearly solidly Buddhist character of the population, the numerical advances, whether by Roman Catholics or by Protestants, were not so striking as in some of the neighbouring lands. In British Malaya there were accessions from Chinese and Indian immigrants. In the portions of Indo-China which by 1914 had come under French control, Roman Catholic Christianity, dating from pre-nineteenth century times, enjoyed a prosperous growth, and that in spite of persecution in the first three-quarters of the century and of the anti-clerical bias of much of the later French administration.

In the vast Chinese Empire Christianity made progress, but at unequal rates in the various sections. Its accessions were mostly in the two decades immediately preceding 1914. They were chiefly in the provinces along the coast and the lower reaches of the Yangtze River, the areas most affected by the impact of the Occident. They were least numerous in the regions farthest from the sea, Tibet, Sinkiang, and Mongolia. Yet no province or outlying dependency was without them. Numerically Roman Catholicism was much stronger than Protestantism, for it had been in the land much longer. However, proportionately Protestantism was growing more rapidly.

In Japan the missionary activity which had been forcibly suspended early in the seventeenth century could not be renewed until past the middle of the nineteenth century. When it was resumed, the discovery was made that Christianity had not been entirely extirpated by the rigours of persistent persecution, but had merely been driven into hiding and had been somewhat reduced in strength. Through the adherence of many of these Christians, Roman Catholicism had an initial high rate of accessions. The Russian Orthodox Church was represented, chiefly through the leadership of a great missionary. However, the major advance was by Protestants, predominantly through missionaries from the United States, and mainly from the intellectual and professional classes most affected by Western learning.

In Korea Roman Catholic Christianity arrived late in the eighteenth century. In spite of recurring persecution of great severity it gained an enduring foothold. The suspension of persecution and the partial conformation to Western cultural patterns which followed the treaties of the 1880's were accompanied by a marked extension of the Christian communities. Protestantism, as in Japan propagated mainly from the United States, prospered more than did Roman Catholicism.

In the huge but thinly settled portions of Asia occupied by Russia, Christianity made notable gains through migration from Europe. It was mostly Orthodox, but there were Roman Catholic and Protestant minorities. There were also Orthodox missions among the animistic aborigines.

This rapid and compact summary will at least serve to show how widely Christianity had been disseminated in the nineteenth century. Nothing to equal it had previously been seen in the history of the faith. Nothing remotely approaching it could be recorded of any other religion at any time in the human scene.

We must note, however, that Christianity did not displace rival cults over as wide areas as it had in some earlier stages of its spread. In this respect it had no achievement comparable to its elimination of the historic faiths of the Mediterranean world in its first five centuries or to its destruction of its rivals in western Europe in what we have termed "the thousand years of uncertainty." Nor did it deal such shattering blows to non-Christian religions for so many millions as it had between A.D. 1500 and A.D. 1800 in Mexico, much of the west coast of South America, and the Philippines. Among non-European peoples its major gains were from animistic or near-animistic folk and against some of the near-primitive types of faith. Here and there, as in some of the islands of the Pacific, it eradicated the antecedent cults. Against the major high religions of Asia, however, it made only slight advances. This may have been in part because of the brevity of the time in which it had to operate. In most of Asia it did not get well under way until the second half of the century. The twentieth and twenty-first centuries might conceivably tell a different story. Yet down to A.D. 1914 the major non-Christian systems of Asia and even of animistic Africa were either substantially intact or had only begun to disintegrate.

More important even than geographic spread is the question of the effect which Christianity had upon its varied environments.

This is much more difficult to determine than the rather obvious fact of the world-wide extension of the faith. Some questions, of extreme importance, can probably not be answered beyond cavil. How far, for instance, if at all, was Christianity responsible for the origin of the scientific method, the closely related development of nineteenth century industry, and the associated renewed expansion of Western peoples which were outstanding features of the period?

That by the discipline which it gave the western European mind through the scholasticism which its theology inspired in the Middle Ages and by the faith to which it contributed in the orderliness, dependability, and rationality of the universe Christianity was one of the sources of the scientific approach seems not only possible but probable. Yet he would be rash who would venture the assertion that it was the essential source. That at times Christian missionaries, most notably David Livingstone, were pioneers in nineteenth century exploration by Europeans is clear. That their Christian faith constituted their driving and sustaining motive seems also incontrovertible. That but for them the geographic discoveries would not soon have been made would be a most dubious generalization. That it was the daring faith bred in the European spirit by Christianity which inspired even seemingly irreligious individuals reared in the milieu of which it was an ingredient to climb unscaled mountains, to search for the North and South Poles, and to embark upon vast industrial undertakings and the building of huge empires is an interesting hypothesis. That it is indubitable truth only the ignorant or the rashly dogmatic would confidently assert. Similarly the situation is too complex to deny or to affirm that Christianity was either a waning or a growing force in the culture of the Occident. Plausible cases can be made for both contentions.

However, although there are many unresolved and probably unresolvable uncertainties, in some phases of culture potent Christian influences can be clearly established.

One of the most obvious of these was the emergence of Christian churches in areas where they had not existed at the dawn of the nineteenth century. This was seen especially in large portions of North America, in New Zealand and much of Australia, in many of the islands of the Pacific, in vast reaches in Africa, and in many sections of India, the Chinese Empire, Japan, Korea, and Siberia.

Another of the well authenticated effects of Christianity was, as in all ages, the transformation to be seen in individual character. In a very large proportion, perhaps in most of its converts, Christianity worked a moral and spiritual change. In some lives, usually the small minority, this was revolutionary. There were those who found satisfaction after a long and agonizing spiritual quest. Others won emancipation from a crippling habit. Some were released from hate. Many were absolved from the fear of the surrounding spirit world. To a few choice souls the Christian faith meant not so much a revolution as an enrichment of insights obtained through nurture in other religions. To some with a keen social conscience the Christian faith brought courage to face apparently impossible odds in fighting entrenched evils or in seeking to build wholesome order in an age of destructive change. To millions who were not fresh converts, but who had behind them generations of Christian heritage, Christianity was also an important formative factor. It entered into the moral and spiritual ideals in which they were nurtured. In a real sense each, no matter what his ancestry, had on his own account to begin the Christian life. For many this was through the processes of prolonged nurture. For others it was by soul-shaking struggles. To all who were genuinely Christian, there were crises along the way brought by decisions which had to be reached, burdens which could not well be avoided, illness, or other misfortune, in the meeting of which the resources of the faith were of major importance.

In the realm of the intellect and of education Christianity made outstanding contributions. Christian missionaries reduced more languages to writing than had been given that expression in all the previous history of the race. For the tongues of the majority of mankind means of writing already existed, but the speech of many millions had not been provided with these facilities until that was done by Christian missionaries of the nineteenth century. These previously illiterate languages, although spoken by only the minority of the race, were more numerous than those which had heretofore been rendered literate. The prime purpose of missionaries in this achievement was the spread and maintenance of the Christian faith. Portions or all of the Bible were translated by nineteenth century missionaries into more languages than had ever any other one book. Missionaries were not content with issuing religious literature. They also put into one or another non-European language much material from the Occident which was not strictly in the field of religion but which they hoped would prove useful to the peoples among whom they laboured. Such were the treatises on international law and the large medical literature prepared for the Chinese.

Never before had any other set of agencies pioneered in education for as many different peoples as did the Christian missions of the nineteenth century. Even Christianity itself, which already had behind it a notable record in education, in this respect surpassed its previous history. This was true of schools of all grades, from the elementary through the university. Christianity stimulated on the one hand the spread among the masses of the rudiments of education and on the other the most advanced training and research, with the pushing forward of the borders of human knowledge into the hitherto unknown. This was seen especially on the geographic frontiers of the advance of western European peoples. As scattered illustrations of these generalizations one remembers the scores of colleges and universities planted by the churches on the westward-moving frontier of white settlement in the United States and Canada; the part of Christian home missionaries in bringing into being inclusive tax-supported public education in some of the newer of the United States; the achievement of Roman Catholics in the United States in the creation of church-controlled systems of education from primary grades through the universities; the fact that in 1914 the large majority of the universities of the United States which were outstanding in their advanced research, although largely or entirely independent of ecclesiastical control, owed their inception to one or another of the churches or to a religious movement; the commanding position held by Oxford and Cambridge, ecclesiastical foundations, in higher education in the British Empire; and the fashion in which Christian missionaries led the way in the creation of schools of Western types in many non-Occidental lands, from some of the smaller islands of the Pacific to the huge continent of Africa and to the ancient lands of northern Africa and of western, southern, and eastern Asia.

From Christianity issued impulses which contributed to the fight against some of the chronic ills which have afflicted mankind. In country after country and among people after people Christian missionaries were pioneers in modern Occidental medicine and surgery. This was notably true in China, where the medical profession of the twentieth century owed its origin and the early stages of its development almost entirely to Protestant missions. The worldwide nursing profession of the nineteenth and twentieth centuries had one of its main sources in the institution of Kaiserswerth inaugurated by a Christian pastor in the attempt to meet the needs of an obscure parish. Missionaries later introduced it into region after region. Both in Occidental and non-Occidental lands, care for the blind, the insane, and the lepers owed much to devoted Christians. Hundreds of hospitals, large and small, in all the continents and in many of the islands of the sea were indebted to the churches for their inception. In China Christians fought the opium traffic and helped some of its victims to emancipation. Negro slavery, the largest scale exploitation of members of one race by another in the annals of mankind, was abolished through movements which had as their chief creators men and women whose consciences were made tender and whose resolution was given persistence and confidence by their Christian faith. On many fronts earnest Christians, numbers of them missionaries, fought the mistreatment of other races by their fellow-Occidentals. They sought, not without success, to ease the shock of the impact of Western culture upon non-Western peoples and to assist the latter to a wholesome adjustment to the impinging culture of the Occident. Christian idealism contributed to the benevolent objectives and programmes of British, Dutch, and American imperialism of the latter part of the period—as it had modified Spanish and Portuguese colonial laws and policies in the sixteenth, seventeenth, and eighteenth centuries. The efforts to curb war which displayed their chief strength in Great Britain and the United States usually were due at the outset to devout men and women who drew their convictions from their Christian faith.

The basic structure of Western civilization was not revolutionized. It was still marked by extreme nationalism and materialism and from time to time was disturbed by wars. It was far from conforming to Christian patterns. Yet Christianity was modifying it both in the Occident and in its outreach in other portions of the globe. By a strange contradiction, some of the chronic ills of mankind, notably slavery and war, attained their acme in the nineteenth and twentieth centuries among peoples which had been long subjected to Christian influences, yet the most vigorous movements which mankind had ever witnessed to free the world of these evils had their rise and development among these very peoples and to a great degree stemmed from Christianity. Whether the culture of the Occident was more or less shaped by Christianity than it had been two centuries earlier is impossible to determine. Christianity was potent within it as it had been since the nominal conversion of western Europe. Not in the centuries which Europeans termed the Middle Ages and when Western peoples numbered only a few millions and were an inconsiderable factor in the life of the race as a whole could Western civilization be properly termed Christian. Now in the day when Europeans had multiplied and had mastered most of the world it could still not accurately be given the appellation of Christian. Yet in both ages Christianity was an appreciable force within the Occident, modifying even though not fully informing every phase of life.

Not only was Western civilization not made over to conform fully to Christian standards. It was also true that in 1914 no non-European people could properly be designated as Christian. In the Philippines and a few of the smaller islands of the Pacific the majority of the population called themselves by that name. Their collective life bore the marks of Christianity, but no phase attained even approximately to Christian standards. In the major non-European peoples those calling themselves Christian were only a small percentage of the total population.

It was clear that Christianity, while powerful in human affairs, was as yet far from remaking mankind into the image of its ideal. Some of the states of the Occident were officially Christian. Several subscribed to Christian principles in their laws, morals, and social institutions. At least one large government, however, had frankly severed a Christian connexion of long standing and in others the drift was in that direction. Professing Christians were more numerous and more widely spread than ever before. Their faith was having a greater effect upon mankind as a whole than in any former period. Yet the trend was towards the situation in the first three centuries in the Græco-Roman world, when Christians were self-conscious minori¿ies, in the world but not fully of it. This was in part due to the nature of Christianity. The goal set forth in the New Testament could probably ne~er be fully attained "within history." Judged by the standards of Jesus and the early Apostles no individual could hope to be perfect this side of the grave.

However, there was that in the Christian faith which forbade Christians ever to rest content short of its high calling. In it, too, was that which encouraged them to strive to attain the exacting goal. They were assured that if not within history, then beyond it, they were to be "filled unto all the fulness of God." They could not be satisfied to leave the world about them to destruction. They might believe that the full realization of the Christian hope by any human society was impossible. Yet they were commanded to love their neighbours. That meant that they must seek to relieve the myriad wants of those about them. Moreover, one of the obligations laid upon them in the New Testament was to teach all nations to observe all that their Lord had commanded them, an injunction which made a duty the attempt to bring all mankind to the standards of the Sermon on the Mount. This was to be their objective and in the endeavour to attain it they were promised the companionship of an unseen all-powerful Presence. With these qualities in its very nature, Christianity, if it were not to deny its genius, must continue to be a leaven in the affairs of men. It was still young. Presumably it had only begun its course. The nineteen centuries during which it had been present were only a small fraction of the total history of the race. If one could judge by its past record, Christianity would continue to spread. In general, it came to the year 1914 on an ascending curve. It was now for the first time almost world-wide in its representation. Much of that was the achievement of the preceding few decades. Christianity was gaining momentum.

In what for the present may seem an anticlimax, we must pause to say something of the effect of the nineteenth century environment upon Christianity. Clearly the Christianity of 1914 was not identical with that of 1800. This was partly because of inner developments within the faith itself, partly because of changes brought by expansion, and partly because of the temper of the times. It is not easy to disentangle the various factors which issued in the modifications, but some of the alterations are obvious.

The main strains of Christianity which were present in 1800 continued.

However, by 1914 what is usually called Protestantism was, in relation to the others, much stronger than at the beginning of the nineteenth century. Indeed, the term Protestantism had become more than ever a misnomer. What was embraced under that designation had never been merely a reaction against Roman Catholicism. It had, rather, been a series of fresh movements which the structure of Latin Christianity had not proved flexible enough to retain. These movements had now been so long separated from the parent stock that they could less than ever be deemed a protest. They were positive affirmations with their own ecclesiastical structures and their characteristic forms of religious experience and expression. The fresh awakenings within Protestantism in the eighteenth and nineteenth centuries were making that wing of Christianity ever more distinct from Roman Catholicism and increasingly an independent set of movements. Protestantism preserved many features of historic Christianity. By clinging to the Bible even more emphatically than did Roman Catholics and the Eastern churches it conserved much of the primitive spirit of the faith. Anglicanism and some phases of Lutheranism held to much of what had been developed by the church of the West in pre-Reformation times. Yet what had come out of the Roman Church at the time of the Reformation was clearly not a waning series of schisms. More and more the main stream of vitality in the Christian movement seemed to be flowing through it. This trend was strengthened by the nineteenth century spread of Christianity. Relatively Protestantism had a greater extension than any other form of the faith. It was ceasing to be so largely what it had been at the outset, a Teutonic expression of the transmitted Latin Christianity. It was becoming world-wide. In the largest of the new nations which arose out of the nineteenth century migrations of European peoples, the United States, Protestantism was dominant. In some of the others, Australia, New Zealand, the Union of South Africa, and, to a somewhat less degree, Canada, it was in the majority. In the traditionally Roman Catholic areas of Latin America and the Philippines it was winning growing minorities. In non-European lands it was making proportionately more rapid gains than was Roman Catholicism. In India, Ceylon, Indo-China, China, and some parts of Africa it was numerically not so strong as Roman Catholicism, but in Japan, Korea, the Netherlands Indies, and several sections of Africa Protestants outnumbered Roman Catholics, and in India and China they were having a greater effect upon the country as a whole. Such major social reforms as the anti-slavery, temperance, and peace movements issued more from Protestant than from Roman Catholic Christianity. In developing educational systems Protestantism was the more potent.

In some of its phases Protestantism was partly conforming to its environment. It was, in general, more inclined to adjust itself to the intellectual currents of the day than were the other main types of Christianity. Although by tradition fissiparous, it was beginning to come together in various co-operative enterprises. These were especially marked on the new geographic frontiers. In the United States, Canada, China, Japan, and India where many forms of Protestantism existed side by side, the trend was towards interpenetration of one variety by another and towards working together in common tasks. Through Protestantism a distinct kind of Christianity was already beginning to emerge in the United States. Here and there were indications of similar trends in Japan, China, and India.

The Roman Catholic Church also showed the effects of the nineteenth century environment. This was in part in a refusal to conform to such tendencies in its *milieu* as civil marriage, secularized education, and the application of some forms of historical method to the Bible and to its own history. It rejected its own "modernists." It was not as subservient to the state as it had been in the preceding three centuries. It affirmed the infallibility of the Pope. That pontiff had far more effective administrative power in the whole of his communion than he had enjoyed for several centuries. The Roman Catholic Church was spreading rapidly, but as a more and more highly co-ordinated body under a centralized authority.

Of the Eastern churches the strongest was that of Russia. The Russian Orthodox Church responded less to the spirit of the times than did either Protestantism or Roman Catholicism. It did not move out of Russia to any great extent. It remained in the position to which Peter the Great had reduced it, ancillary to the power of the Tsar and an instrument for enforcing Tsarist autocracy and assimilating non-Russian peoples to Russian culture.

In many ways 1914 marked no sudden break in the stream of Christian history. Numbers of the movements which had been gathering headway before that year persisted. After 1914 Christianity was still expanding, chiefly by conversions from non-European peoples. It became more nearly evenly distributed over the earth's surface than ever before. Through the development of indigenous leadership it also became more deeply rooted among non-European peoples. It continued to have profound effects, some of them of increasing magnitude, particularly upon non-European cultures in Africa, India, China, and Japan. What we have loosely but with confessed inaccuracy termed Protestantism more and more drew together through various phases of what came to be called the Ecumenical movement and reached out towards all branches of non-Roman Catholic Christianity. It even approached Roman Catholics, although very tentatively, in an attempt at reciprocal understanding and fellowship.

However, after 1914 the advances made by Christianity were accomplished in the face of a succession of storms. As never before, wars and revolutions shook the entire fabric of human life. Civilization the world around was in a stage of violent transition. To the spread of Christianity in that period of man's history, still incomplete, we turn in our next and final volume.

BIBLIOGRAPHY

W HAT is given below is by no means a complete list of the materials used in the writing of this volume. A bibliography of all the works consulted would approximately treble the number of titles here recorded. That would add to the pages quite disproportionately without serving a correspondingly useful purpose. As in the preceding three volumes, only those titles are given which have been cited more than once in the footnotes. For those employed only once, by far the majority of the whole, the necessary bibliographical data are with the citation. Moreover, it has seemed unnecessary, with a few exceptions, to repeat here the various reports of missionary societies which have been referred to. The full list of the materials employed on any topic, whether an individual, an organization, or a movement, can be quickly discovered by turning to the text, with the aid of the index, and consulting the appropriate footnotes. If that is done, it will be seen that heavy reliance has been placed, as in the preceding volumes, upon what historians are wont to term primary sources. Some of these are in reports of societies, some are in autobiographies or narratives by participants, and others are in excerpts from correspondence and journals embodied in biographies. As heretofore, extensive use has also been made of secondary accounts. To ignore either class of material would mean a badly truncated narrative.

Adeney, Walter F., *The Greek and Eastern Churches* (New York, Charles Scribner's Sons, 1928. [Preface, 1908.] Pp. xiv, 634). A scholarly survey.

Aitchison, Charles, *Lord Lawrence and the Reconstruction of India under the Crown* (Oxford, Clarendon Press, 1905, pp. 216). By a friend of Lord Lawrence.

Albaugh, Dana M., *Between Two Centuries. A Study of Four Baptist Mission Fields. Assam, South India, Bengal Orissa and South China* (Philadelphia, The Judson Press, 1935, pp. 245). By a secretary of the American Baptist Foreign Mission Society, based partly on manuscript letters, leaflets, and printed reports.

Allen, W. O. B., and McClure, Edmund, *Two Hundred Years: The History of The Society for Promoting Christian Knowledge, 1698-1898* (London, Society for Promoting Christian Knowledge, 1898, pp. vi, 551). The standard history, based upon records, letter-books, reports, and minutes.

Allgemeine Missions-Zeitschrift (Berlin, 1874-1923). A leading Protestant periodical on missions, founded by Gustav Warneck.

Anderson, Rufus, *History of the Missions of the American Board of Commissioners for Foreign Missions in India* (Boston, Congregational Publishing Society, 1874, pp. xvi, 443). By a former secretary of the board.

Anderson, Rufus, *History of the Missions of the American Board of Commissioners for Foreign Missions to the Oriental Churches* (Boston, Congregational Publishing Society, 2 vols., 1872). Based chiefly upon annual reports, *The Missionary Herald,* other records, and the personal knowledge of the author, a former secretary of the board.

Anderson, William B., and Watson, Charles R., *Far North in India. A Survey of the Mission Field and Work of the United Presbyterian Church in the Punjab* (Philadelphia, The Board of Foreign Missions of the United Presbyterian Church of North America, rev. 2d ed., 1911, pp. 312). A popularly written, official account.

André-Marie, *Missions Dominicaines dans l'Extrême Orient* (Paris, 2 vols., 1865).

Andrews, C. F., *Mahatma Gandhi's Ideas, Including Selections from his Writings* (New York, The Macmillan Company, 1930, pp. 382). Largely composed of quotations and first hand information. Sympathetic to Gandhi, by an intimate Christian friend.

Andrews, C. F., *North India* (London, A. R. Mowbray & Co., 1908, pp. xvi, 243). By a member of the Cambridge Brotherhood, Delhi.

Andrews, C. F., *What I Owe to Christ* (London, Hodder & Stoughton, Ltd., 1932, pp. 311). An autobiography of a famous missionary to India.

Anesaki, Masaharu, *History of Japanese Religion with Special Reference to the Social and Moral Life of the Nation* (London, Kegan Paul, Trench, Trubner & Co., 1930, pp. xxii, 423). A work by a thoroughly competent and distinguished scholar in the field of religion. Himself a Buddhist, he is very fair to Christianity.

Anglo-Egyptian Sudan (London, H. M. Stationery Office, 1920, pp. 174).

Annales de la Propagation de la Foi, recueil periodique. Collection faisant suite aux Lettres Édifiantes (Lyon, 53 vols., 1822ff.). Published by the Association de la Propagation de la Foi. Contains letters from various parts of the mission field.

Annals of the Propagation of the Faith (New York, Society for the Propagation of the Faith, 1838-1923. Then combined with *Catholic Missions* to form *Catholic Missions and Annals of the Propagation of the Faith*).

Annett, E. A., *Conversion in India. A Study in Religious Psychology* (Calcutta, Christian Literature Society for India, 1920, pp. xiii, 195). Scholarly.

Annual Report of the National Bible Society of Scotland (Glasgow, 1861ff.).

Annuario da Archidiocese de Goa para 1914. Coordenado com auctoriscacão do. Exmo e Revd.^mo Snr. Arcebispo Primaz, Patriarcha das Indias Orientaes (New Goa, Arthur & Viegas, 1913, pp. vi, 165, 10).

The Apostolic Carmel, Mangalore. A Retrospect of Sixty Years, 1868-1928. (Reprinted from *Carmela,* 1928, pp. 24).

Arens, Bernard, *Handbuch der katholischen Missionen* (Herder & Co., Freiburg i.B., 1920, pp. xix, 418). A second edition, enlarged, was issued in 1925.

Ashley-Brown, W., *On the Bombay Coast and Deccan. The Origin and History of the Bombay Diocese. A Record of 300 Years' Work for Christ in Western India*

(London, Society for Promoting Christian Knowledge, 1937, pp. xiii, 280). Readable. Most of the story is based upon manuscript archives.

Ashmore, Lida Scott, *Historical Sketch of the South China Mission of the American Baptist Foreign Mission Society, 1860-1920* (Shanghai, Methodist Publishing House, 1920, pp. vi, 239). By a member of the mission.

Asia (New York, 1901ff.). A monthly magazine for a popular constituency.

Attwater, Donald, *The Catholic Eastern Churches* (Milwaukee, Wis., The Bruce Publishing Company, 1935, pp. xx, 308). By a Roman Catholic. Contains excellent bibliographies.

Attwater, Donald, *The Dissident Eastern Churches* (Milwaukee, Wis., The Bruce Publishing Company, 1937, pp. xviii, 349).

[Aubry, J.-B.], *Correspondance du Père J.-B. Aubry des Missions Étrangères, Missionnaire au Kouy-Tchéou, docteur in théologie, ancien directeur au grand séminaire de Beauvois* (Beauvois, 1886). Letters 1875-1882.

Aurelius, *De Kapucijnen en de Missie* (Brasschaat, A de Bièvre [1927?], pp. 151). By a Capuchin.

Ayyar, Rao Bahadur L. K. Anantakrishna, *Anthropology of the Syrian Christians* (Ernakulam, Cochin Government Press, 1926, pp. xvii, 338). The author, among other posts, has held that of superintendent of ethnography in the Cochin state and has been lecturer and reader on ethnography or anthropology at two Indian universities. Is often uncritical.

Bacon, Theodore Davenport, *Leonard Bacon. A Statesman in the Church.* Edited by Benjamin Bacon (New Haven, Yale University Press, 1931, pp. xv, 563). A biography, by a grandson, based largely upon original documents.

Badley, B. H., *Indian Missionary Directory and Memorial Volume* (Lucknow, American Methodist Mission Press, 1876, pp. xii, 279).

Badley, Brenton T., editor, *Visions and Victories in Hindustan. A Story of the Mission Stations of the Methodist Episcopal Church in Southern Asia* (Madras, Methodist Publishing House, 1931, pp. xxv, 842). By a bishop of the Methodist Episcopal Church, long a missionary in India. The several chapters are by authors familiar with the local situations of which they write.

Balangero, Gio. Battista, *Australia e Ceylan. Studi e Ricordi di tredici anni di Missione* (Turin, G. B. Paravia e Comp., 1897, pp. xiv, 386). A kind of missionary autobiography.

The Baptist Missionary Magazine (Boston, 1817-1909).

Barnes, Irene H., *Behind the Pardah. The Story of the C.E.Z.M.S. Work in India* (London, Marshall Brothers, 1898, pp. xii, 264). A popularly written account.

Barton, James L., *Daybreak in Turkey* (Boston, The Pilgrim Press, 2d ed., 1908, pp. 306). By a former missionary to Turkey and a distinguished secretary of the American Board of Commissioners for Foreign Missions.

Beach, Harlan P., and St. John, Burton, editors, *World Statistics of Christian Missions* (New York, The Committee of Reference and Counsel of the Foreign Missions Conference of North America, 1916, pp. 148). Authoritative.

Beard, Augustus Field, *A Crusade of Brotherhood. A History of the American Missionary Association* (Boston, The Pilgrim Press, 1909, pp. xii, 334). The author was a secretary of the American Missionary Association.

Becker, C., *Indisches Kastenwesen und Christliche Mission* (Aachen, Xaverius Verlag, 1921, pp. 164). By the Prefect Apostolic of Assam.

Becker, C., *Im Stromtal des Brahmaputra* (Munich, Salvator-Verlag, 1923, pp. xxix, 512, 2d ed., Aachen, Aachener Missionsdruckerei A.-G. 1927, pp. xx, 584).

Becker, Émile, *Un Demi-siecle d' Apostolat en Chine. Le Révérend Père Joseph Gonnet de la Compagnie de Jésus* (Ho-kien-fou, Imprimerie de la Mission, 1916, pp. xi, 268).

Beckmann, Johannes, *Die katholische Missionsmethode in China in neuester Zeit (1842-1912). Geschichtliche Untersuchung über Arbeitsweisen, ihre Hindernisse und Erfolge* (Missionshauses Bethlehem Immensee [Schweiz], 1931, pp. xvi, 202). A scholarly, well documented impartial study, by a Roman Catholic, based upon an extensive examination of the pertinent printed material.

Berg, Ludwig, *Die katholischen Heidenmission als Kulturträger* (2d ed., Aachen, Aachener Missionsdruckerei, 3 vols., 1927). Carefully supported by references to authorities, which as a rule are standard German experts and missionary periodicals. Warmly pro-Roman Catholic and critical of Protestants.

Berry, Katherine Fiske, *A Pioneer Doctor in Old Japan. The Story of John C. Berry, M.D.* (New York, Fleming H. Revell Company, 1940, pp. 247).

Bickersteth, Samuel, *Life and Letters of Edward Bickersteth, Bishop of South Tokyo* (London, Sampson Low, Marston & Co., 1899, pp. xv, 492). By a brother.

Birks, Herbert, *The Life and Correspondence of Thomas Valpy French, First Bishop of Lahore* (London, John Murray, 2 vols., 1895).

Blackman, Winifred S., *The Fellāhin of Upper Egypt. Their Religious, Social and Industrial Life To-day with Special Reference to Survivals from Ancient Times* (London, George G. Harrap & Co., Ltd., pp. 331). Based upon careful observation.

Blakeslee, George H., editor, *Recent Developments in China* (New York, G. E. Stechert and Company, 1913, pp. xi, 413). Scholarly.

Blodget, Henry, and Baldwin, C. C., *Sketches of the Missions of the American Board in China* (Boston, American Board of Commissioners for Foreign Missions, 1896, pp. 57). By missionaries in that field.

Bonjean, Ch., *Marriage Legislation in Ceylon* (Trichinopoly, The Scottish Press, 1864, pp. xi, 166). By a Roman Catholic missionary in Ceylon.

Boulger, Demetrius C., *Lord William Bentinck* (Oxford, Clarendon Press, 1897, pp. 214).

Bouniol, S., editor, *The White Fathers and Their Missions, with a foreword by Cardinal Bourne (Archbishop of Westminster)* (London, Sands and Co., 1929, pp. 334). A popular account, not especially scholarly.

Bowers, A. C., *Under Head-Hunters' Eyes* (Philadelphia, The Judson Press, 1929, pp. 248). A popularly written account of the work of the American Baptist Foreign Mission Society among the hills in Assam, by one engaged in it.

Braisted, Paul Judson, *Indian Nationalism and the Christian Colleges* (New York, Association Press, 1935, pp. xii, 171). A careful study.

Britton, Roswell S., *The Chinese Periodical Press, 1800-1912* (Shanghai, Kelly & Walsh, 1933, pp. vi, 151). Carefully done.

Brockman, Fletcher S., *I Discover the Orient* (New York, Harper & Brothers, 1935, pp. xii, 211). The autobiography of a leading Young Men's Christian Association secretary in China.

Broomhall, Marshall, *Hudson Taylor's Legacy. A Series of Meditations* (London, China Inland Mission, 1931, pp. xiv, 166). Meditations selected from Hudson Taylor's writings and arranged for daily devotional reading.

Broomhall, Marshall, *The Jubilee Story of the China Inland Mission* (London, Morgan & Scott, 1915, pp. xvi, 386). An official history, well written.

Broullion, *Missions en Chine. Mémoire sur l'État Actuel de la Mission du Kiang-nan, 1842-1855. . . . Suivi de Lettres Relatives a l'Insurrection, 1851-1855* (Paris, Julien, Lanier et Cie, 1855, pp. 487).

Brown, Arthur Judson, *One Hundred Years. A History of the Foreign Missionary Work of the Presbyterian Church in the U. S. A., With Some Account of Countries, Peoples and the Policies and Problems of Modern Missions* (New York, Fleming H. Revell Company, 1937, pp. 1140). An official history by a secretary emeritus of the board.

Buchanan, Claudius, *Memoir of the Expediency of an Ecclesiastical Establishment for British India* (Cambridge, Hilliard and Metcalf, 1811, pp. 96).

Buck, Oscar MacMillan, *India Looks to Her Future* (New York, Friendship Press, 1930, pp. viii, 214). A study book for the churches, in popular style, by an expert on missions who was born in India, the son of a missionary, and spent some time there himself in that capacity.

Burke, James, *My Father in China* (New York, Farrar & Rinehart, Inc., 1942, pp. xiv, 431). A life of W. B. Burke, in narrative, semi-fictional form, but based upon first-hand sources.

Burt, E. W., *Fifty Years in China. The Story of the Baptist Mission in Shantung, Shansi, and Shensi, 1875-1925* (London, The Carey Press, 1925, pp. 127).

Burton, Margaret E., *Notable Women of Modern China* (Chicago, Fleming H. Revell Company, 1912, pp. 271). Sympathetically told.

Butler, William, *From Boston to Bareilly and Back* (New York, Phillips & Hunt, 1886, pp. 517). Partly autobiographical, by the founder of the India mission of the Methodist Episcopal Church.

Cadbury, William Warder, *At the Point of a Lancet. One Hundred Years of the Canton Hospital 1835-1935* (Shanghai, Kelly and Walsh, 1935, pp. xvii, 304). By a superintendent of the hospital.

Caldwell, R., *Records of the Early History of the Tinnevelly Mission of the Society for Promoting Christian Knowledge and the Society for the Propagation of the Gospel in Foreign Parts* (Madras, Higginbotham and Co., 1881, pp. xi, 356).

Cannon, James, III, *History of Southern Methodist Missions* (Nashville, Cokesbury Press, 1926, pp. 356).

Canton, William, *A History of the British and Foreign Bible Society* (London, John Murray, 5 vols., 1904-1910).

The Capuchin Mission Unit (C.S.M.C.), Cumberland, Maryland, *India and Its Missions* (New York, The Macmillan Company, 1923, pp. xxi, 315). Prepared over a period of four years of study by the theological students of the Capuchin Monastery of SS. Peter and Paul, Cumberland, Md. A fairly careful piece of work, usually based upon excellent authorities.

Capuchins Missionnaires. Missions Françaises. Notes Historiques et Statistiques (Paris, Société et Librairie Coopératives St. François, 1926, pp. iv, 86). No author given. A popular summary.

Carey, S. Pearce, *William Carey, D.D., Fellow of Linnæan Society* (New York, George H. Doran Co., preface 1923, pp. xvi, 428). By a great-grandson. A standard biography.

Carter, Thomas, *Rose Harvey, Friend of the Leper* (London, The "Z" [Zenana] Press, no date, pp. ix, 159).

Cary, Otis, *A History of Christianity in Japan* (New York, Fleming H. Revell Company, 2 vols., 1909). The standard account in English, especially of Protestant missions. The first volume deals with Roman Catholic and Greek Orthodox missions, and the second with Protestant missions. The work contains much excellent information, but is not always critical and is defective in the scantiness of its bibliography and of references in footnotes to the sources of its information. The author is a Protestant, but his attitude towards non-Protestant missions is irenic. He was long a missionary in Japan.

Catalogue des Prêtres, Clercs et Frères de la Congrégation de la Mission qui ont Travaillé en Chine depuis 1697 (Peking, 1911).

The Catholic Church in Korea (Hongkong, Imprimerie de la Société des Missions-Etrangères, 1924, pp. 108).

Catholic Directory of India, 1912 (Madras, The Catholic Supply Society, pp. 544).

Catholic Directory of India, 1913 (Madras, The Catholic Supply Society, pp. 532, xxxv).

Catholic Directory of India, 1915 (Madras, The Catholic Supply Society, pp. xxviii, 266).

Catholic Directory of India, 1916 (Madras, The Catholic Supply Society, pp. 581).

Catholic Directory of India, Ceylon and Burma, 76th Annual Issue, 1926 (Madras, The Madras Catholic Supply Co., pp. 554).

The Catholic Encyclopedia (New York, 16 vols., 1907-1913). Written for informative and apologetic purposes.

Catholic Missions (New York, Society for the Propagation of the Faith, 1907ff.).

Caubrière, J. M., editor, *Synthesis Decretalium Sinarum e decretis regionalium synodorum ab anno 1803 ad annum 1910. Habitarum in Sinis, necnon aliquibus documentis ab anno 1784 ad annum 1884 a S.C. de P. Fide editis seu approbatis* (Hongkong, Typis Nazareth, 1914).

Centennial Report of the American Marathi Mission of the A.B.C.F.M. Edited by Alden H. Clark, William Hazen, and Clara Bruce (Ahmednagar, Alden H. Clark, no date, pp. vi, 119, vi, 109, 17).

A Century of Mission Work in Iran (Persia) 1834-1934 (Beirut, The American Press, pp. 171). No date or author. Compiled from longer special papers written for the centenary.

Chamberlain, Mrs. W. I., *Fifty Years in Foreign Fields, China, Japan, India, Arabia* (New York, Woman's Board of Foreign Missions Reformed Church in America, 1925, pp. xv, 292). By one long connected with the foreign enterprise of the Reformed Church in America.

Chandler, John S., *Seventy-Five Years in the Madura Mission* (American Madura Mission, no date, pp. xxii, 471). By one long a member of the mission.

Charles, H., *Jésuites Missionnaires, Syrie Proche Orient* (Paris, Gabriel Beauchesne, 1929, pp. 114).

Chatterton, Eyre, *A History of the Church of England in India since the Early Days of the East India Company* (London, Society for Promoting Christian Knowledge, 1924, pp. xxiv, 353). Based upon the sources.

China Centenary Missionary Conference Records (New York, American Tract Society, no date, pp. xxxvii, 823).

The China Mission Hand-book (Shanghai, American Presbyterian Mission Press, 1896, pp. 335). A useful compilation prepared by the American Presbyterian Mission Press with the aid of several missionaries.

The China Mission Year Book (Shanghai, Christian Literature Society, 1910-1919, 1923-1925). A Protestant publication.

China's Millions (London, 1875ff.). The official periodical of the China Inland Mission.

Chine, Ceylan, Madagascar. Lettres des Missionnaires Français de la Compagnie de Jésus, Province de Champagne (Lille, 1920ff.).

The Chinese Recorder (Published at Foochow, 1867, as *The Missionary Recorder*, at Foochow, 1868-1872, as *The Chinese Recorder and Missionary Journal*, and at Shanghai, 1874-1941. Beginning about 1911 the title was shortened to *The Chinese Recorder*). The standard interdenominational Protestant missionary journal of China.

The Chinese Repository (Canton, 1832-1851). A standard journal edited by missionaries of the American Board of Commissioners for Foreign Missions, containing much valuable information on contemporary China.

The Christian College in India. The Report of the Commission on Christian Higher Education in India (Oxford University Press, 1931, pp. xiii, 388). The commission was constituted by the International Missionary Council, was headed by A. D. Lindsay, and visited India in 1930-1931.

The Christian Endeavour Manual for India, Burma and Ceylon (Agra, The Indian Christian Endeavour Union, 1909, pp. ii, 176, vi).

The Christian Movement in Japan (Tokyo, various publishers, 1903ff.). An annual publication by Protestants.

The Christian Occupation of China. Edited by Milton C. Stauffer (Shanghai, China Continuation Committee, 1922, pp. 13, 468, cxii).

Christie, Dugald, *Thirty Years in the Manchu Capital. In and around Moukden in Peace and War: Being the Recollections of Dugald Christie* (New York, McBride, Nast & Co., 1914, pp. xiv, 303).

Christlieb, M[arie] L[ouise], *Indian Neighbours* (London, Student Christian Movement Press, 1930, pp. 96). All the occurrences narrated happened in one part of an Indian district. They are all facts—although names of places and persons have been changed and the name of the missionary is not given.

Clark, Charles Allen, *Digest of the Presbyterian Church of Korea* (*Chosen*) (Seoul, Korean Religious Book and Tract Co., 1918, pp. viii, 263).

Clark, Charles Allen, *The Korean Church and the Nevius Methods* (New York,

Fleming H. Revell Company, 1930, pp. 278). A doctoral dissertation by a Presbyterian missionary who had lived in Korea for the past twenty-seven years. The study is confined to the Presbyterian Church in Korea.

Clark, Robert, *The Punjab and Sindh Missions of the Church Missionary Society* (London, Church Missionary Society, 2d ed., 1885, pp. viii, 386). By a pioneer member of the mission.

Clemen, Carl, *Der Einfluss des Christentums auf andere Religionen* (Leipzig, A. Deichertsche Verlagsbuchhandlung D. Werner Schall, 1933, pp. 122). A brief treatment of a large subject, well documented, by a professor at the University of Bonn.

Clough, Emma Rauschenbusch, *Social Christianity in the Orient. The Story of a Man, a Mission and a Movement* (New York, The Macmillan Company, 1914, pp. xiii, 409). Largely autobiographical.

Cochrane, Thomas, *Survey of the Missionary Occupation of China* (Shanghai, The Christian Literature Society for China, 1913, pp. 372). By a missionary to China.

Collectanea S. Congregationis de Propaganda Fide seu Decreta Instructiones Rescriptc pro Apostolicis Missionibus (Rome, 2 vols., 1907).

The Concordat Question (Bombay Examiner Press, 1885, pp. 56). No author given. It is a continuation of *The Padroado Question* and is against the padroado.

The Continuation Committee Conferences in Asia 1912-1913. A Brief Account of the Conferences Together with Their Findings and Lists of Members (New York, Chairman of the Continuation Committee, 1913, pp. 488).

Cooksey, J. J., *The Land of the Vanished Church. A Survey of North Africa* (London, World Dominion Press, pp. 107).

Cordes, August, *Heinrich Cordes, der Vater der neueren lutherischen Tamulenmission* (Leipzig, Verlag der Evangelisch-lutherischen Mission, no date, pp. 78).

Cordier, Henri, *Histoire des Relations de la Chine avec les Puissances Occidentales 1860-1900* (Paris, Félix Alcan, 3 vols., 1901-1902). A standard work.

Coste, Pierre, *La Congrégation de la Mission Dite de Saint-Lazare* (Paris, Librairie Lecoffre, J. Gabalda et Fils, 1927, pp. viii, 231). By a Lazarist, based upon standard authorities.

Couling, Samuel, *The Encyclopædia Sinica* (Oxford University Press, 1917, pp. viii, 633). Carefully done, but with the shortcomings of a pioneer work.

Cromer, The Earl of, *Modern Egypt* (New York, The Macmillan Company, 2 vols., 1909). By one of the greatest of British representatives in Egypt.

Culshaw, W. J., *A Missionary Looks at His Job* (London, Student Christian Movement Press, 1937, pp. 144). By a young missionary to India.

Dale, William, *Our Missions in the Far East. A Historical Sketch of the Foreign Missions of the Presbyterian Church of England 1847-1907* (London, The Publications Committee, 1907, pp. 88).

Dallet, Ch., *Histoire de l'Église de Corée* (Paris, Victor Palmé, 2 vols., 1874). By a member of the Société des Missions-Étrangères. Based largely upon documentary reports by missionaries.

Davies, Hannah, *Among the Hills and Valleys of Western China. Incidents of Missionary Work* (London, S. W. Partridge & Co., 1901, pp. 326). By a member of the China Inland Mission.

Davis, J. Merle, *Davis, Soldier Missionary. A Biography of Rev. Jerome D. Davis* (Boston, The Pilgrim Press, 1916, pp. 347).

Davis, N., *A Voice from North Africa* (Edinburgh, Paton and Ritchie, 1844, pp. xvi, 232).

Dean, William, *The China Mission. Embracing a History of the Various Missions of all Denominations among the Chinese with Biographical Sketches of Deceased Missionaries* (New York, Sheldon & Co., 1859, pp. 396). By one of the early Baptist missionaries to the Chinese.

De Bussierre, Le Vicomte M.-Th., *Histoire du Schisme Portugais dans les Indes* (Paris, Jacques Lecoffre, 1854, pp. 363). An anti-Portuguese treatise. Some pertinent documents are included, some in French translation only and some in the original as well.

Demimuid, *Vie du Vénérable Justin de Jacobis, de la Congrégation de la Mission . . . Premier Vicaire Apostolique de l'Abyssinie* (Paris, Ancienne Maison Charles Douniol, 1906, pp. vi, 415).

Descamps, Baron, *Histoire Générale Comparée des Missions* (Paris, Librairie Plon, 1932, pp. viii, 760). Seven other writers have contributed. A standard survey, by Roman Catholic scholars, of Roman Catholic mission history from the beginning, together with chapters on the spread of Protestantism and of some other religions.

Dictionary of American Biography (New York, Charles Scribner's Sons, 21 vols., 1928-1937). The standard work. A monument of careful research.

Documents Relatifs aux Martyrs de Corée de 1839 et 1846 (Hongkong, Imprimerie de Nazareth, 1924, pp. vii, 145).

[Domenge], *La Mission de Vizagapatam par un Missionnaire de Saint François de Sales* (Annecy, J. Niérat, 1890, pp. xvi, 531). Chiefly a history of the mission.

Los Dominicos en el Extremo Oriente. Provincia del Santísimo Rosario de Filipinas. Relaciones publicadas con motivo del Séptimo Centenario de la confirmación de la Sagrada Orden de Predicadores (no date or place of publication, pp. 391). Done by a commission. No names of authors given.

Doolittle, Justus, *Social Life of the Chinese* (New York, Harper & Brothers, 2 vols., 1867). After fourteen years as a missionary in Foochow.

Downie, David, *The Lone Star. A History of the Telugu Mission of the American Baptist Foreign Mission Society* (Philadelphia, The American Baptist Publication Society, 1924, pp. 319). By one who spent many years in that mission.

Dozier, Edwin B., *A Golden Milestone in Japan* (Nashville, Broadman Press, 1940, pp. 184).

Drach, George, editor, *Our Church Abroad. The Foreign Missions of the Lutheran Church in America* (Philadelphia, The United Lutheran Publication House, 1926, pp. 277). An official description of the missions of the various Lutheran bodies of the United States.

Drach, George, and Kuder, Calvin F., *The Telugu Mission of the General Council of the Evangelical Lutheran Church in North America* (Philadelphia, General Council Publication House, 1914, pp. 399). Carefully done.

Drury, A. W., *History of the Church of the United Brethren in Christ* (Dayton, Ohio, United Brethren Publishing House, revised edition, 1931, pp. 832). By one long connected with the church. Based upon personal knowledge and extensive research.

D'Sa, M., *History of the Catholic Church in India* (Bombay, The Lalka Printing and Litho Works, 2 vols., 1910-1922). Not very well articulated: a series of notes taken from various books and put roughly into chronological order.

D'Sa, M., *The History of the Diocese of Damaun* (Bombay, Presidency Printing Press, 1924, pp. 276, iv). The author, a priest, is not always critical, but uses old authorities which he seems to follow fairly closely and often gives the documents or selections from them. ,

Duchaussois, *Sous les Feux de Ceylan chez les Singhalais et les Tamouls* (Paris, Bernard Grasset, 1929, pp. 380). Written by an Oblate of Mary Immaculate. A popular description of Ceylon and of the history and work of the Oblate Mission.

Dwight, Henry Otis, *The Centennial History of the American Bible Society* (New York, The Macmillan Co., 2 vols., 1916). By a secretary of the society.

The East and the West. A Quarterly Review for the Study of Missionary Problems (Westminster, The Society for the Propagation of the Gospel in Foreign Parts, 1903-1927).

Eddy, Sherwood, *A Pilgrimage of Ideas or the Re-education of Sherwood Eddy* (New York, Farrar and Rinehart, 1934, pp. xiii, 336). An autobiography.

Ekvall, Robert B., and others, *After Fifty Years. A Record of God's Working through the Christian and Missionary Alliance* (Harrisburg, Christian Publications, 1939, pp. vi, 278). An official history.

The Encyclopædia Britannica (New York, The Encyclopædia Britannica, 11th ed., 25 vols., 1910, 1911).

The Encyclopædia Britannica (London, The Encyclopædia Britannica, 14th ed., 24 vols., 1929).

The Encyclopædia of Islam (Leyden, E. J. Brill, 1913-1934, 4 vols.). By many different scholars.

Erickson, Lois Johnson, *The White Fields of Japan. Being Some Account of the History and Conditions in Japan of the Mission of the Presbyterian Church in the United States there from 1885 to the Present Day* (Richmond, Presbyterian Committee of Publication, 1923, pp. 207).

Evangeliske Fosterlands-Stiftelsens Årsberättelse för . . . 1913 (Stockholm, Evang. Fosterlands-Stiftelsens Förlags-exp., pp. 284).

The Far Eastern Quarterly (New York, Columbia University Press, 1941ff.).

Farquhar, J. N., *Modern Religious Movements in India* (New York, The Macmillan Company, 1915, pp. xv, 471). A standard work.

Faust, Allen Klein, *Christianity as a Special Factor in Modern Japan* (Lancaster, Steinman & Foltz, 1909, pp. 96). A doctoral dissertation at the University of Pennsylvania.

Favier, Alphonse, *Péking. Histoire et Description* (Peking, Vol. I, Imprimerie des Lazaristes, au Pé-t'ang, Vol. II, new edition, Paris, Desclée, de Brouwer et Cie, 1902). A standard work by a French Lazarist bishop.

Ferguson-Davie, C. E., editor, *In Rubber Lands. An Account of the Work of the*

Church in Malaya (Westminster, The Society for the Propagation of the Gospel in Foreign Parts, 1921, pp. 89).

Fides News Service (Rome, c. 1926ff.). A mimeographed set of news release notes on current happenings in Roman Catholic missions. Compiled in close cooperation with the Association for the Propagation of the Faith.

Findlay, G. G., and Holdsworth, W. W., *The History of the Wesleyan Methodist Missionary Society* (London, The Epworth Press, 5 vols., 1921-1924). An official history, based largely upon the manuscript records of the society.

Fleisch, Paul, *Hundert Jahre luterischer Mission* (Leipzig, Verlag der Evangelisch-luterischen Mission, 1936, pp. xiv, 480). Well done.

The Foreign Mail Annual (New York, Foreign Department of the International Committee of Young Men's Christian Associations).

Forsyth, Robert Coventry, editor, *The China Martyrs of 1900. A Complete Roll of the Christian Heroes Martyred in China in 1900 with Narratives of Survivors* (New York, Fleming H. Revell Company, no date, pp. xii, 516).

Fortescue, Adrian, *The Lesser Eastern Churches* (London, Catholic Truth Society, 1913, pp. xv, 468).

France, Walter F., *Japan* (Westminster, Society for the Propagation of the Gospel in Foreign Parts, 1930, pp. 79). By a former Anglican missionary in Japan.

Freeman, John H., *An Oriental Land of the Free, or Life and Mission Work among the Laos of Siam, Burma, China and Indo-China* (Philadelphia, The Westminster Press, 1910, pp. 200).

Gallo, Luigi, *Storia del Christianesimo nell' Impero Barmano Preceduta dalle Notizie del Paese* (Milan, Boniardi-Pogliani di Ermen, 3 vols., 1862).

Gentili, Fra Tommaso Maria, *Memoire di un Missionario Domenicano nella Cina* (Rome, 3 vols., 1887). The history of the Fukien mission from the beginning to 1886. Much detail, but little perspective. The third volume partly what the author had himself seen.

Gerhard, Paul, *Geschichte und Beschreibung der Mission unter den Kolhs* (Berlin, Buchhandlung der Gossnerischen Mission, 1883, pp. 140).

Gibson, J. Campbell, *Mission Problems and Mission Methods in South China. Lectures on Evangelistic Theology* (New York, Fleming H. Revell Company, Preface 1901, pp. 332). By a distinguished missionary.

Gidney, W. T., *The History of the London Society for Promoting Christianity amongst the Jews, from 1809 to 1908* (London, Society for Promoting Christianity amongst the Jews, 1908, pp. xxx, 672). A centenary history, by a secretary of the society, based upon the society's records.

The Girl Who Learned to See. By One Who Loves India (London, Church of England Zenana Missionary Society, no date, pp. vi, 90). Told in popular style: apparently a true story by an eye-witness.

Gledstone, Frederick F., *South India* (Westminster, The Society for the Propagation of the Gospel in Foreign Parts, 1930, pp. 83). By a missionary in the diocese of Dornakal.

[Gobat, Samuel], *Samuel Gobat, Bishop of Jerusalem, His Life and Work. A Biographical Sketch Drawn Chiefly from His Own Journals* (London, James Nisbet

& Co., 1884, pp. xi, 401). There is a German translation, but containing additional material, published at Basel by C. F. Spittler, 1884, pp. vi, 550).

Goforth, Jonathan, "*By My Spirit*" (London, no date). An account of the revivals in China in which Goforth was the leader or had a large part.

Gogerly, George, *The Pioneers*: *A Narrative of Facts Connected with the Early Christian Missions in Bengal. Chiefly Relating to the Operations of the London Missionary Society* (London, John Snow, no date, pp. 352). Largely personal reminiscences.

Gordon, Andrew, *Our India Mission. A Thirty Years' History of the India Mission of the United Presbyterian Church of North America together with Personal Reminiscences* (Philadelphia, Andrew Gordon, 1888, pp. 516). Partly autobiographical, by the pioneer member of the mission.

Stand und Arbeit der Gossnerschen Mission in Jahre 1905/1906 (Friedenau-Berlin, Gossnersche Mission, 1906, pp. 152).

Greene, Evarts Boutell, *A New-Englander in Japan. Daniel Crosby Greene* (Boston, Houghton Mifflin Company, 1927, pp. x, 374). By a son, a distinguished historian.

Grentrup, Theodorus, *Jus Missionarium* (Steyl, Mission Press, Vol. I, 1925, pp. xiv, 544). An excellent compilation.

Griffis, William Elliot, *A Maker of the New Orient. Samuel Robbins Brown* (Chicago, Fleming H. Revell Company, 1902, pp. 332). Based upon Brown's letters, notebooks and journals, by a close personal friend.

Gützlaff, Charles, *Journal of Three Voyages along the Coast of China in 1831, 1832, & 1833, with notices of Siam, Corea, and the Loo-choo Islands* (London, Frederick Westley and A. H. Davis, 1834, pp. vi, xciii, 450).

Habig, Marion A., *Pioneering in China. The Story of the Rev. Francis Xavier Engbring, O.F.M., First Native American Priest in China, 1857-1895. With Sketches of His Missionary Comrades* (Chicago, Franciscan Herald Press, 1930, pp. 153). Carefully done, largely on the basis of first-hand narratives, by a Franciscan.

Hagspiel, Bruno, *Along the Mission Trail* (Techny, Mission Press, S.V.D., 5 vols., 1925-1927). A travelogue by a member of the Society of the Divine Word.

Hall, Gordon, *Anecdotes of the Bombay Mission for the Conversion of the Hindoos* (London, Frederick J. Williamson, 1836, pp. xi, 246).

Handmann, Richard, *Die Evangelisch-lutherische Tamulen-Mission in der Zeit ihrer Neubegründung* (Leipzig, J. C. Hinrichs'sche Buchhandlung, 1903, pp. x, 477).

Hardy, Arthur Sherburne, *Life and Letters of Joseph Hardy Neesima* (Boston, Houghton, Mifflin Company, 1892, pp. vi, 350). Contains extensive quotations from the letters and other autobiographical writings of Neesima.

Harper, Marvin Henry, *The Methodist Episcopal Church in India. A Study of Ecclesiastical Organization and Administration* (Lucknow, The Lucknow Publishing House, 1936, pp. vii, 222). Carefully done; a doctoral dissertation at the University of Chicago by a Methodist missionary.

Harris, Merriman C., *Christianity in Japan* (Cincinnati, Jennings and Graham, 1907, pp. 88).

Harvard, W. M., *A Narrative of the Establishment and Progress of the Mission to Ceylon and India . . . under the Direction of the Wesleyan-Methodist Confer-*

ence (London, T. Blanshard, etc., 1823, pp. lxxiii, 404). By one of the pioneers.

Hasluck, F. W., edited by Hasluck, Margaret M., *Christianity and Islam under the Sultans* (Oxford, Clarendon Press, 2 vols., 1929). Well documented.

Heeren, John J., *On the Shantung Front. A History of the Shantung Mission of the Presbyterian Church in the U. S. A. in its Historical, Economic, and Political Setting* (New York, The Board of Foreign Missions of the Presbyterian Church in the United States of America, 1940, pp. xiv, 264). Scholarly, by a member of the mission.

Heyworth-Dunne, J., *An Introduction to the History of Education in Modern Egypt* (London, Luzac & Co., c. 1938, pp. xiv, 503).

Hilaire de Barelon, *La France Catholique en Orient durant les Trois Derniers Siècles d'après des Documents Inedits* (Paris, Oeuvre de Saint-François d'Assise, 1902, pp. xxi, 318). Based largely upon manuscript sources.

Hoffmann, Johannes B., *37 Jahre Missionär in Indien. Tröstliche Erfahrungen beim Naturvolk der Mundas der Misserfolg in der Missionierung höherer Kasten und seine Ursachen* (Innsbruck, Verlagsanstalt Tyrolia, 1923, pp. 64). A popular account of the Chota-Nagpur mission, by a Jesuit missionary in the region.

Hole, Charles, *The Early History of the Church Missionary Society for Africa and the East to the end of A.D. 1814* (London, Church Missionary Society, 1896, pp. xxxviii, 677). Very full, based upon extensive and careful research.

Holtom, D. C., *Modern Japan and Shinto Nationalism. A Study of Present-Day Trends in Japanese Religions* (University of Chicago Press, 1943, pp. 178). Based upon the study of original documents, by an outstanding authority on Shinto who tends to emphasize the power of Shinto and its contradiction to Christianity.

Hoole, Elijah, *Madras, Mysore, and the South of India: or a Personal Narrative of a Mission to Those Countries from MDCCCXX to MDCCCXXVIII* (London, Longman, Brown, Green, and Longmans, 2d ed., 1844, pp. xlviii, 443). By an agent of the Wesleyan Missionary Committee.

Howard, Randolph L., *Baptists in Burma* (Philadelphia, The Judson Press, 1931. pp. 168). By a former Baptist missionary to Burma.

Hughes, Lizbeth B., *The Evangel in Burma, being a Review of the Quarter Century 1900-1925 of the Work of the American Baptist Foreign Mission Society in Burma* (Rangoon, American Baptist Mission Press, 1926, pp. 225).

Hulbert, Homer B., *The History of Korea* (Seoul, The Methodist Publishing House, 2 vols., 1905).

Hull, Ernest R., *Bombay Mission-History with a Special Study of the Padroado Question* (Bombay, Examiner Press, no date, Vol. I, 1534-1858, pp. vii, 493, x, Vol. II, 1858-1929, pp. xiv, 521). By a Jesuit, with the express purpose of objectivity on the padroado question, and incorporating many documents, given in English translation.

Hunnicutt, Benjamin H., and Reid, William Watkins, *The Story of Agricultural Missions* (New York, Missionary Education Movement of the United States and Canada, 1931, pp. ix, 180). A study book for adults. Hunnicutt was an agricultural missionary in Brazil and Reid was active in the International Association of Agricultural Missions.

Hunter, Robert, *History of the Missions of the Free Church of Scotland in India and Africa* (London, T. Nelson and Sons, 1873, pp. xii, 387). By a former missionary: based in part upon printed reports.

Huntington, Virginia E., *Along the Great River* (New York, The National Council, Protestant Episcopal Church, 1940, pp. 261). An historical account of the China Mission of the Protestant Episcopal Church, by the wife of a bishop in China.

Huonder, Anton, *Der einheimische Klerus in den Heidenländern* (Freiburg im Breisgau, Herdersche Verlagshandlung, 1909, pp. x, 312). Based upon fairly wide reading.

Hutton, J. E., *A History of Moravian Missions* (London, Moravian Publication Office, 1923, pp. 550).

Hylander, Nils, *Morgonljus. Femtioårigt Missionsarbete på Nutthöljd Jord 1865-1916* (Stockholm, Nordiska Boktryckeriet, 1917, pp. 257).

The India Mission of the Free Church of Scotland. Being Report of the Deputies to India in 1888-9, Opinion of the Missionaries in 1890 and Minute of the Foreign Missions Committee. To be Submitted to the General Assembly of 1891 (Edinburgh, Edinburgh. Press, 1891, pp. vi, 198).

Inglis, James, *Protestant Missionary Directory of India for 1912-1913* (Ajmer, Scottish Mission Industries Co., pp. lxxxviii, 167).

The International Review of Missions (London, 1912ff.). The standard Protestant journal on foreign missions.

International Survey of the Young Men's and Young Women's Christian Associations (New York, The International Survey Committee, 1932, pp. vi, 425). A careful, objective study.

Isaacs, Albert Augustus, *Biography of the Rev. Henry Aaron Stern, D.D., for more than Forty Years a Missionary amongst the Jews* (London, James Nisbet & Co., 1886, pp. 480). Contains large excerpts from Stern's own hand.

J. V. F., *A Quarter-Century of Progress in the Diocese of Quilon 1900-1925. Souvenir of the Episcopal Silver Jubilee of the Rt. Rev. Aloysius Maria Benziger, C.D., D.D., Bishop of Quilon* (Trichinopoly, St. Joseph's Industrial School Press, 1925, pp. 59).

The Jaffna Ecclesiastical Directory for the Year of Our Lord 1875 (Jaffna, St. Joseph's Catholic Press, pp. 53).

The Japan Evangelist (Yokohama [later Tokyo], 1894-1925). An undenominational magazine covering various phases of missionary effort.

Jeffrey, Robert, *The Indian Mission of the Irish Presbyterian Church. A History of Fifty Years of Work in Kathiawar and Gujarat* (London, Nisbet & Co., 1890. pp. 279). Based upon printed and manuscript sources.

Jenks, David, *Six Great Missionaries of the Sixteenth and Seventeenth Centuries* (London, A. R. Mowbray and Co., 1930, pp. vii, 252). Popular, sympathetic account of Roman Catholic missionaries, by an Anglican.

Jessup, Henry Harris, *Fifty-Three Years in Syria* (Chicago, Fleming H. Revell Company, 2 vols., 1910).

Johnston, Jas., *China and Formosa. The Story of the Mission of the Presbyterian Church of England* (London, Hazell, Watson & Viney, 1897, pp. xvi, 400). By a former missionary.

Jones, J. P., editor, *The Year Book of Missions in India, Burma and Ceylon, 1912* (The Christian Literature Society for India, 1912, pp. xvi, 780). Authoritative, by various missionaries and specialists.

Jonquet, Mgr. Bonjean. *Oblat de Marie Immaculée, Premier Archevêque de Colombo* (Nimes, Imprimerie Générale, 2 vols., 1910).

Josson, H., *La Mission du Bengale Occidental ou Archidiocèse de Calcutta. Province Belge de la Compagnie de Jésus* (Bruges, Imprimerie Sainte-Catherine, 2 vols., 1921). Based on careful research, by a Jesuit.

Kagawa, Toyohiko, *Christ and Japan* (New York, Friendship Press, 1934, pp. vi, 150).

Karsten, Hermann, *Die Geschichte der evangelisch-lutherischen Mission in Leipzig* (Güstrow, Opitz & Co., 2 vols., 1893).

Die katholischen Missionen (Freiburg, 1872ff.).

Kawai, Michi, *My Lantern* (Tokyo, Kyo Bun Kwan, no date, pp. 229). An autobiography.

Kaye, John William, *Christianity in India. An Historical Narrative* (London, Smith, Elder & Co., 1859, pp. xvi, 522). Based in part on printed and in part on manuscript material. Confessedly incomplete.

Kennedy, James, *Life and Work in Benares and Kumaon 1839-1877* (New York, Cassell and Company, 1885, pp. xxiii, 392). In part autobiographical.

Kerr, Robert, *Morocco after Twenty-Five Years. A Description of the Country, Its Laws and Customs, and the European Situation* (London, Murray and Evenden, 1912, pp. xv, 364). By the first representative of the Southern Morocco Mission.

Kervyn, Louis, *Méthode de l'Apostolat Moderne en Chine* (Hongkong, 1911). A frank treatment by a Roman Catholic, regarded critically by the official Church.

Kesson, John, *The Cross and the Dragon, or, the Fortunes of Christianity in China* (London, Smith, Elder and Co., 1854, pp. xi, 282).

Koo, Vi Kyuin Wellington, *The Status of Aliens in China* (New York, Columbia University, 1912, pp. 359). Well done.

Kozaki, Hiromichi, *Reminiscences of Seventy Years. The Autobiography of a Japanese Pastor,* translated by Nariaki Kozaki (Tokyo, Christian Literature Society of Japan, 1933, pp. iv, 406). The author was a member of the Kumamoto band, second president of the Doshisha, and long a pastor in Tokyo.

Krapf, J. Lewis, *Travels, Researches, and Missionary Labours during an Eighteen Years' Residence in Eastern Africa* (London, Trübner and Co., 1860, pp. li, 566).

Kuruppu, D. J. B., *The Catholic Church in Ceylon. A Brief Account of Its History and Progress* (Colombo, The "Messenger" Press, 1923, pp. 24).

LaFargue, Thomas E., *China's First Hundred* (Pullman, State College of Washington, 1942, pp. xiv, 176). Based upon extensive research, pleasantly written.

Lansdell, Henry, *Through Siberia* (Boston, Houghton, Mifflin Company, 3d ed., 1882, pp. xxiii, 811). By a deeply religious English traveller who was concerned for prisoners.

Laouënan, Monseigneur, *Lettres sur l'Inde. Publiées par Adrien Launay* (Paris, Librairie Victor Lecoffre, 1893, pp. xii, 296). By an Archbishop of Pondichéry, a member of the Société des Missions-Étrangères.

Latourette, Kenneth Scott, *A History of Christian Missions in China* (New York,

The Macmillan Company, 1929, pp. xii, 930). Based upon extensive research.

Launay, Adrien, *Histoire des Missions de l'Inde Pondichéry, Maïssour, Coïmbatour* (Paris, Charles Douniol, 5 vols., 1898).

Launay, Adrien, *Histoire Générale de la Société des Missions-Étrangères* (Paris, Pierre Tequi, 3 vols., 1894). By a member of the society. Based upon the archives.

Launay, Adrien, *Société des Missions-Étrangères. Martyrs Français et Coréens 1838-1846 Béatifiés en 1925* (Paris, P. Tequi, 1925, pp. xv, 271). By the historian of the society.

Laveille, E., *L'Évangile au Centre de l'Afrique Le P. van Hencxthoven, S.J.* . . . *(1852-1906)* (Louvain, Editions du Museum Lesscanum, 1926, pp. 401).

Lavigerie, Cardinal, *Œuvres choisies de son Éminence le Cardinal Lavigerie Archevêque d'Alger* (Paris, Librairie Poussielque Frères, 1884, 2 vols., pp. iv, 540, 546).

Laymen's Foreign Missions Inquiry (New York, Harper & Brothers, 7 vols., 1933).

Report of the Commission of Appraisal of the Laymen's Foreign Mission Inquiry (New York, 1932, pp. viii, 417). References are not to the printed report but to a reproduction of a mimeographed copy.

Leeder, S. H., *Modern Sons of the Pharaohs. A Study of the Manners and Customs of the Copts of Egypt* (London, Hodder and Stoughton, Ltd., c. 1918, pp. xvi, 355).

Legge, Helen Edith, *James Legge* (London, The Religious Tract Society, 1905, pp. viii, 247).

Lemmens, Leonhard, *Geschichte der Franziskanermissionen* (Münster i.W., Aschendorffschen Verlagsbuchhandlung, 1929, pp. xx, 376). Carefully done, by a Franciscan.

Lemerle, F. Franz, *My Diary, or A Record of Events and Experiences* (Madras, The Examiner Press, 1891, pp. iii. 250). Written 1887-1890, largely at Ootacamund, by one attached to the entourage of the Delegate Apostolic in the East Indies.

Leroy, Henri-Joseph, *En Chine. Au Tché-ly S.-E. Une Mission d'après les Missionnaires* (Lille, Desclée, de Brouwer & Cie, 1900, pp. xl, 458).

Lesourd, Paul, editor, *L'Année Missionnaire 1931* (Paris, Desclée de Brouwer et Cie, pp. 667).

Lewis, Arthur, *George Maxwell Gordon . . . The Pilgrim Missionary of the Punjab. A History of his Life and Work, 1839-1880* (London, Seeley & Co., 1889, pp. v, 397). Containing many long excerpts from Gordon's letters.

Little, Archibald, *Gleanings from Fifty Years in China* (London, Sampson, Low, Marston & Co., no date, pp. xvi, 335).

Little, Mrs. Archibald, *Intimate China. The Chinese as I have seen them* (London, Hutchinson & Co., Ltd., 1899, pp. xv, 615).

Lockhart, William, *The Medical Missionary in China: a Narrative of Twenty Years' Experience* (London, Hurst and Blackett, 1861, pp. xi, 404). By a representative of the London Missionary Society.

Reports of the London Missionary Society (London, 1796ff.).

Louvet, L.-E., *La Cochinchine Religieuse* (Paris, Challamal Ainé, 2 vols., 1885).

Louvet, Louis-Eugène, *Les Missions Catholiques au XIXme Siècle* (Lyon, Œuvre de la Propagation de la Foi, 1895, pp. xvi, 543, 46). Popular account. Must be used with discrimination.

Lovett, Richard, *The History of the London Missionary Society 1795-1895* (London, Henry Frowde, 2 vols., 1899). Based upon the sources.

Lübeck, Konrad, *Die Christianisierung Russlands* (Aachen, Xaveriusverlagsbuchhandlung, 1922, pp. 118). By a Roman Catholic scholar, using a good deal of Russian material, as well as that in western European languages. Objective, scholarly.

Lübeck, Konrad, *Die katholische Orientmission in ihrer Entwicklung dargestellt* (Cologne, J. P. Bachem, 1917, pp. 152). With extensive footnote references to the sources.

Lübeck, Konrad, *Die russischen Missionen* (Aachen, Xaverius-Verlagsbuchhandlung, 1922, pp. 68). Careful and objective, by a Roman Catholic scholar.

The Lutheran World Almanac and Annual Encyclopedia for 1921 (New York, The Lutheran Bureau, 1920, pp. 966).

Lys, Antoine du, *Un Vrai Frère Mineur. Vie et Martyre du bienheureux Jean de Triora béatifié le 27 Mai 1900* (Paris, [1900]).

McFarland, George Bradley, editor, *Historical Sketch of Protestant Missions in Siam 1828-1928* (Bangkok Times Press, 1928, pp. xvii, 386).

MacGillivray, D., editor, *A Century of Protestant Missions in China (1807-1907), Being the Centenary Conference Historical Volume* (Shanghai, American Presbyterian Mission Press, 1907, pp. vii, 677, xl, 52). The sketches were largely compiled by the societies themselves.

Mackenzie, John, editor, *The Christian Task in India* (London, 1929). By various authors.

Mackichan, D., *The Missionary Ideal in the Scottish Churches* (London, Hodder and Stoughton, 1927, pp. 238). A semi-popular series of lectures.

McLeish, Alexander, *Christian Progress in Burma* (London, World Dominion Press, 1929, pp. 100). A careful survey of Protestant effort.

MacMurray, John V. A., compiler and editor, *Treaties and Agreements With and Concerning China, 1894-1919* (New York, Oxford University Press, 2 vols., 1921). A standard compilation.

Macnicol, Nicol, *India in the Dark Wood* (London, Edinburgh House Press, 1930, pp. 224). A popularly written book by an authority on India and missions in India.

Macnicol, Nicol, *The Living Religions of the Indian People* (London, Student Christian Movement Press, 1934, pp. 324).

The Madras Catholic Directory and General Annual Register for the Year of Our Lord 1906. Fifty-Sixth Annual Publication (Madras, Standard Office, pp. vi, 335). More detailed on the archdiocese of Madras, but contains much information as well on the rest of India, Ceylon, and Burma, and some on Siam, Japan, and China.

The Madras Christian College Magazine (Madras, 1883ff.).

Directory of the Diocese of Mangalore For the Year of Our Lord 1925 (Mangalore, Codiabail Press, pp. 105).

Manna, Paolo, *The Conversion of the Pagan World. A Treatise upon Catholic Foreign Missions Translated and adapted from the Italian of Rev. Paolo Manna, M. Ap., by Rev. Joseph F. McGlinchey* (Boston, Society for the Propagation of the Faith, 1921, pp. xix, 303).

Marie, Élie, *Aux Avant-postes de la Chrétienté. Histoire des Instituts Religieux et Missionnaires* (Paris, P. Lethielleux, 1930, pp. xii, 343). Has useful bibliographies.

Marnas, Francisque, *La "Religion de Jésus" (Iaso Ja-kyō) Ressuscitée au Japon dans la Seconde Moitié du XIXe Siècle* (Paris, Delhomme et Briguet, 2 vols., c. 1897).

Marshall, Harry Ignatius, *The Karen People of Burma: A Study in Anthropology and Ethnology* (Columbus, Ohio State University, 1917, pp. xv, 329).

Marshman, John Clark, *The Life and Times of Carey, Marshman, and Ward, embracing the History of the Serampore Mission* (London, Longman, Brown, Green, Longmans & Roberts, 2 vols., 1859). A standard work.

Mathews, Basil, *John R. Mott, World Citizen* (New York, Harper & Brothers, 1934, pp. xiii, 469). A warmly appreciative biography by a personal friend, based upon careful research and upon data provided by Mott.

Mayers, William Frederick, editor, *Treaties between the Empire of China and Foreign Powers* (Shanghai, North China Herald, 5th ed., 1906, pp. xiv, 354). A compilation of documents.

Medhurst, W. H., *China: Its State and Prospects, with Especial Reference to the Spread of the Gospel* (London, John Snow, 1842, pp. xv, 592). By an early Protestant missionary to the Chinese.

Memorias de la Misiones Catolicas en el Tonkin. Written in Italian by Alberto Guglielmoti, translated into Spanish by Manuel Amado (Madrid, Eusebio Aguado, 1846, pp. 320).

Miller, Henry K., editor, *History of the Japan Mission of the Reformed Church in the United States, 1879-1904* (Philadelphia, Board of Foreign Missions, Reformed Church in the United States, 1904, pp. 127).

Milne, William, *A Retrospect of the First Ten Years of the Protestant Mission to China* (Malacca, The Anglo-Chinese Press, 1820, pp. viii, 376). Largely the work of Robert Morrison.

Miner, Luella, *China's Book of Martyrs. A Record of Heroic Martyrdoms and Marvelous Deliverances of Chinese Christians during the Summer of 1900* (Philadelphia, The Westminster Press, 1903, pp. 512). By one who went through the siege in the legations in Peking.

Mishima, Sumie Seo, *My Narrow Isle. The Story of a Modern Woman of Japan* (New York, The John Day Company, 1941, pp. 280). Autobiographical.

Missionaries of the United Church of Canada in Japan, *Fruits of Christian Missions in Japan* (Toronto, The Woman's Missionary Society of the United Church of Canada, no date, pp. x, 260). No separate authors are given.

The Missionary Herald (Boston, 1806ff.). It began as *The Panoplist.* The organ of the American Board of Commissioners for Foreign Missions.

The Missionary Intelligencer (Cincinnati, 1888ff.).

The Missionary Review of the World (Princeton, later New York, 1878-1939). Earlier *The Missionary Review.*

Missiones Catholicae Cura S. Congregationis de Propaganda Fide Descriptae Statistica. Data Statistica Referunter ad diem 30 Juni 1927 (Rome, Typis Polyglottis Vaticanis, 1930, pp. xii, 534). Official and full figures and summary descriptions.

Missions en Chine et au Congo (Bruxelles, 1899ff.). (Beginning with 1909, the Philippines were added to the title.) Published for the Congregation of the Immaculate Heart of Mary.

Modak, S., *Directory of Protestant Indian Christians* (Ahmednagar, 1900, pp. xxvi, 562).

Moidrey, Joseph de, *La Hiérarchie Catholique en Chine, en Corée et au Japon (1307-1914)* (Zi-ka-wei, Imprimerie de l'Orphelinat de T'ou-sè-wè, 1914, pp. ii, 301). Very useful.

Monk, F. F., *A History of St. Stephen's College, Delhi* (Calcutta, Y.M.C.A. Publishing House, 1935, pp. vi, 262).

Montgesty, G. de, adapted from the French by Florence Gilmore, *Two Vincentian Martyrs, Blessed Francis Regis Clet, C.M., Blessed John Gabriel Perboyre, C.M.* (Maryknoll, Catholic Foreign Mission Society of America, 1925, pp. v, 182).

Moody, Campbell N., *The Mind of the Early Converts* (London, Hodder & Stoughton, Ltd., 1920, pp. xii, 310). A stimulating comparison between the early church and the converts in Formosa.

Moore, Herbert, *The Christian Faith in Japan* (Westminster, The Society for the Propagation of the Gospel in Foreign Parts, 1904, pp. 151). Chiefly an account of the Society for the Propagation of the Gospel in Foreign Parts.

Morris, John Hughes, *The Story of Our Foreign Mission (Presbyterian Church of Wales)* (Liverpool, Hugh Evans and Sons, 1930, pp. 105).

Morse, Hosea Ballou, *The Chronicle of the East India Company Trading to China 1635-1834* (Harvard University Press, 5 vols., 1926-1929). Made up largely of documents.

Morse, Hosea Ballou, *The International Relations of the Chinese Empire* (London, Longmans, Green and Company, 3 vols., 1910-1918). A standard work, well documented.

Moyer, Elgin S., *Missions in the Church of the Brethren. Their Development and Effect upon the Denomination* (Elgin, Ill., Brethren Publishing House, 1931, pp. 301). Scholarly.

Mullens, Joseph, *A Brief Review of Ten Years' Missionary Labour in India between 1852 and 1861* (London, James Nisbet and Co., 1863, pp. 196). Compiled from local reports and original letters.

Mullens, Joseph, *Missions in South India Visited and Described* (London, W. H. Dalton, 1854, pp. vii, 191). By a missionary of the London Missionary Society.

Murdoch, John, *Indian Missionary Manual. Hints to Young Missionaries in India* (London, James Nisbet and Co., 1895, pp. xi, 535).

The Near East and American Philanthropy. A Survey Conducted under the Guidance of the General Committee of the Near East Survey by Frank A. Ross, C. Luther Fry and Elbridge Sibley (New York, Columbia University Press, 1929, pp. xiii, 308).

Nevius, John L., *China and the Chinese* (London, Sampson Low, Son, and Marston, 1869, pp. 456). Written after ten years as a missionary in China.

Nisbet, Mrs. Anabel Major, *Day In and Day Out in Korea* (Richmond, Presbyterian Committee of Publication, no date, pp. 199). First hand glimpses by a missionary to Korea.

Nitobe, Inazo, and others, *Western Influences in Modern Japan* (Chicago, University of Chicago Press, 1931, pp. xii, 532). A series of papers originally prepared for foreign delegates to the meeting of the Institute of Pacific Relations held in Kyoto in 1929.

Noble, Mattie Wilcox, compiler and translator, *Victorious Lives of Early Christians in Korea* (Christian Literature Society, [1933], pp. 174). Appeared first in Korean. Translated by the author. Largely brief autobiographies.

Notizie Statistiche delle Missioni di Tutto il Mondo Dipendenti dalla S.C. de Propaganda Fide (Rome, Coi Tipi della S.C. de Propaganda Fide, 1844).

Nottrott, L., *Die Gossnersche Mission unter den Kolhs* (Halle, Richard Mühlmann, 2 vols., 1874, 1888).

Nouvelles Lettres Édifiantes des Missions de la Chine et des Indes Orientales (Paris, 8 vols., 1818-1823).

L'Œuvre de la Propagation de la Foi. Dix Années d'Apostolat Catholique dans les Missions 1898-1907.

Ohm, Thomas, *Indien und Gott. Religions- und Missionskundliche Streifzüge durch Ceylon und Vorderindien* (Salzburg, Anton Pustet, 1931, pp. 276). By a Benedictine.

Oldham, W. F., *India, Malaysia, and the Philippines. A Practical Study in Missions* (New York, Eaton & Mains, 1914, pp. viii, 299).

Oldham, F. F., *Thoburn, Called of God* (New York, The Methodist Book Concern, 1918, pp. 188).

Olichon, Mgr., *Le Baron de Phat-Diem (Histoire d'un Prêtre Tonkinois)* (Paris, Librairie Bloud & Gay, no date, pp. 138).

Our Church's Work in India. The Story of the Missions of the United Free Church of Scotland in Bengal, Santalia, Bombay, Rajputana, and Madras (Edinburgh, Oliphant, Anderson & Ferrier, no date, pp. 128). By various authors, missionaries, each writing of his or her field.

Our Mission in Bengal (Edinburgh, Foreign Mission Committee of the United Free Church of Scotland, 1917, pp. 68).

Our West China Mission (Toronto, The Missionary Society of the Methodist Church, 1920, pp. 475). By various members of the mission.

The Padroado Question (Bombay, The "Examiner Press," 1885, pp. 54). No author given. A well informed argument against the padroado.

Paik, L. George, *The History of Protestant Missions in Korea 1832-1910* (Pyeng Yang, Union Christian College Press, 1929, pp. v, 438, xiii). A doctoral dissertation, carefully documented.

Parker, Kenneth Lawrence, *The Development of the United Church of Northern India* (The University of Chicago Libraries, 1936, pp. 94).

Pascoe, C. F., *Two Hundred Years of the S.P.G. An Historical Account of the Society for the Propagation of the Gospel in Foreign Parts, 1701-1900* (London, published at the Society's Office, 1901, pp. xli, 1429). Very detailed, by an assistant secretary of the society.

Paul, R. C., *History of the Telugu Christians* (Madras, "Good Pastor" Press, 1929, pp. ix, 120). By a local Roman Catholic priest, based upon Kroot's *History of the Telugu Christians, Histoire des Missions Étrangères de l'Inde, The Catholic Expositor of Madras, The Catholic Directory,* and personal knowledge.

Peake, Cyrus H., *Nationalism and Education in Modern China* (New York, Columbia University Press, 1932, pp. xiv, 240). Scholarly.

Penny, Frank, *The Church in Madras. Being the History of the Ecclesiastical and Missionary Action of the East India Company in the Presidency of Madras in the Seventeenth and Eighteenth Centuries* (London, Smith, Elder and Co., 1904, pp. xii, 702). Based upon the documents, chiefly official dispatches and replies of the East India Company.

Il Pensiero Missionario Periodico Trimestrale dell' Unione Missionaria del Clero in Italia (Rome, Unione Missionaria del Clero in Italia, 1929ff.).

Pettee, James H., compiler, *A Chapter of Mission History in Modern Japan, being a Sketch for the Period since 1869 and a Report for the Years since 1893 of the American Board's Mission and the Kumiai Churches in their Affiliated Work* (Tokyo, Seishibunsha, no date, pp. 193, xii).

Philip, P. O., *Report on a Survey of Indigenous Christian Efforts in India, Burma and Ceylon* (Poona, Scottish Mission Industries Co., 1928, pp. 14).

Phillips, C. S., *The Church in France 1848-1907* (London, Society for Promoting Christian Knowledge, 1936, pp. 341).

Phillips, G. E., *The Outcastes' Hope or Work among the Depressed Classes in India* (London, Young People's Missionary Movement, 1912, pp. ix, 134).

Pickett, J. Waskom, *Christian Mass Movements in India. A Study with Recommendations* (Cincinnati, The Abingdon Press, 1933, pp. 382). Based upon a careful, objective study reaching over some years.

Pierson, George P., and Ida G., *Forty Happy Years in Japan, 1888-1928* (New York, Fleming H. Revell Company, 1936, pp. 130).

Piolet, J.-B., and Vadot, Ch., *L'Église Catholique aux Indes* (Paris, Bloud & Cie, 2d ed., 1907, pp. 60).

Piolet, J.-B., *Les Missions Catholiques Françaises au XIXe Siècle* (Paris, Librairie Armand Colin, 5 vols., no date, last vol. to 1902). By various authors.

Pitcher, P. W., *Fifty Years in Amoy or a History of the Amoy Mission, China* (New York, Board of Publication of the Reformed Church in America, 1893, pp. 207). By a member of the mission.

Pitman, Mrs. E. R., *Missionary Heroines in Eastern Lands* (London, Pickering and Inglis, no date, pp. vii, 191). Popularly written biographies of four women missionaries.

Planchet, J.-M., *Les Missions de Chine et du Japon* (Première Année, Peking, Imprimerie des Lazarists, 1916, pp. 492). A useful compilation.

Pons, A., *La Nouvelle Église d'Afrique ou Le Catholicisme en Algérie, en Tunisie et au Maroc depuis 1830* (Tunis, Librairie Louis Namura, no date, pp. xv, 343). By the Protonotary Apostolic in Carthage.

Prakasar, S. Gnana, *XXV Years' Catholic Progress. The Diocese of Jaffna under the Episcopate of Dr. Henry Joulain, O.M.I. 1893-1918* (Jaffna, Industrial School Press Colombogam, 1925, pp. 274). By an Oblate.

Minutes of the Synod of the Presbyterian Church of England, 1876ff.

Proceedings of the Church Missionary Society for Africa and the East (Vol. I, London, 1805, pp. 479).

Proceedings of the General Conference of the Protestant Missionaries of Japan, held at Osaka, Japan, April, 1883 (Yokohama, R. Meiklejohn & Co., 1883, pp. xviii, 468).

Proceedings of the General Conference of Protestant Missionaries in Japan Held in Tokyo October 24-31, 1900 (Tokyo, Methodist Publishing House, 1901, pp. xi, 1048).

Proceedings of the South India Missionary Conference, held at Ootacamund, April 19th-May 5th, 1858 (Madras, The Press of the S.P.C.K., 1858, pp. vii, 342, xxxiii).

Purser, W. C. B., *Christian Missions in Burma* (Westminster, Society for the Propagation of the Gospel in Foreign Parts, 1911, pp. xvi, 246). Admirably done, with chief emphasis upon Anglican missions.

Memoir of the Life and Public Services of Sir Thomas Stamford Raffles . . . by his Widow (London, James Duncan, 2 vols., 1835).

Records of the General Conference of the Protestant Missionaries of China, Held at Shanghai, May 10-24, 1877 (Shanghai, Presbyterian Mission Press, 1878, pp. 3, 492).

Records of the General Conference of the Protestant Missionaries of China Held at Shanghai May 7-20, 1890 (Shanghai, Presbyterian Mission Press, 1890, pp. lxviii, 744).

Reid, J. M., *Missions and Missionary Society of the Methodist Episcopal Church.* Revised and extended by J. T. Gracey (New York, Hunt and Eaton, 3 vols., 1895-1896). Based upon manuscript and printed sources, but without footnote references to the authorities.

Repeticci, Chanoine P., *L'Algérie Chrétienne Esquisse Historique 1830-1930* (Algiers, Librairie a Notre Dame, pp. 264). Contains extensive quotations from source materials.

Report of the Punjab Missionary Conference held at Lahore in December and January, 1862-63 (Lodiana, American Presbyterian Mission Press, 1863, pp. xix, 398).

Reports on the Schemes of the Church of Scotland, 1911 (Edinburgh, William Blackwood & Sons, Ltd., pp. xxxi, 1358).

Revue d'Histoire des Missions (Paris, 1924ff.).

Ricci, Giovanni, *Barbarie e Trionfi. Ossia le Vittime Illustre del San-si in Cina nella Persecuzione del 1900* (Florence, Tipografia Barbèra, 2d ed., 1910, pp. viii, 851). Largely although not exclusively a compilation of original documents.

Ricci, Giovanni, and Porta, Ercolano, *Storia della Missione Francescane e del Vicariato Apostolico del Hunan Meridionale dalle sue Origini ai Giorni Nostri* (Bologna, Stabilimenti Poligrafici Riuniti, 1925, pp. 222). Contains many documents.

Richard, Timothy, *Forty-Five Years in China. Reminiscences* (New York, Frederick A. Stokes Company, Inc., 1916, pp. 384).

Richter, Julius, *Die deutsche Mission in Südindien* (Gütersloh, C. Bertelsmann, 1902, pp. vii, 275).

Richter, Julius, *Die evangelische Mission in Fern- und Südost-Asien, Australien, Amerika* (Gütersloh, C. Bertelsmann, 1932, pp. xii, 488). Readable. Few footnote references to sources, but occasional bibliographies.

Richter, Julius, *Indische Missionsgeschichte* (Gütersloh, C. Bertelsmann, 2d ed., 1924, pp. vi, 570). The standard history of Protestant missions in India. There is an English translation of an earlier edition.

Richter, Julius, *Mission und Evangelisation im Orient* (Gütersloh, C. Bertelsmann, 2d ed., 1930, pp. 294). The standard account of Protestant missions in the Near East. There is an English translation of the first edition, under the title, *A History of Protestant Missions in the Near East* (Edinburgh, Oliphant, Anderson & Ferrier, 1910, pp. 432). Few footnote references to authorities are given and the book is somewhat scanty in bibliography.

Richter, Julius, *Nordindische Missionsfahrten* (Gütersloh, C. Bertelsmann, 1903, pp. 325).

Richter, Julius, *Das Werden der christlichen Kirche in China* (Gütersloh, C. Bertelsmann, 1928, pp. xvi, 584). A readable and comprehensive account, chiefly of Protestantism.

Ritter, H., *A History of Protestant Missions in Japan*. Translated by George E. Albrecht. Revised and brought down to date by D. C. Greene (Tokyo, The Methodist Publishing House, 1898, pp. xv, 446).

Rommerskirchen, Joh., *Die Oblatenmissionen auf der Insel Ceylon im 19. Jahrhundert 1847-1893* (Hünfeld, Verlag der Oblaten, 1931, pp. xi, 247). By an Oblate priest; in its original form a doctoral dissertation (Fulda, Fuldner Actiendruckerei, 1930, pp. ix, 81).

Ross, John, *Mission Methods in Manchuria* (New York, Fleming H. Revell Company, no date, pp. 251). By a missionary pioneer in that region.

Rossillon, Pierre, *Les Moissonneuses du Coromandel, ou Quatre-vingts Ans d'Apostolat dans la Mission de Vizagapatam par les Sœurs de Saint-Joseph d'Annecy* (Paris, Librairie Saint-Paul Chambéry, Direction du Missionnaire Indien, 1933, pp. 219).

Rossillon, P., *Sous les Palmiers du Coromandel* (Lyon, Emm. Vittc, 1926, pp. 334). By a Bishop Coadjutor of Vizagapatam. Vividly told incidents of missionary experiences.

Rutherford, J., and Glenny, Edward H., *The Gospel in North Africa* (London, Percy Lund, Humphries & Co., 1900, pp. 248). The historical section, by Glenny, is by one of the founders of the North Africa Mission.

Rutten, Joseph, *Les Missionnaires de Scheut et leur Fondateur* (Éditions de l'Aucam, Louvain, 1930, pp. 228). A sympathetic account by a Superior General of the congregation. Includes a number of documents.

Ryang, J. S., editor, *Southern Methodism in Korea. Thirtieth Anniversary* (Seoul, Board of Missions, Korea Annual Conference, Methodist Episcopal Church, South, no date, pp. 186, lxviii, 299).

Ryder, Stephen Willis, *A Historical Sourcebook of the Japan Mission of the Re-*

formed Church in America (1859-1930) (York, The York Printing Co., pp. 156).

Saito, Soichi, *A Study of the Influence of Christianity upon Japanese Culture* (Tokyo, The Japan Council of the Institute of Pacific Relations, 1931, pp. iii, 71). By the general secretary of the Tokyo Y.M.C.A.

Sandegren, Herman, *Svensk Mission och Indisk Kyrka. Historisk Skildrung av Svenska Kyrkans Arbete i Sydindien* (Stockholm, Svenska Kyrkans Diakonis-tyrelses Bokförlag. 1924, pp. 280). Excellent.

Schlatter, Wilhelm, *Geschichte der Basler Mission 1815-1915* (Basel, Basler Missions-buchhandlung, 3 vols., 1916). Based especially upon unpublished sources.

Schmidlin, Joseph, *Das deutsche Missionswerk der Gegenwart* (Munster in West-falen, 1929). Carefully done; detailed.

Schmidlin, Joseph, *Katholische Missionsgeschichte* (Steyl, Missionsdruckerei, 1924, pp. xi, 598). A standard work by a distinguished Roman Catholic specialist on missions, with extensive bibliographical notes.

There is an English translation, by Matthias Braun (Mission Press, Techny, Ill., 1933, pp. xiv, 862), which makes additions to the bibliographies, especially of more recent works and works in English, and here and there adds to the text and footnotes. In some portions, therefore, it is fuller and better than the Ger-man original.

Schulze, Adolf, *200 Jahre Brüdermission. II Band, Das zweite Missionsjahrhundert* (Herrnhut, Verlag der Missionsbuchhandlung, 1932, pp. xii, 715). Well docu-mented.

Schwager, Friedrich, *Die katholische Heidenmission der Gegenwart im Zusammen-hang mit ihrer grossen Vergangenheit* (Steyl, Missionsdruckerei, 1907, pp. 446). A standard work.

Scott, J. E., *History of Fifty Years. Comprising the Origin, Establishment, Progress and Expansion of the Methodist Episcopal Church in Southern Asia* (Madras, M.E. Press, 1906, pp. xvi, 367, xv).

Sequeira, Rosario D., *My Ramble Through the Missions of The Diocese of Manga-lore* (Mangalore, Codialbail Press, 1929, pp. 97). By a missionary.

Servière, J. de la, *Histoire de la Mission du Kiang-nan* (Zi-ka-wei, Imprimerie de l'Orphelinat de T'ou-sè-wè, 2 vols., no date). Well documented, by a Jesuit.

Seth, Mesrovb Jacob, *Armenians in India, from the Earliest Times to the Present Day* (Calcutta, published by the author, 1937, pp. xv, 629). Based upon detailed research.

Sharrock, J. A., *South Indian Missions. Containing Glimpses of the Lives and Cus-toms of the Tamil People* (Westminster, Society for the Propagation of the Gos-pel in Foreign Parts, 1910, pp. viii, 312). By a missionary in South India of the Society for the Propagation of the Gospel in Foreign Parts.

Shaw, P. E., *American Contacts with the Eastern Churches, 1820-1870* (Chicago, The American Society of Church History, 1937, pp. 208). Based upon the sources; careful and objective.

[Sherwood, Martha Mary, and Sherwood, Henry], *The Life and Times of Mrs. Sherwood (1775-1851). From the Diaries of Captain and Mrs. Sherwood,* edited by F. J. Harvey Darton (London, Wells Gardner, Darton & Co., 1910, pp. xiv, 519).

Shortland, John R., *The Persecution of Annam: a History of Christianity in Cochin China and Tonking* (London, Burns and Oates, 1875, pp. ix, 430). Based largely upon letters published in *Annals of the Propagation of the Faith* and *Lettres Edifiantes*.

Sigismund Freiherrn von Bischoffshausen, *Das höhere katholische Unterrichtswesen in Indien und die Bekehrung der Brahmanen. Ein Beitrag zur Frage: Wie kann Indien katholisch werden?* (Freiburg im Breisgau, Herder'sche Verlagshandlung, 1897, pp. 86).

Silbernagl, Isidor, *Verfassung und gegenwärtiger Bestand sämtlicher Kirchen des Orients. Eine kanonistisch-statistische Abhandlung.* Second, revised edition by Jos. Schnitzer (Regensburg, G. J. Manz, 1904, pp. xxiv, 396). Well fortified by footnotes. By a Roman Catholic.

Singha, Shoran S., and Shepherd, Arthur P., *More Yarns on India* (London, Edinburgh House Press, 1930, pp. 80). A book of true stories for boys.

Smirnoff, Eugene, *A Short Account of the Historical Development and Present Position of Russian Orthodox Missions* (London, Rivingtons, 1903, pp. xii, 83). By the chaplain to the Russian Embassy in London; based upon careful study of reports of the Chief Procurator of the Holy Synod and of the various missions.

Smith, Arthur H., *China in Convulsion* (Chicago, Fleming H. Revell Company, 2 vols., 1901). By a contemporary Protestant missionary to China.

Smith, Eli, *Researches of the Rev. E. Smi⁻ and Rev. H. G. O. Dwight in Armenia* (Boston, Crocker and Brewster, 2 vols., 1833).

Smith, George, *Henry Martyn* (London, The Religious Tract Society, 1892, pp. viii, 580).

Smith, Judson, *Congregational Missions in the Heavenly Kingdom* (Boston, American Board of Commissioners for Foreign Missions, 1904, pp. 41).

An Abstract of the Annual Reports and Correspondence of the Society for Promoting Christian Knowledge from the Commencement of Its Connexion with the East India Missions, A.D. 1709, to the Present Day (London, F. C. and J. Rivington, 1814, pp. xvi, 730).

Soltau, T. Stanley, *Korea, the Hermit Nation and Its Response to Christianity* (London, World Dominion Press, 1932, pp. 123). By a member of the American Presbyterian Mission, North.

Soothill, Lucy, *A Passport to China* (London, Hodder & Stoughton, Ltd., 1931, pp. xi, 339). A delightfully written account of her life in China, by the wife of W. E. Soothill.

The Spirit of Missions (New York, 1836ff.).

Stauffer, Milton T., *The Christian Occupation of China* (Shanghai, China Continuation Committee, 1922). A very careful, comprehensive survey, by Protestants.

Stevenson, Margaret Sinclair, *Without the Pale. The Life Story of An Outcaste* (Calcutta, Association Press, 1930, pp. x, 87). An account of the Dheds of Gujarāt, by an expert in sociology. It deals chiefly with the rites of the people.

Stewart, Deaconess E. L., *Forward in Western China* (London, Church Missionary Society, 1934, pp. ix, 77). By a missionary in Szechwan.

Stock, Eugene, *The History of the Church Missionary Society: Its Environment, Its Men, and Its Work* (London, Church Missionary Society, 4 vols., 1899-1916). The standard history, by a secretary of the society.

Stock, Eugene, *Japan and the Japan Mission of the Church Missionary Society* (London, Church Missionary House, 2d ed., 1887, pp. 275).

Streit, Carolus, *Atlas Hierarchicus* (Paderborn, Typographia Bonifaciana, 1913, pp. 128, 37, 35). A standard book of reference.

Strong, Esther Boorman, and Warnshuis, A. L., editors, *Directory of Foreign Missions. Missionary Boards, Societies, Colleges, Coöperative Councils, and Other Agencies of the Protestant Churches of the World* (New York, International Missionary Council, 1933, pp. xii, 278).

Strong, William Ellsworth, *The Story of the American Board: An Account of the First Hundred Years of the American Board of Commissioners for Foreign Missions* (Boston, The Pilgrim Press, 1910, pp. xv, 523). A semi-official history.

Strothmann, R., *Die koptische Kirche in der Neuzeit* (Tübingen, J. C. B. Mohr [Paul Siebeck], 1932, pp. 167). Scholarly; based on the sources.

Svenska Missionsförbundets Årsberättelse för . . . 1913 (Stockholm, Svenska Missionsförbundets Exp., pp. 192).

Sword, Victor Hugo, *Baptists in Assam. A Century of Missionary Service, 1836-1936* (Chicago, Conference Press, 1935, pp. 160). Popularly written, but carefully done and based upon wide reading.

Taylor, Mrs. Howard, *Guinness of Honan* (London, The China Inland Mission, 1930, pp. ix, 322). A well written, sympathetic biography of G. Whitfield Guinness, by his sister.

Tennent, James Emerson, *Christianity in Ceylon: Its Introduction and Progress under the Portuguese, the Dutch, the British, and American Missions; with an Historical Sketch of the Brahmanical and Buddhist Superstitions* (London, John Murray, 1850, pp. xv, 345).

Teysseyre, E., *Histoire d'un Héros ou Vie de Monseigneur Galibert* (Paris, Téqui, 3d ed., 1890, pp. xiv, 393).

Thoburn, J. M., *India and Malaysia* (Cincinnati, Cranston & Curts, 1896, pp. 566). The history of the Methodist Episcopal Church in southern Asia by a pioneer missionary and bishop of the church.

Thoburn, J. M., *My Missionary Apprenticeship* (New York, 1887, pp. 425). By the leading figure in the development of the missions of the Methodist Episcopal Church in India and south-eastern Asia.

Thomas, A., *Histoire de la Mission de Pékin depuis l'Arrivée des Lazaristes, jusqu'a la Révolte des Boxeurs* (Paris, Louis Michaud, 1925, pp. 758). Thomas is a pen name. A good many documents are given *in extenso*. The book has a French bias.

Thompson, Virginia, *French Indo-China* (New York, The MacMillan Company, 1937, pp. 517). Based upon extensive reading.

Thompson, Virginia, *Thailand. The New Siam* (New York, The Macmillan Company, 1941, pp. xxxii, 865). Based upon extensive reading.

Thomson, W. Burns, *Reminiscences of Medical Missionary Work* (London, Hodder & Stoughton, Ltd., 1895, pp. xv, 248).

Tobar, Jérôme, translator and commentator, *Kiao-ou Ki-lio.* "*Résumé des Affaires Religieuses.*" *Publié par Ordre de S. Exc. Tcheou Fou* (Shanghai, Imprimerie de la Mission Catholique, 1917, Variétés Sinologiques No. 47, pp. ix, 252).

Tournier, Jules, *La Nouvelle Église d'Afrique. La Conquête Religeuse de l'Algérie 1830–1845* (Paris, Librairie Plon., 6th ed., 1930, pp. vi, 260). Very biased in favour of the Church, but based in part on original documents.

Treat, Payson S., *Diplomatic Relations between the United States and Japan 1853-1895* (Stanford University Press, 2 vols., 1932). Based largely upon unpublished diplomatic documents in the United States Department of State, and with a slight pro-Japanese bias.

Trochu, Francis, *Un Martyr Français au XIXe Siècle. Le Bienheureux Théophane Vénard, Prêtre de la Société des Missions-Étrangères de Paris (1829-1861), d'après sa correspondance, les témoignages de sa cause et de nombreux documents inédits* (Paris, Librairie Catholique Emmanuel Vitte, 1929, pp. xvi, 537). By a warm admirer.

Trollope, Mark Napier, *The Church in Corea* (London, A. R. Mowbray & Co., 1915, pp. 132). By a bishop of that church.

Tucker, Henry St. George, *The History of the Episcopal Church in Japan* (New York, Charles Scribner's Sons, 1938, pp. 228).

Underwood, Horace G., *The Call of Korea. Political-Social-Religious* (Chicago, Fleming H. Revell Company, 3d ed., 1908, pp. 204). By a distinguished Protestant missionary.

Väth, Alfons, *Die deutschen Jesuiten in Indien. Geschichte der Mission von Bombay-Puna (1854-1920)* (Regensburg, Jos. Kösel & Friedrich Pustet, 1920, pp. viii, 260). Carefully done.

Väth, Alfons, *Im Kampfe mit der Zauberwelt des Hinduismus. Upadhyaya Brahma-bandhav und das Problem der Überwindung des höheren Hinduismus durch das Christentum* (Berlin and Bonn, Ferd. Dümmlers Verlag, 1928, pp. 238). Scholarly, sympathetic; by a Jesuit.

Van der Schueren, T., *The Belgian Mission of Bengal* (Calcutta, Thacker, Spink & Co., 1922, 2 parts, pp. 100, 108). By a Jesuit missionary. Accounts of visits to the missions in Chota Nagpur.

Waldmeier, Theophilus, *The Autobiography of Theophilus Waldmeier, Comprising Ten Years in Abyssinia and Forty-Six Years in Syria.* Edited by Stephen Hobhouse (London, The Friends' Bookshop, 1925, pp. xv, 317).

Walsh, James A., *Observations in the Orient. An Account of a Journey to Catholic Mission Fields in Japan, Korea, Manchuria, China, Indo-China, and the Philippines* (Ossining, The Catholic Foreign Mission Society of America, 1919, pp. xiii, 321).

Wanless, Sir William, *An American Doctor at Work in India* (New York, Fleming H. Revell Company, 1932, pp. 200). Largely autobiographical.

Warneck, Gustav, *Abriss einer Geschichte der protestantischen Missionen von der Reformation bis auf die Gegenwart, mit einem Anhang über die katholischen Missionen* (Berlin, Martin Warneck, 10th ed., 1913, pp. x, 624).

Wasson, Alfred W., *Church Growth in Korea* (New York, International Missionary

Council, 1934, pp. xii, 175). A scholarly study, chiefly of the part of the Korean church related to the Methodist Episcopal Church, South.

Watson, Andrew, *The American Mission in Egypt 1854 to 1896* (Pittsburgh, United Presbyterian Board of Publication, 1904, pp. 487). By a member of the mission.

Watson, Charles R., *Egypt and the Christian Crusade* (Philadelphia, The Board of Foreign Missions of the United Presbyterian Church of North America, 1907, pp. xi, 288). A popular survey by a competent missionary to Egypt.

Watson, Charles R., *The Sorrow and Hope of the Egyptian Sudan. A Survey of Missionary Conditions and Methods of Work in the Egyptian Sudan* (Philadelphia, Board of Foreign Missions of the United Presbyterian Church of North America, 1913, pp. xiii, 233).

Wherry, E. M., *Our Missions in India 1834-1924* (Boston, The Stratford Co., 1926, pp. ii, 356). By one long a missionary of the Presbyterian Church, U. S. A., in India.

Williams, Frederick Wells, *The Life and Letters of Samuel Wells Williams, LL.D., Missionary, Diplomatist, Sinologue* (New York, G. P. Putnam's Sons, 1889, pp. vi, 490). A well documented biography, by a son.

Williams, S. Wells, *The Middle Kingdom* (New York, Charles Scribner's Sons, revised edition, 2 vols., 1907). Long a standard work, especially valuable for those portions of Chinese history of which the author was a personal observer and, at times, a participant.

Wilson, Robert Smith, *The Indirect Effects of Christian Missions in India* (London, James Clarke & Co., 1928, pp. 224).

Wischan, F., *Wilhelm Grönning, Missionar im Telugu-Lande in Indien* (Philadelphia, 1891, pp. 301).

Wolff, Joseph, *Researches and Missionary Labours among the Jews, Mohammedans, and other Sects* (London, James Nisbet and Co., 1835, pp. 523).

Wolff, Joseph, *Travels and Adventures of the Rev. Joseph Wolff* (London, Saunders, Otley & Co., 1861, pp. xiii, 601).

World Missionary Conference, 1910 (Edinburgh and London, Oliphant, Anderson & Ferrier, 9 vols., 1910).

Wylie, Alexander, *Memorials of Protestant Missionaries to the Chinese: giving a list of their publications, and obituary notices of the deceased, with copious indexes* (Shanghai, American Presbyterian Mission Press, 1867). By a careful scholar.

Wylie, Mrs. Macleod, *The Gospel in Burmah* (London, W. H. Dalton, 1859, pp. vii, 439).

Wyon, O., *An Eastern Palimpsest. A brief survey of the religious situation in Turkey, Syria, Palestine, Transjordania, Egypt* (London, World Dominion Press, no date, pp. 115). Based upon a special visit for survey and report.

The Year Book of Missions in India, Burma and Ceylon, 1912. Edited by J. P. Jones (The Christian Literature Society for India, 1912, pp. xvi, 780).

Yung Wing, *My Life in China and America* (New York, Henry Holt and Company, Inc., 1909, pp. vi, 286).

Zeitschrift für Missionswissenschaft (Münster i.w., 1911ff.).

INDEX

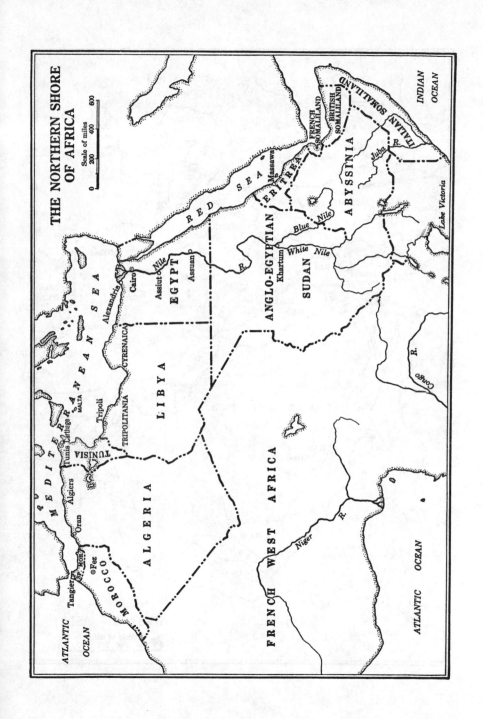

THE NORTHERN SHORE
OF AFRICA

Scale of miles
0   200 400 600

MEDITERRANEAN SEA

ATLANTIC
OCEAN

MOROCCO

SP. MOR.
Tangier
Fez

Oran
Algiers

ALGERIA

TUNISIA
Tunis Carthage
MALTA
Tripoli

TRIPOLITANIA

CYRENAICA

LIBYA

Alexandria
Cairo
Assiut
Assuan
Nile

EGYPT

R.

FRENCH WEST AFRICA

Niger R.

ATLANTIC
OCEAN

RED SEA

Massawa

ERITREA

ANGLO-EGYPTIAN

Khartum
White Nile
Blue Nile

SUDAN

FRENCH
SOMALILAND

BRITISH
SOMALILAND

ITALIAN SOMALILAND

ABYSSINIA

Juba R.

Lake Victoria

Congo R.

INDIAN
OCEAN

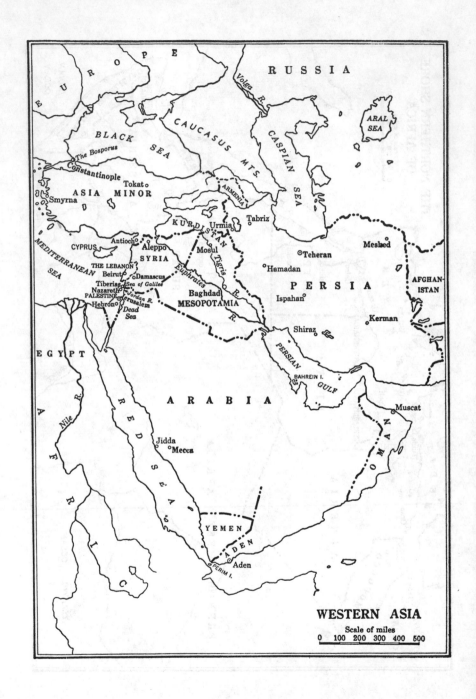

WESTERN ASIA

Scale of miles
0   100 200 300 400 500

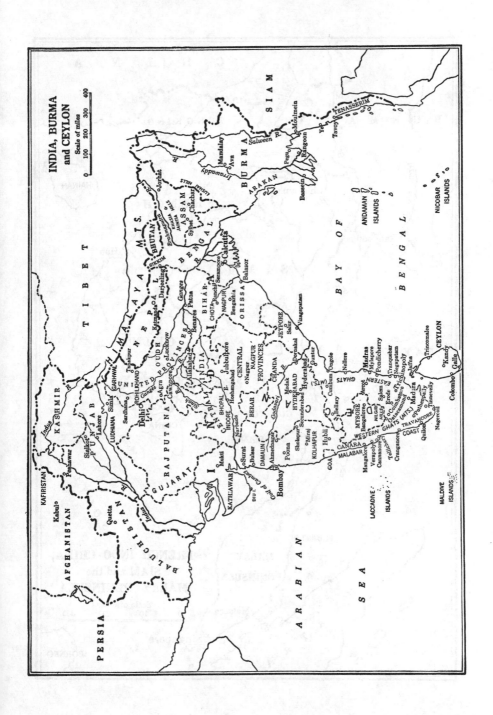

INDIA, BURMA
and CEYLON

Scale of miles

0   100   200   300   400

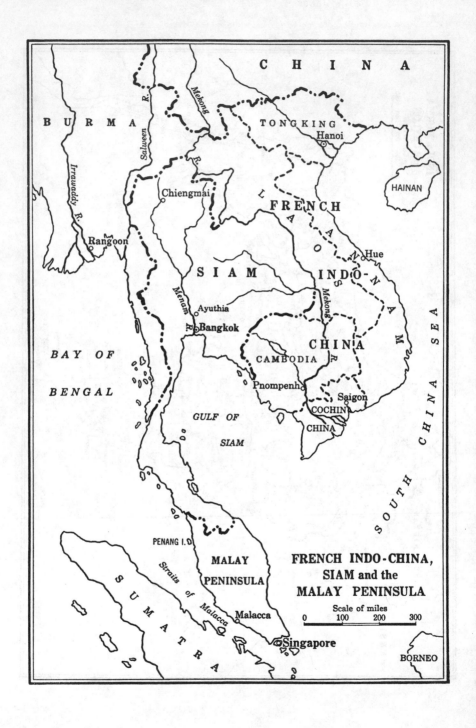

FRENCH INDO-CHINA,
SIAM and the
MALAY PENINSULA

Scale of miles
0   100   200   300

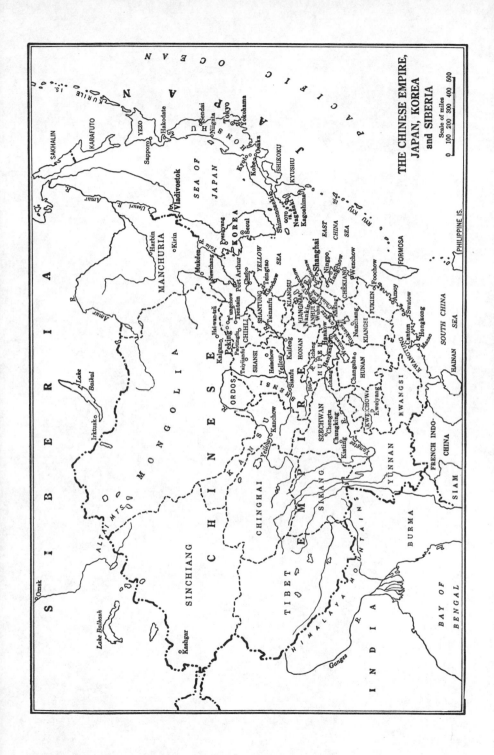

THE CHINESE EMPIRE,
JAPAN, KOREA
and SIBERIA

Scale of miles
0 100 200 300 400 500